Teenage Sexuality, Pregnancy, and Childbearing

Teenage Sexuality, Pregnancy, and Childbearing

Edited by
Frank F. Furstenberg, Jr.,
Richard Lincoln,
Jane Menken

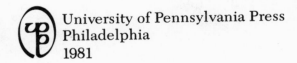
University of Pennsylvania Press
Philadelphia
1981

Library of Congress Cataloging in Publication Data
Main entry under title:

Teenage sexuality, pregnancy, and childbearing.

1. Youth—United States—Sexual behavior—Addresses, essays,
lectures.   2. Premarital sex—United States—Addresses, essays,
lectures.   3. Pregnant schoolgirls—United States—Addresses, essays,
lectures.   4. Teen-age marriage—United States—Addresses, essays,
lectures.   5. Illegitimacy—United States—Addresses, essays,
lectures.   I. Furstenberg, Frank F., Jr.   II. Lincoln, Richard.
III. Menken, Jane.
HQ27.T43   306.7′088055   80-22767

ISBN 0-8122-7787-2
ISBN 0-8122-1107-3 (pbk.)

To Frederick S. Jaffe

Contents

Preface

All of the articles in this volume are reprinted, with permission, from *Family Planning Perspectives*, published bimonthly by The Alan Guttmacher Institute, a nonprofit agency that engages in research, policy analysis, and public education on issues involving family planning and population concerns in the United States. We wish to acknowledge the contribution of the *Perspectives* editorial staff in helping to prepare these articles for publication. Portions of the *Overview* are drawn from a paper by Frank F. Furstenberg, Jr., and Albert G. Crawford entitled "The Social Implications of Teenage Childbearing," published in *Pregnancy: Perspectives for the Health Professional*, edited by Peggy B. Smith and David M. Munford (G. K. Hall and Co.: Boston, 1980).

We are aware that there is a certain amount of redundancy in some of the articles presented here, especially in the introductory material on levels of and trends in adolescent childbearing and in reviews of earlier studies. Except where authors have wished to update their findings, however, we believed it best to publish the articles as they appeared in their original context, primarily for the benefit of those who wish to read them individually rather than in sequence.

Overview

Contrary to popular impression, teenage childbearing in the United States has been on the decline during the past decade. Moreover, the newly discovered "epidemic" of adolescent pregnancy is not recent; elevated levels of teenage childbearing can be traced to the beginning of the baby boom after the Second World War. Nevertheless, the issue does seem to be more salient now than ever before. In this overview, we shall touch on some of the reasons. We intend to look at evidence on the social consequences of teenage childbearing for adolescent parents, their offspring, and members of their family of origin; examine briefly some of the available clues to the determinants of early parenthood; and consider some of the policy initiatives available to prevent premature childbearing or to ameliorate its deleterious effects.

Teenage Childbearing as a Social Issue

Whether we conclude that adolescent fertility is a problem of growing or diminishing significance rests largely on how we define adolescence and how we measure fertility. Table 1 presents an array of natality statistics for teenagers for the period 1950–1977. Depending on which indicator, which specific time period, and which age segment we examine, we may form quite different impressions of the current situation. The statistics can provide either some degree of reassurance or considerable cause for alarm. They demonstrate first that teenage fertility is not a rare or even an unusual event. According to 1977 rates, some 10 percent of women give birth before age 18, and more than 20 percent do so by age 20. Considered in terms of absolute numbers, adolescent (or teenage) childbearing has fallen significantly since the late 1960s and early 1970s. Even among the population younger than 18, there has been a decline recently in the number of births. One explanation for this downward trend is that the number of adolescents is not growing as rapidly as it did up to 1970. As the baby-boom children reached adolescence during the 1960s, an increase in adolescent births was inevitable unless the susceptibility of teenagers to pregnancy decreased enough to offset the numerical increase. Conversely, the teenage population has declined in size in recent years, so that even if adolescent fertility rates had remained constant, the number of births would have fallen. In fact, teenagers, especially 18- and

19-year-olds, are now less likely to have children then they used to be. Their fertility rate (the number of births per 1,000 women in the 15–19-year-old age group), has dropped off sharply since the end of the baby boom 20 years ago. Both these trends—the shrinking pool of teenagers and the decline in their birthrate—are likely to continue in the near future, suggesting that the absolute number of adolescent births may decline still further in the next few years.

If both the numbers and rates of births have fallen, then what has generated the intense concern about early childbearing in the past few years? Is adolescent parent-hood a socially manufactured problem created by the mass media to generate public interest, or by government officials or private agencies in order to extend their social programs? We think not. If we look at the two lower panels of Table 1, we can see the basis for the recent focus of attention on the subject: both the absolute and the relative declines in adolescent fertility have been restricted to married teenagers. Out-of-wedlock childbearing has risen during the same period that marital childbearing among the young has fallen. While most teenagers who have babies are married when the birth occurs, if present trends continue it will not be long before most adolescent births take place outside marriage. In 1955, approximately 85 percent of the births among the under-20 population occurred to married women; by 1977, the proportion was only 56 percent. When these figures are broken down by age, we can see that nonmarital childbearing has risen for both older and younger adolescents. Indeed, nearly 60 percent of 1977 births to females under age 18 took place out of wedlock. For the youngest teenagers, girls under 15, fertility, nearly all of it out of wedlock, increased sharply in the late 1960s and early 1970s, and only recently has declined slightly.

Fertility rates have long differed between blacks and whites in the United States. Table 2 shows that rates in the 1970s have been declining more rapidly for blacks than for whites. In fact, out-of-wedlock birthrates among white adolescents have risen sharply, suggesting that racial differences in sexual activity and pregnancy risks are diminishing. As early childbearing is seen more clearly as a problem affecting the white middle class, more vocal demands for attention and solutions are being heard.

Whether it is justified or not, out-of-wedlock births invariably generate more con-cern about the well-being of the mother and child than births that occur within marriage. (Later we shall show that we should be just as concerned about marital as nonmarital teenage fertility.) In fact, one might argue plausibly that the alarm sur-rounding early childbearing has been largely provoked by moral concern regarding the fact that an increasing number of teenagers are failing to marry when pregnancy occurs. If these teenagers did marry, or continued to drop out of school at the same very high rates that they did in the 1950s and early 1960s, the problem might well have continued to escape public notice. For many years, pregnancy was the primary reason given by young adolescent girls for leaving school. Few school systems encouraged pregnant girls to attend special classes, even when they were provided, and even fewer actively encouraged or aided young mothers to return to school. Because they were no longer visible, it was easy to ignore their plight. However, as the policies of educational institutions were challenged in this area and more pregnant teens con-tinued in school, the number of adolescents affected by early pregnancy became all too visible.

In addition, fewer pregnant teenagers were marrying to legitimate the birth of their child. Martin O'Connell and Maurice J. Moore report in chapter 3 that 71 percent of

Table 1. Selected natality indicators for women under 20, United States, 1950–1977

Age	Year						
	1950	1955	1960	1965	1970	1975	1977
No. of births (in 000s)							
15–19	—	484	587	591	645	582	559
18–19	—	334	405	402	421	355	345
15–17	—	150	182	189	224	227	214
<15	—	5	7	8	12	13	11
Birthrates (per 1,000 women)							
15–19	81.6	90.3	89.1	70.4	68.3	56.3	53.7
18–19	—	—	—	—	114.7	85.7	81.9
15–17	—	—	—	—	38.8	36.6	34.5
<15	1.0	0.9	0.8	0.8	1.2	1.3	1.2
Birthrates by marital status							
Marital (per 1,000 married)							
15–19	410.4	460.2	530.6	462.3	443.7	315.8	—
Out-of-wedlock (per 1,000 unmarried)							
15–19	12.6	15.1	15.3	16.7	22.4	24.2	25.5
18–19					32.9	32.8	35.0
15–17					17.1	19.5	20.7
Ratios of out-of-wedlock births (per 1,000 births)							
15–19	—	142	148	208	295	382	429
18–19	—	102	107	152	224	298	344
15–17	—	232	240	327	430	514	566
<15	—	663	679	785	808	870	882

Sources: DHEW, National Center for Health Statistics, *Vital Statistics*, Vol. 1, 1955, 1960, 1965, 1970 and 1975; ———, "Teenage Childbearing: United States, 1966–1975." *Monthly Vital Statistics Report 26(5)* Supplement (September 8, 1977); ———, "Advance Report, Final Natality Statistics, 1977." *Monthly Vital Statistics Report 27(11)* Supplement (February 5, 1979).

Table 2. Birth rates and out-of-wedlock birthrates for women under age 20, by race, United States, 1950–1977

Age and Race	Year						
	1950	1955	1960	1965	1970	1975	1977
A. Birthrates (per 1,000 women)							
15–19							
White	70.0	79.1	79.4	60.7	57.4	46.8	44.6
Black	163.5*	167.2*	156.1	140.6	147.7	113.8	107.3
18–19							
White	—	—	—	—	101.5	74.4	71.1
Black	—	—	—	—	204.9	156.0	147.6
15–17							
White	—	—	—	—	29.2	28.3	26.5
Black	—	—	—	—	101.4	86.6	81.2
10–14							
White	0.2	0.3	0.4	0.3	0.5	0.6	0.6
Black	5.1*	4.8*	4.3	4.3	5.2	5.1	4.7
B. Rates of out-of-wedlock births (per 1,000 unmarried women)							
15–19							
White	5.1	6.0	6.6	7.9	10.9	12.1	13.6
Black	68.5*	77.6*	76.5*	75.8*	96.9	95.1	93.2

*Rates are for nonwhites.

Sources: See Table 1.

unmarried white teenagers who conceived premaritally married before the birth of the child in 1963–1966. In the most recent period, 1975–1978, only 58 percent elected to marry. Among black teenagers, the percentage fell from 26 to eight.

Even though fewer premarital pregnancies are leading to marriage, more marital first births among whites (nearly half in 1975–1978) are premaritally conceived. As age at marriage has risen, relatively few nonpregnant teenagers are choosing to marry. It seems likely that a high proportion of teenage marriages are being hastened or contracted to legitimate the outcome of teenage conceptions. The changing schedule of family formulation is taken up in greater detail in Section I of the readings, especially in the reports by Beth Berkov and June Sklar and by Martin O'Connell and Maurice J. Moore (chapters 1 and 3).

Part of the concern about early childbearing probably reflects a more general apprehension about the rise in sexual activity among unmarried adolescents. Would increases in the premarital sexual activity of young people still cause public concern even if greater use of contraceptives and abortion resulted in a sharp diminution of out-of-wedlock teenage births? We believe that it would, and that the teenage parent has provided an opportunity for adults to discuss publicly the broader issue of the sexual mores and sexual instruction of the young.

Although we lack good evidence on patterns of sexual behavior among the young prior to the past decade, it is a safe assumption that youth has never even approached the ideal of premarital chastity. Historical records testify that premarital pregnancy has always been common in American society, although there were undoubtedly tremendous regional, religious and ethnic variations in adherence to sexual standards.[1] Those variations still persist, though there is some evidence that they may break down in the future as increasing numbers of adolescents opt for a more liberal sexual code.

In part, changes in adolescent sexual behavior may be a consequence of earlier sexual maturation of both girls and boys. There is good reason to believe that age at menarche fell dramatically during this century.[2] In the United States around 1970, the average age at menarche was just under 13; in many developing areas of the world it is still over 15, and even ranges up to 18.[3] Most of today's young women are therefore capable of becoming pregnant at younger ages. Sexual standards may be changing partly as a response to this pattern of earlier physical maturation.

While we can only speculate about sexual behavior in the past and the future, we have learned a good deal about recent trends through the national surveys conducted by Melvin Zelnik and John F. Kantner. As they show in Table 7 "Sexual and Contraceptive Experience of Young Unmarried Women in the United States, 1976 and 1971" (chapter 4 in this volume), there has been a sharp rise in the proportion of young women who have had sexual intercourse at each age. Noteworthy is the change in sexual patterns among the white women. Although their overall level of coital experience is lower, their rate of increase is faster, suggesting that white adolescents are "catching up" to blacks. As more whites, particularly those from the middle class, are exposed to the risk of pregnancy, the problem of adolescent sexuality will attract wider interest and will command more support for intervention.

Contraception for teenagers is one form of intervention that has received considerable attention. Availability has increased and, as Zelnik and Kantner's studies have shown, contraceptive use by teenagers is indeed preventing a large number of unwanted pregnancies and births. (They estimate that 680,000 additional nonmarital pregnancies per year would occur if it were not for use of contraceptives by teenagers.) It seems likely that the increased availability of abortion has both "permitted" more sexual experimentation and, at the same time, allowed teenagers to escape the consequences of an unwanted birth. However, it is difficult to determine the changes in use of abortion among teenagers because reliable data exist only for the period since its legalization in 1973. Each year since then, nearly one-third of the women obtaining abortions have been teenagers, and the total number of abortions has increased annually.[4] These changes in the availability of abortion and contraception may explain in part why adolescent fertility has declined in the face of increased sexual activity, as well as why proportionately fewer teenagers today marry upon becoming pregnant than did so some years ago. While abortion has served to conceal the growing sexual experience of teenagers, and to mitigate the potentially adverse effects of a rise in the adolescent birthrate, it has also drawn increased attention to teenage sexuality. In no small measure, opposition to abortion has forced attention to an issue that would previously have been swept under the rug. The controversy has pressured the public sector into action when it might have preferred to treat adolescent sexuality as a private concern, relegated to the jurisdiction of local communities, the churches, or the family. Later we will return to a more detailed discussion of the alternatives open to various parties interested in preventing premature parenthood.

The Consequences of Early Childbearing

In suggesting reasons why interest in adolescent pregnancies has mounted, we should not ignore the role of researchers in supplying information both to policy makers and to the general public through the mass media. Until 1970, only scattered studies of teenage parenthood existed. Since then, however, a consistent series of results on the consequences of teenage childbearing has emerged in this burgeoning area of research. Catherine Chilman has produced a comprehensive summary of the literature.[5] Here we only highlight some of the relevant findings.

Much research on the consequences of adolescent childbearing has followed one of two complementary approaches. One describes the life course of women (and men) who became parents as teenagers and the ways in which their experience differs from their peers who chose to or were able to postpone the birth of their first child. Other research has attempted to separate out the experiences *caused* by early childbearing and those that followed from pre-existing circumstances that produced the pregnancy and birth in the first place. Information has come from analyses of small, often nonrepresentative samples of individuals from whom extensive data were obtained (sometimes over a period of years), and from examination of much larger groups of individuals, selected randomly from the total U.S. population, whose responses, usually to structured questions, were much less detailed. The conclusions reached by these quite different routes, where comparable, are reassuringly consistent.

Teenage Childbearing and Health of the Mother and Child

Research has regularly shown that very young mothers and their children are subject to increased health risks during pregnancy and around the time of birth. To our knowledge, however, no studies have attempted to document any longer-term effects.

Higher rates of fetal mortality are found for women under age 20. Infants of teenage mothers have higher mortality rates both in the first month of life (when mortality results primarily from problems existing at birth) and in the remainder of the first year, when environmental conditions play a greater role. The high likelihood of prematurity and low birth weight is a distinct disadvantage for infants of young mothers. Prematurity is a critical factor in infant survival and is implicated in a host of later health problems. Recent data summarized by Wendy Baldwin and Virginia Cain (chapter 17) suggest that this disadvantage to infants can be compensated for, even in the case of very young mothers, by excellent prenatal care, but that longer-term risks to the infant's health are not so easily disposed of.[6]

The recent increase in teenage abortions may have contributed to the reduction in the U.S. infant mortality rate by reducing the number of low-birth-weight infants. The Institute of Medicine of the National Academy of Science, in its report on legalized abortion and the public health, speculates that "it should be possible to prove an effect of increased frequency of teenage abortions on the total proportion of newborns weighing less than 2,500 grams."[7] Data necessary for a thorough analysis are not available, but indirect observation was made by comparing the percentage decline in infant mortality rates between 1970 and 1972 in New York (9.3 percent), California (9.3 percent), and Washington (8.6 percent)—states that had liberalized their abortion laws—and the rest of the United States (6.9 percent). It is therefore possible that increased abortion has led to improved overall health of the infant population.[8]

Teenage Childbearing and Schooling

As one might expect from casual observation, teenage mothers, especially those under 18, are more likely to drop out of school than women who delay their first birth until they are in their 20s.[9] Between one-half and two-thirds of all female high school dropouts cite pregnancy and/or marriage as the principal reasons that they left school.[10] Significantly, the differences between those who drop out and those who do not are not merely a product of the young women's social background—their race, their parents' socioeconomic status, or their academic aptitude or expectations; in fact, early childbearing has a greater detrimental effect on educational attainment than any of these factors. Thus, early parenthood is a major *cause* of low educational attainment, and not just another element in a vicious cycle of poverty.

There is strong evidence that a teenage pregnancy is not merely a convenient excuse to drop out of school. Undoubtedly, an important reason why school-age mothers fail to complete their education lies in the enormous difficulties of simultaneously meeting the demands of schooling and those of child-rearing. However, in at least two studies, a majority of teenage mothers return to high school after delivery.[11] In Frank Furstenberg's Baltimore study, the majority of the mothers also managed to graduate.[12] As one might expect, socioeconomic and family backgrounds influence the likelihood of graduation. Additional childbearing, however, usually brings education to an abrupt halt. With each successive pregnancy, the proportion of dropouts rises. And as James Trussell and Jane Menken show in chapter 15, the likelihood of repeat pregnancies is quite high among teenage mothers.

Marriage, according to some recent evidence, may be a major complicating factor for teenagers. Women who marry as adolescents have an 80 percent chance of dropping out of school, whether or not they have an early birth.[13] Among teenage mothers, those who marry are twice as likely to drop out of high school as those who remain single. These findings are quite surprising and require more of an explanation than that provided by the heavy demands of conflicting roles. Specifically, why should marriage be so much more burdensome than caring for an infant? Preexisting motivations and aspirations appear to play a part. The more educationally ambitious young mothers are more likely both to delay marriage and to postpone further childbearing.[14] Other young mothers, including some with little interest in pursuing careers, opt for marriage and reliance on a spouse rather than preparation for employment. Unfortunately, this choice all too often works out to the women's disadvantage, since so many teenage marriages fail. Marriage may also reduce the woman's chances for additional education because of increased childbearing. Married teenagers are more likely to bear another child shortly after the first birth than those who remain single, thereby reducing even further their chances of meeting the heavy demands of schooling and motherhood.

Early Childbearing and Marriage

A high proportion of teenagers who conceive a child out of wedlock have, at least until rather recently, married before the birth of the child. Although marriage is less likely to follow a teenage pregnancy today, many teenagers still resolve an early pregnancy by a precipitate marriage, or at least by wedding much earlier than they otherwise might have done.

Both early pregnancy and early marriage impair a couple's chance of conjugal stability. Data from census materials and surveys explicitly designed to examine the effect of nuptial and birth timing on marriage duration convincingly demonstrate that women who marry as teenagers are more likely to separate and divorce than those who marry later and conceive after wedlock.[15] The subsequent marriages of women whose first birth was out of wedlock are more likely to be dissolved than those of women who gave birth at the same age but who married prior to delivery. Over the long term, marriages that follow conception are more likely to be dissolved than marriages of nonpregnant brides. Some have argued that the source of marital instability lies more in early marriage than in early childbearing. There is little question that early marriages are less stable than later ones, irrespective of the woman's age at first childbirth or whether that birth occurs after marriage. It is possible, however, that an early first birth may actully promote the stability of an early marriage.[16] The child may provide the couple with a reason to remain married in spite of the many problems associated with early marriage—psychological immaturity, lack of preparation for parental and conjugal roles, and limited socioeconomic achievement.

A significant proportion of young mothers, especially blacks, who separate do not divorce, even by five years after the couple has separated.[17] Furstenberg has attributed this pattern in part to a feeling that there is no need for divorce unless and until another marriage is contemplated.[18] Black women, whatever their age at marriage or childbirth, are far less likely than white women to remarry once the first union terminates. Socioeconomic status and parity may, therefore, be more important determinants of legal divorce and remarriage than the age factors considered here.

There are a number of possible reasons why a premarital pregnancy, particularly one which occurs early in life, lessens the chances of a stable marriage. First, the bonds between the young couple are often only newly formed. Additionally, a marriage in the early teens pulls the young mother away from her family of origin, often sooner than otherwise might have occurred. Many young mothers are both psychologically and economically unprepared to depart from the parental household. Indeed, a substantial minority of those who marry soon after delivery continue to live with their parents, at least for a time. Although these arrangements are partly an adaptation to economic problems, they frequently limit the young parents' commitment to the marriage, particularly when its prospects appear bleak. On the other hand, an early marriage is more likely to last when the mother marries the father of the child rather than another man,[19] perhaps because, in this case, the bond between the parents is strengthened by their common attachment to the child.

A number of studies have demonstrated that economic resources are essential for the survival of a marriage, regardless of the partners' ages.[20] Frequently, early parenthood forces young men and women to leave school and enter the labor market prematurely, thus eroding their prospects of long-term economic advancement.[21] Paradoxically, couples who marry in order to provide for a child conceived out of wedlock typically are separated after a few years because the male finds himself unemployed or in a menial job with little prospect of improving his situation. Thus, it hardly matters whether marriage occurs following an early birth; most of the young women end up with the main responsibility of rearing the child.

Teenage Childbearing and Subsequent Fertility

The earlier a women's age at marriage, the greater her level and pace of subsequent childbearing.[22] Moreover, whatever a woman's age at marriage, a premarital first birth leads to a higher level of fertility.[23] Nevertheless, there is evidence that it is not a *premarital* birth but an *early* birth that eventuates in increased childbearing. The earlier a woman's age at first birth, the greater her fertility for up to 15 years later and the greater the proportion of out-of-wedlock and unwanted births she experiences.[24] The consequences of early childbearing vary little by race or level of educational attainment. In fact, age at first birth accounts for about half of the racial and educational differences in completed fertility. These results suggest a need for birth control services among all adolescents, younger and older, single and married.

It should be noted here that there is little evidence to support the argument advanced by some authors that early childbearing is the inevitable product of generous welfare payments. Several studies have found no relationship between public assistance payments and the level of teenage childbearing.[25] The "broodsow myth" remains popular, however, despite the fact that women on welfare have been shown to regulate their fertility as well as other women when given access to the means of birth control (see chapter 12).[26]

Teenage Childbearing and Occupational and Economic Achievement

Adolescent childbearing seriously injures the young parents'—especially the young mother's—occupational and economic prospects.[27] These consequences are independent of and even more severe than the disadvantages resulting from minority status or poor socioeconomic background.[28] For women, at least, there is evidence that childbearing influences income primarily by curtailing education.[29]

Both Furstenberg[30] (see chapter 12) and Card and Wise[31] (see chapter 13) found that young mothers are in a precarious economic situation—they are more likely to have relatively low incomes and less satisfactory jobs, or to require public assistance. The extremely high proportion of women living in households receiving Aid for Dependent Children who had borne a child as a teenager (61 percent in 1976, accounting for half of AFDC expenditures) attests to the high welfare burden associated with early childbearing (see chapter 7).[32]

In part, the consequences of early childbearing for economic independence may depend on the woman's marital career and on her pattern of childbearing following the first birth. For all teenage parents, irrespective of marital status, child care is essential to their efforts to find stable employment. Thus a kinship network that can provide childcare support is one of the critical conditions determining whether young mothers will work or must rely on welfare.[33] Policy makers have been slow to recognize the important function that can be played by the family in mitigating some of the adverse effects of early childbearing on the young parent.

Long-Term Consequences for the Children of Early Childbearers

For children of teenagers, surprisingly few consequences directly associated with parental age have been found. The children, of course, share in the social and economic disadvantages already described in detail: namely, the greater likelihood of living in a one-parent home, with a parent who is immature, badly educated, poor, or dependent on welfare. Children of teenage parents tend to become adolescent parents themselves; and they appear to be more likely to demonstrate poor cognitive development and to have more problems of social and behavioral adjustment than other children.[34] However, family structure is apparently far more important than the age of the mother in influencing psychological and intellectual growth and maturation. The cognitive development of the child is less likely to be impaired if a teenage mother lives with other adults who share childrearing than if she lives alone. Again, whether or not a supportive network exists may be a critical determinant of the life course of teenage parents and their children.

Determinants of Teenage Childbearing

Once it has been ascertained that teenage childbearing has serious negative consequences, it becomes essential to pinpoint its determinants. In comparison to the relatively well-documented consequences of early parenthood, there is a paucity of information on antecedents. Theories about the etiology of early childbearing have often failed to take into account the fact that parenthood is the result of social process. There has been a tendency to search for psychological or characterological factors that motivate adolescents to enter parenthood prematurely, such as the need for affection, the quest for adult status, resolution of the Oedipal conflict, the desire to escape parental control, or the inability to foresee a more gratifying future. While some of these reasons no doubt apply in some instances, the fact remains that most studies show that only a tiny minority of adolescents become parents because they want to have a child (at least at the time conception occurs). There is little evidence of self-selection for motherhood. Most become pregnant unwillingly and unwittingly, though, to be sure, once conception occurs many are reluctant to terminate the pregnancy by abortion. Adolescents typically have reasons why they want a child once they have become pregnant, but these reasons do not necessarily explain why the pregnancy initially occurred.

Too little research has been done on how and why teenagers begin to have sexual relations. The few existing studies show the powerful influence of peer groups, the difficulty that parents have in communicating and reinforcing their sexual expectations, and the competing interests of young males and females in heterosexual interaction. Clearly, many teenagers are unprepared to assume responsibility for their sexual behavior. This is partly due to the fact that the transition to nonvirginity is seldom premeditated.

It follows, then, that regular use of contraception will be relatively rare among adolescents just beginning to engage in sexual relations. Since most girls or young women do not foresee having intercourse when it first happens, most fail to take the necessary steps to prevent pregnancy. Occasionally, their male partners are equipped with a condom; typically, however, the young men do not have the same interest in contraception. Since they are less affected by the consequences of an early conception. Not surprisingly, then, most studies show that only a minority of teenagers use contraception when intercourse first occurs; and, of course, as time elapses, many nonusers become pregnant. Indeed, as Laurie Schwab Zabin, John F. Kantner and Melvin Zelnik report in chapter 8, half of teenage pregnancies occur in the first six months after intercourse is initiated.

Individuals who do receive family planning information and instruction are much less likely to experience an unplanned pregnancy. Several studies suggest, however, that many teenagers equipped with the means of contraception have difficulty using them over a sustained period. This difficulty is increased because of the intermittent nature of intercourse among teenagers—especially young teenagers—for whom intercourse is often perceived, or rationalized, as unexpected. While psychological factors undoubtedly play an important part in the rate of contraceptive compliance among teenagers, we should recognize that contraception is not easy to use, even for adults, over a lengthy period of time. Accordingly, many adults elect to become sterilized rather than encounter the risks of imperfect use or the perceived dangers associated with the pill or the IUD.

Teenagers do not have that option and are forced to make use of contraceptive methods that at best are technically effective but difficult to use. It is quite likely that if teenagers had to take a pill to become pregnant, early childbearing would quickly vanish as a major social problem. In addition, contraceptives are considerably less accessible to teenagers than to married adults. Legal restrictions against the provision of contraception to minors (at any rate, to "mature" minors) have been relaxed by action of legislatures or, more often, the courts. But many doctors and clinics still refuse to give teenagers contraceptives without their parents' consent. Embarrassment and lack of knowledge about where to go also contribute to unavailability for many teenagers. Many others have mistaken ideas about pregnancy risks—they think they are too young, or have intercourse too seldom or at the wrong time of the month to get pregnant.

Approximately one-third of all teenage pregnancies and one-half of all pregnancies occurring to women under age 18 are terminated by abortion. If pregnancies are generally unwanted, why are abortions not more prevalent? In fact, teenagers turn to abortion much more often than older women who are more experienced contraceptors: one-third of all legal abortions are to teenagers, who represent only one-fifth of the population of reproductive-aged women. In addition, even more than is the case with contraception, abortion is not always an easily available alternative to a teenager with limited means. The Hyde amendment, which has cut off practically all federally subsidized abortions for the poor, has probably affected pregnant teenagers more than any other age group. Even before Hyde went into effect in 1977, many teenagers were denied abortions unless they had the permission of their parents. Although blanket parental consent statutes have since been declared invalid by the Supreme Court, teenagers can still be required to go through a complex and time-consuming court procedure if they wish to obtain an abortion without their parents' knowledge or consent. It is also certain that many teenagers, as do their parents, disapprove of abortion. One suspects, however, that some adolescents who decline the option of having an abortion are not fully aware of the hardships that will be imposed on them as a result of early childbearing, or feel that the price of adolescent parenthood may be offset by the advantages of motherhood.[35]

Prospects for the Future and Implications for Social Programs

In this overview, we have summarized only a portion of the growing body of research on the consequences of teenage childbearing. Despite the diversity of research designs, populations studied, and measures employed, we have observed a remarkable degree of consistency in the results obtained by reseachers. Early childbearing creates a distinctly higher risk of social and economic disadvantages, in great part because it complicates the transition to adulthood by disrupting schooling and creating pressures for early marriage and further fertility. We are disposed to conclude that premature parenthood is one of the social conditions that maintain the cycle of poverty.

This leads us to ask what social measures can be taken to lessen the effects of early and unplanned parenthood. As public awareness of the costs of adolescent childbearing has grown in the past decade, services have developed to equip the young parent to handle the economic and psychological demands of child care. Prenatal services providing medical care to the mother and child, special educational programs permitting the young mother to remain in school during the transition to parenthood, child care services, and contraceptive instruction are but a few measures in an arsenal of social interventions that have been devised by public and private agencies to reduce the adverse effects of early childbearing.

In 1978, the House of Representatives constituted a Select Committee on Population, which chose adolescent childbearing as one of the three main topics it considered in the area of U.S. fertility. Among its recommendations, the Committee urged the allocation of an additional $65 million in funds for family planning projects, in order to increase the number of program sites so that more adolescents at risk of unwanted pregnancy could be served. It called for "changes in service-delivery strategies" to reach more teenagers in need, the elimination of legal impediments and of factors which contribute to "lack of motivation to utilize available services." The Committee specifically recommended greater use of nontraditional approaches to birth control, such as vending machines for condoms and foam.

It asked for federal encouragement of sex education programs run by the schools as well as by private and religious groups. (A recent Gallup survey found that only 40 percent of 13–18-year-old boys and girls had ever had a sex education course in school, and only 30 percent had a course that included instruction in birth control.)[36]

The Committee also urged the federal government to support comprehensive health and social programs for pregnant teenagers and teenage parents. It noted, however, that such comprehensive programs were far more expensive than family planning programs, and were not so clearly successful as preventive programs in dealing with undesirable social outcomes such as dropping out of school.[37]

The Committee was not reconstituted, and there is no substitute group in Congress that considers this area its special interest. However, Congress did approve legislation in 1978 to support a network of comprehensive programs for pregnant teenage parents. The Adolescent Health Services and Pregnancy Prevention and Care Act is designed to coordinate and integrate the disparate services to teenage parents as well as to channel some additional monies to agencies for new programs. Appropriations were $1 million in its first year and $17.5 million in its second year. Assuming that the appropriations are spent, what can we expect the effect of this legislation to be on the well-being of young parents and their children?

While we believe that the bill passed by Congress represents a positive initiative on the part of the federal government, we do not hold out much hope that it will substantially alter the life chances of adolescent parents and their babies. Our research and the findings of others persuade us that the single most important obstacle facing the teenage parent is economic insecurity.

Lack of skills, minimal daycare support, and the uncertainties of the labor market conspire to create an uncertain economic future for teenage parents and their offspring. Unless jobs become more readily available, it is certain that many adolescent mothers will be compelled to turn to public assistance for support. Few are in a position to be fully supported by the child's father, who frequently cannot find work himself. Families are often willing to extend resources when they can to the young mother, but the assistance is unpredictable. Economic disadvantage erodes the possibility of a stable conjugal partnership, and marital breakup in turn jeopardizes the child's life chances.

In pointing to the need for stable and remunerative employment for teenage parents, we are well aware of the potential costs involved. Childcare services, vocational training, and public service jobs are suffering cutbacks for lack of taxpayer support. Given the political climate, it is unlikely that this trend will be reversed in the near future. Indeed, we do not look forward to much change until a labor market shortage develops in this country, an event that may not occur until the latter part of this century, when the fertility declines of recent decades begin to shrink the size of the labor force.

In the meantime, we must look to other strategies for coping with the undesirable consequences of early parenthood. We believe the most promising approach is a much more vigorous campaign to prevent most teenage childbearing, almost all of which is unwanted. There are some encouraging signs.

Schools are gradually introducing sex education courses into the curriculum, a step which is bound to provoke a host of political, ethical, and social problems in the communities involved. Thus far, most such programs are not introduced until high school, after many young people have begun sexual activity; and they do not effectively communicate to the students the risks of pregnancy or how and where they can obtain means to avoid it. (A notable exception, in two high schools in St. Paul, has been described by Laura Edwards.[38] But even here, the effectiveness of the program in preventing pregnancy was much less when it was introduced at the high school level than when it was introduced on a pilot basis in a junior high school.) Nonetheless, as such programs increase, it appears unavoidable that parents will be encouraged, if not pushed, to share the task of providing sexual socialization to the young. Only rarely have family planners directed their attention to educating parents, who are often ill-prepared to provide guidance and instruction to their teenage offspring. It also seems clear that churches, voluntary organizations such as the Scouts, and special interest groups will need to take a more active part in equipping youth with sexual knowledge, decision-making skills and family planning services.

At present, researchers have little to say about the likely success of such public education campaigns in controlling teenage pregnancies, though only the most optimistic planners believe that family planning and sex education and contraceptive services by themselves will reduce adolescent births to an insignificant number. (We assume that the prevalence of sexual activity is not likely to decline in the immediate future, a proposition with which few experts disagree.) Given the many reservations that teenagers have about birth control, the ambivalent feelings that often accompany nonmarital sexuality, and the psychological propensity of many adolescents toward risk-taking, we may expect a substantial, though diminished, rate of premarital pregnancy in years to come.

Teenage pregnancies could probably be reduced sharply however, with the proper mixture of luck and social determination. Only good luck, coupled with an increase in research dollars, will give us a safe contraceptive method more suited to teenagers, for whom sex tends to be episodic and unexpected, than those currently available. The most likely prospect is for a postcoital contraceptive, taken either shortly after intercourse or at the time of expected menses. The Center for Population Research of the National Institute of Child Health and Human Development has announced a stepped-up program of research into such a method, but it is unlikely that a workable method will be generally available for at least 10 years.

Social determination would best be evidenced by facing the fact of increasing sexual activity by unwed teenagers at earlier and earlier ages, and not considering it a social deviation to be treated on a case-finding basis so that those who are still virgins might not be corrupted.

While we have not succeeded in preventing all teenagers from taking up smoking, we have reversed the trend of decades. This was accomplished by a massive educational program in the media and through the schools and private organizations, financed by government and private health and social service agencies. We did not limit ourselves to setting up discreet smoking clinics to which teenagers could go if they felt the urge to smoke or if they were already caught in the toils of tobacco.

Yet, this is exactly how society treats the problem of adolescent pregnancy prevention. With very few exceptions, school sex education programs do not provide young people with specific information that will help them make reasoned judgments about when to begin sexual activity, or about how and where services may be obtained that will help them prevent pregnancy. The programs do not even communicate effectively about the risk of pregnancy in relation to age and the menstrual cycle. Magazines, newspapers, television, and radio do not accompany their antismoking messages with comparable adjurements against sexual risk-taking. Church and youth groups are still more likely to provide proscriptions than prescriptions to avoid pregnancy. In order to avoid corrupting the young and sexually inexperienced, sexual information too often is not given to the teeenager until it is too late to prevent the first pregnancy.

That is why there has been so much emphasis on secondary pregnancy prevention—that is, prescription of birth control after the teenager is known to be sexually active because she has delivered a baby or obtained an abortion or (far less often) because she had displayed the initiative and determination to seek out professional birth control help on her own before beginning sexual activity. (Indeed, it is extraordinary that more than one million teenagers find their way each year to family planning clinics, and that a similar number obtain services from private physicans.)

If the current case-finding approach to adolescent pregnancy prevention continues, society will probably have to face the unpleasant prospect of an increasing number of abortions to teenagers each year as a necessary backup to failed contraception. Such an increase is likely to further stir controversy on the issue of legal abortion. Reasoned debate is not likely to prevail where concern over the morality of abortion is combined with concern over the sexual mores of our youth. Exhortations against sexual experimentation are not likely to reduce sexual activity among young people, and the recent federal legislation to help teenage parents and their babies is not likely to offset the severe economic and social costs of early childbearing. Our best strategy is to prevent as many unwanted pregnancies as possible in the first place. To do this, society will have to make the difficult decision to transmit the knowledge and the means of pregnancy prevention to *all* teenagers—not just those known to be sexually active. There is the chance that some, thereby, may be encouraged to experiment with sex somewhat earlier than they would have done otherwise, although there is no evidence that provision of information about sexual decision-making or contraception encourages teenagers to initiate sexual intercourse earlier than they might have done without such information.

In this brief overview of service needs, we have not given adequate space to the immense complexities of providing programs for adolescents. Generally speaking, most health and social services programs have been tailored to suit the convenience of professionals, not the clients they serve. Teenagers looking for contraceptive information and services have had to seek them out, often against considerable obstacles. At relatively low cost, family planning programs have begun to remove these barriers by making service programs more accommodating to the adolescent lifestyle. More flexible clinic hours, more attractive and congenial settings for service programs, outreach by community workers, subsidized transportation, and peer-based counseling are but a few of the innovations that have been made to reach the teenage population.

When we remember that a decade ago, few programs existed for the teenage population, and two decades ago it would have been unthinkable to equip unmarried adolescents with contraceptives, it should be clear that enormous strides have been made in the prevention of unwanted pregnancy. Though these gains have not come easily, they auger well for a more enlightened approach to teenage sexuality in the future.

References

1. I. L. Reiss, *The Social Contract of Premarital Sexual Permissiveness*, New York, Holt, Rinehart and Winston, 1967; D. S. Smith, "The Dating of the American Sexual Revolution: Evidence and Interpretation," in Michael Gordon, ed., *The American Family in Social-Historical Perspective*, St. Martin's Press, New York, 1973.
2. J. M. Tanner, "Age at Menarche: Evidence on the Rate of Human Maturation," paper read at the second annual general meeting of the British Society for Population Studies, 1975.
3. J. Trussell and R. Steckel, "The Age of Slaves at Menarche and Their First Birth," *Journal of Interdisciplinary History*, **8**, 3 (Winter): 477, 1978.
4. DHEW, Center for Disease Control, *Abortion Surveillance 1972–1978*, published 1973–1979, Atlanta, Georgia.
5. C. S. Chilman, "Social and Psychological Aspects of Adolescent Sexuality: An Analytic Overview of Research and Theory," report prepared for National Institute of Child Health and Human Development, Contract NO1-HD-52821, by the Institute for Family Development, Center for Advanced Studies in Human Services, School of Social Welfare, University of Wisconsin, Milwaukee, 1977.
6. W. S. Baldwin and V. S. Cain, "The Children of Teenage Parents," chapter 17, below.
7. National Academy of Sciences, *Legalized Abortion and the Public Health*, Institute of Medicine Publication 75-02. The National Academy of Sciences, Washington, D.C. 1975.
8. Ibid.
9. C. S. Chilman, 1977, op. cit.; K. A. Moore, L. J. Waite, S. B. Caldwell and S. L. Hofferth, "The Consequences of Age at First Childbirth: Educational Attainment," Working Paper 1146-01, The Urban Institute, Washington, D.C., 1978; J. J. Card and L. L. Wise, "Teenage Mothers and Teenage Fathers: The Impact of Early Childbearing on the Parents' Personal and Professional Lives," chapter 13, below.
10. J. Coombs and W. W. Cooley, "Dropouts: In High School and After School," *American Educational Research Journal*, **5**: 343, 1968; K. A. Moore, L. J. Waite, S. L. Hofferth and S. B. Caldwell, "The Consequences of Age at First Childbirth: Marriage, Separation, and Divorce," Working Paper 1146-03, The Urban Institute, Washington, D.C., 1978.
11. F. F. Furstenberg, Jr., *Unplanned Parenthood: The Social Consequences of Teenage Childbearing*, The Free Press, New York, 1976; K. A. Moore, L. J. Waite, S. B. Caldwell and S. L. Hofferth, 1978, op. cit.
12. F. F. Furstenberg, Jr., 1976, op. cit.
13. K. A. Moore, L. J. Waite, S. L. Hofferth and S. B. Caldwell, 1978, op. cit.
14. F. F. Furstenberg, Jr., 1976, op. cit.
15. Ibid.; J. J. Card, "Long Term Consequences for Children Born to Adolescent Parents," Final Report, prepared for the National Institute of Child Health and Human Development, Contract HD-72820, by the American Institutes for Research, Palo Alto, California, 1978; J. McCarthy and J. Menken, "Marriage, Remarriage, Marriage Disruption and Age at First Birth," chapter 14, below; J. J. Card and L. L. Wise, chapter 13, below; J. Menken, J. Trussell, D. Stempel and O. Babakol, unpublished manuscript, "Marriage Dissolution in the United States: Applications of Proportional Hazard Models."
16. K. A. Moore, L. S. Waite, S. L. Hofferth and S. B. Caldwell, 1978, op. cit.
17. J. McCarthy, "A Comparison of the Probability of the Dissolution of First and Second Marriages," *Demography*, **15**, 3: 345, 1978.
18. F. F. Furstenberg, Jr., 1976, op. cit.
19. M. Sauber and E. Corrigan, *The Six Year Experience of Unwed Mothers as Parents*, Community Council of Greater New York, New York, 1970.

20. J. Bernard, "Marital Stability and Patterns of Status Variables," *Journal of Marriage and the Family,* **28**: 421, 1966; H. Carter and P. C. Glick, *Marriage and Divorce: A Social and Economic Study,* revised edition. Harvard University Press, Cambridge, 1976; J. R. Udry, "Marital Instability by Race, Sex, Education, and Occupation Using 1960 Census Data," *American Journal of Sociology,* **72**: 203, 1966; J. R. Udry, "Marital Instability by Race and Income Based on 1960 Census Data," *American Journal of Sociology,* **72**: 673, 1967.

21. F. F. Furstenberg, Jr., 1976; op. cit.; J. J. Card and L. L. Wise, chapter 13, below.

22. C. F. Westoff and N. B. Ryder, *The Contraceptive Revolution,* Princeton University Press, Princeton, 1977.

23. L. Coombs and R. Freedman, "Premarital Pregnancy, Childspacing, and Later Economic Achievement," *Population Studies,* **24**: 389, 1970.

24. J. Trussell and J. Menken, "Early Childbearing and Subsequent Fertility," Chapter 15, below.

25. P. J. Placek and G. E. Hendershot, "Public Welfare and Family Planning: An Empirical Study of the 'Brood Sow' Myth," *Social Problems,* **21**: 658, 1974.

26. F. F. Furstenberg, Jr., 1976, op. cit.

27. J. J. Card and L. L. Wise, chapter 12, below.

28. J. J. Card, 1978, op. cit.

29. J. Trussell and J. Abowd, "Teenage Mothers, Labor Force Participation and Wage Rates," in J. Menken, J. McCarthy and J. Trussell, *Sequelae to Teenage Pregnancy,* Final Report, National Institute of Child Health and Human Development, Contract NO1-HD-62858, Office of Population Research, Princeton, 1979 (mimeo).

30. F. F. Furstenberg, Jr., 1978, op. cit.

31. J. J. Card and L. L. Wise, chapter 13, below.

32. K. A. Moore and S. B. Caldwell, "The Effect of Government Policies on Out-of-Wedlock Sex and Pregnancy," chapter 7, below.

33. F. F. Furstenberg, Jr., and A. G. Crawford, "Family Support: Helping Teenage Mothers to Cope," chapter 18, below. *Teenage Pregnancy in a Family Context: Implications for Policy,* edited by Theodora Ooms. Temple University Press, Philadelphia, Pa., 1980.

34. W. Baldwin and V. S. Cain, chapter 17, below.

35. F. F. Furstenberg, Jr., 1978, op. cit.

36. G. Gallup, "Teens Claim Sex Education Classes Helpful," Gallup Youth Survey, Princeton, N. J., Oct. 4, 1978.

37. Select Committee on Population, U.S. House of Representatives, *Final Report,* Serial F., U.S. Government Printing Office, Washington, D.C. 1978.

38. L. E. Edwards, M. E. Steinman, K. A. Arnold and E. Y. Hakanson, "Adolescent Pregnancy Prevention Service in High School Clinics." chapter 25, below.

I
Trends and
Their Interpretation

Teenagers today are growing up in a world in which fundamental changes are taking place in sexual attitudes and experience. While continuing the documentation of teenage fertility trends begun in the Overview, the papers in this section take up the question of identifying those aspects of reproductive behavior that have shifted in recent years and assessing their contributions to the declines in overall teenage fertility. The transitions in marriage, marital fertility, nonmarital conceptions, the initiation and frequency of sexual activity, and the use of contraception and abortion are all examined. Controversial views regarding social attitudes and programs that either promote or restrain sexual activity and fertility among teenagers are frequently expressed in these readings. Finally, the future course of fertility and family life is treated in the last two articles.

Teenage fertility has fallen, in large part, according to Beth Berkov and June Sklar, because of changes associated with postponement of marriage (see chapter 1). By the time of their study in the early 1970s, teenage marriage rates had plummeted. They have continued to fall throughout the decade. In addition, fertility within marriage has followed a downward course.

Teenage marital fertility has traditionally been high because many brides entered marriage already pregnant. Since fewer teenagers and their sexual partners are choosing to marry before the birth of the child, marital fertility has fallen. However, it is doubtful that this change accounts completely for the dramatic drop in fertility within marriage. There was also a decline in fertility resulting from declining marital conceptions. Perhaps because married teenagers are older, or because they have become more adept at controlling their fertility through contraception or abortion, they are delivering fewer babies.

The contrast between declining marital fertility and increasing nonmarital fertility begs for further analysis and interpretation. The pioneering work of Melvin Zelnik and John F. Kantner (chapters 4 and 5) offers a wealth of relevant information. Their two studies, carried out in 1971 and 1976, disclose sharp changes: sexual activity among teenagers starts at younger ages and has increased in frequency. The changes are greater for white than for black teenagers (reflecting the much greater level of sexual activity prevalent among black teenagers by 1971). Zelnik and Kantner also found that use both of contraception generally and of the most effective methods in particular increased remarkably in the five years between their surveys. Just published data from these investigators' 1979 survey shows that sexual activity and contraceptive use have continued to increase—but there has been a decline in use of the most effective methods, the pill and the IUD, and a corresponding rise in use of the most unreliable method, withdrawal. Ironically, teenagers, who are generally least vulnerable to health risks from the pill and most vulnerable to unwanted pregnancy, have also been most influenced to give up the pill without substituting another effective method.[1] Perhaps, for this reason, the proportion of sexually active teenagers who became pregnant for the first time remained at about the same level. (Recent analysis of their 1976 study results, not reported in this volume, indicates that the number of subsequent pregnancies did decline over the five-year period; this finding reinforces the conclusion reached in the Overview that birth control information and services are often reaching teenagers too late for effective primary pregnancy prevention.[2]) Despite the decline in marriages entered in order to legitimate births, *fewer* pregnant teenagers are delivering babies out of wedlock. The increase in the availability and choice of abortion and in the use of contraception to prevent repeat pregnancies has reduced the proportion of teenagers who become mothers.

Although, as Zelnik and Kantner show in chapter 6, teenage contraceptive use is preventing a large number of premarital pregnancies (an estimated 680,000 per year), increased and more regular use could further reduce unwanted teenage pregnancies significantly—by about 480,000 if all unmarried teenagers practiced contraception at current levels of effectiveness. If there were greater and more consistent use of the most effective methods, pregnancies would be reduced even further. (They note that teenagers who consistently use the most effective methods are only one-tenth as likely to get pregnant as nonusers.) They discuss in detail both the methods chosen by (or for) teenagers and the need for safe and effective contraceptives acceptable to this age group.

Berkov and Sklar conclude in their article that changing abortion patterns reduced out-of-wedlock births for a time. These findings, however, have never been confirmed on a national level. Earlier and increased adolescent sexual activity has more than offset increases in contraception and abortion to produce sharply rising illegitimacy rates for women under 20. The decline in legitimation has not been an important influence on out-of-wedlock childbearing.

O'Connell and Moore make use of recent data from the Current Population Survey to depict the changing sequence of family formation. In chapter 3, they demonstrate that teenage fertility patterns have sharply diverged from the patterns of women in their early twenties. Showing that first births to women in their teens (especially those 15 to 17) increasingly occur outside of marriage. O'Connell and Moore point to the necessity of rethinking strategies for extending family planning services to the adolescent population, a topic pursued in later sections of this volume.

Opinions, frequently controversial, about the causes and consequences of these changes are expressed throughout these readings. While we do not agree with all the views offered, we present them to dramatize the lack of a consensus among researchers, hindering the development of clear-cut guidelines for policy and program decisions.

An explanation of the rise in teenage sexual activity and illegitimacy is considered basic to deriving policies aimed at reducing adolescent fertility and its consequences. Berkov and Sklar suggest several reasons for increased out-of-wedlock childbearing.

They imply that young girls gamble at forcing a marriage when they become pregnant and that out-of-wedlock births have increased because young men (or their parents) have changed the game, and the gamble is paying off less well. They also imply a belief that declining sanctions against illegitimacy and social welfare programs serve to promote illegitimacy by not *deterring* it. In chapter 2 Phillips Cutright and Frank Furstenberg take them to task for these views. Kristin Moore and Steven B. Caldwell actually examined welfare support in relation to out-of-wedlock childbearing and conclude that availability and high levels of payments of Aid to Families with Dependent Children (AFDC) are not incentives to childbearing (see chapter 7). They do find, on the other hand, that the availability of subsidized family planning programs is related to a reduction in teenage pregnancies. Zelnik and Kantner suggest that because of the rising labor force participation of women, the home, which is left empty during the day, offers an enticing locale and increasing opportunity for sexual activity by the children. Clearly no satisfactory explanation has yet emerged.

Utilizing the Zelnik and Kantner data, Laurie Zabin reports in chapter 8 that because of early age at initiation of intercourse and the associated nonuse of contraception, half of first premarital pregnancies to teenagers occur in the first six months after they begin intercourse; one-fifth occur in the first month. She points out that most teenagers do not seek out contraceptive assistance until they have been sexually active for about a year; and she concludes that programs to prevent adolescent pregnancy will not succeed unless they reach young people before they begin sexual activity. While the figures on timing of pregnancy may be imprecise because of the tendency of adolescents to conceal longer exposure to sexual activity, her general conclusions are consistent with other empirical findings.

Even the most dedicated proponents of widespread contraceptive information and availability for teenagers are aware that their efforts may promote sexual activity, even while they are reducing pregnancy among the sexual active. Most are convinced, however, that so many institutional changes in society are promoting sex at all ages that the need for prevention of the consequences of teenage intercourse must prevail.

The two concluding papers in this section attempt to place our concerns in a larger perspective. The need for acceptable, effective contraception for adolescents is underscored in chapter 9 by Christopher Tietze, who projects the trends in pregnancy, births, and abortions forward from 1978 to 1984 to estimate that, unless contraception increases, close to 40 percent of girls who were 14 in 1978 will have at least one pregnancy before they reach age 20 in 1984.

Finally, in chapter 10, Charles Westoff speculates on the declining fertility and the changing marriage and family patterns of the entire population, reminding us that fertility is, overall, highly controlled in this and other developed countries. Rather than agonizing over high teenage fertility, we may in the future be concerned about the low birthrates at all ages.

References

1. M. Zelnik and J. F. Kantner, "Sexual Activity, Contraceptive Use and Pregnancy Among Metropolitan-Area Teenagers: 1971–1979," *Family Planning Perspectives*, **12**:5, 1980.
2. M. Zelnik and J. F. Kantner, "Second Pregnancies to Premaritally Pregnant Teenagers, 1976 and 1971," *Family Planning Perspectives*, **12**:69, 1980.

Teenage Family Formation in Postwar America

June Sklar and Beth Berkov

Teenagers have come into their own as a demographic force in American society. The total number of Americans of all ages increased by 13 percent—from 179 million to 203 million—between 1960 and 1970. But because of the post-World War II surge in birth rates, the number of Americans aged 15-19 jumped by 46 percent — from 13 million to 19 million during the same period.[1] The teenage population in the United States has continued to expand as the children who were born during the peak baby boom years in the late 1950s have entered the early reproductive ages. By the end of the 1970s and the beginning of the 1980s, when this group moves into the prime childbearing ages of 20-29, it will largely determine future rates of population growth. At the same time that the ranks of the American teenage population are being swelled by the entry of the baby boom cohorts, today's teenagers are also growing up in a period when far-reaching and significant changes appear to be occurring in sexual attitudes and behavior, women's roles and the family. They are also arriving on the reproductive scene at the moment when legal abortion is becoming a realistic option throughout the United States for women who have unwanted pregnancies. These changes presumably are having an impact not only upon the pattern of family formation of today's teenagers, but upon the milieu of family life into which the next generation of children will be socialized as well.

Methods

The significance of the massive demographic shifts and fundamental social changes being experienced by the current crop of teenagers has led us to investigate the manner and rate at which they are presently starting their childbearing ca-

This article is adapted from a paper presented at the 1974 annual meeting of the Population Association of America, held April 18–20, in New York City. The paper was prepared as part of a cooperative project between International Population and Urban Research, University of California, Berkeley, and the California Department of Health. The project is headed by Professor Kingsley Davis and supported by a contract with the National Institute of Child Health and Human Development, Center for Population Research (NIH NICHD-73-2728). The California data were made available through the cooperation of the California Department of Health, in particular George C. Cunningham, Chief, Maternal and Child Health Unit, and Paul W. Shipley, Chief, Vital Statistics Section. We thank Arlene Guerriero and Sarah Lee Tsai for research assistance and Kingsley Davis for his advice and encouragement.

reers, and how this pattern compares with that of previous cohorts. To do this, we used published federal marriage and birth data through 1969. In addition, we used data developed through a joint effort between International Population and Urban Research at the University of California, Berkeley, and the California Department of Health. These data consist of our own estimates of legitimate and illegitimate birthrates for the country as a whole for the period 1965-1971, and the most current marriage, birth, and abortion information available for the State of California. The more recent U.S. data used in this paper come from our larger study of the impact of legal abortion on fertility, reported elsewhere.* For that study, we developed independent estimates of birthrates for all age groups of women in the country for 1965-1971. It was necessary to make special estimates of birthrates for the United States for these recent years because of a long delay in the publication of birth data by legitimacy status for the country as a whole. Our rates are not

---

*See: J. Sklar and B. Berkov, "Abortion, Illegitimacy and the American Birth Rate," *Science*, 1974. At the inception of this study, nationwide data on births by legitimacy status were available only through 1968, and it appeared there would be continued delay in the publication by the National Center for Health Statistics of data for 1969-1971. We obtained, therefore, the more recent data for this study by communicating directly with all states reporting births by legitimacy status in 1968. States that did not officially have a specific legitimacy question on the birth certificate, but nonetheless used the information reported on the birth certificate to infer apparent legitimacy status, were also contacted. Of the states responding to our inquiry, 44 provided adequate information for detailed tabulation. These states accounted for 95.8 percent of all births occurring in the United States in 1968. On the basis of the state data, we developed estimates of birthrates by legitimacy status for the United States as a whole, cross-classified by age, race, geographical region and legal status of abortion in 1970.

directly comparable with those prepared by the National Center for Health Statistics. First, we used inferentially derived birth data by legitimacy status as provided by the states for a number of large states, including California, New York and Massachusetts.† Second, in calculating our rates we considered separated women as unmarried and included them with single, widowed, and divorced women as exposed to the risk of illegitimate childbearing.‡ In the present article we used our study

---

† This yields a larger estimated number of illegitimate births for the entire United States than the federal method because the federal office deals only with data from states which have a legitimacy item on the birth certificate; it extends the experience of these states to other states in the same region where the birth certificate asks no direct questions about legitimacy. The following is a comparison of our estimates of illegitimate births and total births with figures published by the National Center for Health Statistics.

Year	Total births		Illegitimate births	
	Study estimates	Federal estimates	Study estimates	Federal estimates
1965	3,726,448	3,760,358	306,801	291,200
1966	3,599,875	3,606,274	320,081	302,400
1967	3,517,128	3,520,959	338,140	318,100
1968	3,500,112	3,501,564	357,267	339,200
1969	3,590,427	3,600,206	383,893	360,800
1970	3,725,166	3,731,386	424,958	398,700
1971	3,552,698	3,559,000[1]	416,127	na

[1] Provisional.

‡ This yields lower illegitimate and higher marital birthrates than shown by the federal data, particularly for nonwhite women over age 25. The reasons for considering separated women as exposed to the risk of illegitimate childbearing are discussed in B. Berkov and P. Shipley, *Illegitimate Births in California: 1966 and 1967*, California Department of Public Health, Berkeley, 1971.

estimates to trace trends for 1965 and later years. However, in Figures 2 and 3, we show both our study figures and federal figures for 1965 for comparative purposes. Further comparisons between our estimates and the federal estimates appear in our earlier paper.

Overview

The United States has always been a country of relatively early marriage, and teenagers have historically contributed a large part to this early marriage pattern. The trend toward early and teenage marriage intensified from the end of World War II to the early 1960s, during which period there was a concomitant trend toward earlier childbearing. The typical pattern of teenage family formation in the United States between 1940 and 1960 was of early wedlock coupled with early childbearing within wedlock, while illegitimate childbearing among teenagers was relatively minimal. Beginning in the 1960s, however, the incidence of early marriage and early childbearing within marriage among teenagers declined, while the incidence of childbearing outside of marriage rose. By the late 1960s, teenage family formation increasingly occurred outside rather than within marriage. Increased availability of legal abortion apparently reversed temporarily the trend to increased rates of illegitimacy. Evidence from California points to a renewed rise in teenage illegitimate fertility in the early 1970s among whites, although the magnitude of that increase has been lessened by legal abortion.

In order to analyze the trends in teenage family formation, it is desirable to separate them into two main time periods: before and after 1957, the year the baby boom peaked (where necessary, using 1960 census data to indicate the peak).

Table 1. Percent of teenagers ever married, United States and Europe, around 1900

Country	Year	% ever married, aged 15-19	
		Male	Female
United States			
All races	1900	1.0	11.3
White	1900	0.9	10.4
Nonwhite	1900	1.9	17.0
Sweden	1900	*	1.1
Norway	1900	0.4	1.8
Scotland	1901	0.3	1.7
Switzerland	1900	0.1	1.1
Netherlands	1899	0.2	1.1
Denmark	1901	*	1.4
England and Wales	1901	0.3	1.6
Belgium	1900	0.2	2.6
Portugal	1900	0.8	3.5
Finland	1900	0.5	3.5
Spain†	1900	0.5	6.7
France	1901	0.4	6.5
Italy	1901	1.2	8.8

* Less than 0.1 percent.

† Age group is 16-20.

Sources: U.S. Census Office, *Census Reports: 1900*, Vol. II, "Population," Part 2, GPO, 1902, Table 29; and L'Office Permanent de l'Institut International de Statistique, *Annuaire International de Statistique*, I. "Etat de la Population (Europe)," W. P. Van Stockum et Fils, La Haye, 1916, pp. 44-103.

Teenage Family Formation from 1900 To the Peak Baby Boom Years

Americans have traditionally married relatively younger than members of other industrial societies. An important part of this early marriage pattern has been the high proportions of U.S. teenagers entering wedlock, although this has generally been more true for women than for men and for nonwhites than for whites. As early as 1900, more than 10 percent of white and 17 percent of nonwhite U.S. teenage women had ever been married (see Table 1). Among American teenage men, one percent of whites and two percent of nonwhites had ever been mar-

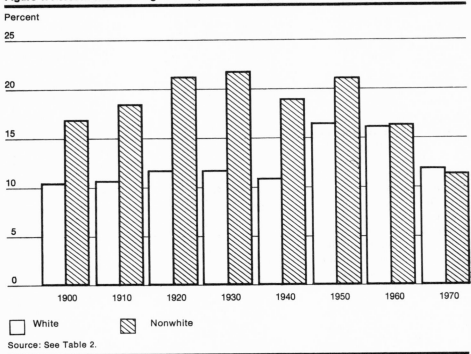

Figure 1. Percent of women aged 15-19, ever married, United States, 1900-1970

Percent

White   Nonwhite

Source: See Table 2.

ried in 1900. These proportions contrast sharply with Western Europe, where the married teenager — man or woman — has always been the exception. In fact, in most of Western Europe around 1900, fewer than four percent of teenage women, and fewer than one percent of teenage men, had ever been married. Only Italy even approached U.S. levels.

The propensity for Americans of both races to wed in their teens remained relatively unchanged until the end of World War II. Following the war, the United States witnessed an increased trend to early marriage that lasted until around 1960. White teenagers were active participants in this trend. As Table 2 and Figure 1 indicate, the proportion of all white women who had ever been married

by ages 15-19 remained relatively stable at 10-12 percent between 1900 and 1940, rising to more than 16 percent in 1950, where it remained through 1960. White teenage men also participated in this trend to increased early marriage after the war. Between 1940 and 1960, the proportion of white men ever-married in their teens rose from two percent to four percent. Nonwhite teenage marriage took a different turn. Among women, the proportion ever-married by their teens remained at a relatively high level of 17-22 percent between 1900 and 1950, and then began descending rapidly. Among nonwhite men, the percent married by the teen ages fluctuated between two percent and four percent through each decade of the century.

Despite their differential participation

in the postwar trend to early marriage, young women of both races, like their elders, displayed an increasing tendency to bear children soon after marriage. Data from Current Population Surveys show that more than two-fifths (42.1 percent) of white women who first married under age 22 in 1940-1944 had a first birth within 18 months of marriage.[2] The proportion rose to 55.9 percent for those marrying in 1950-1954, and to 61.4 percent for those first marrying in 1955-1959. A similar telescoping of the first birth also occurred among white women who delayed marriage until they were 22 or older. Essentially the same results were found for nonwhite women. Not only were women of all ages and races having their first births sooner after marriage than in previous decades, but they were also spacing their second and higher order births more closely than before.[3] What is more, many teenagers were having larger families than previously. Census data show that the number of children ever born to ever-married white women aged 15-19 rose from 548 per 1,000 in 1950 to 725 per 1,000 in 1960.[4] Among ever-married nonwhite teenage women, the figures rose from 917 per 1,000 to 1,247 per 1,000. Similar results are found if we restrict the analysis to women married once and living with their husbands.

The postwar trends in family formation produced a dramatic and virtually uninterrupted rise in the teenage marital birthrate, with the rate reaching a peak of 531 legitimate births per 1,000 married women aged 15-19 in 1960 (see Figure 2). Both white and nonwhite married teenagers participated in this rise, although nonwhites consistently showed higher rates than did whites. Since a substantial proportion of first births occurring to married teenagers are, in fact, premaritally conceived,[5] some of this rise in teenage marital birthrates undoubtedly was due

Table 2. Percent of teenagers ever married, United States, 1900-1970

Year	All races		White		Nonwhite	
	Male	Female	Male	Female	Male	Female
1900	1.0	11.3	0.9	10.4	1.9	17.0
1910	1.2	11.7	1.0	10.7	2.3	18.4
1920	2.1	12.9	1.9	11.8	4.0	21.2
1930	1.8	13.1	1.5	11.8	3.6	21.9
1940	1.7	11.9	1.6	10.9	3.2	19.0
1950	3.3	17.1	3.2	16.5	4.4	21.1
1960	3.9	16.1	3.9	16.1	3.8	16.2
1970	4.1	11.9	4.1	12.0	4.5	11.3

Sources: U.S. Bureau of the Census, *Census of Population: 1900*, Part 2, Table 29; *1910*, Vol. 1, Table 14; *1920*, Vol. II, Table 2; *1930*, Vol. III, Table 5; *1940*, Vol. IV, Part 1, Table 6; *1950*, Vol. II, Part 1, Table 104; *1960*, Vol. I, Part 1, Table 176; *1970*, PC(1)-D1, Table 203, GPO, various years.

to an increasing incidence of 'forced marriage' in which the bride was already pregnant. As data from the Current Population Survey show, the proportion of white women marrying for the first time and giving birth to a first child within only eight months after marriage doubled from about nine percent for women first married in 1940-1944 to 18 percent for women first married in 1955-1959.[6] A similar rise was experienced by nonwhite women.

As may be seen in Figure 3, teenage illegitimate birthrates climbed after World War II as teenagers joined—but did not quite equal — the general rise in out-of-wedlock reproduction that occurred among American women during the postwar period. From about seven illegitimate births per 1,000 unmarried women aged 15-19 in 1940, the incidence of nonmarital childbearing increased during the next decade to about 13 births per 1,000 in 1950, and to about 15 per 1,000 in 1955, where it remained essentially unchanged until the early 1960s. Both white and nonwhite teenagers participated in this trend although, as with marital fertility, non-

Figure 2. Legitimate births per 1,000 married* women aged 15-19, United States, 1940-1971

Legitimate births per 1,000 married women

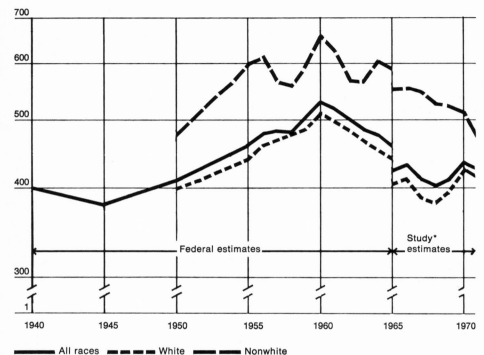

■■■■ All races ■■ ■■ ■■ White ■■■ ■■■ Nonwhite

* Study estimates exclude separated women from married.

Note: Available data plotted every five years 1940-1955 and for each single year thereafter.

Sources: International Population and Urban Research, special estimates of births and birthrates by legitimacy status for the United States, 1965-1971; National Center for Health Statistics, DHEW (NCHS), *Vital Statistics Rates in the United States, 1940-1960,* U.S. Government Printing Office, Washington, D.C. (GPO) 1968, Table 14; and revised estimated legitimate birthrates in the United States, 1950-1969 made available by NCHS in *Vital Statistics of the United States, Vol. 1,* "Natality: 1969," GPO, 1974.

whites displayed consistently higher rates of teenage illegitimacy than did whites.

Despite the relatively rapid rise in out-of-wedlock reproduction after World War II, the incidence of childbearing within marriage among teenagers of both races was at such a high level that the illegitimacy ratio — the percent of all births that are out of wedlock — remained relatively unchanged (see Figure 4). Between 1950 and 1960, the ratio among white teenage mothers rose by only one percentage point — from six percent to seven percent. Among nonwhite teenagers, a relatively high proportion of childbearing had previously been out of wedlock; but even this group saw its illegitimacy ratio rise by only six percentage points — from 36 percent in 1950 to 42 percent in 1960. In sum, among all teenage women giving birth in

Figure 3. Illegitimate births per 1,000 unmarried* women aged 15-19, United States, 1940-1971

Illegitimate births per 1,000 unmarried women

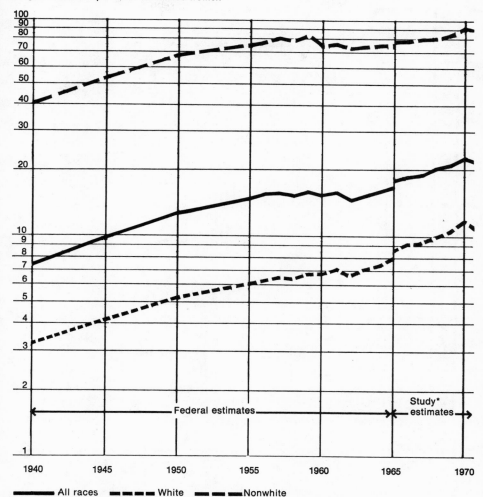

All races ━━━━ White ▰▰▰▰ Nonwhite ▰▰▰

* Study estimates include separated as well as single, widowed and divorced women among unmarried.

Note: Available data plotted every five years 1940-1955 and for each single year thereafter. Data by race not available for 1945.

Sources: International Population and Urban Research, special estimates of births and birthrates by legitimacy status for the United States, 1965-1971; and NCHS, *Trends in Illegitimacy, United States, 1940-1965*, Series P-21, No. 15, GPO, 1968, pp. 4, 25 and 26.

Figure 4. Illegitimate births as a percent of total births to mothers aged 15-19, United States and California, selected years, 1940-1973

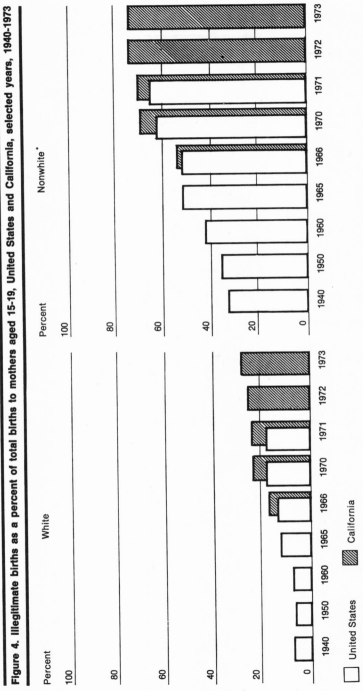

* Black for California.

Note: 1973 California data are provisional estimates based on births processed January through July and September.

Sources: International Population and Urban Research, special estimates of births and birthrates by legitimacy status for the United States, 1965-1971; NCHS, *Vital Statistics Rates in the United States, 1940-1960*, GPO, 1968, Table 28; NCHS, *Trends in Illegitimacy, United States, 1940-1965*, Series P-21, No. 15, GPO, 1968, Table 9; and California Department of Health, Birth Records.

1960, more than 90 percent of the whites and about 60 percent of the nonwhites were doing so within marriage.

With the 1960s, the postwar trend to early marriage and childbearing came to a halt. In fact, the 1960s proved to be a significant turning point for teenage family formation. From the start of the decade, the tendency to early marriage eased off, childbearing came to be delayed by those who did marry, and teenage marital fertility declined markedly. Teenage illegitimacy remained fairly stable in the first half of the 1960s, and then started to rise rapidly. These trends continued into the early 1970s, although the increased availability of legal abortion reduced the level of teenage out-of-wedlock childbearing and appeared also to have reduced teenage marital reproduction, a large part of which is premaritally conceived.

Marriage and Birth Postponement After 1960

The reversal of the tendency to early marriage is evidenced in first-marriage rates. These data, which became available for the U.S. marriage registration area beginning in 1960, show that between 1960 and 1967 first-marriage rates for women declined substantially for all age groups, but most dramatically for teenagers. During this seven-year period, the rate decreased by three percent for all women aged 14 and over (from 87.5 to 85.2 per 1,000 single women), but by 20 percent for teenage women (from 74.6 to 60.0). The first-marriage rate for teenage women turned upward in 1968 and 1969;[7] but it had a considerable distance to climb before again reaching its 1960 level.

As Table 3 shows, in California, where more recent first-marriage rates are available, the rate for women aged 15-44 dropped by 10 percent between 1960 and 1967 (from 112.4 to 100.6 first marriages

Table 3. Estimated first-marriage rates, by age of bride, California, 1960-1972

Year	First marriages per 1,000 single women*			
	15-44	15-19	20-24	25-44
1960	112.4	91.7	220.8	82.3
1961	110.1	89.4	220.3	79.1
1962	104.1	80.7	221.9	76.5
1963	103.2	75.8	229.2	78.6
1964	102.6	74.2	226.1	78.9
1965	100.7	73.6	211.5	81.7
1966	100.3	73.7	202.2	84.8
1967	100.6	70.9	202.6	83.1
1968	105.1	72.4	209.3	86.5
1969	103.3	71.6	198.1	86.7
1970	98.7	67.7	182.3	89.6
1971	90.1	59.2	167.2	86.9
1972	90.8	61.8	163.6	88.0

* Single refers to never-married women. Number of single women estimated by interpolation and projection using census data for 1960 and 1970.

Sources: U.S. Bureau of the Census, *Census of Population: 1960*, Vol. I, Part 6, Tables 94 and 105; *1970*, PC(1)-B6, Table 19; Ibid., PC(1)-D6, Section 1, Table 152, GPO, various years; and California Department of Health, Marriage Records.

per 1,000 single women aged 15-44); but the rate for women aged 15-19 dropped by 23 percent during the same period (from 91.7 to 70.9). With the exception of a slight rise between 1967 and 1968, first-marriage rates for California women, particularly those in the teen ages, continued to drop in 1969 and 1970. In 1971, the teenage rate sank by 13 percent (from 67.7 to 59.2), its sharpest annual decline in the 12 years for which first-marriage rates are available for California. Although the first-marriage rate for California's teenagers rose slightly in 1972, it nevertheless remained at a very low level.

The declining propensity to marry in the teen ages influenced nonwhites more than whites. As Table 2 and Figure 1 show for the United States as a whole, the proportion of nonwhite women ever-married by the teen ages began dropping

Table 4. Estimated marital birthrates for women aged 15-19 and 15-44 in nonabortion states and states with liberalized abortion laws,* by race, United States, 1965-1971

Age and race	Legitimate births per 1,000 married women†							Average annual percent change‡	
	1965	1966	1967	1968	1969	1970	1971	1965-1970§	1970-1971
15-19									
All races	424.1	433.5	411.9	404.6	410.6	435.9	428.2	0.5	—1.8
Abortion	411.5	413.3	400.6	392.7	396.5	415.9	394.4	0.2	—5.2
Nonabortion	430.6	443.8	417.6	410.6	417.6	445.7	444.7	0.7	—0.2
White	407.1	416.7	392.2	386.3	394.1	424.0	420.3	0.8	—0.9
Abortion	394.2	397.3	382.0	376.9	381.7	406.0	386.4	0.6	—4.8
Nonabortion	413.6	426.6	397.3	391.0	400.3	432.8	436.8	0.9	0.9
Nonwhite	549.4	555.3	551.0	531.6	524.2	517.4	482.2	—1.2	—6.8
Abortion	536.3	528.1	529.1	500.1	496.3	482.6	448.2	—2.1	—7.1
Nonabortion	556.3	569.4	562.3	547.8	538.3	534.8	499.1	—0.8	—6.7
15-44**									
All races	136.6	131.0	126.1	123.5	124.9	127.4	120.0	—1.4	—5.8
Abortion	132.4	127.2	122.9	120.5	122.3	123.6	114.0	—1.4	—7.8
Nonabortion	138.8	133.0	127.8	125.0	126.2	129.5	123.2	—1.4	—4.9
White	131.3	126.3	121.9	119.9	121.6	124.2	116.9	—1.1	—5.9
Abortion	127.5	123.1	119.6	117.9	119.8	121.0	111.5	—1.0	—7.9
Nonabortion	133.2	127.9	123.0	120.9	122.5	125.8	119.6	—1.1	—4.9
Nonwhite	186.0	174.7	164.4	155.9	154.8	156.3	147.8	—3.4	—5.4
Abortion	171.5	159.0	148.2	140.8	141.1	143.1	132.9	—3.6	—7.1
Nonabortion	195.3	184.7	174.9	165.8	163.8	165.2	157.9	—3.3	—4.4

* The following states had liberalized abortion laws by 1970: Alaska, Arkansas, California, Colorado, Delaware, Hawaii, Kansas, Maryland, New Mexico, New York, North Carolina, Oregon, South Carolina, Virginia and Washington.

† Married women exclude those who are separated.

‡ Percent change calculated by computer from unrounded estimated rates and will differ slightly from percent change calculated from rounded figures shown above.

§ Calculated assuming a constant rate of change between 1965 and 1970 (i.e., calculated by solving for r in the formula e^{5r} = rate in 1970/rate in 1965).

** Rates calculated by relating legitimate births, regardless of age of mother, to estimated number of married women aged 15-44.

Sources: International Population and Urban Research, special estimates of births and birthrates by legitimacy status for the United States, 1965-1971; see also reference 10.

rapidly after 1950. By 1970, 11 percent had ever been married among nonwhite teenage women, the lowest proportion ever during the century, and approximately half the proportion ever married between 1920 and 1950. Among white women, the proportion ever married by the teen ages remained at a relatively high 16 percent in 1950 and 1960, and then declined to 12 percent in 1970, approximately its prewar level.

Not only did a smaller proportion of teenage women of both races marry during the 1960s than the 1950s, but there is some evidence showing that those who did marry lengthened or at least stopped shortening the time between marriage and first birth. Current Population Survey data on childspacing, which are available only through 1964, show that, among white women who first married under age 22 in 1955-1959, 61.4 percent had had a first birth within 18 months after marriage.[8] For such women marrying in 1960-1964, however, the proportion having their first baby within 18 months after marriage declined slightly to 59.9 percent. Although this is a very small decrease, it was the first time that the data showed any decline since 1940. Women delaying marriage until they were 22 or older, and nonwhite women, also showed some postponement of the first birth in the early 1960s.[9]

The Decline in Marital Fertility and The Rise in Illegitimacy

As one might expect, the decline in teenage marriage and the possible postponement of the first birth by those who did wed were accompanied by declining marital birthrates after 1960. Among white teenagers, the downward trend in the marital birthrate extended through 1968, and turned upward in 1969 and 1970, making this the only group of married women to experience an overall rise in marital fertility between 1965 and 1970 (from 407.1 to 424.0 births per 1,000, see Table 4 and Figure 2). This rise did not continue, however, as the rate declined to 420.3 in 1971. Even with this decline, the white teenage marital fertility rate was higher than it had been in 1965. Nonwhite teenagers, on the other hand, experienced a rapid and virtually uninterrupted decline in legitimate childbearing during the same period, with their rate dropping from 549.4 in 1965 to 482.2 per 1,000 in 1971. Because of the more rapid and consistent drop in the late 1960s and early 1970s among nonwhite married teenagers, the gap in marital fertility between the two races narrowed considerably. Whereas in 1965, the teenage nonwhite marital birthrate was 35 percent higher than that of

the white, by 1971 the difference was only 15 percent.

In the last half of the 1960s, when illegitimacy among women in other age groups either declined or remained unchanged, the teenage illegitimate birthrate rose at an annual average of six percent (see Table 5 and Figure 3). The rate rose from 17.6 to 23.3 illegitimate births per 1,000 unmarried women aged 15-19 between 1965 and 1970. The ascent of teenage illegitimacy characterized both racial groups, but white teenagers showed the greater increase with an annual average rise of seven percent, compared to three percent for nonwhites. Despite the slower rate of increase among nonwhite teenagers, they, as well as older nonwhite women, continued to show far higher rates of illegitimacy than comparable white women.

The strong advance of the teenage illegitimate birthrate in the 1960s did not continue into 1971. From its peak of 23.3 in 1970, the rate dropped to 22.5 in 1971. A comparison of illegitimate fertility in states with and without legal abortion, which we have presented in detail elsewhere, showed that this reversal in trend marked the introduction of legal abortion as an important influence upon the reproductive behavior of American teenagers, as upon all other age groups.[10]

The Impact of Legal Abortion

Beginning in 1967, abortion laws were liberalized in California, Colorado and North Carolina, and by the end of 1970, 15 states had adopted similar legislation.*

---

* Center for Disease Control (CDC), *Abortion Surveillance Report — Legal Abortions, United States, Annual Summary, 1970*, CDC, DHEW, Atlanta, Ga., 1971, Table 21. The 15 states characterized as having liberalized abortion laws in 1970 are those in categories V, VI and VII of this report. The 15 states exclude Georgia, which was in a different category.

Table 5. Estimated illegitimate birthrates for women aged 15-19 and 15-44 in nonabortion states and states with liberalized abortion laws,* by race, United States, 1965-1971

Age and race	Illegitimate births per 1,000 unmarried women†							Average annual percent change‡	
	1965	1966	1967	1968	1969	1970	1971	1965-1970§	1970-1971
15-19									
All races	17.6	18.4	19.2	20.3	21.2	23.3	22.5	5.8	—3.4
Abortion	18.7	19.4	20.6	21.6	22.9	24.7	22.2	5.7	—10.2
Nonabortion	17.1	17.9	18.6	19.6	20.4	22.6	22.7	5.8	0.3
White	8.5	9.1	9.4	10.2	10.7	11.8	10.7	6.7	—8.9
Abortion	9.8	10.4	11.1	12.0	12.8	13.7	11.8	6.9	—14.4
Nonabortion	7.8	8.4	8.6	9.2	9.7	10.8	10.2	6.6	—5.5
Nonwhite	77.7	78.5	80.4	81.7	83.8	91.0	90.3	3.2	—0.7
Abortion	69.5	70.1	71.9	72.2	75.2	80.3	74.1	2.9	—7.8
Nonabortion	82.7	83.7	85.6	87.4	89.1	97.4	100.1	3.3	2.8
15-44**									
All races	22.2	22.2	22.7	23.2	24.1	25.7	24.2	3.0	—5.8
Abortion	23.5	23.7	24.4	25.0	25.9	27.1	23.7	2.9	—12.4
Nonabortion	21.5	21.4	21.7	22.3	23.1	24.9	24.5	3.0	—1.9
White	11.7	12.0	12.6	13.1	13.8	14.5	12.7	4.4	—12.3
Abortion	13.7	14.1	15.0	15.8	16.6	17.1	14.2	4.5	—16.9
Nonabortion	10.6	10.9	11.2	11.8	12.3	13.1	11.9	4.4	—9.1
Nonwhite	72.3	70.3	69.5	68.9	70.0	75.1	74.1	0.7	—1.2
Abortion	65.9	64.6	63.8	62.8	63.8	67.2	61.4	0.4	—8.6
Nonabortion	76.2	73.7	73.0	72.6	73.8	79.9	82.0	1.0	2.6

* The following states had liberalized abortion laws by 1970: Alaska, Arkansas, California, Colorado, Delaware, Hawaii, Kansas, Maryland, New Mexico, New York, North Carolina, Oregon, South Carolina, Virginia and Washington.

† Unmarried women are those single, widowed, divorced or separated.

‡ Percent change calculated by computer from unrounded estimated rates and will differ slightly from percent change calculated from rounded figures shown above.

§ Calculated assuming a constant rate of change between 1965 and 1970 (i.e., calculated by solving for r in the formula e^{5r} = rate in 1970/rate in 1965).

** Rates calculated by relating illegitimate births, regardless of age of mother, to estimated number of unmarried women aged 15-44.

Sources: International Population and Urban Research, special estimates of births and birthrates by legitimacy status for the United States, 1965-1971; see also reference 10.

Although some states had liberalized their laws prior to 1970, it was not until about the middle of 1970 that legal abortion services were widely available in any state. All state abortion laws which had been liberalized prior to 1970 included restrictive provisions. In California, for example, the restrictive provisions of the Therapeutic Abortion Act initially were strictly enforced. By 1970, however, the Act was interpreted much more liberally.* (Cali-

---

* For an analysis of the effects of California's abortion law during 1967-1970 see: E. Jackson, in K. Davis and F. G. Styles, eds., *California's Twenty Million: Research Contributions in Population Policy,* Institute of International Studies, University of California, Berkeley, 1971, p. 228.

fornia's legal abortion rate in 1968-1969, for example, was only 1.9 per 1,000 women aged 15-44, but 19.4 in 1970-1971.[11]) It was not until 1970 that New York, Washington, Alaska and Hawaii adopted the first laws with virtually no restrictive provisions. In 1973, the U.S. Supreme Court eliminated almost all statutory barriers to abortion, although attempts currently are being made to overturn the Court's decision through a constitutional amendment.

As shown in Table 5 and Figure 5, in the five years preceding 1970, a comparison of the trend in teenage illegitimate reproduction indicates no important difference between states with liberalized abortion laws and other states. Both groups of states averaged an annual six percent rise in the rate of teenage nonmarital reproduction. Between 1970 and 1971, however, the states with liberalized abortion laws and those where it was illegal diverged markedly, with teenage illegitimacy dropping 10 percent in the states with liberalized laws, but rising slightly (0.3 percent) in the states where abortion was prohibited. Given the earlier similarity between the two groups of states, this subsequent divergence suggests that legal abortion was a major factor in the nationwide declines in teenage illegitimacy between 1970 and 1971.

The data further show that among states where abortion laws were liberalized, teenage illegitimacy declined most in those having the highest rates of legal abortion use (a reliable indicator, in general, of availability of legal abortion).

For example, in California and New York, where legal abortion rates were among the highest in the country in 1970, teenage illegitimacy declined by 15 and 16 percent, respectively, between 1970 and 1971 (from 24.0 to 20.4 for California, and from 22.4 to 19.0 for New York). By contrast, in the relatively low abortion

use states of Virginia and North Carolina, the comparable declines were four and five percent (from 28.0 to 26.9 for Virginia, and from 35.5 to 33.8 for North Carolina). In Arkansas and South Carolina, where legal abortion rates were the lowest of the states where abortion laws were liberalized, teenage illegitimacy rose by two and three percent, respectively, between 1970 and 1971 (from 28.8 to 29.4 for Arkansas, and from 36.3 to 37.4 for South Carolina).[12]

Unmarried teenage women in both racial groups turned to legal abortion, though with some differences. In states with liberalized abortion laws, both white and nonwhite teenagers showed declines in illegitimacy of 14 percent and eight percent, respectively. By contrast, in the states which prohibited abortions, white teenagers showed a more modest decline of six percent, while nonwhite teenagers showed a rise of three percent. In fact, as we have shown elsewhere, in the states where abortion was illegal, white women of all age groups showed declines of at least five percent, whereas nonwhite women of virtually all age groups showed either little change or small rises.[13] The decline for teenage white women living in states where abortion was prohibited probably reflects their greater use of migratory abortion. With abortion laws liberalized in 15 states in the period affecting 1971 births, it was possible to obtain a legal abortion by traveling to another state. However, a number of constraints — such as ignorance of the legality of abortion in other states and the expense of travel to a state where abortion was legal, coupled with the costs of and concerns about abortion itself — limited the widespread use of migratory abortion. Poor and nonwhite women in general, especially if they were teenagers, probably suffered most from these constraints and thus were unlikely to have resorted to abortion

Figure 5. Estimated birthrates by legitimacy status, women aged 15-19, United States, 1965-1971

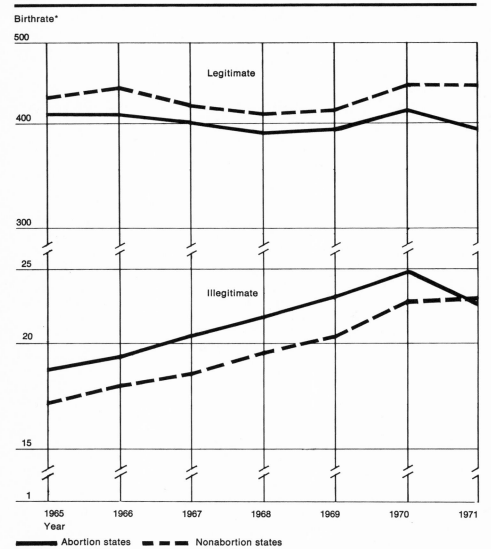

Birthrate*

Year

Abortion states   Nonabortion states

* Birthrates are per 1,000 married (legitimate) and unmarried (illegitimate) women aged 15-19.
Sources: See Tables 4 and 5.

in very great numbers unless it was legal and readily available in their state of residence or very nearby.

In 1971, legal abortion not only influenced teenage illegitimate birthrates but, for white teenagers, marital birthrates as well (see Table 4). White teenagers were the only age and racial group of women to experience rising marital birthrates between 1965 and 1970. Whereas in 1971 their marital fertility continued to rise in states where abortion was prohibited, it declined in states with liberalized abortion laws. Because the fertility of married teenagers reflects the influence of conceptions before marriage, this decline suggests that legal abortion had a depressive influence not only on white teenage marital fertility, but on the incidence of forced marriage as well. Among nonwhite teenagers, whose marital birthrates were declining rapidly for virtually the entire period 1965-1971, a similar difference was not found in 1971 between states where abortion laws were liberalized and where they were not.

On the whole, then, legal abortion was a significant factor in teenage reproduction in 1971. The question naturally arises as to whether the trend in teenage reproductive behavior continued past 1971, and of the role of legal abortion in this trend. We cannot answer this question for the entire country because we were able to develop birth data by legitimacy status only through 1971 for the United States as a whole. Let us turn, therefore, to an examination of more recent information on legitimate and illegitimate births in California. Since 1966, we have been able to examine California's fertility experience on a current basis and we have found that, although changes may occur earlier or be more extreme in California, the California experience tends to reflect what is happening in other large states and in the country generally. The California data thus permit not only a preliminary assess-

ment of the more long-term effects of legalized abortion, but they also allow us to examine the most recently observed patterns of American teenage reproductive behavior.

Persistence of Teenage Illegitimacy: The California Experience

Teenage illegitimacy rates showed a trend in California similar to the rest of the country through 1971, although the state generally had higher rates of teenage out-of-wedlock reproduction.* Because of the more widespread availability of legal abortion in California than in the country as a whole, legal abortion apparently had an even sharper downward impact on nonmarital childbearing in the state in 1971 than was found for the entire nation. The downward impact of legal abortion on white teenage illegitimacy in California began, however, to level off in 1972.[14] Our most recent data, which are estimates for 1973 based on birth counts for the first half of the year, show that this leveling off has continued (see Table 6). After declining 17 percent between 1970 and 1971 (from 17.9 to 14.9 per 1,000), California's white teenage illegitimate birthrate actually rose by nearly three percent in 1972 (to 15.3), and rose again by another three percent in 1973 (to 15.8). Nonwhite teenagers and most older groups of white and nonwhite women showed continued declines in illegitimacy in 1972 and 1973, although these declines were generally of smaller magnitude than had occurred in 1971.

The smaller declines in illegitimacy in California in 1972 and 1973 followed a tendency for the rate of legal abortion use

---

* See Table 5 of this article for U.S. estimates which can be compared with estimates for California shown in Table A of Sklar and Berkov, 1973 (see reference 11).

Table 6. Estimated birthrates, by legitimacy status, race and age of mother, California residents, 1970-1973

Race and age of mother	Illegitimate				Legitimate				All live births			
	1973*	1972	1971	1970	1973*	1972	1971	1970	1973*	1972	1971	1970
All races												
15-44†	21.8	22.0	22.6	27.0	92.5	98.4	109.5	122.1	63.6	67.6	74.7	84.6
15-19	20.8	20.7	20.4	24.1	331.8	333.8	354.7	409.6	53.1	55.2	58.2	68.8
20-24	31.5	31.3	32.8	41.3	184.8	194.2	220.3	247.9	114.1	121.2	137.4	158.0
25-34	21.7	23.5	25.4	29.9	95.4	102.8	114.1	127.6	78.3	84.9	94.3	106.1
35-44‡	5.4	5.4	6.1	7.2	14.5	15.9	18.3	20.7	12.7	13.8	15.9	18.1
White												
15-44†	17.5	17.4	17.7	21.6	93.5	99.2	110.2	122.8	63.5	67.3	74.3	84.1
15-19	15.8	15.3	14.9	17.9	339.8	342.2	364.2	418.1	50.4	52.2	55.1	65.1
20-24	25.0	24.9	26.2	34.2	185.8	195.5	221.3	249.5	114.4	121.8	138.4	159.3
25-34	19.3	20.7	21.9	26.0	95.8	102.8	114.0	127.4	79.3	85.6	94.9	106.8
35-44‡	5.3	5.0	5.5	6.4	14.2	15.3	17.7	20.0	12.5	13.4	15.4	17.5
Black												
15-44†	61.2	65.4	69.1	80.1	82.8	92.3	109.7	126.4	70.8	77.5	87.6	101.6
15-19	78.8	85.5	87.6	102.0	288.1	286.4	330.2	405.2	97.7	105.0	111.8	133.2
20-24	102.6	101.6	106.3	123.5	183.9	192.3	223.2	254.4	136.7	141.1	157.9	182.4
25-34	38.0	42.7	49.2	58.5	70.6	83.9	101.0	117.0	56.9	67.0	80.0	93.6
35-44‡	6.6	8.5	10.0	12.2	14.0	17.4	22.6	26.2	11.0	13.8	17.6	20.6

* Provisional data for 1973 based on births processed January through July and September.

† Rates computed by relating total births, regardless of age of mother, to estimated number of women aged 15-44.

‡ Rates computed by relating births to mothers aged 35 and over to estimated number of women aged 35-44.

Note: Rates are per 1,000 unmarried (illegitimate), married (legitimate) and total women. Unmarried women are those single, widowed, divorced or separated. For methods of estimating percent of women unmarried, see reference 11.

Sources: U.S. Bureau of the Census, *Census of Population: 1970,* "General Population Characteristics, Final Report," PC(1)-B6, California, GPO, 1971, Tables 19 and 22; California Department of Health, Birth Records; and California Department of Finance, population estimates prepared November 1972 and July 1973.

in the state to level off. Among teenagers, legal abortion rates were much higher for unmarried than for married women (41.2 legal abortions per 1,000 unmarried and 25.5 per 1,000 married in the period affecting 1972 births), a differential that also held true for all women of childbearing ages (45.4 unmarried, compared to 11.5 married).[15]

As is true throughout the country, California's rising rates of teenage illegitimacy in the late 1960s were accompanied by declines in marital fertility. White teenagers in California, as in the United States as a whole, showed a marked decline in marital birthrates in 1971, indicating a drop in pregnancy-related marriages associated with increased use of legal abortion.* Like the illegitimate birthrate, the decline in the marital birthrate for white teenagers leveled off in 1972 and 1973 (see Table 6). Throughout the late 1960s and early 1970s, marital birthrates declined more rapidly and more consistently for black than for white teenagers in California. In 1973, the birthrate for married black teenagers was an estimated 288.1 per 1,000; this was 43 percent below the 1966 rate of 504.8, and substantially below the 1973 rate of 339.8 for married white teenagers.

The net effect of sharply declining marital fertility combined with generally rising illegitimate birthrates has meant that in California, and in the country generally, there has been a shift to childbearing outside marriage for teenage women of both races (see Figure 4). In California between 1966 and 1970, the proportion of all births to teenage mothers that were out of wedlock rose from 21.5 percent to 31.0 percent for women of all races; from 16.7 percent to 24.2 percent for whites, and from 53.2 percent to 68.7 percent for blacks. In 1971, the ratio remained essentially unchanged for whites but rose slightly for blacks. In 1972 and 1973, however, the ratios rose for both race groups, and in 1973 we estimated that more than one-fourth of the babies born to white teenagers and almost three-fourths of the babies born to black teenagers were illegitimate.

---

* This inference from the legitimate birthrate trend is supported by marriage data presented for the first time in Table 3 of this article. Table 3 shows that the first-marriage rate for California teenagers declined by 13 percent between 1970 and 1971, its largest annual drop in the 12 years for which first-marriage rates are available for the state. The rate turned up slightly in 1972 (the most recent year for which we have data), indicating that pregnancy-related marriages among California teenagers were showing a trend similar to that of illegitimate births.

The shift in teenage family formation to out-of-wedlock childbearing is even more striking when we look only at women aged 15-19 who become mothers for the first time. In 1966, illegitimate births comprised 18.6 percent of all white teenage first births and 57.6 percent of all black teenage first births. By 1973, the proportions had risen to 30.3 for white first births and 76.5 for black first births.[16]

The movement toward childbearing outside of marriage among California's teenagers is underscored by an examination of the cumulative childbearing experience of specific groups of women as they passed through the teen ages. From the data we have compiled for California in the years 1966-1973, we have been able to estimate cumulative first-birth rates for three successive cohorts of women as they passed through ages 14-19 (see Table 7). The declines in cumulative first-birth rates for the three successive cohorts reflect the declining period birthrates after 1970, a decline which, we have shown, was related to the increasing availability and use of legal abortion. Perhaps the most striking finding shown by the cumulative first-birth rates is that, even after legal abortion became widely available in California, there continued to be a fairly high rate of teenage family formation, particularly family formation outside marriage. The cohort rates also document much earlier childbearing among black than among white teenagers, and the continuation of a much higher level of nonmarital reproduction among black teenagers.

The cohort of women who reached age 14 in 1968 (the most recent cohort we can trace) experienced most of their teenage childbearing after legal abortion became fairly widely available in California. For this cohort, we find that 21.6 percent of the white teenagers became mothers for the first time before age 20, with slightly

Table 7. Estimated cumulative first-birth rates through age 19, for cohorts of California women reaching age 14 in 1966-1968

Race and cohort	Cumulative first-birth rate through age 19		
	Illegit-imate	Legit-imate	All live births
All races			
Age 14 in 1966	8.3	17.8	26.0
1967	8.0	15.5	24.0
1968	8.1	14.3	22.7
White			
Age 14 in 1966	6.3	18.7	25.0
1967	6.1	16.8	22.9
1968	6.1	15.5	21.6
Black			
Age 14 in 1966	34.3	13.4	47.8
1967	33.0	11.2	44.2
1968	32.9	9.8	42.6

Note: Cumulative first-birth rates per 100 women for cohorts were estimated from period first-birth rates by single years of age. The estimated rate for the cohort reaching age 14 in 1968 equals the summation of first-birth rates for resident women age 14 in 1968, 15 in 1969, 16 in 1970, 17 in 1971, 18 in 1972 and 19 in 1973. For each of these years the illegitimate, legitimate and total births were related to the estimated total number of women of the specific age regardless of marital status. The births are those to women reporting themselves as California residents. The estimates of resident women used as denominators attempt to take account of migration in and out of California. Estimates of resident women by single years of age were available for all races and were allocated to white and black in accordance with estimates for the entire age group 15-19.

Sources: California Department of Health, Birth Records; and California Department of Finance, population estimates prepared October 1973.

over one-fourth of these white mothers beginning their childbearing careers outside of marriage. For black women in this cohort, we find that 42.6 percent entered motherhood before age 20, with more than three-fourths of these black mothers beginning their reproductive lives outside of marriage. For women of all races in the cohort reaching age 14 in California in 1968, 22.7 percent became mothers before age 20, with over one-third of these becoming mothers outside of wedlock.[*]

The persistence of out-of-wedlock childbearing at relatively high levels has been accompanied by an increasing tendency among young unmarried mothers to keep their babies. The number of babies adopted by nonrelatives dropped almost 50 percent in California between 1967-1968 and 1971-1972 (from 11,257 to 5,807).[17] Assuming that most of the children adopted by nonrelatives were born out of wedlock, we estimate that the proportion of illegitimate children adopted declined from about 30 percent in 1967 and 1968 to about 15 percent in 1971 and 1972.

What Explains Teenage Illegitimacy Trends?

The rise in teenage illegitimacy in the United States in the late 1960s, and its persistence in California even after legal abortion became widely available in the 1970s, call for an explanation. In this section, we will present our interpretation of some of the causative influences behind this trend.

One might have expected that teenage illegitimacy should have declined in this period. There were highly reliable contraceptives to preclude pregnancy, regardless of frequency of intercourse, and most teenagers knew of the existence of such

[*] The overall proportion of 22.7 percent is about one-fourth below the 30 percent becoming mothers before age 20 estimated for the cohort of California women aged 14 in 1960. We do not have comparable information for earlier cohorts of California women, but the 1960 cohort experienced cumulative first-birth rates not much below peak rates in the postwar baby boom era. (See: J. C. Bowman and J. F. Browne, *California Health Trends — Fertility*, Vol. 5, California Department of Public Health, Dec. 1969, Table E 5.)

contraceptives.[18] Although lack of access is probably one reason why contraceptives were not used regularly, recent studies indicate that there were other important reasons. Some teenage women felt that systematic use of contraception implied advance preparation and planning for intercourse and hence was inconsistent with ` the view that sexual relations should be held under "natural, spontaneous and unplanned" conditions. In addition, some appeared to feel that contraceptives were an unnatural and potentially harmful agent in the body, others that contraceptives were too troublesome and inconvenient, that nearly all of the menstrual cycle is 'safe', or that they were too young to get pregnant.[19]

Another reason given by unmarried teenagers for not using contraceptives was that they either "wanted" to get pregnant or "did not mind" doing so. In a 1971 national sample of teenage women, one-fourth of the blacks and one-third of the whites who had a premarital first pregnancy reported that the pregnancy had been wanted at the time it occurred.[20] One reason for wanting the pregnancy, particularly among white teenagers, probably was the hope that it would result in marriage. Half of the white teenagers who became pregnant before marriage married before resolution of the pregnancy, but among black teenagers only eight percent did so. Although definitive data are lacking, it appears that the traditional method of using pregnancy to induce a man to marry has become less successful in recent years. Teenage girls are increasingly at risk of unwed pregnancy, as evidenced by the rising incidence of premarital intercourse and the declining age of initiation of intercourse.[21] Nonetheless, the recent decline in the teenage marriage rate suggests that for many young girls, the gamble of forcing marriage with a premarital pregnancy has not paid off. This

may well be because, with the development of female-oriented contraceptives, contraceptive responsibility has increasingly shifted to the girl. Not only may the boy feel less obligation toward the girl if she becomes pregnant, but there also may be less pressure from the parents and the community to hold the boy accountable for the pregnancy. With the option of legal abortion increasingly available, there would tend to be even less motivation on everyone's part to hold the boy responsible. Thus, the increasing emphasis on equality in matters related to sex may have resulted in less practical equality.[22] The girl increasingly shoulders the entire burden of pregnancy and child care, while there is little expectation that the boy will marry her or support the child.

Not all teenage women who become premaritally pregnant wish to marry the man who brought about the pregnancy. Young women may see little advantage in such a marriage if, for example, the male partner has few economic or other resources to offer. This may be one reason why more whites than blacks intend their premarital pregnancies, and why more whites than blacks who are premaritally pregnant do marry. Why, however, do so many girls who do not marry go on to become mothers anyway? With the increase in availability of abortion, why do not more teenagers choose this option? In our opinion, at least part of the answer may be found in changes in the penalty and reward structure surrounding childbearing outside of wedlock.[23] In American society, rewards for motherhood have remained strong while penalties against childbearing outside marriage have lessened considerably. Whereas unwed mothers and their children formerly were often treated in cruel and inhumane ways, modern humanitarian attitudes and social welfare programs try to help them overcome their disadvantaged situations. In addition to financial assistance, programs are designed specifically for unmarried pregnant teenagers to provide such necessary services as prenatal and postnatal care, special educational classes, vocational and job training, psychological counseling and special child care facilities for those wishing to attend and complete high school. While few pregnant teenagers receive all or even most of these services, many receive at least some of them.

It is easy to understand why these social programs exist. Once a woman has a child out of wedlock, modern humanitarian attitudes require that the child and its mother be given adequate support and medical care. Although it does not seem likely that teenagers purposely become pregnant in order to take advantage of these benefits, the benefits do lessen the penalties of illegitimate childbearing. Having a baby remains a rewarding experience, and for many young women, there is a lack of viable and satisfying alternatives to motherhood. In this context, the availability of even minimal financial support, coupled with services which lessen the costs and inconvenience of out-of-wedlock childbearing, make more possible the option of motherhood without marriage — an option that frequently is most immediately satisfying. As noted previously, young mothers increasingly are keeping their out-of-wedlock babies.

Despite the effort to give modern care to the unwed mother and her child, it is still true that illegitimate children do not fare as well as legitimate children. Studies have shown that, compared with legitimate children, illegitimate children suffer more frequently a variety of social, economic and health handicaps and are less likely to perform well in school.[24] If this is true for illegitimate children in general, it is even more true for those born to teenage mothers. The handicaps suffered by these children result not so much from the moral opprobrium attached to the label "illegitimate" as from the circumstances in which the children are reared. Very few teenage mothers or fathers are prepared for parenthood, either in terms of emotional or social maturity or of economic capacity. Their deficiencies in this respect can hardly be compensated by the services offered outside the family by social agencies.

References

1. U.S. Bureau of the Census, *Census of Population: 1970, General Population Characteristics, Final Report PC(1)-B1, United States Summary*, U.S. Government Printing Office, Washington, D. C. (GPO), 1972, Table 49.

2. U.S. Bureau of the Census, "Marriage, Fertility and Child Spacing: June 1965," *Current Population Reports*, Series P-20, No. 186, GPO, Aug. 1969, Tables 21 and 22.

3. Ibid.

4. U.S. Bureau of the Census, *Census of Population: 1950, Vol. IV, Special Reports*, Part 5, Chapter C, "Fertility," GPO, 1955, Table 1; and *Census of Population: 1960, Subject Reports*, "Women by Number of Children Ever Born," Final Report PC(2)-3A, GPO, 1964, Table 1.

5. National Center for Health Statistics, DHEW (NCHS), "Interval Between First Marriage and Legitimate First Birth, 1964-66," *Monthly Vital Statistics Report*, National Natality Survey Statistics, Vol. 18, No. 12, Supplement, March 27, 1970.

6. U.S. Bureau of the Census, *Current Population Reports*, 1969, op. cit.

7. DHEW, *Vital Statistics of the United States: Vol. III*, "Marriage and Divorce: 1960," Tables 1-M and 2-15; 1963, Tables 1-6 and 1-16; 1964-1965, Tables 1-7 and 1-17; 1966-1969, Tables 1-7 and 1-15, GPO, various years.

8. U.S. Bureau of the Census, *Current Population Reports*, 1969, op. cit.

9. Ibid.

10. J. Sklar and B. Berkov, "Abortion, Illegitimacy and the American Birth Rate," *Science*, 1974.

11. J. Sklar and B. Berkov, "The Effects of Legal Abortion on Legitimate and Illegitimate Birth Rates: The California Experience," *Studies in Family Planning*, 4:281, 1973, Table 2.

12. J. Sklar and B. Berkov, 1974, op. cit.

13. Ibid.

14. J. Sklar and B. Berkov, 1973, op. cit., Table A, p. 289.

15. Ibid., Table F, p. 291.

16. California Department of Health, provisional data for 1973 based on birth records processed January through July and September (unpublished).

17. California Department of Health, Adoption Services Section, data on relinquishments to public and private agencies and independent nonrelative adoptions, Annual Summary Statistical Reports, 1967-1972 (unpublished).

18. M. Zelnik and J. F. Kantner, "Sexuality, Contraception and Pregnancy Among Young Unwed Females in the United States," in Commission on Population Growth and the American Future, C. F. Westoff and R. Parke, Jr., eds., *Demographic and Social Aspects of Population Growth*, GPO, 1972, p. 357.

19. Ibid.; E. Sandberg and R. Jacobs, "Psychology of the Misuse and Rejection of Contraception," *American Journal of Obstetrics and Gynecology*, 110:227, 1971; M. Diamond, P. Steinhoff, J. Palmore and R. Smith, "Sexuality, Birth Control and Abortion: A Decision-Making Sequence," *Journal of Biosocial Science*, Vol. 5, No. 3, 1973, p. 347; and K. Luker, *Patterns of Pregnancy: Toward A Theory of Contraceptive Risk-Taking*, Yale University, 1974 (unpublished).

20. M. Zelnik and J. F. Kantner, "The Resolution of Teenage First Pregnancies," *Family Planning Perspectives*, 6:74, 1974. Proportions of extramarital pregnancies wanted at the time they occurred calculated from Tables 4 and 7 using as weights proportions married and unmarried at outcome given in Table 3.

21. M. Zelnik and J. F. Kantner, "The Probability of Premarital Intercourse," *Social Science Research*, Vol. 1, No. 3, 1972, p. 335.

22. K. Davis, "Sexual Behavior," in R. K. Merton and R. Nisbet, eds., *Contemporary Social Problems*, 3rd ed., Harcourt, Brace, Jovanovich, New York, 1971, p. 313.

23. B. Berkov, "Illegitimate Fertility in California's Population," in K. Davis and F. G. Styles, eds., *California's Twenty Million: Research Contributions to Population Policy*, Institute of International Studies, University of California, Berkeley, 1971, p. 207.

24. E. Crellin, M. L. K. Pringle and P. West, *Born Illegitimate: Social and Educational Implications*, National Foundation for Educational Research in England and Wales, London, 1971; K. Davis, "The Birth Rate and Public Welfare in California," testimony before the State Social Welfare Board, 1972 (unpublished); and J. Menken, "Teenage Childbearing: Its Medical Aspects and Implications for the United States Population," in C. F. Westoff and R. Parke, Jr., eds., 1972, op. cit., p. 331.

2
Teenage Illegitimacy: An Exchange

Phillips Cutright, Frank F. Furstenberg, Jr.,
June Sklar and Beth Berkov

Phillips Cutright

June Sklar and Beth Berkov's "Teenage Family Formation in Postwar America" provides a valuable analysis of historical trends and unique data on recent fertility rates in California. Their work also highlights deficiencies in national record keeping that should be corrected by the National Center for Health Statistics (NCHS). The authors note that national estimates of illegitimacy over the 1965-1970 period understate the total count of illegitimate births by five to seven percent.[*] There seems to be no good reason for NCHS to continue to omit illegitimacy data from nonreporting states, when a modest effort would allow it to include California, New York City, Massachusetts (at least for some years) and Georgia. Perhaps this new report will, at last, stir NCHS to action.

I have a few objections to the last sections of the article, where the emphasis is

on teenage fertility. Concentration on this age group and the emphasis on the fertility of unmarried teenagers results in little discussion in the text of the main fertility trends in California. The authors' analysis of Table 6 leaves the reader with the impression that illegitimacy rates are not declining rapidly enough — teenagers "persist" in having illegitimate children. However, my reading of Sklar and Berkov's Table 6 would focus on the overall trend in general fertility rates (births per 1,000 women 15-44) in California. Between 1970 and 1973 the general fertility rate (GFR) declined from 84.6 to 63.6. The decline among blacks alone is even more striking — the 1973 GFR for blacks was 70.8, and this is a 30 percent reduction from the 1970 black GFR of 101.6. The 1973 black GFR, if continued over time, will result in a replacement level of new mothers for succeeding black cohorts. Black and white fertility rates in 1973 are even closer to equality of demographic impact on future population size when the higher mortality of blacks than whites is taken into account.

We also see in Table 6 rapid declines in illegitimacy rates among blacks. For example, the black illegitimacy rate for unmarried women 15-44 in 1973 was esti-

---

[*] 1971 data have now been released (NCHS, "Summary Report: Final Natality Statistics, 1971," *Monthly Vital Statistics Report*, Vol. 23, No. 3, Supplement (3), June 7, 1974, Table 11). NCHS estimated 401,400 illegitimate births, about 3.5 percent fewer than the Sklar and Berkov estimate for 1971.

mated at 61.2, down 24 percent from the 1970 level. Among black teenagers the 1973 rate was down 23 births per 1,000 — from the 1970 level — a 23 percent drop. Among white teenagers the rates declined by 12 percent, while the illegitimacy rates among white unmarried women of all ages declined by some 19 percent. These declines are interpreted by Sklar and Berkov as evidence of "persistence."

Sklar and Berkov report a recent increase in, as well as a vast difference between, illegitimacy *ratios* by race. Does the higher illegitimacy ratio among blacks affect their completed fertility? In Table 6 we observe that black marital fertility rates among older women in 1973 were lower than white marital fertility rates at comparable ages. This suggests that high early black illegitimacy is followed by restricted black marital fertility. In spite of the large racial differences in illegitimacy in California there was little racial difference in the general fertility rates of whites and blacks in 1973. Other research has found no impact of illegitimate rather than legitimate first births on the likely completed fertility of either white or black mothers in the United States.* Concern with illegitimacy as a powerful force in raising completed fertility, and thus increasing the rate of population growth, lacks an empirical foundation.

In spite of enormous differences in the poverty status of white and black women in California, the near equality of black and white general fertility rates seems impressive. The likely role of family planning programs in California in helping low-income women control fertility is ignored by Sklar and Berkov.

The authors accept the view that a large proportion of unwed mothers attained

that status because they wanted to have a child. Data supporting this idea come from interviews with unwed mothers and, thus, are subject to retrospective error and rationalization. Had one interviewed the teenagers prior to their pregnancies, I doubt that many would have said they wanted to have an illegitimate child. Further, no evidence exists to show that legitimated premarital pregnancies are the result of deliberate efforts by unmarried girls to trap men into a forced marriage. Sklar and Berkov wonder why teenage illegitimacy exists at all in the face of legal abortion and available contraception. Their policy-relevant answer is that traditional economic sanctions have been reduced with the growth of various welfare programs. But they present no evidence to support the opinion that the trend in teenage illegitimacy is caused by the development of AFDC or related programs. The attractiveness of their opinion has been tested by others, and found wanting.† The authors do not bother to review the work of researchers also concerned with fertility trends. For example, Farley and Cutright emphasize the role of improved health conditions in explaining trends in fertility after 1940.‡ A good deal of the 'mystery' surrounding the postwar

* P. Cutright and O. Galle, "The Effect of Illegitimacy on U.S. Fertility Rates and Population Growth," *Population Studies*, 27:515, 1973.

† P. Cutright, "Illegitimacy and Income Supplements," in R. Lerman and A. Townsend, eds., *Studies in Public Welfare*, Paper N. 12, Pt. I, Joint Economic Committee of the Congress, U.S. Government Printing Office, Washington, D.C. (GPO), 1973, p. 90.

‡ R. Farley, *The Growth of the Black Population*, Markham, Chicago, 1970; P. Cutright, "Illegitimacy in the United States: 1920-1968," in Commission on Population Growth and the American Future, *Social and Demographic Aspects of Population Growth*, C. F. Westoff and R. Parke, Jr., eds., Vol. I of Commission Research Reports, GPO, 1972, p. 375; and P. Cutright, "The Teenage Sexual Revolution and the Myth of an Abstinent Past," *Family Planning Perspectives*, Vol. 4, No. 1, 1972, p. 24.

rise in illegitimacy can be explained without resort to hypothetical effects of the AFDC program.

Concern with illegitimacy sometimes follows from the conviction that an illegitimate birth is a turning point that affects the future course of a woman's life. While illegitimacy does have a number of effects in the short run, research using a large national sample of black and white mothers* found little effect of an illegitimate rather than a legitimate first birth on the status of ever-married mothers some 15-20 years after their first birth.

If, as we have suggested, illegitimacy has only trivial impact on completed fertility and if it also has only small effects on the later marital, economic, labor force and family status of former unwed mothers, one's concern with illegitimacy must rest on other reasons. Perhaps family planners would benefit from a fresh look at the available evidence on the various social, economic and individual effects of illegitimacy.

Frank F. Furstenberg, Jr.

In a generally well-documented and reasoned research report, June Sklar and Beth Berkov in "Teenage Family Formation in Postwar America" skillfully assemble statistics from disparate sources, and build a convincing case that the rates of marital and nonmarital births among teenagers have not followed the same course over the past decade. Marital unions and fertility have decreased while illegitimate births, after an initial decline, have drifted upward. Contrasting the birthrates in states where abortion laws were liberalized before 1973 with those whose statutes were restrictive until then,

Sklar and Berkov demonstrate that availability of abortion has had an immediate and sizeable impact on curbing the rate of teenage fertility. Nevertheless, a specific analysis of California fertility trends indicates that the steep initial decline may not be sustained, especially among white adolescents. In California the rate of illegitimacy for females aged 14-19 increased very slightly after 1971, the period when abortion facilities in the state have become more widespread.

This demographic analysis is informative, but it hardly seems sufficient to bear the weight of the interpretation proffered by the authors. After briefly alluding to a number of possible explanations for the persistence of nonmarital fertility among teenagers, Sklar and Berkov elect to stress the effect that social programs for the unwed mother have had on "lessening the penalties of illegitimate childbearing." The authors maintain that the benefits of these programs have made motherhood outside of marriage a more attractive option. They never explicitly propose to correct the situation by increasing the penalties. They even describe the programs as "necessary." However, the clear implication is that social do-gooders are mucking things up by their humanitarian attitudes which dictate that medical and social services be provided to the unwed mother and her child. One short step behind Sklar and Berkov are the enterprising politician and frustrated taxpayer, only too happy to leap to the conclusion that social programs are at the root of the problem. . . .

Having recently concluded a longitudinal study of the social careers of teenage mothers, let me reassure Sklar and Berkov that the vast majority of teenage parents manage to escape the benefits of medical, educational, vocational and family service programs. At the time of pregnancy, most young mothers expect life to be difficult, and indeed their expectations are more

---

* P. Cutright, "Timing the First Birth: Does it Matter?" *Journal of Marriage and the Family,* **35**:585, 1973.

than borne out by later events. It can hardly be said that those who manage to overcome the perils of early parenthood owe their success to the generous support and assistance provided by the Welfare State.°

If the incentives created by supportive services for childbearing cannot account for the persistence of teenage out-of-wed-lock births, what is the answer? I suggest that Sklar and Berkov reconsider the ex-planations that they passed over so lightly.

Even if the proportion of sexually active teenagers were not increasing, the popu-lation at risk of having an illegitimate child would be growing if the authors are cor-rect in their assumption that marriage has become less attractive as a solution to a premarital conception. A constant rate of premarital pregnancy yields a higher rate of illegitimacy if more couples reject forced marriage. As it becomes more diffi-cult for a teenage male to support a ready-made family, fewer couples will elect to marry quickly following a premarital con-ception.† The social and economic pres-sures which discourage early marital un-ions in the population at large have a similar effect on dissuading couples from entering wedlock should a premarital con-ception occur.‡

We need not assume that the proportion of sexually active teenagers has remained constant. In fact, there is every reason to believe that the incidence of sexual activ-ity has increased within the teenage popu-lation, and the inception of coitus occurs at an earlier age for females now than a decade ago. Both of these changes, espe-cially the latter, place a greater percentage of youth at risk of becoming pregnant. It is not unreasonable to assume, on the basis of the available research, that the rate of intercourse for females (whites in particu-lar) during the teen years has risen sub-stantially. § If only the median age of in-ception of coitus dropped, there would be reason to expect a higher rate of illegiti-mate births. A 16-year-old is far less likely to legitimate a premarital conception than an 18-year-old. Indeed, the earlier timing of premarital pregnancy among black women is an important reason why their rates of illegitimacy traditionally have been so much higher than among whites. Now, white females are beginning to have sex at an earlier age, and this de-clining age of onset may be one reason their rate of illegitimacy has been rising at a more rapid pace.

Sklar and Berkov correctly take note of some of the obstacles to contraceptive use among nulliparous adolescents. While it is true that the barriers to effective contra-ception have been dropping in recent years, it is easy to exaggerate the current state of affairs. Most teenagers know about the pill, but whether they have sufficient knowledge of and easy access to oral con-traceptives is quite another matter.

Finally, it is too early to discount the

° The authors conceivably might be able to make a better case for their argument if they examined the rates of nonmarital fertility in Scandinavian society, but I would suggest even there it would be difficult to prove their thesis. (See, for ex-ample, P. Cutright, "Illegitimacy: Myths, Causes and Cures," *Family Planning Perspectives,* Vol. 3, No. 1, 1971, p. 25.)

† In my study of low-income black adolescent mothers, it was common for young mothers to defer marriage until the father had the prospect of stable employment or to decide not to marry because they foresaw no prospect of receiving economic support from the male. (*Unplanned Parenthood: The Social Consequences of Teenage Pregnancy,* The Free Press, New York, 1976.)

‡ P. Cutright, 1971, op. cit.

§ H. T. Christensen and C. Gregg, "Changing Sex Norms in America and Scandinavia," *Journal of Marriage and the Family,* 32:616, 1970; R. P. Bell and J. B. Chaskes, "Premarital Sexual Ex-perience Among Coeds, 1958 and 1968," *Jour-nal of Marriage and the Family,* 32:81, 1970.

potential influence of abortion on the rate of teenage pregnancy. While California, no doubt, forecasts many social trends, it may be somewhat imprudent to draw conclusions on the basis of a three-year experience with liberalized abortion regulations. The attitudinal and structural barriers to obtaining abortions may survive beyond the point of legislative change. Again, referring to my data collection in Maryland, liberalized abortion regulations did not immediately remove the psychological and ideological misgivings that many women held about abortion. The dire prognostication of Sklar and Berkov is reminiscent of the prediction of some social scientists in the early 1960s that the poor would be unwilling or unable to use birth control.

On the basis of the data presented in their article, it is not at all clear why Sklar and Berkov have chosen to adopt a position of alarmism. If anything, their figures show that the rising rate of illegitimacy among teenagers in the late 1960s has begun to level off by the early 1970s. Their observation of a rise in illegitimacy is based on a negligible increase (less than one birth per thousand) among white teenagers over a two-year period in California. Black teenagers, and women of both races in all other age groups, experience a lower rate of illegitimacy during this same period. Moreover, the national figures presented in their article reveal a pattern of stability as well. Illegitimacy among teenagers increased only imperceptibly from 1970 to 1971 *even* in states with restrictive abortion laws, suggesting that the upward trend of the late 1960s may have begun to abate even before abortion restrictions were removed. The author's explanation of "changes in the penalty and reward structure" seems a bit farfetched when the "increase" in illegitimacy has been confined to a single age group among whites only. If the reward structure were changing, would it not be

reasonable to assume that it would affect women of all age groups? Indeed, a strong case could be made that the presumed shift in economic incentives should have its greatest impact on older multiparous women who have less to lose by an additional birth than an adolescent pregnant for the first time.

The authors might just as well have concluded that the rate of out-of-wedlock pregnancies remained remarkably stable since the late 1960s considering the increased sexual activity, limited protection against pregnancy, and declining availability of marriage as a viable solution to premarital pregnancy. It is only in the past 10 years that we have seriously begun to contemplate the need or desirability of preventing unwanted pregnancies and births among teenagers by means more concrete than moral exhortation. I do not suggest that Sklar and Berkov would have us return to the era of moral exhortation, but the note of alarm which they sound is unwarranted and misleading. If not corrected, it may lead others to expound a policy that would be both regrettable and retrogressive.

June Sklar and Beth Berkov Reply:

The criticisms of both Cutright and Furstenberg reflect considerable confusion as to the nature and purpose of our study. Both attribute to us — and then refute — attitudes, opinions and interpretations we never expressed.

Cutright, for example, objects to our "concentration" on illegitimacy. However, our article was about teenage fertility, a substantial part of which is illegitimate. He claims that illegitimacy is unimportant for population growth and the subsequent career of the unwed mother, but our article says nothing about the impact of illegitimacy per se on population growth. There are many reasons other than population growth for studying illegitimacy.

Among these are its potential effects on the later life of the mother and, more important, on the development of the child. Available data strongly suggest that illegitimate children as a group fare poorly in later life.* These studies, together with cross-cultural and historical analyses of marriage and parenthood, give little basis for reaching what appears to be Cutright's conclusion — that illegitimacy makes little or no difference.† Significantly, he ignores the impact of illegitimacy on the children involved and offers no evidence, other than his own study, that illegitimacy fails to affect the later life of the mother. His study, which we find unconvincing in a number of respects, was confined to an analysis of the timing of the first birth, and applied only to ever-married mothers. Never-married mothers, who comprised six percent of the nonwhite mothers in the sample, did show long-term effects. Furthermore, the measurement of the influence of an illegitimate first birth on the mother was restricted to four items of information at one point in time — whether the mother was head of the family at the time of the survey, whether the family was above or below the poverty line at that time, labor force participation of the mother in 1966, and an approximation of completed fertility. The measurements did not include consideration of lost opportunities, psychological adjustments, health history, years lived in and outside marriage, and the history of support through public agencies — equally im-

portant factors in any analysis of the long-term influence of out-of-wedlock childbearing. That Cutright found little effect in terms of his four indicators is no proof that illegitimacy has no enduring influence on the later life of those women who subsequently marry.

Both Cutright and Furstenberg apparently object to the fact that a high level of teenage illegitimacy persists in California. Cutright points to the decline that our data show in illegitimacy rates between 1970 and 1973, while Furstenberg notes that teenage rates in the early 1970s exhibit a leveling off from the late 1960s. Both ignore our demonstration that all of the decline for white teenagers, and more than half of the decline for black teenagers, had occurred between 1970 and 1971, and was largely the result of the increased availability and use of legal abortion. Cutright does not mention the renewed rise in white teenage illegitimacy and the slower decline in black teenage illegitimacy that occurred between 1971 and 1973, while Furstenberg minimizes these changes by calling them evidence of "stability."

Cutright and Furstenberg overlook the fact that this was not just any three-year period; it was an extremely crucial one in which significant and fundamental changes had already occurred. In this period, for the first time in California, legal abortion was readily available and widely used and contraceptives were more accessible to teenagers than ever before. Yet black teenage illegitimacy, although declining, remained at a high level, while white teenage illegitimacy rose. It is this slower rate of decline in black teenage illegitimacy after 1971 and the renewed rise in white teenage illegitimacy — given the widespread availability of abortion and contraception — which led us to characterize teenage illegitimacy as persisting "at a relatively high level" in California. This characterization is borne out in the

---

* See reference 24 of our article.

† B. Malinowski, "Parenthood, the Basis of Social Structure," in R. L. Coser, ed., *The Family: Its Structure and Functions*, St. Martins, New York, 1964, p. 3; K. Davis, "Illegitimacy and the Social Structure," *American Journal of Sociology*, 45:215, 1939; and K. Davis, "Sexual Behavior," in R. K. Merton and R. Nisbet, eds., *Contemporary Social Problems*, Harcourt, Brace, Jovanovich, New York, 1971, p. 313.

cohort rates we estimated for California women, rates apparently overlooked by our critics in their rush to belittle the question of illegitimacy. For the cohort of women who reached age 14 in the state in 1968 (most of whose childbearing occurred after legal abortion became widely available), six percent of the whites and 33 percent of the blacks bore at least one illegitimate child before their twentieth birthday. Although the six percent for whites is low in comparison to blacks, it is probably considerably above the level for cohorts of white women who reached age 14 before 1960.

In his attempt to minimize the high level of teenage illegitimacy that persists in California, Furstenberg also cites the relatively small rise between 1970 and 1971 in illegitimacy rates for teenagers living in *nonabortion* states. This small rise, he claims, proves that illegitimacy was leveling off, even in the absence of liberalized abortion laws. But he neglects to mention what we took pains to point out — namely, that in states where abortion was prohibited, a sizeable number of women, particularly whites, made use of migratory abortion. It should have been clear to Furstenberg that in the absence of migratory abortion the increase in teenage illegitimacy experienced by the non-abortion states would have been greater than what actually occurred between 1970 and 1971.

Cutright thinks we should have emphasized the convergence of white and black overall fertility in California. Why? The subject of our article is *teenage* family formation, not general fertility. We dealt at some length with the convergence of white and black fertility in a previous article.* Cutright himself chooses to ignore

* J. Sklar and B. Berkov, "The Effects of Legal Abortion on Legitimate and Illegitimate Birth Rates: The California Experience," *Studies in Family Planning*, 4:281, 1973.

the very large gap between white and black teenage illegitimacy that continued in California in 1973; in that year, a little less than two percent of unmarried white teenagers as compared to eight percent of unmarried black teenagers had a baby out of wedlock.

Cutright does not believe that pregnancy is used as a means to precipitate marriage. He gives no evidence to support his belief. We do not agree with his conclusion that the evidence available from retrospective and other studies can be dismissed.

If we had consulted his work, Cutright asserts, the "mystery surrounding the . . . rise in illegitimacy after 1940" could have been cleared up. His own explanation is "improved health conditions." He is welcome to this hypothesis, but we prefer our own explanation, which is a sociological one. Cutright forgets that our explanation of the *persistence* of teenage illegitimacy at relatively high levels in California deals only with changes in the most recent period — i.e., the early 1970s after legal abortion became widely available in the state — not with changes that have occurred over the past three and a half decades. Indeed, birth data by legitimacy status for California do not begin until 1966. "Improved health conditions" cannot possibly explain why teenage illegitimate birthrates rose between 1965 and 1970 in the country as a whole, and why in California, after a sharp drop in 1971, the white teenage rate began a renewed rise in 1972 and 1973.

Neither of our critics seems to grasp our argument about the relationship between contemporary treatment of the unwed mother and the trend in illegitimacy. They interpret us as saying that young women purposely become pregnant in order to take advantage of welfare payments. The only fact to which we called attention was that social and economic support programs have contributed to a *lessening* of the penalties for out-of-wedlock childbearing. This is an obvious fact that no one has questioned, but both our critics fail to see it. They complain that we give no evidence in support of a hypothesis we never presented. Furstenberg has us saying that supportive services have made illegitimacy so "attractive" that teenage mothers have managed to "overcome the perils of early parenthood." He then assures us that this is not so, citing only his unpublished study, which apparently is based on a sample of nonwhite mothers from one hospital in Baltimore, first interviewed in 1966-1967.

The evidence we have reviewed seems to indicate that choosing to have a baby out of wedlock is not determined solely by the availability or level of support services, but also by a consideration of the *total framework* of rewards and punishments perceived by the woman. Contrary to what Furstenberg assumes, this total framework need not be the same for women of all age groups. Indeed, in recent years, it probably has been quite different for younger than for older women. Many teenagers may be experiencing little satisfaction at school and having personal problems at home. For these girls, the willingness to risk pregnancy and, once pregnant, the decision not to seek an abortion may well be influenced by the strong social approval of motherhood and the knowledge that minimal financial and other kinds of educational and community solicitude are available. Furstenberg himself cites the relevance of economic considerations. Referring to his study of low-income black adolescent mothers, he notes that "it was common for young mothers to defer marriage until the father had the prospect of stable employment or to decide not to marry because they foresaw no prospect of receiving economic support from the male." If not from the man, then from where did these young girls expect to obtain their support? Furstenberg gives no answers.

Should the possibility that social and economic programs may be relevant to a causal understanding of teenage illegitimate reproduction be ignored? Furstenberg says yes, not because the possibility is unreal, but because "enterprising politicians and reluctant taxpayers" might draw implications from it. His objection to our "alarmism" reflects his own taboo on any suggestion that welfare programs and illegitimacy might be linked. His view, then, is that it is the policy implication, not the facts, that should determine what will be admitted as causal interpretation. He sees only one stereotyped policy implication from our study, one he terms "regrettable and retrogressive." But a realistic and constructive policy can be developed only with an understanding of causes.

Both commentators fall into the fallacy of believing that illegitimacy can be dealt with relatively easily by contraception and abortion. Yet in California, as already noted, contraceptives are now more easily available than ever before to teenagers. Legal abortion use in the state reached a very high level in 1971-1972 and has remained about the same ever since. There is no basis for expecting California's legal abortion rate to climb much further and there is even some evidence that it may decline. Thus, even with widespread availability of contraception and abortion, it still remains true that teenage illegitimacy in California persists at a high level. Cutright and Furstenberg place their bet on improving the *means* of reducing fertility but completely ignore the problem of what will *motivate* teenage girls to use these means. Our studies indicate that this is a highly simplistic approach to the study of reproductive motivation among teenage girls.

3

The Legitimacy Status of First Births to U.S. Women Aged 15–24, 1939–1978

Martin O'Connell and Maurice J. Moore

Summary

Between 1975 and 1978, more than 60 percent of first births to white teenagers, and 90 percent of first births to black teenagers, were premaritally conceived. Among women aged 20–24 in the same period, only 17 percent of first births to whites, and 56 percent of those to blacks, were premaritally conceived. Since the mid-1950s, the proportion of first births premaritally conceived has risen approximately 100 percent for white teenagers and 50 percent for blacks.

There has been a sharp increase in the rate of premaritally conceived first births to white teenagers that are legitimated by marriage, as well as a decrease in births that are postmaritally conceived. As a result of these trends, about 50 percent of marital first births to white teenagers in the 1975–1978 period were premaritally conceived. Among white women aged 20–24, only 10 percent of comparable births in this period were premaritally conceived. While the proportion of

This article is based on a paper presented at the annual meeting of the Population Association of America, Philadelphia, Apr. 26–28, 1979. The authors have benefited from the helpful comments on earlier drafts of this article by Wendy H. Baldwin and Arthur A. Campbell.

marital births to white teenagers that are premaritally conceived has never been *less* than 15 percent (a level reached in the 1940s), the proportion has never been *greater* than 15 percent (reached in 1967–1970) among comparable women in their early 20s.

Since the mid-1960s, there have been approximately equal proportional declines in the postmarital-first-birth rate among both age-groups. But women aged 20 and older have recorded much larger declines than have teenagers in the rate of first births that take place out of wedlock or are legitimated by marriage. Indeed, the premarital-birth rate has increased among teenagers—especially among those aged 17 and younger, who have also registered a large relative increase in the rate of legitimated births.

After increasing steadily between the early 1940s and the late 1950s (when three-quarters of premaritally conceived first births to whites and one-third of those to blacks aged 15–24 were legitimated by marriage), the percentage of premaritally conceived first births that were legitimated by marriage has declined to a level slightly below that recorded around World War II.

Between 1973 and 1977, about 14 percent of postmarital pregnancies among teenagers were terminated by abortion, compared to nine percent among 20–24-year-olds. However, the proportion of premarital pregnancies among teenagers terminated by abortion was only 37 percent, compared to 50 percent for women in their early 20s. This lower percentage may reflect the fact that access to abortion services is more limited for unmarried teenagers than for older women.

Methodology

Several fertility studies conducted in recent years have included estimates of the incidence of premaritally conceived births in the United States. Studies of teenage fertility undertaken by Zelnik and Kantner[1] and several National Natality Surveys[2] have provided some insight into the changes in the legitimacy status of births over the past decade; but the magnitude of and trends in premarital-conception rates before the mid-1960s remain almost entirely unknown. Both the Growth of American Families Studies of 1955 and 1960 and the National Fertility Studies of 1965, 1970 and 1975 suffered from various restrictions of the survey universe—including those on the age, race and marital status of respondents. These limitations have made it virtually impossible to develop a retrospective fertility time series that is representative of the childbearing experience of all women.[3]

Beginning with the June 1976 Current Population Survey (CPS) of the U.S. Bureau of the Census, questions in the fertility supplement to the CPS have been asked of never-married women in a broad range of childbearing years, as well as of ever-married women.[4] With the inclusion of questions on the month and year of first marriage and first birth, and the raising of the age limit for respondents to 59 years, the June 1978 CPS became a unique tool for exploring changing patterns in legitimacy status of first births for the period 1939–1942 to 1975–1978. In our

analysis of these changes, first births were divided into three groups: premarital births, legitimated births and postmaritally conceived births.

A premarital first birth is defined in this article as a first birth occurring before a woman's *first marriage* (for all ever-married women) or any first birth to a never-married woman. A legitimated first birth is defined as a first birth occurring seven or fewer months after a woman's first marriage. Since the dates of first marriage and first birth are given in the CPS in months and years, misclassifications may occur if a birth and a marriage occurred in the same month and the day of the birth preceded the day of marriage.

Combining the premarital- and legitimated-first-birth categories produces the total number of first births resulting from premarital conceptions. It should be noted that not all legitimated births are the outcomes of forced or "shotgun" weddings. In many cases, it is likely that couples had already agreed to marry before the woman conceived, or realized that she was pregnant.

A first birth resulting from a postmarital conception is defined as a first birth occurring eight months or more after a first marriage. Combining this category with that of legitimated first births produces an estimate of marital fertility. The previously mentioned caveat on the dating of births and marriages also has implications here. If a woman's marriage took place in the same year and month as her first birth, the birth may be misclassified (in either direction). In addition, because of our definition of terms, some out-of-wedlock births to divorced or widowed women are classified as postmarital conceptions. To minimize the methodological problems resulting from the increasing proportions of divorced and widowed women with increasing age, this article will be confined to the childbearing experience of women under 25 years of age at the time of a first birth. Only 5–10 percent of first births to women 25 years

Figure 1. Percentage distribution of first births to women aged 15–19 and 20–24, by legitimacy status of birth, 1939–1942 to 1975–1978

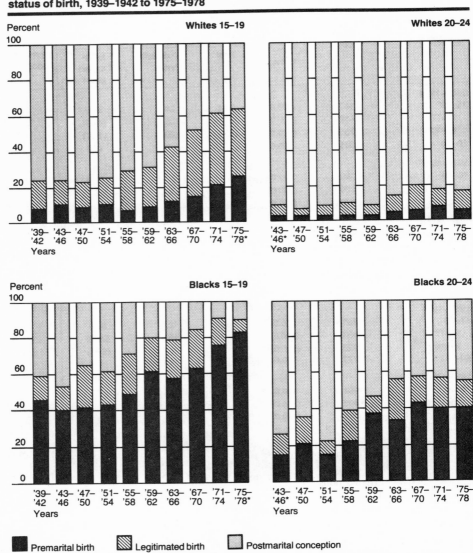

Percent
Whites 15–19

Whites 20–24

Percent
Blacks 15–19

Blacks 20–24

■ Premarital birth   ▨ Legitimated birth   ☐ Postmarital conception

*Data for this age-group are not strictly comparable with those for other periods because a number of women in this cohort are not included in the survey universe. This number is relatively small. See Tables 1 and 2.

of age and older are premaritally conceived, with the trend being slightly upward in recent years.

Data Base

The data in the June 1978 Current Population Survey come from a national probability sample of approximately 54,000 interviewed households. The respondent universe for the fertility and marital-status questions consists of ever-married women 14–59 years old and never-married women 18–59 years old at the time of the survey. Because of these survey design limitations, some of the measures discussed here for the earliest and most recent time periods are not strictly comparable to those in the intervening periods; this qualification is noted where it applies.

To utilize the full range of data in the survey, and provide a substantial base on which to compute rates, the data, except where noted, are presented in four-year periods which run from July of the preceding year to June of the stated year; for example, the 1939–1942 period runs from July 1938 to June 1942.

The Overview

Tables 1 and 2 provide a broad perspective on the changing patterns of the legitimacy of first births to women 15–19 and 20–24 years old. In general, the percentage of first births initiated by premarital conceptions is higher among blacks than among whites; higher among teenagers than among women 20–24 years old; and higher in more recent time periods than in earlier ones.

For teenagers, there are two distinct periods characterized by different trends in the percentage of first births initiated by premarital conceptions (premarital births plus legitimated births). The first period, 1939–1942 to 1951–1954 (which encompasses the World War II period and the early years of the postwar baby boom), shows a fairly constant percentage of first births resulting from

premarital conceptions—about 25 percent for white women and 60 percent for blacks. In this period, out-of-wedlock births accounted for about 10 percent of all first births to whites and 40 percent of first births to blacks (see Figure 1).

With the beginning of the second period in 1955–1958, declines in marital fertility and in marriage rates produced large increases in the percentage of first births that resulted from premarital conceptions. Within less than a generation, the percentage of first births to white teenagers that were due to premarital conceptions doubled from 29 percent in 1955–1958 to 63 percent in 1975–1978; the corresponding proportions for black teenagers increased from 71 percent to 90 percent. There were also large increases in premarital births as a percentage of all first births in this period: from seven percent to 26 percent for white teenagers, and from 49 percent to 83 percent among blacks.

The proportion of first births premaritally conceived is generally higher among 15–17-year-olds than it is among 18–19-year-olds. In the most recent period (1975–1978), 98 percent of all first births to black women aged 15–17 resulted from premarital conceptions; and 93 percent of the births occurred premaritally. Eighty percent of first births to white women aged 15–17 resulted from premarital conceptions; 36 percent were premarital births.

Of about 1.6 million first births to women aged 15–19 in 1975–1978, seven of 10, or approximately 1.1 million, resulted from premarital conceptions. Of these, six in 10 births, or about 620,000, occurred premaritally. Never-married women under 18 years of age at the time of the survey were not included in the sample; therefore, the estimates for women aged 15–17—indeed for the whole teenage sample—should be considered minimum estimates of the number and percentage of first births to 15–19-year-olds that occurred out of wedlock or were conceived premaritally. (Based on recent vital

Table 1. Percentage distribution of first births by legitimacy status, according to period in which first birth occurred, 1939–1942 to 1975–1978; white women

Period and age at 1st birth	No. of 1st births (000s)	%, by legitimacy status				
		Total 1st births	Premaritally conceived			Post- maritally conceived
			Total	Premarital births	Legit- imated births	
1975–1978						
15–19*	1,187	100.0	62.6	26.1	36.5	37.4
15–17*	(432)	(100.0)	(80.3)	(35.5)	(44.8)	(19.7)
18–19	(755)	(100.0)	(52.5)	(20.8)	(31.7)	(47.5)
20–24	1,865	100.0	17.3	7.2	10.1	82.7
1971–1974						
15–19	1,392	100.0	60.6	21.4	39.2	39.4
15–17	(520)	(100.0)	(73.2)	(34.5)	(38.7)	(26.8)
18–19	(872)	(100.0)	(53.1)	(13.6)	(39.5)	(46.9)
20–24	1,987	100.0	18.0	7.7	10.2	82.0
1967–1970						
15–19	1,304	100.0	51.6	15.0	36.6	48.3
15–17	(379)	(100.0)	(68.4)	(25.4)	(43.0)	(31.6)
18–19	(925)	(100.0)	(44.8)	(10.9)	(34.0)	(55.2)
20–24	2,171	100.0	19.9	6.2	13.7	80.1
1963–1966						
15–19	1,361	100.0	42.2	12.2	30.0	57.8
15–17	(433)	(100.0)	(55.7)	(19.9)	(35.8)	(44.3)
18–19	(928)	(100.0)	(35.9)	(8.6)	(27.2)	(64.1)
20–24	1,772	100.0	13.8	4.6	9.2	86.2
1959–1962						
15–19	1,264	100.0	31.4	9.0	22.4	68.6
15–17	(407)	(100.0)	(46.4)	(14.0)	(32.4)	(53.6)
18–19	(857)	(100.0)	(24.2)	(6.6)	(17.6)	(75.8)
20–24	1,804	100.0	9.4	3.2	6.2	90.6

*Total excludes births to women who were never married and were aged 15–17 at the time of the survey.

statistics estimates, there were probably at least 100,000 more out-of-wedlock births to 15–17-year-olds during 1975–1978 than are shown here.[5])

The percentage of all first births to black and white 20–24-year-old women that were premaritally conceived more than doubled between 1951–1954 and 1967–1970, rising from 22 percent to 57 percent among blacks, and from nine percent to 20 percent among whites. However, unlike the pattern among teenage women, no increases can be seen after that period among black women, and a slight decline is evident among whites. For women in this age-group, declines in the rate of childbearing resulting from premarital conceptions have apparently kept pace with declines in fertility within marriage.

Table 1 (continued)

| Period and age at 1st birth | No. of 1st births (000s) | %, by legitimacy status | | | | |
| | | Total 1st births | Premaritally conceived | | | Post-maritally conceived |
			Total	Premarital births	Legit-imated births	
1955–1958						
15–19	1,127	100.0	29.2	7.1	22.1	70.8
15–17	(353)	(100.0)	(43.9)	(12.0)	(32.0)	(56.1)
18–19	(774)	(100.0)	(22.5)	(4.9)	(17.6)	(77.5)
20–24	1,868	100.0	9.9	2.7	7.2	90.1
1951–1954						
15–19	951	100.0	24.5	9.6	14.9	75.5
15–17	(344)	(100.0)	(30.6)	(15.1)	(15.5)	(69.4)
18–19	(607)	(100.0)	(20.9)	(6.4)	(14.5)	(79.1)
20–24	1,752	100.0	8.9	3.4	5.5	91.1
1947–1950						
15–19	953	100.0	22.4	8.9	13.5	77.5
15–17	(263)	(100.0)	(31.6)	(11.4)	(20.2)	(68.4)
18–19	(690)	(100.0)	(19.0)	(8.0)	(11.0)	(81.0)
20–24	2,046	100.0	7.3	2.5	4.8	92.6
1943–1946						
15–19	772	100.0	23.8	9.6	14.2	76.2
15–17	(249)	(100.0)	(35.9)	(17.5)	(18.4)	(64.1)
18–19	(523)	(100.0)	(18.1)	(5.8)	(12.3)	(81.9)
20–24†	1,446	100.0	8.5	2.8	5.7	91.6
1939–1942						
15–19	651	100.0	24.4	8.0	16.4	75.6
15–17	(220)	(100.0)	(25.4)	(9.4)	(16.0)	(74.6)
18–19	(431)	(100.0)	(23.9)	(7.1)	(16.8)	(76.1)
20–24‡	‡	‡	‡	‡	‡	‡

†Data for this age-group are not strictly comparable with those for other periods because a number of women in this cohort are not included in the survey universe. This number is relatively small.

‡Data not available for a large portion of this age-group.

Premarital- and Marital-Fertility Rates

The relative proportions of premarital, legitimated and postmaritally conceived first births are determined by changes in rates of premarital and marital fertility, and by variations in the proportions of married women within each age-group. The distributions shown in Tables 1 and 2 are more clearly understood in the light of first-birth rates which relate the frequency of childbearing by legitimacy status to the appropriate female population at risk.

The average annual first-birth rates by legitimacy status are shown in Tables 3 and 4. Because of the very small bases on which black birthrates are computed (especially for ever-married women), the

Table 2. Percentage distribution of first births by legitimacy status, according to period in which first birth occurred, 1939–1942 to 1975–1978; black women

Period and age at 1st birth	No. of 1st births (000s)	Total 1st births	Premaritally conceived			Post-maritally conceived
			Total	Premarital births	Legit-imated births	
1975–1978						
15–19*	373	100.0	90.1	82.6	7.5	9.9
15–17*	(147)	(100.0)	(97.7)	(92.9)	(4.8)	(2.2)
18–19	(226)	(100.0)	(85.1)	(75.8)	(9.3)	(14.8)
20–24	231	100.0	55.5	40.3	15.2	44.6
1971–1974						
15–19	375	100.0	91.4	75.7	15.8	8.6
15–17	(205)	(100.0)	(94.2)	(80.0)	(14.2)	(5.8)
18–19	(170)	(100.0)	(88.0)	(70.2)	(17.8)	(12.0)
20–24	251	100.0	55.7	40.2	15.5	44.2
1967–1970						
15–19	385	100.0	85.0	62.9	22.1	15.1
15–17	(211)	(100.0)	(89.2)	(70.2)	(19.0)	(10.8)
18–19	(174)	(100.0)	(79.9)	(54.1)	(25.8)	(20.1)
20–24	213	100.0	57.1	42.9	14.2	42.9
1963–1966						
15–19	327	100.0	78.6	58.2	20.4	21.3
15–17	(175)	(100.0)	(89.3)	(72.9)	(16.4)	(10.7)
18–19	(152)	(100.0)	(66.6)	(41.8)	(24.7)	(33.4)
20–24	195	100.0	55.9	32.8	23.1	44.1
1959–1962						
15–19	266	100.0	79.7	61.7	18.0	20.3
15–17	(152)	(100.0)	(89.3)	(75.0)	(14.3)	(10.7)
18–19	(114)	(100.0)	(66.9)	(44.4)	(22.5)	(33.1)
20–24	167	100.0	45.8	36.9	8.9	54.2

*Total excludes births to women who were never married and were aged 15–17 at the time of the survey.

time series of black birthrates is sketchy and discontinuous, and will not be discussed in this section.

Since the data presented in this report are for first births only, the rates are expressed as first births per 1,000 childless women. The premarital-first-birth rate is expressed as the average annual number of premarital births per 1,000 never-married childless women; whereas the legitimated- and postmaritally-conceived-first-birth rates are the average annual number of marital births per 1,000 ever-married childless women; the last two rates taken together constitute the total marital-first-birth rate.

As may be seen in Table 3, the premarital-first-birth rate for teenagers increased sharply during the 1940s, leveled off during the 1950s and early 1960s, but increased after the 1959–1962 period. (The slight decrease in

Table 2 (continued)

Period and age at 1st birth	No. of 1st births (000s)	%, by legitimacy status				
		Total 1st births	Premaritally conceived			Post-maritally conceived
			Total	Premarital births	Legit-imated births	
1955–1958						
15–19	258	100.0	71.2	49.0	22.2	28.8
15–17	(126)	(100.0)	(79.1)	(60.5)	(18.6)	(20.9)
18–19	(132)	(100.0)	(63.9)	(38.0)	(25.9)	(36.1)
20–24	158	100.0	39.2	21.5	17.7	60.8
1951–1954						
15–19	217	100.0	60.9	42.9	18.0	39.2
15–17	(107)	(100.0)	(72.8)	(57.2)	(15.6)	(27.3)
18–19	(110)	(100.0)	(49.0)	(29.0)	(20.0)	(51.1)
20–24	125	100.0	22.2	14.3	7.9	77.8
1947–1950						
15–19	204	100.0	65.5	41.4	24.1	34.5
15–17	(101)	(100.0)	(73.0)	(47.0)	(26.0)	(27.0)
18–19	(103)	(100.0)	(58.5)	(35.9)	(22.6)	(41.5)
20–24	137	100.0	35.3	21.3	14.0	64.7
1943–1946						
15–19	169	100.0	52.6	39.6	13.0	47.3
15–17	(93)	(100.0)	(66.1)	(54.5)	(11.6)	(33.9)
18–19	(76)	(100.0)	(35.3)	(21.2)	(14.1)	(64.8)
20–24†	78	100.0	25.6	14.1	11.5	74.4
1939–1942						
15–19	161	100.0	59.3	45.7	13.6	40.7
15–17	(89)	(100.0)	(68.7)	(58.4)	(10.3)	(31.3)
18–19‡	(72)	(100.0)	‡	‡	‡	‡
20–24§	§	§	§	§	§	§

†Data for this age-group are not strictly comparable with those for other periods because a number of women in this cohort are not included in the survey universe. This number is relatively small.
‡Data not shown when base is less than 75,000.   §Data not available for a large portion of this age-group.

the rate from 10.4 per 1,000 women in 1971–1974 to 10.2 in 1975–1978 probably results from the omission of births to single women under 18 years of age in the survey.)

Table 4 shows the total marital-first-birth rate and its two components, the legitimated- and the postmaritally-conceived-first-birth rates.* Between 1939–1942 and 1951–1954, the postmaritally-conceived-first-birth rate for white teenagers was roughly five times the legitimated rate; the ratio fell to about three to one by 1959–1962; and by 1971–1974, the rates for the two marital-fertility groups were at the same

*Since all *ever-married* women 14 years of age and older were included in the survey universe in June 1978, the total marital, legitimated and postmarital rates shown for the 1975–1978 period do not suffer from the incompleteness which affects the premarital rate.

Table 3. Average annual premarital first-birth rates per 1,000 never-married childless women, according to period in which first birth occurred, 1939–1942 to 1975–1978; by race

Period and age at 1st birth	White No. of women (000s)*	Rate	Black No. of women (000s)*	Rate	Period and age at 1st birth	White No. of women (000s)*	Rate	Black No. of women (000s)*	Rate
1975–1978					**1955–1958**				
15–19†	7,616	10.2	1,148	67.1	15–19	4,332	4.6	521	60.5
15–17†	(4,986)	(7.7)	(799)	(42.9)	15–17	(2,998)	(3.5)	(375)	(50.7)
18–19	(2,630)	(14.9)	(349)	(122.5)	18–19	(1,334)	(7.1)	(146)	(85.6)
20–24	3,182	10.5	392	59.3	20–24	1,438	8.9	180	47.2
1971–1974					**1951–1954**				
15–19	7,204	10.4	967	73.2	15–19	4,036	5.6	469	49.6
15–17	(4,851)	(9.2)	(692)	(59.3)	15–17	(2,746)	(4.7)	(333)	(45.8)
18–19	(2,353)	(12.7)	(275)	(108.2)	18–19	(1,290)	(7.6)	(136)	(58.8)
20–24	2,579	14.9	310	81.5	20–24	1,655	8.9	167	27.0
1967–1970					**1947–1950**				
15–19	6,717	7.3	812	74.5	15–19	4,196	5.1	444	47.3
15–17	(4,489)	(5.4)	(551)	(67.2)	15–17	(2,744)	(2.7)	(306)	(38.4)
18–19	(2,228)	(11.2)	(261)	(90.0)	18–19	(1,452)	(9.5)	(138)	(67.0)
20–24	2,248	15.0	261	87.2	20–24	1,878	6.9	201	36.1
1963–1966					**1943–1946**				
15–19	6,127	6.8	743	64.3	15–19	4,595	4.0	458	36.6
15–17	(4,286)	(5.0)	(547)	(58.1)	15–17	(3,014)	(3.7)	(320)	(39.9)
18–19	(1,841)	(10.9)	(196)	(81.6)	18–19	(1,581)	(4.8)	(138)	(29.0)
20–24	1,801	11.3	197	81.2	20–24‡	2,158	4.6	190	14.5
1959–1962					**1939–1942**				
15–19	4,974	5.7	564	72.7	15–19	4,651	2.8	411	45.0
15–17	(3,456)	(4.1)	(401)	(71.1)	15–17	(3,033)	(1.7)	(279)	(46.6)
18–19	(1,518)	(9.4)	(163)	(76.7)	18–19	(1,618)	(4.8)	(132)	(41.7)
20–24	1,481	9.8	169	91.7	20–24§	§	§	§	§

*Average number of women as of January 1 for each year in period.

†Women who were never married and 15–17 years old at the time of the survey were assumed to be childless. These rates, then, represent minimum estimates of premarital childbearing.

‡Data for this age-group are not strictly comparable with those for other periods because a number of women in this cohort are not included in the survey universe. This number is relatively small.

§Data not available for a large proportion of this age-group.

level—about 240 first births per 1,000 childless ever-married women. An equivalent decline in both the legitimated and the postmarital rates subsequently kept these rates at the same level through 1975–1978 (about 200 per 1,000 women).

There are sharp contrasts between younger and older teenagers in the two component marital-fertility rates. In the 1975–1978 period, the postmarital-birth rate among white 15–17-year-olds was 180 per 1,000

women—less than half the legitimated rate of 411. Among 18–19-year-olds, however, the postmarital-first-birth rate of 212 was one and one-half times the legitimated-first-birth rate of 141.

Although the legitimated-birth rate is high, and has grown in recent years, it is implausible that all women who were pregnant at the time of their first marriage were forced into hasty marriages for the sole purpose of legitimating a child. Given that

Table 4. Average annual marital first-birth rates per 1,000 ever-married childless women, according to period in which first birth occurred, 1939–1942 to 1975–1978; by race

Race, period and age at 1st birth	No. of women (000s)*	Total marital	Legit- imated birth	Post- marital birth	Race, period and age at 1st birth	No. of women (000s)*	Total marital	Legit- imated birth	Post- marital birth
White					**White (contd.)**				
1975–1978					**1951–1954**				
15–19	541	405.3	200.1	205.2	15–19	512	420.4	69.3	351.1
15–17	(118)	(591.1)	(411.0)	(180.1)	15–17	(169)	(433.4)	(79.9)	(353.6)
18–19	(423)	(353.4)	(141.3)	(212.2)	18–19	(343)	(414.0)	(64.1)	(349.9)
20–24	2,101	206.0	22.4	183.6	20–24	1,166	363.0	20.8	342.2
1971–1974					**1947–1950**				
15–19	572	477.7	238.2	239.5	15–19	514	422.2	62.8	359.4
15–17	(135)	(629.6)	(372.2)	(257.4)	15–17	(146)	(399.0)	(90.8)	(308.2)
18–19	(437)	(430.8)	(196.8)	(234.0)	18–19	(368)	(431.4)	(51.6)	(379.8)
20–24	1,976	232.0	25.7	206.4	20–24	1,313	379.7	18.9	360.8
1967–1970					**1943–1946**				
15–19	560	494.2	213.0	281.3	15–19	464	376.1	59.3	316.8
15–17	(121)	(584.7)	(336.8)	(247.9)	15–17	(141)	(365.3)	(81.6)	(283.7)
18–19	(439)	(469.3)	(178.8)	(290.4)	18–19	(323)	(380.8)	(49.5)	(331.3)
20–24	1,584	321.3	47.0	274.3	20–24†	1,232	285.3	16.6	268.7
1963–1966					**1939–1942**				
15–19	546	547.2	186.8	360.4	15–19	427	350.7	62.7	288.1
15–17	(153)	(567.0)	(253.3)	(313.7)	15–17	(141)	(352.8)	(62.1)	(290.8)
18–19	(393)	(539.4)	(161.0)	(378.5)	18–19	(286)	(349.7)	(62.9)	(286.7)
20–24	1,114	379.7	36.6	343.1	20–24‡	‡	‡	‡	‡
1959–1962					**Black§**				
15–19	576	499.1	122.8	376.3	1975–1978	103	335.0	85.0	250.0
15–17	(189)	(463.0)	(174.6)	(288.4)	1971–1974	110	340.9	88.6	252.3
18–19	(387)	(516.8)	(97.6)	(419.3)	1967–1970	90	336.1	83.3	252.8
20–24	989	441.1	28.1	413.1	1963–1966	74	**	**	**
1955–1958					1959–1962	66	**	**	**
15–19	570	459.2	109.2	350.0	1955–1958	77	402.6	90.9	311.7
15–17	(182)	(427.2)	(155.2)	(272.0)	1951–1954	88	306.8	28.4	278.4
18–19	(388)	(474.2)	(87.6)	(386.6)	1947–1950	103	259.7	46.1	213.6
20–24	1,037	438.1	32.3	405.7	1943–1946†	89	188.2	25.3	162.9
					1939–1942‡	‡	‡	‡	‡

*Average number of women as of January 1 for each year in period.

†Data for this age-group are not strictly comparable with those for other periods because a number of women in this cohort are not included in the survey universe. This number is relatively small.

‡Data are not available for a large portion of this age-group.

§Because of the small data base for teenage wives, rates are shown only for ever-married childless women 20–24 years old.

**Data not shown when base is less than 75,000.

the 1973 Supreme Court decisions in *Roe* v. *Wade* and *Doe* v. *Bolton* struck down most state laws restricting abortions, pressures to marry have probably been less in recent years than in the past. The observed increases in the rate of legitimated births may merely reflect an increase in premarital conceptions among couples who already anticipate marriage.[6] In any event, the fact that such a large percentage of young women begin their married life with an already developing family portends, for a great many of them, future emotional and financial strains associated with marital instability.[7]

The first-birth rates for whites 20–24 years old differ widely from the teenage rates. Although the premarital-fertility rates for both age-groups increased during the 1940s (see Table 3), the similarity ends there. While teenage rates bottomed out during the 1950s, and subsequently increased, premarital-birth rates for women in their early 20s continued to rise to a peak in 1967–1970, but declined subsequently.

Regarding postmarital-birth rates, not only are the general trend and the peak period (1959–1962) identical for women 15–19 and 20–24, but the rates for both groups are of comparable magnitudes (see Table 4). The legitimated-birth rates, however, tell a different story: While the legitimated rate for teenagers in the past decade has grown both in magnitude and as a proportion of the overall total marital- birth rate, the legitimated rate for women in their early 20s has fallen substantially, both absolutely and relatively. And whereas the proportion of marital births resulting from premarital conceptions among teenagers has never been *less than* 15 percent (the low point of 15 percent was reached in 1947–1950), in no instance has this proportion been *greater than* 15 percent for women aged 20–24 (that high point was attained in 1967–1970).

The differences in the fertility patterns of the two age-groups are explained in part by their varying degrees of knowledge about and access to contraception and abortion

services, teenagers being relatively disadvantaged in this regard.[8] The table below presents the percentage change in the average annual first-birth rates for white women, for the three categories of births and the total marital rate, from the beginning of the "modern" fertility control period in 1963–1966 through the most recent period, 1975–1978.

Age at 1st birth	Pre-marital	Total marital	Legit-imated	Post-marital
15–19	+50.0*	−24.4	+9.2	−41.9
15–17	(+54.0*)	(+4.3)	(+62.3)	(−42.6)
18–19	(+36.7)	(−34.5)	(−12.2)	(−43.9)
20–24	−7.1	−45.7	−38.8	−46.5

*Represents the minimum percentage change for this period.

During these years, there were uniformly greater declines in marital fertility among women 20–24 than among teenagers. (The premarital-birth rate increased among teenagers—especially younger teenagers—as well as among women aged 20–21.) The postmarital-first-birth rate fell by a greater percentage than the legitimated-first-birth rate (which actually increased substantially among younger teens). Little difference by age was found in the percentage change in the postmarital-birth rate—women of all ages shared about equally in declines in fertility within marriage. These patterns suggest a social diffusion process in which fertility control practices are first adopted by and made available to married and relatively older women, and only subsequently to never-married and younger women.

Legitimation

The effect of changes in the premarital- and legitimated-first-birth rates is shown in Table 5.* The peak periods of legitimation among white women (in all age-groups) occurred in the late 1950s and early 1960s. During this

*Percentages are based on the total number of premaritally conceived first births occurring in each four-year period.

Table 5. Percentage of premaritally conceived first births legitimated by marriage, according to period in which first birth occurred, 1939–1942 to 1975–1978; by race

Period	Age at first birth					
	White				Black	
	15–19	15–17	18–19	20–24	15–19	20–24
1975–1978	58.3*	55.9*	60.4	58.4	8.3*	27.3
1971–1974	64.7	52.9	74.3	56.9	17.3	27.9
1967–1970	70.9	62.9	75.8	68.8	26.0	24.8
1963–1966	71.1	64.3	76.0	66.8	26.0	41.3
1959–1962	71.3	69.8	72.6	65.7	22.6	19.5
1955–1958	75.7	72.9	78.2	72.4	31.1	†
1951–1954	60.9	50.9	69.3	62.2	29.5	†
1947–1950	60.3	63.9	58.0	65.6	36.8	†
1943–1946	59.8	51.1	68.1	67.2‡	24.7	†
1939–1942	67.3	†	69.9	§	22.9	§

*Base excludes premarital births to women who were never married and were aged 15–17 at the time of the survey.

†Data not shown when base is less than 75,000.

‡Data for this age-group are not strictly comparable with those for other periods because a number of women in this cohort are not included in the survey universe. This number is relatively small.

§Data not available for a large portion of this age-group.

period, more than 70 percent of all premaritally conceived births were legitimated. Women aged 18 and 19 generally had the highest legitimation ratios throughout the study period. This is to be expected, since these ages represent a crucial period in the life cycle (which includes graduation from high school and the attainment of legal adulthood). Large numbers of women have traditionally married at these ages, whether or not they were pregnant.

Recent declines in the legitimation of premaritally conceived first births may be traced partly to the declining economic position of young men,[9] which limits their ability to support a family begun unexpectedly.[10] By 1975–1978, both white women aged 15–19 and those aged 20–24 had legitimation ratios below 60 percent; although these were lower than the ratios recorded in the 1960s, they were not very different from those seen during the 1940s. It would appear, then, that young couples today legitimate premaritally conceived births in approximately the same proportion as they did 30 to 40 years ago. However, in view of the higher proportion of conceptions that are currently terminated by legal abortion than was the case in past decades, the interpretation of the legitimation ratio as a moral barometer of the behavior of young couples is rather dubious.

It is highly probable that recent declines in the legitimation ratio have occurred because many women today realize that marriage may not be the solution to a premarital conception; indeed, it is often a precursor of even greater problems and of marital discord.* [11] In fact, research by Furstenberg and Crawford suggests that premaritally

*While a large proportion of women who have a premarital first birth marry shortly after the birth, this proportion has declined sharply in the last two decades. Among white women who had a premarital birth during 1955–1958 at ages 15–24, 36 percent married within one year of the birth; by 1971–1974, the percentage had declined to 24 percent. The proportions of comparable black women marrying in the same time periods were considerably less—23 percent and 10 percent, respectively.

pregnant women who bear a child and *do not* marry often receive considerable emotional and financial support from their families.[12] This often gives them a considerable socioeconomic advantage over premaritally pregnant women who *do* marry and subsequently divorce, as is often the case. Bearing in mind that many teenage births result from premarital conceptions, the advent of legal abortion may not only have affected the legitimation ratio, but may also have contributed significantly to the accelerated decline in first-marriage rates during the 1970s by removing a principal reason for early marriage, namely, a premarital conception.[13]

Also shown in Table 5 are the legitimation ratios for black women. Although the data are sketchy, and indicate no definite trend, they do show that the legitimation ratios for black women are one-third to one-half those for white women. A very sharp decline in the legitimation ratio during the 1975–1978 period, however, resulted in only eight percent of premaritally conceived first births to black teenagers being legitimated, whereas 58 percent of premaritally conceived first births to white teenagers were legitimated.

In analyzing changes in the legitimation ratio, it should be remembered that the increased availability of abortions in recent years has provided a premaritally pregnant woman with a legal and practical alternative to an out-of-wedlock birth or forced marriage. The declines in the legitimated-birth rate were earlier and sharper than the declines in the premarital-birth rate (see Tables 3 and 4). This suggests that the women who obtained abortions would, in the absence of legal abortion, have been more likely to marry and legitimate a premarital conception. Since the women who obtained abortions were apparently more likely to marry, the effect of an increase in the proportion of pregnancies terminated by abortion has been to decrease the legitimated-birth rate relative to the premarital-birth rate (see Table 5).

No one knows how many current abortions

may be attributed to the legalization of abortion in the early part of the 1970s. Thus, there is no way to reconstruct past patterns in the legitimacy status of first births while controlling for the effect of differences in abortion rates over time. For the period 1973–1977, however, Table 6 presents an attempt to approximate the distribution of first live births, first legal abortions and first spontaneous fetal losses for women through 24 years of age.*

Overall, approximately one-third of all teenagers and one-fourth of all women aged 20–24 whose first conceptions had outcomes in this five-year period obtained legal induced abortions. This resulted in an estimated 2.4 million first abortions during 1973–1977, out of about 8.6 million first conceptions which had outcomes in this period. As expected, the older women had a higher proportion of first conceptions resulting in live births (62 percent) than did the teenage group (53 percent); the difference is presumably due to the greater frequency of postmarital intended first conceptions among women aged 20–24 than among teenagers.

Among both teenagers and women in their early 20s, relatively more premarital than postmarital conceptions were terminated by abortions. This finding is quite plausible if one assumes that premarital pregnancies are more likely than postmarital conceptions to be accidental and undesired. With respect to premarital first conceptions, the percentage ending in legal abortions is higher among women in their early 20s (50 percent) than among teenage women (37 percent); the opposite holds for postmarital first conceptions, with 14 percent of teenage wives obtaining an abortion compared to nine percent of

*Not all first births are the outcomes of first conceptions. The distributions shown in Table 6 are based on *first events* occurring in 1973–1977 and are not necessarily the outcomes of *first pregnancies*. For exposition purposes, however, the term "first conceptions" is used in this article.

Table 6. Distribution of first live births, first legal abortions and first spontaneous fetal losses, by age of woman at time of event and legitimacy status at time of conception, 1973–1977*

Type of 1st event	Age<20 Estimated no. (000s)	%	Age 20–24 Estimated no. (000s)	%
Total 1st events	**4,420**	**100**	**4,229**	**100**
Live births	2,349	53	2,638	62
Premarital births	(974)	(22)	(308)	(7)
Legitimated births	(693)	(16)	(279)	(7)
Postmarital births	(682)	(15)	(2,051)	(48)
Legal abortions	1,415	32	1,001	24
Fetal losses	656	15	590	14

Type of 1st event	Age<20 Estimated no. (000s)	%	Age 20–24 Estimated no. (000s)	%
Total premarital 1st events	**3,433**	**100**	**1,515**	**100**
Live births	1,667	49	587	39
Premarital births	(974)	(28)	(308)	(20)
Legitimated births	(693)	(20)	(279)	(18)
Legal abortions	1,274	37	751	50
Fetal losses	492	14	177	12
Total postmarital 1st events	**987**	**100**	**2,714**	**100**
Postmarital births	682	69	2,051	76
Legal abortions	141	14	250	9
Fetal losses	164	17	413	15

*Data are for calendar years.
Note: The detailed computations used to obtain the distribution of fertility events above are obtainable from the authors on request. The sources of the data are as follows: **Birth statistics for 1973–1975:** National Center for Health Statistics, DHEW (NCHS), *Vital Statistics of the United States: Volume I—Natality,* annual volumes, Table 1-52; **data for 1976–1977:** NCHS, "Advance Report, Final Natality Statistics," *Monthly Vital Statistics Report,* Vol. 26, No. 12, 1978, Supplement, Table 2, and Vol. 27, No. 11, 1979, Supplement, Table 2. **First-birth data for 1973–1977:** June 1978 CPS computer printouts. **Abortion estimates for 1973–1977:** J. D. Forrest, C. Tietze and E. Sullivan, "Abortion in the United States, 1976–1977," *Family Planning Perspectives,* **10:**271, 1978, Tables 1 and 3. **Estimated first abortions:** C. Tietze, "Teenage Pregnancies: Looking Ahead to 1984," chapter 8, above. **Fetal loss ratios:** estimated by C. Tietze and J. Bongaarts, The Population Council (personal communication).

wives aged 20–24. Regardless of the type of conception, it seems reasonable to assume that a birth is more likely to be unacceptably disruptive in the lives of teenage women than in the lives of women of greater maturity and personal stability, and that the pregnancy is thus more likely to be aborted. The lower percentage of premarital conceptions ending in abortions among unmarried teenagers may, however, also reflect the teenagers' more limited knowledge of and access to abortion services.[14]

Appendix

Although this study indicates that large increases have recently occurred in the percentage of teenage births resulting from premarital conceptions, widely publicized analyses based on the 1964–1966 and 1972 National Natality Surveys (NNS) have suggested that the proportion of teenage births due to premarital conceptions did not appreciably change between the early 1960s and the early 1970s, and that the increase in premarital births as a proportion of all births occurred not because more births were premaritally conceived, but because fewer were being legitimated.[15]

Table 7 presents data on the legitimacy status of first births from the June 1978 CPS and the NNS of 1964–1966 and 1972. While the NNS data record little dif-

Table 7. Percentage distribution of first births to women aged 15–19 in 1964–1966 and 1972, by legitimacy status of birth, National Natality Survey (NNS) and June 1978 Current Population Survey (CPS)

Legitimacy status	1964–1966		1972	
	NNS	CPS	NNS	CPS
Premarital conceptions	56.7	52.9	59.2	67.5
Premarital births	(24.9)	(25.0)	(40.1)	(32.8)
Legitimated births	(31.8)	(27.9)	(19.1)	(34.7)
Postmarital conceptions	43.3	47.1	40.8	32.5
All 1st births	100.0	100.0	100.0	100.0
Percent of premarital conceptions legitimated	56.1	52.7	32.3	51.4

Source: For NNS, see reference 2.

ference between the two time periods in the percentage of teenage first births resulting from premarital conceptions (57 percent in 1964–1966 and 59 percent in 1972), the CPS data show an increase from 53 percent to 68 percent. In the NNS, the percentage of premaritally conceived births that were legitimated declined from 56 percent to 32 percent, whereas the CPS percentage remained essentially the same in both periods— just over 50 percent. The CPS data, then, present a completely different picture of trends in the legitimacy status of first births in the stated period.

The conflict between the NNS and CPS data apparently arises from the poor response rates in the NNS. Both the 1964–1966 and the 1972 surveys were mail-out/mail-back surveys of marital births during the stated periods and were used in conjunction with vital statistics data on out-of-wedlock births to generate the distribution of first births by legitimacy status. The response rate for women aged 15–19 was 83 percent in the 1964–1966 survey, but only 58 percent in the 1972 survey. On the other hand, in the June 1978 CPS, the response rate for women who would have been 15–19 years old in those periods and had a first birth then was

between 90 and 95 percent. It is highly likely, then, that the NNS nonrespondents tended to be women who had a legitimated birth; therefore, an understatement of the number of legitimated births in the 1972 survey apparently compensated for a rise in the number of out-of-wedlock births during this period (as recorded in the vital statistics system) to produce a 1972 distribution of first births that had a similar percentage premaritally conceived, but a lower percentage legitimated, than was the case in 1964–1966.

References

1. M. Zelnik and J. F. Kantner, "First Pregnancies to Women Aged 15–19: 1976 and 1971," chapter 5, above.

2. P. J. Placek, "Trends in Legitimate, Legitimated by Marriage and Illegitimate First Births: United States, 1964–66 and 1972," paper presented at the annual meeting of the American Statistical Association, San Diego, Aug. 14–17, 1978.

3. C. F. Westoff and N. B. Ryder, *The Contraceptive Revolution,* Princeton University Press, Princeton, N.J., 1977, pp. 3–4.

4. M. J. Moore, "Asking Single Women About Their Children: The Census Bureau's Experience," in S. D. Goldfield, ed., *Proceedings of the Social Statistics Section 1976,* American Statistical Association, Washington, D.C., 1976.

5. National Center for Health Statistics, DHEW (NCHS), *Vital Statistics of the United States, 1975: Volume I— Natality,* U.S. Government Printing Office, Washington,

D.C. (GPO), 1978; NCHS, "Advance Report, Final Natality Statistics, 1976," *Monthly Vital Statistics Report*, Vol. 26, No. 12 (March supplement), 1978; and M. O'Connell, "Comparative Estimates of Teenage Illegitimacy in the United States, 1940–44 to 1970–74," *Demography*, Vol. 17, No. 1, 1980.

6. M. Zelnik and J. F. Kantner, "Sexual and Contraceptive Experience of Young Unmarried Women in the United States, 1976 and 1971," chapter 4, above.

7. J. McCarthy and J. Menken, "Marriage, Remarriage, Marital Disruption and Age at First Birth," chapter 14, above.

8. Select Committee on Population, U.S. House of Representatives, 95th Congress, *Fertility and Contraception in the United States*, GPO, 1979.

9. R. A. Easterlin, "What Will 1984 Be Like? Socioeconomic Implications of Recent Twists in Age Structure," *Demography*, 15:397, 1978.

10. F. F. Furstenberg, Jr., "The Social Consequences of Teenage Parenthood," chapter 12, above.

11. W. H. Baldwin, "Adolescent Pregnancy and Child-bearing—Growing Concerns for Americans," *Population Bulletin*, Vol. 31, No. 2, 1976; and H. B. Presser, "Sally's Corner: Coping with Unmarried Motherhood," *The Journal of Social Issues*, 36:107, 1980.

12. F. F. Furstenberg, Jr., and A. G. Crawford, "Family Support: Helping Teenage Mothers to Cope," chapter 18, above.

13. M. J. Moore and C. C. Rogers, "Some New Measurements of First Marriages, 1954 to 1977," paper presented at the annual meeting of the Population Association of America, Philadelphia, Apr. 26–28, 1979.

14. E. W. Paul, H. F. Pilpel and N. F. Wechsler, "Pregnancy, Teenagers and the Law, 1976," *Family Planning Perspectives*, 8:16, 1976; and L. Ambrose, "Misinforming Pregnant Teenagers," chapter 26, below.

15. C. S. Chilman, *Adolescent Sexuality in a Changing American Society*, DHEW Publication No. (NIH) 79-1426, Washington, D.C., 1979; W. H. Baldwin, 1976, op. cit., p. 8; Select Committee on Population, 1979, op. cit.; chapter 18; and P. J. Placek, 1978, op. cit.

4
Sexual and Contraceptive Experience of Young Unmarried Women in the United States, 1976 and 1971

Melvin Zelnik and John F. Kantner

In the spring and early summer of 1971, a study was conducted with a national probability sample of women 15–19 years of age living in households and in college dormitories in the continental United States. The sampled population included women of all marital statuses and races.* One of the major purposes of that study was to provide for teenagers estimates of the prevalence of premarital intercourse, the use and nonuse of contraception, pregnancy and the manner in which pregnancies were resolved. The study also attempted to determine how knowledgeable teenage women were about contraception and the menstrual cycle.[1]

A similar but independent study was carried out in the spring and early summer of 1976, again with a national probability sample of women aged 15–19 who lived in households in the continental United States. As before, the sampled population covered women of all marital statuses and races.†

This article is an overview from the 1976 study of certain aspects of sexual knowledge, the prevalence of premarital sexual experience, and contraceptive practices. The findings relate to never-married women 15–19 years of age in 1976. Where the data permit, comparisons are made with 1971.‡

The authors acknowledge the invaluable assistance of Judy Gehret, Nelva Hitt and Farida Shah. The 1971 and 1976 studies upon which this article is based were supported by Grant No. HD05255 from the National Institute of Child Health and Human Development, DHEW. Generous assistance also was received from the Ford Foundation and the General Services Foundation.

*The sampling procedures involved stratification by race to ensure a substantial and disproportionate number of interviews with black respondents but not with other nonwhites.

†As with the 1971 study, the sampling procedures used in 1976 involved stratification by race to ensure a substantial number of interviews with black respondents. Following our previous practice, we use the term white to refer to whites plus nonwhites other than blacks.

‡The 1976 study did not include women living in college dormitories. For the sake of comparison, therefore, the 1971 study which included such women has been appropriately retabulated. Another point of difference from our previous practice is the presentation here of the unweighted data when dealing separately with each race. Because of differences in the weighting schemes employed in 1971 and 1976, we prefer to make comparisons from the unweighted data where appropriate. Obviously, in examining distributions for the total population (i.e., whites and blacks combined), weighted estimates must be employed since blacks are disproportionate-

Table 1. Percent of never-married women aged 15-19 who have ever had intercourse, by age and race, 1976 and 1971

Age	Study year and race											
	1976					1971					% increase 1971-1976		
	All	White		Black		All	White		Black		All	White	Black
	%	%	N	%	N		%	N	%	N			
15-19	**34.9**	**30.8**	**1,232**	**62.7**	**654**	**26.8**	**21.4**	**2,633**	**51.2**	**1,339**	**30.2**	**43.9**	**22.5**
15	18.0	13.8	276	38.4	133	13.8	10.9	642	30.5	344	30.4	26.6	25.9
16	25.4	22.6	301	52.6	135	21.2	16.9	662	46.2	320	19.8	33.7	13.9
17	40.9	36.1	277	68.4	139	26.6	21.8	646	58.8	296	53.8	65.6	16.3
18	45.2	43.6	220	74.1	143	36.8	32.3	396	62.7	228	22.8	35.0	18.2
19	55.2	48.7	158	83.6	104	46.8	39.4	287	76.2	151	17.9	23.6	9.7

Note: *In this and subsequent tables:* Base excludes those for whom no information was obtained on intercourse; this amounted in 1971 to 1.2 percent of the never-married blacks and 1.3 percent of the whites; and, in 1976, to 0.9 percent of the blacks and 0.7 percent of the whites. Percentages for whites and blacks are computed from unweighted data (Ns in tables); percentages for total sample are computed from weighted data and thus may sometimes appear to be inconsistent with figures by race. Figures for 1971 differ from earlier published reports because they exclude women living in group quarters. Except where indicated, the base excludes women who did not respond to the question analyzed in the table.

Although restriction of the discussion to unmarried women greatly simplifies the exposition, it can lead in some instances to biased or misleading estimates. For example, a valid estimate of the prevalence of premarital intercourse or premarital pregnancy among a cohort of women must include ever-married as well as never-married women. A companion piece to this article examines premarital intercourse and pregnancy among the total sample—the ever-married as well as the never-married (see chapter 5).

There are two differences between the 1971 and 1976 studies which may have a minor bearing on the findings. In the

1971 study, age eligibility** was determined at the time the household was screened; young women whose age at last birthday was 15–19 were eligible to participate in the study. Although interviewing usually proceeded immediately after screening, screening itself extended over a 3–4 month interval. As a result, the respondents represented more than 60 months of births, but no events could occur to them at an age greater than their reported current age. In the 1976 study, age eligibility was based on having been born between March 1956 and February 1961, with those born between March 1956 and February 1957 classified as age 19, those born between March 1957 and February 1958 as age 18, and so forth. As a result of this procedure, respondents represent exactly 60 months of births. However, since interviewing occurred over a four-month span, recent events could have occurred to a respondent at

ly represented in the samples. The weights for the 1971 sample were computed from the 1970 census counts of females aged 14–18, by single years of age and race, for each of the 45 geographical and residential strata of the sampling scheme. The weights for the 1976 sample were computed for each respondent, incorporating PSU, SSU, segment, household and eligible selection probabilities plus adjustments for household screening and interview nonresponse.

** In both studies, the sole criterion of eligibility was age, with the restriction that only one eligible female could be selected (randomly) from any one household.

an age greater than her age at the time eligibility was established.* While we do not regard this as a serious matter, the two samples are not strictly comparable in respect of age.

The other difference between the two studies is in the manner of asking some of the questions. In the 1971 study, questions presumed to be more "sensitive" were included in a self-administered questionnaire; in 1976, all questions were asked by an interviewer. While the two procedures might have a differential impact on the quality of the answers, it is our impression that such impact is negligible. The procedure used in 1976 allows for greater complexity in the design of the questionnaire, making it possible to tie events together more satisfactorily. The presumed price for this is some loss of privacy for the informant, but as will become apparent in discussing the results of a randomized response procedure used in reference to one of the most sensitive issues, that concerning sexual experience, respondents appear to be remarkably candid in their answers to the direct question on sexuality as asked by the interviewer.

Prevalence of Premarital Intercourse

Evidence from a number of studies indicates that the level of sexual activity among young Americans has been in-

---

*For example, a respondent born in March 1960 is classified in the study as age 15, since her birth date falls between March 1960 and February 1961. If such a respondent were interviewed any time after March 1976, she would have turned 16, although still classified as 15. This could produce anomalous results in some instances; thus, if she first had intercourse in May 1976, her age at first intercourse would be 16. Such anomalies can occur only for respondents whose birth dates fall in the earlier months of the years as here bounded and would be of importance only for events which occurred to them after attaining their survey age.

creasing. Much of this evidence comes from studies of selected groups, particularly of high school and college students. A decade or so ago, some students of adolescent behavior believed that it was not sexual behavior that was changing but merely the willingness to talk frankly about it. This view has faded in the face of a steady escalation of the rates of premarital intercourse. It was claimed that the great change in sexual mores occurred after World War I, and that since the mid-1920s, the sexual revolution has been essentially a revolution in candor. There are no satisfactory data for accurately tracing the trend in premarital sexual activity. Data presented by Catherine Chilman suggest that, for white females at any rate, the rise has been especially sharp since the late 1960s.[2] The data from the two surveys presented here show a continued increase during the 1970s—a trend that was foreshadowed in the 1971 survey.[3]

As Table 1 and Figure 1 show, 35 percent of the unmarried teenagers interviewed in 1976 had experienced sexual intercourse, as compared to 27 percent of a comparable group in 1971—an increase in prevalence of 30 percent. Since the number of teenagers increased over the five years, the absolute growth in prevalence was even greater. The increase in premarital sexual experience occurred between 1971 and 1976 for both blacks and whites at each year of age. The proportionate change is about the same for both races at age 15, but is two times greater overall for whites than for blacks. As a result, although blacks continue to show higher rates of prevalence than whites, the relative differences are smaller in 1976 than in 1971. In total, 63 percent of unmarried black teenagers interviewed in 1976 report having had sexual intercourse, as compared to 31 percent of comparable whites. By age, the proportion sexually

Figure 1. Percent of never-married women aged 15–19 who have ever had intercourse, by age, 1976 and 1971

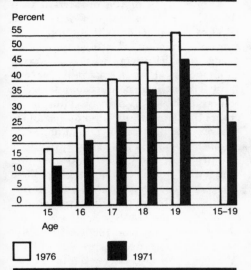

Age

☐ 1976   ■ 1971

Table 2. Percent of sexually experienced never-married women aged 15–19 who had intercourse only once, by age and race, 1976

Age	Race				
	All	White		Black	
	%	%	N	%	N
15-19	14.8	14.3	379	12.7	410
15-17	19.9	18.4	206	18.4	217
18-19	8.6	9.3	173	6.2	193

experienced rises in 1976 from 18 percent at age 15 to 55 percent at age 19. The increase in the prevalence of intercourse is accompanied by a slight downward shift, averaging four months, in the age at first intercourse.*

The increase of 30 percent in the level of premarital sexual activity between 1971 and 1976—with due allowance for sampling errors, minor elements of noncomparability in the two samples, and a possible increase in candor over the five years—represents clear evidence that more young women are today engaging in premarital intercourse than in years past.† Whether the change in behavior is indicative of a sexual revolution or evo-

lution is a matter for individual judgment, as is the issue of whether the change is desirable or deplorable. Clearly, however, a substantial fraction of American female teenagers engage in premarital intercourse.

Among those young women who, in 1976, report that they have experienced intercourse, most have had it more than once. As Table 2 shows, only 15 percent have had intercourse only one time (comparable data do not exist for 1971). Not surprisingly, those aged 15–17 were more likely to have had intercourse only once than were older adolescents. Blacks and whites are very similar in this respect.

Validation of the Estimate

Studies of this type, which rely on the respondent's candor, inevitably raise questions about the truthfulness of the responses. The most frequently raised question about the 1971 study concerned the validity of the data on the prevalence of premarital sexual intercourse. While that was and is a legitimate question, there was no definitive way of answering it. The overall quality of the data from the 1971 study and its internal consistency suggest that the data on premarital sexual activity were reasonably good, but no stronger defense for the estimates can be made.

The 1976 study included an application of the randomized response tech-

---

*This phenomenon is examined in detail below (see Table 8 and discussion).

†The conclusion that there has been a marked increase in the prevalence of sexual experience among teenage women holds when the comparisons are standardized for age.

nique (RRT) to provide another estimate of the proportion of respondents who had experienced intercourse.* Basically, the RRT is a procedure for arriving at an estimate of the level of some form of (usually sensitive or clandestine) behavior among a group of respondents without revealing to the interviewer whether they have or have not engaged in that behavior. In effect, the respondent "plays a game" that determines whether he or she will answer a sensitive or an innocuous question without the interviewer knowing which question is being answered. The rules of the game determine the probability of the selection of the sensitive question. The respondent simply answers yes or no to the question determined by the game. The interviewer, who does not know which question is being answered, records only a yes or no answer. Given the known probability of selection of the sensitive question and the proportion of yes answers, it is possible to arrive at an estimate of the proportion who are responding affirmatively to the sensitive question, i.e., who have engaged in that behavior. The estimation procedure depends upon knowing for the innocuous question the distribution of expected yes and no answers.†

The estimate of the proportion who have had intercourse provided by the RRT is 44.1 percent, with a standard error of 1.6 percent. The unweighted estimate from the direct question on sexual intercourse, 41.8 percent,‡ falls comfortably within the 95 percent confidence interval of 40.9–47.3 percent. Thus, it appears that a direct question on sexual intercourse addressed to young unmarried women 15–19 years of age in 1976 elicits truthful responses. To the degree that the initial question on sexual intercourse has been answered truthfully, it seems reasonable to assume that subsequent questions on other aspects of sexual behavior have been answered truthfully also.

Knowledge of Risk

The 1971 study indicated that fewer than two out of five unmarried women 15–19 years of age had a generally correct notion about the period of greatest risk of conception during the menstrual cycle. Only 16 percent of blacks correctly perceived that the period of greatest

---

* Ideally, when the RRT is used, the total sample should be randomly split into two groups; one group should be asked the direct question (of interest) and the other should be subjected to the RRT. Each group would thereby provide an independent estimate of the behavior in question. If the RRT provides an unbiased estimate and is consistent with the population estimate derived from responses to the direct question, then the validity of the latter is supported. Unfortunately, the RRT procedure provides an estimate of a population parameter; it does not provide any information (about the behavior of interest) at the individual level. Thus, respondents subjected to the RRT cannot be included when the behavior of concern is related to individual characteristics. To prevent that "loss" of cases, this study did not follow the ideal but costly procedure of splitting the sample. Instead, all unmarried respondents were asked both a direct question on whether they had ever had intercourse and subjected to the RRT.

† For further discussions see: J. R. Abernathy, B. G. Greenberg and D. G. Horvitz, "Estimate of Induced Abortion in Urban North Carolina," *Demography*, 7:19, 1970.

‡ This percentage, which is based (as is the estimate from the RRT) on an unweighted combination of the data for both races, is greater than the value shown in Table 1 for the weighted total. There is no way to weight the RRT responses. However, if the RRT calculation is made separately for each race, the results again are very close to those obtained by the direct question:

Race	Percent who had intercourse		
	RRT	(SE)	Direct
White	33.6	(±2.0)	30.8
Black	64.1	(±2.6)	62.7

risk is about two weeks after the period begins, in contrast to 40 percent of the whites (see Table 3). Among whites, there was a direct relationship between age and knowledge of the period of risk, and those who were sexually experienced were more knowledgeable than those who were not. On the other hand, blacks showed no variation in knowledge by age, and those with sexual experience were no more knowledgeable than those without such experience.

Proportionately more of the teenage respondents in 1976 know the time of greatest risk than was the case in 1971; however, the increase is small, especially for whites. Overall, 41 percent of unmarried women 15–19 years of age in 1976 have a correct notion of the period of greatest risk—up by only three percentage points from 1971. As in 1971, sexually experienced whites are better informed about the risk of pregnancy than their age peers who have not had intercourse. Among blacks, misinformation is widespread and bears little relationship to sexual experience or age. The continued high level of misinformation and ignorance about the period of greatest risk during the menstrual cycle may be surprising in light of the attention that has been given in recent years to sex education.

Sex Education

In an attempt to determine how effective sex education is in informing women about the menstrual cycle, each respondent was asked if she had ever had any formal classroom instruction in sex education and, if so, whether the course included information about the monthly menstrual cycle.* Table 4 shows, for those who had a course that included such information and for those who didn't, the proportions who know the pe-

riod of greatest risk of conception.† The data in Table 4 indicate that those who have had a sex education course in which the menstrual cycle was discussed are more knowledgeable than those who have not had such a course, but the differences are not great. Only a little over one-fourth of blacks who have had a course correctly identify the period of greatest risk during the menstrual cycle, and slightly fewer than half of the whites who have had a course can correctly identify that period. We do not know much about the competence of the instruction, or about the duration or content of these courses; but these data do suggest that, as in other areas of education, the transfer of knowledge in formal settings may be likened to carrying water in a basket.

The Geography of Sex

Has premarital sex among young women become more common because the opportunities for it have increased? The automobile, assorted wayside attractions, by-the-hour motels, in short, the world of a mobile teenage society, removes adolescents from the purview of concerned adults. In an earlier time, parental influence was palpable if not pres-

*If a respondent reported that she had not had formal classroom instruction in sex education in school, she was asked if she had ever had such a course somewhere else. Of those who reported having had a course in sex education, more than 90 percent said they had had the course in school.

†The table does not include a breakdown by sexual intercourse status, since for both blacks and whites the proportions having had a course that covered the menstrual cycle were not very different for the sexually active and the sexually inactive. Among blacks, 75 percent of the sexually experienced had had such a course in comparison with 70 percent of those who hadn't had intercourse; for whites, the figures were 67 and 64 percent, respectively.

Table 3. Percent of never-married women aged 15-19 who correctly perceived the time of greatest pregnancy risk within the menstrual cycle, by age, race and sexual experience, 1976 and 1971

Age	Race and sexual experience																	
	All			White						Black								
	Total	Experienced	Not experienced	Total		Experienced		Not experienced		Total		Experienced		Not experienced				
	%	%	%	%	N	%	N	%	N	%	N	%	N	%	N			
1976																		
15-19	40.6	47.3	36.9	43.9	1,194	53.2	365	39.8	829	23.5	646	24.0	405	22.8	241			
15	29.5	33.5	28.6	30.5	272	40.5	37	28.9	235	22.7	132	17.6	51	25.9	81			
16	33.5	42.8	30.3	39.8	289	50.8	65	36.6	224	18.0	133	17.4	69	18.8	64			
17	47.0	51.7	43.7	48.0	271	51.0	98	46.2	173	26.6	139	28.4	95	22.7	44			
18	49.2	52.7	46.3	52.6	215	57.0	93	49.2	122	22.3	139	23.1	104	20.0	35			
19	48.6	46.7	51.1	56.5	147	59.7	72	53.3	75	29.1	103	29.1	86	29.4	17			
1971																		
15-19	37.6	41.6	36.1	40.2	2,624	50.2	562	37.5	2,062	16.0	1,333	16.3	681	15.8	652			
15	28.6	32.8	28.0	29.5	640	41.4	70	28.1	570	16.1	341	14.4	104	16.9	237			
16	34.0	35.3	33.7	36.7	659	41.4	111	35.8	548	15.4	319	15.6	147	15.1	172			
17	38.7	41.6	37.6	42.7	644	51.8	141	40.2	503	16.3	295	16.8	173	15.6	122			
18	44.5	46.7	43.2	48.9	395	56.2	128	45.3	267	15.0	227	16.9	142	11.8	85			
19	48.5	45.8	50.8	54.6	286	55.4	112	54.0	174	18.5	151	17.4	115	22.2	36			

Table 4. Percent of never-married women aged 15-19 who correctly perceived the time of greatest pregnancy risk within the menstrual cycle, by age, race and exposure to sex education, 1976

Age	Race and exposure to sex education												
	All			White						Black			
	Total	Had course	No course*	Total		Had course		No course*		Total		Had course	No course*
	%	%	%	%	N	%	N	%	N	%	N	%	N	%	N
15-19	40.6	44.6	31.8	44.0	1,199	47.6	786	37.3	413	23.5	650	26.3	475	16.0	175
15-17	36.7	41.3	27.5	39.5	836	43.0	532	33.2	304	22.4	407	24.8	298	15.6	109
18-19	49.1	51.3	43.3	54.6	363	57.1	254	48.6	109	25.5	243	28.8	177	16.7	66

*Includes a small number who had a sex education course which did not discuss the menstrual cycle.

Table 5. Percent distribution of sexually experienced never-married women aged 15-19, according to place of occurrence of selected episodes of intercourse, by race, 1976

Place of occurrence	Episode of intercourse and race								
	First			Only once			Most recent		
	All	White (N= 323)	Black (N= 348)	All	White (N= 53)	Black (N= 51)	All	White (N= 324)	Black (N= 350)
Respondent's home	16.3	15.2	20.7	12.4	15.1	21.6	23.0	22.8	26.0
Partner's home	41.6	44.0	38.5	41.5	35.8	51.0	51.2	50.0	44.8
Relative/friend's home	21.4	19.8	21.0	24.8	24.5	15.7	11.6	13.0	9.7
Motel/hotel	5.2	2.2	13.5	0.6	0.0	5.9	6.4	3.4	16.0
Automobile	9.5	11.1	4.9	13.8	17.0	3.9	6.1	8.3	2.6
Other	6.0	7.7	1.4	6.9	7.6	1.9	1.7	2.5	0.9
Total	100.0	100.0	100.0	100.0	100.0	100.0	100.0	100.0	100.0

ent in the parlors and on the porches of small-town America, and it was represented by proxy on Main Street and in the corner store. Whether this is fact, romantic reconstitution or some of both, there is a pervasive belief that control of the young has become seriously weakened in a society in which children are more and more at large and the home is less and less the center of their activities. The situation is exemplified by solemn mayors announcing that it is 11 p.m. and asking worried parents at their TVs the question many cannot answer.

The geography of premarital sex has received little attention from those who study such matters, perhaps because they feel that they know where such acts occur, or perhaps also because of the conviction that it doesn't really matter since love, whether of the durable or disposable variety, will find a way. In the 1976 survey, each sexually active respondent was asked where sexual intercourse occurred the first time and the most recent time. For those who had intercourse only once, of course, first and most recent are the same events. More than three out of four white and black respondents report that they have had intercourse in their own or their partner's home, or in the home of a friend or rela-

tive, regardless of whether it was the first, most recent, or only time that they have had intercourse (see Table 5). The partner's home is especially favored. If intercourse does not occur in someone's home, then blacks are more likely to go to a motel or hotel; whites, on the other hand, are more likely to have intercourse in an automobile or "elsewhere," which translates generally as some part of the "great outdoors"—an option somewhat less open to blacks, who are more urban.

The changes in locale between first and most recent intercourse are in the direction of increased use of either the respondent's or the partner's home, and less reliance on the home of a friend or relative. With few exceptions, place of intercourse shows no systematic variation by current age, although with increasing age, blacks tend to place greater reliance on motels, and whites, decreasing reliance on the automobile, both in regard to first and last intercourse. There is a high degree of consistency among blacks in the locale of the first and most recent intercourse.* From half to two-thirds have had sex in the same kind of

---

*These observations pertain only to those who had intercourse more than once.

Table 6. Percent distribution of sexually experienced never-married women aged 15-19, according to frequency of intercourse in the four weeks preceding interview, by age and race, 1976 and 1971

No. of times	Race and age								
	All			White			Black		
	15-19	15-17	18-19	15-19	15-17	18-19	15-19	15-17	18-19
1976				(N=378)	(N=206)	(N=172)	(N=404)	(N=214)	(N=190)
0	47.6	51.0	43.5	49.2	53.4	44.2	49.3	55.1	42.6
1-2	25.4	30.1	19.6	21.2	24.3	17.4	29.2	28.5	30.0
3-5	11.7	10.3	13.4	12.2	10.7	14.0	14.1	10.8	17.9
≥6	15.3	8.6	23.5	17.4	11.6	24.4	7.4	5.6	9.5
Total	100.0	100.0	100.0	100.0	100.0	100.0	100.0	100.0	100.0
1971				(N=528)	(N=299)	(N=229)	(N=641)	(N=392)	(N=249)
0	39.6	41.5	37.7	38.3	39.8	36.2	40.1	42.4	36.6
1-2	30.2	34.5	25.7	30.1	34.4	24.5	34.0	33.9	34.1
3-5	17.4	15.4	19.5	17.6	15.4	20.5	17.6	16.6	19.3
≥6	12.8	8.6	17.1	14.0	10.4	18.8	8.3	7.1	10.0
Total	100.0	100.0	100.0	100.0	100.0	100.0	100.0	100.0	100.0

place. Whites exhibit a greater tendency than blacks to change locales, except where the first encounter occurred at the partner's home (not shown).

A closer examination of where sex takes place, taking account of the female's age at the time, reveals that the initiation of sex among those under age 13 occurs most often in the girl's home; at age 13, the home of a friend or relative becomes the most likely place; from age 14 on, the partner's home becomes increasingly important so that from age 17 on, half or more of all first sexual encounters occur there (not shown). The partner's home is the most likely place for the most recent intercourse to have occurred regardless of the girl's age at the time.[*] The girl's home becomes increasingly important as the locale for the most recent intercourse as her age increases. Thus, for four out of five sexual-

ly experienced unmarried females who have had more than one encounter with sex, the choice seems to lie in the answer to "my place or your place?" with his place having the edge.

"Home" is an elastic and dynamic concept. Not only has there been a sharp increase in single-person households and households containing an unmarried couple, but more and more homes are in effect zero-person households during much of the time. It is thus often a relatively easy matter to find a home that is reliably vacant at an opportune time. It is no more than ironic speculation, but one wonders to what extent the upsurge in employment among married women that has helped to reduce their own fertility may have been a factor in the sexual liberation of their children.

Frequency of Intercourse

The 1971 study revealed that most never-married, sexually experienced teenage women had intercourse infrequently. As

---

[*]Excluding those who have had intercourse only once.

Table 7. Percent distribution of sexually experienced never-married women aged 15-19, according to number of partners ever, by age and race, 1976 and 1971

No. of partners	Age and race								
	All			White			Black		
	15-19	15-17	18-19	15-19	15-17	18-19	15-19	15-17	18-19
1976				(N=372)	(N=203)	(N=169)	(N=398)	(N=213)	(N=185)
1	50.1	54.0	45.3	52.9	54.7	50.9	40.2	47.9	31.3
2-3	31.4	31.5	31.3	28.0	31.0	24.2	42.0	35.7	49.2
4-5	8.7	8.4	9.1	7.8	6.4	9.5	11.8	11.7	11.9
≥6	9.8	6.1	14.3	11.3	7.9	15.4	6.0	4.7	7.6
Total	100.0	100.0	100.0	100.0	100.0	100.0	100.0	100.0	100.0
1971				(N=541)	(N=308)	(N=233)	(N=648)	(N=400)	(N=248)
1	61.5	66.5	56.1	61.6	66.5	54.9	61.4	64.2	56.9
2-3	25.1	22.7	27.7	22.9	20.8	25.7	28.9	27.8	30.6
4-5	7.8	5.9	9.9	8.5	6.5	11.2	6.9	6.0	8.5
≥6	5.6	4.9	6.3	7.0	6.2	8.2	2.8	2.0	4.0
Total	100.0	100.0	100.0	100.0	100.0	100.0	100.0	100.0	100.0

measured by the frequency of intercourse during the month preceding the survey, approximately two in five abstained. Race made no difference. Teenagers in 1976 appear even more abstemious (see Table 6). About half of the never-married, sexually experienced respondents had not had intercourse during the month prior to the survey, and fewer than three in 10 had had intercourse as many as three times in the month.* Thus, the increase since 1971 in the proportion of young unmarried women who have had sex has not been paralleled by an increase in the frequency of such behavior among the initiated. Blacks and whites are very similar with respect to degree of sexual activity; whites who had sex at all during the reference period had it somewhat more often.

*The data shown in Table 6 include those who have had intercourse only once. Most of them had that experience more than four weeks prior to the survey. When they are removed from consideration, the modal frequency is still zero for both blacks and whites.

The Male Partner

Most sexually experienced unmarried women in the 1971 survey tended to confine themselves to one partner (see Table 7 and Figure 2). Whites and blacks were quite similar except that whites were considerably more likely than blacks to have had six or more partners. By 1976, both whites and blacks at each age show less exclusivity in the choice of sexual partners. The change in general is greater among blacks than among whites. Thus, whereas in 1971 more than 61 percent of sexually experienced whites and blacks had had only one partner, in 1976 this was true of only 53 percent of comparable whites and 40 percent of blacks.

Such an increase in the number of partners might occur if intercourse were beginning at younger ages than was true five years before—that is, if the period of sexual experience was lengthened. The median age at first intercourse has declined by about four months (see Table 8), but it is unlikely that this could be the entire explanation. We have no other

Figure 2. Percent of sexually experienced never-married women aged 15–19, by number of partners ever, 1976 and 1971

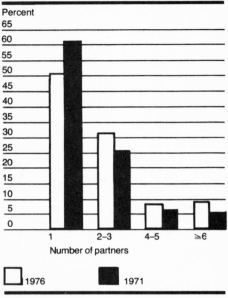

Percent

Number of partners

☐ 1976   ■ 1971

clues as to this rather substantial increase except possibly an increase in the tendency to postpone marriage.

Whatever the reason, it appears that proportionately more unmarried female teenagers are having intercourse; they are initiating sex earlier; and, on the average, they have had more partners, but without any increase in frequency of sexual activity. Perhaps the reason that coital frequency has not increased is that more partners mean that relations are somewhat less established.

The male partner at first intercourse is generally two to three years older than the female (not shown). More than 85 percent of the first partners of black teenage females are themselves teenagers; for whites, the figure is 73 percent.

As might be expected, the partner at the most recent intercourse is older than

the partner at first intercourse. More than half of the most recent partners, regardless of race, are 20 years of age or older. This high proportion of older males is due in part to the predominance of 18- and 19-year-old females among the sexually experienced. However, even among women 17 years of age and younger, a little over one-quarter of the black male partners, and nearly one-third of the white, are 20 or older. What is important is the fact that older males are more difficult to reach with organized programs than are younger ones, most of whom are still in school.*

Initiation of Sex

The decline in age at first intercourse from 16.5 to 16.2 years (as shown in Table 8)—a decline which occurs at virtually each age—is consistent with the apparent general relaxation in sexual behavior that we have observed both in the increase in the proportion who have had intercourse and in the relative increase in number of partners.

The initiation of sex bears no relation to the age at menarche for whites, but does show some systematic tendency for blacks, among whom the earlier the age of menarche, the earlier sex begins.

Nearly two-fifths of respondents first experienced intercourse during the summer (not shown).

Contraceptive Prevalence

From a strictly demographic point of view, the significance of sexual activity depends upon whether it occurs at a time

---

*If we include male partners of age 19, since most of these, too, are out of high school, the proportion of girls who were 17 years of age or younger at most recent intercourse and whose partner was 19 or older was nearly 50 percent for both races.

Table 8. Median age at first intercourse of sexually experienced never-married women aged 15-19, by age and race, 1976 and 1971

Age	Median age, by race											
	1976						1971					
	All	White		Black			All	White		Black		
		Age	N	Age	N			Age	N	Age	N	
15-19	16.2	16.3	378	15.6	405		16.5	16.5	549	16.0	667	
15	14.7	14.8	38	14.2	51		14.7	14.8	67	14.5	103	
16	15.5	15.6	68	15.4	71		15.9	15.9	109	15.5	140	
17	16.4	16.3	100	15.7	93		16.4	16.5	137	16.1	173	
18	16.8	17.1	96	16.3	105		17.2	17.3	126	16.7	140	
19	17.1	17.3	76	16.2	85		18.0	18.2	110	16.8	111	

Table 9. Percent of sexually experienced never-married women aged 15-19, according to contraceptive use status, by age and race, 1976 and 1971

Age	Race and use status														
	All				White					Black					
	Never	Some-times	Al-ways	Last* time	Never	Some-times	Al-ways	Last* time	N	Never	Some-times	Al-ways	Last* time	N	
1976															
15-19	25.6	44.5	30.0	63.5	24.1	45.8	30.2	64.8	378	25.0	46.1	28.9	58.3	408	
15	38.0	32.5	29.5	53.8	36.8	31.6	31.6	55.3	38	47.1	27.4	25.5	35.3	51	
16	30.9	38.7	30.5	56.3	36.8	33.8	29.4	50.0	68	21.1	35.2	43.7	69.0	71	
17	29.4	41.4	29.3	61.8	25.2	45.5	29.3	64.6	99	32.3	46.2	21.5	57.0	93	
18	20.8	49.1	30.1	70.3	20.8	47.9	31.3	71.9	96	17.9	47.2	34.9	66.0	106	
19	15.1	54.4	30.5	68.8	9.1	61.0	29.9	74.0	77	16.1	64.4	19.5	55.2	87	
1971															
15-19	17.0	64.6	18.4	45.4	18.3	62.0	19.7	45.1	548	16.3	67.3	16.4	41.6	669	
15	32.9	47.4	19.7	29.9	36.8	42.6	20.6	29.4	68	27.2	51.4	21.4	31.1	103	
16	20.6	58.9	20.5	38.8	20.2	58.7	21.1	38.5	109	21.8	64.8	13.4	34.5	142	
17	12.2	70.8	17.0	45.2	14.0	68.4	17.6	46.3	136	11.0	68.6	20.4	44.2	172	
18	13.0	70.1	16.9	48.8	13.5	68.3	18.2	47.6	126	11.4	72.3	16.3	48.9	141	
19	14.6	66.4	19.0	55.3	15.6	62.4	22.0	56.9	109	13.5	76.6	9.9	46.8	111	

*"Last time" includes always-users plus sometimes-users who used contraception at time of last intercourse.

when conception can occur; this, in turn, depends a very great deal on whether and how effectively contraception is employed. Contraceptive use among U.S. teenage women as revealed by the 1971 study was irregular and, except at the older ages, heavily reliant on such conventional methods as the condom and withdrawal and, among blacks, the douche.[4] Most sexually experienced teenage women had used contraception at some time, but at the time of their last intercourse, fewer than half were protected against the risk of conception.

Figure 3. Percent of sexually experienced never-married women aged 15–19 who used contraception at last intercourse, by age, 1976 and 1971

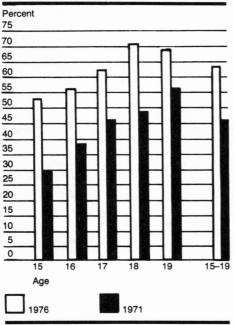

Age

☐ 1976   ■ 1971

As may be seen in Table 9 and Figure 3, that picture has changed remarkably since 1971.* For both races, and at all ages, there has been an increase in the percentage of sexually experienced unmarried women who have always used contraception. For all ages, this category of users is up 53 percent for whites and 76 percent for blacks—very substantial increases. Such a change in the regular-

ity of use produces a dramatic rise also in the proportions who were protected at their last intercourse†—from 42 to 58 percent for blacks and from 45 to 65 percent for whites. Even the younger respondents, those aged 17 and *under* in 1976, are more likely to have used contraception at last intercourse than were those *over* 17 in 1971.‡

Moderating this picture of improved contraceptive practice is the fact that the proportion of those who have never used contraception has increased also, though by only nine percentage points. If we remove those cases who have had intercourse only once,§ for whom the use or nonuse of contraception is essentially a chance matter,** the proportion who have never used contraception is only slightly diminished. Some suggestion of what may be going on comes from a comparison of the methods of contraception that were being used in these two periods.

---

†Always-users plus those sometime-users who used contraception at time of last intercourse.

‡Percent who used contraception at last intercourse:

Age	White	Black
15-17 (1976)	58.0	55.8
18-19 (1971)	51.9	48.0

§This can be done for 1976 but not for 1971.

**The proportion of those who had intercourse only once and who used contraception is about the same as the proportion of users at first intercourse among those who had subsequent episodes of intercourse. If, as some theorize, the use of contraception is a function of the "commitment" to sex, i.e., to the incorporation of sex into the "self-image," it would seem from the evidence here regarding the early use of contraception that the commitment develops subsequent to sexual initiation. This, indeed, is the view propounded by Constance Lindemann, who sees more frequent sex as indicative of commitment with a self-concept to match, leading not only to more contraception but, ultimately, to the use of medical methods of birth control which require the user to bear witness to her behavior before various authority figures (see reference 6).

---

*Information on the use of contraception in 1971 was obtained by means of a self-administered questionnaire with no interchange necessary between the respondent and interviewer. In 1976, this information was obtained by direct question, but the use of cards with lettered response categories required the respondent merely to indicate a letter which corresponded to her answer.

Table 10. Percent of ever-contracepting never-married women aged 15-19, according to methods ever used, by age and race, 1976 and 1971

Methods ever used	Age and race								
	All			White			Black		
	15-19	15-17	18-19	15-19	15-17	18-19	15-19	15-17	18-19
1976				(N=288)	(N=142)	(N=146)	(N=307)	(N=147)	(N=160)
Pill	58.8	45.1	72.9	55.6	43.7	67.1	72.3	63.3	80.6
Foam, jelly, cream	9.5	4.4	14.8	10.1	5.6	14.4	6.8	4.8	8.8
IUD	5.1	2.5	7.8	5.6	3.5	7.5	6.8	3.4	10.0
Diaphragm	1.8	1.3	2.4	2.4	2.1	2.7	0.3	0.7	0.0
Condom	39.3	41.2	37.4	42.7	44.4	41.1	28.7	34.0	23.8
Douche	9.1	6.8	11.4	7.3	4.9	9.6	17.9	14.3	21.2
Withdrawal	30.0	39.1	20.7	35.8	43.7	28.1	12.4	15.0	10.0
Rhythm	14.4	14.3	14.5	15.3	15.5	15.1	6.2	6.1	6.2
Other	0.3	0.1	0.5	0.0	0.0	0.0	1.0	0.7	1.2
1971				(N=451)	(N=248)	(N=203)	(N=565)	(N=342)	(N=223)
Pill	26.9	17.4	36.3	23.1	13.7	34.5	32.0	25.2	42.6
Foam, jelly, cream	10.2	7.7	12.7	10.0	8.1	12.3	12.4	9.6	16.6
IUD	2.8	1.7	3.8	1.8	0.8	3.0	7.3	5.8	9.4
Diaphragm	3.2	2.6	3.8	3.1	3.2	3.0	4.1	3.2	5.4
Condom	60.6	61.6	59.7	59.4	61.3	57.1	65.3	64.6	66.4
Douche	32.0	32.0	32.0	24.8	25.0	24.6	54.5	53.8	55.6
Withdrawal	64.3	62.9	65.6	74.1	75.0	72.9	45.8	45.0	47.1
Rhythm	5.5	5.6	5.5	6.4	6.8	5.9	1.1	0.3	2.2
Other	0.1	0.2	0.0	0.2	0.4	0.0	0.0	0.0	0.0

Methods of Contraception

A change in the prevalence of contraceptive use would be expected if there were a shift in the mix of contraceptive methods toward more use of such noncoitally related methods as the IUD or birth control pills. These methods, with reasonable continuity of use, would tend to increase the amount of regular use and, thus, the extent of contraceptive use on any given occasion. That appears to be what happened. Table 10 shows that among contraceptors, use of the pill more than doubled between 1971 and 1976. Use of the IUD, still a relatively

unimportant method of contraception in 1976, increased substantially also. The condom, douche and withdrawal, the big three in 1971, all suffered great losses in popularity among contraceptors. There was also a relatively large increase in the use of rhythm, due in part perhaps to more specific questioning about this method in 1976 than in 1971. Though rhythm is not highly regarded as an effective method of contraception, particularly when its use is combined with incorrect information about the timing. of ovulation, rhythm users are much better informed on the time of greatest pregnancy risk than those using

Table 11. Percent distribution of ever-contracepting never-married women aged 15-19, according to method most recently used, by age and race, 1976 and 1971

Method	Age and race								
	All			White			Black		
	15-19	15-17	18-19	15-19	15-17	18-19	15-19	15-17	18-19
1976				(N=287)	(N=141)	(N=146)	(N=306)	(N=146)	(N=160)
Pill	47.3	36.4	58.5	43.6	35.5	51.4	59.8	52.8	66.2
IUD	3.4	2.4	4.3	4.2	3.5	4.8	4.9	2.7	6.9
Condom	20.9	27.6	14.2	22.6	27.7	17.8	17.0	25.3	9.4
Douche	3.5	3.8	3.2	1.7	2.8	0.7	7.2	6.9	7.5
Withdrawal	16.9	24.7	9.0	18.5	25.5	11.6	5.9	8.2	3.8
Other	8.0	5.1	10.8	9.4	5.0	13.7	5.2	4.1	6.2
Total	100.0	100.0	100.0	100.0	100.0	100.0	100.0	100.0	100.0
1971				(N=448)	(N=247)	(N=201)	(N=560)	(N=339)	(N=221)
Pill	23.8	15.4	32.1	20.1	11.7	30.3	27.5	21.8	36.2
IUD	1.5	0.6	2.3	0.7	0.0	1.5	3.9	2.7	5.9
Condom	32.1	40.6	23.7	30.8	38.1	21.9	37.9	43.1	29.8
Douche	5.8	6.6	5.0	2.9	2.4	3.5	12.3	13.9	10.0
Withdrawal	30.7	31.8	29.7	39.5	42.1	36.3	13.2	15.3	10.0
Other	6.1	5.0	7.2	6.0	5.7	6.5	5.2	3.2	8.1
Total	100.0	100.0	100.0	100.0	100.0	100.0	100.0	100.0	100.0

Figure 4. Percent of sexually experienced never-married women aged 15–19, according to method used at last intercourse, 1976 and 1971

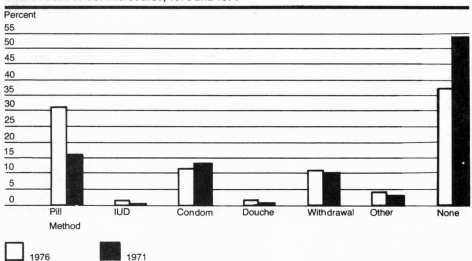

Table 12. Percent distribution of sexually experienced never-married women aged 15-19, according to method used at last intercourse, by age and race, 1976 and 1971

Method	Age and race								
	All			White			Black		
	15-19	15-17	18-19	15-19	15-17	18-19	15-19	15-17	18-19
1976				(N=378)	(N=205)	(N=173)	(N=408)	(N=215)	(N=193)
Pill	31.2	21.6	42.9	30.4	21.9	40.5	35.3	30.7	40.4
IUD	2.2	1.3	3.4	2.9	2.0	4.0	2.5	0.9	4.1
Condom	12.6	15.2	9.3	13.2	14.2	12.1	9.8	13.5	5.7
Douche	2.3	2.4	2.3	1.1	1.5	0.6	5.1	4.6	5.7
Withdrawal	10.6	14.9	5.4	12.2	15.6	8.1	3.4	4.7	2.1
Other	4.5	3.0	6.3	5.0	2.9	7.5	2.2	1.4	3.1
None	36.6	41.6	30.4	35.2	41.9	27.2	41.7	44.2	38.9
Total	100.0	100.0	100.0	100.0	100.0	100.0	100.0	100.0	100.0
1971				(N=551)	(N=314)	(N=237)	(N=674)	(N=420)	(N=254)
Pill	15.1	7.7	23.0	13.4	6.0	23.2	13.6	9.5	20.5
IUD	0.8	0.2	1.4	0.4	0.0	0.9	2.1	1.2	3.5
Condom	14.4	17.3	11.2	14.7	18.2	10.1	16.0	16.0	16.1
Douche	1.7	2.1	1.3	0.5	0.6	0.4	3.1	3.8	2.0
Withdrawal	10.3	9.4	11.3	12.9	12.4	13.5	3.9	4.8	2.4
Other	2.9	2.4	3.4	2.9	2.6	3.4	2.5	2.1	3.1
None	54.8	60.9	48.4	55.2	60.2	48.5	58.8	62.6	52.4
Total	100.0	100.0	100.0	100.0	100.0	100.0	100.0	100.0	100.0

other methods or those who have never used contraception.[*]

The data in Table 10 refer to ever-use, which is a montage of experience over time with various methods. Table 11 shows current contraceptive practice as measured by most recent use of any method. The sharp decline in use of conventional contraception and the growth in use of oral contraception is even more clearly brought out in this table. Be-

[*]Percent having correct idea of period of greatest risk, 1976:

Method ever used	Total	White	Black
Rhythm	77.3	75.6	36.8*
Other	47.6	55.3	24.5
None	37.3	40.4	20.8

*N<20.

tween 1971 and 1976, pill use doubled, while use of the condom declined by 27 percent among whites and by 55 percent among blacks. Condom and withdrawal, which used to account for more than half of contraceptive use among blacks and 70 percent among whites, now together capture 23 percent of black and 41 percent of white contraceptive use. Only in the youngest ages do these two methods account for as much or more use than orals. Both lose popularity rapidly among older women.

Table 12 and Figure 4 show the same trend in choice of method at last intercourse. Only 45 percent of teenagers used *any* method at last intercourse in 1971, and just 16 percent used the pill and IUD. In 1976, on the other hand, 63 percent used a method at last intercourse

Figure 5. Percent distribution of sexually experienced never-married women aged 15–19, by age at first intercourse and timing of first use of contraception, according to race, 1976 and 1971

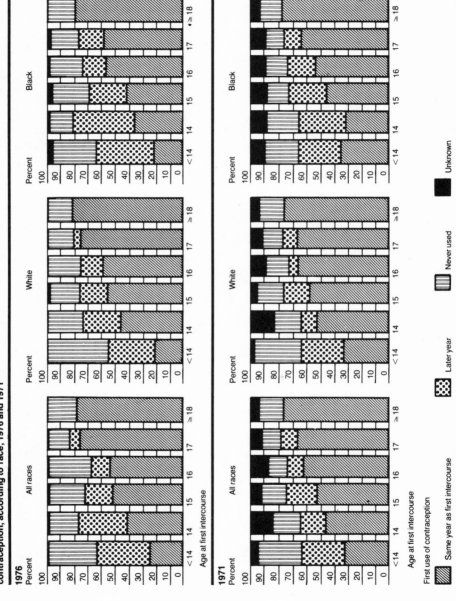

and one-third used the pill and IUD. This is greater than pill and IUD use in 1973 among *married* women of reproductive age, and two-thirds the level of such use among married women aged 15-24.[5] It is notable, too, that the decline in condom, douche and withdrawal seen for ever-use and most recent use among contraceptors is not apparent for most recent intercourse when all sexually active teenagers are considered. This is because there is a smaller proportion using these methods in 1976, but using them with greater regularity.

As we have seen, many sexually experienced teenagers are relatively inactive sexually. Although oral contraception is generally considered to be best-suited to women who have regular and frequent intercourse, it is very popular among teenage women generally—including those who have sex only occasionally. It might be asked whether those who have used pills but are not currently sexually active tend to discontinue oral contraception to a greater extent than those who continue to be active. That is, does infrequent intercourse discourage continued use? The answer is yes—to some extent. About one-third of those whose most recent method was the pill and who did not have intercourse in the four weeks before the interview stopped using the pill; while only about one-sixth of the women who were sexually active during that period discontinued use. However, it is most notable that two-thirds of the sexually experienced but inactive women *did* continue to take their pills.

First Use

The older the teenager at the time of first intercourse, the more likely it is that she will commence contraception at the same time she begins to have sex (see Figure 5. Comparisons between 1971 and 1976 are complicated by the proportionately greater number of cases in the earlier year for which the data on age at first use were deficient. Nevertheless, there is no evidence that the gap between age at first intercourse and age at first use of contraception has narrowed in the last five years. The proportion of teens of each race who delay use (including those who have yet to start use) appears to be about as great as or greater today at each age of sexual initiation than it was in 1971. The only compensatory factor at work (as we shall see) is that delayed contraception is often better contraception.

First Method

The theory which holds that an upgrading of contraceptive practice, i.e., a progression from nonuse to conventional to medical methods, follows increasing commitment to sex[6] would predict that the distribution by method last used would differ from the distribution by first method used. Theory aside, it is simply easier for more knowledgeable and older girls to negotiate the institutional obstacles that regulate access to the most effective modes of contraception.* In view of these considerations, it is surprising to observe that although most recent use† is characterized by

---

*Another factor in adoption of effective methods is pregnancy. The 1971 survey showed that teenagers often adopted the most effective methods of contraception following pregnancy. The effect of pregnancy on contraceptive use would, in those cases where it occurs, tend to augment the aggregate effect of increased sexual commitment. In some cases, of course, pregnancy may destroy or prevent the development of a sense of commitment.

†Those who had intercourse only once are excluded from this discussion since their contraceptive practice, whatever it was, could not change.

Table 13. Percent distribution of ever-contracepting never-married women aged 15-19,* according to first and most recently used method, by race and use at first and last intercourse, 1976

Method	Race and timing of use																	
	All						White						Black					
	First method			Most recent method			First method			Most recent method			First method			Most recent method		
	(1) Used first time	(2) Not used first time	(3) Total	(4) Used last time	(5) Not used last time	(6) Total	(7) Used first time	(8) Not used first time	(9) Total	(10) Used last time	(11) Not used last time	(12) Total	(13) Used first time	(14) Not used first time	(15) Total	(16) Used last time	(17) Not used last time	(18) Total
							(N= 130)	(N= 134)	(N= 264)	(N= 223)	(N= 42)	(N= 265)	(N= 119)	(N= 156)	(N= 275)	(N= 211)	(N= 68)	(N= 279)
Pill	21.5	57.2	39.7	53.9	36.6	51.1	20.0	50.8	35.6	50.7	23.8	46.4	46.2	73.7	61.8	65.9	57.3	63.8
IUD	0.1	2.5	1.3	4.0	2.4	3.7	0.0	3.0	1.5	4.9	2.4	4.6	1.7	3.9	2.9	4.7	7.4	5.4
Condom	40.6	18.4	29.3	14.8	27.6	16.9	42.3	24.6	33.3	16.6	35.7	19.6	27.7	10.3	17.8	13.3	17.6	14.3
Douche	3.6	0.7	2.1	3.6	2.5	3.5	0.0	0.7	0.4	1.4	2.4	1.5	13.5	1.9	6.9	8.1	1.5	6.5
Withdrawal	21.1	13.4	17.2	16.7	18.0	16.9	26.9	11.9	19.3	18.8	16.7	18.5	6.7	5.8	6.2	4.7	5.9	5.0
Other	13.1	7.8	10.4	7.0	12.9	7.9	10.8	9.0	9.9	7.6	19.0	9.4	4.2	4.5	4.4	3.3	10.3	5.0
Total	100.0	100.0	100.0	100.0	100.0	100.0	100.0	100.0	100.0	100.0	100.0	100.0	100.0	100.0	100.0	100.0	100.0	100.0

*Excludes those who had intercourse only once.

somewhat more pill and IUD use and less condom use than is first use, the difference is not as great as might be expected (see Table 13, cols. 3 and 6).° Moreover, the difference is due to those who used contraception the first time they had intercourse. On that occasion, this group put major reliance on the condom and withdrawal. Even at·that, a surprisingly large proportion of those who used contraception at first intercourse used either the pill or the IUD. This is especially true of blacks (see Table 13, col 13), among whom 48 percent used these methods—more than twice the percentage for comparable whites.

The contrasting first method profiles, depending on whether or not contraception was used at first intercourse (cols. 1 and 2), are puzzling. One might argue that those who fail to use at first intercourse would be those with less interest in contraception; of this group, about one-third do in fact remain never-users. However, those who fail to use the first time, but do so subsequently, reveal a remarkably sophisticated initial methods profile. In fact, the group that had had some sexual experience by the time they first used contraception started off with more effective methods than did those who used contraception at first intercourse. This difference in quality of initial contraception between those who do and do not delay first use does not appear to be solely a matter of differences in the age at which contraception begins or of pregnancies which lead to adoption of improved contraception. The method profiles at first use were retabulated to include only those who were never pregnant (not shown). The superior quality of the first-use profile of those who delayed first contraception is still evident, although slightly diminished.

The effect on the first-method distribution produced by removing cases that have experienced pregnancy is greatest for delayed contraceptors (since they experience about three times as much pregnancy as those who begin to use contraception right away) and for blacks (since their pregnancy prevalence is about twice that of whites). The differences in choice of a first method between first-time users and those who delayed adoption of contraception hold when examined by age at first contraception (not shown).

Before attempting an interpretation of these differences in first contraception, let us add one more piece to the puzzle— the contraception employed by those who have had intercourse only once. Only about one in seven sexually experienced unmarried women fall into this group. Just under half used contraception on that one occasion, the same proportion of users as we find among those who continue to be sexually active. Fewer than 10 percent of those who contracepted used the pill, less than half the figure for the more sexually experienced who used contraception at first intercourse. More than three out of five used the condom, compared to two out of five among those who continued to have sex. Thus, the contraceptive practice of 'one-timers' is of a much poorer quality than that of the group which in our discussion thus far has shown the least sophisticated profile.†

° Most recent use occurred at a somewhat older age on average. There is little overlap between the two groups, i.e., cases in which most recent use could be the same event as first use.

† Percent who used contraception at first intercourse, 1976:

Method	Had inter-course once	More than once
Pill	9.7	21.5
Condom	61.7	40.6
Douche	4.0	3.6
Withdrawal	16.4	21.1
Other	8.2	13.2
Total	100.0	100.0

The one-timers presumably are the least sexually committed among those who have had intercourse. Next to them, the least sexually committed teens, at least at the time of adoption of a contraceptive method, are those who used contraception at first intercourse. By definition, those who did not begin to use contraception right away were sexually experienced by the time they did; those who began contraception at their first intercourse were sexually inexperienced at that time.

It would appear that the facts conform rather well to Lindemann's theory that the less committed a young woman is to sex, the less likely she is to use contraception and the more likely, if contraception is used, that it will be a method such as the condom that does not involve much positive action or acknowledgement on her part.[7] It appears, therefore, that the greater the presumed sexual commitment, the greater the efficacy of initial contraceptive practice. Those most inclined to rely initially on male methods, particularly the condom, are those who have had the least sexual involvement, i.e., who have had sex only once. About half this group used no contraception the first time. Also reliant on conventional contraception as their first method, but to a lesser extent, are those who have had intercourse more than once and contracepted the first time they had intercourse. However, when contraception is delayed, the first method used is much more likely to be a medical method. This difference in the quality of contraception between those who delay first use and those who do not is not a matter of age at the time contraception is adopted or of experience with pregnancy, although pregnancy is frequently a stimulus to more effective contraception. What the theory does not account for is the never-users who have had intercourse more than once.

Sources of Contraception

The major change since 1971 in contraceptive practice is the massive shift to oral contraception. The shift can be observed among both races and is substantial at all ages. In Table 14, we show the source from which prescriptions for the pill were first obtained. Whereas there is a wide diversity of outlets for conventional contraceptives, prescriptions for orals in almost all cases are obtained either from a private physician in his office or from a clinic or other medical facility. Not surpisingly, both sources figure prominently, with blacks showing somewhat greater resort to clinic facilities and whites to private physicians.[*] This extraordinary reliance by unmarried teenage women on organized clinics for oral contraception contrasts with the preference for the private MD shown by most married women.[†] It is their unmarried status rather than age that accounts for the popularity of the clinic among unmarried teenage women. Although the numbers are small in some instances, there is no apparent trend by age in the

---

[*]If the respondent went for her prescription to a doctor in his private office, it is likely that she would give 'private physician' as her source. If she saw a doctor in a clinic or hospital, she may have been confused as to her proper response. Since we did not probe this matter deeply, we cannot resolve the possible ambiguity.

[†]Married women in the present survey who have used pills obtained their first prescription overwhelmingly from a private physician. Some of them, of course, may have been unmarried at the time. The married woman's preference for the private physician over the clinic is found in other studies also. See, for example: J. E. Anderson, L. Morris and M. Gesche, "Planned and Unplanned Fertility in Upstate New York," *Family Planning Perspectives*, 9:4, 1977. The data from their study are not strictly comparable with the figures in Table 14, since 'source' is more broadly defined and refers to a wider array of methods. To have focused on the first 'prescription' for 'orals' presumably would have given even greater prominence to the role of the physician.

Table 14. Percent distribution of sexually experienced never-married women aged 15-19 who ever used oral contraception, according to first source of prescription, by age and race, 1976

Source	Age and race								
	All			White			Black		
	15-19	15-17	18-19	15-19 (N=160)	15-17 (N=62)	18-19 (N=98)	15-19 (N=222)	15-17 (N=93)	18-19 (N=129)
Doctor	54.1	52.9	54.8	55.6	53.2	57.1	42.3	43.0	41.9
Clinic	45.2	45.3	45.2	43.8	45.2	42.9	57.7	57.0	58.1
Other	0.7	1.8	0.0	0.6	1.6	0.0	0.0	0.0	0.0
Total	100.0	100.0	100.0	100.0	100.0	100.0	100.0	100.0	100.0

percentages reporting the clinic as the source from which they got their prescription.

The large-scale utilization of clinics by teenagers may help to account for the increase in the use of oral contraception by teens in recent years, since it has been documented that enrollment in clinics by teenagers rose from 453,000 in 1971 to 1.1 million in 1975.[8]* Since passage of the Family Planning Services and Population Research Act of 1970, federal funds supporting the provision of family planning services have more than doubled.[9] During this period, there has also been a significant liberalization of laws and policies affecting teenagers' access to contraceptive services.[10]

Differences in contraceptive practice among teenage pill users bear little relation to the source from which they first obtained their prescriptions. Among whites, slightly more than 70 percent of those who had ever used the pill had used it at last intercourse, regardless of source. This lack of difference by source was true for blacks also, among whom 65 percent who had ever used the pill had used it at last intercourse.

Summary

Data gathered in two nationwide surveys made in 1971 and 1976 provide an opportunity to examine recent changes in prevalence of sexual experience and in contraceptive use among unmarried women aged 15-19. Confining the analysis to unmarried (i.e., never-married) women is a data processing expedient which introduces minor distortions into the findings without, it is believed, altering major conclusions. To have included ever-married women in this analysis† would have increased the level of estimated premarital sexual activity, since the vast majority of the married had had intercourse before marriage. The effect on contraceptive practice is harder to judge. Many marriages are precipitated by pregnancy which results either from the failure to use contraception at all, or from ineffective use. On the other hand, the stable courtship arrangements which often precede marriage are associated, or were in 1971, with better than average contraception.

With respect to sex and contraception, the following findings are most salient:
• Between 1971 and 1976, there was, for both races and at all ages, an increase

---

*Unfortunately, the 1971 and 1976 surveys cannot be compared, since in the earlier survey the source question referred to all methods and asked about source *ever* used.

†They were included in the survey and will be analyzed subsequently.

among unmarried teenage women in the prevalence of premarital intercourse. The validity of the prevalence estimate for 1976 is confirmed by the use of an indirect estimating procedure which is believed to elicit true responses to sensitive questions.

• Knowledge of the time of greatest risk of conception during the menstrual cycle (which is relevant to the use of coitally related methods of contraception) was relatively poor in both 1971 and 1976. Sex education courses helped somewhat; however, among whites (but not blacks) experience and maturity were the better teachers. It is possible that sex education had other, and for this study, unmeasured effects on the use of contraception, the management of pregnancy and other aspects of sex and reproduction.

• Most sexual encounters take place in the home of the girl or her male partner. The older the girl, the more likely it is to be the partner's home.

• Along with increased prevalence of sexual experience, there has been a fairly substantial increase in the number of partners with whom teenage women have ever been involved. This is not a necessary consequence of more sex, and may be related to some stretching of the premarital period by a reduction in the age at first intercourse, as well as by greater postponement of marriage.

• At first intercourse, male partners tend to be teenagers themselves. The most recent partner, on the other hand, tends to be out of his teens and thus, presumably, somewhat harder to reach through programs that are based on some form of institutional catchment.

• The median age at first intercourse, which declined by a few months for both blacks and whites, bears some relationship to the age of menarche among blacks, but not among whites.

• First intercourse among unmarried teenage women is seasonal—summer being the time, apparently, when temptation and opportunity peak together.

• Contraceptive practice among unmarried teenage women improved significantly between 1971 and 1976. The proportions of sexually active unmarried women who always used contraception and who used it at the time of last intercourse increased. This improvement was moderated to some extent by a concurrent though smaller growth in the proportion who never used contraception. These changes appear to have been fostered by changes in the types of contraceptives being used.

• Many more young women used the pill and IUD in 1976 than in 1971. Along with this increase in use of the most effective medical methods, there has been a substantial decline in the use of the three methods—condom, douche and withdrawal—which were most prominent in 1971. Only among very young teenagers are these the methods of choice.

• Oral contraception is more popular among blacks at every age than among whites. It is, however, for both races, the most popular method.

• The gap between first intercourse and first use of contraception that was observed in 1971 has not narrowed significantly. Those who delay the use of contraception are much more likely than those who do not to have had a pregnancy.

• Seemingly, the more committed to sex a young woman is, the more sophisticated is her initial use of contraception. There are striking differences in the first-use profiles of those who have sex only once, those who continue to have sex but use contraception from the start and those who delay the use of contraception. For these three groups, pill use as the first method goes from less than 10 percent, to over 20 percent, to over 50 percent, respectively; while condom use declines from 62, to 41, to 18 percent. Experience with pregnancy and age at first use of contraception cannot explain these differences.

• About half of the unmarried teenage women who have used oral contraception got their original prescription from a clinic rather than from a private physician. This contrasts with the practice of older, married women, who rely much more on the private MD for contraception.

• Whether the first prescription for pills is obtained from a private physician or from a clinic makes little difference in continuation or effectiveness of subsequent use. The importance of the clinic for contraception among unmarried teenage women therefore seems to lie in increasing access to oral contraception by unmarried teens.

Data from two national surveys indicate that the prevalence of sexual intercourse is on the rise among young unmarried women in the United States. Although the majority of female teenagers have not had intercourse, the magnitude of that majority appears to be diminishing, so that more than one-half of those aged 19 in 1976 have had intercourse. The surveys also reveal that more of the sexually active are using contraception, they are using the more effective methods, and they are using all methods with greater regularity. Although the increasing use of the pill and the IUD among teenagers should help prevent undesired pregnancy, questions may also be raised about the desirability of early and continued use of these contraceptives because of known and suspected increased risk of serious side effects, such as thromboembolic disease with use of orals, as well as delay and possible im-

pairment of fertility following discontinuation of pill use.

Some will see in these data cause to lament the passing of the old ways; others will see the beginning stages of a happier, better adjusted society. Some will argue that changes are inevitable and will propose various ways of dealing with them; others will advocate one scheme or another for turning the tide. Exhortations or simplistic tinkerings, however, can be expected to have little if any effect. In Japan and the People's Republic of China, there appears to be little premarital intercourse, at least among those under age 20. But both societies are very different from the United States, and in ways presumably related to behavior of young people. The methods of contraception that are growing in popularity among American teenagers generally accompany an established pattern of sexual activity. What is more, it is of no little sociological significance that most sexually active young unmarried women in the United States are engaging in that behavior either in their own homes or in the homes of their partners. This, perhaps, is more telling evidence of the establishment of sexual activity than any number of statistics.

References

1. For the major findings of the 1971 study, see: M. Zelnik and J. F. Kantner, "Sexuality, Contraception and Pregnancy Among Young Unwed Females in the United States," in Commission on Population Growth and the American Future, *Demographic and Social Aspects of Population Growth*, C. F. Westoff and R. Parke, Jr., eds., Vol. 1 of Commission Research Reports, U.S. Government Printing Office, Washington, D.C., 1972, p. 355; ———, "Probability of Premarital Intercourse," *Social Science Research*, 1:335, 1972;———, "Sex and Contraception Among Unmarried Teenagers," in C. F. Westoff, *Toward the End of Growth*, Prentice-Hall, Englewood Cliffs, N.J., 1973, p. 7; ———, "The Resolution of Teenage First Pregnancies," *Family Planning Per-*

spectives, 6:74, 1974; ———, "Attitudes of American Teenagers Toward Abortion," *Family Planning Perspectives,* 7:89, 1975; J. F. Kantner and M. Zelnik, "Sexual Experience of Young Unmarried Women in the United States," *Family Planning Perspectives,* Vol. 4, No. 4, 1972, p. 9; ———, "Contraception and Pregnancy: Experience of Young Unmarried Women in the United States," *Family Planning Perspectives,* 5:21, 1973; and F. Shah, M. Zelnik and J. F. Kantner, "Unprotected Intercourse Among Unwed Teenagers," *Family Planning Perspectives,* 7:39, 1975.

2. C. S. Chilman, "Possible Factors Associated with High Rates of Out-of-Marriage Births Among Adolescents," University of Wisconsin-Milwaukee, School of Social Welfare, 1976.

3. M. Zelnik and J. F. Kantner, "Probability of Premarital Intercourse," 1972, op. cit.

4. J. F. Kantner and M. Zelnik, "Contraception and Pregnancy . . . ," 1973, op. cit.

5. C. F. Westoff, "Trends in Contraceptive Practice: 1965-1973," *Family Planning Perspectives,* 8:54, 1976.

6. C. Lindemann, *Birth Control and Unmarried Young Women,* Springer, New York, 1975.

7. Ibid.

8. The Alan Guttmacher Institute (AGI), *Data and Analyses for 1976 Revision of DHEW Five-Year Plan for Family Planning Services,* New York, 1976.

9. AGI, *11 Million Teenagers,* Planned Parenthood Federation of America, New York, 1976, p. 46.

10. E. W. Paul, H. F. Pilpel and N. F. Wechsler, "Pregnancy, Teenagers and the Law, 1976," *Family Planning Perspectives,* 8:16, 1976, Table 1.

5

First Pregnancies to Women Aged 15–19: 1976 and 1971

Melvin Zelnik and John F. Kantner

In a previous article, we compared various aspects of the sexual behavior and contraceptive practices of never-married women 15-19 years of age in 1976 and 1971.[1] This article focuses on pregnancy, especially premarital first pregnancy, its prevalence, the ways in which it is resolved, whether contraception is used at the time the pregnancy occurs, and whether the pregnancy is intended.* Our findings here are for *all women 15-19 years of age, the ever-married as well as the never-married.* Here again, comparisons will be made between 1976 and 1971 where the data permit. To facilitate those comparisons, we will utilize the same groupings used in an earlier analysis of the 1971 data on first pregnancies.†[2]

*While the greatly increased availability and accessibility of legal and medically safe abortion may lessen the impact of first pregnancy on the lives of young women, especially young unmarried women, (because of the dangers of births and illegal abortions averted), we believe this event still influences considerably their future decisions and options. Any reduction in the availability of legal abortion (as the result of recent congressional action and Supreme Court decisions) could again increase the impact of first pregnancy on the lives of the young women involved. First pregnancies constitute about 80 percent of the pregnancies that occurred to both the 1976 and 1971 samples.

†The data reported from the two surveys are on events that occurred at any age in any year up to the time of the survey, when the respondents were 15-19 years of age. The figures shown here for 1971 differ somewhat from those shown in the earlier analysis (see reference 2) because that earlier article included the college dormitory sample.

The authors acknowledge the invaluable assistance of Judy Gehret, Nelva Hitt and Farida Shah. The 1976 and 1971 studies upon which this article is based were supported by Grant No. HDO5255 from the National Institute of Child Health and Human Development, DHEW. Generous assistance also was received from the Ford Foundation and the General Services Foundation.

Both the 1976 and 1971 data are derived from national probability sample surveys of ever-married and never-married women 15-19 years of age living in households in the continental United States. The sampling procedures for both studies involved stratification by race to ensure substantial numbers of interviews with black respondents. The fieldwork for the 1976 study was carried out under contract by the Research Triangle Institute and provided 2,193 completed interviews. The fieldwork for the 1971 study was carried out under contract by the Institute of Survey Research, Temple University, and yielded a total of 4,392 completed interviews. The 1971 study also included a separate national probability sample survey of women 15-19 years of age living in college dormitories. To provide comparability with the 1976 sample, the authors have excluded these women from the tabulations shown here for 1971. (For additional information on the two studies, see chapter 4.)

Premarital Sexual Experience

As of 1971, three out of every 10 women aged 15-19 had experienced sexual intercourse while unmarried; by 1976, four in 10 had had such premarital intercourse (see Table 1).* The increase in premarital sexual experience occurred for both marital status and racial groups. The percentage increase was considerably greater for whites (41 percent) than for blacks (19 percent).

If all other factors had remained the same, the substantial increase in the prevalence of premarital sexual experience among teenage women between 1971 and 1976 might have been expected to result in an increase in premarital pregnancy. Over the same period, however, these same young women reported a dramatic increase in overall contraceptive use, in use of the most effective methods, and in more regular use of all methods—changes which, other things being equal, should have led to a decrease in premarital pregnancy.[3]

Before beginning the analysis, we must note here that the quality of the 1976 data on pregnancies among blacks

is questionable. Estimates derived from the 1976 survey data on children ever born, on births in 1975 and on abortions in 1975 were compared with external independent national data, themselves of varying quality and completeness. (For example, the national data on births are more complete and detailed than the data on legal abortions, especially by race and age.)† The comparisons suggest that our survey data for whites are reasonably accurate; differences between estimates derived from our survey data and the national data appear to be largely or entirely explicable by the fact that the sample represents women living in households in 48 states, whereas the national data represent all women in 50 states, whether they live in households, group quarters or institutions.

For blacks, however, the comparisons present a different picture. Estimates from our survey of the number of births in 1975 and of children ever born are somewhat higher than are shown in the external national data; whereas our survey estimate of the number of abortions obtained by blacks in 1975 is much too low. It is possible that some of the black survey respondents reported pregnancies that were terminated by abortion as ending in live births. However, the deficit in the survey data on abortions considerably exceeds the overreporting in the survey of live births. We believe that most of the overreporting of births among blacks occurred because this segment of our sample is not representative of all blacks 15-19 years of age; whereas the underreporting of pregnancies terminated by abortion may be a reflection

---

*The figures shown in Table 1 for the never-married differ slightly from figures published earlier (see chapter 4). In the previous article, the estimates were computed from unweighted sample data, whereas these estimates are based on weighted sample data. The weights for the 1971 sample were computed from the 1970 census counts of females aged 14-18, by single years of age and by race, for each of the 45 geographical and residential strata of the sampling scheme. The weights for the 1976 sample were computed by marital status, race and age group (15-17 years and 18-19 years) from Current Population Survey data, adjusted by exclusion of those living in group quarters (as of 1972, inmates of institutions are not included in the Current Population Survey), and exclusion of the populations of Alaska and Hawaii. (See: U.S. Bureau of the Census, "Marital Status and Living Arrangements: March 1976," *Current Population Reports*, Series P-20, No. 306, 1977.)

---

† The data on births are from the National Center for Health Statistics; data on children ever born, from the Census Bureau; and data on abortions, from the Center for Disease Control and The Alan Guttmacher Institute.

Table 1. Percent of women aged 15–19 at interview who had ever experienced premarital intercourse, by current marital status and race, United States, 1976 and 1971

Marital status	1976			1971		
	Total	White	Black	Total	White	Black
All	40.9	37.2	64.3	30.1	26.3	54.1
N	2,178	1,482	696	4,341	2,924	1,417
Ever-married	80.2	79.2	90.5	57.9	55.9	78.3
N	292	250	42	369	291	78
Never-married	36.1	31.7	62.3	26.8	22.7	52.4
N	1,886	1,232	654	3,972	2,633	1,339

Note: *In this and subsequent tables based on the 1971 and 1976 surveys:* Base excludes those for whom no information was obtained on premarital intercourse. Percentages for whites, blacks and totals are computed from weighted data; absolute numbers shown in italics are unweighted sample Ns. "White" includes the relatively small number of races other than black. Except where indicated, the base excludes women who did not respond to the question analyzed in the table.

of the ambivalent attitude about abortion that has been noted in the young black population.[4]

Given the incompleteness of the national data on abortions, and the fact that the college dormitory population is not represented in the survey, we cannot determine the extent to which abortions among blacks are underreported in the survey. It appears that our reports on abortions to blacks represent only about 20-30 percent of the actual number. This would be the case not only for those abortions occurring in 1975, the year for which the comparison was made, but probably also for the cumulative number of abortions obtained by respondents up to the time of the survey.

These defects in the quality of the data for blacks have different implications at different points in the ensuing discussion. We shall attempt wherever possible to indicate how these defects affect the data we present, but we are not able to specify the magnitude of the errors. An additional problem arises in considering changes between 1971 and 1976, since indications of change are affected not only by errors in the 1976 survey, but also by whatever error resides in the 1971 survey data. Our continuing inves-

tigation of the quality of the survey data includes the 1971 study. Data on abortions are less available and of poorer quality for years prior to 1971 than for more recent years. At the same time, it is likely that far fewer young black women were able to obtain abortions (at least, legal abortions) up to 1971 than in the 1971-1976 period, during which time several states liberalized their abortion laws, and the Supreme Court (in 1973) overturned most restrictive state abortion laws. Thus, whatever underreporting of abortions exists in the 1971 study would be expected to have a relatively small impact on the findings of that study.

Many of the 1976 survey data on blacks, such as those dealing with prevalence of premarital sexual activity* and use of contraception, appear to be valid. The errors we have described affect the picture of pregnancy and its outcome for blacks. These defects probably are not unique to our data, although we are not aware of other studies that have attempt-

---

*Thus, the respondents' direct answers on sexual activity were validated by a randomized response technique test (see chapter 4).

Table 2. Percent of women aged 15–19 at interview who experienced a premarital first pregnancy, among all women, among women who had premarital intercourse and among women who had a first pregnancy, by race, 1976 and 1971

| Women aged 15–19 | Percent experiencing a first premarital pregnancy | | | | | |
| | 1976 | | | 1971 | | |
	Total	White	Black	Total	White	Black
All	11.6	9.3	25.4	9.0	6.4	25.5
N	2,175	1,481	694	4,341	2,924	1,417
Had premarital intercourse	28.3	25.2	39.5	29.8	24.3	47.1
N	1,022	576	446	1,477	731	746
Had first pregnancy	78.7	73.5	93.7	74.3	65.5	94.6
N	419	233	186	614	265	349

ed such comparisons with external data as we have made here.

Premarital First Pregnancy

As may be seen in Table 2, there was an increase in the proportion of all 15-19-year-old white women who had experienced at least one premarital pregnancy up to the time of interview—from 6.4 percent of those surveyed in 1971 to 9.3 percent of those questioned in 1976. However, among those young white women who had had premarital intercourse, the proportion experiencing a premarital pregnancy remained at about the same level.* In effect, the proportion of premaritally sexually active whites increased between 1971 and 1976, but the proportion who became premaritally pregnant remained the same, so that an increase occurred in the proportion of all white women aged 15-19 who experienced a premarital pregnancy. Thus, for whites, the risk of a premarital pregnancy

among the sexually active has remained essentially the same (see appendix).

The proportion of all black women who had ever experienced a premarital pregnancy appears to have remained constant between 1971 and 1976, whereas the proportion of the sexually experienced who had ever had a premarital pregnancy declined. However, both of these rates for 1976 are undoubtedly too low as a result of the underreporting by never-married blacks of abortions and, thus, of the pregnancies themselves.† Given the uncertainty of these rates (as well, perhaps, as of the rates for 1971) we cannot make a definitive statement about the amount or direction of change among blacks between 1971 and 1976. It is notable, however, that the rates among blacks in 1976, although underestimated, remain considerably higher than the rates for whites.

Table 2 shows also that by 1976 almost 80 percent of all first pregnancies among teenagers had been conceived out of wedlock: over 90 percent of first preg-

---

*The lack of a decline is somewhat surprising in light of data previously presented on changes in contraceptive practices (see chapter 4). We intend to examine and in a subsequent article report in greater detail on the use of contraception prior to and subsequent to a first premarital pregnancy.

†Some women who aborted their first unreported pregnancy may have had a subsequent reported pregnancy while still unmarried; but this could not have occurred among all of them.

Table 3. Percent distribution of women aged 15–19 at interview who had a premarital first pregnancy, by changes in marital status before and after pregnancy outcome, according to race, 1976 and 1971

Timing of change in marital status	1976			1971		
	Total (N=336)	White (N=160)	Black (N=176)	Total (N=512)	White (N=178)	Black (N=334)
Total	100.0	100.0	100.0	100.0	100.0	100.0
Married before outcome*	28.0	36.5	8.8	35.4	52.2	8.5
Not married before outcome	72.0	63.5	91.2	64.6	47.8	91.5
Married after outcome	9.2	9.4	8.6	10.6	12.3	7.8
Never married*	62.8	54.1	82.6	54.0	35.5	83.7

*Includes currently pregnant women.

Table 4. Percent distribution of premarital first pregnancies to women aged 15–19 at interview who were unmarried at outcome, by type of outcome and race, 1976 and 1971

Outcome of pregnancy	1976			1971		
	Total (N=249)	White (N=86)	Black (N=163)	Total (N=392)	White (N=86)	Black (N=306)
Total	100.0	100.0	100.0	100.0	100.0	100.0
Live birth	46.0	27.4	75.6	59.2	44.3	71.6
Stillbirth	1.3	1.4	1.2	0.3	0.0	0.5
Miscarriage	11.1	14.9	5.0	7.4	7.6	7.3
Induced abortion	30.6	44.9	7.9	17.7	32.9	5.0
Currently pregnant	11.0	11.4	10.3	15.4	15.2	15.6
Plans to marry before outcome	8.4	**	**	19.0	**	20.7
No plans to marry before outcome	91.6	**	**	81.0	**	79.3

Note: In this and subsequent tables, a double asterisk signifies N<20.

nancies among blacks, and almost 75 percent of those among whites. While these proportions represent very little change for blacks, they do represent an increase for whites.

Change in Marital Status

Table 3 shows that during the five-year period there was a substantial reduction in the proportion of whites who had ever resolved a premarital pregnancy by marriage prior to pregnancy outcome; the percentage declined from 52 among those interviewed in 1971 to 37 among those surveyed in 1976.* Nor were

*The data in Table 3 include, for both 1976 and 1971, women who had never been married at the time of the survey, and who were currently pregnant for the first time. Some of these women might have married after the survey but before the pregnancy ended. Very few of them, in fact, had plans to marry before the baby was born (proportionately fewer in 1976 than in 1971, as may be seen in Table 4); their inclusion in the data for both years does not, we believe, distort differences over time or by race.

whites more likely in 1976 than in 1971 to marry after the premarital pregnancy ended—indeed, there appears to have been a small decline.° Among blacks, there is almost no change between the 1971 and 1976 interviews in the likelihood of marriage before or soon after the outcome of a premarital first pregnancy. Whatever errors exist in the 1976 data in regard to reporting of abortions are likely to have only a small impact on this distribution, and undoubtedly work in the direction of causing a small overestimate of the proportion who marry while premaritally pregnant. Although the gap is somewhat narrower in 1976 than in 1971, there remain substantial differences between blacks and whites in the proportion who marry before the outcome of a premarital first pregnancy.

Outcome of Premarital Pregnancy

What are the outcomes of premarital first pregnancies, and did these outcomes change between 1971 and 1976? Table 4 shows the percent distribution of the outcomes of premarital first pregnancies ever experienced among women who were unmarried at the time of outcome (including as an outcome those who were "currently pregnant"). In this table, more than at any other place in this analysis, the deficiency in the reporting of black abortions renders the data for blacks questionable. We confine our discussion, therefore, to the outcomes of pregnancies among whites.

°The hesitancy to conclude that the decline was real reflects the small numbers of cases involved. Those who married after the outcome of the premarital first pregnancy married at any time subsequent to that outcome; some, in fact, had an intervening second or even third premarital pregnancy. Obviously, with the passage of time, more women who are unmarried at the outcome of their premarital first pregnancy will marry.

In 1971, more than two in five premarital first pregnancies among whites ended in live births; whereas in 1976, only about one in four pregnancies had this outcome. By contrast, in 1971, two in five pregnancies among whites ended in induced or spontaneous abortions, but in 1976, three in five so terminated. Since Table 4 includes those pregnant at interview, the final distribution could be expected to differ slightly. Looking exclusively at premarital first pregnancies (among whites) that have terminated in births or induced or spontaneous abortions sharpens the picture of change, as may be seen below. This is because proportionately more unmarried whites were pregnant at the 1971 survey.

Pregnancy outcome	1976 (N=77)	1971 (N=71)
All	100.0	100.0
Live birth	30.9	52.2
Stillbirth	1.6	0.0
Miscarriage	16.8	9.0
Induced abortion	50.7	38.8

Premarital Pregnancy and Intent

Among those teenagers who, by 1976, had had at least one premarital pregnancy and were still unmarried at the outcome of that pregnancy (or were pregnant for the first time and still unmarried at the time of interview), fewer than one-fourth had intended to become pregnant, about the same level as reported in 1971 (see Table 5).† At the same time, only one-fifth of those who had not intended the pregnancy reported that they had been regularly contracepting to prevent

---

†The underreporting of abortions among blacks probably results in a slight overestimation of the proportions of black intended pregnancies. Thus, the small increase in intended pregnancies shown for blacks is probably spurious.

1

Table 5. Percent distribution of premarital first pregnancies to women aged 15–19 at interview who were unmarried at outcome, for all pregnancies and pregnancies that ended in live births, by pregnancy intention and race, 1976 and 1971

Pregnancy intention and contraceptive use	1976			1971		
	Total	White	Black	Total	White	Black
Pregnancies	(N=249)	(N=86)	(N=163)	(N=370)	(N=77)	(N=293)
All	100.0	100.0	100.0	100.0	100.0	100.0
Intended	23.2	19.3	29.2	21.8	18.2	24.5
Not intended	76.8	80.7	70.8	78.2	81.8	75.5
Used contraception	18.8	23.5	10.2	13.4	13.3	13.5
Did not use	81.2	76.5	89.8	86.6	86.7	86.5
Live births	(N=148)	(N=25)	(N=123)	(N=254)	(N=38)	(N=216)
All	100.0	100.0	100.0	100.0	100.0	100.0
Intended	36.4	44.8	31.5	22.5	21.9	22.8
Not intended	63.6	55.2	68.5	77.5	78.1	77.2
Used contraception	14.3	**	11.5	12.8	8.8	14.9
Did not use	85.7	**	88.5	87.2	91.2	85.1

it. While this is perhaps a surprisingly low level of contraceptive practice among those who wish to avoid pregnancy, it nevertheless represents an improvement in preventive efforts since 1971. The increase in contraceptive use appears to be restricted to whites, among whom use nearly doubled over the five-year period.

The 1971 survey did not collect information on the birth control method that was used by contraceptors at the time conception occurred, and the number of cases included in the 1976 survey is too small to allow for a breakdown by race. However, of those surveyed in 1976 who had not intended to become pregnant and had been 'regularly' contracepting, 36 percent had used the pill, 25 percent had relied on condoms and 39 percent had employed foam, withdrawal, douche or rhythm. Forty-one percent of those contracepting said that they had thought there was a "good chance" they might become pregnant when they did in spite of their efforts at prevention; 55 percent of the nonusers had thought they were likely to become pregnant. Most of those who had taken the pill did not think that there was a good chance they would become pregnant, while most users of other methods did think pregnancy was likely.

The lower half of Table 5 shows the reproductive intentions of those teenagers whose first pregnancies ended in live births. A higher proportion of these pregnancies were intended than of all premarital pregnancies (36 percent as compared with 23 percent). This difference is due primarily to the tendency for many unintended pregnancies to be resolved through abortion. Such is also the probable explanation of the increase from 22 percent to 36 percent between 1971 and 1976 in the proportion of out-of-wedlock first births which resulted from intended pregnancies.* If the pregnancy was not intended, there was a greater tendency after 1971 to resort to abortion. Although some pregnancies

---

*The change is striking only among whites, but it must be remembered that abortions (virtually all of which are of unintended pregnancies) are seriously underestimated among blacks in the 1976 data.

Table 6. Percent distribution of out-of-wedlock live births resulting from first conceptions to women aged 15–19 at interview, by disposition of baby and race of mother, 1976 and 1971

Disposition	1976			1971		
	Total (N=148)	White (N=25)	Black (N=123)	Total (N=259)	White (N=39)	Black (N=220)
All	100.0	100.0	100.0	100.0	100.0	100.0
In mother's household	93.3	87.2	96.8	85.6	72.2	92.4
With relatives or friends	1.0	2.9	0.0	4.7	5.8	4.2
Adopted	2.6	7.0	0.0	7.6	18.4	2.0
Dead	3.1	2.9	3.2	2.1	3.6	1.4

that end as live births may be declared intended retroactively, this tendency is unlikely to alter the conclusions regarding change between the 1971 and 1976 surveys.

It is equally appropriate to run the percents the other way, i.e., to ask what were the outcomes among those who intended and among those who did not intend to become pregnant. For blacks the data are questionable. The results for whites (below) indicate that whether or not the pregnancy was intended seems to make a very large difference in the outcome:

Pregnancy outcome	Intended (N=17)	Not intended (N=69)
Live birth	63.4	18.8
Stillbirth	0.0	1.7
Miscarriage	5.9	17.1
Abortion	11.8	52.7
Currently pregnant	18.9	9.7

The relatively higher rate of miscarriage among those who did not intend to become pregnant may suggest that some of these events were actually induced abortions or that deliberate attempts were made to miscarry.

Disposition of Out-of-Wedlock Births

Approximately 18 percent of babies born live to unmarried whites surveyed in

1971 had been given up for adoption; another six percent were living with relatives or friends of the mother (see Table 6). In contrast, only six percent of babies ever born to unmarried blacks were living apart from their mothers. This same pattern is repeated among respondents surveyed in 1976; but the differences are less pronounced than in 1971, largely because of the decrease in the proportion of white babies placed for adoption. This decline in adoptions is consistent with the view that because of the greater availability of abortion, more of the babies born to white adolescents (including those born out of wedlock) are wanted and so remain with their mothers.

Marriage After Pregnancy Outcome

The reduced likelihood of early marriage among premaritally pregnant whites illustrated in Table 3 is seen again in Table 7. Of all white teenagers in 1971 who had ever been premaritally pregnant (exclusive of those pregnant at the time of the survey) and who had remained unmarried through the outcome of the pregnancy, 30 percent had married by the time of the survey. By contrast, only 17 percent of the comparable group interviewed in 1976 had married by the time of that survey. This reduction in the

Table 7. Percent of women aged 15–19 at interview, unmarried at outcome of premarital first pregnancy who married subsequently, by outcome and race, 1976 and 1971

Outcome	1976			1971		
	Total	White	Black	Total	White	Black
Total	14.3	16.7	10.5	19.3	30.3	10.0
N	223	77	146	332	71	261
Live birth	16.7	25.6	11.5	21.2	41.3	10.8
N	148	25	123	259	39	220
Baby living with mother	14.5	19.5	11.9	18.5	43.2	8.5
N	140	21	119	236	28	208
Stillbirth/miscarriage/abortion	11.8	12.8	5.2	14.8	18.4	5.5
N	75	52	23	73	32	41

likelihood of marriage for whites occurred whatever the outcome of the pregnancy. Whereas 41 percent of the whites who had had an out-of-wedlock live birth had married by 1971, only 26 percent had done so by 1976. Similarly, among those who had given birth out of wedlock to a baby who had remained in the mother's household,° 43 percent had married by 1971, but only 20 percent by 1976. Among those who had had a stillbirth or an induced or spontaneous abortion, the percent who subsequently married declined from 18 percent to 13 percent over the five-year period.

For both blacks and whites, outcome of pregnancy is related to the likelihood of marriage. In 1976, those who had ever delivered a live baby were twice as likely to have married subsequently as those who had had some other pregnancy outcome. There is also a large difference by race—whites were about twice as likely to have married as blacks, whatever the pregnancy outcome. Between 1971 and

1976, the rates for blacks remained remarkably stable.†

Postmarital Outcome

Although the proportion of premaritally pregnant whites who married before the outcome of their first pregnancy declined from 52 percent to 36 percent between 1971 and 1976, whites were still four times more likely to marry before the outcome than blacks (see Table 3). Among those surveyed in 1971, as Table 8 shows, there were only small differences by race in the pregnancy outcomes of those who married between the first pregnancy and its outcome. The number of cases is too small to show the distribution of outcomes for blacks surveyed in 1976 but by inference (since the distribution for whites is very similar to the distribution for the total group), there appear to be only small differences by race in pregnancy outcomes. The differences in the distributions for 1971 and 1976 also seem small (except that among those interviewed in 1976, a larg-

---

°We do not know where the child was living between the time of birth and the time of survey. Thus, in some instances, the child may have been living with the mother up to the time of marriage, and in others, may have been returned to the mother's household following the marriage.

---

†Sixty-six percent of mothers whose child was living with them and who married following the birth married the putative father of the child by 1976 as compared with 60 percent in 1971.

Table 8. Percent distribution of premarital first pregnancies to women aged 15–19 at interview who married prior to pregnancy outcome, according to pregnancy outcome and intention at time of conception, by race, 1976 and 1971

Outcome and intention	1976			1971		
	Total	White	Black	Total	White	Black
Pregnancy outcome	(N=87)	(N=74)	(N=13)	(N=120)	(N=92)	(N=28)
All	100.0	100.0	**	100.0	100.0	100.0
Live birth	82.2	81.2	**	74.4	74.0	76.7
Stillbirth	0.0	0.0	**	0.6	0.7	0.0
Miscarriage	2.5	2.7	**	3.0	2.8	5.8
Abortion	1.2	1.4	**	0.0	0.0	0.0
Currently pregnant	14.1	14.7	**	22.0	22.5	17.5
Pregnancy intention	(N=87)	(N=74)	(N=13)	(N=117)	(N=90)	(N=27)
All	100.0	100.0	**	100.0	100.0	100.0
Intended	58.3	59.6	**	49.3	50.0	42.0
Not intended	41.7	40.4	**	50.7	50.0	58.0
Used contraception	7.7	6.8	**	17.0	15.8	**
Did not use	92.3	93.2	**	83.0	84.2	**

er proportion of pregnancies ended in live births and relatively fewer respondents were pregnant at time of interview). However, whereas 51 percent of the women who married prior to outcome did not intend the pregnancy in 1971, 42 percent did not in 1976. Among those who did not intend the pregnancy, there also was a decline, from 17 percent in 1971 to eight percent in 1976, in the proportion who had used a birth control method at the time they conceived.

Among those women surveyed in 1976 who had a live birth, 36 percent did not intend the pregnancy, in contrast to 49 percent in 1971 (not shown). Thus, in 1976, women who had ever become premaritally pregnant but had married prior to the outcome of the pregnancy differed from those who had remained unmarried at the outcome in that relatively more of the former had intended to become pregnant, fewer had used contraception even when the pregnancy was not intended

and (especially among whites) more had carried the pregnancy to term. *

We have no information, for 1971, as to whether or not those who married wed the men responsible for the pregnancy. In 1976, a minimum of 76 percent of the women who married while pregnant married the man responsible for the pregnancy and at least three percent married someone who was not responsible for the pregnancy. The remaining 21 percent married the last person with

---

*We cannot account for the relatively low rate of miscarriage, both in 1971 and in 1976, among women who conceived premaritally but who married prior to the outcome of the pregnancy. It might, of course, be argued that unmarried pregnant women who miscarry do not 'need' to marry. Aside from the fact that miscarriage could just as easily follow marriage as precede it (assuming "shotgun" marriages are not all delayed until the very late months of pregnancy), this argument should lead us to expect a relatively high rate of miscarriage among the never-married. However, neither among those surveyed in 1971 nor in 1976 is this the case (see Table 4).

whom they had had intercourse prior to the marriage, an unknown proportion of whom were the responsible males.

Postmarital Pregnancy

As with women who married prior to the outcome of a premarital pregnancy, the distributions of postmarital first pregnancies remained unchanged between 1971 and 1976 (see Table 9).° At the same time, there is a decrease over the five-year period in the proportion who did not intend the pregnancy. This decrease conforms with the decline in unintended pregnancy that has been observed in recent years among married women generally, and is apparently due less to increased utilization of abortion than to improved contraceptive practice, since the birthrate declined for this group of women[5] and our data show that the use of abortion increased very little.

Just as in 1971, then, in 1976 the proportion of first pregnancies that is unintended declines progressively from 77 percent of women who conceive premaritally and are unmarried at outcome (Table 5), to 42 percent of those who conceive premaritally but marry before the outcome (Table 8), to 16 percent among those who conceive after marriage (Table 9). A similar reduction occurs in the proportion of women who do not intend to become pregnant but do

Table 9. Percent distribution of postmarital first pregnancies to women aged 15–19 at interview, according to pregnancy outcome and intention at time of conception, 1976 and 1971

Outcome and intention	1976	1971
Pregnancy outcome	(N=83)	(N=102)
All	100.0	100.0
Live birth	58.8	57.9
Stillbirth	0.0	1.6
Miscarriage	14.7	12.1
Abortion	1.3	0.0
Currently pregnant	25.2	28.4
Pregnancy intention	(N=83)	(N=101)
All	100.0	100.0
Intended	84.1	73.0
Not intended	15.9	27.0
Used contraception	**	18.8
Did not use	**	81.2

not use contraception to prevent it— from 62 percent to 38 percent to 12 percent (not shown). The proportion of postmarital pregnancies ending in a live birth that was intended (82 percent) is very similar to the proportion of all postmarital pregnancies that was intended (Table 9).

All First Conceptions

Among women 15-19 years of age in 1976, about 15 percent had ever experienced one or more pregnancies. Of first pregnancies, close to 80 percent occurred prior to marriage. In 1971, by comparison, about 12 percent of women aged 15-19 had ever experienced a conception, with 74 percent of the first conceptions occurring prior to marriage (not shown in tables). Table 10 shows a decline in the proportion of all first pregnancies ending in live births and an increase in the proportion ending in abortion. If we exclude those women who

°In 1971 abortions were reported only by women who had never been married by the time of the pregnancy outcome. In 1976, however, not only did the never-married report abortion as an outcome, but so did a small number of those who conceived postmaritally and of those who conceived premaritally but married prior to outcome. While these abortions are very few in number and are reported only by whites, such reports give credence to the overall accuracy of reporting of abortions by whites.

Table 10. Percent distribution of all first pregnancies to women aged 15–19 at interview, according to pregnancy outcome and race, 1976 and 1971

Outcome	1976			1971		
	Total (N=419)	White (N=233)	Black (N=186)	Total (N=614)	White (N=265)	Black (N=349)
All	100.0	100.0	100.0	100.0	100.0	100.0
Live birth	56.8	50.1	76.0	62.8	58.9	71.9
Stillbirth	0.7	0.6	1.0	0.7	0.8	0.4
Miscarriage	9.9	11.7	4.9	7.5	7.8	6.8
Abortion	17.9	21.7	6.7	8.5	10.3	4.3
Currently pregnant	14.7	15.9	11.4	20.5	22.2	16.6

Table 11. Percent distribution of all first pregnancies and of first pregnancies ending in live births to women aged 15–19 at interview, according to pregnancy intention and race, 1976 and 1971

Pregnancy intention and contraceptive use	1976			1971		
	Total	White	Black	Total	White	Black
Pregnancies	(N=419)	(N=233)	(N=186)	(N=588)	(N=253)	(N=335)
All	100.0	100.0	100.0	100.0	100.0	100.0
Intended	43.9	47.2	34.4	42.7	48.6	29.2
Not intended	56.1	52.8	65.6	57.3	51.4	70.8
Used contraception	17.2	20.2	10.3	14.9	15.3	14.3
Did not use	82.8	79.8	89.7	85.1	84.7	85.7
Live births	(N=269)	(N=128)	(N=141)	(N=394)	(N=149)	(N=245)
All	100.0	100.0	100.0	100.0	100.0	100.0
Intended	55.2	65.7	35.0	44.3	52.3	29.1
Not intended	44.8	34.3	65.0	55.7	47.7	70.9
Used contraception	11.0	10.4	11.6	15.7	15.3	16.1
Did not use	89.0	89.6	88.4	84.3	84.7	83.9

were currently pregnant for the first time at time of interview, 79 percent of all first pregnancies of known outcome had ended in a live birth by 1971, compared with 66 percent by 1976.

While the proportion of all first conceptions (of known outcome) ending in live births has declined, there has been a corresponding increase in the proportion ending in abortion—from 11 percent in 1971 to 21 percent in 1976—again, excluding the currently pregnant. (The figure for 1976 is on the low side because of the underreporting of abortions by blacks.) For whites, the proportion of all first conceptions of known outcome ter-

minated by abortion doubled, from 13 percent in 1971 to 26 percent in 1976. Among whites, the ratio of first pregnancies that ended in abortions to those ending in live births increased by two and one-half times—from 17.5 percent in 1971 to 43.2 percent by 1976 (not shown in tables).

Table 11 shows little change between 1971 and 1976 in the proportion of all pregnancies that were intended, and only a modest increase in the use of contraception to prevent those unintended pregnancies. However, the proportion of live births that were intended rose from 44 percent to 55 percent over the five-

Table 12. Percent distribution of all live births and legitimate births to women aged 15–19 at interview that resulted from first conceptions, according to whether conceived or born prior to marriage, by race, 1976 and 1971

Birth status	1976			1971		
	Total	White	Black	Total	White	Black
Live births	(N=269)	(N=128)	(N=141)	(N=403)	(N=153)	(N=250)
All	100.0	100.0	100.0	100.0	100.0	100.0
Conceived prior to marriage	77.9	68.9	95.1	76.3	66.6	94.8
Born prior to marriage	45.9	25.5	85.1	45.2	23.6	86.2
Born after marriage	32.0	43.4	10.0	31.1	43.0	8.6
Conceived after marriage	22.1	31.1	4.9	23.7	33.4	5.2
Legitimate live births	(N=121)	(N=103)	(N=18)	(N=144)	(N=114)	(N=30)
All	100.0	100.0	100.0	100.0	100.0	100.0
Conceived prior to marriage	59.1	58.3	**	56.8	56.2	62.2
Conceived after marriage	40.9	41.7	**	43.2	43.8	37.8

Table 13. Percent of sexually experienced women aged 15–19 at interview who had a live birth resulting from a premarital first conception, according to marital status at birth, by race, 1976 and 1971

Marital status at birth	% who had live birth, by race					
	1976			1971		
	Total	White	Black	Total	White	Black
	(N=1,022)	(N=576)	(N=446)	(N=1,477)	(N=731)	(N=746)
All	15.9	11.9	30.4	19.3	14.5	34.0
Unmarried at birth	9.4	4.4	27.2	11.4	5.1	30.9
Married at birth	6.5	7.5	3.2	7.9	9.4	3.1

year period, reflecting the impact of increased utilization of induced abortion to terminate unintended pregnancy.

If we restrict our attention to those live births that resulted from first conceptions, we find very little change between 1971 and 1976 in the proportions conceived prior to or subsequent to marriage, or in the proportion of legitimate live births conceived prior to or subsequent to marriage (see Table 12).

Births to Premaritally Sexually Active

We noted earlier that among white teenagers who had ever had premarital intercourse, the proportion who experienced a premarital first pregnancy did not change appreciably between those sur-

veyed in 1971 and 1976 (although it may have declined among blacks—see Table 2). Table 13 presents data on changes that occurred over the five-year period in the proportions of premaritally sexually active teenagers who ever gave birth as the result of such premarital first pregnancies. Twenty-seven percent of blacks with premarital sexual experience interviewed in 1976 had ever had an out-of-wedlock birth, as compared with 31 percent of those interviewed in 1971; among whites the decline was from 5.1 percent to 4.4 percent.* There was also a

---

*These results are consistent with the results shown in the appendix regarding the rate of illegitimacy among sexually active unmarried women derived from official registration data on illegitimacy.

decline among whites who conceived premaritally, but married before the birth, from 9.4 percent of those surveyed in 1971 to 7.5 percent of those questioned in 1976; among sexually experienced blacks, however, there was virtually no change over the pe riod.

Thus, while the use of contraception to prevent pregnancy barely kept pace with the increasing proportion of sexually active young women, the increased utilization of abortion led to a decrease in the level of out-of-wedlock child bearing among those who had premarital sexual experience. Why the greatly increased and more regular use of the most effective contraceptive methods did not reduce the level of premarital pregnancy among the sexually experienced teenage population needs more detailed analysis. We plan to explore this relationship in a subsequent article.

Summary and Conclusions

We have examined various aspects of teenage first pregnancy based on data from two national samples of young women surveyed in 1971 and in 1976. Because of differences by race in pregnancy-related behavior, the analysis was carried out separately for blacks and for whites.

Comparable data on pregnancies among young women are not available from outside sources. However, it is possible to compare our data on the two principal outcomes of pregnancy—live birth and abortion—with other national figures. With respect to whites, the survey data agree reasonably well with these other sources, whereas for blacks, the 1976 data include slightly more births and considerably fewer abortions than would be expected.

Bearing in mind these general comments regarding the validity of the survey data, especially the underreporting of abortions obtained by blacks, we can summarize the main findings relating to pregnancy and its outcome that arise from a comparison of the two surveys as follows:

• Between 1971 and 1976 the proportion of white teenagers who had ever been pregnant increased in rough proportion to their increased rates of sexual activity (Tables 1 and 2). Thus, among sexually active whites, there was no change in the incidence of pregnancy. During this same period, there was reported an impressive improvement in contraceptive use, regularity of use and use of the more effective methods. Why this improvement did not result in a pregnancy decline requires more detailed analysis.

• Blacks are much more likely than whites to experience premarital intercourse (Table 1) and more likely to become premaritally pregnant (Table 2).

• In 1976 more than seven in 10 first pregnancies that had ever occurred to teens had been premaritally conceived—nine in 10 pregnancies to blacks and more than six in 10 to whites (Table 3). Between 1971 and 1976, the percentage of first pregnancies conceived out of wedlock among whites rose by about one-third; such a rise would be expected, since premarital sexual activity increased sharply while the marriage market remained sluggish.

• Very few premarital first pregnancies among teenagers who did not marry before the outcome were intended; yet only a minority of either race reported that they had used a method of contraception at the time the pregnancy occurred (Table 5). Some nonusers unrealistically discounted their chances of becoming pregnant; but over half of the nonusers who unintentionally became pregnant thought there was a "good chance" that conception might occur. At least part of the explanation for this seemingly irrational behavior may be a low degree of confidence by teenagers in the most available ("drugstore") methods. This explanation is substantiated by the fact that even among those using contraceptives—except for those using the pill—most of the teenagers thought they had a good chance of becoming pregnant.

• Increasingly, out-of-wedlock births, both to blacks and whites, are the outcome of intended pregnancies (though most remain unintended). More than one in three babies ever born out of wedlock to the 1976 respondents resulted from intended pregnancies, in contrast to the one in five ever born to the 1971 sample (Table 5). The most probable cause of the change is the increase in the proportion of unintended pregnancies that are terminated by abortion.

• The relation of intention to the outcome of the pregnancy is what one would expect: Respondents who did not marry before the outcome report proportionately more unintended pregnancies than intended pregnancies as terminating in miscarriages and abortions. Such reports are especially striking among whites, fewer than one in five of whom reported unintended pregnancies as ending in live births, compared with more than three in five who reported intended pregnancies as ending in this manner.

• Among whites surveyed in 1971, premarital pregnancy spurred many to marry; but those questioned in 1976 were less likely to do so. More than half of whites interviewed in 1971 married before the outcome of their premarital first pregnancy; by 1976 this proportion had declined to about one-third. Interposing marriage between a premarital pregnancy and its outcome was relatively rare among blacks surveyed in 1971, and their behavior in this regard did not

change as of the 1976 survey (Table 3).

• Not only have premaritally pregnant whites shown a diminished tendency to marry *before* the outcome of their first pregnancy, but they also appear to have become less inclined toward marriage *after* the outcome. The probable explanation of this trend is that many more premarital first pregnancies are now being resolved through abortion, thus removing one of the chief arguments for early marriage. Those who do marry following the pregnancy outcome tend to be those who have had out-of-wedlock births rather than those with no live issue (Table 7).

• For a pregnant white teenager who did *not* marry before the outcome of her pregnancy, the most frequent outcome among those questioned in 1976 was the combination of abortion and miscarriage—up by nearly 20 percentage points since 1971 (Table 4). In both 1976 and 1971, the overwhelming proportion of blacks reported electing to have their babies. However, we know that in 1976, blacks overreported births and underreported abortions.

• The rate of illegitimacy, calculated so as to take account of the level of sexual activity (thus referring to those truly exposed to the risk of pregnancy rather than to all young women), has declined markedly for blacks and is marginally lower for whites than it was in 1971 (see appendix). The steady increase in the total number of out-of-wedlock births and in the conventional illegitimacy rate, as reported in official statistics, reflects changes in the number of sexually active young unmarried women rather than a greater likelihood of childbirth among teenagers at risk. The apparent paradox of rising illegitimacy together with improved contraception and increased abortion is not a real paradox, but rather an incomplete observation.

• Adoptions of babies born out of wed-lock have declined; proportionally more mothers are keeping their babies even though most are the result of unintended pregnancies (Table 6). The strategy of encouraging adoption in place of abor-tion that is being advocated by anti-abortion groups appears to be bucking a clear trend that is going in the opposite direction. In any event, neither in 1971 nor in 1976 was adoption a major outlet for out-of-wedlock first births to teenag-ers: If they had the baby, they kept it.

• Pregnant brides are more likely to car-ry the pregnancy to term than women who remain unmarried until after the outcome of the premarital pregnancy; and proportionately fewer of their preg-nancies are reported as unintended (Ta-bles 4 and 8).

• The highest proportion of intended pregnancies (eight in 10) is found among those whose first pregnancy comes after marriage (Table 9). Relatively more of these postmarital pregnancies are in-tended among those interviewed in 1976 than in 1971, but there is no change over the five-year period in the distribution according to pregnancy outcome. Im-proved use of contraception appears to have reduced the prevalence of unin-tended pregnancy in this group. How-ever, when conception, whether intend-ed or not, occurs subsequent to marriage, the pregnancy typically is carried to term.

• As for all live births among teenagers, there is remarkable stability over the five years in the relationship between the timing of first conceptions and births and the timing of marriage: In both sur-veys, about three-fourths of live births were conceived prior to marriage, and six in 10 of these conceptions resulted in out-of-wedlock births (around nine in 10 among black mothers; close to four in 10

among whites—see Table 12). It is not immediately obvious why the propor-tions of births conceived—and deliv-ered—prior to marriage has not changed. The change in contraceptive behavior over the five-year period—more use, more regular use and use of more effec-tive methods—might have been expect-ed to bring about a decline in these pro-portions. So should the increased availa-bility and utilization of legal abortion. On the other hand, the increase in pre-marital sexual activity, the earlier timing of initiation of intercourse, and the de-cline in the popularity of marriage as a response to premarital pregnancy, could be expected to increase the proportions. In fact, between the 1971 and 1976 sur-veys, the timing patterns of births did not change at all. The principal effect of more and better contraception and freer availability of abortion seems to have been to achieve a reduction in the il-legitimacy rate and to reduce the pres-sure for pregnancy-induced marriages among those who are sexually active (Ta-ble 11). Otherwise, the pathways to par-enthood, in or out of wedlock, appear to remain as before.

• In both the 1971 and 1976 studies, we have shown some of the ways in which young women in our society are con-fronting the questions of sex and repro-duction. However, defining the dimen-sions of the sexual and reproductive be-havior of female teenagers does not nec-essarily explain that behavior. Some fur-ther insight can be expected as the analy-sis advances to a consideration of other variables associated with the behavior described here. But we expect that there will still be much that remains inexplica-ble or, at least, unclear. Far more study is required before we can hope to explain and understand the sexual and reproduc-tive behavior of young Americans.

References

1. M. Zelnik and J. F. Kantner, "Sexual and Contraceptive Experience of Young Unmarried Women in the United States, 1976 and 1971," see chapter 4, above.

2. ——, "The Resolution of Teenage First Pregnancies," *Family Planning Perspectives*, 6:74, 1974.

3. Chapter 4.

4. ——, "Attitudes of American Teenagers Toward Abortion," *Family Planning Perspectives*, 7:89, 1975.

5. S. J. Ventura, "Teenage Childbearing: United States, 1966-1975," *Monthly Vital Statistics Report, Natality Statistics*, National Center for Health Statistics, DHEW, Vol. 26, No. 5, Supp., 1977.

Appendix:

Teenage Illegitimacy & Abortion 'Measures'

Because all teenage women are not sexually active and the proportion who are changes over time, several standard demographic measures (e.g., the illegitimacy rate and the abortion rate) can be very misleading when applied to teenagers, especially if the rates are compared over time or between racial groups.

Illegitimacy Rate

The illegitimacy rate is conventionally defined as the number of out-of-wedlock births to unmarried women in an age group per 1,000 unmarried women in that age group. For the age group 15–19 years, the illegitimacy rate declined for blacks from 99.1 per 1,000 in 1971 to 95.1 in 1975, but increased for whites over the same period, from 10.3 to 12.1.[1] Based on this measure, the probability of teenagers having an out-of-wedlock birth in 1975 was greater for whites but lower for blacks than in 1971.*

While the unmarried population may satisfactorily approximate those at risk of having an out-of-wedlock birth at older ages, when most unmarried women may be presumed to be sexually active, rates so computed can be misleading for teenagers, a significant proportion of whom are not sexually active and,

therefore, not at risk of having an illegitimate birth. In effect, the illegitimacy rate as conventionally computed measures the combined effect of two risks—the risk of having an out-of-wedlock birth among those unmarried women who are sexually active, and the risk of an unmarried woman being sexually active. Quite simply, the illegitimacy rate can be expressed in the following manner:†

$$\frac{\text{Out-of-wedlock births}}{\text{All unmarried women}} =$$

$$\frac{\text{Out-of-wedlock births}}{\text{Sexually active unmarried women}} \times \frac{\text{Sexually active unmarried women}}{\text{All unmarried women}}$$

Clearly, then, differences in illegitimacy rates, whether between two populations or for the same population over time, may be due either to differences in the risk of having an illegitimate birth among the sexually active or to differences in the proportion who are sexually active.

The data in text Table 1 show a 35 percent increase between 1971 and 1976 in the proportion of never-married 15–19-year-olds who were sexually experienced. Since the officially reported illegitimacy rate for blacks has declined, while the proportion of never-married who are sexually active has increased, the illegitimacy rate among sexually active blacks obviously must have declined even more than among 15-19-year-olds. But what about whites, for whom the official illegitimacy rate

---

*The events referred to here are those that occurred in these two years to women who at the time of occurrence were 15–19 years of age. 1975 is the most recent year for which such data are available; 1971 coincides with the date of our first survey.

---

†The right-hand side of the equation could in principle be broken down further.

increased between 1971 and 1976, as did the proportion sexually active?

An approximate answer to that question can be obtained by dividing the illegitimacy rate by the proportion sexually active. Thus, the illegitimacy rates given above for 1971 and 1975 are divided by the proportion of sexually active never-married women.* The results shown below indicate that for both blacks and whites, there was a decline between 1971 and 1975 in the proportion of sexually active teenagers who bore children out of wedlock.

Illegitimacy rates per 1,000 unmarried women and per 1,000 sexually active unmarried women 15–19 years of age, by race, 1975 and 1971

Year	All		Sexually active	
	Black	White	Black	White
1975	95.1	12.1	157.7	40.5
1971	99.1	10.3	189.1	45.4

Thus, the illegitimacy rate as usually computed shows an increase for whites between 1971 and 1975 and a decrease for blacks over the same period. This difference occurs because there were increases in the proportion of both black and white teenagers who were sexually active—with the increase relatively greater for whites than for blacks; and there were declines among sexually active whites and blacks in the likelihood of having a birth out of wedlock—with the decline proportionately greater for blacks than for whites. A decrease in the risk of an out-of-wedlock birth among the sexually active is not inconsistent with stable (or even increasing) rates of premarital pregnancy among the sexually active, since the former is affected by abortion whereas the latter is not.

Abortion Rate

The abortion rate is conventionally defined as the number of abortions obtained by women at any given age per 1,000 women of that age. A recent article gives abortion rates in 1973 of 20.6 for whites under age 20 and 43.8 for nonwhites,[†2] yielding a ratio of the nonwhite to white abortion rate of 2.1:1. Presumably, then, nonwhites under 20 years of age were twice as likely as whites to resort to abortion.

However, a substantial proportion of the women 15–19 years of age are not sexually active and therefore not at risk of having an abortion, but nevertheless are included in the denominator of the abortion rate. Moreover, the proportion not sexually active differs between whites and nonwhites. Even among the sexually active, only those who are pregnant are in fact at risk of abortion. In effect, the abortion rate can be expressed as follows:

$$\frac{\text{Number of abortions}}{\text{All women}} = \frac{\text{Number of abortions}}{\text{Pregnant women}} \times$$

$$\frac{\text{Pregnant women}}{\text{Sexually active women}} \times \frac{\text{Sexually active women}}{\text{All women}}$$

The third term on the right hand side of the equation gives the risk of being sexually active among all women; the middle term accounts for the risk of pregnancy among sexually active women; and the first term gives abortions to pregnant women—i.e., a more refined rate of abortion since it pertains more precisely to those who are in fact at risk of abortion.

The risk of being sexually active is estimated by assuming that 10 percent of the population aged 15–19 are ever-married and all of these women are sexually active, and that among the 90 percent who are never-married, the proportion sexually active as of 1973 is that value obtained by linear interpolation between the proportions reported in our 1971 and 1976 surveys.‡ Our estimate of the risk of

---

*Data from the 1971 and 1976 surveys; 1975 obtained by linear interpolation. We ignore the distinction between never-married and unmarried. The survey data applied to the white illegitimacy rates refer to whites and "others," while the survey data applied to the nonwhite illegitimacy rates refer to blacks; this is of little consequence.

†These rates were computed by relating the estimated average number of abortions to young women under age 20 (including those to young women under age 15) over the three-year period 1972–1974 to women aged 15–19 in 1973.

‡The population figures are those given in reference 2. Our estimate of sexual activity for blacks is applied to the nonwhite population, and our estimate of sexual activity for whites and others is applied to the white population.

pregnancy in 1973 is crude and approximate, probably even more so than our estimate of the proportion of all teenagers who were sexually active in 1973. For illustrative purposes, however, the approximations will serve.

To estimate the number of pregnancies among sexually active teenagers in 1973, we add the number of live births occurring that year to women aged 15–19 to estimates of the number of abortions that year to white and nonwhite women under 20 years of age based on the total number of abortions reported in 1973 to the Center for Disease Control (CDC) and distributed by the percent distributions given by CDC.[3] The live births and abortions that occurred in 1973 are assumed to equal pregnancies conceived in 1973.* Dividing this number by the number estimated to be sexually active that year gives the risk of pregnancy among the sexually active.

If we now divide the conventional abortion rate by the rate of sexual activity among all women and by the rate of pregnancy among the sexually active, we get the abortion rate among the pregnant. The resulting figures are 310 per 1,000 pregnant women for whites and 280 per 1,000 pregnant women for nonwhites.

─────────────────────

*We recognize that conceptions resulting in births occurred earlier than conceptions resulting in abortions, and we do not include miscarriages and stillbirths in our estimates of pregnancy. While these would affect the overall total number of pregnancies, they should not affect the relationships between black and white pregnancies which we are examining here.

The ratio of the nonwhite rate to the white rate is below 1, which would imply that among those actually at risk of abortion—i.e., pregnant women—nonwhites are slightly less likely than whites to obtain an abortion.

We would be reluctant to argue from these approximate data that pregnant white teenagers are more likely to resort to abortion than are pregnant nonwhites 15–19 years of age. However, this exercise, we believe, shows how the conventional abortion rate, when applied to teenagers, distorts the actual risk of obtaining an abortion; since it reflects not only differential recourse to abortion but very substantial differences by race in the probability of sexual activity and pregnancy.

The refinements introduced here to the conventional abortion rate do not depend on or involve our survey data on abortion. The only survey data used in the process are the estimates of the prevalence of sexual activity, which we believe to be reasonably accurate.

References

1. National Center for Health Statistics, DHEW (NCHS), "Final Natality Statistics, 1971," Monthly Vital Statistics Report, Vol. 23, No. 3, Supplement (3), 1974; NCHS, "Final Natality Statistics, 1975," Monthly Vital Statistics Report, Vol. 25, No. 10, Supplement, 1976.

2. C. Tietze, "Legal Abortions in the United States: Rates and Ratios by Race and Age, 1972–1974," Family Planning Perspectives, 9:12, 1977.

3. Center for Disease Control, DHEW, Abortion Surveillance, Annual Summary, 1973, Atlanta, 1975.

6

Contraceptive Patterns and Premarital Pregnancy Among Women Aged 15–19 in 1976

Melvin Zelnik and John F. Kantner

We have, in two previous articles, presented comparative data on the premarital sexual and contraceptive[1] and pregnancy-related[2] behavior of two groups of 15–19-year-old American women—one surveyed in 1971 and the other in 1976. In summary, the data show
● an increase in the prevalence of premarital sexual activity;
● an increase in the proportion of never-married sexually experienced teenagers who have always used contraception, and a smaller increase in the proportion who have never used contraception;
● among never-married contraceptors, an increase in the regularity of contraceptive use and in the use of more effective methods; but
● no change among sexually active whites, and only a small decline among blacks,* in the proportion who have ever been premaritally pregnant.

Thus, the data on contraceptive practices indicate that sexually active young women interviewed in 1976 were better protected against pregnancy than were comparable young women interviewed in 1971; but the data on premarital pregnancies do not show any change over the period in the proportions who had experienced a pregnancy up to the time of interview. This does not mean that improved contraception did not affect the incidence of pregnancy. But we cannot make the detailed comparisons of contraceptive use and pregnancy between the two surveys needed to explain the apparent contradiction.† However, the

The authors acknowledge the invaluable assistance of Judy Gehret, Nelva Hitt and Farida Shah. The 1976 study on which this article is based was supported by Grant No. HD05255 from the National Institute of Child Health and Human Development, DHEW. Generous assistance also was received from the Ford Foundation.
The data are derived from a national probability sample survey of ever-married and never-married women 15–19 years of age living in households in the continental United States. The sampling procedure involved stratification by race to ensure a substantial number of interviews with black respondents. The fieldwork was carried out under contract by the Research Triangle Institute and provided 2,193 completed interviews.

*The decline for blacks may in fact be spurious (see chapter 5).

†The number of questions in the 1971 study on contraceptive use were far fewer and less detailed and specific than those asked in 1976. In addition, data on contraceptive use among the ever-married surveyed in 1976 refer specifically to the premarital state, whereas for 1971 the data cannot be split into premarital and postmarital segments.

1976 data alone, although far from perfect, do permit us to examine in far greater detail than we could from the 1971 survey the relationship of contraceptive use and premarital pregnancy.*

In this article, premaritally sexually active teenagers are classified by contraceptive-use status as "always-users," "never-users" or "sometimes-users" of contraception. This classification refers to contraceptive behavior up to the time of a premarital pregnancy, or if the teenager has never been pregnant premaritally, up to interview or marriage.†

We have noted previously that about 28 percent of teenagers (25 percent of whites and 40 percent of blacks) who have had premarital intercourse have ever experienced a premarital pregnancy.[3] Table 1 shows how these proportions vary widely according to contraceptive-use status (classified in the manner noted above). Roughly similar proportions—about three in 10—report that they are always-users and never-users, while about four in 10 say they have used a method sometimes. Blacks

are about one and one-half times more likely than whites to be never-users.

Most important, the data in Table 1 show a strong negative correlation between contraceptive use and continuity of use, and pregnancy: Fifty-eight percent of never-users experienced a premarital pregnancy, compared to 24 percent of sometimes-users and only 11 percent of always-users. The difference in premarital pregnancy between regular use and nonuse of contraception is more striking for blacks than whites,‡ but the basic pattern is the same. For all teenagers, contraceptive use makes a substantial difference: Never-users are five times more likely to become pregnant than always-users, and two and one-half times more likely than sometimes-users.

We examine the association of preg-

---

*About 40 percent of the women 15–19 years of age in 1976 had experienced premarital intercourse; 80 percent of those who were married had had intercourse before marriage, compared to 36 percent of those still unmarried. This article applies only to premarital behavior. Thus, a respondent who was married at interview and who had had premarital intercourse, but had never used contraception while unmarried, is classified as a never-user whether or not she used contraception after marriage.

In discussing the contraceptive practices of premaritally sexually active women, we have removed from the analysis those women who have had premarital sexual intercourse only one time and thus cannot exhibit *patterns* of contraceptive use. In doing so we are undoubtedly excluding some who will continue to be sexually active; but we have no way of distinguishing between those who will continue such activity and those who will be sexually abstinent for some extended period of time. These "one-timers" represented 13.3 percent of all premaritally sexually active women, with remarkably little variation by race or current marital status.

---

† In our previous article, contraceptive-use status of never-married sexually active teenagers referred to contraceptive behavior up to the time of the survey. Over time, the sometimes-user group will increase as some never-users adopt contraception and as some always-users accidentally or intentionally fail to use it. The slippage into sometimes-use is a potential source of confusion if the proportions ever and never pregnant are computed for each contraceptive-use category, since pregnancy itself is likely to lead to a change from one category to another. Imagine, for example, that every nonuser of contraception who becomes pregnant starts to use contraception after the pregnancy ends, and that every regular and consistent user of contraception who becomes pregnant stops using it after she becomes pregnant. In such a situation, the proportion ever pregnant among never-users and always-users would be zero since all who become pregnant would end up as sometimes-users. And the results would tell us little about contraceptive practices prior to pregnancy or about the relationship between use and pregnancy.

‡ Blacks who reported always-use were somewhat less likely than comparable whites to have been pregnant perhaps because a larger proportion used the more effective medical methods, while black never-users were more likely to have experienced pregnancy perhaps because of earlier initiation of intercourse and, therefore, greater exposure to risk (see chapter 3, Tables 8 and 12).

Table 1. Percentage distribution of young women with premarital sexual experience,* by contraceptive-use status, and percent ever premaritally pregnant for each status, according to race

Contraceptive-use and pregnancy status	Total %	Total N	White %	White N	Black %	Black N
Always-use	26.9	228	27.7	135	23.8	93
Ever pregnant	10.9		11.2		9.6	
Sometimes-use	42.1	343	44.6	215	33.3	128
Ever pregnant	23.9		22.6		30.0	
Never-use	31.0	312	27.7	147	42.9	165
Ever pregnant	58.0		52.2		71.2	
Total	100.0	883	100.0	497	100.0	386

*This and subsequent tables refer to women with premarital sexual experience who were aged 15-19 in 1976.

Table 2. Percentage of young women who used contraception at first intercourse, by age at first intercourse and race

Age at 1st inter-course	Total %	Total N	White %	White N	Black %	Black N
All	38.7	878	40.2	496	33.5	382
<15	24.5	237	23.8	97	25.8	140
15-17	40.9	564	42.0	338	36.2	226
18-19	54.8	77	54.1	61	**	16

Note: In this and subsequent tables, a double asterisk indicates N<20.

nancy and contraceptive use in somewhat greater detail below. We continue to base contraceptive-use status on behavior up to pregnancy, marriage or the survey while at the same time subsuming the categories of always-, sometimes- and never-use under two more general categories. So that the reader may follow the presentation more easily, the scheme we use is outlined as follows:

I. Used contraception at first intercourse
   a) and always used it prior to pregnancy, marriage or survey
   b) but did not always use it prior to pregnancy, marriage or survey

II. Did not use contraception at first intercourse
   a) but used it prior to pregnancy, marriage or survey
   b) and never used it prior to pregnancy, marriage or survey

In terms of contraceptive-use status, Ia corresponds to always-use, IIb corresponds to never-use and Ib plus IIa corresponds to sometimes-use.

Used Contraception at 1st Intercourse

Almost 40 percent of all teenage women with premarital sexual experience used contraception the first time they had intercourse, with the proportion somewhat higher for whites than for blacks (see Table 2). There is a clear positive relationship between age at first intercourse and the likelihood of using contraception at that event: Fifty-five percent of those who first had intercourse at ages 18 or 19 used a contraceptive at that initial event—more than two times the proportion of those who first had intercourse before age 15.

Such a relationship may be related to changes in circumstances over time as well as to a direct effect of age at first intercourse and such concomitants as greater education and sophistication. That is because all young women who initiated intercourse at ages 18 or 19 began sex shortly before the survey, while those who started at younger ages had that experience at varying intervals preceding the survey. For example, the current 15-year-old whose first intercourse occurred at age 14 began sex shortly before interview, while the 19-year-old who initiated sex at 14 began sex five years before the survey. It is probable that a 14-year-old in 1970 and in 1975 faced quite different situations regarding the availability and accessibility of contraception, for example.

If age at first intercourse were the sole factor accounting for the use of contraception at initial intercourse, we would expect that among those who began sex before age 15, the proportion using contraception at first intercourse would not vary with current age. On the other hand, if the calendar year in which intercourse first occurred is important—for example, because of the increased availability of contraceptives to teenagers in recent years—there should be variation by current age, with currently younger women having different rates of initial use than older women. The data in Table 3 show that for both races (reading down the columns), age at first intercourse remains positively associated with contraceptive use at that initial event. For blacks, and possibly for whites who began sex before age 15 (though here, the Ns are small), there appears to be an increase in use over time (reading across the rows); while for whites who initiated intercourse between ages 15 and 17, the year that sex began appears to make little difference. These data are consistent with reports indicating that in recent years contraceptives have become more available to younger teenagers,[4] and that expansion

Table 3. Percentage of young women who used contraception at first intercourse, by age at first intercourse and current age, according to race

Age at 1st intercourse	Current age			
	15-17		18-19	
	%	N	%	N
Total				
<15	26.7	148	20.6	89
15-17	41.7	230	40.4	334
18-19	na	na	54.8	77
White				
<15	25.7	64	20.2	33
15-17	42.1	137	42.0	201
18-19	na	na	54.1	61
Black				
<15	28.7	84	21.3	56
15-17	39.8	93	33.7	133
18-19	na	na	**	16

Note: In this and subsequent tables, na=not applicable.

Table 4. Percentage of young women practicing contraception at first intercourse who used a medical method of contraception, by age at first intercourse and race

Age at 1st intercourse	Total		White		Black	
	%	N	%	N	%	N
All	25.1	326	20.1	198	46.6	128
<15	23.1	59	12.6	23	41.1	36
15-17	21.9	225	16.8	143	46.5	82
18-19	40.8	42	38.1	32	**	10

of family planning services in organized clinic programs has increased availability proportionally more for blacks than for whites.°

°DHEW's National Reporting Service for Family Planning Services shows that between 1972 and 1976, the number of teenagers under age 18 served in organized family planning clinics increased by 89 percent, compared to a 55 percent increase for those aged 18 and 19. Services to black teenagers increased by 69 percent and to white teenagers by 65 percent.

Table 5. Percentage of young women practicing contraception at first intercourse who are always-users of contraception, by initial method and race

Initial method	Total		White		Black	
	%	N	%	N	%	N
All	69.7	327	69.1	198	72.2	129
Medical	87.3	100	92.4	39	78.0	61
Nonmedical	63.8	227	63.2	159	67.1	68

Table 6. Percentage distribution of always-users of contraception, by initial method and race

Initial method	Total (N=228)	White (N=135)	Black (N=93)
Medical	31.6	26.9	51.3
Nonmedical	68.4	73.1	48.7
All	100.0	100.0	100.0

What methods were adopted by those who used a contraceptive the first time they had intercourse? Table 4 shows that one-quarter of all those who used contraception at first intercourse used a medical method (pill, IUD or diaphragm)—one-fifth of whites and nearly one-half of blacks. Again, there is a clear positive association between the age at which intercourse begins and the likelihood of adopting a medical method at initiation.*

---

*However, it must be remembered that those using a medical method at first intercourse represent only about one-tenth of all sexually active teenagers who have had premarital intercourse. It would be desirable to look at use of medical methods at initiation by current age to see the effect of changes over time. This is only one of a number of important questions concerning contraceptive and pregnancy behavior that we cannot attempt to answer because of the small number of sample cases that would be involved. Some of the differences we do tabulate involve Ns that are fairly small. The reader should view these with caution, especially where the differences are not great.

Those who use contraception at the time of first intercourse can be subdivided into two groups: those who continue to use a method at every subsequent act of intercourse up to pregnancy, marriage or survey (always-users); and those who do not (sometimes-users). Having considered all of those who used a contraceptive at first intercourse, we now consider, briefly, each of the two subgroups.

Always-Users

Table 5 shows that about seven in 10 of both whites and blacks who used a contraceptive at first intercourse reported that they always used a method. Although regularity of use does not vary with race, there are considerable differences depending on whether the first method used was medical or nonmedical: Eighty-seven percent of those who used a medical method of contraception at first intercourse continued to use contraception regularly, compared to 64 percent of those who started with a nonmedical method. Both blacks and whites who started with a medical method were more likely to continue use than those who started with a nonmedical method; but whites who started with a medical method were more likely to continue use than comparable blacks. However, black always-users were much more likely than whites to start with a medical method: Fifty-one percent of black always-users began with a medical method, in contrast to 27 percent of the white always-users (see Table 6).

Over time, one-quarter of the always-users changed the type of method employed between first and most recent contraceptive use.† One-third of those

---

†Most recent use refers to time of pregnancy, or last intercourse preceding marriage or interview.

Table 7. Percentage distribution of initial method of contraception employed by always-users, according to most recent method used, by race

Initial method	Most recent method			N
	Medical	Nonmed-ical	All	
Total				
Medical	94.0	6.0	100.0	84
Nonmedical	34.3	65.7	100.0	144
All	53.2	46.8	100.0	228
White				
Medical	93.2	6.8	100.0	36
Nonmedical	35.2	64.8	100.0	99
All	50.8	49.2	100.0	135
Black				
Medical	95.8	4.2	100.0	48
Nonmedical	28.6	71.4	100.0	45
All	63.1	36.9	100.0	93

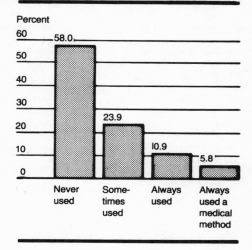

Figure 1. Percentage of sexually active young women who ever had a premarital pregnancy, by contraceptive-use status

who started with a nonmedical method switched to a medical method; whereas only one in 16 of those who began with a medical method shifted to nonmedical contraception (see Table 7). As a result, 53 percent of always-users were using a medical method at most recent use, compared to 32 percent at first use (see Table 6); and the racial difference that had prevailed at first use declined, so that 51 percent of the whites were using a medical method at last use, as compared to 63 percent of the blacks.

Table 1 showed that 10 percent of black always-users and 11 percent of white always-users had ever experienced a premarital pregnancy. However, there are substantial differences in the proportions of always-users who ever became pregnant, depending on whether they were using a medical or nonmedical method of contraception: Thus, 17 percent of always-users who employed a nonmedical method (at time of pregnancy or last intercourse preceding marriage

Table 8. Percentage of always-users who became premaritally pregnant, by method and race

Method	Total		White		Black	
	%	N	%	N	%	N
All	10.9	228	11.2	135	9.6	93
Medical	5.8	128	6.1	69	4.9	59
Nonmed-ical	16.6	100	16.4	66	17.7	34

or survey) experienced a pregnancy, three times the proportion of those who used a medical method (see Table 8).* Even more striking (as comparison of Tables 8 and 1 shows), the proportion of never-users who became pregnant (58 percent) is 10 times that of always-users who employed a medical method (6 percent). Among blacks, the proportion is

---

*Of those always-users who became pregnant, 29 percent were using a medical method at the time of pregnancy and 71 percent were using a nonmedical method.

Table 9. Percentage distribution of young women who used contraception at first intercourse but not consistently thereafter, by whether ever premaritally pregnant, by whether pregnancy was intended, and, if not, by whether contraception was used at time of conception, according to race

Pregnancy status, intent, and use of contraception	Total (N= 98)	White (N= 63)	Black (N= 35)
Never pregnant	66.8	70.8	47.8
Ever pregnant	33.2	29.2	52.2
Intended pregnancy	38.9	39.0	**
Did not intend	61.1	61.0	**
Used medical method	2.3	**	**
Used nonmedical method	13.2	**	**
Did not use	84.5	**	**
Total	100.0	100.0	100.0

15 times greater, and among whites, nine times greater.

In summary:

• Use of contraception at first intercourse, and especially use of a medical method, is associated with more consistent use of contraception.

• One-third of always-users who start intercourse using a nonmedical method switch to a more effective medical method later, while almost all who begin with a medical method continue to use medical contraception.

• Those who consistently use a medical method are one-third as likely to become pregnant as those who use a nonmedical method, and one-tenth as likely to get pregnant as those who use no method.

Used at Initiation, but Not Always

As indicated in Table 5, 36 percent of those who used a nonmedical method at first intercourse subsequently failed to use contraception consistently, compared to just 13 percent of those initially using a medical method. Table 9 shows that among those who used contraception at first intercourse but not consistently thereafter,* one-third—half of the blacks and three in 10 of the whites—became pregnant. Six out of 10 of those who became pregnant reported that they did not intend to become pregnant, but the overwhelming majority of them—more than eight in 10—were not using contraception at the time pregnancy occurred.

No Contraception at 1st Intercourse

Just as we divided those who used contraception at first intercourse into two groups according to whether they continued to practice contraception consistently, we now divide teenagers who did not use contraception at first intercourse into those who did† and those who did not use any method subsequently (prior to a pregnancy, marriage or the survey).

Table 10 shows that almost half of the young women who did not use a method at first intercourse but adopted contraception later began with a medical method. This compares to just one-quarter adopting a medical method among those who began intercourse and contraception concurrently (see Table 4). The difference does not stem merely from the fact that those who delay contraception until some time after initiation are older than those who begin sex and contraception at the same time. Comparison of Tables 4 and 10 shows that at each age of first intercourse, the

---

*This group represents 28 percent of the sometimes-users shown in Table 1.

†This group represents 72 percent of the sometimes-users shown in Table 1.

Table 10. Of young women who delayed use of contraception,* percentage who began with a medical method, by age at first intercourse and race

Age at 1st intercourse	Total		White		Black	
	%	N	%	N	%	N
All	47.5	241	45.0	151	59.8	90
<15	46.0	67	39.4	36	67.8	31
15-17	48.4	158	47.1	102	55.1	56
18-19	**	16	**	13	**	3

*That is, did not use contraception at first intercourse but did use it prior to pregnancy, marriage or survey.

Table 11. Mean number of years between first intercourse and first use of contraception for those who delayed use of contraception,* by method and race

Age at 1st intercourse	Method					
	All		Medical		Nonmedical	
	No. yrs.	N	No. yrs.	N	No. yrs.	N
Total						
<15	1.4	65	1.8	34	0.9	31
15-17	0.5	156	0.6	78	0.4	78
18-19	na	na	na	na	na	na
White						
<15	1.2	36	**	13	0.8	23
15-17	0.5	101	0.6	47	0.3	54
18-19	na	na	na	na	na	na
Black						
<15	1.7	29	1.7	21	**	8
15-17	0.6	55	0.7	31	0.5	24
18-19	na	na	na	na	na	na

*See Table 10.

proportion who start contraception with a medical method is greater among those who delay contraception than among those who use it at sexual initiation. In fact, among both blacks and whites who had intercourse before age 15 and who did not initially use contraception, the proportion starting with a medical method is as high as that among those who began intercourse and contraception at ages 18 or 19. Thus, the higher level of initial use of medical contraception among those who start to contracept after they begin to have intercourse is not due to an older age at first use of contraception.

Of obvious importance is the length of the interval between first intercourse and first contraception. As may be seen in Table 11, there was an average of 1.4 years between first intercourse and first contraception for those who initiated sex before age 15; whites tended to adopt a method somewhat sooner (1.2 years) than blacks (1.7 years). Those adopting a medical method waited an average of 1.8 years, while those adopting a nonmedical method waited only 0.9 years.

The young women who began intercourse between ages 15 and 17 waited just half a year to begin to contracept;

there is no difference in this respect between blacks and whites or between those adopting a medical and nonmedical method. We have no information on the frequency of intercourse during the interval between sexual initiation and the adoption of contraception.°

Twenty percent of those who delayed contraception became pregnant following the adoption of some method (22 percent of the blacks and 20 percent of the whites). Of those who became pregnant, nearly three-quarters did not intend the pregnancy (see Table 12). But of

°It should be pointed out that those who had intercourse in this interval and remained nonpregnant but subsequently began to use contraception are categorized as sometimes-users, while those who had unprotected intercourse and did become pregnant are classified as never-users.

Table 12. Percentage distribution of young women who delayed use of contraception,* by whether ever premaritally pregnant, by whether pregnancy was intended, and, if not, by whether contraception was used at time of conception, according to race

Pregnancy status, intent, and use of contraception	Total (N= 245)	White (N= 152)	Black (N= 93)
Never pregnant	**79.7**	**79.9**	**78.5**
Ever pregnant	**20.3**	**20.1**	**21.5**
Intended pregnancy	27.6	23.7	45.3
Did not intend	72.4	76.3	54.7
Used medical method	16.8	16.6	**
Used nonmedical method	13.9	14.6	**
Did not use	69.3	68.8	**
Total	100.0	100.0	100.0

*See Table 10.

Table 13. Percentage distribution of premaritally pregnant young women, by whether contraception had ever been used prior to pregnancy, according to race

Use of contraception before pregnancy	Total (N= 316)	White (N= 151)	Black (N= 165)
Ever used	41.9	47.6	28.7
Never used	58.1	52.4	71.3
Total	100.0	100.0	100.0

these, seven in 10 were not using any method at the time they conceived.

In summary, about one in five young women who started contraception at the time they initiated sex, but then failed to use contraception consistently, had an unwanted pregnancy, whereas about one in seven who delayed contraception until some time after initiating sex had an unwanted pregnancy (derived from Tables 9 and 12). This difference appears to be due mainly to the fact that those who began use later were more likely to use a more effective medical method.

Never Used Contraception

As shown in Table 1, 28 percent of whites and 43 percent of blacks with premarital sexual experience had never used contraception prior to pregnancy, marriage or the survey. Slightly more than one-half of the white never-users had experienced a premarital pregnancy,

as had seven in 10 of the black never-users. Of those never-users who had become pregnant, 66 percent of the whites and 72 percent of the blacks reported they did not intend to become pregnant (not shown in tables).

Following the outcome of the pregnancy, a very high proportion of eligible never-users ° did in fact adopt contraception, and almost all of them adopted a medical method. Thus, seven in 10 of the black never-users who became pregnant began to contracept subsequent to the pregnancy outcome, and virtually all of these adopted a medical method. Six in 10 whites adopted contraception after the pregnancy outcome, and nine in 10 adopted a medical method.† At the same time, one-fourth of the ever-pregnant

°Eligible refers to those with a definite first pregnancy outcome while still unmarried. Thus, those who married while pregnant for the first time, and the never-married who at interview were currently pregnant for the first time, are excluded. We have not examined the postpregnancy behavior of the other contraceptive-use groups because of small Ns (see Table 16).

We have not computed the lag between the outcome of the pregnancy and the first use of contraception for never-users, since we have no way of knowing when sexual relations were resumed following the outcome of the pregnancy.

†If those who did not resume sexual activity following pregnancy outcome are removed from the base, there is no difference between blacks and whites in the proportion adopting contraception.

never-users continued to be sexually active without using contraception (not shown).

The Premaritally Pregnant

So far, our discussion of the use of contraception in relation to premarital first pregnancy has focused on the proportion of sexually active young women who ever became pregnant. In Table 13, we show for those who were premaritally pregnant whether contraception had ever been used prior to the time pregnancy occurred.* The table shows that the bulk of premarital first pregnancies occur to that portion of the sexually active teenage population who do not use contraception before they become pregnant. Comparing Table 1 with Table 13, we see that 31 percent of sexually active teenagers are never-users, and that these comprise 58 percent of those who had a premarital pregnancy. Among blacks, 43 percent are never-users, comprising 71 percent of those who had a premarital pregnancy; among whites, the proportion of never-users is 28 percent, or 52 percent of those who had a premarital pregnancy.

What proportion of all premarital pregnancies were reported as intended? Table 14 shows that seven in 10 premarital pregnancies occurring to both whites and blacks were not intended.† However, only one in five of those who did not intend the pregnancy were using contraception when conception occurred; whites were somewhat more

---

*This does not mean that those who had ever used a method prior to the pregnancy were in fact using one at time of conception.

†These tabulations include the always-users who became pregnant, none of whom intended the pregnancy.

Table 14. Percentage distribution of premaritally pregnant young women, by whether pregnancy was intended and, if not, by whether contraception was used at time of conception, according to race

Pregnancy intent and use at time of conception	Total (N= 316)	White (N= 151)	Black (N= 165)
Intended pregnancy	28.8	28.3	29.8
Did not intend	71.2	71.7	70.2
Used medical method	7.4	8.5	4.9
Used nonmedical method	13.7	17.0	6.0
Did not use	78.9	74.5	89.0
Total	100.0	100.0	100.0

Table 15. Percentage of premaritally pregnant young women who married while pregnant, by whether or not pregnancy was intended, according to race

Pregnancy intent	Total		White		Black	
	%	N	%	N	%	N
All pregnancies	26.9	316	34.8	151	8.7	165
Intended	43.7	96	57.0	47	14.5	49
Did not intend	20.1	220	26.1	104	6.2	116

likely to have been using a method than blacks.

Overall, almost three in 10 young women who became premaritally pregnant married while pregnant. Those who intended the pregnancy were twice as likely to marry before the outcome as those who did not intend the pregnancy (see Table 15). Whether or not the pregnancy was intended, whites who conceived premaritally were four times more likely to marry while pregnant than were comparable blacks.

In Table 16, we show the postpregnancy contraceptive behavior of all those who had a first pregnancy outcome

Table 16. Percentage distribution of premaritally pregnant eligible* young women, by use of contraception subsequent to pregnancy outcome, according to race

Contraceptive use after pregnancy	Total (N= 214)	White (N= 75)	Black (N= 139)
Used a method	**71.8**	**70.8**	**73.3**
Medical	83.0	79.6	88.3
Nonmedical	17.0	20.4	11.7
Did not use	**16.2**	**12.5**	**22.1**
Not sexually active	**12.0**	**16.7**	**4.5**
Total	100.0	100.0	100.0

*Refers to those who had a definite first pregnancy outcome while still unmarried.

Table 17. Percentage of premaritally pregnant white young women who were using contraception at time of conception, by pregnancy outcome, for all first pregnancies and for all unintended first pregnancies

Pregnancy intent	Pregnancy outcome					
	All		Abortion		Other	
	%	N	%	N	%	N
All first pregnancies	18.2	151	27.1	38	14.5	113
All unintended first pregnancies	25.4	104	27.8	37	23.9	67

while still unmarried. Seventy-two percent used contraception after the pregnancy outcome, and 83 percent of these contraceptors used a medical method. On the other hand, 16 percent continued to be sexually active but did not use any method after the outcome. Whites and blacks do not differ in the degree to which they use contraception, but blacks appear more likely to use a medical method. However, whites seem to be less likely to resume sex following the

outcome of the pregnancy (at least over the short run) than blacks.*

Contraception and Abortion

One area the previous discussion has not touched upon is the association—if any—between abortion and prior contraceptive use. Are young women who become premaritally pregnant and obtain an abortion more or less likely to have used contraception at the time of conception than those who give birth or miscarry? In Table 17, we provide two comparisons between women whose pregnancy ended in abortion and women with all other outcomes.† The first comparison involves all first premarital pregnancies; the second, all first premarital pregnancies that were reported as unintended.‡ When all first pregnancies are considered, those young women having an abortion are seen to be almost twice as likely to have been contracepting at the time pregnancy occurred (27 percent) as those with some other pregnancy outcome (14 percent). When we exclude from consideration those who were deliberately not contracepting because they intended to become pregnant, i.e., consider only unintended pregnancies, the difference narrows but still contradicts the assertion that those who obtain an abortion are less likely to have been contracepting at time of conception than those whose pregnancies have some

---

*The qualifications are made here because of the small Ns involved.

†Included as an outcome is current pregnancy, since all of the pregnant women reported that they planned to have the baby.

‡ Because of a deficit, noted in a previous article, in the reporting by blacks of pregnancies terminated by abortion, data in Table 17 refer to whites only (see chapter 5, above).

other outcome.[*] Thus, although a substantial majority of young unmarried women who became pregnant and had an abortion were not contracepting at the time they became pregnant, they were no less likely, and were probably more likely, to be contracepting than young women who became pregnant unintentionally and did not have an abortion.

In summary, four in 10 of those who became premaritally pregnant had practiced contraception at some time prior to their pregnancy. Although seven in 10 did not want to get pregnant, only two in 10 of this group were using any method at the time of conception. However, following the pregnancy, eight in 10 of those who resumed sexual activity adopted a method, and eight in 10 of these chose a medical method. Those who intended to get pregnant were more than twice as likely to marry in the course of pregnancy as those for whom the pregnancy was unintended. The data strongly suggest that teenagers are *not* using abortion as a substitute for contraception. More teenagers who obtained abortions than who gave birth or had other pregnancy outcomes were practicing contraception at the time they became pregnant.

Conclusion

When we recognize that eight in 10 of those teenagers who have an unwanted pregnancy are not in fact using any method when the pregnancy occurs,[5] it becomes somewhat easier to understand

---

[*]The pregnancies referred to in Table 17 all occurred premaritally, but the outcomes are premarital and postmarital. It is not surprising, but perhaps worth noting, that virtually all of the pregnancies that eventually ended in abortion were reported as unintended pregnancies.

why the level of premarital pregnancy continues to remain as high as it does in spite of increased and more regular use of contraception by teenagers.

It is clear that if a sexually active young woman uses a contraceptive regularly, she runs a relatively low risk of becoming pregnant (11 percent), and if she uses a medical method of contraception regularly, she runs an even lower risk (six percent). It also is the case that a sexually active young woman who never uses a method is exceedingly likely (58 percent) to become pregnant.

Although four in 10 sexually active young women initiate use of contraception prior to a pregnancy, one-third of these do not continue to use it consistently, even though most say they do not want to get pregnant. We cannot be certain what their reasons are for not continuing use. Misinformation about the real risk of unprotected intercourse when the partners are young and sex occurs seldom and episodically; the inappropriateness of long-term methods in the face of episodic sexual encounters, and embarrassment over obtaining coitus-dependent methods like. condoms from unsympathetic druggists; differential availability of methods and services, especially to younger teenagers; or a need to dare the fates—all are among the many diagnoses and speculations that have been made. (We are currently analyzing the reasons proffered by the teenage respondents to our study, and will present the results in a future article.) It is a fairly safe assumption that sexual activity among adolescents is unlikely to decline. If unintended premarital pregnancies are to be reduced, it seems to us that it will be necessary to increase the proportion who use contraception and who use it consistently. This would require increased availability and accessi-

Figure 2. Number of premarital pregnancies experienced by 15-19-year-olds in 1976, and number that would have occurred a) if no contraception had been used and b) if all who did not want a baby had consistently used contraception

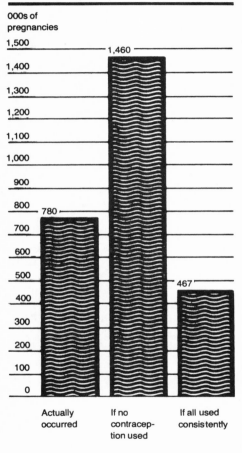

000s of
pregnancies

Actually
occurred

If no
contracep-
tion used

If all used
consistently

methods like condoms and foam. Better information about pregnancy risk—in a form that teenagers can absorb and will believe—would also be needed if teenagers are to recognize the importance of consistent contraceptive use before they have the unfortunate experience of an unintended pregnancy. In addition, given the inexperience of teenage users, and a likelihood of contraceptive failure greater than that among married adults, accessible backup abortion services would undoubtedly still be needed for teenagers who continue to have unintended pregnancies but wish to avoid unintended births. Recent federal and state legislation restricting the availability of abortion under Medicaid will especially handicap low–income teenagers who have unintended pregnancies.

Some of the data presented in this article may be disheartening to those alarmed over the magnitude of teenage pregnancy. Certainly, these findings leave no room for complacency. But they do show that many teenagers *are* using contraception, are using effective methods and are using them regularly.[6] And they show that use of contraception—even less than perfect use—makes a considerable difference in reducing the probability of an unintended pregnancy. Service providers should realize that the teenage pregnancy problem would be far greater than it now is if contraceptive services had been less available to sexually active teenagers than they were. The fact that considerable effort is still needed should not cause us to lose sight of the fact that many sexually active teenagers have availed themselves of services and, as a result, have not become pregnant.

In 1976, a little more than one million 15–19-year-olds experienced a pregnan-

bility of contraceptives through clinics, physicians and drugstores, as well, perhaps, as through nonthreatening neighborhood-based peer networks—especially for distribution of nonphysician cy.* About 77 percent, or 780,000, of these pregnancies occurred premaritally. Based on the data from our study, it is probable that an additional 680,000 premarital pregnancies would have occurred (for a total of 1,460,000 premarital pregnancies) if no unmarried sexually active teenagers had used contraception.† These additional unwanted teenage pregnancies would have had to be resolved through more abortions, more out-of-wedlock births and more shotgun marriages. The social, psychological and economic consequences of unwanted pregnancies to teenagers, to their progeny and to society have been amply documented.

On the other hand, if all the teenagers who did not intend to give birth had been consistent users of contraception, there would have been about 467,000 premarital pregnancies (half of them intended)—313,000, or 40 percent, fewer than the 780,000 premarital pregnancies that actually occurred.‡ In other words, the difference between no use of contraception and always-use (by those who do not want to conceive) is about one million pregnancies.

These calculations, crude as they are, give an approximate idea of the number of premarital pregnancies that are now being averted through family planning efforts, and of the number that could be prevented if policy makers, educators and service providers were able to increase the number of teenagers who use contraception regularly and effectively to prevent unwanted conception.

References

1. M. Zelnik and J. F. Kantner, "Sexual and Contraceptive Experience of Young Unmarried Women in the United States, 1976 and 1971," chapter 4, above.

2. ——, "First Pregnancies to Women Aged 15–19: 1976 and 1971," chapter 5, above.

3. Ibid., Table 2.

4. E. W. Paul, H. F. Pilpel and N. F. Wechsler, "Pregnancy, Teenagers and the Law, 1976," *Family Planning Perspectives*, 8:16, 1976.

5. Chapter 5, Table 11.

6. Chapter 4.

*Based on the following: **For births**: National Center for Health Statistics, DHEW, "Final Natality Statistics, 1976," *Monthly Vital Statistics Report*, Vol. 26. No. 12, Supplement, 1978. **For abortions**: totals from 1976 Alan Guttmacher Institute national survey, and percent to 15-19-year-olds, from Center for Disease Control, DHEW, *Abortion Surveillance: Annual Summary, 1976*, Atlanta, 1978. Involuntary fetal loss estimated to be 10 percent of total abortions plus births.

†Assuming that the 780,000 premarital pregnancies occurred to young women with the same contraceptive-status profile as that found in our study population, and that each contraceptive-status group had contributed to the total number of premarital pregnancies in the same proportion as found in our study.

‡This is presuming that each contraceptive-status group had the same proportion of wanted pregnancies as in our study population, and that the level of contraceptive protection among those who did not want to get pregnant was the same as among the always-users in our study population.

7
The Effect of Government Policies on Out-of-Wedlock Sex and Pregnancy

Kristin A. Moore and Steven B. Caldwell

Of all children born out of wedlock, at least 60 percent end up on welfare. They represent over 30 percent of all children receiving Aid to Families with Dependent Children (AFDC), and the proportion is rising.[1] In fact, the proportion of all births occurring outside of marriage has been increasing steadily, from five percent in 1960 to 14 percent in 1975.[2] Concern over these trends has led to speculation that governmental policies may have encouraged them. It is frequently argued that the provision of welfare support for children born outside of marriage encourages women to become pregnant outside of marriage, or at least discourages marriage among women who do become pregnant while unwed.[3] The existence of AFDC is also sometimes alleged to encourage teenagers to become pregnant in order to form their own households and thus escape parental control and conflict.[4] In addition, it is

suggested that the provision of contraceptive services and abortion encourages promiscuity and carelessness among unmarried people.[5] Such beliefs seem to constitute the basis for much of the opposition to government policies in the area of welfare support.

Several governmental programs are of particular relevance in this connection. AFDC provides welfare support for low-income families. The size of the monthly benefit and the ease of obtaining benefits vary from state to state. Do states with generous, easily available benefits encourage—or fail to discourage—childbearing among unmarried women? Some states refuse to provide AFDC if there is a father in the home—even if he is unemployed. Does absence of coverage for unemployed fathers reduce the likelihood of marriage and thus encourage out-of-wedlock childbearing? Does the availability of abortion in a state reduce the likelihood that premaritally pregnant women will carry pregnancies to out-of-wedlock births? Does abortion encourage contraceptive carelessness, thus increasing the rate of pregnancy? Does the availability of subsidized family planning services decrease the probability of conception among the unmar-

This article summarizes some of the findings of research conducted under DHEW grant number 014B-7502-P201. Copies of the complete report, *Out-of-Wedlock Pregnancy and Child-bearing*, can be obtained for $7.50 from the Urban Institute, Social and Economic Status of Women, 2100 M Street, N.W., Washington, D.C., 20037.

ried, or does it rather enable or even encourage earlier initiation of sexual activity among unmarried females with no decline in the probability of conception? The research reported here represents an attempt to evaluate empirically whether government programs have consequences other than those officially intended.

Data and Methodology

The data are derived from a survey of a national probability sample of 1,479 black and 3,132 other (referred to as white henceforth) females aged 15-19 in 1971 living in households or college dormitories. The survey was conducted by John F. Kantner and Melvin Zelnik. A number of descriptive reports based on the data have already been published.[*6] Respondents were questioned about their sexual and reproductive attitudes and histories, as well as their personal and family backgrounds. Only eight percent of the respondents had ever been married, but 28 percent reported having had sexual intercourse; nearly 14 percent reported having been pregnant at some time. Since women aged 15-19 bear more than half of all out-of-wedlock children—and probably even larger proportions of those who are unwanted and those who end up requiring welfare— this is an appropriate data base for examining the issues described above.

Three transitions are examined, each for a different eligible subpopulation:
• first intercourse among virgins;

• first pregnancy among the sexually experienced; and
• pregnancy outcome (abortion, marriage or out-of-wedlock birth) among those who conceive premaritally.

The analysis is based on multiple regression with dichotomous dependent variables that are set equal to one if a transition takes place and zero if no transition takes place. For example, if first intercourse occurs during a particular year in the life of a female who is a virgin at the beginning of the year, the dependent variable equals one. If intercourse does not take place, the dependent variable equals zero. Similarly, if a first pregnancy occurs during a year to a young woman who is sexually experienced, the dependent variable equals one, and zero otherwise. Since we hypothesize that age and race each interact in major ways with other influences on sexual activity and pregnancy, separate regressions were performed by age (years 12-15[†] and 16-18) and race for the first two transitions.

The number of young women who reported premarital pregnancies is, of course, considerably smaller than the total number in the initial sample. Of the 4,611 teenagers in the Kantner-Zelnik 1971 study, only 520 represent premarital conceptions. Because of the diminished sample size, analyses were conducted on the entire sample of premaritally pregnant teenagers, rather than on separate age and race groups. Three possible outcomes of a premarital conception were analyzed: marriage prior to birth; abortion; and live out-of-wedlock

---

[*] In 1976, Kantner and Zelnik fielded a second nationwide study of female adolescent sexuality, contraception and pregnancy; one report from this study (on sexuality and contraception) has been published. However, the results were published too late to be considered in this research. (See chapter 4, above.)

[†] We assumed that all respondents were nonmarried virgins at age 11. Each cohort was then aged forward to the point at which they had initiated sexual activity and had experienced a pregnancy. (See: K. A. Moore and S. B. Caldwell, reference 1, p. 92.)

Table 1. Summary of results of multiple regression analyses of individual data indicating probability of transition to sexual activity and to pregnancy among U.S. women aged 15–19, by age and race, circa 1971

Variable	Whites		Blacks	
	12-15	16-18	12-15	16-18
Transition to sexual activity				
Older age	+	+	+	+
Higher education of father or father substitute	0	−	−	−
Higher education of mother or mother substitute	0	0	0	0
Recency of birth cohort	+	+	+	0
More frequent church attendance	−	−	−	−
Respondent Catholic	0	0	0	0
Nonintact family of origin	+	+	+	+
Respondent lives on Pacific coast	+	+	0	−
Farm background	−	0	0	0
Rural residence	−	−	−	−
Central city residence	+	+	+	+
High abortion availability	0	0	0	0
High AFDC benefits	0	+	0	0
High AFDC acceptance rate	0	−	−	0
High unmet family planning need	0	0	0	0
Transition to pregnancy				
Older age	+	0	+	0
Higher education of father or father substitute	0	0	0	0
Higher education of mother or mother substitute	−	−	−	0
Recency of birth cohort	0	0	−	0
High importance of religion to respondent	0	+	0	0
Respondent Catholic	0	0	+	+
Nonintact family of origin	0	0	0	+
1–2 years' intercourse experience	+	+	+	0
Ever used contraception	0	0	0	0
Urban/rural residence	0	0	0	0
High abortion availability	0	0	0	0
High AFDC benefits	0	0	−	0
High AFDC acceptance rate	0	0	0	0
High unmet family planning need	0	0	0	+

Note: In this and subsequent tables: + = positive association; − = negative association; 0 = no statistically significant association.

Source: K. A. Moore and S. B. Caldwell, reference 1, Tables 37 and 39.

birth.* Clearly, these are not independent analyses. Their value lies in their ability to supplement one another.

Public policy variables were added to each respondent's computer record to represent governmental programs in her state of residence at about (or a little before) the time of the survey. (See inset for definitions of these variables.)

First Intercourse

To test the hypothesis that liberal public policies encourage sexual activity, measures of the availability of legal abortion and of subsidized family planning services in the respondent's state of residence were included in the analysis. Measures of the level of welfare benefits and of the rate of acceptance of welfare applications in the respondent's state of residence were also included to test the hypothesis that generous welfare policies encourage sexual activity by providing an income cushion in case of premarital pregnancy. As shown in the top deck of Table 1, no consistent pattern emerges indicating that public policies affect the initiation of sexual activity, although several weak associations can be found both in support of and against these hypotheses.

High AFDC benefits are associated with a higher probability of first intercourse among older white virgins; however, a high AFDC acceptance rate is related to a *lower* probability of first intercourse among older whites and among younger blacks. In addition to this inconsistency, subsequent analyses with these data (and with a related state-level data set) have produced *no* positive associations between welfare generosity and the probability of conception (see bottom deck of Table 1) or between wel-

*Miscarriages were dropped from the sample after no patterns in the occurrence of this outcome were detected.

AFDC benefit level. AFDC (yearly amount paid in state to a family with four recipients, July 1971) divided by 1969 median family income in state

AFDC acceptance rate. AFDC applications accepted in state in 1971, divided by AFDC applications in state in 1971

AFDC unemployed father program. Whether state AFDC program covered unemployed father, 1970:
0 = no program in respondent's state of residence
1 = program exists in respondent's state of residence

Family planning availability. Percent of need for subsidized family planning services met in state, 1969 (based on estimate of need in J. G. Dryfoos, "Women Who Need and Receive Family Planning Services: Estimates at Mid-Decade," Family Planning Perspectives, 7:172, 1975):
1 = 0-10% of need met
2 = > 10-20% of need met
3 = > 20% of need met

Abortion availability. Availability in 1971 (a compound of abortion .rates, ratios, laws and amount of time that passed since liberalizing legislation):
1 = liberal
2 = intermediate
3 = restrictive

Table 2. Summary of results of multiple regression analyses of individual data indicating probability of abortion, marriage or out-of-wedlock birth among premaritally pregnant U.S. women aged 15–19, circa 1971

Variable	Direction of association, by pregnancy outcome*		
	Abortion	Marriage	O-W birth
Older age	0	0	0
College-educated father or father substitute	+	0	–
Pregnancy desired	–	+	–
Recency of pregnancy (calendar year)	+	0	0
High importance of religion to respondent	–	0	0
Respondent Catholic	0	0	0
Respondent white	+	+	–
Nonintact family of origin	0	0	0
Urban/rural residence	0	0	0
High abortion availability	+	0	–
High AFDC benefits	–	0	0
High AFDC acceptance rate	0	0	–
AFDC unemployed father program	0	0	–

*All ever-pregnant respondents included in the same regression.

Source: K. A. Moore and S. B. Caldwell, reference 1, Table 41.

fare benefit levels and the probability of an out-of-wedlock birth (see Table 2). This suggests that the single instance of a positive association between welfare generosity and early sexual experience may be an artifactual finding (especially since one would expect welfare benefits which are paid only for children to have more of an effect on pregnancy than on sexual activity).

The top deck of Table 1 also shows that the availability of subsidized family planning services in 1969* was not relat-

ed to the initiation of sexual activity in any of the age-race groups. Nor was the availability of legal abortion found to be associated with a greater probability of sexual experience among any of the subgroups.

Other Factors and First Intercourse

Kantner and Zelnik have observed that more recent birth cohorts are experiencing first intercourse at earlier ages.[†7]

---

*In 1969, relatively few unmarried teenagers were served by organized family planning clinics.

†For example, 18.0 percent of 15-year-olds in 1976 compared with 10.9 percent in 1971 had initiated sexual activity; among 16-year-olds, 25.4 percent in 1976 had done so, compared with 21.2 percent in 1971.

Such a change means that much larger populations are at risk of pregnancy, abortion, forced marriage, out-of-wedlock childbearing and venereal disease.

No full measure of social class is available, but as Kantner and Zelnik found in their 1971 study,[8] we also found that, by and large, those teenagers with less-educated fathers began sexual activity at earlier ages. Later initiation of sexual experience was noted among whites, and among teens who attended church regularly, or who lived on a farm, or who came from intact families. Neither Catholic identification nor the educational level of the mother was found to be related to age at first intercourse.[9]

Pregnancy

The hypothesis that generous AFDC benefits and high AFDC acceptance rates would be associated with a greater incidence of pregnancy was not supported by our research. As the bottom deck of Table 1 shows, no indication of such a relationship was found. In addition, no association was found between the availability of legal abortion and a higher probability of pregnancy, thus arguing against the contention that abortion encourages contraceptive carelessness.

On the other hand, the availability of subsidized family planning services was found to be negatively related to the occurrence of pregnancy among older black teens. The availability of family planning services was measured using data prepared for the U.S. Office of Economic Opportunity showing the percent of unmet need for family planning services in a state in 1969. Our analysis shows that there was a significantly lower annual probability of pregnancy among older teenage black women living in states with the most subsidized family planning services. (This finding

is not replicated among the other subgroups.) Given the frequently lower income of blacks in the United States, it seems reasonable to assume that older black teenagers are somewhat overrepresented among users of subsidized family planning services and thus are more affected by their availability than whites. It is important to note that although family planning availability is *not* related to a greater likelihood of premarital sex, it does seem to be related to a *lower* incidence of conception, at least among older black teenagers.

Other Variables Affecting Conception

It has also been maintained that the education of the mother (or mother substitute) affects the probability of conception among teenagers, since young women with better educated mothers should be more knowledgeable about sex, reproduction and contraception. Our analysis confirms this argument; the likelihood of conception is lower for teenagers with better educated mothers, as is shown in the bottom deck of Table 1. This variable does not seem to be a proxy for social class, however, since the education of the father or father substitute was not found to be related to pregnancy. In addition, the probability of pregnancy is higher when there is no mother (or substitute) in the home, or when the respondent is not aware of the educational attainment of the woman designated as her caretaker. The probability of conception is also higher among blacks, among teenagers who did not live in intact families when they were aged 10-15, and among teens aged 15 or older.

Older white teenagers who regard their religion as important to them, and black Catholics, are just slightly more likely to become pregnant. Not surprisingly, longer exposure to sexual intercourse is also positively associated with a higher annual probability of conception. Little impact from individual contraceptive use was documented, probably because of the lack of detail in the variable available for analysis and because of the sporadic and ineffective use of contraceptives among adolescents. *

Outcome of a Premarital Conception

Once a premarital conception has occurred, decisions about continuing or terminating the pregnancy must be made. It seems reasonable to assume that policy variables would have the greatest impact at this time. What impact does governmental policy actually have on pregnancy outcome?

As Table 2 shows, in states having relatively generous AFDC benefit levels, the probability of abortion is significantly lower. The probability of marriage in order to legitimate a birth and the probability of having a child out of wedlock are both slightly (but not significantly) higher. On the other hand, states with high AFDC acceptance rates were found to have a significantly lower proportion of out-of-wedlock births. There is, then, *no statistically significant evidence linking welfare availability with the probability of carrying an out-of-wedlock pregnancy to an out-of-wedlock birth.*

AFDC coverage of unemployed fathers seems to be a program with rather direct relevance to the probability of marriage among many couples faced with a premarital pregnancy. Young women residing in states with such a program do have a slightly (but not significantly) higher probability of marriage—but a considerably (though still not significantly) higher probability of undergoing abortion as well. Consequently, presence of an unemployed father program is associated with a significantly lower incidence of out-of-wedlock childbearing. One would expect more marriages in the presence of such a program because it allows young couples to marry and receive AFDC payments if the father is unemployed. The higher incidence of abortion was not predicted and may well be an artifact of a simultaneous occurrence of liberal abortion policies and AFDC coverage of unemployed fathers.

Table 2 also shows that wide availability of legal abortion has a strong, statistically significant impact on pregnancy outcome. Even in a 1971 data set, the impact of changes in abortion laws over time can be noted. When the outcomes of pregnancies occurring before 1970 are compared with those pregnancies occurring in 1970 and 1971, we find that the abortion outcome is twice as frequent in the later time period, and that there is about a six percent decline in the proportion of pregnancies that terminate in live births.[†] There is also a slight (but nonsignificant) decline in the proportion of pregnant teenagers who marry, but this change seems to be outweighed by the impact of abortion, since there is a net reduction in the probability of a live out-of-wedlock birth. The importance of change over time in abortion laws is further emphasized by another variable added to the current data set.

Respondents were assigned a code for

---

*Kantner and Zelnik found that in 1971, only 18 percent of sexually experienced, never-married teenage women reported that they always used contraception, and 17 percent never used it. In addition, those who reported ever use of a method relied heavily on withdrawal, the condom and douche. (See: J. F. Kantner and M. Zelnik, "Contraception and Pregnancy . . . ," 1973, reference 6.)

[†]See chapters 4, 5, and 6.

the kind of abortion law existing in their state of residence in 1971. An abortion outcome was much more frequently reported by females residing in those states in which abortion was legal and available, and in states where abortion was somewhat restricted but fairly available (if only by virtue of geographic propinquity to a state in which abortion was easily available). The impact of a high abortion rate is felt on both the marriage and the out-of-wedlock variables. Apparently, abortion availability slightly reduces the probability of a forced marriage, and has a significant effect in reducing the probability of an out-of-wedlock birth.

Other Variables Affecting Outcome

Overall, among those teenagers who became premaritally pregnant, pregnancy outcome was most strongly affected by four factors. As noted, young women living in states with relatively liberal policies were significantly more likely to obtain abortions and, correspondingly, were less likely to bear a child out of wedlock or to marry to legitimate the pregnancy. As Table 2 shows, young women with college-educated fathers were also significantly more likely to obtain abortions. On the other hand, young women who desired their pregnancies were especially likely to marry. Black teenagers were far less likely to marry or obtain abortions, and thus were much more likely to carry their pregnancies to term outside of marriage.

Since this analysis was conducted on the entire sample of premaritally pregnant teenagers, a variable for respondent's race appears for the first time. The differences captured by this particular variable dwarf those captured by all other independent variables. Premaritally pregnant blacks are considerably less likely than whites to obtain an abortion,[*] and are also much less likely to marry before the birth. Thus, a markedly greater proportion of black teenagers end up delivering infants outside of marriage.

Analysis of State Aggregate Data

To supplement the 1971 survey of 4,600 teenagers, an analysis of the variation in out-of-wedlock birthrates among states in 1974 was also conducted. One purpose was to see whether state programs and certain socioeconomic characteristics seemed to affect the overall out-of-wedlock birthrates of the *states* in the same way as they did out-of-wedlock childbearing among the *individuals* in the Kantner-Zelnik survey. The measurement of variables as they affect individuals was cruder, and many factors could not be measured at all in the state-level analysis.

The results of this analysis as summarized in Table 3 strengthen the impression that public welfare policies do *not* act as economic incentives to childbearing outside of marriage. Neither AFDC benefit levels nor AFDC acceptance rates are associated with the out-of-wedlock birthrates of blacks or whites.

Abortion availability is negatively associated with white out-of-wedlock birthrates, but shows no statistically significant association with black rates.

---

[*]These data refer to the period prior to the 1973 Supreme Court decisions on abortion, when legal abortion was much less accessible to young, poor and black women. Data on abortions at a later period, 1972-1974, show that the abortion rate among black teenagers (31.1) was 2.2 times higher than the rate for white teenagers (14.1). While the marital status of these teenagers was not provided, it can be assumed that a majority of them were unmarried. (See: C. Tietze, "Legal Abortions in the United States: Rates and Ratios by Race and Age, 1972-1974," *Family Planning Perspectives*, 9:12, 1977.)

Table 3. Summary of results of multiple regression analysis of state-level data indicating probability of impact on out-of-wedlock birthrates among U.S. women aged 15–44, by age and race, 1974

Variable	Direction of association, by race and age					
	Whites			Blacks		
	15-19	20-24	15-44	15-19	20-24	15-44
High AFDC benefits	0	0	0	−	0	0
High AFDC acceptance rate	0	0	0	0	0	0
High abortion availability	−	−	−	0	0	0
Family planning availability	0	0	0	−	0	0
Age of consent for contraception ≥ 18	0	na	na	+	na	na
Age of consent for abortion ≥ 18	0	na	na	0	na	na
AFDC unemployed father program	0	0	0	0	0	0
AFDC unborn child coverage	0	0	0	0	0	0
Medicaid abortion coverage	0	0	0	0	0	0
Median educational attainment	0	0	0	0	0	0
% of work force unemployed	0	0	0	−	0	0
% of females 15–34 employed	0	0	0	0	0	0
Female earnings	0	0	0	+	0	0
Female/male earnings ratio	0	0	0	0	0	0
% of state in SMSAs	0	0	0	0	0	0
% of state Catholic	0	0	0	0	0	+

Note: na = not applicable.

Source: K. A. Moore and S. B. Caldwell, reference 1, Table 43.

Since we know that nonwhites obtain nearly 30 percent of the abortions performed in the United States, it seems surprising that abortion availability is not related to black out-of-wedlock rates. This is probably due to the lack of race- and age-specific abortion data for states

and to understatement of the unmarried population denominator in our data.* We do find that existence of a state law limiting family planning services to women aged 18 or older is associated with significantly higher out-of-wedlock fertility among black teenagers. In addition, there is a negative association between the availability of subsidized family planning services and black teenage out-of-wedlock fertility, but no association with white rates. It seems probable that the availability of subsidized family planning services is most important to black teenagers, because of their frequently disadvantaged income position.

Overall, measures of attitudes, social controls, alternatives to childbearing and motivations for pregnancy and childbearing were not related to the out-of-wedlock birthrate at the state level. Decisions regarding sexuality and reproduction are intensely personal, however, and are better addressed at the individual level. One value of the state-level analysis is that it explores whether individual decisions add up to anything. That is, can an aggregate effect of contextual variables be identified? The variables of primary interest here are, of course, the public policy variables, and from our analysis, it does not appear that AFDC benefits encourage out-of-wedlock childbearing. In addition, subsidized family planning relates to lower black teenage out-of-wedlock fertility, while abortion availability predicts lower white out-of-wedlock fertility. It is reassuring that on these crucial questions,

---

*Estimates of the unmarried population were obtained by applying 1970 state marriage proportions to 1974 state estimates of population. Among whites, the proportion unmarried grew only slightly between 1970 and 1974, but among blacks it increased significantly. The effect, therefore, is to overestimate the out-of-wedlock birthrates for blacks.

the two complementary approaches are in accord.

Discussion and Conclusions

Certainly the most important policy conclusion to be drawn from these analyses is that the level of AFDC ,benefits and the AFDC acceptance rate do not seem to serve as economic incentives to childbearing outside of marriage for either blacks or whites. In addition, the availability of contraception and abortion does not seem to encourage the individual to initiate sexual activity. However, the availability of subsidized family planning services does seem to lower pregnancy rates, especially among black teenagers; and the availability of abortion does seem to reduce substantially the incidence of out-of-wedlock childbearing among those who are premaritally pregnant, especially for whites.

Knowledge and information about conception and contraception seem to be important as well. The educational attainment of the mother (or mother substitute) is assumed to affect the amount of information a young woman has; it was found that females with relatively poorly educated mothers were more likely to become pregnant. Further, states which prohibited the provision of family planning services to teenagers had significantly higher out-of-wedlock birthrates among blacks aged 15-19 (almost 20 more births per 1,000 unmarried females of that age group). Even when services are available, however, use of contraception among the young, unmarried population frequently seems to be erratic and ineffective. Provision of better services and more information to those who want them seems to be an important policy goal.

It is also essential to recognize that although most unmarried people do not report that they desire pregnancy, some do. The latter are unlikely to seek abortions and are likely to marry before the birth. Information about the difficulties of early and single parenthood should also be made more available to this group, even though those who do ·not wish to become parents premaritally will be most motivated to take advantage of birth control information and services.

Personal and family life style also seem to be important explanatory factors. An intact family of origin and religious commitment seem to reduce the probability of sexual activity and pregnancy. Social and cultural factors are pertinent as well. For example, more recent birth cohorts, whites on the Pacific coast, and blacks are more likely to be sexually active, even after controlling for other factors.

It is crucial to acknowledge that most of the variance remains unexplained. In addition, the measurement of policy variables is crude. Ideally, such measurement should capture the type of government policy in force (which may differ from the policy on the books) in the respondent's state or local community at the time the respondent is making her decision about sex or pregnancy.

Other variables, not available in these data sets, also merit exploration. No really good retrospective measures of family income and social status were available, and it would be desirable to include some measures of these important factors. In addition, a number of personal attributes are probably very important influences. For example, we still don't know the dynamics of the conception process among those not intending or desiring conception. What is the role of peer group pressure? How do sex-role attitudes affect the use of contraception and the desire for pregnancy? We also know little about the values, motivations and expectations of unmarried males. Certainly, the decision to be sexually active and to use contraception is made through an interactive process. How do unmarried males perceive their roles and responsibilities?

In many ways, our results are still descriptive. We know that the education of the father affects the likelihood that a young unmarried woman will become sexually experienced, but that among the sexually active, it is the education of the mother that affects the probability of pregnancy. Later, it is having a college-educated father that affects the likelihood that a premaritally pregnant female will obtain an abortion. The decision-making processes that underlie these associations are undoubtedly extremely complex. We can count offspring of unmarried people and estimate other important statistics, such as the proportion sexually active and the proportion having abortions, but we have little idea of what *causes* or *explains* the numbers. Even at this point, we do not have a handle on the decision-making process at the level of the individual person or couple.

The focus and the central task of this research has been to explore whether public welfare policies affect the occurrence of out-of-wedlock childbearing. Our data indicate that the answer to this question is that welfare benefits do *not* appear to provide an economic incentive that encourages the bearing of children outside of marriage. To answer the question of what really motivates or explains such childbearing requires a great deal of further, sophisticated and detailed analytic research.

References

1. K. A. Moore and S. B. Caldwell, *Out-of-Wedlock Pregnancy and Childbearing*, Urban Institute, Washington, D.C., 1976, pp. 78-79.

2. National Center for Health Statistics, DHEW, "Advance Report: Final Natality Statistics, 1975," *Monthly Vital Statistics Report*, Vol. 25, No. 10, 1976, Table 12.

3. J. Sklar and B. Berkov, "Teenage Family Formation in Postwar America," chapter 1, above.

4. Ibid.; and L. Connolly, "Little Mothers," *Human Behavior*, Vol. 4, No. 6, 1975, pp. 17-23.

5. R. Marshall, quoted in *Planned Parenthood-World Population Washington Memo*, Mar. 1, 1977, p. 3.

6. M. Zelnik and J. F. Kantner, "Sexuality, Contraception and Pregnancy Among Young Unwed Females in the United States," in Commission on Population Growth and the American Future, *Demographic and Social Aspects of Population Growth*, C. F. Westoff and R. Parke, Jr., eds., Vol. 1 of Commission Research Reports, U.S. Government Printing Office, Washington, D.C., 1972, p. 355; J. F. Kantner and M. Zelnik, "Sexual Experience of Young Unmarried Women in the United States," *Family Planning Perspectives*, Vol. 4, No. 4, 1972, p. 9; ————, "Contraception and Pregnancy: Experience of Young Unmarried Women in the United States," *Family Planning Perspectives*, 5:21, 1973; M. Zelnik and J. F. Kantner, "The Resolution of Teenage First Pregnancies," *Family Planning Perspectives*, 6:74, 1974; F. Shah, M. Zelnik and J. F. Kantner, "Unprotected Intercourse Among Unwed Teenagers," *Family Planning Perspectives*, 7:39, 1975; and M. Zelnik and J. F. Kantner, "Attitudes of American Teenagers Toward Abortion," *Family Planning Perspectives*, 7:89, 1975.

7. M. Zelnik and J. F. Kantner, "The Probability of Premarital Intercourse," *Social Science Research*, 1:335, 1972; and ————, "Sexual and Contraceptive Experience of Young Unmarried Women in the United States, 1976 and 1971," chapter 4, above.

8. J. F. Kantner and M. Zelnik, "Sexual Experience of Young Unmarried Women . . . ," 1972, op. cit., Table 4, p. 11.

9. Ibid.

8

The Risk of Adolescent Pregnancy in the First Months of Intercourse

Laurie Schwab Zabin, John F. Kantner and Melvin Zelnik

Summary

Life-table analysis of data on 544 sexually active women aged 18–19 years at interview in 1976 shows that nearly one-fifth become pregnant within six months after beginning sexual intercourse. Half of all initial premarital teenage pregnancies occur in the first six months of sexual activity, and more than one-fifth in the first month. Those who conceive soon after initiation of intercourse have longer periods of exposure in which to become pregnant again. Thus, more than three-fifths of the premarital pregnancies after the first one that occur among whites, and over two-fifths of those among blacks, are contributed by young women who initially conceive within six months after first coitus.

Early age at initiation of intercourse appears to be a key factor in explaining high risk of pregnancy. The data show

This article is based on the 1976 National Survey of Young Women, which was supported by grant no. HD-05255 from the National Institute of Child Health and Human Development, DHEW. Assistance was also received from the Ford Foundation. The authors gratefully acknowledge the assistance of Judy Gehret and Young J. Kim.

that despite some adolescent subfecundity, which might be thought to protect younger sexually active teenagers, those who first have intercourse at age 15 or younger are nearly two times more likely to get pregnant in the first 1–6 months of sexual activity than are those who wait to have intercourse until they are 18 or 19. This is largely because those who first have intercourse at early ages are less likely to use contraception: Two-fifths of those who begin sexual activity at age 15 or younger are never-users, compared to just one-quarter of those who first have intercourse at ages 18 or 19. The positive relationship of age at initiation of coitus with contraceptive use is much stronger among blacks than whites.

Within two years after commencing sexual activity, two-thirds of those who have never used contraception become pregnant—nearly twice the proportion reported for the entire sample. One-quarter of never-users who get pregnant over the two-year period do so in the first month.

Not only does use of contraception diminish the risk of pregnancy, but it also tends to spread that risk more evenly over time. The proportion of the risk which is experienced in the first month of exposure is inversely related to the effectiveness of the method employed, so that a very high proportion of the risk to noncontraceptors is experienced in the first month after initiation of coitus. Because of the relatively greater likelihood of nonuse of contraception at early ages, young age at initiation of intercourse has a profound effect on the risk of adolescent pregnancy. Because blacks are more likely to initiate sexual activity at earlier ages than whites, their pregnancy rates are higher. Overall, however, risks per month of exposure are similar for blacks and whites; observed differences in pregnancy rates are due largely to the duration of sexual exposure.

Whatever programs are designed to address the problem of teenage pregnancy, whether educational or medical, must include the period prior to sexual activity if they are to prevent that large proportion of pregnancies that occurs shortly after the onset of coitus.

The Study

This article is a preliminary report based on a larger study of the risk of pregnancy to adolescents.[1] Our purpose is to find out more about the risks of conception associated with the early months of sexual activity. Little has been done to provide birth control information and services to teenagers early in their sexual careers. This is partly because it is difficult to identify those who are in need of services in their first months of exposure to the risk of pregnancy, and partly because society is ambivalent about providing such instruction to young people who are not yet sexually experienced, lest it imply social approval of their sexual activity. A more accurate understanding of the risk to which young women are exposed in their first months of coitus might not change the reluc-

tance of society to instruct the young, but it should make it possible to estimate how many teenage pregnancies could be prevented by services programmed to intervene before months of unprotected intercourse have passed. Furthermore, to the extent that decisions to engage in sexual intercourse and to use or not use contraception are rational decisions, the same information could have implications for individual young women and for the professionals who serve them.

Our immediate objective, therefore, was to explore the risks of conception in the first two years of intercourse. In addition, we wanted to investigate the extent to which those risks are affected by the age at which first intercourse occurs, and by patterns of contraceptive use.

Since our interest was not only in the risk of conception, but also in the distribution of that risk over time, the basic analytic tool utilized in the study was the life table. The data source we used provides information on necessary events in the sexual histories of young women, with dates and ages, so that a chronology of intercourse, contraception, pregnancy and marriage could be developed. The National Survey of Young Women, carried out in 1976, is a stratified probability sample of 15–19-year-olds living in households in the continental United States.[2] A subsample of premaritally sexually active respondents who were 18 or 19 years old at the time of the interview has been used for the analysis that follows, whether or not they subsequently married. This subsample includes 216 black and 328 white teenagers. By restricting the subsample to the two oldest age-groups, we were able to use teenage histories which were almost complete. By utilizing life-table methodology in which respondents are included up to the time of pregnancy, marriage or interview, we were able

Table 1. Estimated cumulative percentage of women aged 18–19* who have ever had a first premarital pregnancy, by number of months following first intercourse, according to race

Months after 1st intercourse	% of women, by race		
	Total (N=526)	White (N=322)	Black (N=204)
1	7.5	6.9	12.8
6	17.4	17.4	25.8
12	22.2	23.1	31.8
18	31.9	34.4	39.8
24	34.8	37.8	43.3

*In this and subsequent tables, data are based on sexually active women aged 18–19 at the time of interview in 1976.

Note: In this and subsequent tables, total Ns are weighted for age, race and marital status, while Ns for blacks and whites are unweighted.

to make maximum use of information about the early months of exposure, even for those whose first coital experience had been fairly recent.

Respondents were asked to recall the dates of their first intercourse, first use of contraception and first use of the pill or the IUD, and the dates of pregnancies and marriage. They were asked what methods of contraception they had ever used, including a wide range of more or less effective nonmedical methods. Limitations of the data have made it necessary to combine many methods into one category of nonmedical contraception that includes the diaphragm as well as the condom, rhythm, foam, withdrawal and douche, and to restrict the category of medical contraception to the pill, the IUD and sterilization. Sterilization was used by only one respondent, and the IUD, by only a few; the vast majority of those who employed medical methods used the pill.

The data do not give us a continuous monthly estimate of the frequency of intercourse during the 24 months under study; we assume that the evidence of low frequency reported by all age-

groups for the month before the interview indicates a general pattern of intermittent and sporadic sexual activity. The risks of pregnancy we will report, therefore, are not strict life-table probabilities per month of exposure, since, except for the first month, we cannot be sure how many of the young women actually engaged in coitus in any given month. What we are reporting is the probability of a first premarital conception in a given number of months after *onset* of coitus.

The risk of a premarital pregnancy has been calculated by using the interval between first coitus and marriage, premarital pregnancy or the interview, whichever was first to occur. Thus, within the limits of the interview frame, all premarital pregnancies are recorded, along with the length of time after first intercourse that they occurred. All first premarital conceptions have been included, whatever the young women's marital status at the time of pregnancy outcome.

Timing of First Premarital Conception

Of all respondents in the subsample, 7.5 percent have become pregnant within one month after first intercourse (see Table 1). In the first six months, that proportion rises to 17 percent. In the first year, it is 22 percent, and by the end of two years, 35 percent.

When the entire two-year period of exposure is considered, the *distribution* of the risk of pregnancy is seen to be reasonably similar for whites and for blacks (except in the first month, when the risk for blacks is nearly twice as great).* The pattern of increasing cumulative risk for the two racial groups is also similar, rising very sharply through six months of

---

*The pregnancy rates for black teenagers are probably underestimated because of the underreporting by blacks of pregnancies that were terminated by abortions (see chapter 5, above).

exposure, then increasing gradually and steadily.

There are several reasons why a disproportionately high level of risk should be concentrated in the first month of exposure. In the first place, that is the only month in which it is certain that all the respondents had intercourse. Because of the episodic nature of sex among many teenagers, in any other month some, and possibly many, of the respondents were not sexually active. Second, in all comparable studies, the first month of exposure has been shown to select the most fecund women—even among married women, who may be assumed to be more consistently exposed to the risk of pregnancy. The most fecund women become pregnant most rapidly, leaving behind a less fecund, less accident-prone group, who have a lower rate of conception. In addition, among our sample of teenagers, more and more of those who continued to have intercourse after their first experience adopted a contraceptive method. The risk of pregnancy for the group as a whole in the later months is therefore somewhat lower. By two years after first intercourse, 90 percent of all respondents who have never become pregnant have used some method of contraception.[3]

It has been suggested that some respondents who became pregnant, in attempting to recall the date of their first experience of intercourse, might have mistakenly advanced that time up to the date at which they conceived. Such a systematic error would have the effect of heaping pregnancies in the first month of exposure. We have tested the data to see whether there is any evidence of such heaping by calculating the frequencies of coitus that would be associated with fecundability in the ranges experienced by the noncontraceptors in our sample. The implied frequencies are not at all unreasonable. This leads us to

Table 2. Estimated cumulative percentage of all first premarital pregnancies among women aged 18–19, by number of months following first intercourse, according to race

Months after 1st intercourse	% of pregnancies, by race		
	Total (N=212)	White (N=109)	Black (N=103)
1	21.9	20.2	25.2
6	49.6	49.5	50.5
12	61.2	62.4	61.2
24	84.3	88.1	78.6

believe that there is no evidence for this kind of heaping. If there is any error of this kind, its effect is likely to be slight.*

The concentration of risk in the first month that is suggested in Table 1 is highlighted when we look at all first premarital conceptions over the teen years—not simply those during the first 24 months after first intercourse—to determine what proportion of all such conceptions those in the first month represent. Table 2 shows that 22 percent of all adolescent first conceptions occur in the

---

* If we assume a fertile period of 48 hours per cycle, the risk reported here for white noncontraceptors in their first month of intercourse is associated with frequencies of approximately 1–2 coital experiences per month. (See: H. Leridon, *Human Fertility: The Basic Components*, trans. by J. Helzner, University of Chicago Press, Chicago, 1977.) For blacks, the risk is higher and is associated with frequencies of 2–3 per month. If we assume a fertile period of 72 hours per month, the associated frequencies drop to under one exposure for whites and 1–2 for blacks. (We know that the frequency cannot be below one, since the first month is the only one in which all girls must have been sexually active.) Even if a minimal fertile period of only 24 hours is assumed, maximum frequency for blacks need not exceed five. Any of these estimates are plausible, but the two-day fertile period and associated frequencies are probably the most reasonable estimate. Thus, the estimated fecundability of the sample appears to be compatible with reasonable values of the relevant parameters. The authors are grateful to Frank Furstenberg, Jr., for raising the question about heaping, and to Christopher Tietze for suggesting a method for testing it.

first month of coital activity; 50 percent occur before six months have passed. The findings are quite similar for both racial groups.

The importance of these early conceptions is clear. In the first place, services have rarely been designed to reach young women before they become sexually active. Younger adolescents especially are likely to delay use of contraceptives until they have been sexually active for a year or more, and use of the most effective medical methods for even a longer period.[4] Data from family planning clinics show that teenage clients are likely to be sexually active for 1–2 years before ever seeking professional birth control help.[5] For too many, that is too late. What is more, those who have first conceptions soon after initiation of intercourse are at a relatively high risk of having additional pregnancies because of their rapid return to the pool of young people exposed to risk. Of the premarital conceptions of second order and above among respondents in this study, 64 percent of those among whites and 44 percent of those among blacks are contributed by young women who initially conceive within six months after first coitus. These women account for a disproportionate share of adolescent pregnancies. This is not unexpected, since pregnancy and childbirth require time; those who conceive early make maximum use of their exposure time for reproduction. Similarly, many who conceive premaritally in the first month and then marry go on to have additional marital conceptions during their teen years. Moreover, the adverse social and health consequences of unplanned adolescent pregnancy and childbirth are not limited only to those women who conceive premaritally. Therefore, the prevention of early first conceptions can have far-reaching consequences for the teenagers, their offspring and society.

Age at First Intercourse

The increase in sexual activity among teenagers implies that the age of first intercourse is becoming younger.[6] This makes it of interest to know what effect age at first intercourse has on the risks we have described. Three groups of ages of coital onset were examined in order to see whether youthful coitus increased the probability of conception by month. We were aware that there might be an observable effect of postmenarcheal subfecundity operating in the other direction. To explore the effects of physical maturation on the risk of pregnancy in early adolescence, life tables were constructed based on the gynecological age* of the respondent at first intercourse (not shown). Those tables indicate that the number of respondents who initiated coitus close to menarche is small. In general, those who begin intercourse at an early age also experience early menarche. For that reason, the interval between menarche and first intercourse is generally two or three years even for girls whose first intercourse takes place at 13 or 14 years of age.[7]

Among white respondents, there are no conceptions in the first year of exposure among those who initiate coitus within a year of menarche; the probability of conception is higher for those who start intercourse more than a year after menarche. Among blacks who begin coitus within one year of menarche, there are a few conceptions. But for blacks as well as whites, the probability of conception is higher for those who start two years after menarche.

These preliminary results suggest that although the effects of subfecundity are visible, they are very brief, and much weaker than other effects that increase

---

*Gynecological age is a measure of the interval between menarche and first coitus.

Table 3. Estimated cumulative percentage of women aged 18–19 who have ever had a first premarital pregnancy, by number of months following first intercourse, according to race and age at first intercourse

Months after 1st intercourse	% of women, by race and age at first intercourse								
	Total			White			Black		
	≤15 (N=177)	16–17 (N=251)	18–19 (N=98)	≤15 (N=92)	16–17 (N=156)	18–19 (N=74)	≤15 (N=85)	16–17 (N=95)	18–19 (N=24)
1	9.1	7.8	4.6	7.6	7.7	4.1	15.3	11.6	8.3
6	20.7	17.9	11.4	19.7	17.9	13.3	28.2	25.7	16.7
12	24.1	23.5	16.6	22.0	25.7	18.4	36.5	30.2	16.7
18	33.2	34.4	16.6	32.6	38.9	18.4	46.1	36.9	16.7
24	36.7	36.6	16.6	36.5	41.6	18.4	49.7	39.8	16.7

the risk to younger starters. Immaturity has a negligible impact on the risk of pregnancy, however, when we look at respondents with low *chronological* ages at first intercourse. This effect is probably due in large measure to the positive correlation between age at first intercourse and age at menarche. Even those teenagers whose sexual activity begins at an early age have usually passed the immediate postmenarcheal period before the onset of coitus. Thus, lack of physical maturity cannot be relied upon to reduce the risk of pregnancy to which these young teenagers are exposed.

Not only is little protection conferred by subfecundity on the youngest starters, but there is also a strong age effect in the opposite direction. Those who begin intercourse early run a higher risk of pregnancy in the first month of exposure and throughout the rest of the two-year period. As Table 3 and Figure 1 indicate, the direct effect of younger age at first intercourse on pregnancy risk is clearer for blacks than for whites.* In the early months of exposure, blacks who com-

mence intercourse at age 15 or younger have a higher risk of pregnancy than those who begin coitus at 16 and 17, and close to twice the risk of those who wait until later. The difference becomes

Figure 1. Estimated cumulative percentage of women aged 18–19 who have ever had a first premarital pregnancy, by number of months following first intercourse, according to age at first intercourse

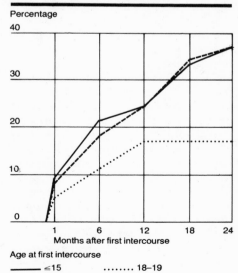

Percentage

Months after first intercourse

Age at first intercourse
——— ≤15   ········ 18–19
----- 16–17

*Life-table figures for later months must be used cautiously because there are few respondents who begin intercourse at ages 18–19 who are exposed more than 12 months. The figures become very unreliable when based on too small a sample.

greater as the months go by. Among whites, there is a similar but less consistent difference between early and later starters; those who begin coitus at ages 16 and 17 do not show risks midway between those for younger and older starters. Rather, they seem to share the high risks of the youngest group; for some exposure periods, their risks are even higher.

For *both* whites and blacks, the message is clear: The youngest starters, far from being protected by immaturity from the risk of conception, are at the greatest risk of pregnancy in the early months of exposure. Clearly, the longer duration of their exposure should add to their total number of pregnancies. But the life table tells us that even when duration of exposure is controlled, the youngest starters have a higher probability of becoming pregnant than do those who postpone sexual activity.

Contraceptive Use

Contraceptive use is the major mechanism through which this differential risk comes about. Table 4 shows the distribution of respondents by contraceptive-use status up to first pregnancy, marriage or interview, according to race and age at first intercourse. Two-fifths of those who begin intercourse at age 15 or younger are never-users; the proportion declines with increasing age to one-quarter of those who start sexual activity at ages 18 or 19. Conversely, the use of both medical and nonmedical methods increases with rising age at first coitus. The relation of contraceptive use with age at first intercourse is much stronger for blacks than for whites: Fifty-eight percent of blacks who begin intercourse at age 15 or younger are never-users, compared to just 20 percent of those who start sexual activity at ages 18 or 19. For

whites, the proportion only declines from 36 percent to 28 percent.

Because of the obvious impact of contraceptive use on the risk of pregnancy in the early months of exposure, it is of interest to examine the way in which the practice of contraception alters that risk. Life-table methodology presents certain difficulties in analyzing the impact of contraceptive use if that use does not begin at the same time as intercourse. This analysis focuses on respondents who always used a method from first coitus, and on those who never used contraception; it touches briefly on some of the effects of ever-use of medical and non-medical methods.* Although respondents who always used a method and those who never did represent extreme cases, they include considerable numbers of young women.

Among those who have never practiced contraception up to the time of pregnancy, marriage or interview, the risk of pregnancy is extremely high: As shown in Table 5, by the end of two years after first intercourse, about two-thirds of the never-users have conceived; this is almost twice the proportion of the entire sample who become pregnant over the same time span (see Table 1). About one-quarter of never-users who

---

*There are methodological problems in measuring the effects of contraception through life-table analysis because a life table requires a single point of entry in time. The results described above for racial and age-groups established that point as the month of first intercourse. However, contraception and intercourse begin at different times for many of the young women in the sample. They begin simultaneously only for the select group who have used a method from first coitus. The experience of these respondents cannot be generalized to all users, even users of the same methods, since initiation of contraception at first intercourse may imply a different level of caution, a different regularity of use, and possibly a higher level of information among these users.

conceive during those two years do so in the first month—one-fifth of white never-users and nearly two-fifths of blacks. Over the two-year period, however, the pregnancy risks for whites and blacks tend to converge, so that by the end of that time, similar proportions of whites (66 percent) and blacks (70 percent) have become pregnant. High as these risks are, they may be understated, since we do not make allowances for respondents who abstain from sexual activity once they have begun.

At the other extreme are the young women who report that they have consistently used a method from first intercourse. This group includes those who have only used a medical method, those who have only used a nonmedical method and those who have used both ("mixed" method users) but have always been protected. As Table 6 shows, only about one-tenth of the always-users become pregnant during two years of exposure. Blacks who practice contraception consistently and who have ever used a medical method (medical and mixed method users) contribute almost nothing to the pregnancy risk. Whites do not do as well, but they do fare better than those who practice contraception only sporadically.° Respondents of both races who re-

---

° The always-users of both medical and nonmedical methods (the mixed category) might have been expected to show a pregnancy risk between those of the two other groups, but instead they show the lowest risk of all. This is in part a result of our method of classification: To survive the use of one method and become a user of another takes time. Therefore, if nonmedical use comes first, inclusion in this mixed category implies a period of exposure during use of a nonmedical method without a pregnancy; this in turn implies that we are dealing with a selective group of highly effective nonmedical method users. Apart from this necessary result of the method of classification, it is still true that those who adopt a medical method after using a nonmedical method appear to have a low risk of pregnancy.

Table 4. Percentage distribution of women aged 18–19 by use of contraception before pregnancy, marriage or interview, according to race and age at first intercourse

Race and age at 1st intercourse	% of women, by contraceptive use				N
	Never	Non-medical only	Medical ever	Total	
Total					
Total	32.4	25.4	42.2	100.0	541
≤15	40.1	21.5	38.4	100.0	187
16–17	31.4	25.7	42.9	100.0	254
18–19	25.0	29.9	45.1	100.0	100
White					
Total	31.9	27.6	40.5	100.0	326
≤15	36.2	25.5	38.3	100.0	94
16–17	31.2	28.0	40.8	100.0	157
18–19	28.0	29.3	42.7	100.0	75
Black					
Total	45.6	15.8	38.6	100.0	215
≤15	58.1	12.9	29.0	100.0	93
16–17	40.2	16.5	43.3	100.0	97
18–19	20.0	24.0	56.0	100.0	25

Table 5. Estimated cumulative percentage ever premaritally pregnant among women aged 18–19 who have never used contraception prior to pregnancy, marriage or interview, by number of months following first intercourse, according to race

Months after 1st intercourse	% of women, by race		
	Total (N=194)	White (N=102)	Black (N=92)
1	16.9	13.8	26.2
6	39.0	37.3	48.8
12	48.6	47.6	57.1
18	64.7	66.3	67.4
24	65.9	66.3	70.2

port having always used a method have only one-sixth the cumulative risk of never-users by the end of two years; blacks have one-eighth the risk† and whites one-fifth the risk (see Table 5).

---

† Note our earlier caution about the probable underestimation of pregnancies among blacks.

Table 6. Estimated cumulative percentage ever premaritally pregnant among women aged 18–19 who have always used a contraceptive method, by number of months following first intercourse, according to race and type of method used

Months after 1st intercourse	% of women, by race and type of method used											
	Total				White				Black			
	Total	Non-medical	Medical	Mixed	Total	Non-medical	Medical	Mixed	Total	Non-medical	Medical	Mixed
	(N=142*)	(N=52)	(N=42)	(N=40)	(N=90*)	(N=34)	(N=23)	(N=27)	(N=52*)	(N=18)	(N=19)	(N=13)
1	3.3	5.7	4.2	0.0	3.3	6.0	4.3	0.0	1.9	5.6	0.0	0.0
6	6.5	10.8	7.0	2.2	8.3	12.1	9.5	3.8	3.9	11.5	0.0	0.0
12	8.9	14.0	12.8	2.2	12.0	18.0	17.1	3.8	6.3	11.5	6.9	0.0
18	10.7	15.5	12.8	5.8	14.3	18.0	†	10.3	9.0	19.5	6.9	†
24	10.7	15.5	12.8	5.8	†	†	†	†	9.0	†	6.9	†

*These Ns are larger than the sum of those for the contraceptive-use columns because we have information on regularity of use for a few respondents for whom method data are incomplete.

†Ns are too small to permit analysis.

Never-use is a special case of a more general category of nonuse, a category which refers in this study to all those who initiate coitus without contraception. When nonusers begin to contracept they drop out of that category, and finally only the never-users remain. Predictably, the risks for nonusers are lower than those for never-users because nonusers include many young women who go through an early period of nonuse but have time to adopt contraception without a pregnancy.

As Table 7 and Figure 2 show, the risk of pregnancy to the large group of nonusers is high, especially in the early months. Those who adopt medical contraception are least likely to get pregnant, and their pregnancy risk is spread out almost linearly over time. Their risk of conception in the first month after they begin use is only one-fifteenth as high as the risk nonusers experience in that time period. The differential decreases, however, with time. By the end of two years, nonusers have a cumulative risk less than four times that of users of medical methods.

Thus, use of contraception, especially of medical methods, not only diminishes the risk of pregnancy, but also tends to spread that risk more evenly over time. The proportion of the risk that is experienced during the first month is inversely related to the effectiveness of the method employed (see bottom row of Table 7): Twenty-three percent of the nonusers who become pregnant within 24 months conceive in the first month, compared to 14 percent of those using a nonmedical method and just six percent of medical method users.[*]

[*]It should be noted that in this analysis, the same respondent may appear in more than one use-status category. For example, if she began intercourse with no method, then adopted a nonmedical method and then switched to a medical method, she will appear in all three columns at the appropriate month since entry into that category.

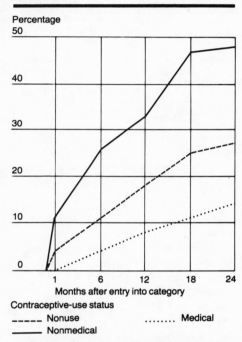

Figure 2. Estimated cumulative percentage of women aged 18–19 who have ever had a first premarital pregnancy, by number of months following entry into a contraceptive-use category, according to contraceptive-use status

Percentage

Months after entry into category

Contraceptive-use status

– – – – Nonuse   .... Medical

——— Nonmedical

The proportions of nonmedical method users who become pregnant during each time period are predictably between those of nonusers and medical method users. Pregnancy risks to black and white users of nonmedical methods are parallel. The risk is spread over time, but not as smoothly as it is for users of medical methods. The ratio of the percent pregnant in the first month to the percent pregnant in 24 months is higher for those who employ nonmedical methods than for users of medical methods: More of the risk is experienced more rapidly. At the end of two years, the cumulative pregnancy risk for nonusers is 48 percent, compared to 27 percent for

Table 7. Estimated cumulative percentage of women aged 18–19 who have ever had a first premarital pregnancy, by number of months following entry into a contraceptive-use category, according to race and contraceptive-use status

Months after entry into category	% of women, by race and contraceptive use								
	Total			White			Black		
	Non-use (N= 315*)	Non-medical (N= 198*)	Med-ical (N= 207*)	Non-use (N= 181)	Non-medical (N= 146)	Med-ical (N= 128)	Non-use (N= 134)	Non-medical (N= 52)	Med-ical (N= 79)
1	11.2	3.7	0.7	10.3	4.2	0.8	18.3	4.0	0.0
6	25.6	11.3	3.6	25.2	12.4	3.5	36.2	11.7	7.9
12	32.7	17.7	7.9	32.6	20.4	8.4	43.6	15.5	14.5
18	46.6	24.7	11.2	49.0	28.7	10.3	53.1	23.9	21.0
24	48.4	26.5	13.6	50.7	30.8	14.1	56.0	29.3	23.4
$\frac{\text{Mo. 1}}{\text{Mo. 24}}$ X 100	23.1	14.0	5.7	20.2	13.8	5.6	32.6	13.6	0.0

*These Ns add to more than 544 because respondents can appear in more than one category.

those employing nonmedical methods, and 14 percent for those using medically prescribed contraceptives.

Table 8 shows the percentage of *all* first premarital pregnancies that occur to nonusers and users of medical and nonmedical contraception, according to the number of months following first intercourse. Twenty-one percent of the pregnancies among medical method users occur in the first six months, compared with 45 percent of the pregnancies among nonmedical method users and 58 percent of those among nonusers.

We saw in Table 2 that the distributions are similar by race. This racial similarity echoes a finding which appears throughout this study: Despite the differences in age of first intercourse and contraceptive usage that have been reported, the overall risk of first premarital pregnancy *per month of exposure* is similar for whites and blacks (except for a discrepancy for noncontraceptors in the very first month, which has yet to be explained). A similarity is observed within various age and contraceptive groups as

Table 8. Estimated cumulative percentage of all first premarital pregnancies among women aged 18–19, by number of months following first intercourse, according to contraceptive-use status

Months after 1st intercourse	% of pregnancies, by contraceptive use			
	Total (N= 212)	Non-use (N= 134)	Non-medical (N= 45)	Medical (N= 33)
1	21.8	26.2	20.3	6.4
6	49.6	58.4	44.9	21.2
12	61.2	70.4	56.6	30.5
24	84.4	88.5	86.0	64.4

well as when the total racial samples are compared. Differences in observed pregnancy rates for the two racial groups are due largely to their differential durations of sexual activity; when exposure is controlled, their risks are not significantly different.

Early age at first intercourse is, of course, related to duration of exposure. Furthermore, early age at first intercourse, largely through its relationship with nonuse of contraception, has a profound effect on the risk of pregnancy. As we noted in the discussion of Table 4, contraceptive use is associated with age at initiation of intercourse, especially among blacks. Correspondingly, younger age at first intercourse is associated with a relatively high risk of pregnancy. Again, the association is especially pronounced among young blacks (see Table 3); the majority of those who begin intercourse at age 15 or younger never use a birth control method (prior to pregnancy, marriage or interview), whereas the majority of those who begin intercourse at older ages do become users of contraception, especially medical methods (see Table 4).

We noted in the discussion of Table 1 that those who begin sexual activity in the early teen years not only are at the greatest risk of pregnancy over time, but also are disproportionately more likely to conceive in the first 1–6 months after initiation of intercourse. This is the period when they are least likely to have available the information and services that they need to prevent pregnancy.

Policy and Program Implications

This article offers an unsettling insight into why the problem of teenage pregnancy appears to remain intractable in the face of increasing provision of contraceptive services. Programs aimed at preventing adolescent pregnancy typically provide contraceptive services and counseling *after* adolescents have begun sexual activity. In fact, family planning clinics report an average lag of a year or more between the time a young woman first has intercourse and the time she comes to a clinic for services. Her visit is often precipitated by the suspicion of pregnancy rather than by the onset of coitus. Clearly, teenagers are being

reached too late; despite the increase in clinic services and growing utilization of them by young people, more than one million teenagers continue to get pregnant each year.

Few programs have tried to reach young women before they become sexually active with information on the risks of pregnancy, methods of preventing pregnancy, and places where birth control services may be obtained. The disproportionately high risk of pregnancy in the early months of sexual activity documented above tells us that programs that do not make contact with teenagers until some months after intercourse begins will miss a great many of the premarital pregnancies they are intended to prevent.

Furthermore, since *young* adolescents are the least likely to utilize contraception, and since the relative risk of pregnancy in the early months of intercourse is highest for nonusers, it is the young adolescent who runs the greatest risk of conceiving shortly after initiating intercourse. That has disturbing implications: It is unlikely that women in their early teens will get the information they need in time to avoid the consequences of unprotected coitus unless it is presented to them through their homes, the media and the schools. But educating young, sexually inexperienced women about sex and contraception is still a highly charged issue. Since we now know that programs will fall short of their goals if they do not reach teenagers early, some way must be found to resolve the ambivalence of a society which seeks to prevent adolescent pregnancy but fears the effects of early reproductive education. Up until now, initiatives aimed at the young and the sexually inexperienced are precisely those that have encountered the most opposition.

Perhaps one reason that parents have

been concerned about sex education programs in the schools is their timing. Parents perceive, quite correctly, that young women mature at very different rates: For some, sex education may seem inappropriate, while for others, it is already too late. It may be that sex education should not be geared to the chronological age of students but might better depend upon their level of pubertal development. The benchmark of menarche may be a good one—an appropriate point to introduce the basic biology which the data in this article indicate is not understood by many young women even after they become involved in sexual activity. Reached at a time close to menarche, the young women would probably show a high level of interest, and the benefits of such education would come in time to prevent many adolescent conceptions. With the right preparation of the parent population, an initiative which grouped young women of like maturity would probably encounter less opposition than a broadside of sex education which might be launched too early for many of them, and too late for those who needed it most.

While we cannot conclude from these data exactly what the content of new initiatives should be, we must conclude that neither education nor service can await the initiation of intercourse. Timing is crucial.

References

1. L. S. Zabin, "Pregnancy Risk to Adolescent Girls in Early Years of Intercourse," dissertation, School of Hygiene and Public Health, The Johns Hopkins University, Baltimore, 1979.

2. M. Zelnik and J. F. Kantner, "Sexual and Contraceptive Experience of Young Unmarried Women in the United States, 1976 and 1971," chapter 4 above; and——, "First Pregnancies to Women Aged 15–19: 1976 and 1971," chapter 5 above.

3. L. S. Zabin, unpublished data.

4. M. Zelnik and J. F. Kantner, "Contraceptive Patterns and Premarital Pregnancy Among Women Aged 15–19 in 1976," chapter 6, Tables 2 and 11.

5. C. A. Akpom, K. L. Akpom and M. Davis, "Prior Sexual Behavior of Teenagers Attending Rap Sessions for the First Time," Family Planning Perspectives, 8:203, 1976; and D. S. F. Settlage, S. Baroff and D. Cooper, "Sexual Experience of Younger Teenage Girls Seeking Contraceptive Assistance for the First Time," Family Planning Perspectives, 5:223, 1973.

6. M. Zelnik, Y. J. Kim and J. F. Kantner, "Probabilities of Intercourse and Conception Among U. S. Teenage Women, 1971 and 1976," Family Planning Perspectives, 11:177, 1979.

7. L. S. Zabin, "Pregnancy Risk to Adolescent Girls . . .," 1979, op. cit.; and F. Furstenberg, Jr., L. Gordis and M. Markowitz, "Birth Control Knowledge and Attitudes Among Unmarried Pregnant Adolescents," Journal of Marriage and the Family, 31:34, 1969.

9

Teenage Pregnancies: Looking Ahead to 1984

Christopher Tietze

About 1.1 million teenagers are giving birth, obtaining abortions or having miscarriages or stillbirths each year; another 200,000 are getting pregnant as teenagers, although the pregnancy outcome doesn't occur until they are past 20. Few teenage pregnancies are intended; most occur outside of wedlock. The adverse health, social, psychological and economic consequences of such pregnancies have received widespread publicity. Girls just turning 14, many of whom are beginning to risk pregnancy because they have become biologically fecund and have initiated sexual activity, will be 20 years old in 1984. Just how Orwellian is their adolescent reproductive future likely to be? How many will become mothers, obtain abortions, get pregnant while still in their teens? Aside from the very few 14-year-olds who have already been pregnant, this is entirely an open question. If legal barriers (e.g., parental notification or consent laws) reduce the accessibility of contraception to teenagers, or if the proportion sexually active increases, or if more adolescents initiate sexual activity at younger ages, teenage pregnancies will be likely to increase. On the other hand, if teenagers' contraceptive practices improve, if fewer become sexually active, or if initiation of sex is postponed, the number of pregnancies should be smaller.

In this analysis, we seek to estimate how many of today's 14-year-olds are likely to experience one or more pregnancies, births, abortions and miscarriages before they reach age 20, assuming that there is no change in the level or timing of sexual activity among teenagers, or in their use of contraception or abortion.

The Current Picture

First, what is the reproductive picture among teenagers today? Data from the National Center for Health Statistics indicate that 570,672 live births to women under the age of 20 were registered in 1976, the most recent year for which statistics are available.[1] Of these, 442,540 were first births. This is the number of teenagers who became mothers for the first time.

In the same year, a total of 1,179,300 abortions were reported to The Alan Guttmacher Institute's annual survey of abortion providers.[2] About 32 percent of these abortions—some 378,500—were obtained by teenagers, according to data

Table 1. First live births, first legal abortions, and first spontaneous fetal losses, by age at event: numbers, annual rates and cumulative rates per 1,000 women aged 14–19

Completed years of age	Number			Annual rate			Cumulative rate		
	Live births	Legal abortions	Fetal losses	Live births	Legal abortions	Fetal losses	Live births	Legal abortions	Fetal losses
≤14	11,321	15,800	3,800	5.5*	7.6*	1.9*	5.5	7.6	1.9
15	29,561	28,000	8,700	14.1	13.3	4.2	19.6	20.9	6.1
16	63,459	47,300	17,400	30.9	23.0	8.5	50.5	43.9	14.6
17	93,656	60,100	24,700	45.2	29.0	11.9	95.7	72.9	26.5
18	116,151	85,200	31,800	55.3	40.5	15.1	151.0	113.4	41.6
19	128,392	77,600	33,400	60.6	36.6	15.8	211.6	150.0	57.4
<20	442,540	314,000	119,800						

*Per 1,000 girls 14 years of age.

from the Center for Disease Control (CDC).[3] The CDC also has data on teenage abortions by single year of age, from 26 states that provided about three-quarters of all reported teenage abortions.[4] Extrapolating from these data, and assuming that all abortions to women under 15 were first abortions, and that the proportion of first abortions declined five percentage points with each year of age (to 75 percent at age 19),[5] we estimate that in 1976, 314,000 first abortions were obtained by women under 20 years of age at the time of the abortion.

The total number of miscarriages and stillbirths that occur annually to teenagers is estimated at 20 percent of the number of live births plus 10 percent of the number of legal abortions, or about 152,000 in 1976, of which some 120,000 were first events.

Thus, about 1,100,000 pregnancies ending in births, abortions, miscarriages or stillbirths occurred to teenagers in 1976, and about 876,000 of these were first events. In addition, however, some conceptions which occurred to teenagers in 1976 were not terminated until after the young women's 20th birthday. Ages at termination can be converted into ages at conception by means of formulas.* Application of these "de-aging" formulas results in estimates of an additional 164,300 live births, 28,500 abortions, and 36,000 miscarriages or stillbirths that occurred after age 20, but resulted from pregnancies conceived at age 19.

Thus, the grand total of pregnancies conceived prior to age 20 is about 1,330,000. Illegal nonmedical abortions probably totaled fewer than 10,000 in 1976 among women of all ages[6] and may, therefore, be ignored in our computations.

---

*Births and abortions are separated for each year of age, by quarter (Q1-Q4). X indicates the number of events during the year of age under consideration; Y is the number one year younger; and Z is the number one year older.

$Q1 = (30X + 7Y - 5Z)/128$

$Q2 = (34X + Y - 3Z)/128$

$Q3 = (34X - 3Y + Z)/128$

$Q4 = (30X - 5Y + 7Z)/128$

Births occurring during the first three quarters of each year are moved to the preceding year (when they were conceived); abortions are moved back only a single quarter, since the average abortion is assumed to occur three months from conception. (The formulas were suggested to the author by Nathan Keyfitz.)

The Road Ahead

Looking once more at the approximately two million girls just turning 14, we can estimate the proportion who, if current rates continued, would experience one or more live births, legal abortions, miscarriages or stillbirths before their 20th birthday. Our estimate is based on single-year age-specific rates of *first* births, abortions and spontaneous fetal losses, cumulated through age 19, as shown in the last three columns of Table 1 for cohorts of 1,000 women. By age 20, about 21 percent of all women would have experienced at least one live birth; 15 percent would have obtained at least one legal abortion, and six percent would have had at least one miscarriage or stillbirth.

Age-specific rates of *first pregnancies* are required in order to estimate the proportion of women who would experience one or more pregnancies prior to their 20th birthday. To compute these rates, it is necessary to *include* pregnancies conceived before age 20 but terminated after age 20, and to *exclude* those first events (births, abortions, spontaneous fetal deaths) in each category that were preceded by one or more such events in another category. Two simplifying assumptions have been made:

• All pregnancies prior to age 15 occur at age 14.
• No woman experiences more than one first event per year of age.

In addition, two alternative assumptions have been made about the likelihood of subsequent pregnancies after the first:

• The first assumption is that pregnancy rates per 1,000 sexually active women in any given year of age are independent of pregnancy experience in earlier years.
• The alternative assumption is that pregnancy rates are reduced by one-half

Table 2. Annual and cumulative first pregnancy rates per 1,000 women aged 14–19, under alternate assumptions: no influence of prior pregnancies on subsequent pregnancies (Ass. 1) and subsequent pregnancy rate reduced by one-half after the first pregnancy (Ass. 2)

Completed years of age	Annual		Cumulative*	
	Ass. 1	Ass. 2	Ass. 1	Ass. 2
14	29	29	29	29
15	41	44	70	73
16	58	66	128	139
17	72	82	200	221
18	74	87	274	308
19	66	78	340	386

*At end of year of age, i.e., exact age equals age shown in stub plus one year.

after the first pregnancy. (This assumption seeks to take into account Melvin Zelnik's and John Kantner's finding that use of contraception among unmarried teenagers increases dramatically after the first pregnancy.[7] Among the young women they surveyed, 79 percent of those who had had an unintended first pregnancy had never previously practiced contraception, and 65 percent of those who had used birth control employed nonmedical methods; the proportions were reversed, however, after the outcome of a first pregnancy, when 82 percent of those who resumed sexual activity were using contraception, and 83 percent of these were using a medical method.)

Estimates of sexually active teenagers were obtained from the 1976 nationwide survey by Zelnik and Kantner,[8] with an appropriate correction to include ever-married women.[9] The computation of cumulative first pregnancy rates (under the assumption that pregnancy rates are independent of prior pregnancy experience) was carried out as shown in the appendix.

Appendix Table A. Computation of cumulative first pregnancy rates per 1,000 women aged 14–19

| Completed years of age | Estimated no. of 1st events, by age at conception* | | | Sum of 1st events (cols. 1-3) | 000s of women | | Sexually active women per 1,000 total women | | | 1st events per 1,000 sexually active women (cols. 4÷6) | 1st pregs. per 1,000 women | |
| | Live births | Legal abortions | Fetal losses | | Total | Sexually active | Total | With prior pregs.† | Without prior pregs.† | | Annual | Cumulative‡ |
	(1)	(2)	(3)	(4)	(5)	(6)	(7)	(8)	(9)	(10)	(11)	(12)
14	30,900	21,400	8,300	60,600	2,066	u	na	na	na	na	29	29
15	54,600	32,700	14,200	101,500	2,099	399	190	29	161	254.4	41	70
16	86,700	50,300	22,400	159,400	2,053	573	279	70	209	278.2	58	128
17	111,400	67,000	29,000	207,400	2,072	945	456	128	328	219.5	72	200
18	126,700	85,000	33,800	245,500	2,102	1,142	543	200	343	215.0	74	274
19	125,300	76,500	32,700	234,500	2,120	1,444	681	274	407	162.4	66	340
≤20	535,600	332,900	140,400	1,008,900	12,512	u						

*These numbers are different from those in the first three columns of Table 1, which show events by the woman's age at the pregnancy outcome. Thus, pregnancies conceived during adolescence but not terminated until after age 20 are shown here, but not in Table 1.

†At beginning of year of age.   ‡At end of year of age; exact age equals age shown in stub plus one year.   Note: na = not applicable; u = unavailable.

Table 2 shows the proportion of young women who could be expected to become pregnant at least once by the completion of each year of age from ages 14 through 19 under our alternative assumptions (no influence of prior pregnancies on subsequent pregnancies, and reduction of the pregnancy rate by half after the first pregnancy). Thus, from 20 to 22 percent would experience at least one pregnancy before their 18th birthday, and before they reached age 20, 34-39 percent would become pregnant.

Implications

Do these estimates mean it is inevitable that before they are 20 years of age, 21 percent of today's 14-year-olds will give birth, 15 percent will obtain a legal abortion, six percent will have a miscarriage or stillbirth, and 34-39 percent will experience at least one pregnancy? Certainly not. As Kantner and Zelnik have pointed out, it would be possible to reduce the number of premarital pregnancies by 40 percent if all young people were to use contraception and use it consistently.[10] If most used medical methods, the pregnancy rate would be reduced even more sharply. Studies of married women have shown that there is great variation in the effectiveness with which individuals use a method, with relatively young women less effective users than older, more experienced women.[11] If sex education courses for young people at the junior high school level included instruction in birth control, some of this discrepancy could probably be eliminated. With sexual activity among young people apparently continuing to increase and beginning at ever earlier ages, it is inevitable, however, that a substantial number of teenagers will continue to have unwanted pregnancies. The tendency toward limiting access to abortion through Medicaid restrictions and requirements of parental notification for minors could result in increasing the proportion of unwanted and out-of-wedlock births among adolescents 18 years of age and younger.

The often crippling health, psychic, economic and educational consequences of such births for young adolescents and their progeny do not need documentation here. Suffice it to say that 1984 may or may not contain the chilling overtones of Orwell's famous book as regards the reproductive lives of today's 14-year-olds. Much of the answer may depend on the actions, or inaction, of their seniors.

Appendix

The computations to obtain the rates seen in Table 2, above, are carried out as shown in Appendix Table A:

Step 1. Add numbers of first live births, first legal abortions, and first spontaneous fetal deaths (cols. 1-3). Enter in col. 4.

Step 2. Divide sum of 1st events (col. 4) by the number sexually active (col. 6). Enter in col. 10.

Step 3. To obtain first pregnancies prior to age 15 per 1,000 women, divide col. 4 by col. 5. Enter in col. 8 at 15 years and in col. 11 at 14 years.

Step 4. To obtain women entering age 15 without prior pregnancy, subtract col. 8 from col. 7. Enter in col. 9.

Step 5. To obtain first pregnancies, multiply col. 9 by col. 10. Divide by 1,000, round off to units, and enter in col. 11.

Step 6. To obtain women entering age 16 with prior pregnancies, add cols. 8 and 11 at age 15. Enter in col. 8 at age 16.

Step 7. Repeat steps 4-6 for successive years of age.

Step 8. Cumulate entries in col. 11 through age 19. Enter in col. 12.

References

1. National Center for Health Statistics, DHEW, "Advance Report: Final Natality Statistics, 1976," *Monthly Vital Statistics Report*, Vol. 26, No. 12, Supplement, 1978, Table 2.

2. The Alan Guttmacher Institute, *Abortion 1976-1977: Need and Services in the United States, Each State and Metropolitan Area*, New York, 1979.

3. Center for Disease Control, DHEW, *Abortion Surveillance, Annual Summary, 1976*, Atlanta, 1978, Table 6.

4. Ibid., Table 7.

5. C. Tietze, "Repeat Abortions: Why More?" *Family Planning Perspectives*, 10:286, 1978.

6. P. C. Glick and A. J. Norton, "Marrying, Divorc-ing, and Living Together in the U.S. Today," *Population Bulletin*, Vol. 32, No. 5, 1977, Table 12.

7. M. Zelnik and J. F. Kantner, "Contraceptive Patterns and Premarital Pregnancy Among Women Aged 15-19 in 1976," chapter 6, Tables 14 and 16.

8.——, "Sexual and Contraceptive Experience of Young Unmarried Women in the United States, 1976 and 1971," chapter 4, above.

9. U.S. Bureau of the Census, "Marital Status and Living Arrangements: March 1976," *Current Population Reports*, Series P-20, No. 306, 1977, Table 1.

10. Chapter 6, above.

11. B. Vaughan, J. Trussell, J. Menken and E. F. Jones, "Contraceptive Failure Among Married Women in the United States, 1970-1973," *Family Planning Perspectives*, 9:251, 1977.

10
Some Speculations on the Future of Marriage and Fertility

Charles F. Westoff

Twenty-six of the world's 33 industrialized countries—including the United States—are currently experiencing extremely low fertility, and some are rapidly approaching zero population growth. In at least five (Austria, Britain, East and West Germany and Luxembourg), there are already more deaths than births. If we project current trends,[1] these five countries are likely to be joined in about 1980 by Belgium, Denmark, Czechoslovakia, Hungary, Norway and Sweden. By 1990, negative population growth should also occur in Bulgaria, Finland, Greece, Italy and Switzerland; by 2000, France and the Netherlands should be added to the list. The populations of the remaining countries in Europe should begin to decline in subsequent decades. Collectively, the population of Europe and the Soviet Union should begin to decline around the year 2000. Deaths should outstrip births in the United States by about 2020, when the population should reach about 250 million.

This projected decline implies a total fertility rate of 1.5 births per woman over her reproductive lifetime. Although such low fertility has never existed for an actual cohort of women (the lowest on record is 1.8 for women born in 1907 in England and Wales), an argument can be made that because of the development of modern contraceptive technology and the increasing availability of legal abortion, such a low level is quite possible over sustained periods of time.

The question of obvious policy significance is what really will happen in the future. Fertility in the United States is already very low. The birthrate is 15.3 per 1,000 population, and the death rate is 8.8. The total fertility rate is below 1.9 births per woman (projected from current rates to a lifetime total). Were it not for a net legal immigration of about 400,000 per year, the growth rate would be 6.5 per 1,000 population. With immigration included, it is about 8.5 per 1,000 population. Even with continued immigration at that volume, such below-replacement fertility means that the population will stop growing in about 50

This article is adapted from the Charles C. Moskowitz Memorial Lecture, "Fertility Decline in the United States and Its Implications," delivered at New York University and published in *Demographic Dynamics in America*, Free Press, New York, 1977, and from a paper, "On the Predictability of Fertility," delivered at the meeting of the United Nations Ad Hoc Group of Experts on Demographic Projections, Nov. 7-11, 1977, United Nations, New York.

years at about 250 million and will then begin to decline. If the current rate continues, a total of 245 million in the year 2000 may be expected, a far cry from the 300 million anticipated by the President in a message to Congress only eight years ago. But such projections assume the continuation of this rate of fertility. Is fertility likely to rise or decline? The honest answer is that nobody knows; only more or less plausible speculations can be advanced. Back in the late 1930s, there was also a very low fertility level, and some expressions of apprehension about the prospect of impending decline were heard. Such concerns disappeared rapidly with the war and the ensuing baby boom. How do we know that another baby boom is not in store? Not long ago, some demographers were talking about a second baby boom, a kind of echo effect of the first one. They believed that a large number of babies could be expected as the products of the first baby boom reached the age of parenthood.[2] This has not yet occurred because the extremely low fertility rates have outweighed the increase in the numbers of young people.

Predictions of another baby boom have come as well from some economist-demographers who believe that as the children born during the recent years of declining birthrates come of age and enter the labor force, they will enjoy a competitive advantage and brighter prospects because of their smaller numbers.[3] They are, therefore, expected to marry earlier and have more children because their incomes will be relatively higher and their futures more promising. The empirical evidence for this hypothesis is essentially the relationship observed between previous increases in the number of births over time and declining cohort fertility. The small cohorts of the 1930s experienced high fertility in the 1950s, whereas those born during the baby boom of the 1950s are experiencing low fertility in the 1970s. If the cycle is repeated, those born in the 1970s will produce another baby boom toward the end of the century.

Although attractive because of its theoretical grounding, this method of forecasting leads to an expectation of cyclical patterns for which there are only two historical examples. What is more, no similar evidence has yet been adduced for other countries. Even for the United States, this theory ignores what appears to be a massive postponement of marriage. A steady decline since 1960 in the proportion of women marrying at ages 20-24 may be the unrecognized beginning of a radical change in the family as we know it. Even more important, perhaps, the theory does not take into account the changing status and role of women in our society. The assumption that the future increase in the demand for labor which will result from smaller cohorts entering the labor force will automatically translate into higher fertility ignores the very real changes in women's attitudes toward work (the supply of labor includes female labor also), marriage and childbearing.

There is also a seemingly irreversible change: The technology of fertility control has improved tremendously in the past 15 years and is widely diffused throughout the population. Virtually all American married couples use contraception if they are not pregnant, trying to get pregnant, or sterile. Among those currently using contraception in 1975, three out of four had either been sterilized or were using the pill or the IUD.[4] Abortion is now widely available, and further technological developments in fertility control (e.g., to enable the predetermination of sex of offspring) are on the horizon. We are fast approaching the perfect contraceptive society in which unwanted births will become nonexistent, although teenage childbearing will still be a major social problem.

Another sustained baby boom does not seem likely when such social changes are taken into account. But what fertility can we expect? For one thing, annual fertility rates should become more volatile, more responsive to short-term fluctuations in the economy. Perfect control of fertility does not imply that couples will *want* no more than one or two children; in theory, they could just as easily opt for twice that number. But larger family size in the future does not seem likely. The historical trends all point in the downward direction. The one exception, the baby boom, was not created by a return to the large families of the 19th century, but by a movement away from spinsterhood, childless marriage and the one-child family, and by a bunching together of births at early ages. Only a minor part of the baby boom can be attributed to increases in the proportions having three or more births. The decline in births that occurred in the 1960s was almost entirely due to a decrease in the number of unplanned births.[5] The accelerated decline since 1970 no doubt continues this trend but includes a reduction in the number of planned births as well. Some observers argue that the low fertility of recent years reflects primarily the postponement of births and that the postponed births will be made up in the next few years.[6] The decline in total expected family size (the number of children that women in surveys say they expect to have) does not substantiate this view. There has been some postponement, and modest increases in fertility during 1977 suggest that some of this postponement is now being made up. However, there is now increasing evidence to support the view that "later means fewer," and low fertility at one level or another seems here to stay.

Marriage and the Family

If we look closely at current social trends and their demographic outcomes, we see signs that the institution of marriage may be changing in still new ways that will cause fertility to decline to new lows. The theory that the historical demographic transition will terminate in a magical balance of births and deaths at low levels may be more aesthetic than realistic. The current evidence from the United States, and from two Scandinavian countries that historically seem to be in the avant-garde of social change in the developed world, reveals a significant constellation of social and demographic changes:

• *Marriage.* Radical changes in marriage patterns are both cause and consequence of declining fertility. In the United States, the proportion not married by ages 20-24 increased from 28 percent in 1960 to 43 percent by 1976.[7] In Denmark, this figure rose between 1970 and 1975 from 44 to 59 percent.[8] In Sweden, the number of marriages declined by 30 percent between 1966 and 1975.[9]

• *Cohabitation.* It is estimated that in the United States, nearly one million unmarried couples were living together in 1976—about two percent of *all* couples living together. This proportion will undoubtedly increase.[10] In Denmark, about one-quarter of *all* women 18-25 are living with a man to whom they are not married. The number of such relationships increased by half between 1974 and 1976, from 200,000 to 300,000 couples.[11] In Sweden recently, about 12 percent of all couples living together (ages 16-70) were not married.[12] The intriguing question is whether we are witnessing a postponement of marriage with an institutionalization of trial marriage or a more basic change that will eventually alter the institution itself.

• *Divorce.* It is abundantly clear from our very high divorce rate that the traditional concept of one partner forever has disappeared for growing segments of our society. A recent estimate indicates that one-third of all U.S. children will spend a significant amount of time with a divorced or separated parent.[13]

• *Remarriage.* Since such a high proportion of divorced persons remarry, there seems little reason to think of divorce as a reflection on the institution of marriage itself. But we also see signs of change here. In the United States, the remarriage rate, which has steadily increased over recent decades, has started to decline. (In Sweden, it has declined by about 50 percent since 1965.) A higher proportion of second marriages now seem headed for divorce. Cohabitation is not limited to the young premarital state; one is increasingly aware of middle-aged and even older divorced persons living together without the formality of marriage. There are more and more "nonfamily" households consisting of individuals either living alone or sharing quarters with one or more unrelated persons. Such nonfamily households accounted for nearly one-half of the entire increase in the number of households between 1970 and 1976.[14]

• *Illegitimacy.* In the United States, there was a record high proportion of out-of-wedlock births (14.2 percent of all births) in 1975.[15] In Denmark, the proportion of births out of wedlock doubled in a decade—to 18.8 percent in 1974;[16] in Sweden, the number tripled, so that out-of-wedlock births now comprise about one-third of all births.[17]

One could argue that all of these changes simply mean that formal marriage in the sense of a legal contract is just going out of style, at least in the early stages of "coupling," and that the rate of living together in monogamous unions is basically not changing. Indeed, research in Denmark suggests that cohabitation is for some an institutionalization of experimental or trial marriage. In a sample survey of unmarried Danish couples, about one-third said that they regarded living together as a period of experimentation, and about one-seventh indicated that it was economically advantageous; but one-quarter simply rejected the idea of the necessity of the legal formality.[18] At any rate, it seems reasonable to infer that such informal arrangements will hardly contribute to increasing fertility and that there will probably be less stability in the early (more fertile) years of marriage than in past generations. As an observer of the Danish scene concludes, these changes "make marriage a less 'weighty' commitment than formerly."[19]

Women's Status

All of these trends that seem to be depressing reproduction, separating sex from reproduction, and weakening the permanence of marriage are tied in one way or another to the growing economic independence of women as well as to the diminishing influence of religion in our lives. There has been a substantial increase in the proportion of women employed outside the home. The proportion of U.S. women in the prime childbearing years (20-34) who are working has increased from less than two-fifths in 1960 to about three-fifths in 1976; and it is projected to reach about two-thirds by 1990.[20] The International Labor Organization projects that three-fifths of European women of reproductive age will be participating in the labor force by the year 2000.[21]

There is a considerable body of research literature on the relationship between fertility and women's work. Much of it is ambiguous about the causal sequences involved and there are certainly institutional childcare arrangements that facilitate a mother's working. Nevertheless, there is little doubt that women's work and fertility are negatively related on the whole, and that the future will probably see increasing proportions working.

The increasing equality of the sexes, however, still has a long way to go in the economic sphere. Although educational differences between the sexes have greatly diminished and more and more women are working, there is still a wide gap in economic status between men and women. Women are concentrated disproportionately in less remunerative jobs and are paid less in the same jobs. Among year-round full-time U.S. workers who received income in 1975, the earnings of women 20–44 years of age were 61 percent of those of men.[22] (Significantly, that ratio remains unchanged at different levels of education.)

Nonetheless, the future trend of women's economic status seems fairly clear. Increasing proportions of women will have the option of financial independence, although genuine economic equality is probably generations away. (Indeed, such equality may never materialize, although it may be approximated to some significant degree.) But imagine the consequences for marriage and fertility of a society in which men and women are economically equal and independent!

The institution of marriage will lose yet another part of its sociological foundation. For centuries, men have exchanged some of the financial rewards, social status and security associated with their employment and income for the sexual, companionate and maternal services of women. This is hardly a romantic view of the relationship, but it does go a long way toward explaining the universality and historical persistence of marriage. But consider a social system in which just as many women as men are engineers, bank presidents, corporation executives, doctors, lawyers and salespersons. What exactly will be the motivation of women to enter the legal partnership of marriage? Sex and companionship are certainly available without the commitment implied by marriage. Given the·ease of divorce and the growing acceptability of simply living together, does it not seem probable that traditional forms of marriage will diminish even further than they have already?

One of the remaining sociological rationales for marriage is the bearing and raising of children, but with the retreat from parenthood that seems to be in process, even this age-old function seems shaky. If current first-order birthrates were to continue, about 30 percent of women would never have any children, an unprecedented but not totally implausible development. There is now evidence that childlessness within marriage is increasing. The proportions of ever-married women aged 25–29 who had not yet given birth increased from 12 percent in 1965 to 22 percent by 1976.[23] Moreover, if the large increase in out-of-wedlock births that has occurred in Sweden in recent years as a consequence of unmarried couples' living together is any indication of a diminishing taboo on having children out of wedlock, then even this function of marriage may be weakening. It seems significant that in the United States in 1975, the greatest increase in out-of-wedlock births occurred among white women 20–29 years old. At the same time, the birthrate reached a new low.[24]

Thus, demographic trends, more particularly the decline of fertility, can be regarded as both a cause and a consequence of changes in the family. The decline of childbearing can be construed as freeing women for economic equality with men, which in turn makes marriage and childbearing less of an automatic social response. The future seems less and less compatible with long-term traditional marriage.

Future Growth

If this is a reasonable interpretation of the evidence and if this diagnosis is even approximately correct, then fertility in the United States and other developed countries seems destined to fall to very low levels, probably below replacement. Several countries such as France and some East European nations already seem very uncomfortable with this trend. How, then, is society going to sustain the level of reproduction necessary to replace one generation with the next? Such questions are not new; they were raised more than 40 years ago during the depths of the Depression, when birthrates had fallen sharply and an impending decline in population was projected. At that time there was speculation by at least one serious sociologist that society would develop professional breeders, that reproduction would become the specialized function of a category of women who would be paid for their childbearing services.[25] The products of such specialists would be raised in special child-care institutions in the absence of conventional family arrangements.

This all has a ring of science fiction about it, and, of course, World War II and the subsequent scramble to the suburbs, universal marriage and the baby boom made the whole speculation seem ludicrous in retrospect. Yet, given current trends, it is not difficult to visualize a society in which perhaps one-third of women never have any children, which would mean that the remaining two-thirds would have to reproduce at an average rate of three births per woman to maintain replacement. Under such circumstances, there is little doubt that some types of financial incentives to encourage childbearing will have to be implemented, as they already have been, in mild form, in many European countries. And my guess is that there will have to be considerable public investment in underwriting such incentive systems. There is no clear evidence that the trivial baby bonuses, maternity care benefits and various employment benefits that have been legislated in European countries have had any appreciable impact on the birthrate. It is difficult to imagine well-paid women with little interest in childbearing being attracted by a few hundred dollars' worth of miscellaneous benefits. There may very well have to be a serious investment in child-care institutions and a willingness to subsidize reproduction on a large scale.

There is an alternative to subsidizing reproduction in order to meet the consequences of negative natural increase, and that is immigration. Assuming that our economy can remain strong enough to attract immigrants, the desired rate of population increase could be achieved through the manipulation of immigration quotas, a practice not unknown in our past. Since the supply of potential immigrants to the United States typically exceeds existing quotas, the qualifications for immigration could be set fairly high to bring in persons with training in skills in short supply in our economy. This concept already exists in our immigration law. From the economic point of view, such a practice would be highly rewarding, since the capital costs of education and training would have been borne by other countries. From the social point of view, however, to depend entirely on importing our population deficit would have many of the problems that we associate with the assimilation of immigrants in our past: e.g., different customs and languages, additional minority group problems, and hostility of many native citizens (50 percent of the public in 1971 thought that immigration should be reduced[26]). It is instructive that other countries confronted with such questions have opted primarily for programs to raise the fertility of their native populations. The recent labor migrations in Europe, and the resulting difficulty of accommodating large numbers of foreign workers in countries with labor shortages, have been an experience that the receiving countries are not likely to forget if it comes to the more basic question of supplementing population growth.

Also, is seems unlikely that the current volume of illegal migration (whatever its magnitude may actually be) will be permitted to continue indefinitely, and in any event, it could hardly be rationalized as a substitute for native fertility.

Thus, immigration does not seem a basic long-term solution if the rate of natural increase falls and remains radically below replacement. If current fertility rates were to continue beyond the time zero population growth was reached, our net legal immigration volume would have to be about doubled in order to avoid population decline.

This whole discussion is predicated on the assumption that governments will not look kindly on negative population growth or, for that matter, even a sustained period of below-replacement fertility prior to zero population growth. It is obvious that negative population growth cannot be sustained indefinitely although some of our citizens appear not to be averse to returning to a population

about half our current size, which was the level experienced around 1920.* We know very little about the short-run consequences of negative population growth; the long-run consequences are clear.

Conclusions

So what does it all add up to? Americans are having fewer children than ever before, and there do not seem to be any forces in view that will reverse this trend. Better contraception is available and is being used, and abortion is more or less available. The demographic result is a declining rate of population growth and an expectation that zero population growth may be reached in 50 years if not sooner. Estimates for a total population as low as 250 million are now in vogue. The age composition will change significantly with an increase in the proportions of individuals of working age and aged 65 and older, and with a decrease in youth.

In general, as we have explained elsewhere, the social, economic, environmental and political consequences of these demographic changes seem desirable.[27] There are some concerns about the implications of an older population, but sooner or later such change is inevitable as population growth slows. At any rate, the reduction of growth means less pressure on the environment and resources and an opportunity to invest economic growth in improving the quality of life. From the standpoint of the economy, there will be more workers and fewer dependents, and per capita income will be higher. From the standpoint of government, there will be an opportunity to invest public resources in better education

---

*See, for example, various statements of Negative Population Growth, Inc.

and to improve the level of government services generally.

The future of marriage and the family is less clear. The divorce rate continues at a high level, the marriage rate is low, and there seems to be a massive postponement of marriage in the making. Increasingly, young men and women are living together without the added commitment of marriage; illegitimacy rates will probably continue to increase. Whether increasing proportions will never marry or will just marry at a later age is unknown. Although it seems ironic, if not ludicrous—in view of our concerns about growth of only a few years ago—to be thinking about the possible need in the near future to *maintain* replacement fertility, there are reasons to believe that some subsidization of reproduction may eventually become necessary. The problem has already arisen in more than one European country, and the social trends apparent in the United States today all seem to point in that direction.

References

1. J. Bourgeois-Pichat, "The Economic and Social Implications of Demographic Trends in Europe up to and Beyond 2000," *Population Bulletin of the United Nations*, No. 8-1976, 1977, p. 34.

2. W. Brass, "Perspectives in Population Prediction: Illustrated by the Statistics of England and Wales," *Journal of the Royal Statistical Society*, 137:532, 1974; R. A. Easterlin, "The American Baby Boom in Historical Perspective," National Bureau of Economic Research, New York, 1962; R. Lee, "Demographic Forecasting and the Easterlin Hypothesis," *Population and Development Review*, 2:459, 1976. See also N. Keyfitz, "On Future Population," *Journal of the American Statistical Association*, 67:361, 1972, who suggests a great amount of variability around replacement.

3. R. Lee, 1976, op. cit.

4. C.F. Westoff and E.F. Jones, "Contraception and Sterilization in the United States, 1965-1975," *Family Planning Perspectives*, 9:153, 1977.

5. C.F. Westoff, "The Decline of Unplanned Births in the United States," *Science*, 191:38, 1976.

6. J. Sklar and B. Berkov, "The American Birth Rate:

Evidence of a Coming Rise," *Science*, 189:693, 1975.

7. P.C. Glick, "Social Change and the American Family," in National Conference on Social Welfare, *Social Welfare Forum, 1977*, Columbia University Press, New York, 1978.

8. L. Roussel, "Démographie et Mode de Vie Conjugale au Danemark," *Population*, 32:339, 1977.

9. F. Prioux-Marchal, "Le Marriage en Suède," *Population*, 29:824, 1974; and J. Bourgeois-Pichat, 1977, op. cit., p. 64.

10. P. C. Glick, 1977, op. cit.

11. L. Roussel, 1977, op. cit.

12. F. Prioux-Marchal, 1974, op. cit.

13. P. C. Glick, 1978, op. cit.

14. Ibid.

15. National Center for Health Statistics, DHEW (NCHS), "Advance Report: Final Natality Statistics, 1975," *Monthly Vital Statistics Report*, Vol. 24, No. 10, Supplement, 1976.

16. L. Roussel, 1977, op. cit.

17. F. Prioux-Marchal, 1974, op. cit.

18. L. Roussel, 1977, op. cit.

19. Ibid.

20. U.S. Bureau of Labor Statistics, "New Labor Force Projections to 1990," *Special Labor Force Reports*, report no. 197, Washington, D.C., 1976.

21. Estimated from graphic figures in J. Bourgeois-Pichat, 1977, op. cit., p. 70.

22. Calculated from U.S. Bureau of the Census, "Characteristics of the Population below the Poverty Level: 1975," *Current Population Reports*, Series P-60, No. 106, 1977.

23. U.S. Bureau of the Census, "Fertility of American Women: June 1976," *Current Population Reports*, Series P-20, No. 308, 1977, Table 19.

24. NCHS, 1976, op. cit.

25. K. Davis, "Reproductive Institutions and the Pressure for Population," *The Sociological Review*, 29:289, 1937.

26. D. M. Wolman, "Findings of the Commission's National Public Opinion Survey," in Commission on Population Growth and the American Future, *Aspects of Population Growth Policy*, R. Parke, Jr., and C. F. Westoff, eds., Vol. VI of Commission Research Reports, U.S. Government Printing Office, Washington, D.C. (GPO) 1972, p. 491.

27. The Commission on Population Growth and the American Future, *Population and the American Future*, GPO, stock no. 5258-0002, 1972.

II
The Consequences of
Early Parenthood

Despite mounting concern over the fate of the pregnant adolescent, the young parents and their children, surprisingly little was known until recently about the consequences of early childbearing except through anecdote. A classic description was provided by Arthur Campbell in 1968:

> The girl who has an illegitimate child at the age of 16 suddenly has 90 percent of her life's script written for her. She will probably drop out of school, even if someone else in her family helps to take care of the baby; she will probably not be able to find a steady job that pays enough to provide for herself and her child; she may feel impelled to marry someone she might not otherwise have chosen. Her life choices are few, and most of them are bad. Had she been able to delay the first child, her prospects might have been quite different.[1]

This statement offers both a summary of the life course of the young teenage mother and a proposition that early childbearing is the cause of a host of later problems. It was realized at the time that both summary and proposition were speculative, although culled from informed observation. Especially uncertain was the causation proposition. Since it was well known that pregnant adolescents and young mothers are disproportionately drawn from disadvantaged backgrounds, whether early parenthood precipitated difficulties or whether both resulted from already existing unfavorable economic and social circumstances remained undetermined. Answers to this troublesome question continue to be needed, not as academic exercises, but to inform policy and program decisions intended to alleviate the predicament of young mothers, fathers, and their offspring.

The articles in this section expand the description given here and in the Overview of the consequences of early childbearing for parents and their children. They draw on a variety of sources and methodologies to examine the health, social, marital, fertility, and economic experiences of teenage parents. Two of the data sets described in chapter 12, Furstenberg's Baltimore study of adolescent mothers and their classmates, and the Project TALENT study (analyzed in chapter 13 by Josefina Card and Lauress Wise) of a national sample of boys and girls in high school in 1960, are especially significant. They both followed groups of adolescents, selected prior to any childbearing experiences, for a number of years. This approach offered opportunities for pioneering work in separating true consequences of teenage birth from sequelae that are determined primarily by the same socioeconomic and other background characteristics that may make early parenthood more likely. In both cases, the young parent could be compared, later in life, to his or her peers whose experience was similar up to the event of pregnancy and childbirth. The results show that divergent experiences subsequent to the first birth depend substantially on the age of the parents. There is good reason, then, to believe that postponement of childbearing can improve the life chances of young women and men.

These two data sets have the disadvantage of being quite restricted, the first to a rather small sample in a single inner-city area, and the second to a single group—those in high school in 1960. It is therefore important to note that the results of the studies that are limited to description of later careers according to age at first birth are consistent with those of the Baltimore and Project TALENT studies.

Taken as a whole, the research lends firm support to the proposition that early childbearing is disadvantageous to the teenage parents and involves high social and economic costs for individuals and society. One of the repeated findings concerns the role of education. For many years the question of whether pregnancy causes low education, or whether on the contrary low educational performance or aspiration leads to pregnancy has been a subject of intense debate. Card and Wise found that when prior school performance is controlled, the young parents are more likely to curtail education than those whose childbearing is postponed. Zelnik and Kantner, in the previous section, contributed to relevant information that fewer than one quarter of pregnant teenagers wanted to have a child. Taken together with studies of the economic consequences of teenage childbearing (indicating lack of education as the primary cause of low income), these and other studies lead inevitably to the conclusion that programs geared toward helping young parents further their studies may help alleviate the deleterious consequences of early childbearing.

What about the children of teenage parents? Wendy Baldwin and Virginia Cain, in their review of a broad spectrum of studies (chapter 17), find few consequences for the child that are directly related to parental youth. Indeed, even the well-documented increased risk of perinatal morbidity and mortality of infants born to teenage mothers may be reversed with excellent prenatal care. (Increased health risks continue in the first year of life, however, especially if there is no adult other than the teenage mother to care for the child.) Rather, it is poor socioeconomic status that is the villain in most cases. Since young parents are disproportionately drawn from the poor and less well educated, and since early childbearing often leaves the parents poor and poorly educated, their children are the victims of these circumstances rather than of parental age per se.

What can be done to aid parents and children? The importance of family support networks is emphasized in chapter 18 by Frank Furstenberg and Albert Crawford, and in the studies cited in this section by Baldwin and Cain. These investigations do not suggest that special programs should be designed for the children of teenage parents. Indeed, such categorical programs would not only be inappropriate, but could be damaging insofar as they stigmatize the children. Rather, these findings strongly suggest that the appropriate program intervention is with the young parents—starting before the birth and extending well beyond it—to prevent the health, educational, and economic hardships that are transmitted to the children through the handicaps imposed on the young parents.

Reference

1. A. A. Campbell, "The Role of Family Planning in the Reduction of Poverty," *Journal of Marriage and The Family,* 30:238, 1968.

11
The Health and Social Consequences of Teenage Childbearing

Jane Menken

Teenage childbearing is associated with a long list of adverse health and social consequences for young mothers and their infants. Yet, as of 1968 (the most recent year for which detailed data are available), one-fourth of 20-year-old girls had had at least one baby while in their teens. One-sixth of births in that year were to girls in their teens; a third of these — 200,000 infants — were born to mothers 17 or younger,[1] and two-fifths of these 200,000 were born out of wedlock.[2] What is more, as birthrates and illegitimacy rates have declined, since the beginning of the 1960s, the proportion of all babies born to teenagers has risen appreciably,[3] and teenage illegitimacy rates have continued stubbornly to increase.[4]

Childbearing at any age is a momentous event for a woman. For the teenager, however, it is often accompanied by problems quite different from and far less benign than those experienced by older mothers.

For the very young mother, the risks that her baby will be stillborn, or die soon after birth, or be born prematurely or with a serious physical or mental handicap are much higher than those for women in their twenties. Early childbearing is also associated with high parity and short birth intervals, compounding the already high risks to the life and health of the young mother and her infant. Moreover, bearing a first child while in her teens is likely to be a critical and highly adverse turning point in a young woman's life.[5] This is particularly true if the baby is conceived out of wedlock (as are nearly six in 10 of all first births to 15-19-year-olds[6]) or born out of wedlock (as are 27 percent of births to this age group[7]). In Arthur Campbell's words:

> The girl who has an illegitimate child at the age of 16 suddenly has 90 percent of her life's script written for her. She will probably drop out of school, even

This article is adapted from a paper, "Teenage Childbearing: Its Medical Aspects and Implications for the U.S. Population," in the Research Reports of the Commission on Population Growth and the American Future, Volume I: *Demographic and Social Aspects of Population Growth*, C. F. Westoff and R. Parke, Jr., eds., U.S. Government Printing Office, Washington, D.C., 1972.

The author acknowledges the assistance of Mary Grace Kovar and Arnold Nelson of the National Center for Health Statistics and Marion Howard of the Research Utilization and Information Sharing Project, who were extremely helpful in providing information for this review. Mindel Sheps, Dorothy Nortman and Norman Ryder commented on an early version.

Table 1. Births, by Legitimacy Status and Color, for Total Population and for Teenagers, 1961 and 1968

	Births (in thousands)					Percent of Total Births			
	Total	<15	15-17	18-19	<20	<15	15-17	18-19	<20
All									
1968	3502	10	193	398	601	0.3	5.5	11.4	17.2
1961	4268	7	178	424	609	0.2	4.2	9.9	14.3
Percent change	−18.0	27.4	8.5	−6.1	−1.3				
White									
1968	2912	3.1	121	306	430	0.1	4.2	10.4	14.7
1961	3601	2.8	125	347	475	0.1	3.5	9.6	13.2
Percent change	−19.1	10.9	−3.2	−12.9	−9.4				
Nonwhite									
1968	589	6.4	72	93	171	1.0	12.1	15.8	28.9
1961	667	4.7	53	77	135	0.7	7.9	11.6	20.2
Percent change	−11.7	37.3	36.3	20.8	27.2				

	Out-of-Wedlock Births (estimate, in thousands)					Percent of Total Out-of-Wedlock Births			
All									
1968	339	7.7	78	80	166	2.3	23.0	23.6	48.9
1961	240	5.2	45	48	98	2.2	18.8	20.0	41.2
Percent change	41.2	48.1	72.7	66.7	68.7				
White									
1968	155	1.9	28	39	69	1.2	18.3	25.1	44.6
1961	91	1.4	16	20	37	1.5	17.0	22.6	41.1
Percent change	70.4	35.7	83.2	95.0	84.2				
Nonwhite									
1968	184	5.8	49	42	97	3.2	26.9	22.4	52.5
1961	149	3.8	30	27	61	2.5	19.9	18.4	40.8
Percent change	23.3	52.6	66.9	55.6	59.2				

Sources: DHEW, *Vital Statistics of the United States, Vol. I — Natality, 1968,* Tables 1-26, 1-41 and 1-51; 1961, Tables 2-9 and 2-12.

if someone else in her family helps to take care of the baby; she will probably not be able to find a steady job that pays enough to provide for herself and her child; she may feel impelled to marry someone she might not otherwise have chosen. Her life choices are few, and most of them are bad. Had she been able to delay the first child, her prospects might have been quite different. . . . [8]

While the main focus of this article is on the medical aspects of teenage childbearing, some consideration will also be given to the social consequences to parent and child, and to what little is known about the social and economic conditions which may influence teenage childbearing.

Teenage Births and Birthrates

As the U.S. birthrate declined in the last decade, births to teenagers became a larger proportion of all births (see top deck of Table 1). In 1968, 17 percent of all births were to teenagers, compared to 14 percent in 1961. The increase was sharpest among nonwhites, among whom

29 percent of births in 1968, compared to 20 percent in 1961, were to teenagers. The concentration of out-of-wedlock births at young ages is even more striking (see bottom deck of Table 1): Nearly half of all out-of-wedlock births in 1968 were to teenagers, compared to 41 percent in 1961. These changes were only partly due to increases in the numbers of teenagers in the population. An additional factor was the relative change in birthrates in the various age groups. Women 20 and older experienced greater declines in birthrates during the period 1961-1968 than did 15-19-year-olds.[9]

A slightly different perspective is obtained by examining the proportion of women bearing a child while in their teens, rather than the proportion of total births that occur to young mothers. The data presented in Table 2 show that, for women born in the United States between 1940 and 1951, the proportion who became mothers by the time they reached their eighteenth birthday declined by 25 percent — from 12.5 percent of girls born in 1939 to 9.4 percent of girls born 11 years later. A similar reduction occurred in the proportion starting their reproductive lives by age 20 — from 33.8 percent of girls born in 1939 to 25.9 percent of girls born nine years later — a decline of 23 percent. Despite this downward trend, the table shows that almost 26 percent of the latest cohort for which data are available bore a child before age 20, and more than one-fourth of these mothers had at least two children.

Table 3 shows that between 1961 and 1968 illegitimacy rates (births per 1,000 single women) declined slightly for all age groups except for 15-19-year-olds. While teenagers did not have the highest rates of illegitimacy of all age groups (single women aged 20-34 had much higher rates), more of them — 89 percent in 1969 — were unmarried than in any other

Table 2. Percent of Birth Cohort Having at Least One Live Birth by Age 18 and Age 20: U. S. Birth Cohorts, 1939-1950

Cohort Born During Fiscal Year	Percent Becoming Mothers by Age		Percent of Mothers Having at Least Two Live Births by Age	
	18	20	18	20
1940	12.5	33.8	18.5	34.6
1941	12.2	33.2	18.7	34.9
1942	11.5	31.9	19.0	34.5
1943	10.9	30.0	19.2	34.0
1944	11.0	30.0	19.3	33.6
1945	10.8	29.4	19.8	32.6
1946	10.8	29.4	19.3	31.0
1947	9.1	25.8	17.8	27.5
1948	9.5	26.4	17.8	27.0
1949	9.4	25.9	17.0	25.7
1950	9.4		16.2	
1951	9.4		14.8	
Percent Decline	24.8	23.4	20.0	25.7

Sources: Derived from cumulative birthrates by live-birth order and exact age of mother, *Vital Statistics of the United States, Vol. I — Natality: 1968*, Table 1-17; *1967*, Table 1-17; *1966*, Table 1-18; *1965*, Table 1-18; *1964*, Table 1-19. Also, P. K. Whelpton and A. A. Campbell, "Fertility Tables for Birth Cohorts of American Women," *Vital Statistics — Special Reports*, Vol. 51, 1960, Part 1, Table 2, p. 78.

Table 3. Estimated Illegitimacy Rates* by Age of Mother: United States 1961-1968

Year	15-44	15-19	20-24	25-29	30-34	35-39	40-44
1968	24.1	19.8	36.1	39.4	27.6	14.6	3.7
1967	24.0	18.7	38.6	41.4	29.8	15.3	4.0
1966	23.6	17.5	40.8	44.4	32.1	16.9	4.3
1965	23.4	16.7	38.8	50.4	37.1	17.0	4.4
1964	23.4	16.5	40.0	50.1	41.4	15.0	4.0
1963	22.5	15.3	39.9	49.4	33.7	16.1	4.3
1962	21.5	14.9	41.8	46.4	27.0	13.5	3.4
1961	22.6	16.0	41.2	44.8	28.9	15.1	3.8

Source: *Vital Statistics of the United States, 1968, Vol. I — Natality*, Table 1-25.
* Number of out-of-wedlock births per 1,000 single women in specified group.

Table 4. Percent of First Births Conceived Out of Wedlock for Women Aged 15-19 and 15-44, by Color: United States, 1964-1966 National Natality Survey

	Age of Mother at First Birth					
	15-19			15-44		
	Total	White	Non-·white	Total	White	Non-white
Number of First Births (in Thousands)	442	348	94	1,180	1,008	171
Percent of First Births Which Were:						
Illegitimate	24.0	15.0	57.3	14.5	9.3	45.5
Born Less than 8 Months after Marriage	32.2	33.9	26.0	18.5	17.7	22.6
Conceived Out of Wedlock	**56.2**	**48.9**	**83.3**	**33.0**	**27.0**	**68.1**
Percent of Legitimate First Births Which Were Conceived Out of Wedlock	42.4	39.9	60.8	21.6	19.5	41.6
Percent of First Births Which Were Conceived Out of Wedlock and Were Later Legitimized by Marriage	57.2	69.3	31.1	55.9	65.6	33.3

Source: Unpublished data, National Center for Health Statistics, 1964-1966 National Natality Survey.

age group.[10] Together, these factors result in a situation where close to half the mothers delivering infants out of wedlock are teenagers.

Illegitimate births represent a large proportion of total births to teenagers. In 1968, 40 percent of births to mothers aged 15-17 and 20 percent to 18-19-year-olds were illegitimate, compared to eight percent of births to 20-24-year-olds, and about four percent of births to women in the 25-34-year age group.[11] Standard vital statistics data do not indicate the number of out-of-wedlock conceptions that are legitimized by marriage. However, a National Natality Study conducted in 1964-1966 by the National Center for Health Statistics (NCHS) included date of marriage in the information obtained from a sample of over 2,500 mothers of legitimate first-born children.[12] Table 4 summarizes some of the findings. Fifty-six percent of first-born children to girls aged 15-

19 were conceived prior to marriage.* The lower proportion of out-of-wedlock-conceived births among whites (49 percent) than among nonwhites (83 percent) may reflect differences in the availability of abortion. The data show a much greater probability for whites who deliver a premaritally conceived infant to marry before the birth occurs. Similar but more detailed results for Detroit in 1960 show that the proportion of births conceived out of wedlock which were legitimized increased from age 14 to age 17.[13]

Medical Aspects

The medical literature generally discusses reproductive loss at specified stages on the continuum of development of the fetus

---

* This assumes that births occurring within eight months of marriage were premaritally conceived.

and infant: fetal mortality, perinatal mortality (from 28 weeks of gestation through the first week of life), neonatal mortality (first 28 days of life) and postneonatal mortality (28 days through one year). The latter two are components of the standard measure of infant mortality, that is, deaths in the first year of life. These distinctions are important here in that fetal, perinatal and, to a lesser extent, neonatal mortality appear to be caused primarily by factors related to the *pregnancy* itself, while postneonatal mortality is attributed more often to environmental causes. The risks of reproductive loss vary with the age and parity of the mother. These two factors, while usually rising together, have quite different biologic interpretations: Age is a rough indicator of whether a young pregnant woman has reached full physical maturity or of whether the reproductive effectiveness of the older woman has begun to decline. Parity, on the other hand, reflects previous experience with the reproductive process.[14] The combination, parity at a certain age, is a result of the timing of births (the age at first birth and the rapidity with which subsequent ones occur).

Sociological interpretations of the age relationship are also plausible. The risk of childbearing at certain ages may be correlated with the risk of reproductive loss. Few data, however, are available to distinguish between the biological and sociological interpretations.

Mortality and Maternal Age

To study the relationship of infant mortality to maternal age, it is necessary either to match a sample of infants' death certificates to infants' birth certificates or to request further information from the families. As a result, there have been only a handful of large-scale studies.

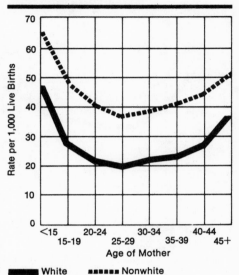

Figure 1. Infant Mortality of White and Nonwhite Infants by Age of Mother: United States, 1960 Birth Cohort

Age of Mother

▬▬ White   ■■■■■ Nonwhite

Source: Working Group, "Relation of Nutrition to Pregnancy in Adolescence," in *Maternal Nutrition and the Course of Pregnancy*, Committee on Maternal Nutrition, Food and Nutrition Board, National Research Council, National Academy of Sciences, Washington, D. C., 1970, Table 3, p. 144.

Those in the United States and United Kingdom have shown consistently that the infant mortality rate is extremely high for mothers younger than 15, declines to a minimum in either the early or late twenties and increases fairly sharply thereafter.[15] Figure 1 illustrates this with data from a matched birth certificate/infant death certificate study.[16] This NCHS investigation succeeded in matching birth and death certificates for 94 percent of the nearly 110,000 children born in 1960 who died before reaching their first birthday.[17] The shapes of the curves are similar but, at all ages, the infant mortality rate is considerably higher among nonwhites than among whites.

Figure 2. Neonatal and Postneonatal Mortality of White and Nonwhite Infants by Age of Mother: United States, 1960 Birth Cohort

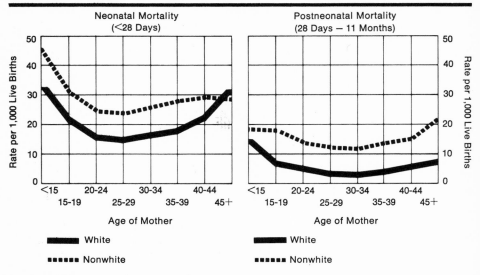

Source: Working Group, "Relation of Nutrition to Pregnancy in Adolescence," 1970, op. cit.

When mortality among infants born to mothers younger than 20 is compared to the mortality of those whose mothers are aged 20-30, it can be seen that the differences are far greater in the first month of life than in the remainder of the first year (see Figure 2). In other words, just after birth, when biologic factors related to the pregnancy are the primary determinants of survival, risks to infants of young mothers are much higher than those to infants of older mothers in both color groups.

Postneonatal death rates are high and differences by color are least in mothers younger than 15, suggesting large and negative environmental influences for infants of the youngest mothers, regardless of color. It is well-documented that postneonatal mortality rates have declined over the past 30 years more rapidly than have neonatal mortality rates, mainly the result of declining death rates from infectious disease.[18] However, for nonwhites the relative improvement in mortality conditions has occurred much more slowly. In 1960, at almost all ages, postneonatal mortality accounted for approximately one-fourth of the infant deaths in each maternal age group among whites, but closer to one-third of the deaths among nonwhites. Sam Shapiro and his colleagues examined infant mortality within the postneonatal period according to the age (in months) of the infant at death.[19] They found that the rates for whites and nonwhites increasingly diverged during the first four months. At that point, nonwhite infant mortality was three times that of whites.

Infant mortality by legitimacy status of the pregnancy was derived for the period 1964-1966, again by the NCHS, using data from the National Natality Survey and the National Infant Mortality Study.[20] Except for nonwhites aged 25-29, the rates shown in Figure 3 follow the age-pattern already described: The infant mortality rates for the out-of-wedlock births exceed those for legitimate births, and this differential increases with age. (The single exception is for nonwhites younger than 20 years, where the proportion of infants surviving the first year of life is greater for out-of-wedlock births.)

No U.S. data are available to reveal the mortality experience of infants conceived out of wedlock. However, it was found in England and Wales in 1949 that neonatal mortality among single live births was 16.4 per 1,000 for legitimate births, 22.4 per 1,000 for births occurring in the first nine months of marriage and 27.0 per 1,000 for out-of-wedlock births.[21] It is distinctly possible that these figures are at least partially the result of the age distribution of women conceiving premaritally, but they do suggest increased risks to infants whose conception precedes marriage.

Fetal death ratios (the number of reported fetal deaths of over 20 weeks' duration divided by total live births) for women younger than 20 are somewhat elevated when compared to women aged 20-29, but women over 30 are clearly subject to a far higher risk of not carrying their pregnancy to full term.[22] Again, nonwhites are exposed to higher risks at all ages. The fetal loss rate is greater for out-of-wedlock pregnancies in all age and color groups except for nonwhites under 15, for whom the ratio for pregnancies classed as legitimate is 45.6 per 1,000 live births compared with 29.0 for out-of-wedlock births. At all other ages, the differential in the ratio for legitimate vs. out-of-wedlock births is much greater for whites than nonwhites. What proportion of these reported fetal deaths is the result of induced abortion is unknown.

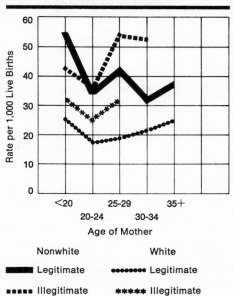

Figure 3. Infant Mortality Rates by Color of Child and Legitimacy Status by Age of Mother: United States, 1964-1966

Source: "Infant Mortality Rates by Legitimacy Status: United States, 1964-1966," National Center for Health Statistics, *Monthly Vital Statistics Report,* Vol. 20, No. 5, 1971, Table 2, p. 3.

These preliminary results demonstrate that, at all stages of pregnancy and infancy examined, the very young mother is exposed to greater risks of losing her baby than her somewhat older counterparts.

Influence of Parity

Risks of reproductive loss are highest for young women who have already had several live births and for older women. Data on fetal death rates for 1960-1961 show that the risks for young mothers at all parities are high, and increase rapidly with parity after the first birth (see Table 5).

Neonatal death certificates for infants

Table 5. Average Fetal Death Rates per 1,000 Live Births and Fetal Deaths, by Birth Order and Age of Mother: United States, 1960-1961

Birth Order	Age of Mother						
	All Ages*	15-19	20-24	25-29	30-34	35-39	40-44
First	15.5	13.8	13.0	17.8	30.0	46.6	60.2
Second	11.2	12.2	9.4	10.7	14.6	21.0	32.2
Third	13.2	16.3	11.3	11.5	14.5	21.4	32.2
Fourth	16.0	23.1	14.4	13.9	15.8	21.9	31.0
Fifth	19.1	47.3	17.3	16.2	18.7	23.8	33.0
Sixth and over	28.8	72.7	23.3	22.4	25.2	31.6	43.4
Total	**15.8**	**13.7**	**11.9**	**14.2**	**19.0**	**26.8**	**38.5**

Source: S. Shapiro, E. Schlesinger and R. E. L. Nesbitt, Jr., *Infant, Perinatal, Maternal and Childhood Mortality in the United States,* Harvard University Press, Cambridge, Mass., 1968.
* Includes data for age groups under 15 years and 45 years and older.

Table 6. Neonatal Mortality Rates per 1,000 Live Births, by Birth Order and Age of Mother: United States, January-March 1950

Birth Order	Age of Mother						
	All Ages	15-19	20-24	25-29	30-34	35-39	40-44
First	19.1	21.2	16.6	17.3	24.1	28.7	30.9
Second	17.8	28.1	18.2	14.3	16.1	20.3	25.3
Third	19.7	35.3	22.0	17.7	16.9	19.8	26.4
Fourth	21.1	45.2	24.9	19.6	18.8	21.5	23.6
Fifth and over	26.9	68.8	35.8	25.5	25.5	26.1	28.0
Total	**20.0**	**23.8**	**19.0**	**17.6**	**20.0**	**23.6**	**27.2**

Source: S. Shapiro, E. Schlesinger and R. E. L. Nesbitt, Jr., *Infant, Perinatal, Maternal and Childhood Mortality in the United States,* Harvard University Press, Cambridge, Mass., 1968.

born in the first three months of 1950, when matched to the infants' birth certificates, reveal a distinct pattern among white infants.[23] For parities beyond the first, the neonatal death rate for infants of 15-19-year-old mothers is quite high, declines for those in the twenties and then rises again after age 30 (see Table 6). There is no simple age pattern for nonwhites but neonatal mortality for both groups among young mothers rises rapidly with each parity after the first birth.

Similar U.S. data for the postneonatal period are not available. A series of studies following all children born in 1949 and 1950 in England and Wales[24] shows that, in the age period between four weeks and six months, the mortality rate for all parities follows the same pattern as for the neonatal rates displayed in Table 6.[25] At any maternal age, mortality increases with birth order after the first. In the last half of the first year, observed mortality is highest in infants of the youngest mothers. This pattern in postneonatal mortality holds for all socioeconomic groups, although the *level* of mortality rises as the socioeconomic level declines.[26] Less detailed findings of an inverse relationship between mortality and occupation exist for fetal and neonatal mortality in areas of the United States.[27] The British Perinatal Mortality Survey, which studied all stillbirths and infants born alive in a single week in England and Wales in 1958, found similar inverse relationships between social class and the perinatal mortality rate (defined as stillbirths and deaths in the first week).[28]

In North Carolina, a study of perinatal mortality (defined as fetal deaths plus neonatal mortality) for mothers under 20 has indicated that mortality is highest when the mother is younger than 15, dips at age 16, and then declines slightly with each additional year to age 20.[29]

Summary of Mortality Risks

Young women — particularly multiparous young women — and older women run an especially high risk that their babies will die at birth or soon after. Table 7 summarizes the evidence of the risk of mortality for infants of mothers in these given age groups compared to the risk to infants of mothers aged 20-24. Infant mortality for white mothers under 15 is over twice as high as for mothers in their early twenties. For younger mothers, the relative risk of fetal or neonatal death climbs as parity rises, so that neonatal mortality of the infants born to women younger than 20 who already have had three live births (last line) is 90 percent higher than

of infants of older mothers. The reverse situation holds for older mothers. Apparently, a mother who delivers a child after age 40 is more likely to have a liveborn child who survives the neonatal period if she has already had previous live births.

Birth Intervals

Girls who have a first child at an early age tend also to bear their subsequent children in rapid succession.[30] There may be a selection process by which girls who are more fecund, or who have less access to abortion or contraception, or who are less effective users of contraception, may tend to marry and/or become pregnant early in their sexual experience. There is also some evidence that marriage at an early age is related to education and religion, two variables which have been associated with fertility in almost every study of the subject.[31] Short birth intervals have been linked to increased rates of stillbirth, prematurity, and neonatal and postneonatal deaths.[32]

Prematurity

The increased risk of prematurity may be the most important medical aspect of teenage pregnancy.[33] The infant's maturity at birth is usually gauged by birth weight, although there are different developmental levels for the same weight in different populations.[34] It has been estimated that "the risk of death in the first year of life among infants who weigh 2500 grams or less at birth is 17 times the risk among infants weighing 2501 grams or more."[35] This has been verified in two national studies, one of neonatal mortality in 1950 and the other of mortality in the first year of life in 1960.[36] At all birth weights under 2500 grams, the neonatal mortality rate was lower in 1960 for non-

Table 7. Mortality Rate for Specified Age Groups Relative to the Rate for Infants of Mothers Aged 20-24, by Color

	White			Nonwhite		
Rate for Women	(< 15)	(15-19)	(40-44)	(< 15)	(15-19)	(40-44)
Rate for Women	(20-24)	(20-24)	(20-24)	(20-24)	(20-24)	(20-24)
United States, 1960						
Infant Mortality	2.2	1.3	1.3	1.6	1.2	1.1
Neonatal Mortality	2.2	1.3	1.4	1.8	1.2	1.2
Postneonatal Mortality	2.8	1.4	1.1	1.3	1.3	1.0
United States, 1964-66						
Infant Mortality						
Legitimate Births	na	1.3*	1.3†	na	1.7*	1.1†
Illegitimate Births	na	1.2	‡	na	1.2	‡
United States, 1967						
Fetal Death Ratios						
by Parity						
First	na	1.0	4.8	na	0.8	3.9
Second	na	1.2	3.5	na	1.2	3.9
Third	na	1.3	3.0	na	1.4	3.4
Fourth	na	1.4	2.3	na	1.5	2.6
United States, 1950						
Neonatal Mortality						
Rates by Parity						
First	na	1.3	1.9	na	1.0	
Second	na	1.6	1.5	na	1.3	
Third	na	1.8	1.1	na	1.4	
Fourth	na	1.9	0.9	na	1.9	

Sources: "Infant Mortality Rates by Legitimacy Status: United States, 1964-1966," *Monthly Vital Statistics Report*, Vol. 20, No. 5, 1971, Table 2, p. 3; J. Loeb, *Weight at Birth and Survival of the Newborn, by Age of Mother and Total Birth Order, United States, Early 1950*, National Center for Health Statistics, Series 21, No. 5, 1965; S. Shapiro, E. Schlesinger and R. E. L. Nesbitt, Jr., *Infant, Perinatal, Maternal and Childhood Mortality in the United States*, Harvard University Press, Cambridge, Mass., 1968; Working Group, "Relation of Nutrition to Pregnancy in Adolescence," in *Maternal Nutrition and the Course of Pregnancy*, Committee on Maternal Nutrition, Food and Nutrition Board, National Research Council, National Academy of Sciences, Washington, D.C., 1970.

* Age group includes all mothers aged less than 20 years.

† Age group includes all mothers aged 35 or more years.

‡ Numerator does not meet standards of reliability or precision.

na = not available.

whites than for whites, implying that developmental maturity was not the same at a given birth weight for these two groups. Postneonatal mortality, however, was lower for whites than for nonwhites at all birth weights; the risk of postneonatal mortality for a white infant weighing more than 2500 grams at birth was little more than one-third that for a nonwhite infant.[37]

The percentage of infants weighing less than 2500 grams was greatest among very young mothers, and has been increasing for nonwhites since 1950 (see Table 8). In 1950, the percentage of in-

Table 8. Percent of Low Birth Weight Infants, by Age of Mother and Color: United States, January-March 1950 and 1967

Age of Mother	Total			White			Nonwhite		
	Jan.-Mar. 1950*	1967	Difference	Jan.-Mar. 1950*	1967	Difference	Jan.-Mar. 1950*	1967	Difference
< 15	15.1	17.2	+2.1	15.9	12.5	−3.4	14.7	19.5	+4.8
15-19	9.0	10.5	+1.5	8.0	8.5	+0.5	12.0	15.7	+3.7
20-24	7.3	7.7	+0.4	6.9	6.7	−0.2	9.6	13.2	+3.6
25-29	6.7	7.2	+0.5	6.5	6.5	0.0	8.4	11.8	+3.4
30-34	7.2	7.9	+0.7	7.0	7.0	0.0	8.8	12.6	+3.8
35-39	7.7	9.1	+1.4	7.5	8.3	+0.8	9.0	13.3	+4.3
40-44	7.7	9.6	+1.9	7.5	9.1	+1.6	8.9	12.2	+3.3
≧ 45	6.1	8.6	+2.5	5.7	8.1	+2.4	7.4	10.8	+3.4
Total	**7.4**	**8.2**	**+0.8**	**7.0**	**7.1**	**+0.1**	**9.7**	**13.6**	**+3.9**

Source: H. Chase, "Trends in 'Prematurity': United States, 1950-1967," *American Journal of Public Health*, 60:1978, 1970, Table 8.
* Excludes all live births recorded in Massachusetts.

fants of low birth weight increased greatly for young mothers of higher parity.[38] One hypothesis explaining the increasing frequency of low birth weight is that since 1950 there has been great effort to prolong "pregnancies which gave indication of terminating prematurely."[39] This could decrease fetal losses while increasing prematurity rates and tending to increase neonatal mortality.

Prematurity may be strongly associated with socioeconomic status. The 1963 National Natality Survey found that the relationship between the proportion of infants weighing less than 2500 grams and maternal age was similar to that shown in Table 8. When women were classified by family income, however, the differences in the proportion born prematurely varied little by age within any income group,[40] although a much larger proportion of women under 20 were in the lower income groups than were older women. In a study of infants liveborn in Baltimore between 1961 and 1965[41] birth weight was found to be related more,

within each color group, to the trimester of pregnancy in which prenatal care began than to age, parity or socioeconomic status per se. However, the timing of prenatal care was highly correlated with socioeconomic status in this study. Those running the greatest risk of having an infant of low birth weight were unmarried black women who received no medical care, were younger than 15, were delivering their first child and were in the lowest socioeconomic category of the study. Just under 30 percent of infants born to mothers in this group are expected to weigh less than 2500 grams.

Increased mortality risk is only one of the dangers facing infants of low birth weight. Prematurity has also been linked to such conditions as epilepsy, cerebral palsy and mental retardation, and to higher risks of deafness and blindness.[42] In addition, studies of developing infants tested over a period of years for intelligence, motor development and similar traits showed improved scores as birth weight increased.[43]

Other Problems

Various studies are not conclusive about the relationship of age of the mother to the intelligence of the child as well as to physical and mental handicaps. Benjamin Pasamanick and Abraham Lilienfeld found the risk of mental retardation was high for children of mothers younger than 20, and Raymond Illsley and others found that IQ increased with maternal age.[44] But, in another study, at each age the scores decreased with parity of the mother; this led one team of investigators to conclude that the difference in intelligence is due to the difference between families rather than within a family as the mother ages.[45] In considering the two high-risk groups of mothers — mothers younger than 20 and those older than 35 — another study linked increased risks of congenital defects—such as intracranial or spinal injury, breathing difficulties and clubfoot — for first births to the young mothers. In addition, this study noted an increased risk of epilepsy for the first two parities among mothers younger than 20 years of age.[46]

Thus, whether because of biologic or environmental factors that affect the infant directly or indirectly through prematurity, the infant born to a teenage mother has a much higher risk than infants of somewhat older mothers of suffering specific severe handicaps.

Maternal Mortality

Maternal mortality rates have undergone radical and rapid declines over the last 30 years. In 1940, the rate was 376 per 100,000 live births; in 1968 it was 25. For whites, the rate dropped from 320 to 17 and for nonwhites from 774 to 64.[47] Although a large and rapid decline has occurred, nonwhite maternal mortality is nearly four times that of whites. Rates are lowest for women younger than 30 but increase rather sharply thereafter. Color differences in mortality increase steadily with maternal age.[48] Mortality among nonwhites is lowest (40.9 per 100,000 births) for women under 20 years of age, while for whites the rate for women aged 20-24 is slightly lower (11.0) than that of younger women (15.1). For women younger than 20 years, the color difference in maternal mortality is to a large extent due to differences in the death rates from three causes: toxemia (excluding abortion — 12.6 for nonwhites vs. 3.4 for whites), abortion with sepsis (7.8 vs. 1.8) and ectopic pregnancy (2.4 vs. 0.7). The rates for toxemia and for abortion with sepsis are approximately 50 percent higher for teenagers than for women 20-24 in each color group.

Complications of Pregnancy

The complications of pregnancy most frequently mentioned for young mothers are toxemia, prolonged labor and iron-deficiency anemia. Poor diets, late or inadequate prenatal care, and emotional and physical immaturity may well be contributing factors. Biologic immaturity appears to be a problem while the mother is still growing.[49] However, the now voluminous literature on the pregnant teenager overwhelmingly points toward social rather than medical problems as the primary concern.[50]

This rather uniformly negative review ends with a single favorable relationship involving teenage pregnancies. A cooperative study carried out in the United States, Greece, Wales, Yugoslavia, Brazil, Taiwan and Japan estimated that "women having their first child when aged under 18 years have only about one-third the breast cancer risk of those whose first birth is delayed until the age of 35 years or more."[51]

Social Aspects

An immediate consequence for pregnant adolescents is the often permanent disruption of schooling. One-third of 154 school systems with 12,000 or more students queried in 1968 by the Educational Research Service required girls to leave school as soon as it was known that they were pregnant.[52] An additional one-fifth forced them to leave well before the end of pregnancy. In 1970, a survey of 17,000 school systems found that scarcely one-third made any provisions for the education of pregnant school girls.[53] In Buffalo, of 123 girls excluded from school in 1963-1964 because of pregnancy, "101 wished to return to school and of these, 67 could not do so because of difficulties in making arrangements for care of their infants."[54]

Mothers who deliver babies out of wedlock represent a large segment of teenage mothers. Cutright estimated that, in 1966, 64 percent of white infants and 6.4 percent of nonwhite infants born out of wedlock were adopted. He also speculated that few, probably less than 10 percent, were legitimized by later marriage.[55] The problems of illegitimacy are beyond the scope of this article. Clearly, however, many teenage mothers must encounter them.

Meanwhile, the outlook for the premaritally pregnant is not auspicious. They represent a large proportion of teenage brides; estimates range from at least 25 percent of brides younger than 20 to more than half of 15-17-year-old brides.[56] A long-term study of a sample of white couples who had a first, second or fourth baby in Detroit in 1961 has described subsequent economic, social and demographic variables among the families.[57] The premaritally pregnant, who composed approximately one-fifth of the sample, were found in 1961, and still in 1965, to be economically disadvantaged in terms of occupation, income and assets when compared to other couples. This was not accounted for by shorter marital duration or younger age at marriage.[58] Neither was it accounted for by status of the parental families. In addition, the marital dissolution rate was higher for the premaritally pregnant (9.4 percent) than for other couples in the study (3.3 percent). This and other studies have shown that, in general, the divorce rates for teenage marriages are very high.[59] Furthermore, women who marry or have their first child very early in life tend to add children rapidly. For example, a 1965 study of child-spacing compares cumulative births by successive intervals since first marriage for women younger than 22 at marriage and for those who married at older ages.[60] Among women married between 1960 and 1964, the average number of children four years after marriage was 1.51 for the younger women as compared to 1.24 for women at least 22 years old at marriage. Similar findings come from the 1960 Census for narrower marital age categories.[61]

The only study found that examined the fertility experience of teenagers, irrespective of marital status, was carried out by J. Philip Keeve and his coworkers in a Middle Atlantic metropolitan county recently.[62] All birth certificates of infants born to mothers aged 12-19 and delivering between January 1, 1958 and December 31, 1967 were scrutinized. Successive births to the same mother were located and cohort fertility tables according to age at first birth constructed. For both color groups, the birthrates were higher in the inner city than in the surrounding county. Actual parity was underestimated since later births to girls who either married, left the area or delivered elsewhere could not be located by a study of this type. The data suggest that these girls were well on their way to having large and closely spaced families. Joe Wray examined exactly this situation, finding evidence that large family size is linked with decreased growth and intelligence as well as increased child mortality among the children, further evidence of problems linked to teenage childbearing.[63]

The Individual and Society

Two interrelated problems are clearly delineated here. First, infants of young mothers, especially very young ones, are subject to higher risks of prematurity, mortality and serious physical or intellectual impairments than children of older mothers. For mothers younger than age 18—and especially for those younger than 15 — biological as well as social influences appear to be important. For the teenager 18 and older the social aspects appear to affect pregnancy outcome most critically. Second, mothers and, perhaps, fathers and children are more likely to be disadvantaged in the socioeconomic sense and to find themselves in unstable family situations than those in families who postpone childbearing at least until the mother is in her early twenties. There is also an increased likelihood of high fertility. Demographic analyses indicate that, at any given time, the number of children a woman has borne is inversely related to her education and to other socioeconomic variables.[64] The evidence presented here supports the speculation that the clustering of highly fertile women in these groups may, at least partially, result from early childbearing.

The sequelae of early childbearing must concern anyone interested in the welfare of individuals. For society as a whole, the number of infants who have been born under circumstances deleterious to their development is a source of concern. These considerations of the welfare of individual human beings, and secondarily of society, surely overwhelm the question of population size. However, we should note that:

• If, at the 1968 level of population and age-specific birth and death rates, no births occurred to teenagers younger than 18, and if this reduced the birthrate among 15-19-year-olds by 30 percent, the population in 50 years would be five percent smaller than it would be if the teenage birthrates remained constant.

• If all births to teenage mothers were postponed, 75 percent until ages 20-24, and the remainder until 25-29, the population would be 6.6 percent smaller.

• If all teenage births were eliminated, the result would be a population 15.1 percent smaller than the size projected with unchanged rates. The net reproduction rate would be reduced from 1.16 to just over the stationary population value of 1.00.[65]

It seems reasonable to speculate that if postponing a first birth also reduces the rapidity with which successive ones occur, birthrates at older ages might also be reduced by postponing a large proportion of teenage births.

Any action with respect to preventing the sequelae of teenage childbearing must start from the belief that these are not inevitable consequences, totally dependent upon innate differences between women who have children while they are young, and the infants of these women, and women who postpone this activity, and their infants. The necessary assumption is that once a pregnancy occurs, the probabilities of prematurity, infant mortality and the social consequences can be altered, or that postponement of childbearing will itself alter these probabilities.

Age, in itself, may not be a direct causative factor in many of the problems associated with teenage pregnancy after a girl has reached full physical maturity at about age 18. Even if childbearing is postponed beyond age 20, unless social and economic conditions change for these young people, they may encounter the same difficulties at a later age. However, postponement of parenthood may increase the chances that these changes will occur.

References

1. U.S. Department of Health, Education and Welfare (DHEW), *Vital Statistics of the United States, 1968, Vol. I-Natality*, U.S. Government Printing Office, Washington, D.C. (GPO), 1970, Tables 1-49 and 1-51.

2. Ibid., Tables 1-26 and 1-51.

3. Ibid.; DHEW, *Vital Statistics of the United States, 1961, Vol. I-Natality*, GPO, 1963, Tables 2-9 and 2-12.

4. DHEW, 1970, op. cit., Table 1-25.

5. N. B. Ryder, "Nuptiality as a Variable in the Demographic Transition," paper presented at annual meeting of the American Sociological Association, 1960; H. B. Presser, "The Timing of the First Birth, Female Roles and Black Fertility," *Milbank Memorial Fund Quarterly*, 49:329, 1971; E. Pohlman, "The Timing of First Births: A Review of Effects," *Eugenics Quarterly*, 15:252, 1968.

6. Derived from unpublished data from the National Center for Health Statistics (NCHS), National Natality Survey, 1964-1966.

7. DHEW, 1970, op. cit., Table 1-26.

8. A. Campbell, "The Role of Family Planning in the Reduction of Poverty," *Journal of Marriage and the Family*, 30:236, 1968.

9. DHEW, 1970, op. cit., Table 1-6.

10. U.S. Bureau of the Census, "Fertility Indicators: 1970," *Current Population Reports*, Series P-23, No. 36, GPO, 1971, Table 11, p. 23; For complete discussion of illegitimacy, see: P. Cutright and O. Galle, "Illegitimacy: Measurement and Analysis," Vanderbilt University, Nashville, Tenn., 1966 (mimeo).

11. DHEW, 1970, op. cit., Table 1-26.

12. NCHS, 1964-1966, op. cit.

13. W. Pratt, "A Study of Marriages Involving Premarital Pregnancies," doctoral dissertation, University of Michigan, Ann Arbor, Mich., 1965.

14. E. Siegel and N. Morris, "The Epidemiology of Human Reproductive Casualties, with Emphasis on the Role of Nutrition," in Committee on Maternal Nutrition, Food and Nutrition Board, ed., *Maternal Nutrition and the Course of Pregnancy*, National Research Council of the National Academy of Sciences, Washington, D.C., 1970, p. 5.

15. Cf., e.g., Report of the Working Group, "Relation of Nutrition to Pregnancy in Adolescence," Committee on Maternal Nutrition, Food and Nutrition Board, 1970, op. cit., p. 163; J. A. Heady, C. Daley and J. N. Morris, "Social and Biological Factors in Infant Mortality, II. Variations of Mortality with Mother's Age and Parity," *Lancet*, 1:395, 1955.

16. Report of the Working Group, ibid.

17. H. Chase, "Infant Mortality and Weight at Birth: 1960 United States Birth Cohort," *American Journal of Public Health*, 59:1618, 1969.

18. S. Shapiro, E. Schlesinger and R. E. L. Nesbitt, Jr., *Infant, Perinatal, Maternal and Childhood Mortality in the United States*, Harvard University Press, Cambridge, Mass., 1968, p. 10.

19. Ibid., p. 23.

20. NCHS, "Infant Mortality Rates by Legitimacy Status: United States, 1964-1966," *Monthly Vital Statistics Report*, Vol. 20, No. 5, 1971.

21. J. A. Heady and J. N. Morris, "Social and Biological Factors in Infant Mortality. Variation of Mortality with Mother's Age and Parity," *Journal of Obstetrics and Gynaecology of the British Empire*, 66:577, 1959.

22. DHEW, *Vital Statistics of the United States, 1968, Vol. II — Mortality*, GPO, 1970, Part A, Table 3-4.

23. J. Loeb, *Weight at Birth and Survival of the Newborn, by Age of Mother and Total Birth Order, United States, Early 1950*, NCHS, Series 21, No. 5, 1965.

24. J. A. Heady and J. N. Morris, 1959, op. cit.; S. L. Morrison, J. A. Heady and J. N. Morris, "Social and Biological Factors in Infant Mortality. VIII. Mortality in the Postneonatal Period," *Archives of the Diseases of Children*, 34:101, 1959.

25. S. L. Morrison, J. A. Heady and J. N. Morris, ibid.

26. Ibid.

27. S. Shapiro, E. Schlesinger and R. E. L. Nesbitt, Jr., 1968, op. cit., p. 66; H. Chase, "The Relationship of Certain Biologic and Socio-Economic Factors to Fetal, Infant and Early Childhood Mortality. II. Father's Occupation, Infant's Birth Weight and Mother's Age," New York State Department of Health, Albany, N. Y., 1962 (mimeo).

28. D. Baird and A. M. Thompson, "General Factors Underlying Perinatal Mortality Rates," in N. Butler and E. Alberman, eds., *Perinatal Problems*, E. & S. Livingstone, London, 1969, Table 29, p. 27.

29. J. F. Donnelly, J. R. Abernathy, R. N. Creadick, C. E. Flowers, B. G. Greenberg and H. B. Wells, "Fetal, Parental, and Environmental Factors Associated with Perinatal Mortality in Mothers under 20 Years of Age," *American Journal of Obstetrics and Gynecology*, 80:663, 1960.

30. U. S. Bureau of the Census, "Childspacing," *U. S. Census of Population: 1960, Subject Reports*, Final Report PC(2)-3B, GPO, 1968, and "Marriage, Fertility and Childspacing, June, 1965," *Current Population Reports*, Series P-20 No. 186 GPO, 1969.

31. L. Bumpass, "Age at Marriage as a Variable in Socio-economic Differentials in Fertility," *Demography*, 6:45, 1969.

32. J. Wray, "Population Pressure on Families: Family Size and Childspacing," in Study Committee of the Office of the Foreign Secretary of the National Academy of Sciences, ed., *Rapid Population Growth*, Johns Hopkins Press, Baltimore, Md., 1971, p. 403.

33. S. Shapiro, E. Schlesinger and R. E. L. Nesbitt, Jr., 1968, op. cit., p. 47.

34. Ibid.

35. H. Chase, "Trends in 'Prematurity': United States, 1950-1967," *American Journal of Public Health*, 60:1967, 1970.

36. J. Loeb, 1965, op. cit.; H. Chase, "Infant Mortality and Weight at Birth . . . ," 1969, op. cit.

37. H. Chase, ibid., p. 1620.

38. J. Loeb, 1965, op. cit.

39. H. Chase, *International Comparisons of Perinatal and Infant Mortality. The United States and Six West European Countries*, NCHS, Series 3, No. 6, 1967, p. 28.

40. M. Kovar, *Variations in Birth Weight, Legitimate Live Births, United States, 1963*, NCHS, Series 22, No. 8, 1968.

41. G. Wiener and T. Milton, "Demographic Correlates of Low Birth Weight," *American Journal of Epidemiology*, 91:260, 1970.

42. A. Lilienfeld and B. Pasamanick, "Association of Maternal and Fetal Factors with the Development of Epilepsy. 1. Abnormalities in the Prenatal and Paranatal Periods," *Journal of the American Medical Association*, 155:719, 1954; A. Lilienfeld and E. Parkhurst, "A Study of the Association of Factors of Pregnancy and Parturition with the Development of Cerebral Palsy. Preliminary Report," *American Journal of Hygiene*, 53:262, 1951; B. Pasamanick and A. Lilienfeld, "Association of Maternal and Fetal Factors with the Development of Mental Deficiency. 1. Abnormalities in the Prenatal and Paranatal Periods," *Journal of the American Medical Association*, 159:155, 1955; M. Vernon, "Prematurity and Deafness: The Magnitude and Nature of the Problem among Deaf Children," *Exceptional Children*, 33:289, 1967; I. D. Goldberg, H. Goldstein, D. Quade and E. Rogot, "Association of Perinatal Factors with Blindness in Children," *Public Health Reports*, 82:519, 1967.

43. G. Wiener, "The Relationship of Birth Weight and Length of Gestation to Intellectual Development at Ages 8 to 10 Years," *Journal of Pediatrics*, 76:694, 1970; L. C. Eaves, J. C. Nuttall, H. Klonoff and H. G. Dunn, "Developmental and Psychological Test Scores in Children of Low Birth Weight," *Pediatrics*, 45:9, 1970; C. M. Drillien, "School Disposal and Performance for Children of Different Birthweight Born 1953-1960," *Archives of Diseases of Childhood*, 44:562, 1969; G. Wiener, R. Rider, W. Oppel, L. Fischer and P. Harper, "Correlates of Low Birth Weight: Psychological Status at Six to Seven Years of Age," *Pediatrics*, 35:434, 1965; S. H. Clifford, "High Risk Pregnancy I. Prevention of Prematurity the *Sine Qua Non* for Reduction of Mental Retardation and Other Neurological Disorders," *New England Journal of Medicine*, 271:243, 1964.

44. B. Pasamanick and A. Lilienfeld, "The Association of Maternal and Fetal Factors with the Development of Mental Deficiency: II. Relationship to Maternal Age, Birth Order, Previous Reproductive Loss and Degree of Deficiency," *American Journal of Mental Deficiency*, 60:557, 1956; R. Illsley, "The Sociological Study of Reproduction and Its Outcome," in S. A. Richardson and A. F. Guttmacher, eds., *Childbearing:*

Its Social and Psychological Factors, Williams and Wilkins, Baltimore, Md., 1967.

45. R. G. Record, T. McKeown and J. H. Edwards, "The Relation of Measured Intelligence to Birth Order and Maternal Age," and "The Relation of Measured Intelligence to Birth Weight and Duration of Gestation," *Annals of Human Genetics,* 33:61 and 71, 1969.

46. H. B. Newcombe and O. G. Tarendale, "Maternal Age and Birth Order Correlations," *Mutation Research,* 1:446, 1964.

47. U. S. Bureau of the Census, *Statistical Abstract of the United States, 1971,* GPO, 1971, Table 73, p. 55.

48. DHEW, *Vital Statistics of the United States, 1967, Vol. II — Mortality,* 1969, op. cit., Part A, Table 1-15.

49. Report of the Working Group, 1970, op. cit.; O. Stine and E. Kelley, "Evaluation of a School for Young Mothers: The Frequency of Prematurity among Infants Born to Mothers under 17 Years of Age, According to the Mother's Attendance of a Special School During Pregnancy," *Pediatrics,* 46:581, 1970.

50. For additional references see: National Library of Medicine Literature Search of Index Medicus, "The Pregnant Adolescent: Medical, Psychological and Social Care, January, 1967 through April, 1970."

51. B. MacMahon, P. Cole, T. N. Lin, C. R. Lowe, A. P. Mirra, B. Ravnihar, E. J. Salber, V. G. Valoaras and S. Yuasa, "Age at First Birth and Breast Cancer Risk," *Bulletin of the World Health Organization,* 43:209, 1970.

52. "Pregnant Teenagers," *Today's Education,* Vol. 59, 1970.

53. Ibid.

54. U. Anderson, R. Jenss, W. Mosher and V. Richter, "The Medical, Social and Educational Implications of the Increase in Out-of-Wedlock Births," *American Journal of Public Health,* 56:1866, 1966.

55. P. Cutright and O. Galle, 1966, op. cit.

56. U. S. Bureau of the Census, "Childspacing," 1968, op. cit., and "Marriage, Fertility and Childspacing, June, 1965," 1969, op. cit.; W. Pratt, 1965, op. cit.; P. Cutright and O. Galle, ibid.

57. R. Freedman and L. Coombs, "Childspacing and Family Economic Position," *American Sociological Review,* 31:631, 1966.

58. L. Coombs, R. Freedman, J. Friedman and W. Pratt, "Premarital Pregnancy and Status Before and After Marriage," *American Journal of Sociology,* 75:800, 1970; L. Coombs and R. Freedman, "Pre-marital Pregnancy, Childspacing, and Later Economic Achievement," *Population Studies,* 24:389, 1970.

59. L. Coombs and Z. Zumeta, "Correlates of Marital Dissolution in a Prospective Fertility Study: A Research Note," *Social Problems,* 18:92, 1970.

60. U. S. Bureau of the Census, "Marriage, Fertility and Childspacing . . . ," 1969, op. cit.

61. U. S. Bureau of the Census, "Childspacing," 1968, op. cit.

62. J. P. Keeve, E. Schlesinger, B. Wight and R. Adams, "Fertility Experience of Juvenile Girls: A Community-Wide Ten-Year Study," *American Journal of Public Health,* 59:2185, 1969.

63. J. Wray, 1971, op. cit.

64. U. S. Bureau of the Census, "Fertility Indicators: 1970," 1971, op. cit.

65. The projection program appears in E. van de Walle and J. Knodel, "Teaching Population Dynamics with a Simulation Exercise," *Demography,* 7:433, 1970.

12
The Social Consequences of Teenage Parenthood

Frank F. Furstenberg, Jr.

In recent years, there has been an upswing in social concern about early childbearing—that is, teenage parenthood has become less socially acceptable as it has become more publicly visible. Unfortunately, this surge of interest has not been matched by an expansion of information about the problem, or by the development of effective programs to help resolve it.

The widespread conviction that early childbearing precipitates a number of social and economic problems is founded, however, on surprisingly little evidence. Systematic research on the consequences of adolescent parenthood is virtually nonexistent. Nor is the narrow scope of existing studies on the consequences of adolescent parenthood their most serious shortcoming. The major defect is their failure to contrast the experiences of young mothers with those of their peers who avoid early parenthood.

Moreover, most existing research on the careers of adolescent mothers has concentrated on the immediate postpartum experience, offering little or no information on the long-range impact of the pregnancy.

In this article, we describe some of the findings of a six-year study of some 400 young adolescent mothers, their partners, progeny and parents. We explore when, how and why childbearing before the age of 18 jeopardizes the life prospects of the young mother and her child; and we compare the experiences of the young mothers to those of a peer group who managed to avoid premature parenthood.

The Baltimore Study

Between 1966 and 1968, interviews were conducted with every adolescent under the age of 18 and never before pregnant who registered at the prenatal clinic of Baltimore's Sinai Hospital.° A total of

This article is adapted from selected chapters of *Unplanned Parenthood: The Social Consequences of Teenage Childbearing*, The Free Press, Macmillan, 1976. The study on which the book and article are based was supported by the Maternal and Child Health Service, DHEW, Contract No. MC-R-420117-05-0.

°The study was originally conceived as a relatively short-term evaluation of the effectiveness of a special 'comprehensive' program for pregnant teenagers as compared to the hospital's regular prenatal program. The pregnant teenagers were assigned on a

Table 1. Design of the Baltimore study, 1966–1972

Interview schedule	Interview dates	Participants	Attempted interviews	Completed interviews*	
				No.	%
Time 1: during pregnancy	1966–1968	Adolescent mothers	404	404	100
		Grandmothers	379	350	92
Time 2: one yr. after delivery	1968–1970	Adolescent mothers	404	382	95
Time 3: three yrs. after delivery	1970	Adolescent mothers	404	363	90
		Classmates	361	268	74
Time 4: five yrs. after delivery†	1972	Adolescent mothers	404	331	82
		Children of adolescent mothers	331	306	92
		Classmates	307	221	82

*This category includes a small number of interviews that were excluded from the analysis because of a large amount of missing or falsified information.
†Interviews were also obtained with about one-third of the fathers at this time.

404 interviews were conducted.† Interviews were also completed with 350 (87 percent) of the mothers of the pregnant teenagers.

Only two of the adolescent mothers indicated unwillingness to participate in the study. Our population consisted almost exclusively of women residing in low-income households. Since Sinai was easily accessible to the black community in northwest Baltimore and many blacks could not afford private medical care, the women in our study were predominantly

random basis to either the special program or the regular clinic. Although there were some significant short-term differences in the two programs' effects on later fertility, the differences were largely attenuated after the first year, both because the special program was not geared to long-term assistance for the adolescent mothers and their children, and because the regular clinic program included many of the same services provided by the special program. Eventually, the study was broadened to become a six-year longitudinal study of the consequences of adolescent parenthood. In this article, no distinction is made between the young mothers who attended the special and the regular prenatal clinics.

†Details of the methodology may be found in Chapter 2 (p. 19) of *Unplanned Parenthood*.

black. However, the participants turned out not to be very different from the sample we might have expected had it been drawn from the entire population of pregnant adolescents who delivered a child in Baltimore during the period of the study.

The adolescent mothers were interviewed three times subsequently: one year after the child was born, again in 1970, and once again in 1972 when the child was about five years old.

Interviews were also attempted in 1970 with 301 of the former classmates of the adolescent mothers—women who had not become pregnant in early adolescence—in order to have a basis for assessing the impact of the very early pregnancy on the career of the young mother. We were able to contact more than 70 percent of the designated sample and to interview most of those whom we were able to locate. Only seven percent of the classmates we located refused to participate in the study. The classmates were reinterviewed in 1972.

We also attempted to follow up all of the fathers who could be located. How-

Table 2. Percent distribution of adolescent mothers and classmates by selected characteristics, Baltimore, 1966–1972

Characteristic	Adolescent mothers (N = 323)	Classmates (N = 221)
Age at Time 4*		
<20	11	12
20	17	19
21	30	24
22	26	26
≧23	15	19
Mean age	21.2	21.1
Race at Time 4*		
Black	91	87
White	9	13
Living arrangements of unmarried adolescents at Time 1		
Lived with both parents	51	59
Lived with mother	38	32
Lived with father	3	2
Lived with neither parent	8	7
Education of mother when present in home at Time 1†		
High school graduate	22	45
Not high school graduate	78	55
Education of father when present in home at Time 1†		
High school graduate	17	41
Not high school graduate	83	59
Occupational status of parents		
One or both skilled	20	27
Mother working	60	66
Neither parent working	20	7
Welfare status during childhood†		
No	76	83
Yes	24	17
Marital status at Time 1†		
Single	81	98
Married	19	2

*Five years after delivery.

†Information for adolescent parents was supplied at the first interview. The classmates reported the information at the second follow-up, three years after the adolescent mothers' delivery.

Note: Percents may not add to 100 because of rounding.

ever, we managed to find only slightly more than half of the 260 men for whom we had some residential information. Interviews were completed for only 33 percent of the fathers, over half of whom were residing with the young mothers and their children when the interviews took place.

In addition, interviews were attempted with all the firstborn children of the adolescent mothers and with the classmates' children who were at least 42 months old in 1972.° The attrition of the samples over the study period is summarized in Table 1.

In the original sample of pregnant adolescents, only 13 percent were white. At the completion of the study, the sample was even more homogeneous: Only nine percent of the women interviewed in the five-year follow-up were white. The whites who remained in the sample, no doubt, were not representative of all white adolescent mothers or even of those who originally entered the prenatal clinics at Sinai.

Table 2 compares the family backgrounds of the young mothers and their former classmates. With the exception of the educational achievement of their parents, the two samples accorded rather well. Like the young mothers, the classmates came mostly from working- and lower-class homes. Before their first child was born, the young women who found their way into the study population could not have been easily differentiated from their peers who managed to avoid such an early pregnancy. Premarital pregnancies even during adolescence had occurred among many of the classmates as well. Nearly half (49 percent) of

---

°Results of the study of the children are not reported in this article. They are discussed in Chapter 10 (p. 195) of *Unplanned Parenthood*.

them acknowledged at Time 4 (six years after initiation of the study) one or more pregnancies before marriage; about half occurred during adolescence, and one in three happened before the classmates turned 18. Thus, comparisons between the classmates and young mothers probably slightly understate the impact of an early and unplanned pregnancy on the subsequent life course, because some of the classmates shared this experience with the young mothers. In the analysis that follows, we subdivide the classmates by their premarital pregnancy experience wherever this breakdown affects the reported findings.

Becoming Pregnant

Most theories about the etiology of out-of-wedlock pregnancy, while differing significantly in their particulars, rest on the assumption that the unwed mother becomes pregnant because she is motivated, consciously or unconsciously, to have a child outside of marriage.

An alternative, but equally plausible, assumption is that most women who become unwed mothers do not engage in sexual activity for the purpose of becoming pregnant, but rather are initially recruited into the ranks of unwed motherhood without possessing any advance commitment. The data collected from the adolescents in the Baltimore study afforded an opportunity to examine the process leading up to unplanned pregnancy.

All of the young mothers in our study had initiated sexual intercourse by their early or mid-teens. About half of their classmates were sexually active by age 16, and 77 percent were no longer virgins before they reached the age of 20. (The proportions sexually active in this predominantly black population were similar to those found among U.S. black

teenagers of the same age by Kantner and Zelnik in the 1971 Johns Hopkins Study of Teenage Sexuality, Contraception and Pregnancy.[1]) It would appear, then, that in their sexual practices, the young mothers did not sharply diverge from their classmates or from the larger population of black adolescents.

Dating not only provided the adolescent with the opportunity, but often made it necessary for her to engage in sexual relations. Approximately one-fifth of the abstainers from sex compared to six percent of the nonvirgins did not date at all in early adolescence. Frequent dating over a long period of time is eventually accompanied by sexual intercourse, and few adolescents are able to remain sexually active for long before pregnancy occurs. We observed this pattern among the young mothers, who were unusually socially active at an early age. (At the time they conceived, nearly two-thirds of the adolescent mothers were going out at least several times a week.) Four out of five became pregnant within two years following the onset of intercourse, which typically occurred at age 15.* In addition to the likelihood that fecundity was low in this youthful population, a sporadic pattern of intercourse helped to reduce the probability of conception. Two-fifths of the young mothers indicated that they had had intercourse as frequently as once a week, and fewer than one-fifth had relations several times a week or more. These self-reports sug-

---

*This same pattern was evident among the classmates. They became sexually active several years later, but by age 20, half of those who had been sexually active in their teens had experienced a premarital pregnancy. Zelnik and Kantner reported almost identical figures. Nearly half of the black adolescents who had intercourse during their teens became pregnant before age 20. (See: M. Zelnik and J. F. Kantner, "The Resolution of Teenage First Pregnancies," *Family Planning Perspectives*, 6:74, 1974.)

gest an unsteady pattern of sexuality, and imply the lack of an advance commitment to becoming pregnant.*

Other studies have found that a majority of both adult and adolescent black women did not approve of premarital relations.[2] The data collected from our study were consistent with these findings. A substantial proportion of the pregnant adolescents and their parents disapproved of premarital sex. Nearly half of the mothers of the pregnant teenagers stated that they thought it was "very wrong" for a girl to have sexual relations before she married, and another quarter said they felt it was "somewhat wrong." The adolescents' views on premarital sex closely resembled those of their parents. Nearly half of the teenagers stated that it was very important for a woman to wait until marriage to have sex.

Undeniably, there was an obvious discrepancy between the words and the deeds of the respondents. Many of the parents and the youths were paying allegiance to a sexual code to which they were unable to adhere. This ambivalence made it especially difficult for these women to deal with the consequences of their sexual behavior.

Few of the adolescents in this population believed that they would or should marry before their early twenties. In the meantime, they were repeatedly provid-

*The figures on sexual activity also correspond to the incidence reports collected by Zelnik and Kantner. The respondents in their sample had a very low frequency of sexual activity, too. (See: M. Zelnik and J. F. Kantner, "Sexuality, Contraception and Pregnancy Among Young Unwed Females in the United States," in Commission on Population Growth and the American Future, *Demographic and Social Aspects of Population Growth*, C. F. Westoff and R. Parke, Jr., eds., Vol. 1 of Commission Research Reports, U.S. Government Printing Office, Washington, D.C., 1972, p. 355.)

ed with opportunities for sexual experience. While direct information on their boyfriends' views about premarital sex was not available, it is safe to assume that the men's views were considerably more permissive than those of the adolescent mothers. By age 14, two-thirds of the males were sexually active, and they reported more frequent and more varied sexual patterns than the females. It is not surprising, then, that when the pregnant teenagers were asked why a female begins to have sexual relations, the most common response was inability to successfully resist pressure from the male. It would be naive to believe the female is invariably the innocent and exploited victim of her boyfriend's dishonorable intentions. Nonetheless, under different circumstances, many women probably would wait at least until their late teens to begin having sexual relations. Only one-quarter of the adolescents thought that a female should have relations before age 18.

The young mothers invoked a number of justifications that permitted them to depart from their ideal norms. Seeing themselves as persuaded or coerced by their boyfriends was obviously one such rationalization. Another was the notion that "everyone else is doing it." (Indeed, this observation is nearly correct, and it is a testimony to the tenacity of ideal norms that they can survive at all in the face of widespread violation.) Another rationalization helped to offset the fear that negative consequences would result from sexual activity, namely, the belief, shared by most participants in our study, that they could avoid "getting caught." A number mentioned that they did not think it was possible to become pregnant "right away." Others thought that if they had sexual relations only "every once in a while," they would not become pregnant.* Finally, their behavior had a self-reinforcing quality. Because many were not yet fecund, as time went on they became increasingly convinced that they would not become pregnant. The longer they went without conceiving, the more likely they were to assume greater risks.

Fewer than one in four of the teenagers' mothers admitted that they had known that their daughters were having sexual relations prior to the pregnancy. As a check on whether the parents were misrecollecting their previous observations, those with other adolescent daughters residing in the home were asked if those children were sexually active. Only 16 percent of the parents suspected, or made a statement to the effect, that their nonpregnant teenage daughters were currently having sexual relations. Extrapolating from the figures provided by Kantner and Zelnik[3] on the incidence of sexual relations among teenagers, we found the mothers' estimates so low as to suggest that the parent has a certain stake in remaining misinformed. By so doing, she is able to preserve the fiction that her daughter is "staying out of trouble." This, in turn, releases her from the responsibility of having to take some action to prevent a pregnancy from occurring. Since most of the mothers did not know what measures to take even if they were aware of their child's sexual activity, they preferred to keep themselves uninformed.

---

*The study of Zelnik and Kantner documented in depressing detail the woefully inadequate knowledge of the reproductive process possessed by adolescents. In their study, fewer than one-third of the respondents could correctly state the time of the month when the risk of pregnancy is greatest. It is a reasonable assumption that the young women in our sample would not have fared as well as the average adolescent in that national study. (See: M. Zelnik and J. F. Kantner, "Sexuality, Contraception and Pregnancy . . . ," 1972, op. cit.)

So long as sexuality is safeguarded from public view, it poses little danger to either mother or daughter. Paradoxically, the techniques for concealment ultimately increase the risk of pregnancy. But it is important to recognize that from the point of view of the adolescent, using contraception may be extremely costly because it involves open acknowledgement of sexuality and thereby increases the threat of public exposure. Therefore, it was not surprising to find that prior to pregnancy, experience with birth control was quite limited.

Birth Control Knowledge, Experience

Most of the adolescents had some limited knowledge of birth control. Almost all were aware that drugs and devices to prevent conception existed; only six percent were unable to identify any method of birth control, and most were able to mention at least two or three techniques. This information, usually acquired from casual conversations with relatives and friends or through the mass media, was, however, extremely superficial. The young women tended to be most aware of those forms of birth control to which they had least access and about which they had only limited practical knowledge. Over 80 percent mentioned the pill as a "method of keeping you from having babies," but only two women had ever used oral contraceptives. In both instances, the pills had been borrowed from their mothers.

Whatever practical knowledge and experience the adolescents had with birth control was confined largely to "getting the boy to use something." More than half of these respondents (37 percent of the total sample) had had some experience with condoms. As with the other methods, however, experience for the most part had been sporadic; only 15 percent of the women reported that condoms had been used more or less regularly when relations occurred. There are many reasons for such irregular use, but by far the most common (mentioned by 54 percent of the users) was that the boyfriend was either unprepared or unwilling most of the time.

Parental Help

The lower class family is, if anything, even more puritanical and prudish about sexual matters than families with higher incomes.[4] Despite this, 59 percent of the mothers in our study had frequently attempted to talk to their daughters about sex, and 92 percent had had at least occasional discussions on the subject. It seems that most talks, however, involved the mother's admonishing her daughter not "to get mixed up with boys" or to do anything she would "be sorry for later."

Slightly more than 61 percent of the mothers and 45 percent of the daughters said that birth control had been explicitly discussed in the family. Quite clearly, however, most of the instruction was casual and oblique. Rarely were the adolescents told about effective contraceptive devices.

Even when the mothers did recognize the need for specific instruction, they could not offer much assistance. They were frequently poorly informed themselves, and at the time of the study in 1966, there was no place that a mother could send or take her teenage daughter for information. Thus, it is understandable that most mothers, if they provided instruction at all, were inclined to give only general advice and admonitions. Nevertheless, this limited instruction apparently had a definite impact. Fifty-two percent of the adolescents from families in which both the mother and the daughter reported discussing birth control had had some experience with contraception, compared to 23 percent from families in which no guidance was given. Moreover, the young mothers' reports revealed that the specific content of the discussion had a decided effect on whether or not birth control was practiced. If the mother had counseled her daughter to use a specific method (typically, she urged her daughter to insist that the male use a condom), the adolescent was more likely to have had some birth control experience. However, when contraceptive instruction was extremely vague, its effect on the adolescent's behavior was hardly greater than that of no instruction.

Apparently, then, the family can and does play a part in transmitting expectations about birth control use. In addition to imparting specific information, parents may promote contraceptive use for quite another reason. In raising the issue of contraception, the mother reveals an explicit awareness that her daughter is or may be having sexual relations. The adolescent, in turn, is allowed to acknowledge her own sexuality and hence may regard sex less as a spontaneous and uncontrollable act and more as an activity subject to planning and regulation.

The nature of the teenage couple's relationship greatly influenced whether and how often birth control was used. The single most important factor was the extent of involvement between the adolescent and her sexual partner. Contraception was much more likely to be practiced by couples who had a stable romantic relationship. Indeed, of those women who were still "going with" the fathers of their unborn babies at the time of the initial interview, nearly twice as many had attempted contraception as those whose relationships had been broken off for one reason or another.

Attitudes Toward Pregnancy

Only nine percent of the sample said that they had deliberately failed to use contraception in order to get pregnant. It is perhaps not surprising, therefore, that pregnancies were greeted by most adolescents and their parents with astonishment. Three-quarters of the adults reported that they were "very surprised" to learn their daughters were pregnant. A large number of the adolescents related this same feeling of disbelief.

Usually a feeling of despair accompanied the initial reaction of astonishment. Only one adolescent in five indicated that she had been happy about becoming pregnant. And even these women qualified their responses by saying that they felt "kind of good" or "sort of happy" about getting pregnant. Another fifth of the sample reported mixed feelings about becoming pregnant or indicated that they had not been affected much one way or the other. Three-quarters of the expectant mothers said they wished they had not become pregnant, and three-fifths stated their first reactions in unambivalently negative terms. Half of them could not bring themselves to tell their parents of the pregnancy for several months. More often than not, the adolescents never actually told their parents; the mothers learned about it elsewhere or detected it on their own.

By the time of first interview, 70 percent of the teenage parents indicated that they were feeling less negative about the pregnancy than they had been initially. However, fewer than one-third described themselves as "very happy"—scarcely an indication that parenthood was preceded by a commitment. Virtually the only women in the sample who were unambivalently positive about impending parenthood were to be found among the 20 percent who had married

by the time of the first interview. More than three times as many married as single women (51 percent versus 14 percent) classified their feelings as positive. It seems, then, that adolescents view pregnancy more favorably when it enhances, or at least does not diminish, their prospects for marriage. Yet even the married women retained many misgivings about becoming parents.

The classmate interviews conducted in 1970 provided some information on how unmarried, sexually active women in their late teens feel before conception about the possibility of having a child. In general, the sentiments of the sexually active classmates who had conceived corresponded to the retrospective reactions of the adolescent mothers at the initial interview. In each case, about two-thirds indicated that they had not wished to become pregnant.

Regardless of their feelings about becoming pregnant in the immediate future, few of the sexually active classmates at risk were using contraception on a regular basis. Although the interviews with the classmates were conducted in 1970, three years after the young mothers became pregnant, and the classmates accordingly were several years older than the young mothers had been at the time of the initial interviews, little had changed in the interim. Like the adolescent mothers, more than half (53 percent) of the classmates were leaving matters to chance; and many, no doubt, were soon to become premaritally pregnant. (By this time, more than two-thirds of the adolescent mothers were using contraception.)

Getting Married

Unwed motherhood is not the only possible consequence of premarital teenage pregnancy. Only one-third of premarital pregnancies to teenagers result in out-of-wedlock births; about half are terminated by induced or spontaneous abortion.[5]

Traditionally (although increasingly less so), marriage has been a popular so-

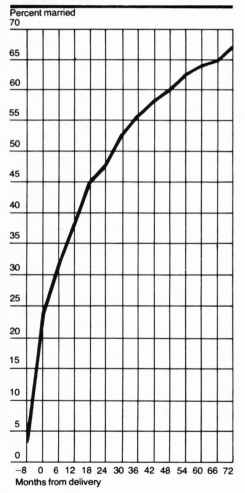

Figure 1. Percent of adolescent mothers married,* by months from delivery, Baltimore, 1966-1972

Percent married

*Cumulative probability using life table procedure.

lution to impending parenthood for the adolescent pregnant for the first time. We looked at the marriage patterns of the adolescent mothers who were interviewed at the five-year follow-up interview in 1972. Only three percent had been married at the time of conception, but nearly 20 percent had wed by the time of their first visit to the prenatal clinic, and by delivery nearly one-quarter of the mothers were married (see Figure 1). All but a few of these women had married the father of the child. By the five-year follow-up, just 36 percent of the young mothers remained single.

Of those who married, more than one-third had done so by the time of delivery, three-fifths by the one-year follow-up, and three-quarters within two years after delivery. These statistics underscore how significant the pregnancy was in determining the timing of matrimony, and strongly suggest that were it not for the birth, most of the marriages would not have taken place when they did.

The marriage patterns of the adolescent mothers and their classmates differed sharply. By age 18, only 21 percent of the classmates were married, as compared to 41 percent of the young mothers. The difference was sharper still for marriages that occurred among women not yet 18—30 percent versus 11 percent. Had the pregnancy not occurred, many fewer of the young mothers obviously would have married before the age of 18.

Premarital pregnancy was not a covert tactic used by the teenage mothers to bring about marriage. Most who married did so with obvious reluctance. Only one in three felt that the timing of her marriage corresponded with her wishes for the future. Fewer than one in three of those who were married by the five-year follow-up had wed at the age they considered to be most desirable. At the three-year follow-up, approximately two-thirds of those who were married claimed, in retrospect, that under normal circumstances they would have chosen to marry at a later age.

If most of the marriages that came about after conception were indeed forced, how can we explain the fact that some women succumbed to the pressure to marry while others resisted? The young mothers who had higher educational and career aims were more reluctant to jeopardize their plans by an early marriage. Indeed, only 10 percent of the most educationally ambitious students married before delivery, compared to 43 percent of the least ambitious, and a greater proportion were still single at the five-year follow-up (47 percent versus 23 percent). Similarly, the women who married early were less able students, and by their own accounts did not perform well in the classroom. Two-fifths of the women who married before delivery characterized themselves as "poor" or "so-so" students. By comparison, only one-third of the young mothers who deferred marriage and one-quarter of those who never married described their academic abilities in such negative terms.

The marriage rate began to rise sharply as the young mothers reached their late teens. By this time, they had had a chance to complete their education and to gain some working experience. More important, the fathers were beginning to find steady employment, suggesting that the economic situation of the males was an important determinant in the decision to wed and in the timing of marriage.

The Economics of Marriage

Two-thirds of the single teenagers indicated during their pregnancy that there was at least a good chance that they would eventually marry the father of the child. Even a year after delivery, half of those women who were still single reaffirmed this intention.

These projected marriages took place among nearly half of the young mothers who were unmarried at the time of conception. Indeed, of all the marriages that occurred during the study period (involving two-thirds of the sample), 70 percent were between the teenager and the father of her child.

Most of the participants in our study, however, wanted to marry the father of the child only *if* and *when* they thought he would be capable of supporting a family. Although direct evidence on the attitudes of the male was lacking, his willingness to marry the mother perhaps depended on similar considerations.[6]

Marriage was much more likely to occur during the prenatal period if the father held a full-time job. Among the men working full-time, 34 percent married before delivery; whereas the rate of prenatal marriage among the unemployed males was only four percent. This helps to explain why a large number of marriages occurred in the two years following delivery. By this time, a higher proportion of the males were in their late teens or early twenties, and many had obtained a job; similarly, the young mothers often had completed their schooling, and a number were employed. Only 31 percent of those 15 or younger at conception ultimately married the father of the child, compared to 53 percent of the 17-year-olds. The boyfriends of the younger women more often were school dropouts and were less likely to find steady jobs than the other fathers.

Conjugal Careers

Most of the young mothers found it difficult to resist matrimony for very long. After a year or two of protracted courtship negotiations, many women simply decided that it was time to "give it a try." Although their chances for success were minuscule, it is not surprising that they were willing to assume the risks, given their problematic and often deteriorating economic situations.

Figure 2. Percent of adolescent mothers and classmates* separated,† by number of months from marriage date, Baltimore, 1966-1972

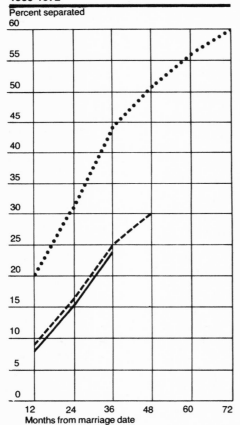

Percent separated

Months from marriage date

●●●●●●● Adolescent mothers
------- Classmates
――――― Classmates not premaritally pregnant

*Probability not reported when base <10.
†Cumulative probability using life table procedure.

Other studies have shown consistently that premarital pregnancy greatly increases the probability of eventual marital dissolution.[7] The mothers in this study proved no exception. Figure 2 shows the mortality of marriages entered into by the young mothers and their classmates. Among the former, marriages that took place during the study had less than an even chance of surviving beyond the first four years. About one-fifth of the marriages broke up within one year and nearly one-third were dissolved within two years. Three out of five of the marriages were destined to break up within six years.

By any standard, these rates are incredibly high. Carter and Glick[8] reported that in a population of white women married for at least 10 years by 1960, about 13 percent of the marriages had dissolved; the figure for nonwhites, 28 percent, was high, but still less than half that for teen mothers in our sample.

The rate of marital breakup among the classmates was only about half as great as the rate for the adolescent mothers during the first three and one-half years of marriage. After two years of marriage, the mothers had already experienced a higher proportion of marital dissolution (32 percent) than the classmates had after four years of marriage (30 percent). When the classmates who had married after conception were separated out, the differences were even more striking, as Figure 2 shows. Among those who had not conceived premaritally, the probability of the marriage breaking up within the first two years was half that calculated for the adolescent mothers. Apparently, the mothers were especially disadvantaged in marriage because their pregnancies had occurred earlier in adolescence than those of the classmates, raising the possibility that marrying young in itself reduces conjugal stability.

Resources and Marital Stability

Almost all existing studies show that economic resources are strongly linked to marital stability. The willingness of black women to work at menial jobs that are poorly paid, dirty and irregular creates a double problem in the family. The husband feels that his role as provider is being undercut; his wife, at the same time, is likely to resent his inability to support the family.

There is every reason to suspect that this situation was common within our sample. Most of the married men were young, inexperienced and unskilled. More than one out of every four women explicitly attributed the failure of her marriage to her husband's inability to support his family. As a rough measure of their earning potential, we classified husbands as lower status if they had not completed high school and held an unskilled job. High school graduates and/or skilled workers were classified as higher status. This crude index turned out to be the single best predictor of marital stability. Among the lower status males, the probability of separation within two years of the wedding date was .45, while it was only .19 for the men classified as higher status.

This finding strongly suggests that the most important link in the chain between an unplanned pregnancy and later marital failure is the weak economic position of the male who fathers a child out of wedlock or marries a single mother. Most of these men have a low earning potential before they ever wed. An ill-timed marriage may further limit their prospects for economic advancement by compelling them to terminate school and enter the labor force under less than favorable circumstances. Consequently, the fathers of unscheduled children are hard-pressed to find good jobs.

One way of putting this speculation to the test is to compare the economic status of the men who married the classmates with the spouses of the young mothers. There was a noticeable difference in status level between the two groups of men, especially after we separated out the couples who married following a premarital pregnancy. Half the husbands of the young mothers were in the higher socioeconomic category, as compared to three-fifths of the spouses of the premaritally pregnant classmates and 85 percent of the husbands of those classmates who married before becoming pregnant.

The Aftermath of Marital Experience

Although our study spanned only five years in the lives of the young mothers, our data suggest that a substantial proportion of the separated women will be permanently disinclined to marry as a result of their first unsuccessful attempt. Only one-fifth of the women whose marriages were no longer intact at Time 4 were divorced, although over half had been separated for two or more years, providing ample time for a formal termination of the marriage. Most remained technically married even after four or more years of separation. The majority showed no inclination to divorce although they no longer considered their marriages to be binding.

The major reason for the low incidence of divorce among the sample, apparently, is that few of the young women had current plans to marry again. However, women like those in our study also face certain objective barriers to remarrying. Most of the adolescent mothers had at least two children by the time their marriages broke up, a situation which presents a formidable challenge to the earning power of potential mates.

Table 3. Cumulative probability of subsequent pregnancies among adolescent mothers, by marital status at Time 4 (1972)

Mo. of exposure	Total	Ever-married	Never-married
2nd pregnancy	(N = 319)	(N = 199)	(N = 120)
12	.23	.29	.15
24	.43	.52	.28
36	.55	.66	.38
48	.62	.73	.44
60	.66	.76	.51
3rd pregnancy	(N = 210)	(N = 150)	(N = 55)
12	.27	.26	.32
24	.39	.41	.35
36	.47	.52	.47
48	.56	.60	.40*

*Too few women for calculation of probability.

To add to her difficulties, the young mother usually has limited economic assets to contribute to a new marriage.

Ironically, most of the young mothers who managed to avoid single parenthood by marrying either before or shortly after delivery ended up as single parents several years later. And many of these women no doubt will never remarry. Therefore, it might be said that once an unplanned pregnancy occurs in adolescence, it hardly matters whether the young mother marries. In time, she may be almost as likely as the unwed mother to bear the major, if not the sole, responsibility for supporting her child.

Further Childbearing

Although some teenagers welcome a second child soon after the first, even when the initial pregnancy was unplanned, the second child more often represents a major setback to the future plans of the young mother, damaging especially her prospects of economic self-sufficiency. Existing evidence seems to support the prevailing belief that a pregnancy in early adolescence signals the beginning of a rapid succession of unwanted births. Al-though estimates vary, depending on the experiences of the women following the first birth, most published studies show that at least one-half of teenage mothers experience a second pregnancy within 36 months of delivery.[9]

Explanations of why adolescent mothers often become pregnant again shortly after the birth of the first child have been based largely on speculation. Not surprisingly, the commentaries are reminiscent of the disputes over the etiology of unplanned parenthood. One school of writers argues that the high parity of teenage parents is consonant with their cultural aspirations and life-styles. They become pregnant again primarily because they want additional children.[10] Sharply diverging from this position are the researchers who contend that childbearing patterns reflect not parental aspirations but the availability of resources for controlling unwanted pregnancies. These authors assert that more family planning services would sharply reduce repeat pregnancies.[11]

Family Size Expectations and Behavior

Nearly all of the first pregnancies to the mothers in our study were unplanned, and most were unwanted at the time conception occurred.* One year after delivery, the entire sample was asked when they planned to have their next child: Only six percent said they hoped to become pregnant again "soon"; at three years after delivery, only seven percent said they were hoping to have another child at the time. Had the young mothers been successful in implementing their

*Nine percent said that prior to the conception, they had not used contraception because they wanted to become pregnant. Twenty-three percent said that they had wished to become pregnant at "some time" when they engaged in sexual relations.

childbearing aims, the rate of second pregnancies during the study, particularly in its early years, would have been extremely low.

In fact, the gap between family size intention and experience was considerable. A year after the birth of the first child, almost 80 percent of the sample hoped to wait at least three more years before becoming pregnant again. Fewer than half of them managed to realize this goal. Not only did many women experience timing failures in the birth of their second child, but within five years after delivery, some women had already reached or exceeded the total number of children they wanted to have ever, although they were still in their early twenties. Asked at the time when they would like to have their next child, more than one-quarter of the young mothers declared "never."

Figure 3 shows that within five years of delivery of their first child, 30 percent of the adolescent mothers had become pregnant again at least twice. (Within this subgroup, a substantial proportion—10 percent of the entire sample—had had at least three additional conceptions.) Thirty-seven percent of the respondents had one further pregnancy during the study period, and the remaining third had not conceived again. As some indication of the unacceptability of the repeat conceptions, the rate of abortion rose sharply with increased parity, though most of the reported pregnancies came to term.

Table 3 presents a life table of the cumulative probability of becoming pregnant a second and a third time. Nearly all of the ever-married women were running well ahead of their desired family size schedules. Very few of the single women expressed a desire to have another child before marrying, yet most became pregnant again out of wedlock.

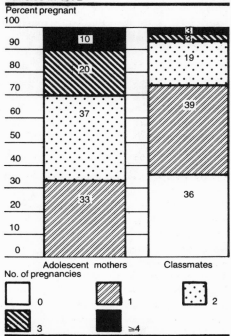

Figure 3. Percent of adolescent mothers and classmates pregnant, by number of pregnancies in 1972

Within the total sample, nearly one woman in four became pregnant again within 12 months of the birth of the first child. By three years, half of the women with two children had become pregnant a third time. Only one woman in five who had become pregnant a second time within three years after delivery reported she had been hoping for a second child; half stated that they had not wanted to become pregnant again. Only 10 percent of those with three pregnancies had been planning to become pregnant a third time. In fact, most of the young mothers in our sample were not able to regulate their fertility to conform to their desires.

When the classmates were first interviewed in 1970, when they were about 19, nearly two-thirds had never been pregnant and almost all who had become pregnant had done so in the preceding 24 months. Two years later, slightly over half of the single classmates and four-fifths of those who were married had conceived at least once. Still, they were well behind the adolescent mothers in number of pregnancies. By this time, two-thirds of the young mothers had had at least two pregnancies, and nearly one-third had had three or more. By contrast, only one-quarter of the classmates had become pregnant more than once, and only six percent had conceived three or more times. The young mothers who never married had, on the average, 1.09 more pregnancies than the single classmates; the difference among the marrieds was 0.66.*

Education and Childbearing Patterns

The women in our study most highly committed to education and those who returned to school immediately following the delivery of their first child were much less likely to experience a second conception in the 12-month period after the birth. Even after four years, the women who returned to school had lower rates of second pregnancy than those who did not.

Two-fifths of the women who quit school after their first child was born had at least two more pregnancies, while only one-quarter of the women who returned to school had an equally high rate of reconception. This was especially true for the unmarried.† Women may defer

---

*Given equal fecundity, the classmates were somewhat more inclined to resort to abortion, although this tendency perhaps reflected the increased availability of abortion in the later years of the study.

†Half of the unmarried dropouts had at least two more conceptions during the study, as compared to only 11 percent of those who returned to school.

childbearing in order to attain their educational goals, but they may also discontinue their educations when they fail to prevent an unwanted pregnancy. Accordingly, we found (even holding educational ambition constant) that women remain in school (at least until graduation) if they are able to defer further childbearing.

It is often said that public assistance encourages childbearing out of wedlock because it provides a means of supporting additional children for unmarried women. The "broodsow myth," as Placek and Hendershot [12] so aptly labeled it, received no confirmation from our data. The welfare mother was not significantly more likely to become pregnant again after she went on relief than the young mother who was not receiving public assistance. Among the single mothers, 42 percent of those on welfare three years following delivery became pregnant again within the next two years, as compared to 38 percent of the women who were not on relief. Among the ever-married women, the difference was somewhat larger, 50 percent versus 38 percent, but was still relatively trivial.

The similarity in fertility of the welfare and the nonwelfare groups suggests that there is no reason to single out the welfare mother as incapable of regulating her childbearing. She does about as well as her peers who are not on welfare.

Birth Control Experience

A substantial shift in knowledge and sentiments about contraception took place between the gestation period and the one-year follow-up. A year after delivery, the adolescent mothers were much more likely to endorse birth control; they had fewer reservations about the effectiveness of contraception, and they were much more confident about the safety of birth control pills. The patterns of change had as much to do with general experience acquired during pregnancy as with participation in the prenatal clinics.

Initial use of birth control was high—88 percent of the young mothers practiced contraception during the year after their first child was born. Only two (four percent) of the nonusers reported that their abstention resulted from their desire to become pregnant again.

However, among those who began to practice contraception after the birth of their first child, more than one-third had abandoned birth control after one year; nearly two-thirds by two years. By the five-year follow-up, only about one woman in five had used contraception continuously during the entire study. If those women who never used birth control are included, the figure drops still lower (see Table 4).

All of the young women had attended one of the Sinai programs which offered contraceptive information and services. The relatively low rate of contraceptive continuation after exposure to the clinic programs is typical of the rates reported from family planning programs for pregnant and postpartum adolescents throughout the country.[13] Most participants discontinue contraceptive use after a short period. Typically, at least one woman in three discontinues birth control within one year. The experience of the young mothers in our study was consistent with these findings.

Overall, women who wed were much less likely to use birth control at any given point in the study. Six months after delivery, more than one-fifth of the ever-married women who had begun using contraception stopped; one-tenth of the single women did likewise. Close to half of the women who married during the study had stopped using contraception

Table 4. Cumulative probability of birth control continuation among adolescent mothers at Time 4 (1972)

Mo. in clinic program	Total (N = 380)	Users only (N = 331)
12	.56	.64
24	.33	.38
36	.25	.29
48	.20	.24
60	.19	.22

by two years after delivery, while more than three-quarters of the single women were still practicing birth control. Therefore, the rate of continuation was about twice as high for the women who remained single. It is little wonder that the rates of pregnancy diverged so sharply in the two populations.

Women with high educational goals and women who returned to school were more likely to adopt some method of contraception following delivery and to practice it more faithfully thereafter than dropouts and women with low educational ambitions. However, even single women who returned to school or went to work and explicitly expressed a desire not to become pregnant again discontinued contraceptive use at a substantial rate. Three years after delivery, more than half of these young mothers had stopped using birth control.

Reasons for Contraceptive Termination

At each follow-up, the young mothers who had stopped using contraception were asked why they had abandoned birth control. As may be seen in Table 5, it was rare for a young mother to indicate that she had done so in order to become pregnant. Just as uncommon was explicit expression of a casual or indifferent attitude toward the prospect of pregnancy. Even when combined, the women in these two categories never constituted

Table 5. Percent distribution of adolescent mothers reporting various reasons for discontinuation of contraception at Times 2, 3 and 4 (1968–1972)

Reason	Time 2 (N = 96)	Time 3 (N = 137)	Time 4 (N = 76)
Desired pregnancy	6	9	15
Didn't care	16	7	8
Little or no sex	10	7	4
Personal reservations	4	8	8
Problem with method	51	58	55
Other	13	12	11

Note: Percents may not add to 100 because of rounding.

more than about one-fifth of those who discontinued. Few women were deliberately attempting to become pregnant again during the follow-up years.

As Table 5 shows, only a small proportion stated that they did not need to use birth control because they engaged in little or no sexual activity. A few cited personal (mostly religious or moral) reservations about contraception. But by far the most common explanation for terminating use (reported by more than half of those who discontinued) was that specific problems had arisen with the method of contraception they were using. In some instances, women mentioned physical problems that they had encountered from the outset — a heavy menstrual flow, nausea, pain or weight gain; but more often they referred to the fear of negative side effects — sterility, cancer or thrombosis. From their comments, it is obvious that many had become frightened by reports in the mass media about the hazards of oral contraceptives or intrauterine devices.

Postpartum contact with the hospital was decidedly linked to contraceptive continuation. Discussions with the staff about how the birth control method was working out were especially critical for continued use. The number of discussions was related directly to the rate of continuation. Follow-up sessions provided an opportunity for the young mother to bring up problems she was having in using birth control, and gave her a chance to allay anxieties about physical reactions to the method of contraception. The discussions also reinforced the resolve to use birth control, countering the inclination to take risks. Many of the mothers needed this reinforcement in order to put up with the initial discomfort or inconvenience of using birth control methods.

After the first year, follow-up was very infrequent. It was up to the mothers to take the initiative in making contact. Few did, and those who continued to visit the clinic were a highly selective group consisting mainly of the single women who had remained in school. Consequently, this group had the highest rate of contraceptive continuation.

In view of the importance of follow-up, why did the clinics not make a greater effort to maintain contact with former participants? In the first place, the problem of maintaining commitment to birth control use was not foreseen by the individuals who designed the program. It was taken for granted that if the young mother wanted to prevent a subsequent pregnancy and was given contraceptive instruction, she would use birth control effectively until she was prepared to have another child. Her ability to use contraception was greatly overestimated, and the staff did not foresee the problems that arise when birth control is practiced by the inexperienced and wary. Finally, the program was designed to provide services in the prenatal and early postpartum periods, and it was not sufficiently flexible to extend services beyond the first year. Clearly, this "inoculation approach" did not work out very well.

Early Parenthood and Schooling

Between one-half and two-thirds of all female dropouts cite pregnancy and/or marriage as the principal reason for leaving school.[14]

The policy of the U.S. Office of Education that every pregnant adolescent has a right to continue her education[15] has not as yet led to the creation of facilities and supportive services to ensure that right.[16] Opportunities for school-age parents vary enormously throughout the country. In some localities, teenagers are pressured to leave school as soon as it is known that they are pregnant, and no alternative education is provided. In other areas, special services are offered to the teenager who becomes pregnant, and she is encouraged to continue her education at home or in separate facilities for pregnant adolescents. Finally, an increasing number of school districts are permitting the expectant mother to attend regular classes.

While some educators justify their exclusion of pregnant teenagers on the ground that only special educational programs can meet their particular needs, relatively few programs of this nature exist. In 1967, there were 35 such programs throughout the country. By 1972, as a result of governmental efforts, the number had climbed to about 225, but these programs were serving only one out of five pregnant students.°[17]

As may be seen in Table 6, five years after delivery, the adolescent mothers in our sample were split almost evenly between women who had dropped out and those who had graduated from high school. Before terminating, nearly half

---

°There are no official estimates, but Shirley A. Nelson, director of the Consortium on Early Childbearing and Childrearing, estimates that by the beginning of 1975, there may have been 350 programs reaching one pregnant student in three.

Table 6. Percent distribution of adolescent mothers and of classmates premaritally pregnant (PMP) and not premaritally pregnant, by educational achievement at Time 4 (1972)

Education	Adolescent mothers (N= 323)	Classmates	
		PMP (N= 113)	Not PMP (N= 107)
Not high school graduate	51	18	11
Never returned	23	0	0
Returned, no longer in school	20	14	9
Returned, still in school	8	4	2
High school graduate	49	82	89
Never returned	7	0	0
Returned, no longer in school	33	65	62
Returned, still in school	9	17	27

of the dropouts had made some attempt to complete their schooling, and 16 percent of the nongraduates were still enrolled in school.

It is obvious that pregnancy was not being used as a convenient excuse to drop out of school; 70 percent of the sample resumed school after delivery. It is equally apparent that teenage parenthood per se is not an insurmountable barrier to educational achievement; half of the sample completed high school, others were close to graduating at the five-year follow-up, and a small minority had gone past high school.

Yet, against the young mothers' own educational goals, their achievements did not measure up quite so well. All but 10 adolescents reported that they hoped to complete high school, and nearly half looked forward to some type of higher education. While many conceded that in all likelihood these aspirations would not be realized, 84 percent still expected to complete high school, and over one-quarter anticipated finishing some higher education. A large number of the young mothers failed to reach their expected goals.

By contrast, nine out of 10 of the classmates had completed high school by the time of the five-year follow-up, and one-fifth of those who had not graduated were still in school. More than one-quarter of the classmates had obtained some amount of higher education. Perhaps it was merely coincidence, but after five years the classmates had achieved almost exactly the level of education that the young mothers in the initial interview had stated that they expected to reach by that time. This comparison indicates that the impact of pregnancy on educational achievement was substantial. On the average, the adolescent mothers had had approximately two fewer years of schooling than the classmates by the five-year follow-up.

Our evidence consistently showed that the young mothers as a group were not conspicuously incompetent or disaffected students. Three out of four were at the grade level appropriate to their age. The great majority reported that they enjoyed school, did moderately well and wanted to return to school after delivery. Most did in fact return to school after their child was born. At the same time, ambition, academic performance and family expectations all were highly predictive of whether the young mother remained in school until graduation. Most of those who did drop out had been marginal students before becoming pregnant, and probably some of them would have left school even if they had managed to avoid early parenthood. But nearly half of the dropouts were at least

moderately able students and were unequivocally committed to obtaining a high school diploma.

If the first pregnancy disrupts the educational career of the young mother, additional childbearing generally brings it to an abrupt halt. With each successive pregnancy, the proportion of dropouts rose, and among those women who had three or more subsequent pregnancies, 85 percent had left school before obtaining a high school diploma. In contrast, only one-third of the young mothers who did not become pregnant again during the course of the study failed to complete high school. In most instances, multiparae managed to complete high school only if their schooling had ended before the birth of the second child.

Economic Career of the Young Mother

The stereotype of the unwed mother as a welfare dependent serves to remind the public of the costs of a disorderly family career. Whether or not this stereotype is accurate is a separate issue. But to verify this assertion one must do more than show that a large number of women who are economically dependent have a history of premarital pregnancy.

At the five-year follow-up, we asked the young mothers how much money they had received during the past year and where they had gotten it. One-quarter of the respondents had obtained most, if not all, of their income from working. Welfare barely edged out income from spouse as the second most common source of support.

Four types of support—self-support, welfare, husband's income and economic partnership in marriage—encompassed all but about four percent of the women. Half the respondents were currently employed. About two-thirds of these women carried the major burden of supporting the family. In total, three out of five young mothers either were self-supporting or were nonworking women married to wage-earning males. These young mothers were clearly in an economically precarious position. Nearly half were living below the 1972 poverty level of $4,275 for a nonfarm family of four.

The classmates reported an almost identical number of income sources. However, they were more likely to be working (63 percent versus 48 percent) and were more often completely self-supporting if they worked. At the five-year follow-up, only 15 percent of the classmates were receiving welfare payments, and only five percent depended completely on public assistance. This figure was just one-third as great as the proportion of adolescent mothers who obtained all of their income from welfare.

The dissimilarity between the groups became even more visible when we subdivided the classmates according to whether or not they had experienced a premarital pregnancy. While one-third of the young mothers were receiving at least one-fifth of their income from welfare, only four percent of the classmates who had not conceived premaritally relied at all on public assistance. Moreover, a much higher proportion of the classmates who had not had a prenuptial conception contributed substantially to their own support (70 percent versus 45 percent) through employment.

In addition, the median annual per capita income of the classmates who had not conceived before marriage ($1,000) was two-thirds greater than that of the young mothers ($600).

The young mothers divided evenly into those who worked and those on welfare. Almost two-thirds were on welfare at some time during our study. At the last follow-up, two-fifths of the women were

receiving relief, so that 36 percent of the women who had had welfare experience were no longer on the rolls. Most of the women who were on welfare at the five-year follow-up were not long-term recipients. Slightly more than one-half of this group had been on welfare for more than 12 months, and only one-third had been on welfare for 30 months.

Past work experience was not a shield against economic dependency when employment terminated. Five years after delivery, the young mothers who had been working at previous points in the study were just as likely to be on relief, if they did not then hold jobs, as were those who had no past employment record. Going on welfare is a specific response to unemployment, not a reflection of unwillingness to seek work; it is not motivation but jobs that are lacking. The vast majority of young mothers on assistance expressed an unequivocal desire to work if given the opportunity: 79 percent indicated that they would take a job immediately if offered one. Moreover, three-quarters indicated that they would be content to find an 'unskilled' job, and very few expected to be hired for a job for which they were not then qualified. Almost two-thirds of the mothers on welfare stated that lack of child care facilities was the reason that they were unable to work.

Welfare mothers generally had large families and young children, a circumstance that decreased their ability to make use of child care options since it was difficult to arrange for care for several young children outside the home. Moreover, welfare mothers were less likely than working women to report that a relative in the home or nearby would be available if a job opened up. Most of the working mothers in our sample were able to call upon relatives to care for their children. Fewer than one-quarter had to resort to babysitters or day-care facilities. Since day-care arrangements are costly, it would seem that a supportive kinship network is one of the critical factors in determining whether a young mother is forced to rely on welfare.

Work Patterns

At the time of the first interview, only five percent of the adolescents were employed, and in most instances they held either part-time or irregular jobs. A year after delivery, one in four held a regular job. More than one-third were working by the three-year follow-up, and at the last interview, just under one-half of the mothers were working—almost all (89 percent) of them full-time. About three-quarters of the women who were not employed at the five-year follow-up were available for work. At that time, 43 percent of the young mothers who had not had an additional child had been employed steadily for the past two years, as compared to only about 10 percent of the multiparous women. Indeed, over half of the young mothers with at least two children had never worked during the five years of the study. Marital status was largely irrelevant to work patterns when childbearing was held constant.

Larger family size, of course, further complicates the already difficult problem of arranging for child care. The presence of a young child presents a further barrier to employment. Two-thirds of the women were working if they had no child younger than four. By contrast, only 20 percent of the mothers were employed when their youngest was not yet two. Having an additional child, however, regardless of his or her age, may deter employment. Since welfare benefits increase with each child, many women in our study found it impossible to locate a job that provided significantly

more income than public assistance, especially if they lacked education and experience.

Managing Motherhood

From the three follow-up interviews and information from hospital records, we constructed a fairly complete history of mother-child separations. Formal separations were relatively rare, and in only a few cases were they permanent. Five years after delivery, just four of the young parents (one percent of the sample) had elected to give up their children for adoption. In addition to these cases, approximately 10 percent of the children were known to have lived apart from their mothers at one or more points during the study. At the time of the last interview, 21 children (6.8 percent of the 307 who were still alive) were not residing with their mothers.

A large number of mothers reported that another individual shared with them the responsibilities of caring for the child. Slightly fewer than half of the mothers said that they alone were the principal caretaker.

A single factor accounted almost completely for the pattern of caretaking that was established five years after the delivery. Only five percent of the women who were working reported that they were the principal caretaker; while nearly all (82 percent) of the nonworking mothers said that they took care of their children most of the time. The longer a woman had worked, the more likely she was to turn over child care responsibilities to someone else, particularly to a person who resided outside the home.

Most of the women who were not the principal caretaker managed to spend a good deal of time with their children. Our data indicate that the full-time mothers spent an average of only 10 hours a week more with their oldest child than did the mothers who shared child care with someone else. Once again, our findings appear to conflict with the argument that adolescent mothers prefer to entrust their maternal responsibilities to another person.

Relatively few of the young mothers could be classified by any standard as rejecting parents. Although most of the adolescents had negative reactions to becoming pregnant, 85 percent of them were rather content with motherhood after the child was born.

On the basis of our tentative results, it would be unreasonable to claim that adolescent mothers adjust to parenthood as easily as women who become pregnant when they are more mature. Our findings do, however, challenge the assumption that early parenthood usually leads to childrearing problems.

Paternal Involvement

More than three-fifths (63 percent) of the fathers were maintaining relations with their children at the five-year follow-up. While only one-fifth were actually living with their children, another fifth saw the children at least once a week, and the remaining fifth visited their children on an irregular basis.

A relatively high proportion of the couples who had never married maintained cordial relations — 30 percent of the unmarried fathers who lived outside the home visited regularly. However, none of the children saw their fathers regularly, and only seven percent had even occasional contact, if the mother had married a man other than the father.

Our data provide little support, however, for the contention that the absence of the father from the home adversely influences the mother's adaptation to parenthood. Neither marriage pattern

nor paternal involvement was related to either maternal commitment or performance as reported in the five-year follow-up interview.

Social Policy and the Teenage Parent

In our investigation we discovered a sharp and regular pattern of differences in the marital, childbearing, educational and occupational careers of the adolescent mothers as compared to their classmates. The young mothers consistently experienced greater difficulty in realizing life plans; a gaping disparity existed between the goals they articulated in the first interview and their experiences following delivery. In contrast, we found that the classmates, especially those who did not become pregnant premaritally during the five years of our study, had a far better record of achieving their immediate objectives in life. The early pregnancy created a distinct set of problems for the adolescent parent that forced a redirection of her intended life course. In particular, we established a number of links connecting early childbearing to complications in marriage, to disruption of schooling, to economic problems and, to some extent, to problems in family size regulation and childrearing as well.

One of the most impressive findings was the diversity of responses to a common event. Although virtually all the participants in the study were low-income black females in their mid-teens who were premaritally pregnant for the first time, the outcome at the five-year follow-up was enormously varied. Whether we look at their decision to wed, their marital stability, subsequent childbearing, work and welfare experience or methods of childrearing, the young mothers were very dissimilar.

Some women had been able to repair

the disorder created by an untimely pregnancy by hastily marrying the father of the child. When these marriages were successful, the situation of the young mothers closely resembled that of the former classmates who had delayed marriage and childbearing until their early twenties. Other young mothers developed innovative styles of coping with the problems caused by early parenthood. Rather than repair their family careers, they rearranged them, putting off marriage indefinitely and resuming their educations. When able to restrict further childbearing and make child care arrangements, these women often managed to achieve economic independence by the time the study ended. Still other participants were not so successful in coping with the problems caused by precipitate parenthood. Their prospects of achieving a stable marriage were damaged by the early pregnancy, and they were having great difficulty supporting a family on their own. Poorly educated, unskilled, often burdened by several small children, many of these women at age 20 or 21 had become resigned to a life of economic deprivation.

Explaining Divergent Careers

Every solution to adolescent parenthood has one element in common: Each is an attempt to cope with the characteristic problems occasioned by early childbearing. Coping strategies, however, simultaneously have the potential for problem producing and problem solving.

Nevertheless, some coping strategies typically work out better than others. For example, young mothers who married the father of their child, restricted their childbearing and graduated from high school generally were able to minimize the disruptive effects of the unscheduled pregnancy.

Without question, the women who overcame many of the problems created by an unplanned pregnancy were more capable and committed than those who negotiated less successfully the course of their later lives, but we must not fall into the trap of concluding that the personal limitations of the young mothers explain why so many had difficulty in completing school, finding rewarding employment, maintaining stable marriages or restricting childbearing. This reasoning is merely another version of what might be designated the "fallacy of supermotivation." When they possess 'genuine' drive or a 'real' desire to succeed, women/blacks/the blind/ex-cons/ the mentally retarded are able to accomplish their goals. The socially advantaged need only be motivated; the disadvantaged must be supermotivated.

Almost all the young mothers in our study wanted to complete high school, but most were not so inspired to achieve educationally that they were prepared to remain in school whatever the difficulties encountered or the sacrifices required. Similarly, with few exceptions, the young mothers wished to avoid a rapid repeat pregnancy, but few were so anxious not to conceive that they continued to use birth control methods when events in their lives made contraception difficult or frightening.

Even if all the participants in the study had been "supermotivated," most would nonetheless have experienced severe difficulties in achieving their immediate life objectives. There was not a sufficient supply of highly eligible males to marry the young mothers; caretakers and day-care facilities were not available to care for the children of many of those who wished to return to school or enter the labor market; and there was a shortage of stable and remunerative jobs whose benefits equaled the income received from public assistance.

The few white women in our study,

the adolescents from two-parent families and the mothers in their late teens tended to be slightly favored when it came to marrying the father of the child, completing school or obtaining work. However, these social attributes provided only a marginal advantage and seemed to have little more than a temporary influence on the life course of the adolescent mother.

Social Programs

The old saying that an ounce of prevention is worth a pound of cure may be hackneyed but it is also true. While the classmates who avoided an unplanned pregnancy were not necessarily destined to lead lives free of social and economic turmoil, their circumstances at the five-year follow-up were clearly better than those of the young mothers. Yet there was, when we began this study, and still is today, a conspicuous lack of programs designed to reduce the pool of recruits to early parenthood. The general approach to social problems in American society is *reactive* rather than preventive. This posture might be understandable if preventive strategies were difficult to devise, but this excuse hardly seems to apply in the case of adolescent parenthood. We possess both the know-how and the techniques to reduce the incidence of early pregnancy and limit the number of adolescent mothers. Sex education, family planning programs and abortion counseling and services, while imperfect strategies, can be effective preventive measures.

Despite some encouraging trends in recent years, one cannot help but be discouraged by the timidity of the approach toward prevention. Essentially, we still cling to the notion that provision of family planning services should be as cautious, unobtrusive and inconspicuous as possible. Even though a clear majority of

Americans favor birth control services for the sexually active teenager and endorse sex education in the schools, some institutional resistance and a great deal of institutional inertia have blocked the development of widespread and intensive sex education and family planning service programs for teenagers. Few populations are as potentially accessible to these services as are school-age youth. Yet school systems have been avoided, bypassed and ignored as sites for pregnancy prevention programs.

In our discussion of the process of unplanned parenthood, we observed that potential recruits to early parenthood are reluctant to plan for sexuality or to take measures to avoid conception once they become sexually active; often they are tacitly encouraged to deny the possibility that their sexual actions may have negative consequences. Although a more open and accepting view of premarital sexual behavior is developing in American society, vestiges of the puritanical past persist. Family planners are still hesitant to reach out aggressively to the population they purport to serve.

What we have said about the need for publicizing contraceptive information applies as well to abortion counseling and services. Although many of the young mothers in our study were at least equivocal in their attitudes toward abortion as a solution to an unplanned pregnancy, they seemed poorly acquainted, even in the 1972 interview, with the specific procedures for arranging an abortion. Education about the alternatives to adolescent parenthood must be part of any realistic prevention program. In order to exercise these options, the teenager who becomes pregnant must have easy access to counseling. Here again, the school is a potential site for pregnancy testing, counseling and referral programs, and school health personnel should be trained for these purposes.

Perhaps the most prominent feature of existing intervention programs is their crisis orientation. Most programs are designed to supply emergency aid to help the young mother get through the prenatal or early postpartum period. Such programs are based on an ill-conceived notion that early parenthood is an affliction from which one recovers in time. The young mothers in our study were aided during pregnancy but abandoned when they became parents. And they were by no means unique.[18] Most programs cease to offer services at the point where many of the gravest problems arise for the adolescent mother.

Educational, vocational, medical or contraceptive programs are certain to fail unless they continue to provide services for as long as the need for services exists. In discussing the weakness of the contraceptive program provided by Sinai Hospital, we made reference to the ideology of inoculation. Most programs for the adolescent parent are based on the premise that short-term assistance will have a long-term impact. We discovered that short-term services produce short-term effects.

If we are to have any hope of influencing the career directions of adolescent parents, it is not enough to be present when plans are formed at important junctures in the life course; we must be available to ensure that these aims are implemented. Career plans are not binding contracts; they are subject to constant renegotiation as new considerations arise. It is far less critical to convince the young mother to stay in school, to use contraception or to look for a job than it is to help her realize these objectives. As the young mother encounters unforeseen obstacles, it may be necessary or convenient for her to reevaluate her initial goals. The formerly firm decision not to have a second child may weaken when she enters a new relationship, loses her job or merely has difficulty practicing contraception. It is not simply that commitments lose strength over time, but that people's ability to act on their commitments may vary as circumstances in their lives change. Accordingly, unless programs for the adolescent mother extend past the early postpartum period, they are bound to have disappointing results.

Regrettably, the delivery of services often is geared more to the convenience of the professional than to the needs of the client. For example, the trend toward specialization among professionals has led to a high degree of fragmentation in service programs. While there has been some encouraging movement toward the creation of comprehensive programs for the adolescent parent, the fact remains that segmentation of services continues to be more the rule than the exception. Educational programs typically do not offer day-care facilities, contraceptive clinics, job counseling and employment placement or pediatric and medical care. At best, several forms of assistance are provided under one roof, and weak ties are formed with agencies that can provide supplementary services.

One solution to the problem of service fragmentation is to make the assistance program mobile, as has been done with some family planning clinics. If these programs do remain stationary, then at least transportation should be provided from schools or day-care centers to them.

There can be little doubt from our results that the fate of the young mother and her child hinges partly on the situation of the child's father. If existing services do not actively discourage his participation, they provide few incentives to attract him. Practitioners are continually amazed by the interest unwed fathers show in their children. If programs were predicated on that interest, they might witness more of it.

Even worse than the fragmentation of services is the paucity of aid provided by programs for the teenage parent. We can point to few programs that come close to reaching a majority of the population in need of services, and those that do usually offer only token assistance. Educational programs reach, at most, one-third of school-age mothers. Family planning programs for teenage mothers are broader based, but have only brief contact with participants; their influence is usually temporary. The two services most needed, day-care facilities and job placement programs, are in short supply.

Without greatly expanding the scope of services, we are not likely to counter successfully the adverse effects of early parenthood. In particular, we cannot expect to modify the life course of the adolescent parent without providing substantial economic assistance, preferably in the form of stable employment for one or both parents; child care in order to permit parental educational and economic participation; and family planning services to prevent additional unplanned pregnancies.

Early parenthood destroys the prospect of a successful economic and family career not because most young parents are determined to deviate from accepted avenues of success or because they are indifferent to, or unaware of, the costs of early parenthood. The principal reason that so many young mothers encounter problems is that they lack the resources to repair the damage done by a poorly timed birth.

What would happen if service programs made it easy, not difficult, for women to restore order in their lives following an unplanned pregnancy? Let us imagine that there were truly comprehensive and extended services for young

parents and their children. Suppose, for example, that family planning programs to prevent unplanned pregnancies and to counsel women who did have unwanted conceptions were established in the schools. Suppose that a woman who elected to bring her pregnancy to term would be granted a child care allowance to purchase day-care services or to pay a relative or friend to care for her child while she completed her education or entered the labor force. And whether or not she remained in school, took a job or assumed full-time child care responsibilities, the young mother would receive an income sufficient to meet the needs of her family. Furthermore, suppose the father were invited to join special educational or job-training programs or were provided with a steady job. Our results indicate that under conditions of economic security, most fathers would contribute to the support of the family and willingly maintain a relationship with their children.

If the limited family planning program such as the one offered to the participants in our study had a modest degree of success, consider the possible effects of a more extensive service that maintained regular contact with participants over a period of years. While we cannot assume that such a program would completely eliminate unwanted conceptions, we can feel certain that a clinic that made more vigorous efforts to anticipate problems before they occurred, that reached out to participants when they encountered difficulties in using contraception, and that was prepared to establish a long-standing relationship with its clients would help to reduce drastically the number of unplanned births.

Providing easy access to social resources means that such resources will be used more readily. When services are difficult to utilize, they assist primarily the relatively privileged and the super-motivated. The privileged are in the best position to use them; the supermotivated are able to overcome barriers that normally discourage use. Making programs easy to use inevitably means that personal advantage plays a lesser part in determining who benefits from the provision of services.

References

1. J. F. Kantner and M. Zelnik, "Sexual Experience of Young Unmarried Women in the United States," *Family Planning Perspectives*, Vol. 4, No. 4, 1972, p. 9.

2. I. L. Reiss, *The Social Context of Premarital Sexual Permissiveness*, Holt, Rinehart & Winston, New York, 1967; L. Rainwater, *Behind Ghetto Walls*, Aldine, Chicago, 1970; H. Rodman, "The Lower-Class Value Stretch," *Social Forces*, 42:205, 1963; and C. E. Bowerman et al., *Unwed Motherhood: Personal and Social Consequences*, Institute for Research in Social Science, University of North Carolina, Chapel Hill, 1966.

3. J. F. Kantner and M. Zelnik, "Contraception and Pregnancy: Experience of Young Unmarried Women in the United States," *Family Planning Perspectives*, 5:21, 1973.

4. L. Rainwater, *Family Design: Marital Sexuality, Family Size and Contraception*, Aldine, Chicago, 1965.

5. National Center for Health Statistics, DHEW (NCHS), "Advance Report: Final Natality Statistics, 1974," *Monthly Vital Statistics Report*, Vol. 24, No. 11, Supplement 2, 1976 (for births); E. Weinstock, C. Tietze, F. S. Jaffe and J. G. Dryfoos, "Abortion Need and Services in the United States, 1974-1975," *Family Planning Perspectives*, 8:58, 1976 (for number of abortions); Center for Disease Control, DHEW, *Abortion Surveillance, Annual Summary 1974*, Atlanta, 1976 (for percent of abortions to teenagers); NCHS, 1972 U.S. National Natality Survey, unpublished data from P. Placek (for proportion of legitimate births to teenagers conceived before marriage); and C. Tietze and J. Bongaarts, The Population Council, for assumptions about number of miscarriages (10 percent of abortions, 20 percent of births).

6. H. Pope, "Negro-White Differences in Decisions Regarding Illegitimate Children," *Journal of Marriage and the Family*, 31:756, 1969; E. Liebow, *Tally's Corner*, Little, Brown, Boston, 1967; D. A.

Schulz, *Coming Up Black: Patterns of Ghetto Socialization*, Prentice-Hall, Englewood Cliffs, N.J., 1969; and R. Staples, ed., *The Black Family: Essays and Studies*, Wadsworth, Belmont, Calif., 1971.

7. H. T. Christensen, "New Approaches in Family Research: The Method of Record Linkage," *Marriage and Family Living*, 20:38, 1953; ———, "Cultural Relativism and Premarital Sex Norms," *American Sociological Review*, 25:31, 1969; ———, "Timing of First Pregnancy as a Factor in Divorce: A Cross-Cultural Analysis," *Eugenics Quarterly*, Vol. 10, No. 1, 1963, p. 119; T. P. Monahan, "Premarital Pregnancy in the United States," *Eugenics Quarterly*, Vol. 7, No. 3, 1960, p. 140; S. H. Lowrie, "Early Marriage: Premarital Pregnancy and Associated Factors," *Journal of Marriage and the Family*, 27:49, 1965; and L. C. Coombs and Z. Zumeta, "Correlates of Marital Dissolution in a Prospective Fertility Study: A Research Note," *Social Problems*, 18:92, 1970.

8. H. Carter and P. C. Glick, *Marriage and Divorce: A Social and Economic Study*, Harvard University Press, Cambridge, Mass., 1970.

9. S. A. Ricketts, *Contraceptive Use Among Teenage Mothers: Evaluation of a Family Planning Program*, Ph.D. dissertation, University of Pennsylvania, Philadelphia, 1973.

10. O. Lewis, *The Study of Slum Culture — Backgrounds for La Vida*, Random House, New York, 1968.

11. F. S. Jaffe and S. Polgar, "Family Planning and Public Policy: Is the Culture of Poverty the New Cop-Out?" *Journal of Marriage and the Family*, 30:228, 1968.

12. P. J. Placek and G. E. Hendershot, "Public Welfare and Family Planning: An Empirical Study of the 'Brood Sow' Myth," *Social Problems*, 21:658, 1974.

13. L. V. Klerman and J. F. Jekel, *School-Age Mothers: Problems, Programs, and Policy*, Linnet, Hamden, Conn., 1973; and S. A. Ricketts, 1973, op. cit.

14. J. Coombs and W. W. Cooley, "Dropouts: In High School and After School," *American Educational Research Journal*, 5:343, 1968.

15. S. P. Marland, Jr., "U.S. Commissioner of Education's Statement on Comprehensive Programs for School-Age Parents," *Sharing*, Mar. 1972.

16. Children's Defense Fund, *Children Out of School in America*, Cambridge, Mass., 1974.

17. M. Howard, *Multi-Service Programs for Pregnant School Girls*, Children's Bureau, Washington, D.C., 1968.

18. L. V. Klerman and J. F. Jekel, 1973, op. cit.

Teenage Mothers and Teenage Fathers: The Impact of Early Childbearing on the Parents' Personal and Professional Lives

Josefina J. Card and Lauress L. Wise

Summary

Young people who become parents while in their teens are much more likely than their classmates who postpone childbearing to have their education truncated. Teenage childbearing results in greater educational deficits for the young mothers than for the young fathers, who do not have to go through the experience of pregnancy and are generally less responsible for the early care of the child. Nevertheless, both the adolescent mothers and fathers have substantially less education than their classmates. The younger the parent at birth, the greater the educational setback. What is more, the negative impact of early childbearing on education remains when the teenage parents are matched with classmates who were not parents in their teen years for academic aptitude and achievement, socioeconomic status, race and educational expectations at age 15, before any of the young people have had a child. Thus, early childbearing appears to be a direct cause of truncated schooling, independent of other influences.

Apparently because of their relatively low educational attainment, adolescent parents are much more likely than their classmates to hold low-prestige jobs. For the teenage mothers, at least, reduced occupational attainment also means lower income and greater job dissatisfaction than is experienced by their classmates.

The spouses of young women and men who have children as teenagers are also more likely to have lower educational and occupational attainment than the spouses of classmates who postpone childbearing until their 20s or later.

Through age 29, the adolescent parents—when matched with their classmates for socioeconomic status, race, academic achievement and aptitude, and educational expectations at age 15 (before the adolescent birth)—also have more children than their classmates who have waited to begin childbearing until their 20s. Indeed, by the time they are 29, the teenage parents have already exceeded their family size preferences, while their classmates have not.

The article is based on a study directed by Dr. Card pursuant to Contract HD-62831 from the National Institute of Child Health and Human Development, DHEW. The detailed report is available for $5.00 from the authors at AIR, P.O. Box 1113, Palo Alto, Calif., 94302. The authors acknowledge the assistance of David E. Gross, who wrote the computer programs to analyze the data, Warren B. Miller and Harriet B. Presser.

Not surprisingly, the adolescent parents are also more likely than their classmates to have their first child out of wedlock, and to be relatively young at the time of first marriage.

For all of these reasons, perhaps, those who give birth as teenagers are more likely than their classmates by age 29 to have experienced unstable marriages, and to have been married several times.

All of the differences between adolescent parents and their classmates are greater for the young mothers than for the young fathers, and for those who give birth in the early teens (before expected high school graduation) than for those who give birth in the later teen years. The differences between teenage parents and their classmates diminish but remain when socioeconomic status, race, and academic achievement, aptitude and expectations are controlled.

Background

Widespread concern about the negative social, economic and health impacts of teenage parenthood has led to a number of research efforts to improve our understanding of the nature and extent of these consequences.[1] This article is based upon one such investigation, in which data from a large prospective nationwide study (Project TALENT) of high school boys and girls were analyzed to document the long-term and short-term impact of adolescent childbearing on the parents' future educational, occupational, marital and childbearing lives.[2] Because of the character of the Project TALENT data base, it has been possible to look at these consequences for the young father as well as for the young mother (who has been the focus of almost all previous studies), and to look at some of the consequences net of such confounding antecedents as race, socioeconomic status, and academic

aptitude, expectations and achievement.

The study findings are generalizable to all Americans who were in high school in 1960. The TALENT sample includes data for both adolescent childbearers and a comparison group of high school classmates. Data covering a 15-year period are analyzed, and consequences of adolescent childbearing are assessed at three different points in the parents' lives—one, five and 11 years after high school, when they were approximately 19, 23 and 29 years old.

Data and Method

The TALENT population is a sample of all Americans who attended grades 9, 10, 11 and 12 in the spring of 1960.* A nationwide random sample of 375,000 students from 1,225 senior and junior high schools—stratified by ownership, region of the country, retention ratio and school size—participated in TALENT. The participating students constituted approximately 4.5 percent of all U.S. students in these grades. The initial testing took two full days. Included were 25 tests of cognitive abilities, 10 personality and 17 interest measures, and some 400 questions on family and home characteristics, study habits, and educational and occupational plans for the future.

Three follow-up studies were conducted, one, five and 11 years after the participants' expected date of high school graduation. The follow-up questionnaires included questions about educational experiences and plans, occupational or job-related experiences and plans, and such personal history items as marital status, family size and community activities. In this article, the data are

---

*The study sample does not include individuals who never reached grade 9, and findings reported here may not be generalizable to this small subgroup of people.

analyzed as if they came from three independent cross-sectional studies of the same population rather than from a single longitudinal study of one sample.*

It is important to note that this study documents the educational, occupational, marital and fertility consequences of a teenage birth for young mothers and fathers who first became parents in the late 1950s and early 1960s. Significant social changes have occurred since that time. Among them: a higher proportion of teenagers sexually active and earlier initiation of sexual activity, increased availability of abortion, and a greater emphasis on outside-the-home concerns for women. All these cultural changes could conceivably alter the consequences of adolescent childbearing for today's teenagers. It is our belief, however, that the consequences of adolescent childbearing will remain basically similar to those documented in this article for as long as education and childbearing continue to be mutually exclusive activities, especially for the young mother.

---

*Rates of response to the mail follow-ups fell off each year, from a high of 62 percent for the 12th grade cohort at the one-year follow-up to a low of 22 percent for the ninth grade cohort at the 11-year follow-up. In order to correct for bias due to attrition, each mail data-collection was followed by an intensive effort to locate and collect data from a special sample of about 4.5 percent of nonrespondents. About 80 percent of these nonrespondents were found and interviewed at each follow-up. A system of weights has been devised to recapture a nationally representative sample for each grade cohort/follow-up period. (For a more thorough description of the TALENT data base, see: L.L. Wise, D.H. McLaughlin and L.J. Steel, *The Project TALENT Data Bank Handbook,* The American Institutes for Research, Palo Alto, 1977.) Because the special samples at the three follow-up periods were drawn independently of one another, separate weights (corrections for attrition) had to be calculated for each grade cohort/follow-up period. This is the reason that the analyses reported below treat the data as though they came from three independent, nationally representative samples.

To study the consequences of adolescent childbearing, a subset of relevant variables was extracted from the TALENT data base. These were:
• age at birth of first child;
• educational, occupational, marital and family-related characteristics at one, five and 11 years after high school (modal ages 19, 23 and 29); and
• a set of demographic, cognitive, social and psychological characteristics hypothesized to be antecedent both to adolescent childbearing and to the outcome variables studied.

The antecedent characteristics were obtained from the original 1960 data base; the independent and outcome variables were obtained from the follow-up data bases.

The study sample analyzed here was drawn from members of the grade 9 cohort for whom five and/or 11-year follow-up data were available, and includes all respondents who became parents before their 20th birthday, plus a representative sample of classmates (the comparison group) who were not parents as of their 20th birthday. Because members of the study sample started to participate in TALENT when they were about 15 years old (in grade 9), their demographic, cognitive, social and psychological characteristics were measured prior to their early parenthood. Thus, the study is prospective, with control data available from a period before the first birth.

All data reported are weighted, i.e., they represent projected means and percentages for the entire cohort of men and women who were in grade 9 in 1960.

Educational, Occupational Differences

Consistent with findings of previous studies,[3] the TALENT data show that adolescent childbearers did not complete as many years of schooling as their classmates. Table 1 shows the relative

Table 1. Mean educational score* five and 11 years after expected high school graduation, by age of parent at birth of first child

Age at 1st birth	Years out of H.S.			
	5 years		11 years	
	Mothers	Fathers	Mothers	Fathers
<17	3.0	4.2	3.7	4.5
17	3.5	4.7	3.7	4.6
18	4.6	4.8	4.1	4.8
19	5.1	5.0	5.1	5.5
20–24	6.0	5.8	6.3	6.5
25–29	7.3	7.0	7.0	7.0
No child at 29	7.3	7.4	7.1	7.4

*A score of 12 indicates a doctoral degree or equivalent; 8, a college graduate; 7, some college; 6, post-high-school but noncollege training; 5, a high school graduate; 3, completed grade 11; 2, completed grade 10; 1, completed grade 9.

educational achievement of male and female students five and 11 years after the date of their expected high school graduation. There is a direct linear relationship between age at first birth and amount of education at both periods (correlation = .28 for males and .54 for females at age 29). Adolescent childbearers, especially teenage mothers, had much lower educational attainment than their classmates.

Occupational differences also are striking (not shown in tables). At one and five years after high school (when they were about 19 and 23 years old), more males who had been adolescent fathers were working than was true of their classmates (e.g., one year after school, virtually all of the adolescent fathers were working, compared to three-quarters of those who had no child by age 29). However, 11 years after high school, when the two groups were about 29 years old, there were no longer any significant differences. More than nine out of 10 in both groups were working. For males, apparently, parenthood leads to early entrance into the labor force

(presumably to support the new family) to the exclusion, however, of continued schooling. By 11 years after high school, most men who have not been teenage fathers have completed their education and joined the labor force. Thus, there is no longer any difference in the percentages of men working according to age at birth of first child, but the educational differences remain (see Table 1).

A reverse pattern is found for women. At one and five years after high school, fewer adolescent mothers than their classmates were working (e.g., one year after leaving school, only about one-third of the teenage mothers were working compared to about two-thirds of their classmates). However, after 11 years, female adolescent childbearers were more likely to be working than their classmates who gave birth between the ages of 20 and 29. Following childbearing, women tend to drop out from the labor force, or fail to enter it. Thus, fewer female adolescent childbearers than their classmates are working one and five years after high school. Eleven years afterward, it is the women who have become parents at ages 20–29 who have young children in the home; as a result, their labor force participation rates drop below those of the adolescent childbearers. Thus, women tend to drop out of school and/or the labor force at whatever age they become mothers.

In the long term, the young mothers suffer more than the young fathers. Adolescent mothers have less prestigious jobs, have lower incomes, and are less satisfied with their jobs than their classmates at all time periods studied, even though the young mothers' labor force participation rates do catch up with (and indeed surpass) those of their classmates as the latter begin their childbearing years. This is because occupational achievement is a function not only of time spent in the labor force, but also of time spent in school. Since adolescent childbearing tends to truncate the number of years a young woman spends in school, it remains persistently difficult for the young mother ever to match her classmate in job prestige or income, however many future years she spends working. The teenage father suffers relatively less truncation of education, so the effects on his job position and income are less severe.

Eleven years after high school, adolescent childbearers were significantly overrepresented (p <.01 for males; p <.001 for females) in the blue-collar job categories, and underrepresented in the professions, reflecting, apparently, their divergent educational attainment. In addition, adolescent parents generally occupied jobs of lower prestige* than did their classmates, and the difference was more pronounced among teenage mothers than teenage fathers.

Similarly, the income of teenage mothers was significantly lower at five and 11 years after high school than the income of their classmates. However, by 11 years after high school, there was no significant difference in income between the adolescent fathers and their classmates. It should be noted, however, that the adolescent fathers start off with relatively higher paying union jobs. At 11 years after high school, their classmates' investments in education have only begun to be reflected in increased income. It may be expected that as time goes on, the classmates' income will surpass that of the less educated teenage fathers.

Adolescent mothers were significantly

*Rated according to an updated version of the NORC Job Prestige Scale. (See: A.J. Reiss, Jr., O.D. Duncan, P.K. Hatt and C.C. North, *Occupations and Social Status*, Free Press of Glencoe, New York, 1961.)

less satisfied with their jobs than were their classmates (p <.05). About 25 percent of the former group were in the lowest job-level category of "laborer" (e.g., domestic servants, nurses' aides). In contrast, only three percent of their classmates held jobs in this category. No relationship was found between job satisfaction and age at birth of first child among the men studied. This is consistent with findings that differences in education, income and job prestige between adolescent parents and their classmates are less pronounced among men than women.

The contrast between men and women is not surprising, considering that women bear the child and, in most cases, accept greater responsibility than males for rearing it. Indeed, when teenagers have children, it is generally easier for the young father than the teenage mother to walk away altogether from the responsibilities of parenthood.

Marital Differences

Among both men and women, adolescent childbearing was strongly associated (correlation >.70) with a young age at first marriage; what is more, far more adolescent mothers and fathers than their classmates were single at the time of conception and birth of their first child. The young fathers were more likely than the teenage mothers to be single at the conception and birth of their child. Thus, when the father is very young, marriage is unlikely to occur, probably because the mother is as young or even younger, and/or because the father is perceived as incapable of supporting the family.[4]

Adolescent parents are likely to marry individuals who have significantly lower educational and occupational attainment than their classmates' spouses. The difference is especially pronounced for the

Table 2. Number of living children, and preferred and expected family size, five and 11 years after expected high school graduation, by age of parent at birth of first child

Age at 1st birth, and years out of H.S.	Family size					
	Actual		Preferred		Expected	
	Mothers	Fathers	Mothers	Fathers	Mothers	Fathers
5 years						
<17	2.4	2.5	u	u	u	u
17	2.2	2.3	u	u	u	u
18	2.0	2.3	u	u	u	u
19	1.9	1.9	u	u	u	u
20–24	1.2	1.2	u	u	u	u
25–29	0.0	0.1	u	u	u	u
11 years						
<17	3.1	3.3	2.4	2.2	3.3	3.8
17	3.0	2.5	2.4	2.2	3.1	2.8
18	2.9	2.8	2.5	2.5	3.1	3.0
19	2.5	2.5	2.6	2.3	2.7	2.8
20–24	2.2	2.2	2.6	2.4	2.5	2.5
25–29	1.5	1.4	2.2	2.2	2.1	2.1

Note: u = unavailable.

spouses of teenage mothers. Eleven years out of high school, fewer than 10 percent of adolescent mothers' husbands had received college degrees, compared to more than 40 percent of their classmates' husbands. The teenage mothers' husbands also had significantly less prestigious jobs than did the spouses of their classmates.

The proportion of teenage parents who were separated or divorced was higher than that of their classmates at all time periods. In part, this finding is attributable to the greater number of years that the younger parents were exposed to marriage (and, thus, to the greater potential for marital disruption that existed). However, when age at first marriage was controlled, the association between age at first birth and subsequent separation or divorce held up.*

In keeping with the above findings on marital status, it was found that adoles-

cent childbearers had been married a greater number of times than their classmates. This was true for both sexes and at both five and 11 years after high school.

Number of Children

Adolescent parents had a greater number of children than their classmates at both five and 11 years after high school, as Table 2 shows. (This finding does not reflect completed family size, since respondents were only 29–30 at the time of the 11-year follow-up.) Given the reproductive head start of the young-parent group, the finding is not too surprising. Parents who began their reproductive

---

*The correlation between these two variables increased from .13 to .14 for males, and decreased slightly from .17 to .14 for females (all correlations, $p<.01$).

careers between the ages of 15 and 19 had an average of 2.1 children at the time of the five-year follow-up, when they were about age 23. Their classmates who began their reproductive careers between ages 20 and 24 averaged about the same number (2.2 children) at the 11-year follow-up, when they were about age 29 and a comparable number of years into their reproductive careers. Thus, the pace of childbearing for both adolescent childbearers and their classmates giving birth in the early 20s is roughly comparable over the first half-dozen years following the first birth. Nevertheless, although the adolescent parents want the same number of children as their classmates (a little over two children each), they expect to have more than they want, while the classmates expect to have a number corresponding to their preference. These expectations are not unrealistic, considering that the teenage parents, with higher fertility at the same age, already have as many as or more children than they want.

Cause or Effect?

The unfavorable educational, marital, economic and fertility sequelae experienced after the first birth by adolescent parents are clear and striking. But what is cause and what is effect? To what extent are the negative outcomes and the early childbirth itself both the result of differences in characteristics between the teenage parents and their classmates *before* the early birth took place? Table 3 shows that in grade 9, when they were about 15 years of age, the boys and girls who later became teenage parents already had lower socioeconomic status, lower academic abilities, and lower educational expectations than their classmates. Since these three characteristics are all highly related to subsequent life chances, and since edu-

cational achievement and fertility planning success are key variables affecting other outcomes (e.g., career success and marital stability), we have chosen to investigate whether the lower educational attainment and higher achieved fertility of adolescent parents might be caused by prior differences in these characteristics rather than by early childbearing.

In order to investigate this question, the seven age-at-first-birth groups were combined to yield four groups (age at first birth <18, 18–19, 20–24, and no children at age 24), and a set of matched samples was constructed for these four groups. The matching procedure consisted of finding, for each of the TALENT participants in the youngest childbearing group (<18), the one individual in each of the other three groups who was most similar in academic ability, socioeconomic status, educational expectation in ninth grade, age (relative to grade in 1960) and race. Table 4 compares the resultant samples according to these key characteristics. Clearly, the matching procedure was successful in producing samples that did not differ significantly.

Differences among the matched samples on three key outcome variables were assessed:

• the probability of receiving a high school degree;
• the probability of receiving a college degree; and
• the number of children born.

These outcome variables were chosen for detailed analysis not only because of the strength of their relationship with early childbearing, as seen above, but also because exact dates of receipt of degrees and births of children were available in TALENT, allowing for an analysis of trends in these outcome variables for the different matched samples.

(text continued on page 221)

Table 3. Selected background characteristics of respondents at grade 9 (age 15), by age of parent at birth of first child

Age at 1st birth	% black		Socioeconomic status*		Academic aptitude †		Educational expectation (in 9th grade)‡	
	Mothers	Fathers	Mothers	Fathers	Mothers	Fathers	Mothers	Fathers
<17	29.2 ±7.1	20.6 ±11.5	89.2 ±1.6	95.9 ±3.4	358.2 ±17.1	379.6 ±22.6	3.6 ±0.2	3.0 ±0.2
17	18.9 ±4.7	18.2 ±11.3	91.7 ±1.1	93.8 ±3.0	387.0 ±12.2	370.1 ±32.1	3.9 ±0.1	3.6 ±0.4
18	10.2 ±2.8	9.5 ± 5.3	91.2 ±0.8	92.5 ±1.9	407.1 ± 8.2	358.8 ±22.0	3.9 ±0.1	4.0 ±0.2
19	12.0 ±2.7	7.0 ± 3.2	93.8 ±0.8	94.6 ±0.8	422.3 ± 7.6	424.3 ±12.9	3.8 ±0.1	3.3 ±0.2
20-24	20.1 ±2.3	19.5 ± 2.9	96.2 ±0.6	96.2 ±0.8	460.6 ± 6.4	424.0 ± 8.3	3.0 ±0.1	2.9 ±0.1
25-29	5.5 ±1.3	8.0 ± 1.3	99.4 ±0.6	98.5 ±0.5	493.2 ± 6.2	437.9 ± 5.6	2.7 ±0.1	2.8 ±0.1
No child at 29	7.2 ±1.4	8.2 ± 1.3	99.4 ±0.6	98.6 ±0.5	488.4 ± 6.1	466.9 ± 6.1	2.7 ±0.1	2.7 ±0.1

*Socioeconomic status (SES) was scored as a composite of the following items: "(a) If your family has bought (or is buying) your home, what is its present value? (b) Please make the best estimate you can of your family's total income for the last year (1959). (c) How many books are in your home? (d) How many of the following articles are in your home … automatic washer, automatic clothes dryer, etc.? (e) Which of the following comes closest to describing the work of your father (or the male head of your household)? (f) Mark the one answer indicating the highest level of education your father reached. (g) Mark the one answer indicating the highest level of education your mother reached." SES scores for the TALENT grade 9 sample ranged from 65 to 128 for males and from 64 to 125 for females, with a mean/standard deviation of 96.9/10.7 for males and 96.3/10.2 for females.

†Academic aptitude was scored as a composite of student scores on the following TALENT tests: mathematics, mathematics information, vocabulary, English, reading comprehension, creativity and abstract reasoning. Scores for the TALENT grade 9 sample ranged from 50 to 784 for males and from 24 to 748 for females, with a mean/standard deviation of 432/119 for males and 455/111 for females.

‡Scores range from 1 (definitely will go to college full time) to 5 (definitely will not go to college full time).

Table 4. Comparison of matched samples on selected characteristics, by age of parent at birth of first child

Age at 1st birth	No. of cases		% black		Socioeconomic status		Academic aptitude		Educational expectation		Age in Mar. 1960 (in months)	
	Mothers	Fathers	Mothers	Fathers	Mothers	Fathers	Mothers	Fathers	Mothers	Fathers	Mothers	Fathers
<18	391	74*	21.2	12.1	89.3	90.5	422.4	409.1	3.7	3.4	178.1	177.2
18–19	391	141	15.6	7.8	89.0	88.7	423.2	411.5	3.6	3.3	178.4	175.2
20–24	391	141	18.4	9.2	89.0	90.3	422.0	408.6	3.6	3.3	178.5	176.4
No child at 24	391	141	16.4	11.3	89.1	90.2	422.7	409.4	3.5	3.4	178.1	176.2
Standard deviation	na	na	na	na	7.7	7.5	105.4	104.9	1.4	1.2	7.1	7.1

*For males, the number in the <18 group was much smaller, so each case was matched to two cases in each of the other groups; however, for seven of the cases, only one satisfactory match could be found.

Note: na = not applicable. The matched samples are representative of students whose characteristics are similar to those of adolescent childbearers. They are no longer representative of the *whole* student population. The case weights, designed to achieve estimates for the whole population, are thus inappropriate for these analyses. The unweighted percentages and means for the adolescent childbearers differ slightly from the weighted percentages and means.

Table 5. Percentage of respondents in matched samples who received a high school diploma, by age of parent at birth of first child and age diploma was awarded

Age diploma received	Age at 1st birth							
	Mothers				Fathers			
	<18	18-19	20-24	No child at 24	<18	18-19	20-24	No child at 24
17	13.7	42.0	47.0	50.7	31.9	36.2	47.5	49.6
18	21.9	72.8	87.6	89.7	57.4	70.2	82.3	89.4
19	26.1	75.7	93.4	95.0	63.1	73.0	90.1	94.3
20	29.0	76.3	94.2	96.0	63.1	73.8	91.5	94.3
21	32.2	76.8	94.2	96.0	63.1	73.8	92.2	96.5
22	34.6	77.3	94.2	96.0	66.0	73.8	92.2	96.5
23	36.7	78.1	94.7	96.3	66.0	74.5	92.2	96.5
24	38.5	78.9	94.7	96.3	67.4	74.5	92.2	96.5
25	41.4	78.9	94.7	96.3	67.4	74.5	93.6	96.5
26	44.1	79.9	94.7	96.3	67.4	74.5	93.6	96.5
27	46.4	79.9	95.3	96.3	68.1	78.0	93.6	96.5
28	48.3	80.5	95.8	96.6	68.1	78.7	93.6	96.5
29	49.9	81.5	96.0	96.6	69.5	79.4	93.6	97.2

Note: The maximum 95% confidence interval for these data is $\pm.05$ for females, $\pm.11$ for males in the <18 group, and $\pm.08$ for males in the other groups.

Table 6. Percentage of respondents in matched samples who completed college, by age of parent at birth of first child and age degree was awarded.

Age degree awarded	Age at 1st birth							
	Mothers				Fathers			
	<18	18-19	20-24	No child at 24	<18	18-19	20-24	No child at 24
20	0.0	0.0	1.3	0.8	0.0	0.7	0.0	0.0
21	0.0	0.3	5.0	10.3	2.2	3.6	8.8	5.1
22	0.3	1.1	6.9	18.5	2.2	6.6	12.4	12.4
23	0.3	1.3	6.9	20.3	3.6	6.6	13.1	15.3
24	0.5	1.3	7.4	21.4	5.1	7.3	14.6	16.8
25	0.8	1.3	7.7	22.2	6.6	8.0	15.3	20.4
26	0.8	1.3	7.9	22.2	6.6	8.8	16.8	24.8
27	1.3	1.6	7.9	22.4	9.5	9.5	17.5	28.5
28	1.3	1.8	7.9	22.4	9.5	9.5	17.5	29.2
29	1.6	1.8	7.9	22.4	10.9	9.5	17.5	29.2

Table 7. Average number of living children reported by respondents in matched samples, by age of parent at birth of first child and current age

| Current age | Age at 1st birth | | | | | | | |
| | Mothers | | | | Fathers | | | |
	<18	18-19	20-24	No child at 24	<18	18-19	20-24	No child at 24
17	1.11	na	na	na	1.22	na	na	na
18	1.42	0.40	na	na	1.45	0.36	na	na
19	1.82	1.11	na	na	1.69	1.12	na	na
20	2.06	1.37	0.25	na	1.96	1.26	0.15	na
21	2.28	1.66	0.53	na	2.15	1.57	0.44	na
22	2.42	1.89	0.84	na	2.24	1.80	0.63	na
23	2.54	2.04	1.20	na	2.36	1.97	1.03	na
24	2.67	2.21	1.51	na	2.51	2.14	1.37	na
25	2.82	2.33	1.71	0.20	2.65	2.31	1.61	0.19
26	2.91	2.43	1.88	0.31	2.77	2.42	1.87	0.30
27	2.99	2.52	2.01	0.45	2.83	2.53	2.06	0.48
28	3.05	2.57	2.11	0.63	2.87	2.56	2.14	0.66
29	3.08	2.61	2.16	0.71	2.88	2.59	2.18	0.76

Table 5 shows the proportions of mothers and fathers in each sample receiving a high school diploma, and the ages at which the diploma was received. Only one-fifth of women who had a birth before age 18 received their diplomas at age 18, compared to nearly three-fourths of those whose first child was born when they were 18 or 19 and nine-tenths of those who had no children before age 20. By age 29, about half of the youngest childbearers had obtained diplomas, compared to nearly all of those who postponed childbearing until their 20s. The differences among the men, who did not have to go through pregnancy and were probably less responsible for early care of the child, are somewhat less striking, although still substantial. It is notable that the youngest teenage fathers were less likely than comparable mothers to go back and get their diplomas if they had not done so by age 19.

It is important to note that virtually all of the men and women who did not have children before age 20 received high school diplomas. The adolescent parents had the same level of academic ability, the same racial and socioeconomic background, and even the same expectations regarding college. Yet a high proportion of the adolescent childbearers did not complete high school and were therefore apparently severely handicapped with respect to future educational and (presumably) occupational attainment.

Table 6 shows the proportion of women and men in each of the matched samples who completed college, and the age by which the college degree was awarded. Almost none of the women who bore children before age 20 completed college, compared to more than one-fifth of those who did not have children by age 24. Equally striking differences between the teenage fathers and those who postponed childbearing are apparent. It is clear from the data in this table that having children as early as ages 20–24 erodes the likelihood of finishing college before age 30, especially among women.

It appears reasonable to conclude that early childbearing truncates the number of years that an individual would otherwise spend in school. Many other studies[5] have shown the importance of education in determining job prestige and income in later life. Thus, adolescent childbearing, by cutting short the number of years an individual would otherwise spend in school, is likely to disrupt the normal route to adult achievement.

What about the fertility-related consequences of adolescent childbearing? Trends in family size over ages 17–29 for matched samples of women and men are shown in Table 7. Differences at age 29 between men who became fathers before they were 18 and those who began parenthood at ages 18–19 are only marginally significant ($p=.10$) because of the small number of males in the former group. All of the other differences, however, are highly significant. The figures show family size to be leveling off by age 29; thus, it seems reasonable to conclude that completed family size for these samples will be consistent with trends documented through age 29. These results are also consistent with findings of other investigators[6] that early childbearing is associated with higher subsequent fertility. It is notable that by age 29, the adolescent parents have already had (as they expected) more children than they considered ideal; while the classmates' fertility remains lower than their ideal and expected family size (see Table 2). In addition, these results show that such relationships persist even when important antecedents of high fertility—such

as race, socioeconomic status and academic aptitude—are controlled. Because they have longer reproductive careers, adolescent childbearers have more children than their classmates coming from similar family backgrounds and possessing similar academic abilities.

References

1. W. Baldwin and V. Cain, eds., *Teenage Childbearing: Recent Research on the Determinants and Consequences*, U.S. Government Printing Office, Washington, D.C., 1980 (in press).

2. J.J. Card, *Consequences of Adolescent Childbearing for the Young Parent's Future Professional and Personal Life*, American Institutes for Research, Palo Alto, Calif., 1977.

3. H. B. Presser, "Social Consequences of Teenage Childbearing," in Baldwin and Cain, 1980, op. cit.; T. J. Trussell, "Economic Consequences of Teenage Childbearing," chapter 16, below; F. Furstenberg, *Unplanned Parenthood*, The Free Press, New York, 1976, Chapter 7; K. A. Moore and L. J. Waite, "Early Childbearing and Educational Attainment,"*Family Planning Perspectives*, 9:220, 1977; and G. E. Hendershot and E. Eckard, "Unwanted Teenage Childbearing and Later Life Chances: Evidence from the National Survey of Family Growth," paper presented at the annual meeting of the Eastern Sociological Society, Philadelphia, Apr. 2, 1978.

4. F. Furstenberg, 1976, op. cit., Chapter 4.

5. O.D. Duncan, D.L. Featherman and B. Duncan, *Socioeconomic Background and Achievement*, Seminar Press, New York, 1972.

6. J. Trussell and J. Menken, "Early Childbearing and Subsequent Fertility," chapter 15, below; J. Menken, "The Health and Demographic Consequences of Adolescent Pregnancy and Childbearing," in Baldwin and Cain, 1980, op. cit.; and S. Bonham and P. J. Placek, "The Relationships of Maternal Health, Infant Health and Sociodemographic Factors to Fertility," *Public Health Reports*, 93:283, 1978.

14
Marriage, Remarriage, Marital Disruption and Age at First Birth

James McCarthy and Jane Menken

There is increasing awareness and more extensive documentation of the serious problems subsequent to adolescent childbearing, especially for the teenage mother. Correlates of teenage motherhood that have been identified by recent studies include lower educational attainment, reduced income and assets, increased childbearing, shorter birth intervals and higher divorce rates.[1] Yet only very general information is available on the marriage patterns of women who bear their first child while they are still in their teens. In this article, we investigate the marital careers of a sample of teenage mothers and compare them with the careers of women who began their reproductive lives at a later age. We consider the context and timing of the first marriage in relation to the first birth, the duration and stability of the first marriage, the likelihood of remarriage after dissolution of the first marriage and, finally, the stability of second marriages.

Examination of the consequences of early childbearing is conceptually difficult. The problem of causal inference is particularly complex, since the independent effect of an early birth cannot always be identified. Women who have children at early ages are different in

many ways from those who delay the start of childbearing. Two contrasting causal mechanisms have been proposed to explain the observed differences. One hypothesizes that teenage mothers are different to begin with, and that the socioeconomic forces which push them into early childbearing will create problems throughout their later lives. The alternative suggests that early motherhood itself is sufficient to ensure that adolescent childbearers will never be like women who become mothers at a later age, not because they were different to start with, but because that first birth has consequences which influence the rest of their lives. Tests of these competing hypotheses are not always possible given the limitations of available data. In this article, therefore, for the sake of precision, we consider the correlates, rather than the consequences, of early childbearing.

This article is based on a paper presented at the annual meeting of the American Public Health Association, Los Angeles, Oct. 15–19, 1978. The data are from Cycle I of the National Survey of Family Growth, conducted by the National Center for Health Statistics, DHEW. The research was supported by Contract No. NO1-HD-62858 awarded by the National Institute of Child Health and Human Development, DHEW.

In addition to the causal argument, one must also consider the confounding association of early childbearing and early marriage. Adverse consequences have been reported for both; however, in considering the long-term consequences, early childbearing appears to be the more restrictive and the more irreversible of the two. One could, presumably, end an early marriage and reclaim the social position of a single teenager more easily if no children were involved. At any rate, to separate accurately the effects of age at marriage from those of age at first birth, a sample large enough to cross-classify women by their ages at each event and to allow sufficient cases for analysis would be needed. Even the data source for this article—the 1973 National Survey of Family Growth (NSFG), which obtained data from nearly 10,000 respondents—is not large enough. Therefore, we will concentrate on demonstrating the association between age at first birth and later marital events, while acknowledging that some of the age-at-first-birth effects may not be independent of age at marriage.

Data and Methods

The 1973 NSFG is based on a national sample of 9,797 women who were either ever-married or who were single and had at least one of their children living with them at the time of the survey. In addition to information on fertility and contraceptive behavior, the NSFG obtained complete marriage histories, including the date of the beginning and end of each marriage, as well as data on the date of separation (defined as the date the couple last lived together), divorce and widowhood. Since no information on single, nulliparous women was obtained, patterns of entry into first marriage not preceded by pregnancy and factors leading to nonmarital conception of first births were not explored. Because

of the very small number of pregnancies and first births among women who were divorced or separated at the time of their first birth, such women were also excluded from the analysis.

In addition, since the data are retrospective, it is to be expected that out-of-wedlock births, premarital conceptions and marriage dissolutions were underreported.[*]

Since women in a cross-sectional survey are interviewed at various marriage durations and in different marital statuses, many of the resulting marriage histories obtained are incomplete. We have, therefore, for this article, employed standard single- and multiple-decrement life tables, in order to combine complete and incomplete histories in one analysis.[†]

---

[*] In other research using NSFG data, one of the authors compared the out-of-wedlock fertility reported in the survey with vital statistics for the same periods and found that, contrary to expectation, the survey did not lead to an underestimate of out-of-wedlock fertility. However, there is a suspicion that first births after which the child was given up for adoption were underreported in the survey data used, since only a handful of infants were reported as never having lived with the mother. Therefore, the results of our study must be interpreted as referring only to those mothers whose infants remained in their care. Unfortunately, there is no adequate way to estimate the completeness of reporting of marriages or marriage dissolutions, since the registration systems in the United States are seriously incomplete. (See: J. Menken, "Fertility Rates by Marital Status: A Comparison of Vital Statistics and Retrospective Survey Derived Rates," unpublished manuscript, 1979.)

[†] Life-table methods consider all individuals exposed to the risk of relevant events at each duration. Duration of exposure-specific rates are then computed by considering the frequency of events that actually occurred at each duration and comparing them to the total person-years of exposure at that duration. These rates can then be combined to estimate, for example, the proportion of marriages that have dissolved within one, two or three years of their start. (See: B. Vaughan, J. Trussell, J. Menken and E. F. Jones, "Contraceptive Failure Among Married Women in the United States, 1970–1973," *Family Planning Perspectives*, 9:251, 1977.)

Table 1. Cumulative percentage, by duration since conception, of women who marry after out-of-wedlock conception leading to a live birth, according to woman's race and age at conception, 1973 NSFG

Months since conception or birth	Age at conception								
	Total*			White			Black		
	<20	≥20	Total	<20	≥20	Total	<20	≥20	Total
A. Months since conception	(N=2,258)	(N=581)	(N=2,839)	(N=799)	(N=282)	(N=1,081)	(N=1,449)	(N=295)	(N=1,744)
1	10.6	22.6	13.5	13.2	26.2	16.6	3.1	5.7	3.5
2	26.1	41.2	29.7	32.6	47.2	36.4	8.3	12.1	8.9
3	41.0	54.0	44.1	50.7	60.8	53.3	14.9	22.3	16.1
4	51.4	66.4	55.0	62.4	74.1	65.5	21.6	31.4	23.2
5	56.9	72.4	60.6	68.1	79.4	71.1	26.7	41.4	29.1
6	61.7	76.4	65.2	73.0	83.7	75.7	31.5	44.2	33.6
7	64.5	79.5	68.1	76.0	86.6	78.7	34.0	48.8	36.5
8	66.6	80.4	69.8	77.6	87.3	80.1	37.0	50.4	39.2
9	68.0	81.1	71.1	79.0	88.1	81.4	38.3	50.9	40.4
B. Months since presumed birth (if not married by 9th month)									
12	37.8	41.2	38.4	43.7	41.1	43.2	32.5	41.9	33.8
24	53.1	55.0	53.4	57.6	52.9	56.8	49.3	59.4	50.7
36	65.2	60.9	64.6	71.5	58.7	69.3	58.9	66.0	59.9

*In this and subsequent tables, total includes nonwhites other than blacks.

Our analysis focused on the 8,085 women who had had at least one birth and on the subset of 7,439 women who had also been married at least once.

Marriage After Nonmarital Conception

A woman who becomes pregnant while single and decides to have the baby has two options—she can either marry or have a birth out of wedlock. Panel A of Table 1 shows that 71 percent of all women surveyed who had out-of-wedlock conceptions marry by the time the baby is born. Women who conceived while they were under the age of 20 are less likely to marry during the following nine months than are women who were 20 or older at the time of conception (68 percent compared with 81 percent).

White women are twice as likely as black women to marry within nine months of conception (81 percent compared with 40 percent). Eighty-eight percent of white women who conceived at age 20 or older, compared with 79 percent of those whose conceptions occurred at younger ages, married in time to avoid an out-of-wedlock first birth. Among black women, the equivalent probabilities are far lower: 51 percent and 38 percent. Older black women are less likely than younger white women to marry within nine months of conception.

Figure 1 shows that the proportion married continues to rise fairly rapidly after the nine months following conception. By the end of four years after conception, 78 percent of black women and 95 percent of white women are married.

Panel B of Table 1 shows the probability of marriage *following* an out-of-wedlock birth (assuming that all births take place nine months after conception). These results present age-at-conception and racial patterns which are quite different from those seen in panel A. Thirty-eight percent of the women who have had an out-of-wedlock first birth

Figure 1. Cumulative percentage, by duration since conception, of women who marry after out-of-wedlock conception leading to a live birth, according to woman's race and age at conception

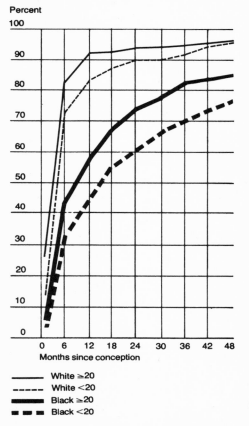

Percent

Months since conception

——— White ≥20
- - - - - White <20
━━━ Black ≥20
■ ■ ■ Black <20

get married within 12 months of that birth and 53 percent marry in the first 24 months of motherhood, with very little difference by age at first birth. Considering only those who conceived before age 20, whites are more likely than blacks to marry after an out-of-wedlock first birth. For those who conceived at age 20 or older, no large differences are observed in marriage patterns after an out-of-wedlock first birth. When age groups are compared within racial groups, we find that blacks who gave birth at early ages are somewhat slower to marry than those who postponed childbearing, whereas marriage apparently occurs sooner among the younger than the older white mothers.°

Marriage Duration

Table 2 takes the marriage date rather than the conception date as the starting point of the analysis. The issue addressed is, how long has the couple had to establish the marriage relationship before the responsibilities of parenting are added? Since the numbers in this table are considerably larger than those in Table 1, a more detailed age breakdown is possible. There are substantial age-at-first-birth and racial differences in the percentage of first births that are premaritally conceived (that is, births that occur within seven months of marriage).

In each category, white women are considerably less likely than black women to have been married seven months or less at their first birth. For example, among those who gave birth at age 18-19, 43 percent of blacks and only 18 percent of whites had been married for

———

°These results are based on quite small samples for the white population (78, 84 and 78 in each age-at-first-birth category report that birth as nonmarital) and should be confirmed with larger samples.

Table 2. Cumulative percentage, by duration of marriage, of marital first births according to woman's race and age at first birth

Months of marriage	Age at 1st birth											
	Total				White				Black			
	14-17 (N= 859)	18-19 (N= 1,527)	≥20 (N= 3,870)	Total* (N= 6,266)	14-17 (N= 470)	18-19 (N= 1,029)	≥20 (N= 2,924)	Total* (N= 4,425)	14-17 (N= 385)	18-19 (N= 492)	≥20 (N= 905)	Total* (N= 1,790)
1	1.9	1.0	0.2	0.6	0.9	0.7	0.1	0.3	3.1	1.6	0.7	1.5
2	6.0	2.4	0.6	1.8	1.8	1.4	0.5	0.6	10.9	4.6	2.0	4.7
3	10.0	4.3	1.3	3.3	3.9	2.3	0.7	1.3	17.1	8.7	3.5	7.9
4	16.3	6.7	2.2	5.3	7.5	3.6	1.3	2.4	26.7	13.6	5.4	12.3
5	22.2	10.4	3.6	7.9	11.8	5.3	2.0	3.7	34.8	21.5	9.2	18.2
6	29.9	17.3	5.7	12.0	19.2	9.9	3.6	6.6	42.9	33.1	13.2	25.1
7	40.3	26.0	8.2	17.1	29.2	18.0	5.5	10.8	53.8	43.1	17.7	32.5
8	48.6	34.2	11.3	22.2	37.9	26.6	8.3	15.6	61.6	50.6	21.7	38.3
9	54.0	39.2	14.2	26.0	45.1	31.8	11.3	19.6	64.5	55.5	24.4	41.6
12	69.5	60.2	29.8	43.0	63.2	61.7	31.0	42.2	79.1	71.6	43.2	58.7
24	94.1	90.3	62.2	73.9	95.4	91.8	62.2	72.7	95.1	92.3	70.0	81.5
36	98.4	97.2	78.9	86.4	99.0	97.6	78.2	85.0	97.2	97.4	81.8	89.4
48	99.2	98.5	88.0	92.5	99.6	99.2	88.0	91.9	98.2	98.2	89.0	93.5

*Includes women who reported a marital first birth at age 13 or younger.

seven months or less. Thus, although black women are less likely than whites to report nonmarital conception followed by marriage, for a much higher percentage of their marital first births than is the case among whites, marriage follows conception. The percentage of first births that are premaritally conceived declines sharply as age at first birth rises. Forty percent of marital first births to women aged 14-17 at first birth occur within seven months of marriage, compared with 26 percent of those to women aged 18-19, and eight percent of those to women 20 and older. Marital births are over five times more likely to be premaritally conceived among whites whose first birth occurred at ages 14-17 than among those whose first birth was at age 20 or older. Among black women, they are three times more likely to be premaritally conceived.

Dissolution of First Marriage

How does marriage dissolution relate to age at first birth? Although a marriage may be dissolved either through the death of a spouse or by voluntary break-up, we are interested here only in voluntary dissolution through separation or divorce. In order to present the pattern of voluntary dissolution in a form which is independent of the pattern of widowhood, multiple-decrement life tables were calculated.* Although, in a legal sense, the date of a divorce decree defines the end of a marriage, many couples separate without obtaining divorces. It has been shown that blacks are more likely to separate than whites, but

*The numbers reported come from the associated single-decrement table with voluntary dissolution as the exit of interest.

Table 3. Percentage of women who separate within five and 15 years of marriage, by woman's race, age at birth of first child and timing of first birth

Timing of 1st birth and years since marriage	Age at 1st birth				White				Black			
	Total											
	14-17	18-19	≥20	Total*	14-17	18-19	≥20	Total*	14-17	18-19	≥20	Total*
Total	(N= 1,449)	(N= 1,854)	(N= 4,115)	(N= 7,455)	(N= 538)	(N= 1,098)	(N= 2,981)	(N= 4,623)	(N= 906)	(N= 749)	(N= 1,090)	(N= 2,776)
5	20.5	12.6	4.4	8.6	17.1	11.4	3.9	7.2	30.5	20.4	11.5	20.3
15	43.6	28.8	13.9	21.7	39.3	26.8	12.4	19.0	57.0	43.5	34.6	44.7
Premarital	(N= 590)	(N= 327)	(N= 245)	(N= 1,189)	—	—	—	(N= 198)	(N= 521)	(N= 185)	(N= 185)	(N= 986)
5	27.8	32.3	23.5	28.3	—	—	—	27.6	33.4	27.4	24.3	29.9
15	54.6	51.8	41.6	50.6	—	—	—	45.3	53.5	49.7	43.3	55.8
Marital premaritally conceived	(N= 416)	(N= 524)	(N= 444)	(N= 1,389)	(N= 178)	(N= 272)	(N= 246)	(N= 697)	(N= 237)	(N= 249)	(N= 196)	(N= 686)
5	21.5	15.4	5.8	13.9	18.3	15.2	5.4	12.3	33.3	17.0	8.2	20.6
15	42.6	29.9	20.0	30.4	39.5	29.2	17.1	26.3	62.3	34.8	36.3	42.1
Postmaritally conceived	(N= 443)	(N= 1,003)	(N= 3,426)	(N= 4,877)	(N= 292)	(N= 757)	(N= 2,678)	(N= 3,728)	(N= 148)	(N= 243)	(N= 709)	(N= 1,104)
5	15.8	8.6	3.6	5.6	16.0	8.0	3.4	5.3	15.4	15.7	8.9	11.3
15	39.2	25.0	12.6	17.5	38.7	23.6	11.6	16.4	45.1	44.2	31.7	36.4

*Includes women who report a first birth at age 13 or younger.

Note: In this and subsequent tables, dash indicates N too small for analysis.

are substantially less likely to obtain a legal divorce.[2] Thus, using divorce as the operational definition of dissolution yields results which are interesting mainly because of the information they conceal: namely, that the racial differences in dissolution probabilities are substantially smaller when divorce is used as a measure of marital breakup than when separation is used.

Since we are interested in social differences in marriage and fertility behavior, and not in variations in the use of legal forms of marriage dissolution, the date the couple last lived together is the more appropriate definition of the end of a marriage.

As may be seen in Table 3, black women in every age and birth-timing category are more likely to separate than are white women in the same category. Both black and white women whose first birth was out of wedlock are more likely to separate than are those whose first birth occurred within marriage. Half of all women whose first birth was out of wedlock are separated within 15 years of marriage, as compared with about one-sixth of those whose first birth was conceived after marriage. Whether a birth was premaritally or postmaritally conceived appears to affect, over the long term, the probability of separating within categories of age at first birth. Fifteen years after marriage, one-fifth of all women whose first marital birth at 20 years of age or older was premaritally conceived have separated, compared with only one-eighth of women in the same age group who had a postmarital conception. Within racial categories, greater differences are associated with age at first birth rather than with timing of first birth in relation to marriage. The relative advantage of a late rather than an early first birth is greater for whites than for blacks. Considering the probability

of separating only by age at first birth and race, whites whose first birth was at ages 14-17 are three times more likely to separate within 15 years than are those whose first birth was at age 20 or over. Comparable blacks are only two-thirds more likely to separate. In terms of reducing the likelihood of marriage dissolution, the probable benefit of delaying childbearing is, in effect, considerably smaller for black women than for white women.

The Likelihood of Remarriage

As may be seen in Table 4, black women are less likely to remarry after a separation than white women (only 33 percent of blacks remarry within 10 years after separation, compared with 83 percent of whites). Among both whites and blacks, those who first gave birth at age 20 or older are consistently less likely to remarry after separation than others, regardless of timing of conception. Those whose first birth was out of wedlock are less likely to remarry than those whose first birth occurred within marriage. None of these differences, however, is as great as the racial differential.

Dissolution of Second Marriages

While age at first birth may well precipitate both first marriages and dissolutions of first marriages, one might expect it to be less closely associated with later marital events. However, Table 5 indicates that both black and white women whose first birth occurred when they were under the age of 20 are more likely to separate after a second marriage than are older mothers. As shown in other research on marriage-order differences and marriage dissolution,[3] the racial patterns of dissolution of second marriages are quite different from those of first mar-

Table 4. Percentage of women who remarry within five and 10 years of separation, by woman's race, age at first birth and timing of first birth

Timing of 1st birth and years of separation	Age at 1st birth											
	Total				White				Black			
	14-17	18-19	≥20	Total*	14-17	18-19	≥20	Total*	14-17	18-19	≥20	Total*
Total	(N= 621)	(N= 542)	(N= 605)	(N= 1,784)	(N= 181)	(N= 254)	(N= 325)	(N= 763)	(N= 439)	(N= 286)	(N= 275)	(N= 1,013)
5	55.6	66.5	45.9	57.1	72.5	74.5	59.0	67.6	24.1	28.4	11.7	21.8
10	68.9	80.7	65.1	70.8	85.1	89.8	75.7	82.7	38.1	36.3	20.7	33.1
Premarital	(N= 262)	(N= 137)	(N= 81)	(N= 491)	—	—	—	(N= 69)	(N= 244)	(N= 107)	(N= 60)	(N= 421)
5	29.8	53.6	37.8	38.2	—	—	—	59.2	19.7	30.9	16.8	21.3
10	42.2	60.4	37.8	50.1	—	—	—	72.4	33.5	38.4	32.5	33.9
Marital, premaritally conceived	(N= 175)	(N= 138)	(N= 79)	(N= 397)	—	—	—	(N= 142)	(N= 120)	(N= 79)	(N= 52)	(N= 254)
5	66.3	70.1	38.0	62.1	—	—	—	76.0	28.9	27.7	17.5	28.1
10	75.0	84.6	59.4	72.3	—	—	—	88.3	45.4	30.7	17.5	37.5
Postmaritally conceived	(N= 184)	(N= 267)	(N= 445)	(N= 896)	(N= 109)	(N= 165)	(N= 278)	(N= 552)	(N= 75)	(N= 100)	(N= 163)	(N= 338)
5	65.6	68.8	53.2	60.8	70.0	73.4	60.1	66.5	32.6	26.9	9.1	19.3
10	81.5	83.6	67.9	76.0	86.6	89.0	76.4	83.1	41.9	36.9	19.1	29.2

*Includes women who report a first birth at age 13 or younger.

riages. Black women and white women are almost equally likely to separate within the first five years of a second marriage—just over 21 percent of black women and just under 21 percent of white women do so. Thus, age at first birth appears to have a more important association with dissolution of second marriages than does race.*

It should be noted that the mean age at second marriage is over 25 for all age-at-first-birth and race categories (not shown).

Discussion and Conclusions

This article has documented the marital careers of mothers in relation to their age at first birth and their marital circumstances at the time of that birth in order to examine the short-range and long-range patterns associated with early childbearing. These are the principal findings:

• A nonmarital pregnancy is more likely to lead to an out-of-wedlock birth rather than to a marital birth if the mother is under 20 than if she is 20 or older at conception. The age differences are not as large, however, as the racial differences: White women are far more likely than black women to legitimize a nonmaritally conceived birth.

• Large proportions of black and white women and of older and younger mothers marry during the period *following* an out-of-wedlock birth. Fifty-eight percent and 53 percent, respectively, of white women who have had an out-of-wedlock first birth before and after age 20, marry in the two years following that birth. For comparison, using census data, we have

Table 5. Percentage of women who separate within five and 10 years after second marriage, by woman's race and age at first birth

Race and years of marriage	Age at 1st birth		
	<20	≥20	Total
Total	(N=614)	(N=267)	(N=881)
5	23.1	16.1	21.0
10	31.7	25.2	29.7
White	(N=355)	(N=198)	(N=553)
5	23.2	16.6	21.1
10	30.8	26.0	29.2
Black	(N=258)	(N=68)	(N=326)
5	23.6	9.8	20.6
10	37.3	16.6	33.1

estimated the proportions of all single 18-year-olds and of single 20-year-olds who married in the subsequent two years, for 1960 and 1970, the two census years that represent best the experience of the women in the NSFG sample: Forty percent of white 18-year-olds in 1960, and 32 percent in 1970, married by age 20, while 46 percent of 20-year-olds in 1960, and 37 percent in 1970, married by age 22.†

For black women, the comparison is far more striking. The NSFG data yield estimates of 49 percent of those who had an out-of-wedlock first birth under age 20 and 59 percent of those who had such a birth at age 20 or older marrying within the subsequent two years. The comparison figures include other nonwhites in 1960, but are restricted to blacks in 1970.

---

*Although sample sizes are too small for firm conclusions to be drawn, these data suggest that in the older age-at-first-birth category, black women may be less likely to separate than white women.

†These estimates were derived under the assumption that marriage rates estimated from proportions ever-married by single year of age held true for the two years following the census. (For data, see: U.S. Bureau of the Census, *Census of Population: 1970, Detailed Characteristics, United States Summary*, Final Report PC(1)-D1; and U. S. Bureau of the Census, *Census of Population: 1960, Detailed Characteristics, United States Summary*, Final Report PC(1)-1D.)

Thirty-three percent of all black 18-year-olds in 1960 and 28 percent in 1970 married in the two-year periods which followed, while among 20-year-olds, 35 percent and 31 percent did so. A recent study of a small group of young teenage mothers and their peers in Baltimore found that giving birth out of wedlock accelerated marriage.[4] The investigator suggests that poor economic circumstances and low educational aspirations pressured these young women into early marriage. Although our data offer no information on the factors leading to rapid marriage, they do support the generalization of this finding to all age and racial groups; namely, an out-of-wedlock birth, especially to a teenager, and even more especially to a black teenager, hastens entry into marriage.

• The younger the age at first birth, the more likely it is that the first marriage will dissolve. This relationship holds true regardless of the marital circumstances of the first birth. Previous research indicates that marriages that legitimize a nonmarital conception are more likely to fail than those in which the bride is not pregnant. The present study indicates that a far stronger association exists: If a first birth occurs at a young age, the marriage is more likely to dissolve.

• White women are more likely than black women to remarry. The racial differences in remarriage far outweigh any age-at-first-birth effects. Women who had a first birth when they were 20 or older are less likely than those who gave birth at younger ages to remarry, but this finding may well be due to the fact that these women are older when their first marriages end and, therefore, in an age group in which marriage rates are lower for all women.

• The association of dissolution of *second marriages* with age at first birth is striking for several reasons. 1) Women who had a first birth prior to or during their first marriage are more likely to have their second marriage dissolve if the first child was born before the mother's 20th birthday. Since the mean age at second marriage is at least 25 in all age-at-first-birth and racial groups, we do not attribute this finding to youthfulness at the second marriage. 2) The racial difference in marital dissolution is greatly diminished in second marriages. 3) The dissolution rates for second marriages, as compared with first marriages, are substantial. For black women, the dissolution rates of first and second marriages differ little after five years; for white women, however, they are higher in second marriages than in first marriages.

These results must be interpreted with some caution because they relate to the lifetime histories of women under the age of 45 in 1973. Trends over time are not examined in this study, and any changes that may have taken place in the previous five years are not considered here. With these caveats in mind, the findings may be summarized briefly.

It has been well documented that women who deliver their first child when they are teenagers are far more frequently unmarried at the time of birth than are their older counterparts. Most of them, however, whatever their age at first birth, will marry within a year after that birth. These women may well be choosing the best of the options available to them. However, if their goal is family stability, it is not met. Marriages following a teenage birth, or in which there is a teenage birth, have high dissolution rates, as do marriages that follow an out-of-wedlock birth. Even if women remarry, those who experienced a teenage birth have a much higher risk of having that marriage dissolve than do those who postponed childbearing beyond age 20.

Whether or not women who experience early childbearing are different to begin with cannot be answered here. We have found, however, that early childbearers carry with them, throughout the years when families are being formed and children raised, problems associated with their early childbearing that lead to more marriages and more marital dissolutions. To the extent that marriage may be chosen as the best of alternatives (none of which may be particularly attractive), policies which help to establish and expand programs of education, day care and financial help to these young women and their families may help stabilize the lives that they can build for themselves and their children.

References

1. J. J. Card and L. L.Wise, "Teenage Mothers and Teenage Fathers: The Impact of Early Childbearing on the Parents' Personal and Professional Lives," chapter 13, above; L. C. Coombs and R. Freedman, "Premarital Pregnancy, Childspacing and Later Economic Achievement," *Population Studies,* 24:389, 1970; J. Trussell and J. Menken, "Early Childbearing and Subsequent Fertility," chapter 15, below; L. L. Bumpass, R. R. Rindfuss and R. B. Janusik, "Age and Marital Status at First Birth and the Pace of Subsequent Fertility," *Demography,* 15:75, 1978; and L. C. Coombs and Z. Zumeta, "Correlates of Marital Dissolution in a Prospective Fertility Study: A Research Note," *Social Problems,* 18:92, 1970.

2. J. McCarthy, "A Comparison of the Probability of the Dissolution of First and Second Marriages," *Demography,* 15:345, 1978.

3. Ibid.

4. F. F. Furstenberg, Jr., "The Social Consequences of Teenage Parenthood," chapter 12, above.

15
Early Childbearing and Subsequent Fertility

James Trussell and Jane Menken

Summary

Women who begin childbearing early in their reproductive careers—especially if they give birth as teenagers—subsequently have children more rapidly, have more children, and have more unwanted and out-of-wedlock births than women who postpone childbearing. These conclusions apply within racial, educational and religious subgroups. The widely noted racial and educational differences in fertility are in large measure attributable to differences in age at first birth. Thus, 56 percent of the black-white difference in childbearing within 10 years after the first birth, and 65 percent of the educational difference, can be attributed to a lower age at first birth among blacks. It is notable that the pace of childbearing is more rapid among blacks than among whites only after first births which occurred before 1965. The federally subsidized family planning

The authors are indebted to Hannah Kaufman, who prepared the computer programs and produced the tables upon which the article is based. The research was supported by Contract No. NO1-HD-62858 awarded by the National Institute of Child Health and Human Development, DHEW.

program, which offered widespread access to modern family planning services to millions of poor and black Americans for the first time, may deserve much of the credit for reversing the earlier trend.

Unlike differences between racial and educational subgroups, the difference between Catholics and Protestants in the subsequent pace of childbearing increases when age at first birth is controlled. If Catholics and Protestants had the same age distribution at first birth, the difference between them in fertility 10 years after the first birth would be 18 percent higher than it actually is.

The association of a younger age at first birth with an increased likelihood of having unwanted births is especially notable among blacks. Even when age at first birth is controlled, blacks report much higher proportions of all births as unwanted, largely because they report much higher proportions of first births as unwanted. Similarly, a younger age at first birth is associated with a greater likelihood among blacks than among whites of having births out of wedlock. In each age group, this risk is at least five times greater. About half the racial difference in the proportions of births out of wedlock can be attributed to a difference in the proportion of out-of-wedlock births among first births, and half to a difference in the proportion among subsequent births.

It is notable that marital status at the time of the first birth has relatively little effect on subsequent fertility.

Although women whose first birth occurs at ages 18 and 19 have somewhat lower subsequent fertility than those whose first birth occurs at ages 15-17, both age groups exhibit a much more rapid pace of later childbearing than women who postpone the first birth until their 20s. Thus, the older teenager should not be neglected in programs designed to stem unwanted teenage births.

The Study

Adolescent childbearing and its consequences have engaged widespread and increasing public concern. Yet, remarkably little is known about the social, economic or demographic impact of teenage births on the young parents, their children or the community. Much of the available information refers to age at marriage. It is well known that the younger the age at marriage, the more rapid the pace and the higher the level of subsequent fertility.[1] Whatever the age at marriage, the fertility of couples is greater when the first child is premaritally conceived than when it is conceived after marriage.[2] However, the proportion of first births that occur out of wedlock—especially among teenagers, and particularly black teenagers—is high, making it difficult to generalize results from the available studies to never-married as well as ever-married women.

Another problem afflicts many studies, even those which do not limit their target population to ever-married women.

Several *associations* between age at first birth and measures of success have been discovered. For example, age at first birth is positively *associated* with educational attainment, but it is difficult to determine which is the cause and which is the effect, or whether both are determined by other factors.[3] One recent study, which controls for educational achievement and aptitude before the first birth, does offer some persuasive evidence that it is early childbearing that *causes* curtailment of formal education, rather than vice versa.[4]

This article focuses on the relationship between age at first birth and the pace and components of subsequent childbearing. Although we cannot demonstrate cause and effect conclusively, we can be sure that, by definition, the childbearing experience of all women is identical until the birth of the first child. (The same cannot, of course, be said of their sexual experience.) We will examine several questions in detail:

• Is a younger age at first birth associated with a more rapid pace of subsequent childbearing? If so, does this association hold within racial, educational and religious subgroups?

• Is the pace of subsequent childbearing affected by the status of the first birth, e.g., by whether it is a wanted or unwanted birth, or a marital or out-of-wedlock birth?

• Is a younger age at first birth associated with a higher proportion of unwanted or out-of-wedlock childbearing?

• Is there a time trend in these relationships?

Data and Methodology

The analysis is based upon Cycle I of the National Survey of Family Growth (NSFG) conducted by DHEW's Nation-

al Center for Health Statistics (NCHS).*
In order to examine the relationship between age at first birth and the pace of
subsequent childbearing, it is important
to compare women at similar stages in
their life cycle. For example, it would be
inappropriate to compare the average
fertility completed at age 30 by different
age-at-first-birth groups, since duration
of exposure to risk would vary. Thus, a
woman whose first child is born when
she is 16 has 10 more years in which to
have children than the woman who first
becomes a mother at age 26. We have regarded the age at first birth as the origin
of a woman's fertility experience. Hence,
the appropriate comparison points are
those at an equal duration since the first
birth. Specifically, we compare the
childbearing experiences of women
three, five, 10 and 15 years after their
first birth. Because of the nature of the
sample, very few women could be observed for the longer durations. Hence,
life-table procedures have been employed to ensure that the experience of
all women with first births is included.†

---

*The NSFG was designed to provide information
about fertility, family planning intentions and activity, and other aspects of maternal and child health
which are closely related to childbearing. Data on
each of these topics were collected in personal interviews with approximately 9,800 women aged 15–44
who had ever been married or had not been married
but had children of their own living in the
household. Interviews were conducted between
July 1973 and February 1974, and centered on September 13, 1973. Respondents were selected by a
multistage, area probability, cross-sectional sampling of households in the continental United
States. Attached to each respondent's record is a
weight indicating the number of women in the target population she is supposed to represent. It
should be emphasized that the statistics reported
here are not representative of all U.S. women who
have had a first birth, since unmarried women with
no children living with them were not interviewed.

Two variables had to be inferred from
data collected in the interview:
• The first is the legitimacy status of
each birth. Births conceived while the
woman was married were coded as *postmaritally conceived*. So that our results
would conform with previous work, we
considered all children born more than
eight months after marriage as postmaritally conceived, while those born eight
or fewer months after marriage were
considered *premaritally conceived*. This
procedure slightly overstates the proportion of births postmaritally conceived.
Births which occurred to women after
termination of a marriage were coded
out-of-wedlock unless the conception
occurred before the end of the marriage.
All other births were coded out-of-wedlock.
• The second inferred variable was related to reproductive intentions, i.e.,
whether the birth was wanted or unwanted, and, if it was wanted, whether it

---

†Separate life tables were computed for each parity
in order to obtain the probabilities of having a birth
of any particular order (second, third, . . . twelfth)
within three, five, 10 and 15 years following the
birth of the first child. Summing across orders while
holding the duration constant yields the average
number of births occurring within a given duration
after the first birth. For example, the average number
born within five years is given by the sum of the
probability of a second birth plus the probability of
a third birth, etc., within that time period. The addition of one birth (the first) yields the average fertility
completed within any given duration. The components of the fertility completed within each duration
are also of interest; specifically, one may decompose
the total births into those which are unwanted, timing failures and timing successes, or into those
which are postmaritally conceived, out-of-wedlock
or legitimated by marriage. In these cases, a multiple-decrement life table is computed; each component comprises a separate decrement. The only difference occurs in the treatment of the first birth; the
proportion of first births of each status is added to
the subsequent fertility of the same status to yield
the average total number in each component.

was successfully timed. The exact procedure for such a determination is described exhaustively elsewhere;[5] the definitions are broadly consistent with those used previously.[6] The important fact is that the determination is made from the mother's retrospective description of her own attitude at the time of each conception.*

In each table, the results are based upon the weighted contribution of individual women included in the sample in order to replicate more nearly the experience of all U.S. women. Estimates based on an unweighted sample of fewer than 20 women are omitted, and those based on 20-50 women are enclosed in parentheses. Weighted and unweighted sample sizes by race, age, first-birth cohort and legitimacy status of first birth are not shown but may be obtained from the authors on request.

Complete marital histories were obtained early in the interview, before any questions about children were asked. Dates of all marriages and their terminations, and birth dates of the respondent and all her children were recorded, so that the age and marital status of the woman at each birth (or conception) could be calculated.† We suspected that some low-parity out-of-wedlock births were not reported, especially if the in-

---

* It should be noted that the sum of the timing success, timing failure and unwanted components does not equal the average completed fertility because some births could not unambiguously be assigned; this (very small) residual, indeterminate category may be obtained by subtracting the sum of the components from the total.

† In our analysis, 99 women, or 1.12 percent of women who had a first birth after their 13th and before their 30th birthday, were eliminated because they reported two consecutive live births less than six months apart, thus throwing the validity of the entire record into doubt.

Table 1. Percentages of marital first births that were premaritally conceived, by race and age of mother, 1964–1966 NCHS Natality Followback Survey* and 1973 NSFG

Race of mother	Age of mother					
	15-19		20-24		25-29	
	%	N	%	N	%	N
White						
NCHS	39.9	350	12.4	476	4.0	131
NSFG	39.5	191	13.2	301	9.6	83
Nonwhite						
NCHS	60.8	97	38.1	54	**	14
NSFG	59.2	237	22.6	129	(13.2)	39

*See: M.G. Kovar, "Interval from Marriage to First Birth," paper presented at the annual meeting of the Population Association of America, Atlanta, Apr. 16-18, 1970.

Note: In this and subsequent tables, a double asterisk indicates that estimates (omitted) are based on an unweighted sample of fewer than 20 women; estimates based on 20-50 women are enclosed in parentheses.

fant never lived with the mother or if the mother later married. In other cases, either marital or birth dates might have been altered to conceal nonmarital conceptions. We therefore sought an independent source of data against which to check our findings.

The NCHS conducted the Natality Followback Survey of married mothers shortly after they delivered infants in 1964–1966. The NCHS investigators were able to estimate the proportions of first births that were premaritally conceived. Table 1 shows these results, by race and age of the mother at first birth, from the Natality Followback Survey and from the 1973 NSFG. Since the numbers of births in both studies are rather small, the proportions are subject to large sampling errors. However, the Followback Survey, taken soon after the birth, and the NSFG, taken 7–9 years later, yield strikingly and surprisingly similar values. There is, however, no similar source of data against which to check the

Table 2. Percentage distribution of first births by legitimacy status,* according to race, first-birth cohort and mother's age at first birth.

Race, cohort and status	Age at 1st birth					
	<30	12-14	15-17	18-19	20-24	25-29
Whites						
1950-1954						
OW	4	**	7	6	3	**
Legit	12	**	26	19	6	**
PM	84	**	66	75	91	**
1955-1959						
OW	5	**	13	5	3	3
Legit	13	**	32	23	7	5
PM	82	**	55	72	90	92
1960-1964						
OW	6	**	13	6	4	2
Legit	18	**	37	30	12	4
PM	76	**	50	64	84	94
1965-1969						
OW	8	**	21	14	4	2
Legit	20	**	53	29	15	8
PM	72	**	25	57	81	90
1970-1973						
OW	6	**	16	8	4	3
Legit	19	**	37	38	14	4
PM	75	**	47	55	82	93
Blacks						
1950-1954						
OW	49	(86)	66	43	25	**
Legit	20	(0)	19	28	15	**
PM	31	(14)	15	29	60	**
1955-1959						
OW	40	(68)	61	40	28	12
Legit	26	(32)	25	30	30	8
PM	34	(0)	14	30	42	80
1960-1964						
OW	46	(92)	63	47	33	26
Legit	19	(2)	22	25	17	13
PM	35	(6)	14	28	50	61
1965-1969						
OW	55	(92)	80	53	35	32
Legit	18	(4)	13	29	14	5
PM	27	(4)	7	18	51	63
1970-1973						
OW	56	(100)	85	54	33	25
Legit	16	(0)	12	22	17	6
PM	28	(0)	3	24	50	69
Total	100	100	100	100	100	100

*In this and subsequent tables, OW = out of wedlock; Legit = legitimated; PM = postmaritally conceived.

Note: Percentages may not add to 100 because of rounding.

reporting of out-of-wedlock births in the NSFG. Nevertheless, on the whole, the comparison strengthens our belief in the quality of the data, despite our lingering suspicion that low-parity out-of-wedlock births were underreported by whites.

Legitimacy Status of First Births and Pace of Subsequent Childbearing

Estimated percentages of first births according to legitimacy status are shown in Table 2 for first-birth cohorts extending from 1950-1954 to 1970-1973. In every time period, the proportion of children born out of wedlock decreases and the proportion postmaritally conceived increases with increasing age at first birth. The proportion born out of wedlock falls more steeply according to age at first birth among blacks than among whites. At the same time, in every time period and age-at-first-birth group, blacks are considerably less likely than whites to have first births that were postmaritally conceived. Among blacks, the proportion of premaritally conceived legitimated births increases with age at first birth through ages 18-19 and then decreases; among whites, this proportion decreases steadily with age at first birth.

Table 3 shows that with very few exceptions, completed fertility decreases with increasing age at first birth, however long ago the first birth has occurred. Three years after the first birth, women who had the birth at ages 15-17 have .13 more children than those who had their first birth at ages 20-24.° By 15 years,

---

°We chose the 20-24-year-olds as our 'older mother' comparison group because it was unusual for women in this study to postpone childbearing beyond age 25. Similarly, we chose the 15-17-year-olds, rather than those under 15, as our 'younger mother' comparison group because we wished to base our discussion on the experience of a more representative age group.

Table 3. Number of children ever born, by years since first birth and legitimacy status of first birth, according to mother's age at first birth

Yrs. since 1st birth and status	Age at 1st birth					
	<30	12-14	15-17	18-19	20-24	25-29
3 years						
Total	1.68	1.51	1.79	1.70	1.66	1.58
OW	1.56	1.49	1.63	1.60	1.48	1.29
Legit	1.79	**	1.92	1.75	1.73	1.83
PM	1.67	**	1.81	1.70	1.67	1.58
5 years						
Total	2.16	2.14	2.35	2.21	2.12	1.97
OW	2.06	1.98	2.26	2.05	1.87	1.48
Legit	2.31	**	2.47	2.29	2.21	2.28
PM	2.14	**	2.32	2.21	2.12	1.97
10 years						
Total	2.89	3.46	3.32	3.02	2.78	2.43
OW	3.08	3.09	3.38	3.04	2.78	2.11
Legit	3.15	**	3.38	3.21	2.87	2.80
PM	2.81	**	3.25	2.94	2.77	2.43
15 years						
Total	3.24	4.29	3.82	3.40	3.07	2.55
OW	3.61	3.90	3.94	3.46	3.35	2.36
Legit	3.63	**	3.95	3.62	3.31	2.96
PM	3.10	**	3.68	3.31	3.03	2.53

Table 4. Number of children ever born, by years since first birth, period when first birth occurred and legitimacy status of first birth, according to mother's age at first birth

Yrs. since 1st birth, period and status	Age at 1st birth					
	<30	12-14	15-17	18-19	20-24	25-29
3 years						
Before 1965						
Total	1.75	1.56	1.86	1.78	1.72	1.62
OW	1.58	1.57	1.65	1.66	1.44	(1.35)
Legit	1.94	**	2.06	1.90	1.88	(2.05)
PM	1.73	**	1.85	1.76	1.72	1.61
1965 or later						
Total	1.55	1.38	1.62	1.53	1.55	1.54
OW	1.54	(1.39)	1.62	1.54	1.53	(1.20)
Legit	1.56	**	1.65	1.49	1.56	(1.64)
PM	1.55	**	1.56	1.54	1.55	1.54
5 years						
Before 1965						
Total	2.25	2.25	2.43	2.32	2.19	2.03
OW	2.12	2.11	2.31	2.15	1.87	(1.48)
Legit	2.51	**	2.62	2.47	2.44	(2.46)
PM	2.21	**	2.38	2.29	2.18	2.03
1965 or later						
Total	1.94	1.74	2.07	1.93	1.93	1.87
OW	1.94	(1.72)	2.14	1.91	1.84	(1.49)
Legit	1.94	**	2.07	1.92	1.85	(2.12)
PM	1.94	**	1.91	1.95	1.96	1.87

this differential has risen to .75 children. Looking only at completed fertility, however, tends to mask the magnitude of the difference in *subsequent* childbearing because the first birth is included in the total. During the first three years, women whose first birth occurred at ages 15–17 have .79 additional children on average; while those entering motherhood at 20–24 have only .66—a difference of 20 percent. Women whose first birth occurred at ages 15–17 have an average of .97 additional births between the fifth and 10th years after the first, and .50 additional births between the 10th and 15th years; while those who were 20–24 when they first became mothers have .66 and .29 additional births, respectively, during the same durations. In

other words, between the fifth and 10th years after the first birth, the younger mothers have 47 percent more children, and between the 10th and 15th years, 72 percent more than the older mothers. In all, after 15 years, the overall difference in subsequent childbearing (.75 births) rises to 36 percent. Results for ages 18–19 lie between those for ages 15–17 and 20–24.

Curiously, during all durations up to and including 10 years, women have more children if their first is premaritally conceived but later legitimated than if it is either postmaritally conceived or born out of wedlock. As Table 4 indicates, however, this peak is much more pronounced among women who bore their

Table 5. Number of children ever born, by years since first birth, race and legitimacy status of first birth, according to mother's age at first birth

Yrs. since 1st birth, race and status	Age at 1st birth					
	<30	12-14	15-17	18-19	20-24	25-29
5 years						
Whites						
Total	2.15	**	2.35	2.21	2.11	1.97
OW	2.02	**	2.35	2.12	1.76	**
Legit	2.28	**	2.41	2.23	2.22	(2.34)
PM	2.13	**	2.30	2.21	2.11	1.97
Blacks						
Total	2.22	2.20	2.36	2.21	2.17	1.80
OW	2.10	2.12	2.22	1.95	2.07	1.87
Legit	2.49	**	2.74	2.56	2.13	(2.03)
PM	2.22	**	2.51	2.30	2.25	1.75
10 years						
Whites						
Total	2.85	**	3.26	2.97	2.77	2.45
OW	3.04	**	3.57	3.05	2.74	**
Legit	3.08	**	3.26	3.11	2.91	(2.75)
PM	2.80	**	3.19	2.92	2.75	2.44
Blacks						
Total	3.19	3.34	3.46	3.31	2.95	2.22
OW	3.13	3.31	3.25	3.03	2.98	2.47
Legit	3.49	**	3.87	3.78	2.65	(2.95)
PM	3.09	**	3.82	3.33	3.05	2.05
15 years						
Whites						
Total	3.16	**	3.73	3.32	3.04	2.55
OW	3.49	**	4.15	3.39	3.13	**
Legit	3.52	**	3.78	3.47	3.39	(2.89)
PM	3.08	**	3.60	3.27	3.01	2.54
Blacks						
Total	3.75	4.20	4.07	3.88	3.47	2.32
OW	3.70	4.16	3.81	3.49	3.68	2.87
Legit	4.10	**	4.59	4.41	2.99	(3.21)
PM	3.59	**	4.42	3.99	3.59	2.10

conceived are also more pronounced for first births which occurred before 1965 than for those which occurred after that date. Women whose first birth occurred before 1965 at ages 15–17 had 20 percent more births in the next five years than those aged 20–24 at first birth; the corresponding figure after 1965 is 15 percent.[*]

It is notable that once age at first birth is controlled, no differences are found in the pace of subsequent childbearing—before or after 1965—whether the first birth was perceived as unwanted, a timing failure or a timing success (data not shown in tables).

One of the more interesting of our findings is revealed in Table 5. Once age at first birth is controlled, there is almost no difference between blacks and whites in the pace of subsequent childbearing until 10 years after the first birth.[†] Even at 10 years, controlling for age at first

___

[*]We chose 1965 as the dividing line because we wanted some measure of difference before and after the advent of massive increases in the proportion of women using highly effective methods of contraception. In addition, the need for a sufficient number of cases in all time periods necessitated the choice of a date not too close to the time of the survey. The date 1965 was a compromise, but an extremely revealing one. Other choices were tried and yielded results which were qualitatively the same.

[†]Most tables which show racial differentials in fertility are tabulated for currently married women only. Our tables follow all women who had a first birth until the time of interview. The lack of differentials by race before 10 years might, therefore, be attributable to the known higher marital separation rates among blacks. (See: J. McCarthy, Princeton University, Office of Population Research, "Social and Demographic Differences in Marital Dissolution," unpublished manuscript, 1978.) We computed two additional sets of life tables in which women were removed from observation at the time of separation or divorce, respectively, instead of at the time of interview. Although subsequent fertility was slightly higher in these marital fertility tables, the racial differentials were only trivially widened.

first child before 1965. For those whose first birth occurred in 1965 or later, no systematic relationship between the legitimacy status of the first birth and the pace of subsequent childbearing is found once age at first birth is controlled. The differentials by age at first birth when that birth was postmaritally birth removes most of the black-white difference in completed fertility. If blacks had the same age pattern of entry into motherhood as whites, then they would experience exactly three births instead of the 3.19 actually observed. Expressed in this way, a lower age-at-first-birth distribution among blacks accounts for 56 percent of the black-white difference in the pace of childbearing within 10 years after the first birth. It is important to note that the racial difference is not large, even when age at first birth is not controlled. Indeed, blacks who postpone motherhood until ages 25–29 have the lowest subsequent fertility of all age-race groups. Table 5 also shows that whites who report an out-of-wedlock birth before age 20 have higher subsequent fertility than blacks in the same category.

It has been traditionally assumed that the pace of childbearing is more rapid among blacks than among whites. Table 6 shows that this assumption holds only for first births occurring before 1965. Blacks who have had a first birth before 1965 display somewhat higher subsequent fertility than comparable whites five years later in each age-at-first-birth category under age 25. However, after 1965, the pattern is reversed; the pace of subsequent childbearing is more rapid among whites. Moreover, the differential between blacks and whites is of sufficient magnitude to overwhelm the opposite influence of a younger age-at-first-birth distribution among blacks; when all ages at first birth (under age 30) are combined, blacks actually have slightly lower completed fertility within three years (not shown) and five years after their first birth. Although we cannot be certain of the cause of this reversal, we would credit, at least in part, the growth of federal involvement in subsidized family planning programs in the late

Table 6. Number of children ever born within five years after the first birth, by period when first birth occurred, race and legitimacy status of first birth, according to mother's age at first birth

Period, race and status	Age at 1st birth					
	<30	12-14	15-17	18-19	20-24	25-29
Before 1965						
Whites						
Total	2.23	**	2.42	2.30	2.18	2.03
OW	2.04	**	(2.35)	(2.21)	(1.74)	**
Legit	2.46	**	2.55	2.39	2.46	**
PM	2.20	**	2.36	2.28	2.17	2.03
Blacks						
Total	2.37	2.36	2.45	2.41	2.34	1.95
OW	2.20	2.29	2.28	2.07	2.13	(2.01)
Legit	2.68	**	2.87	2.83	2.30	(2.12)
PM	2.40	**	2.53	2.50	2.47	1.90
1965 or later						
Whites						
Total	1.94	**	2.07	1.95	1.94	1.88
OW	1.96	**	(2.36)	(2.01)	(1.76)	**
Legit	1.94	**	2.07	1.89	1.87	(2.16)
PM	1.94	**	1.86	1.97	1.96	1.88
Blacks						
Total	1.88	(1.81)	2.07	1.83	1.85	1.52
OW	1.92	(1.79)	2.05	1.79	1.93	(1.70)
Legit	1.94	**	2.09	2.03	1.70	**
PM	1.77	**	(2.41)	1.67	1.85	1.42

1960s and early 1970s, through which effective, modern means of contraception were made available and accessible to poor and black people on a large scale for the first time. Nevertheless, the changes in the pace of subsequent fertility have not been great enough to alter the observed differentials in overall *birthrates* between blacks and whites, since both before and after 1965, the proportions who had entered motherhood by any given age were still much higher for blacks than for whites. For example, among women who were aged 20–24 in 1965, 47 percent of whites but 58 percent of blacks had had at least one child. The corresponding figures for 1973 are 37 percent and 60 percent.[7]

Table 7. Number of children ever born, by years since first birth, current education of mother and legitimacy status of first birth, according to mother's age at first birth

Yrs. since 1st birth, education and status	Age at 1st birth					
	<30	12-14	15-17	18-19	20-24	25-29
3 years						
<H.S.						
Total	1.75	1.56	1.85	1.75	1.70	1.54
OW	1.68	1.58	1.71	1.76	1.57	(1.38)
Legit	1.90	**	1.97	1.80	1.89	(1.89)
PM	1.73	**	1.85	1.73	1.70	1.52
H.S.						
Total	1.64	**	1.67	1.66	1.64	1.60
OW	1.43	**	1.45	1.48	1.40	(1.32)
Legit	1.76	**	1.83	1.75	1.74	(1.73)
PM	1.64	**	1.71	1.65	1.65	1.61
>H.S.						
Total	1.64	**	1.31	1.66	1.67	1.57
OW	1.33	**	(1.28)	(1.32)	(1.49)	**
Legit	1.60	**	**	1.50	1.61	(1.90)
PM	1.66	**	**	1.81	1.69	1.57
10 years						
<H.S.						
Total	3.18	3.58	3.42	3.20	2.92	2.48
OW	3.32	3.19	3.46	3.25	3.13	(2.81)
Legit	3.45	**	3.47	3.49	3.33	(2.90)
PM	3.05	**	3.36	3.11	2.83	2.43
H.S.						
Total	2.78	**	3.04	2.89	2.76	2.42
OW	2.78	**	3.21	2.94	2.52	(1.88)
Legit	3.03	**	3.12	3.14	2.85	(2.93)
PM	2.73	**	2.85	2.78	2.77	2.41
>H.S.						
Total	2.66	**	2.62	2.80	2.71	2.42
OW	2.36	**	(2.69)	(2.40)	(2.37)	**
Legit	2.63	**	**	2.67	2.58	(2.73)
PM	2.67	**	**	2.94	2.73	2.43

Education has proven to be a powerful predictor of contraceptive use and effectiveness of use, as well as of completed fertility. There are real problems, however, in specifying the causal mechanism, because education, like income, but unlike race, changes over time. While for some, an unexpected birth at a young age may result in truncation of their education, others seem clearly to make educational and childbearing decisions simultaneously. Although we cannot hope to sort out the question of causality with the approach or data used in this article, we nevertheless present results in Table 7 stratified by the mothers' educational attainment at the time of the survey in 1973.

The table shows that 10 years after the first birth, there are pronounced differences in family size according to the mothers' educational attainment. These differences remain, although they are reduced, when age at first birth is controlled. If mothers who were not high school graduates had had the same distribution of ages at first birth as those who had gone beyond high school, then by the 10th year after their first birth they would have had an average of 2.84 children instead of the 3.18 actually observed. Hence, 65 percent of the difference in the fertility of these two educational groups can be attributed to differences in age at first birth. For ages at first birth above 18, the subsequent childbearing experience of high school graduates appears to be virtually identical, through the next 10 years, with that of women who went on to college. The most pronounced differences according to educational attainment are seen among women whose first birth occurred at ages 15–17; these are the women for whom a first birth was most likely to have been a factor in curtailing further achievement. Those who did drop out of school were launched at an early age on a career of childbearing, while those who managed to go back to school after having a child were likely to have been motivated in directions incompatible with having a large number of children. It is possible, however, that the causality runs in the opposite direction: Those with few children were better able to go back to school. These patterns hold for first births that occurred before and after 1965 with one exception: Before 1965, women whose first birth took place when they were 18 or 19 showed little difference in subsequent fertility by educational attainment. After 1965, their fertility dropped with increased education from 2.08 to 1.86 to 1.56 children.

As Table 8 demonstrates, Catholics are likely to have a larger number of children than Protestants after each duration following the first birth, even when age at first birth is controlled. In contrast to its effect on the racial and educational differentials, controlling for age at first birth accentuates rather than mitigates the religious differential; thus, if both Catholics and Protestants had the same age-at-first-birth distributions, the observed differential 10 years after the first birth would be increased by approximately 18 percent.* There is no relationship between the legitimacy status of the first birth and the pace of subsequent childbearing among Catholics and non-Catholics.† Nevertheless, as is the case in all the tabulations we have shown, women who bear children early have more children at the end of every duration following the first birth.

---

*The answer varies depending upon which distribution is chosen as the standard. When the Catholic distribution of age at first birth is the standard, the differential increases by 24 percent; with the Protestant as the standard, the differential increases by 12 percent. Eighteen percent is the average of the two yields.

†This finding of no association between the legitimacy status of the first birth and the pace of subsequent childbearing contrasts with the faster pace observed among whites whose first birth was legitimated (see Table 5). The apparent paradox results from the relative overrepresentation of Catholics (with higher fertility within each duration- and age-at-first-birth category) among women whose first birth was legitimated.

Table 8. Number of children ever born, by years since first birth, religion and legitimacy status of first birth, according to mother's age at first birth (whites only)

Yrs. since 1st birth, religion and status	Age at 1st birth					
	<30	12-14	15-17	18-19	20-24	25-29
3 years						
Catholic						
Total	1.77	**	1.92	1.83	1.77	1.66
OW	1.54	**	**	(1.71)	(1.48)	**
Legit	1.85	**	(1.98)	1.83	1.81	**
PM	1.77	**	1.95	1.84	1.77	1.66
Protestant						
Total	1.64	**	1.78	1.66	1.61	1.53
OW	1.52	**	1.72	1.58	(1.34)	**
Legit	1.74	**	1.86	1.68	1.70	**
PM	1.63	**	1.75	1.66	1.61	1.53
5 years						
Catholic						
Total	2.29	**	2.51	2.39	2.28	2.09
OW	2.05	**	**	(2.24)	(2.01)	**
Legit	2.41	**	(2.55)	2.36	2.42	**
PM	2.28	**	2.54	2.43	2.27	2.12
Protestant						
Total	2.09	**	2.28	2.15	2.04	1.90
OW	1.99	**	2.33	2.04	(1.64)	**
Legit	2.20	**	2.33	2.19	2.08	**
PM	2.07	**	2.24	2.15	2.05	1.89
10 years						
Catholic						
Total	3.09	**	3.53	3.25	3.07	2.62
OW	3.18	**	**	3.09	(3.39)	**
Legit	3.22	**	(3.38)	3.22	3.23	**
PM	3.06	**	3.60	3.29	3.04	2.68
Protestant						
Total	2.76	**	3.20	2.90	2.62	2.34
OW	3.05	**	3.62	3.03	(2.43)	**
Legit	3.01	**	3.21	3.08	2.64	**
PM	2.70	**	3.10	2.83	2.62	2.30

Table 9 shows the numbers of births which are timing successes, timing failures and unwanted ever. It can clearly be seen that the younger the age of the mother at the time she bears her first child (excluding ages 12–14, for which the numbers are very small), the greater the proportion of her children that are unwanted. Since fertility increases with

Table 9. Number of children ever born, by years since first birth, race and success of reproductive intention, according to mother's age at first birth

Yrs. since 1st birth, race and success of reproductive intention	Age at 1st birth					
	<30	12-14	15-17	18-19	20-24	25-29
3 years						
Whites						
Total	1.67	**	1.81	1.69	1.66	1.59
Timing success	0.91	**	0.83	0.82	0.95	0.98
Timing failure	0.60	**	0.67	0.65	0.57	0.52
Unwanted	0.16	**	0.28	0.19	0.13	0.08
% unwanted	9.36	**	15.47	11.46	7.70	5.02
Blacks						
Total	1.69	1.68	1.73	1.71	1.68	1.49
Timing success	0.56	0.33	0.44	0.58	0.68	0.63
Timing failure	0.58	0.64	0.59	0.63	0.55	0.43
Unwanted	0.47	0.51	0.62	0.44	0.37	0.33
% unwanted	28.10	30.58	36.01	25.99	21.96	22.33
5 years						
Whites						
Total	2.14	**	2.34	2.20	2.11	1.97
Timing success	1.17	**	1.11	1.07	1.22	1.19
Timing failure	0.72	**	0.79	0.79	0.69	0.64
Unwanted	0.24	**	0.41	0.31	0.19	0.13
% unwanted	11.14	**	17.59	14.28	8.80	6.60
Blacks						
Total	2.21	2.19	2.35	2.20	2.16	1.80
Timing success	0.77	0.44	0.70	0.78	0.88	0.75
Timing failure	0.68	0.73	0.70	0.72	0.64	0.52
Unwanted	0.67	0.79	0.85	0.62	0.55	0.44
% unwanted	30.25	36.09	36.15	27.94	25.63	24.51
10 years						
Whites						
Total	2.85	**	3.26	2.97	2.77	2.44
Timing success	1.52	**	1.54	1.44	1.55	1.47
Timing failure	0.87	**	0.97	0.93	0.84	0.74
Unwanted	0.43	**	0.69	0.56	0.34	0.23
% unwanted	15.00	**	21.18	18.92	12.32	9.24
Blacks						
Total	3.19	3.34	3.46	3.30	2.95	2.22
Timing success	1.10	0.85	1.07	1.13	1.16	0.93
Timing failure	0.81	0.90	0.84	0.85	0.76	0.56
Unwanted	1.13	1.20	1.40	1.16	0.88	0.61
% unwanted	35.37	35.80	40.54	35.04	29.99	27.63

Table 9 (continued)

Yrs. since 1st birth, race and success of reproductive intention	Age at 1st birth					
	<30	12-14	15-17	18-19	20-24	25-29
15 years						
Whites						
Total	3.16	**	3.72	3.32	3.04	2.55
Timing success	1.66	**	1.74	1.60	1.67	1.51
Timing failure	0.93	**	1.07	0.99	0.89	0.76
Unwanted	0.54	**	0.85	0.68	0.44	0.27
% unwanted	17.01	**	22.77	20.59	14.56	10.47
Blacks						
Total	3.75	4.19	4.06	3.88	3.47	2.32
Timing success	1.25	1.01	1.28	1.24	1.30	0.96
Timing failure	0.89	1.08	0.91	0.96	0.84	0.57
Unwanted	1.41	1.55	1.70	1.48	1.15	0.64
% unwanted	37.71	36.92	41.95	38.15	33.17	27.61

Note: Columns may not add to totals because a small proportion of responses were indeterminate.

younger age at first birth, the higher *proportion* of unwanted births reported at each younger age produces an even greater increase in the *number* of unwanted births among women who begin childbearing early. For example, among blacks considered 10 years after the birth of their first child, there is a difference of 10.6 in the percent of unwanted children, a difference of .51 in the total number born, and a difference of .52 in the number unwanted, between those who were aged 15–17 at their first birth and those who were 20–24. Thus, the younger black women have 17 percent more children but 59 percent more unwanted children. For white women, the comparable figures are 18 percent and 103 percent.

Blacks report a much higher proportion of unwanted children than do whites, even when age at first birth is controlled. Thus, even though (once age at first birth is controlled) blacks have the same number of children as whites at three and five years after the first birth, and moderately more 10 and 15 years later, blacks report two to four times as many unwanted births. Moreover, at all durations, the decrease in the proportions of unwanted children with rising age at first birth is steeper for whites than for blacks.°

° This result may be due, in part to differential *reporting*; blacks may have a greater propensity to report births as unwanted, even if they want additional births *later*. At the suggestion of Frank Furstenberg, we did test one form of reporting bias. He hypothesized that reporting would be affected by the *current* marital status of the woman; a currently married woman would be less likely to report previous births as unwanted. Since relatively fewer blacks than whites are currently married, this type of differential reporting could lead to a spurious racial differential. We retabulated Table 9 for only those women who were currently married (data not shown). The results are qualitatively identical: Blacks experience 2–4 times as many unwanted births even when age at first birth and duration since first birth are controlled. As before, the proportion unwanted declines as age at first birth rises.

Table 10. Percentage distribution of first births by success of reproductive intention, according to race and mother's age at first birth

Race and success of reproductive intention	Age at 1st birth				
	<30	15-17	18-19	20-24	25-29
Whites					
Timing success	53	46	45	57	61
Timing failure	39	41	45	37	35
Unwanted	7	12	9	6	3
Indeterminate	0	0	1	0	0
Blacks					
Timing success	31	20	31	42	46
Timing failure	38	38	43	35	32
Unwanted	27	38	23	21	16
Indeterminate	4	4	3	2	7
Total	100	100	100	100	100

Note: Percents may not add to 100 because of rounding.

It is possible that the large racial difference in the proportion of unwanted births is due to a much higher incidence of out-of-wedlock first births among blacks, many of which may be reported as unwanted. To test this hypothesis, we recomputed Table 9 for only those women whose first birth was postmaritally conceived. The results (not shown) are qualitatively identical. The proportion unwanted among both blacks and whites falls slightly, but blacks still experience two to three times as many unwanted births when age at first birth and duration are controlled.

In part, the reason for this difference is that in all age groups, the proportion of *first* births reported as unwanted is much higher among blacks than among whites. For example, as can be seen in Table 10, 38 percent of first births to black women who bore their first child at ages 15–17, but only 12 percent of births to comparable white women, were reported as unwanted. Even at ages 20–24, this differ-

ence persists; black women reported 21 percent and white women, six percent, of their first births as unwanted. If blacks experienced the same proportion of unwanted first births as whites, at 10 years after the first birth, the proportion of all births reported as unwanted by blacks whose first births occurred at ages 15–17 would fall from 40.5 percent (as in Table 9) to just 32.9 percent. Viewed in this way, the higher proportion of *first* births that were unwanted accounts for 39 percent of the difference between blacks and whites in the proportions of *all* births that were unwanted; the estimates for age-at-first-birth categories 18–19, 20–24 and 25–29 are 26 percent, 30 percent and 33 percent, respectively. Hence, we conclude that about a third of the racial difference in proportions unwanted can be attributed to the proportions of first births that are unwanted.

When the same analysis is performed for first births which occurred before and after 1965, the percentage of succeeding births that are unwanted remains much higher for blacks than whites in both time periods. The steep gradient in proportions unwanted by age at first birth remains in both time periods for whites, but disappears among blacks whose first birth occurred after 1965. However, when age at first birth is controlled, the proportion unwanted remains the same before and after 1965 (data not shown).

Table 11 shows that the same type of pattern as was found in the analysis by reproductive intent emerges when total fertility is decomposed by legitimacy status. Among both whites and blacks, and for all durations since the first birth, a younger age at first birth is associated with a greater proportion of all children born out of wedlock. The proportion born outside of marriage drops within each age-at-first-birth category as the number of years since first birth increases; but even after 15 years, 41 percent of all births among black mothers whose first child was born when they were aged 15–17 are out of wedlock. The *proportions* mask the higher *numbers* of out-of-wedlock births among mothers who had their first child early. Black women whose first birth occurred at ages 15–17 had 17 percent more children 10 years later than those whose first birth occurred at ages 20–24, but 119 percent more children born outside of marriage.

The high proportion of births out of wedlock among blacks can be attributed partly to the high proportion of first births that occur outside of marriage. As seen in Table 12, 70 percent of first births to blacks but only 14 percent of those to whites were out of wedlock when the women were aged 15–17 at first birth; at ages 20–24, the percentages were 31 and four, respectively. Blacks continue to bear children out of wedlock at a faster rate than whites. If out-of-wedlock births to blacks occurred at the same rate as comparable births to whites for 10 years after the birth of the first child, then among women whose first birth occurred at ages 15–17, only 26.6 percent of all births would occur outside of marriage, as compared to the 42.6 percent observed. Thus, about half of the racial difference in the proportions of all births that are out of wedlock can be attributed to differences in the proportions of first births that are out of wedlock, and half to the rate of out-of-wedlock childbearing after the first birth. A similar analysis for other age-at-first-birth categories confirms this estimate.

These conclusions hold when separate analyses are performed for first births which occurred before and after 1965 (not shown in tables). The major difference between the two time periods is a vast increase in the proportion of out-of-wedlock births within each age-at-first-birth category. For example, five years after a first birth which occurred at ages 15–17 and after 1965, 65 percent of black births and 14 percent of white births were out of wedlock, compared to 43 percent of black births and eight percent of white births that occurred following a first birth before 1965. This pattern contrasts with that seen in the analysis of unwanted births, since the proportion of unwanted births remained roughly the same in both time periods once age at first birth was controlled.

Conclusions

Younger ages at first birth are strongly associated with a faster pace of subsequent childbearing and, thus, a higher level of completed fertility, and with higher proportions of children unwanted and born out of wedlock. These conclusions hold within racial, educational and religious subgroups. A large proportion of the widely noted racial and educational fertility differentials can be explained by age at first birth.

One of the unexpected findings of this study is that marital status at the time of first birth has relatively little effect on subsequent fertility. Black women (and white women as well, except for those aged 12–14 at motherhood) whose first birth is out of wedlock do not later bear children more rapidly than women of the same age whose first child was born into a marriage. However, we suspect that the estimate of subsequent childbearing among white women whose first birth was out of wedlock is biased because white respondents may have been more likely either to omit a first birth that was outside of marriage or to report a marriage before the birth.

These results have important implications for family planning policies and

Table 11. Number of children ever born, by years since first birth, race and legitimacy status of all births, according to mother's age at first birth

Yrs. since 1st birth, race and status	Age at 1st birth					
	<30	12-14	15-17	18-19	20-24	25-29
3 years						
Whites						
Total	1.68	**	1.81	1.69	1.66	1.59
OW	0.08	**	0.19	0.10	0.04	0.03
Legit	0.18	**	0.36	0.28	0.11	0.05
PM	1.43	**	1.26	1.31	1.51	1.51
% OW	4.49	**	10.39	6.08	2.60	1.90
Blacks						
Total	1.69	1.68	1.73	1.71	1.68	1.49
OW	0.69	1.26	0.95	0.65	0.43	0.29
Legit	0.23	0.15	0.25	0.29	0.21	0.09
PM	0.77	0.26	0.53	0.76	1.04	1.11
% OW	40.60	75.32	55.13	38.19	25.69	19.81
5 years						
Whites						
Total	2.15	**	2.34	2.21	2.11	1.97
OW	0.09	**	0.22	0.12	0.05	0.03
Legit	0.18	**	0.38	0.29	0.12	0.05
PM	1.88	**	1.75	1.80	1.94	1.89
% OW	4.02	**	9.27	5.28	2.39	1.63
Blacks						
Total	2.22	2.19	2.36	2.21	2.17	1.80
OW	0.82	1.47	1.15	0.77	0.51	0.34
Legit	0.25	0.18	0.28	0.31	0.22	0.09
PM	1.15	0.53	0.93	1.13	1.44	1.38
% OW	36.84	67.24	48.84	34.78	23.36	18.65
10 years						
Whites						
Total	2.85	**	3.26	2.97	2.77	2.45
OW	0.11	**	0.28	0.15	0.06	0.03
Legit	0.19	**	0.40	0.31	0.13	0.06
PM	2.55	**	2.59	2.51	2.58	2.36
% OW	3.80	**	8.44	5.11	2.20	1.31
Blacks						
Total	3.19	3.34	3.46	3.31	2.95	2.22
OW	1.06	1.93	1.47	0.98	0.67	0.41
Legit	0.28	0.24	0.31	0.33	0.23	0.09
PM	1.86	1.17	1.67	2.00	2.05	1.71
% OW	33.13	57.84	42.62	29.66	22.59	18.59

Table 11 (continued)

Yrs. since 1st birth, race and status	Age at 1st birth					
	<30	12-14	15-17	18-19	20-24	25-29
15 years						
Whites						
Total	3.16	**	3.73	3.32	3.04	2.55
OW	0.12	**	0.32	0.17	0.07	0.03
Legit	0.20	**	0.41	0.31	0.13	0.06
PM	2.84	**	3.00	2.84	2.84	2.47
% OW	3.95	**	8.61	5.09	2.30	1.26
Blacks						
Total	3.75	4.19	4.06	3.88	3.47	2.32
OW	1.19	2.31	1.65	1.05	0.78	0.44
Legit	0.28	0.27	0.32	0.33	0.24	0.09
PM	2.28	1.61	2.10	2.51	2.46	1.78
% OW	31.73	55.11	40.52	27.07	22.46	19.10

Note: Columns may not add to totals because of rounding.

programs. While we have not proved that early childbearing *leads* to a more rapid pace of childbearing or to larger numbers of unwanted or out-of-wedlock births, the analysis suggests that postponing childbearing past the age of 20 might prove beneficial both to the woman and to her children. If women do have first births in the teen years, our analysis shows, their subsequent childbearing is rapid, regardless of their marital status, and their ability to control the number and timing of births is lower than it would be if they postponed childbearing until their 20s. Although the differentials five years after the start of childbearing appear to have diminished in the period since 1965 for whites, and are not large in absolute terms for blacks, it remains to be seen whether early childbearers can as successfully curtail their fertility as those who become mothers at older ages. The present evidence suggests that these young women are still, therefore, a group in need of special attention and help.

Table 12. Percentage distribution of first births by legitimacy status of first birth, according to race and mother's age at first birth

Race and status	Age at 1st birth				
	<30	15-17	18-19	20-24	25-29
Whites					
OW	6	14	8	4	3
Legit	17	35	27	11	5
PM	77	51	65	85	92
Blacks					
OW	50	70	48	31	23
Legit	20	19	26	18	9
PM	30	12	26	50	69
Total	100	100	100	100	100

Note: Percents may not add to 100 because of rounding.

In addition, in contrast to studies which suggest that childbearing is not a serious problem biologically for 18–19-year-olds and that attention should focus on women 17 and younger,[8] our work suggests that in social terms, 18–19-year-olds, who indeed experience somewhat lower subsequent fertility and fewer unwanted births than younger women, are still a higher risk group than women whose first birth occurs after age 20. Any program geared to enable young women to have the children they want to bear should not neglect the older teenager.

References

1. C. F. Westoff and N. B. Ryder, *The Contraceptive Revolution,* Princeton University Press, Princeton, N.J., 1977, pp. 284–285; and U.S. Bureau of the Census, *Census of Population, 1970. Subject Reports, Final Report PC(2)–3B, Childspacing and Current Fertility,* U.S. Government Printing Office, Washington, D.C. (GPO), 1975.

2. L. Coombs and R. Freedman, "Premarital Pregnancy, Childspacing, and Later Economic Achievement," *Population Studies,* 24:389, 1970.

3. K. A. Moore and L. J. Waite, "Early Childbearing and Educational Attainment," *Family Planning Perspectives,* 9:220, 1977.

4. J. J. Card and L. L. Wise, "Teenage Mothers and Teenage Fathers: The Impact of Early Childbearing on the Parents' Personal and Professional Lives," chapter 13, above.

5. B. Vaughan, J. Trussell, J. Menken and E. F. Jones, "Contraceptive Efficacy Among Married Women in the United States: 1970–1973," *Vital and Health Statistics,* Series 11, Appendix D, 1979.

6. N. B. Ryder and C. F. Westoff, *Reproduction in the United States, 1965,* Princeton University Press, Princeton, N.J., 1971, pp. 241–244; and C. F. Westoff and N. B. Ryder, 1977, op. cit., pp. 249–253.

7. R. L. Heuser, *Fertility Tables for Birth Cohorts by Color, United States, 1917–1973,* National Center for Health Statistics, GPO, 1976.

8. J. Menken, "Health and Demographic Consequences of Adolescent Pregnancy and Childbearing," in W. Baldwin and V. Cain, eds., *Teenage Childbearing: Recent Research on the Determinants and Consequences,* GPO, 1980.

16
Economic Consequences of Teenage Childbearing

James Trussell

Economists since the time of Malthus have attempted to unravel the interrelationship between fertility and various economic variables, primarily income. These analyses have concentrated mainly on two aspects of the economic determinants and consequences of fertility decisions: the macroeconomic impact of fertility on development and growth[1] and, more recently, the home economics approach, which employs microeconomic models to analyze fertility decisions.[2]

Unfortunately, neither the findings nor the approaches of previous analyses of the economics of fertility are particularly helpful in determining the economic effects of teenage childbearing. Moreover, the consequences of teenage childbearing, per se, except perhaps for the medical consequences, have been neglected by disciplines other than economics. Ideally, we should like to find the economic difference to the individual woman and to society if the woman becomes pregnant or does not become pregnant while a teenager. We may call the microeconomic consequences the economic differential between two average women, identical except that one became pregnant while still in her teens.

The impact of many such pregnancies produces a macroeconomic effect.

The new household economics postulates economic models of individual fertility decisions as well as other decisions of consequence, including marriage and suicide.[3] The approach, however, would claim neither that all children are wanted nor that all individuals can calculate costs, many in the future, without error. It seems unlikely that the bulk of teenage fertility is planned[4] or that teenagers can calculate costs very well. Nevertheless, the costs of teenage childbearing must be matched against the benefits, if any. Such benefits might include the satisfaction of being a mother, the comfort

The author thanks Rachel Thurston for invaluable help in locating and interpreting the mass of data used in preparing this paper. Bryan Boulier, Ansley Coale, Thomas J. Espenshade, Jane Menken, Norman Ryder and Charles Westoff each provided thoughtful criticisms and comments. The editorial help of Winifred Procter is appreciated. The article is adapted from a paper presented at a conference on Research on the Consequences of Adolescent Pregnancy and Childbearing, cosponsored by the Center for Population Research of the NICHD/NIH and The Alan Guttmacher Institute, Bethesda, Md., Oct. 29-30, 1975.

of conforming to some social norm, and the pleasure of procreating.

Direct Effects on Future Earnings

A woman's earnings can be viewed as a product of the wage rate available to her if she works and the extent of her labor force participation.[*] In this section, we will consider the effect of teenage childbearing on both variables. Though there have been many studies of women's labor force participation and their wage rates, none have been concerned with the impact of the timing of the first child per se. Recent studies of the determinants of wage rates are based upon models of human capital formation.[5] To the extent that the wage rate commanded is a function of the human capital stock accumulated by the individual, a sequence of positive net investment gives rise to growing earning power over the life cycle. When market skills are eroded by depreciation, net disinvestment occurs.

Two distinct sources of human capital accumulation, formal schooling and learning by doing (formal or informal on-the-job training), have long been recognized; and measures of schooling and length of work experience are usually included in wage equations.[†] Variables other than schooling and work experience, such as marital status, health, geographic region and mobility, often have been found to have explanatory power. The primary impact of teenage childbearing on wages is likely to operate through the two sources of human capital formation, though perhaps in opposite ways. Education is likely to be curtailed by pregnancy, especially if it occurs in high school. On the other hand, the woman may enter the labor market earlier and thus acquire more labor market experience. Another possible effect, particularly for husbands, is that those who have children early may also have to take jobs which offer less on-the-job training (i.e., jobs which have higher wage rates in the present rather than deferred higher wages in the future). Moreover, their opportunity to search for higher paying jobs may be curtailed by child-care responsibilities.

Attempts have been made to sort out these relative effects, using data from the 1967 Survey of Economic Opportunity (SEO).[‡][6] Since these data do not include the length of work experience, potential work experience has been used as a proxy.[§] Such a proxy overstates women's work experience and therefore biases the estimated experience coefficient downward. Equating potential and actual work experience is not the only source of error; further error arises from the assumption that all individuals start school at the same age and advance one grade with each passing year. Since

[*] Actually, the employment rate and not the labor force participation rate is the relevant variable, since a woman can be in the labor force but also be unemployed.

[†] Most such equations are empirically estimated by regression techniques.

[‡] The SEO was conducted by the Bureau of the Census at the request of the Office of Economic Opportunity. In 1966, 30,000 households (18,000 white and 12,000 drawn from areas with a high concentration of nonwhites) were surveyed; in 1967, the people living in the locations chosen in 1966 (not necessarily the same families) were reinterviewed. Questions about labor force experience and participation, income, wages and health were asked. The fertility history is quite complete; dates of birth of first, second, next to last and last child were asked of ever-married women or women with their own children in the household; moreover, the number of children ever born is available for such women. More information is available from the SEO clearinghouse at the University of Wisconsin. The *SEO Newsletter* contains an index to all known research using the SEO data.

[§] Age minus six years minus years of education.

Figure 1. Ratio of wage at age 30 if school is terminated at ages 15–22 compared to wage at age 30 if school is terminated at age 16,* by race

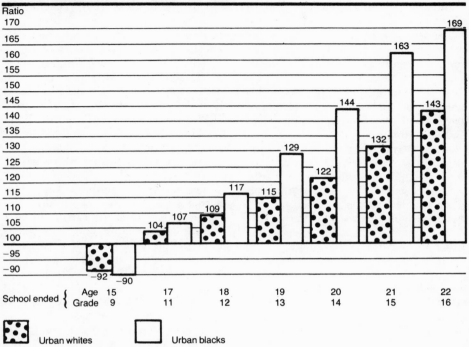

Urban whites   Urban blacks

*Assuming high school education completed at age 18.

Source: See reference 6, Table 2. Calculated according to personal characteristics wage regressions for urban women, assuming same number of children at age 30; same proportion working part-time; same proportion in each marital status; same proportion with health problems; same degree of mobility; and same distribution by size of urban area.

among those aged 16, only 68.0 percent of white females, 63.4 percent of white males, 52.4 percent of black females and 46.5 percent of black males are in the modal grade for their age group, substantial error is introduced even into the measure of potential work experience. As a rough attempt to handle the problem of lost experience, the number of children born to the female has been controlled. A further potential source of bias is the fact that the wage equation is based only upon the experience and characteristics of women who have earnings (specifically, in the week preceding the survey). Nonetheless, from the wage equations based on personal characteristics of the women (e.g., age and education), we can derive the wage women would receive at age 30 if they left school after completing different grades, but are otherwise alike at age 30. Figure 1 shows the results of such calculations, assuming that grade 12 is completed at age 18. A year of education is more important than a year of work experience, other things being equal. Further, the trade-off between work and experience is more pronounced for urban blacks than for urban whites.

What if education is held constant? Does teenage childbearing affect the accumulation of earning power beyond the effect on work experience? Though the question cannot be answered for teenagers, investigators have found that the number of children affects the wage rate only by reducing work experience.[7] Inclusion of a number-of-children variable does not add significantly to the explanatory power of the regression. This finding is important, since it is derived from the National Longitudinal Survey of Work Experience (NLS), which contains detailed work histories of a large sample of women 30-44. With this data file available, there is no need to use a less precise proxy for work experience.[*]

Labor Force Participation Rates

No study of female labor force participation rates (LFPR) has included the age of first childbearing as an independent variable. Much, however, is known about the general effect of children on the labor force participation of women. In a monumental study of the economics of labor force participation, it was found that LFPR of women is highly dependent upon the presence and ages of children in the household.[8] In general, the younger the ages of the children, the lower is the proportion of women in the labor force. This inverse relationship is especially pronounced for children under the age of six. Moreover, it is well known that even if marriage cohort and the time of last birth are controlled, LFPRs vary inversely with the total number of children. Data from the child-spacing volume of the 1960 census, shown in Table 1, illustrate this relationship.

These data indicate that if age at first marriage and number of children are held constant, then the earlier the first child is born, the greater is the labor force participation rate of women in 1960. Of white women who were married during 1945-1949 and who had two children, 36.4 percent whose first child was born before 1950 but only 30.2 percent whose first child was born after 1950 were working in 1960; similar results hold for women with three or more children. Hence, there is some indication that earlier childbearing leads to

---

[*] The NLS is a study of the labor market experience of four groups in the U.S. population: men 45-59 years of age, women 30-44 years of age, and young men and women 14-24 years of age. For convenience, these groups have been labeled men, women, boys and girls, respectively. Women were interviewed in 1967, 1969, 1971 and 1972; a brief questionnaire was mailed to them in 1968. Girls were interviewed annually from 1968 through 1973. Each cohort was represented by a national probability sample of approximately 5,000 individuals. The shrinkage of the samples has been very small; 88 percent of women and 86 percent of girls, respectively, were interviewed in the last scheduled survey. It has been decided that the surveys will be continued for five more years by means of a short telephone interview. There are to be two biennial surveys of this type for each cohort; and, if this experience is favorable, a final face-to-face interview is scheduled for the end of the five-year period.

The data collected on labor market experience and human capital formation are quite extensive. Information on the current school-enrollment status of girls has been collected at every survey. Thus, movement in and out of the formal educational system can be discerned. There is also an index of high school quality; high school curriculum, field of specialization in college, and amount of scholarship aid in college illustrate the kinds of information collected.

The fertility history of older women is inadequate. The month and year of entry of the first child into the family are included in the tapes, but one cannot be sure whether the child is the woman's own. Similarly, the number of children ever born is not asked specifically; it can only be estimated indirectly from answers to several questions. The year of birth of the first child is not asked of girls, nor is their fertility history adequate.

higher rates of labor force participation. Such a conclusion is admittedly very weak, since the data may simply be measuring a babysitter effect, as noted in the study cited above (see reference 8). Although the youngest children of the two groups of women were the same age, the oldest children of the women who had had their first births at younger ages would be older, and could function as babysitters, thereby freeing the mothers for work. If we control for the ages of all children by comparing the cohort of 1950-1954 with the cohort of 1945-1949 (bottom panel of Table 1), we see that the women who married between 1950 and 1954, and therefore had their first child and subsequent children at younger ages, also had higher labor force participation rates. These rates, however, are only marginally higher, and comparison of two different marriage cohorts captures women at different points in their life cycle.

On the other hand, an extensive economic analysis that used the NLS data to examine the timing of births and women's LFPR[9] found that the age of first childbearing was positively related to the rate of labor force participation if wife's and husband's education, income, number of children and age were held constant. Since in another regression in the same study, the age of first childbearing and wife's education were found to be strongly and positively correlated, omission of this control from Table 1 might explain the contradictory results.

Human capital theory predicts a strong positive association between years of school completed and labor force participation rates. Primarily, more education increases a woman's expected market wage and encourages her to substitute time in the labor market for time she might otherwise spend in the home. Moreover, additional education gives

Table 1. Labor force participation rates (LFPR) in 1960 per 1,000 white ever-married women whose most recent birth occurred 1950-1954

First child born	No. of children	LFPR for marriage cohort	
		1950-1954	1945-1949
<1950	≥3	na	332
	2	na	364
1950-1954	≥3	300	284
	2	335	302
	1	457	416

Source: U.S. Bureau of the Census, *Census of Population: 1960. Subject Reports: Childspacing*, PC(2)-3B, U.S. Government Printing Office, Washington, D.C., 1968, p. 180.   Note: na = not applicable.

opportunities for more stimulating work, and the psychic income derived from work is undoubtedly an important component of real income. Such expectations are supported by empirical tests.

One study has shown that for various age and sex groups in the U.S. population, there exists a strong positive relationship between labor force participation rates and educational attainment.[10] Hence, we see that education is positively related not only to wage rates but also to labor force participation rates. It is important, therefore, to determine whether teenage pregnancy curtails the number of years of education completed by the female.

Education

It is often difficult to distinguish between variables that are clearly antecedent and those that are clearly consequent in order to establish unambiguously the causal connection and temporal sequence of events. Hence, it is difficult to determine whether early pregnancy curtails a woman's formal educational experience or whether her education has been terminated prior to childbearing. Undoubtedly, for many women, espe-

Table 2. Percent distribution of U.S. women by years of school completed, according to age at first birth and race, Survey of Economic Opportunity (SEO), 1967

Age and race	No. of women (000s)	% by years of school completed					
		Total	0-4	5-8	9-11	12	≧13
All races							
All ages	45,272	100.0	4.8	22.6	20.8	36.1	15.6
13-15	1,325	100.0	14.5	43.3	30.0	10.6	1.6
16-17	4,680	100.0	6.2	33.5	40.5	17.5	2.2
18-19	9,023	100.0	4.5	24.5	26.2	38.7	6.1
20-21	9,230	100.0	4.6	21.0	18.6	41.5	14.2
≧22	21,014	100.0	4.2	18.8	14.5	38.4	24.1
White							
All ages	40,885	100.0	4.0	22.1	20.2	37.6	16.1
13-15	807	100.0	13.3	47.1	28.5	9.3	1.7
16-17	3,760	100.0	5.4	33.3	41.6	17.8	1.9
18-19	8,063	100.0	3.5	24.6	25.7	40.1	6.0
20-21	8,473	100.0	3.8	20.7	18.6	42.6	14.3
≧22	19,782	100.0	3.7	18.5	14.3	39.3	24.3
Black							
All ages	3,984	100.0	11.9	28.6	27.2	22.5	9.9
13-15	510	100.0	16.9	37.1	32.0	12.9	1.2
16-17	881	100.0	9.2	33.7	36.9	17.3	3.0
18-19	897	100.0	11.4	23.9	31.2	26.9	6.8
20-21	684	100.0	13.0	25.9	19.2	29.7	12.4
≧22	1,012	100.0	11.4	25.8	18.3	23.0	21.4

Source: See reference 11, Table 3.

Note: Percents may not add to 100 because of rounding.

cially those with eight or fewer years of education, the negative relationship between age of first childbearing and years of education is merely associative, and early pregnancy cannot be interpreted as causing low educational achievement. Nevertheless, as analysis of the 1967 SEO data has shown, and as can be seen in Table 2, age of first childbearing and educational attainment are strongly associated.[11] Furthermore, since pregnancy and motherhood have been among the primary reasons for dropping out of school, it would appear that Table 2 displays more than simple association. Among those women with very low educational attainment, only the very young childbearers are distinct; 15 percent who became mothers at 13-15 years, but only six percent at most of those who became

mothers at any other age, had four or fewer years of schooling. The proportion of women who went on to college increased from two percent of those who gave birth at the earliest ages of childbearing to 24 percent of those who became mothers at 22 years of age or later. The proportion of women who completed high school also rose with increased age at motherhood. Only 18 percent of women who bore children below age 18 ever completed high school compared to 57 percent of those who initiated childbearing at 18 or older. There is very little difference between whites and blacks; for ages at first childbearing above 18, the differential between whites and blacks is sharp, with more than three times as many of the latter completing four or fewer years of school and a much smaller percentage completing 12 years. The sample includes only ever-married mothers, so that mothers who had not married by the time of the survey are excluded. A more straightforward approach would be to survey school districts directly, and several investigators have done so, with minimal results. One such study, which examined 153 school districts in the continental United States in cities with populations of 100,000 or more, found that statistics concerning teenage pregnancy and marriage, even in these large school districts, are inadequate.[12] Nevertheless, the study found that there had been a definite shift in policy in the major cities since 1940 to accommodate a higher percentage of young women who were married, were mothers or were pregnant. In general, when such students were permitted to attend school, they attended regular classes; however, there was a tendency to assign them to adult evening school.

A later study, which surveyed by questionnaire the administrators of various agencies in 150 U.S. cities with populations of 100,000 or more, found that the officials of almost half the cities were unable to provide information on the population of teenage mothers and the number of live births to women under 20 years of age.[13]

Forced exclusion from public schools of teenagers who are mothers or who are married or pregnant is now illegal. These students cannot be excluded from regular classes except at their own request.[*]

Therefore, one obstacle to educational achievement has been eliminated. It is still not known, however, what proportion of such women will continue to attend school. One study in Philadelphia followed 100 girls, 17 years of age or younger and in their first pregnancy, from September 1967 to September 1970.[14] During pregnancy, 61 dropped out of school. Of the 61, however, 24 continued to attend school in a special program for pregnant schoolgirls begun in early 1968. Only 33 percent of the 61 are known to have returned to school following delivery, although the percentage was higher (56 percent) among those attending a special teenage obstetrical clinic. Another study, of 180 girls younger than 19 years of age who registered for prenatal care at the Yale-New Haven Hospital from 1967 to 1969, found that at the time of registration, 83 percent were still in school.[15] Moreover, 77 percent either had been graduated or were enrolled two months postpartum.

Effect on Children and Husbands

The effect of early childbearing on the husband and father has not been analyzed, but several studies made in the Detroit area are suggestive.[16] The data were derived from interviews in 1962 with 1,113 married women who had had a first, second or fourth birth in July 1961. These women were reinterviewed in 1962, 1963 and 1966.[†] The effect of

---

[*] Title IX of the Educational Amendments of 1972, effective July 12, 1975. (See: *Federal Register*, 40:24142, 1975.)

[†] The Detroit Family Growth Study analyses are based on interviews with women in the Detroit metropolitan area in 1962, selected to constitute a probability sample of all married white women in the area who had had a first, second or fourth birth in July 1961. This panel was reinterviewed three times, mainly by telephone, in the fall of 1962, 1963 and 1966. Those pregnant at the final interview were later reinterviewed, so that all birth data are based on completed pregnancies. Eighty-five percent of women in the original sample were interviewed all four times. The data contain extensive information on pregnancy histories, family size expectations, and a wide range of social and economic variables.

Table 3. Percent distribution of premaritally pregnant couples (PMP) and non-PMP couples by years of school completed by husband, according to length of first birth interval and husband's age at marriage, Detroit, 1962-1966

Length of interval and age	% by years of school completed by husband					
	Total	<9	9-11	12	13-15	≧16
All couples						
Total (N=1,053)	100	7	22	36	17	18
PMP couples (N=208)	100	8	37	34	14	7
Non-PMP couples						
<one year (N=342)	100	6	13	41	20	20
≧one year (N=503)	100	7	21	34	18	20
Husband 16-19 years old at marriage						
Total (N=144)	100	10	41	36	12	1
PMP couples (N=56)	100	4	50	39	5	2
Non-PMP couples						
<one year (N=37)	100	22	24	40	14	0
≧one year (N=51)	100	8	45	29	18	0
Husband 20-22 years old at marriage						
Total (N=394)	100	4	23	42	20	11
PMP couples (N=90)	100	3	34	37	20	6
Non-PMP couples						
<one year (N=117)	100	2	17	50	20	11
≧one year (N=187)	100	6	22	40	19	13
Husband >22 years old at marriage						
Total (N=515)	100	8	15	31	18	28
PMP couples (N=62)	100	19	31	24	13	13
Non-PMP couples						
<one year (N=188)	100	5	9	36	20	30
≧one year (N=265)	100	7	16	30	17	30

Source: See reference 23, Table 10.

premarital pregnancy and the length of the childspacing interval on later economic achievement was investigated. The sample of wives was divided according to whether their first birth had resulted from a premarital pregnancy (PMP), had occurred within one year of marriage (short spacers), or had occurred more than a year after marriage (long spacers). In 1961 and 1966, long spacers had both higher family incomes and greater family assets than short spacers, who in turn were substantially better off economically and earned more than couples whose first child had been premaritally conceived. These results held when husband's income alone was analyzed, indicating that the wife's income or work experience was not the important determinant of the differential across groups. If marriage duration, or age at first birth, or current age, was held constant, differences between short and long spacers disappeared.

However, the PMP couples suffered a substantial disadvantage. Their income differential disappeared only if education and marriage duration were controlled; moreover, with such controls, their unfavorable asset position was only reduced, not eliminated. Hence, the husband's education at the time of premarital pregnancy is particularly important. Table 3 shows that long and short spacers differed very little in years of schooling completed by the husband, but among couples with a premarital pregnancy, the husband had had markedly fewer years of schooling. The PMP couples were much more likely to have been married at an early age; they were on the average 1.7 years younger at marriage than the others, and many were so young that marriage may have interrupted their education. Thirty-seven percent of the husbands whose wives were pregnant before marriage, but only 18 percent of the other husbands, started but did not complete high school. Husbands of PMP wives were only one-third as likely as other husbands to have finished college.

Interruption of education by early marriage does not, however, entirely explain the lower educational achievement of the husbands of PMP wives, because in only one-quarter of the cases were they under age 20 at marriage. As with mothers, the link between educational achievement and early childbearing and marriage seems to function in opposite ways for different segments of the sample. Among one group, pregnancy leads to dropping out of school, perhaps because of the necessity for marrying young. Among the other group, factors predisposing to little education or resulting from it are also conducive to premarital pregnancy.

While the structure of this analysis and the limitations of the data preclude direct assessment of the effect of early childbearing on later economic achievement, early childbearing does appear to

Table 4. Percent of U.S. women living in poverty, by age at first birth and race, SEO, 1967

Age and race	No. of women	No. in poverty	% in poverty
All races			
All ages	45,272	6,467	14.3
13-15	1,325	410	30.9
16-17	4,680	1,084	23.2
18-19	9,023	1,430	15.8
20-21	9,230	1,327	14.4
≥22	21,014	2,216	10.5
White			
All ages	40,885	4,929	12.1
13-15	807	160	19.8
16-17	3,760	733	19.5
18-19	8,063	1,087	13.5
20-21	8,473	1,065	12.6
≥22	19,782	1,884	9.5
Black			
All ages	3,984	1,461	36.7
13-15	510	246	48.2
16-17	881	342	38.8
18-19	897	327	36.5
20-21	684	251	36.7
≥22	1,012	295	29.2

Source: See reference 11, Table 2.

have a negative impact on income and assets, although it is not clear whether this effect results only from reduced educational attainment.

Public Aid and Income

As a recent study has shown, the incidence of poverty rises substantially as the age at which women become mothers falls.[17] This pattern, shown in Table 4, holds for both whites and blacks. A very real possibility exists, however, that the causation runs the other way. Perhaps the poor are more likely to become pregnant when young, thereby curtailing their education and perpetuating a cycle of poverty. A study published in 1972 estimates that 60 percent of white, and 80 percent of nonwhite, children born out of wedlock in 1964-1966 were delivered by women below the near-poverty line.[18] Another investigator reported that in 1967, medical expenses were paid from public funds for 52 percent of white out-of-wedlock births, but only for 10 percent of white legitimate births.[19] The corresponding figures for blacks are 76 percent and 40 percent, respectively. Neither of these studies controls for age at birth; but the bulk of out-of-wedlock births in 1974 (53 percent) occurred to young women below the age of 20.[20] While the findings of neither study are conclusive, both lend support to the hypothesis that poverty leads to early childbearing. It would appear, moreover, that illegitimacy imposes an additional cost upon the public.

Investigators who made a nationwide survey of the sexual, contraceptive and pregnancy experience of a representative sample of teenagers found that at every age from 15 to 19, unmarried girls from poor families were more likely to have had intercourse than unmarried girls from nonpoor families, and that the poor knew less about the risks of pregnancy than the nonpoor.[21] They also reported that the poor were less likely to use contraception, although among those who did, the black poor were more likely than the black nonpoor to use effective methods.[22] Thus, it appears fairly certain that poor teenagers are going to become pregnant more often than nonpoor teenagers.

Other investigators have found that the social background of the family of origin of the couples whose first child was premaritally conceived did not account for their disadvantaged position after marriage, and that those couples were not drawn from lower status groups.[23] This finding may be a result of their sample: Poor women are less likely to marry if they become pregnant, and unmarried women were not included in the sample.

Unwanted Children and Illegitimacy

Excess costs of unwanted children over those of wanted children have, however, been demonstrated. A longitudinal study of 120 Swedish children, born after an application by the mother for therapeutic abortion was refused, found markedly higher social pathology among these children than among a control group.[24] A British study has estimated that the excess public expenditure for supplementary benefits, child care and sickness benefits, and temporary accommodations is substantial for the out-of-wedlock and average unwanted child.[25] Although equivalent studies for a U.S. population have not been conducted, it would appear that children of teenage mothers, to the extent that they are disproportionately unwanted, would constitute a heavy social cost. An American sociologist reported recently that the percentage of planned first births rose steadily with age of childbearing from 19 percent in the age group 15-19 to 44 percent among women aged 20-23, and to 70 percent among women 24-29 years of age.[26] While unplanned births are not necessarily unwanted, these findings suggest that children of younger mothers may be disproportionately unwanted.*

Are any excess costs attributable to a birth solely because it occurs outside

---

*It may prove difficult to find an operational definition of 'unwanted' for unmarried young women which is as neat and precise as the one for married women developed in the Indianapolis survey and refined in the National Fertility Studies. Births to married women were judged to be unwanted if they constituted excess fertility. By this definition, few young women could have unwanted births. Nevertheless, births to unmarried young women could very well be unwanted in the literal sense of the word, and the motivation for delaying pregnancy will undoubtedly prove to be as powerful a predictor for young unwed women as it has for older women who want no more children ever.

marriage? As previously noted, the expenses of out-of-wedlock childbirth are more likely to be paid for from the public coffers than are those of childbirth inside marriage.[27] However, unless out-of-wedlock births cost more in terms of real resources, regardless of their source of financing, they would create no excess social costs. Whether bearing a child out of wedlock affects subsequent educational attainment and economic achievement is not known. The excess social costs of an out-of-wedlock child compared with one born inside marriage have not been quantified either. Nevertheless, because out-of-wedlock births comprise a large proportion of births to teenagers (36 percent in 1974),[28] the question should be addressed.

Early and Subsequent Childbearing

It has been established that the earlier the age of first marriage, the greater is cumulated fertility;[29] data from the 1970 census indicate that the differential is quite large.[30] The same result almost certainly holds for age at first birth, although the census does not tabulate cumulated fertility by duration of time elapsed since first birth in this manner. Preliminary data from the 1973 National Survey of Family Growth, shown in Table 5, reveal the strong inverse association between completed fertility and age at first birth.[31] (Unfortunately, there is no life-cycle control such as current age, or time since first birth or marriage cohort.)

In addition, several small studies have found that the incidence of repeat pregnancies among teenage mothers is quite high. In one study, it was estimated that between 29 percent of mothers in a special program and 53 percent of mothers in a control group became pregnant again within two years.[32] In another

Table 5. Number of children ever born, additional births expected, and total births expected per 1,000 mothers under 45 years of age, according to age of mother at first birth, National Natality Survey (NNS), 1972, and National Survey of Family Growth (NSFG), 1973

Age	% of mothers	Children ever born	Additional births expected	Total births expected
NNS (N=2,818)				
All mothers	100.0	2,245	788	3,033
Age at 1st birth				
<18	10.4	2,633	760	3,393
18-19	19.2	2,346	780	3,126
20-21	21.3	2,284	822	3,106
22-24	25.6	2,026	878	2,904
25-29	18.5	2,112	742	2,854
≥30	4.9	2,498	439	2,937
NSFG (N=21,201)				
All mothers	100.0	2,682	339	3,022
Age at 1st birth				
<18	12.6	3,439	327	3,766
18-19	24.1	2,896	328	3,224
20-21	23.6	2,728	322	3,050
22-24	23.4	2,443	344	2,787
25-29	13.6	2,100	394	2,494
≥30	2.7	1,756	388	2,144

Source: See reference 31, Table 12.

Note: Percents may not add to 100 because of rounding.

study, it was reported that 20 percent of teenage mothers became pregnant a second time an average of 14.5 months after the first birth; two years later, more than 40 percent were found to have become pregnant again.[33] If early childbearing causes higher completed fertility, and if higher fertility imposes heavier social costs, then this indirect effect should be included in an accounting of costs. Early childbearing may, however, simply reflect higher fecundability (or inept contraceptive practice); higher fecundability, which cannot be directly measured, may cause the observed association between early and greater childbearing.

Maternal mortality rates, although very low in recent years, are higher for teenagers than for mothers in their early twenties.[34] Maternal morbidity rates are also considerably higher, especially among very young teenage mothers.[35] Fetal, neonatal and postneonatal mortality have been found to be significantly higher when the mother or pregnant woman is a teenager than when she gives birth in her twenties.[36] And surviving infants of young mothers are subject ro relatively high risks of morbidity, including permanent neurological and other defects, ascribed largely to the increased likelihood of low birth weight among the offspring of young mothers.[37] Clearly, there are increased medical costs involved in these increased risks, as well as the social and individual costs involved in lost work experience by the mother. While some of the increased health risks of teenage pregnancy and childbearing are certainly biological, it is not clear from existing research how much of these increased risks is due to age alone, and how much to socioeconomic factors.[38]

Research Needs

Although little is known with certainty about the economic effects of teenage pregnancy and childbearing, minor refinements of existing methodology could yield useful results without enormous cost or effort. Data from both the Survey of Economic Opportunity and National Longitudinal Survey have yet to be mined fully. The SEO data have the twin advantages of being surprisingly clean and containing rather complete fertility histories, but they have the disadvantage of becoming increasingly dated; data from the NLS are much less clean and contain paltry fertility information. However, the NLS data are rela-

tively current; the NLS cohort of women aged 14-24 in 1967 provides an ongoing opportunity to analyze childbearing and labor market decisions as they occur. Several answers could be provided by analyzing these data, including:
• the effect of early childbearing on the wage rate;
• the effect of early childbearing on the labor force participation rate; and
• the effect of early pregnancy on the probability of dropping out of high school.

References

1. A. J. Coale and E. Hoover, *Population Growth and Economic Development in Low Income Countries,* Princeton University Press, Princeton, N.J., 1958; S. Enke, *Economics for Development,* Prentice-Hall, Englewood Cliffs, N.J., 1963; ———, "Birth Control for Economic Development," *Science,* 164: 798, 1969; ———, "The Economic Aspects of Slowing Population Growth," *Economic Journal,* Mar. 1966; S. Enke and R. G. Zind, "Effects of Fewer Births on Average Income," *Journal of Biosocial Science,* 1:41, 1969; S. Enke and H. Leibenstein, "An Exchange of Comments on Leibenstein's Paper 'Pitfalls of Benefit-Cost Analysis of Birth Prevention,'" *Population Studies,* 64:115, 1970; E. Hagen, "Population and Economic Growth," *American Economic Review,* June 1959; A. Hansen, "Economic Progress and Declining Population Growth," *American Economic Review,* Vol. 24, No. 1, Part 1, 1939; and H. Leibenstein, *Economic Backwardness and Economic Growth,* Chapman and Hall, London, 1957.

2. G. Becker, "An Economic Analysis of Fertility," in National Bureau of Economic Research, *Demographic and Economic Change in Developed Countries,* Princeton University Press, Princeton, N.J., 1960, pp. 209-231; G. Becker and H. G. Lewis, "On the Interaction Between the Quantity and Quality of Children," *Journal of Political Economy,* 81:S279, 1973; J. Blake, "Are Babies Consumer Durables?" *Population Studies,* 22:5, 1968; G. G. Cain and A. Weininger, "Economic Determinants of Fertility: Results from Cross-Sectional Aggregate Data," *Demography,* 10:205, 1973; H. Leibenstein, "An Interpretation of the Economic Theory of Fertility: Promising Path or Blind Alley?" *Journal of Economic Literature,* 12:457, 1974; E. Mueller, "Economic Motives for Family Limitation," *Population*

Studies, 26:383, 1972; T. P. Schultz, "A Preliminary Survey of Economic Analysis of Fertility," *American Economic Review*, 63:71, 1973; and J. Simon, "The Effect of Income on Fertility," *Population Studies*, 23:327, 1969.

3. G. Becker, "A Theory of Marriage: Part I," *Journal of Political Economy*, 81:813, 1973; ———, "A Theory of Marriage: Part II," *Journal of Political Economy*, 82:511, 1974; and D. Hamermesh and N. Soss, "An Economic Theory of Suicide," *Journal of Political Economy*, 82:83, 1974.

4. H. B. Presser, "Early Motherhood: Ignorance or Bliss?" chapter 22, below.

5. T. Johnson, "Returns from Investment in Human Capital," *American Economic Review*, Sept. 1970; and J. Mincer, "The Distribution of Labor Incomes: A Survey with Special Reference to the Human Capital Approach," *Journal of Economic Literature*, 8:1, 1970.

6. R. Oaxaca, "Male-Female Wage Differentials in Urban Labor Markets," *International Economic Review*, 14:693, 1973.

7. J. Mincer and S. Polachek, "Family Investments in Human Capital: Earnings of Women," *Journal of Political Economy*, 82:576, 1974.

8. W. Bowen and T. A. Finegan, *The Economics of Labor Force Participation*, Princeton University Press, Princeton, N.J., 1969.

9. S. G. Ross, "The Timing and Spacing of Births and Women's Labor Force Participation: An Economic Analysis," National Bureau of Economic Research Working Paper #30, Washington, D.C., 1974.

10. W. Bowen and T. A. Finegan, 1969, op. cit.

11. L. A. Bacon, "Early Motherhood, Accelerated Role Transition and Social Pathology," *Social Forces*, Mar. 1974.

12. G. C. Atkyns, "Trends in the Retention of Married and Pregnant Students in American Public Schools," *Sociology of Education*, 41:57, 1968.

13. H. M. Wallace, E. M. Gold, H. Goldstein and A. C. Olgesby, "A Study of Services and Needs of Teenage Pregnant Girls in the Large Cities of the United States," *American Journal of Public Health*, 63:5, 1973.

14. H. O. Dickens, E. H. Mudd, C.-R. Garcia, K. Toman and D. Wright, "One Hundred Pregnant Adolescents, Treatment Approaches in a University Hospital," *American Journal of Public Health*, 63:794, 1973.

15. A.-M. Foltz, L. Klerman and J. Jekel, "Pregnancy and Special Education: Who Stays in School?" *American Journal of Public Health*, 62:1612, 1972.

16. L. Coombs and R. Freedman, "Premarital Pregnancy, Childbearing and Later Economic Achievement," *Population Studies*, 24:389, 1970; and R. Freedman and L. Coombs, "Childspacing and Family Economic Position," *American Sociological Review*, 31:631, 1966.

17. L. A. Bacon, 1974, op. cit.

18. P. Cutright, "Illegitimacy in the United States: 1920-1968," in Commission on Population Growth and the American Future, *Demographic and Social Aspects of Population Growth*, C. F. Westoff and R. Parke, Jr., eds., Vol. 1 of Commission Research Reports, U.S. Government Printing Office, Washington, D.C. (GPO), 1972, p. 375.

19. B. Berkov, "Illegitimate Fertility in California's Population," University of California, Berkeley, 1971 (unpublished manuscript).

20. National Center for Health Statistics, DHEW (NCHS), "Advance Report: Final Natality Statistics, 1974," *Monthly Vital Statistics Report*, Vol. 24, No. 11, Supplement 2, 1976.

21. J. F. Kantner and M. Zelnik, "Sexual Experience of Young Unmarried Women in the United States," *Family Planning Perspectives*, Vol. 4, No. 4, 1972, p. 9.

22. J. F. Kantner and M. Zelnik, "Contraception and Pregnancy: Experience of Young Unmarried Women in the United States," *Family Planning Perspectives*, 5:21, 1973.

23. L. Coombs, R. Freedman, J. Freidman and W. Pratt, "Premarital Pregnancy and Status Before and After Marriage," *American Journal of Sociology*, 75:800, 1970.

24. H. Forssman and I. Thuwe, "One Hundred and Twenty Children Born After Application for Therapeutic Abortion Refused," *Acta Psychiatrica Scandinavia*, 42:71, 1966.

25. W. A. Laing, *The Costs and Benefits of Family Planning*, Population and Economic Planning, (PEP), London, 1972.

26. H. B. Presser, 1974, op. cit.

27. B. Berkov, 1971, op. cit.

28. NCHS, 1976, op. cit.

29. L. Bumpass, "Age at Marriage as a Variable in Socio-Economic Differentials in Fertility," *Demography*, 6:45, 1969; and J. Busfield, "Age at Marriage and Family Size: Social Causation and Social Selection Hypotheses," *Journal of Biosocial Science*, 4:117, 1972.

30. U.S. Bureau of the Census, *Census of Population: 1970. Subject Reports: Women by Number of Children Ever Born*, Final Report PC(2)-3A, GPO, 1973.

31. G. S. Bonham and P. J. Placek, "The Impact of Social and Demographic, Maternal Health and Infant Health Factors on Expected Family Size: Preliminary Findings from the 1973 National Survey of Family Growth and the 1972 National Natality Survey," paper presented at the annual meeting of the Population Association of America, Seattle, Apr. 17-19, 1975.

32. J. B. Currie, J. F. Jekel and L. V. Klerman, "Subsequent Pregnancies Among Teenage Mothers Enrolled in a Special Program," *American Journal of Public Health,* **62:**1606, 1972.

33. C. M. Drillien, "School Disposal and Performance for Children of Different Birthweight Born 1953-1960," *Archives of Diseases of Childhood,* **44:**562, 1969.

34. NCHS, *Vital Statistics of the United States, 1974, Vol. II, Mortality,* GPO, 1978.

35. D. Nortman, "Parental Age as a Factor in Pregnancy Outcome and Child Development," *Reports on Population/Family Planning,* No. 16, Aug. 1974, Figure 10.

36. NCHS, *Vital Statistics . . . ,* 1976, op. cit.

37. NCHS, *Vital Statistics of the United States, 1974, Vol. 1, Natality,* GPO, 1978.

38. J. A. Menken, "The Health and Social Consequences of Adolescent Pregnancy and Childbearing," paper presented at the Conference on Research on the Consequences of Adolescent Pregnancy and Childbearing, Bethesda, Md., Oct. 29-30, 1975.

17

The Children of Teenage Parents

Wendy Baldwin and Virginia S. Cain

Summary and Introduction

Teenage childbearing is associated with adverse, pervasive and long-lasting social and economic consequences for the young parents, especially adolescent mothers, who, at very young ages, also appear to be at higher risk of maternal morbidity and mortality.[1] Insofar as lower education and income and greater marital instability adversely affect the environment in which teenagers bring up their children, it might be expected that the life chances of their children would also be adversely affected. However, until recently, few studies have attempted to assess directly the impact of teenage parenthood on these children.[2] The relation of mother's age and child outcome can be viewed as the relation between becoming a mother as an adolescent and the outcome for subsequent children— regardless of the mother's age at their birth— or restricted to those children born while the woman is under age 20. This article addresses only the latter situation.

Recent research sheds light on the physical and developmental effects of teenage childbearing on the offspring. Most earlier studies highlighted the relationship of young maternal age with increased risk of low-birthweight babies and perinatal infant mortality.[3] The newer findings suggest that these phenomena are almost entirely functions of the quality of prenatal care received by the teenage mother. However, while excellent prenatal care of the teenager may result in the birth of a healthy infant, the subsequent health of her child may be severely jeopardized by early parenthood. All analyses show deficits in the cognitive development of children (especially male children) born to teenagers; much, but not all, of the effect results from the social and economic consequences of early childbearing. Less consistent effects are found for the children's social and emotional development and school adjustment. The children of teenage mothers are relatively likely to spend a considerable part of their childhood in one-parent households; and they are more likely themselves to have children while still adolescents. Adverse impacts can be observed long into the children's lives. A possible mediating factor between young maternal age and its impact on the child is family structure—that is, adverse effects are most likely to occur when the teenage mother raises her child without help from the father or her own parents.

This article is based on research conducted under the auspices of the Center for Population Research. The samples and methods employed in the individual studies are summarized in the appendix. The studies differ widely in terms of original purpose, measures available for analysis, age of the children when studied and racial, residential, economic and other characteristics of the sample. Data were collected at different times, and in two cases reflect the experiences of other countries. No one project may be viewed as definitive, but each makes a contribution to the delineation of how early childbearing affects the children of adolescent parents.

Physical Health

Previous research has pointed out the apparent increase in risks to the mother's and baby's health as a result of the young age of the mother. This increase is noted especially for second-order and higher order births. Using data for the period 1950–1967, Helen Chase has shown that the percentage of babies who are of low birth weight (under 2,500 grams) is much higher for those born to adolescents, and higher as well for babies of black or other nonwhite mothers.[4] Jane Menken, reviewing an analysis of the 1960 U.S. birth cohort data, shows increased risk of infant mortality associated with young maternal ages, and some increased risk for children of mothers over age 40. Menken remarks, "Just after birth, when biologic factors related to the pregnancy are the primary determinants of survival, risks to infants of young mothers are much higher than those to infants of older mothers in both color groups."[5] Such data have increased interest in unraveling the factors which tie maternal age to infant outcomes. Are many adolescents too biologically immature to produce healthy babies? Are inadequate prenatal care and nutrition among pregnant teenagers responsible for the risks observed?

Birgitte Mednick's study of 9,125 births in an urban Danish hospital around 1960 found that children born to younger mothers—including young adolescents—had lower rates of stillbirth and neonatal mortality than those born to older mothers, and that general indicators of health for both the mother and child in the perinatal period were also better (see Table 1, and Figure 1).[6] It is unlikely that differences in social class could explain this observation, since the adolescent mothers were from a lower socioeconomic group than were the older mothers. Also, since most teenagers in the catchment area were delivered in this program, it is unlikely that the program selected only teenagers highly motivated to get good prenatal care. These young women (aged 14 to 19) were drawn into a system of excellent prenatal care and, while apparently at high risk during pregnancy, had outcomes superior to those of older women.

Is this finding unique? A study of American women found similar results when high-quality prenatal care was provided. The results of the Collaborative Perinatal Project (CPP) indicated that the perinatal mortality rates were lowest for the children of young white adolescents and increased with age of mother.[7] Howard Sandler also examined the relationship between mother's age and baby's health and behavior, based on 1974–1976 birth data from Nashville General Hospital, a county hospital serving primarily low-income patients.[8] Mothers between the ages of 13 and 39 were categorized into 12 age-groups ranging from 13–14-year-olds to 25–39-year-olds. As may be seen in Table 2, no consistent or significant differences in neonatal outcomes were found between age-groups.* Next, the behavioral characteristics of the infants of adolescent mothers were compared with those of older mothers. Table 3 shows Brazelton scores, which are social and neurological assessments taken two days after birth, for children of adolescent and postadolescent mothers. Again, when the quality of medical care was

---

*Some of these age-groups were combined for presentation in Table 2.

Table 1. Pregnancy outcome variable scores,* by mother's age,† Copenhagen, 1959–1961

Mother's age	Pregnancy complications (1)	Delivery complications (2)	Neonatal physical status (3)	One-year physical status (4)	One-year motor development (5)
10–15	2.43	4.84	3.98	7.12	2.45
16–17	3.06	5.28	4.73	7.79	2.45
18–19	3.29	5.20	4.91	8.05	2.33
20–24	4.09	5.97	5.57	8.35	2.83
25–29	4.65	6.48	5.70	8.47	3.07
30–34	4.98	6.73	5.79	8.40	3.16
35–39	5.98	6.78	5.99	7.81	3.08
≥40	5.72	7.39	6.32	7.46	3.63

*Score is a composite indicating both number and severity of problems; the higher the score, the worse the health status.

†Only those variables which vary systematically with mother's age are presented.

Source: See reference 6.

maintained, babies born to adolescents did as well as babies born to older mothers. This study does not, however, show that adolescent obstetric patients fare better than older mothers. Younger adolescent women, pregnant for the first time, experienced more stress during pregnancy than did older women, regardless of parity (not shown).*

A study by Barry Lester also focused on Brazelton scores and found that babies of teenage mothers tested two days after birth were significantly more likely to be underaroused or overaroused than babies of older mothers; these differences were found in both a Florida and a Puerto Rico sample.

*This study has shown length of labor and parity to be related to drug dosage given prior to delivery. Primiparous women and women experiencing a long period of labor received stronger and larger doses of drugs. But as adolescents are likely to be both primiparous and in labor for a shorter period of time, the relationship between predelivery drug usage and age of mother is unclear. However, a clear relationship exists between the mother's usage of drugs and the infant's behavior. The usage and timing of such drugs is subsequently related to decrements in Brazelton scores. Drug dosage should be considered in viewing the effect of maternal characteristics on neonatal behavior.

Although the Brazelton scores of the babies of teenage mothers fell within the normal range, Lester emphasizes that these infants could face serious problems in the future. This is because of the likelihood that the stress of teenage motherhood could affect the interaction between mother and child so as to exaggerate the differences found soon after birth. Both samples were drawn from low-income populations.[9] Sixty-six percent of the adolescent mothers in the Florida group were unmarried, and most were black; while only nine percent were unmarried in the Puerto Rico sample of whites. In Florida, obstetric risk scores were higher for babies born of teenage mothers; this was not the case in Puerto Rico. Lester concludes that "analysis of Brazelton scores showed that when teenage mothers were matched for obstetric history and perinatal risk factors and further divided into high and low obstetric risk groups, infants of teenage mothers show scores comparable to infants of older mothers." Age of mother did not have an independent effect on behavioral outcomes. Obstetric risk was viewed as a function of the environment in which adolescent childbearing took place rather than as a function of age per

Figure 1. Stillbirth, neonatal and perinatal infant mortality rates per 1,000 births, by age of mother, Copenhagen, 1959–1961

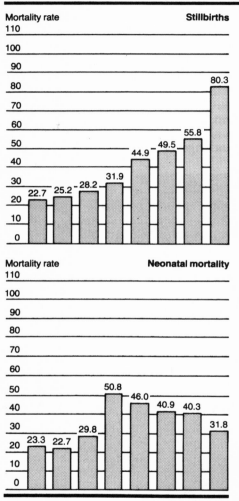

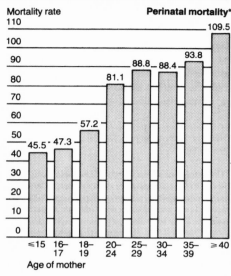

*Includes all fetal loss and deaths up to 28 days.
Source: See reference 6.

se. Thus, the differences between the findings for Florida and Puerto Rico could be due to the different sociocultural contexts in which childbearing occurred. In Puerto Rico, where early marriage and childbearing are accepted as part of normal adolescent development within this socioeconomic group, teenage mothers are likely to experi-

ence less stress. Other studies of adolescent pregnancy and delivery outcome have also suggested that problems associated with adolescent pregnancy may be due to factors other than mother's age, particularly, the quality of prenatal care.[10]

These studies all point to the heavy influence of nonbiological factors—especially the quality of prenatal care—on the relationship between mother's age and risk to the newborn. While encouraging the development of programs to provide such care, this research does not tell us what is the minimum increment in prenatal care programs that is needed, whether urban university-based programs can be translated to suburban or rural environments, what is the cost of such services in a variety of environments and whether taxpayers and policy-makers would view these expenses as cost-effective.

A corollary to the question of cost-effectiveness is the long-term impact of adolescent childbearing, even when perinatal risks are reduced. Both the Sandler and Mednick studies followed children longitudinally and found a somewhat different picture when later health status was assessed. The Danish data showed that at one year of age the children of adolescents did not fare worse than children of mothers in their 20s (see columns 4 and 5, Table 1), but that this relationship was strongly influenced by family structure. The babies of adolescent mothers who were raising the child alone were clearly worse off in terms of their physical health status score (mean 9.2) than those raised by the teenage mother and father (mean score 8.5) or the teenage mother and grandmother (7.6).[11] Sandler found an effect of mother's age on the mother-infant interaction observed at one, three, six and 12 months of the child's age. The older mothers spent more time talking to and looking at their babies than did the younger mothers and these positive social interactions between the mother and child were associated with higher scores on tests of the baby's motor and mental development at nine months (not shown).

Both studies point to the influence of the mother's age on the child's early development as transmitted through the environment. The Danish data show young maternal age, given high quality prenatal care, to be a benefit in terms of perinatal outcome. This early advantage is only maintained at one year, however, when the social environment is optimal. The Tennessee data show differences in the ways teenage and older mothers behave with their babies and differences in child development at later stages even when perinatal outcome has been good.

Cognitive Development

Two other studies focus on whether there is a lasting effect on a child's cognitive development associated with the mother's age at birth. Jeanne Marecek

Table 2. Mean physiological characteristics of infants, by mother's age, Nashville, 1974–1977

Mother's age	Birth weight (kg)	Birth length (cm)	Apgar 1-minute	Apgar 5-minute
13–14	3.05	49.33	7.00	8.33
15–16	3.19	50.52	8.07	9.62
17–18	3.10	49.47	8.12	9.45
19–20	3.11	49.29	8.43	9.48
21–24	3.19	50.26	7.77	9.49
25–39	3.01	49.71	9.50	10.00

Source: See reference 8.

found babies of black urban adolescent mothers to be slightly less well off when their development was measured by the Bayley Scales of Infant Development (at eight months of age), the Stanford-Binet test (at age four) and the Wechsler Intelligence Scale for Children (WISC) and Wide Range Achievement Tests (at age seven).[12] A similar pattern was found by Joy Dryfoos and Lillian Belmont using the total Collaborative Perinatal Project (CPP) data file and studying only seven-year-olds (see Table 4).[13] Regression analyses by Dryfoos and Belmont based on the Health Examination Survey (HES) data confirm small but significant effects of maternal age on IQ and also show a persistence of this effect over the three and one-half years between tests.

A study conducted by Frank Furstenberg in Baltimore included an assessment of preparation for school, the Preschool Inventory (PSI), among children aged 42–60 months.[14] The sample was composed primarily of children of urban, low-income, black adolescents. The children's scores, standardized for the child's age, were somewhat lower than the scores of the children of a sample of the adolescents' classmates who began childbearing at a later age, and were considerably lower than groups of middle-class black and white children and working-class white children. *Within* the sample of children of adolescent mothers, no relationship was found between mother's age and child's cognitive development. Children of mothers younger than 16 did as well as those of mothers aged 16–18. The amount of time the mother spent with the child was inversely related to the child's PSI score. The children of unmarried mothers who were not employed scored lower than those whose mothers worked outside of the home or were continuing their education, thus sharing the childrearing responsibilities with another adult. Generally, the working mothers and mothers attending school were economically advantaged when compared to the mothers who were not employed. In this study, as in others, the socioeconomic status of the mother was closely linked to her child's cognitive test scores. A further explanation, also suggested by other research, is that the child benefits from having an older, more experienced caretaker. Generally, the caretaker is the child's grandmother or other close relative who is likely to be concerned about the child's development and to provide more than just custodial care. Such an arrangement also provides at least two adult figures with whom the child has contact. The positive influence of more than one caretaker on the child's development is borne out by the finding that the children of mothers who married the child's father, and remained married during the study period, scored higher than children in other family situations. However, children whose mothers were unmarried and were working or going to school (who, therefore, had other caretakers besides their mothers) did nearly as well as the children of married mothers.

In sum, various analyses show a considerable relationship between a mother's age and her child's cognitive development. When background characteristics are controlled, a significant effect remains which is to the disadvantage of the children of adolescents. While statistically significant, the effect on measures of aptitude is small and may be trivial in terms of later achievement.

Social-Emotional Development

The relationship between mother's age and her child's social and emotional development is less well-defined than the relationship between age and cognitive development. Furstenberg used doll-play to measure efficacy, trust, self-esteem and ability to delay gratification among children aged 42–60 months; he found no major or consistent effect of having been born to an adolescent mother. When differences between subgroups of the adolescent sample were analyzed, however, a pattern did emerge. Children of mothers who married the child's father and remained married to him scored higher on the social-emotional development measures than other children. Initially, it was thought that the ability of the father and the child to maintain a stable relationship was the key factor in the child's development. However, among the children who did not reside with their fathers, the amount of father's involvement was not related to the child's scores. Additional analyses indicated that children of economically secure families scored higher on the efficacy and trust measures. This finding held true within the single-parent families. Children of unmarried mothers who completed high school and were not on welfare scored higher than more economically disadvantaged children. Furstenberg's study suggests that the factor in the intact families which influenced the child's social and emotional development was the economic advantage afforded by the two-parent household. Parents in these households were generally better educated and more regularly employed.

Marecek focused on the social and emotional behavior of children when the children were four and seven years of age.[15] The CPP data included measures of the child's interactions with a psychological tester who was administering IQ tests, as well as reports from the child's primary caretaker concerning the child's behavior at home. Maternal

Table 3. Mean infant's Brazelton Neonatal Behavioral Assessment Score, by mother's age, Nashville, 1974–1977

Brazelton Scale	Mother's age	
	13–19.5	19.6–39
Initial state	2.26	2.42
Predominant state 1	4.03	4.21
Predominant state 2	4.77	4.96
Interactive processes	2.31	2.38
Motoric processes	1.83	1.67
Organizational pro-cess: state control	2.10	2.00
Organizational pro-cess: physiological response to stress	1.87	1.83

Note: Scores on the first three items of the scale range from (1) deep sleep, to (3) moderate activity to (6) crying; initial state refers to the period two minutes before stimulation of the infant is begun; the predominant states refer to the periods during examination and stimulation of the infant. For the last four items on the scale, a normal score is 2.
Source: J. McLaughlin, H. Sandler, K. Sherrod, P. Vietze and S. O'Connor, "Social-Psychological Characteristics of Adolescent Mothers and Behavioral Characteristics of the First-Born Infants," paper presented at NICHD workshop, Bethesda, Md., Jan. 1979.

Table 4. Mean Wechsler Intelligence Scale for Children (WISC) full-scale IQ, for the Health Examination Survey (HES) and Collaborative Perinatal Project (CPP), by mother's age at birth of index child

Mother's age	HES		CPP (age 7)
	Cycle II (ages 6–11)	Cycle III (ages 12–17)	
14–17	94.41	91.46*	90.96
18–19	95.56	97.87	94.44
20–24	99.75	100.03	97.09
25–29	101.97	101.29	97.31
30–34	102.23	102.16	96.29
35–39	102.67	100.52	96.70
40–44	99.39	100.43	96.56
≥45	93.33	89.25	97.26

*Cycle III mean includes two cases with mothers aged 13 years.
Note: For description of HES and CPP, see appendix, p. 42.
Source: See reference 13.

age had little effect on the child's behavior at age four, but by age seven a number of effects were found: Children born to mothers younger than 18 exhibited greater overactivity, hostility, resistiveness and lack of impulse control. Dryfoos and Belmont, using Cycle II of the Health Examination Surveys, however, found no relationship between mother's age and child's social and emotional behavior.[16]

Overall, the effect of the mother's age on her child's social and emotional development is not as clear as it is on her child's cognitive development. It does seem that when an effect of young maternal age was present, it was negative and often was not evident until the child was nearing school age. Again, evidence suggests that the effect does not result from the mother's age at birth directly, but rather is transmitted through other factors associated with early childbearing, such as educational and economic disadvantage and greater likelihood of marital breakup.

School Achievement

Considering that the children of adolescent mothers are generally found to have lower IQ scores and, possibly, greater social adjustment problems, what is the likelihood that such children will be successful in school, which requires both intellectual achievement and social adjustment? Two studies have examined children's success in school. Kingsley Davis and Amyra S. Grossbard, using a subsample from the HES Cycle II data, studied 10- and 11-year-olds from intact families. Within the group of teenage mothers, financially disadvantaged children did significantly more poorly in school, as measured by grade repetition and reading scores, than those more economically secure.[17]

Sheppard Kellam, in his longitudinal study of 1,242 children and their families in a low-income, urban, black community, found that the children (who entered school in 1966) who were born to mothers 17 years old or younger were less likely to adapt to school,

Table 5. Mean WISC scores for 7-year-old black children in Philadelphia CPP sample, by sex of child and mother's age at first birth

Mother's age	WISC score					
	Full-scale IQ		Verbal IQ		Performance IQ	
	Male	Female	Male	Female	Male	Female
<18	87.7	89.3	87.3	87.6	90.5	93.0
18–19	90.2	92.2	88.7	90.4	93.7	95.5
20–25	92.1	90.6	90.4	89.1	95.4	94.0

Source: See reference 12.

as rated by their first-grade teachers, than were children born to older mothers.[18] When measures were taken 10 years later, mother's age at birth was not found to have a *direct* effect on the 16-year-old children's psychiatric symptom rating. However, failure to adapt to school at age six *was* strongly related to more intense psychiatric symptoms as a teenager. Thus, adolescent childbearing appears to affect the child's teenage emotional adjustment indirectly through its effect on early adaptation to school. As in the Mednick and Furstenberg studies, the negative effect of having an adolescent mother was ameliorated by the presence of either a father or a grandmother in addition to the mother in the household.[19]

An unanticipated result of Kellam's and one other investigator's research was a differential effect of young maternal age on the cognitive and emotional development of male and female children. Kellam's finding that first-grade adaptation problems were associated with psychiatric symptoms 10 years later was particularly strong for boys.[20]

Marecek's analysis of Stanford-Binet IQ scores for four-year-old black children found no effect of young maternal age on girls' scores, but a marginally significant effect on boys' scores.[21] Further evidence of this trend was found in the WISC scores of the seven-year-old black children, where differences between the effects on male children and on female children reached statistical significance. Separate analyses of the verbal

and performance scores indicated that age of mother was related to both verbal and performance scores among boys but only to verbal IQ among girls (see Table 5).

Lasting Effects

A study by Josefina J. Card, based on the Project TALENT data (a longitudinal national survey of 375,000 teenagers in grades 9–12 in 1960) looked at educational, occupational and social differences between children born to adolescent mothers and children born to older mothers.[22] This analysis showed a number of differences that were the result of different social and economic characteristics of children of younger as compared to older mothers. Even with these factors controlled, the children of younger mothers showed decrements in terms of cognitive development, were more likely to live in one-parent homes and also showed more early childbearing themselves as compared to children of older mothers.

In a longitudinal study of a representative sample of mothers in three boroughs of New York City, Harriet Presser assessed the social and demographic consequences of a woman's having a first birth during her teenage years versus postponing it until she is in her 20s.[23] Presser found the best predictor of an adolescent first birth was the subject's mother's age at first birth. That is, the child of a teenage mother was at relatively high risk of becoming a teenage mother herself.

Marital Disruption

The studies cited earlier suggest that the long-term health, cognitive and social and emotional development of the children of teenage mothers was improved if the child was brought up in a household with more than one parent. Do the children of teenage parents have a relatively high risk of spending a considerable part of their childhood in one-parent households?

More than four in 10 adolescent mothers are unmarried; and among those who marry, separation and divorce rates are high. Many unwed teenage mothers marry soon after the birth. But these marriages, too, suffer high rates of disruption, and the relationship of young age at first marriage and an increased risk of divorce or separation persists into second marriages. Jane Menken and James McCarthy have analyzed the 1973 National Survey of Family Growth, a national probability sample of women aged 15–44 who were ever married or were single and living with at least one of their natural children.[24] They found that the younger the mother at the time of her first birth, the greater the likelihood that the child will spend at least some of the years up to age eight in a single-parent (i.e., mother-alone) household. Children born to young mothers are much more likely to be born out of wedlock than those born to older women, and first-born children are more often born out of wedlock than are those born later. Also, the likelihood of being born out of wedlock is much higher for black than for white children. This life-table analysis was done separately for the periods 1965–1969 and 1970–1973; it shows that for the earlier period, 32 percent of first-born children of white women younger than 18 had lived in a single-parent household by age two, and by age eight the proportion had risen to 59 percent (see Table 6). The likelihood of ever residing in a single-parent family was considerably greater for black than for white children. Some researchers are making special efforts to analyze patterns of fam-

Table 6. Percentage of first-born children living in single-parent households, by mother's race and age at child's birth, and child's age, 1965–1969

Child's age	Mother's race and age			
	White		Black	
	<18	>25	<18	>25
2	32	5	85	42
8	59	11	92	46

Source: See reference 23.

ily structure. Such patterns are extremely complex, and extend far beyond the definition of families as intact or not. (For example, Kellam found 86 different combinations of adults in his 1967 family interviews with mothers or mother-surrogates of first-grade children.[25]) Recognition of this complexity is especially important if, in fact, a key issue is whether the mother is alone or not. Clearly, many nonintact families include other adults. Kellam's longitudinal analysis showed that when the study child was in first grade, mothers who had begun childbearing as teenagers were more likely to be living in mother-alone families than were older mothers. Interestingly, if the study child was a first-born, there was no difference in the likelihood of the mother living at home with no other adults; but the other adult was likely to be the maternal grandmother for the teenage mothers and the child's father for the older mothers. In this study, teenage mothers who had two children were at the greatest risk of living in homes where there were no other adults. Whether this was because the grandparents were unable to accommodate a daughter and her two children, or because of a preference on the part of mothers of two to live alone, is not answered.

There were strikingly different patterns of marital stability over time. Married teenage mothers were twice as likely to separate or divorce as were those who gave birth in their

20s. If a marital disruption occurred, the father was likely to leave earlier in the child's life if the mother gave birth as a teenager than if she were older. The effects of early motherhood on the child continued into the teens: The child of a postadolescent mother was more likely at age 16 to be living in a mother-father household (or in a household with the mother and another adult) than was the child of an adolescent mother. Refusal rates for the second interview were higher among adolescents than nonadolescents—possibly part of their pattern of less participation in social organizations—and so these observations should be taken as suggestive of future research directions on the evolution of family structure. Many other studies have documented the high rates of disruption of teenage marriages.[26] Presser found that 34 percent of the 15–19-year-old mothers who were married before the birth of their first child were separated or divorced by the time of the third interview, when the child was between four and six years old.[27]

Conclusion

There is an intriguing pattern of relationship of adolescent childbearing to child development. Previous debates on the role of biological and environmental factors, especially prenatal care, have not been totally resolved, but the evidence is strong for the predominant influence of prenatal care on neonatal outcome. The fact that some programs show no negative effect—and even some positive effect—of young age is persuasive, but raises additional research and policy issues involving the level and cost of prenatal care required to compensate for the high risk involved in early childbearing. Studies that show decrements in infant health after the neonatal period urge us to look at the context of childrearing. Research on the role of family structure strongly suggests that the presence of adults other than the young mother in some way mitigates the deleterious health and other effects on the child associated with teenage childbearing. These findings suggest the need to elaborate better the division of child-care responsibility, the role of support networks and other interpersonal resources available to the young mother and her child. Present research has not dealt with the interrelationships of maternal characteristics and the availability and use of familial supports; we need to know more about why some adolescent mothers have familial or other supports available, and why some choose to accept those resources and others do not. The Family Impact Seminar has elaborated on many of these issues in its report *Teenage Pregnancy and Family Impact.*[28]

The effects of adolescent motherhood are observed in their children over many years; such long-term effects are consistent with findings from research on the effects of early childbearing on the teenage mother. These effects are persistent and color the general atmosphere in which a child develops: reduced education and occupational attainment of the mother, increased welfare dependency, higher fertility and marital disruption.[29] Higher rates of marital instability result in significantly larger proportions of time spent in one-parent families for the children of adolescent mothers than for the children of older mothers.

Research on the children of teenage mothers has focused on the effects on cognitive development, in part because of the availability of data. These effects, while statistically significant, are not startlingly large; but they, too, are persistent. The apparent relationship of early childbearing of the mother with early childbearing of her offspring is disturbing since it implies some generational effect. Do the large numbers of births to adolescents in recent years mean future waves of early childbearing? No one knows for sure, especially since there is little evidence to speak to the effects of intervention programs.

These data do not suggest that meliorative programs should focus directly on the children of teenage parents. Most of the observed adverse consequences to the children appear to result from the truncated education, and the poor employment and marriage prospects of the teenage mother. The research presented here, while not specifically evaluating service programs, suggests that one way to help the children of adolescents is to improve the educational and employment opportunities of the teenage parents and to encourage the supporting role of other adult family members.

Do these diverse studies fit into a coherent picture? They strongly support the view that there are effects of early motherhood on some important areas of early child development. They offer no support for a biological model of explanation of these effects; rather, the avenues through which effects are likely to operate are social and economic. The role of family structure is apparently an important one. These studies were not begun to study family structure nor, in most cases, to study adolescent childbearing; but the findings are consistent, conceptually sound and empirically compelling. They answer many questions, but raise many more. Not the least of these questions is whether researchers will look further at the interrelationship of personal characteristics of the mother and the role of family structure, and at the influence of public policy and social programs on the family careers of young mothers.

In the coming years we are likely to see a reduction in the number of births to adolescents, given declining birthrates and numbers of teenagers. This slackening in the numbers of people involved in adolescent childbearing should give us some time to advance our knowledge base and develop thoughtful social policies and service programs. It would be most unfortunate if we lost sight of the babies born to adolescents in the past decade who will be reaching childbearing age in the next decade.

Appendix

The studies reported here have all received support from the Center for Population Research, NICHD. Detailed final reports of these studies will be available when the projects are completed. A brief description of each follows:

• **Birgitte Mednick** of the University of Southern California is studying the consequences of family structure for the child's and the mother's development using data from the Danish Longitudinal Perinatal study. The 9,125 subjects included in the study were drawn from a Danish birth cohort including all deliveries taking place at the State University Hospital, Rigshospitalet, in Copenhagen within a two-year period from 1959 to 1961. The mothers and the children were subjected to regular and thorough medical examinations during pregnancy and the first year of the child's life. A variety of subsequent outcome measures are available for a subsample of the original subjects.

• **Howard Sandler** of George Peabody College has studied the effects of adolescent pregnancy on mother-infant relationships. Data were collected at the Nashville General Hospital, the county hospital for the indigent, between 1974 and 1977. Information for this study is available for women aged 13–39 and their children. Data were collected prenatally for 85 percent of the sample, and the children of adolescent mothers (aged 14–19) in their first pregnancy were compared with the children of older mothers (aged 20–26) on a variety of measures taken during the neonatal state. In addition, a prospective study of child abuse and neglect provided extensive measures of the mothers' experience with life stress and adjustments to stress. This subproject included observational data on interaction between mother and child at one, three, six and 12 months following birth.

• **Barry Lester** of Children's Hospital Medical Center, Boston, carried out a study of the relationship between teenage pregnancy and neonatal behavior. In this study, the principal measure of behavior is the Brazelton Neonatal Behavioral Assessment Scale applied to two-day-old infants. The study population comprises two groups: 1) 155 babies born at the Shads Teaching Hospital, University of Florida Medical School, and 2) 156 babies born at the Hospital Municipal, San Juan, Puerto Rico. In addition to the Brazelton Scale, complete medical histories of mother and baby, birth weight, and one- and five-minute Apgar scores are available for each infant. A total of 311 babies were studied, 62 of them born to women under age 18. The mothers had low incomes, and the Florida mothers were part of a medical care program for the indigent.

• Several studies used two large national data bases or subsets of those data bases: One source was the Collaborative Perinatal Project (CPP), supported by the National Institute of Neurological Diseases and Stroke, National Institutes of Health. The purpose of the CPP was to define parameters of fetal wastage, assess etiological factors and identify areas for further research or intervention. Fifteen medical centers participated, all university-affiliated, and data were collected on almost 56,000 pregnancies, beginning in 1959. Follow-up extended to age seven for the index child.* A second source was The Health Examination Surveys (HES), supported by the National Center for Health Statistics (NCHS). Data were collected at 40 locations across the United States on the physical and psychological characteristics of the civilian noninstitutionalized population in several nationwide surveys. The initial phase of the project, Cycle I, examined adults. Cycle II includes data on 7,119 children between the ages of six and 11 during 1963–1965. Cycle III provides data on 6,765 youths between the ages of 12 and 17 in 1966–1970. Further descriptions of the Sur-

veys can be found in NCHS publications (Series 1).

Jeanne Marecek of the Institute for the Continuous Study of Man examined the consequences of teen childbearing in a low-income, predominantly black, urban population. The data base was the Philadelphia CPP. Intellectual development was measured at eight months by the Bayley Scales of Infant Development, at four years by the Stanford-Binet and at seven years by the Wechsler Intelligence Scale for Children (WISC). Behavioral profiles were completed by the CPP testers at eight months, four and seven years. The scholastic achievement of the seven-year-olds was measured by the Wide Range Achievement Test.

A study by **Joy Dryfoos** of The Alan Guttmacher Institute and **Lillian Belmont** of Columbia University focused on the differences with respect to intelligence, achievement and personality adjustment between children of youthful mothers and other children of the same age. This study makes use of Cycles II and III of the HES and total CPP data on children seven years old. Measures of intellectual development and achievement included the Goodenough Draw-a-Person Test and the Wide Range Achievement Test. Social and emotional development were assessed by responses to a parent's questionnaire and responses to a questionnaire administered to the child which contained many of the same items. Behavioral observations were also made by the psychologist administering the tests. A final measure of the social and emotional development of the child was based on school problems as reported by the school.

A study by **Kingsley Davis** and **Amyra Shechtman Grossbard** of the University of Southern California examined the relationship between mother's age and child's intellectual development and school performance using the Cycle II HES data. A subsample of 1,750 10- and 11-year-old boys and girls from families with both parents present

*See reference 7.

was selected. Cycle II contains data on children's intellectual development as measured by the Vocabulary and Block Design subtests of the WISC and school performance as measured by grade repetition and reading scores.

• **Sheppard Kellam** of the University of Chicago studied the social, psychological and psychiatric consequences, over time, of teenage childbearing for the teenage mother, the children born to teenage mothers, and families containing women who began childbearing as teenagers. The project analyzed data collected for the Social Psychiatry Study Center's longitudinal communitywide study of children (ages 6–16) and their families in a black, urban, low-income Chicago community. The study sample consisted of 1,242 children who entered the first grade in 1966, over 200 of whom were born to teenage mothers. Over 500 of the mothers in the study began childbearing as teenagers.

• **Frank F. Furstenberg, Jr.,** of the University of Pennsylvania, in a longitudinal study of unmarried teenage mothers living in Baltimore (funded by the Maternal and Child Health Service of DHEW), investigated the relationship of young maternal age to children's cognitive, social and emotional development. Interviews were conducted during 1966–1968 with 404 mothers under 18 years old who were pregnant for the first time. Follow-up interviews were conducted with the mothers at one year, three years and five years after delivery. For comparison, classmates of the adolescent mothers were also interviewed at the three- and five-year follow-up. Interviews were conducted with the children of the study mothers and their classmates at the five-year follow-up. The children's cognitive development was measured by the Preschool Inventory, a test of school readiness; social-emotional development was assessed through doll-play designed to tap efficacy, trust, self-esteem and ability to defer gratification.

• In an analysis of Project TALENT data,

Josefina J. Card of the American Institutes for Research (AIR) studied the long-term consequences of early childbearing for adolescent mothers and their children. In 1960, TALENT, an AIR project sponsored by DHEW's Office of Education, gathered extensive demographic, cognitive and sociopsychological data from a nationwide sample of 375,000 students in grades 9–12. The progress of the personal and professional lives of a sample of these individuals was followed at one, five and 11 years after the date of their expected high school graduation, when they were approximately 19, 23 and 29 years old. Follow-up data from TALENT participants who gave birth as teenagers were compared with similar data from participants who postponed childbearing until their 20s or later.

• In a longitudinal study of mothers in three boroughs of New York City, **Harriet Presser** of the University of Maryland assessed the sociological and demographic consequences of a woman's having a first birth during her teenage years versus postponing it until her 20s. The population from which the sample was drawn was stratified by mother's age, marital status and race to assure a distribution for the sample that was representative of the three New York City boroughs.

• **Jane Menken** of the Office of Population Research, Princeton University, and **James McCarthy** of the Department of Population Dynamics, The Johns Hopkins University School of Hygiene and Public Health, studied the household contexts in which children spend their lives up to age 18, focusing on the differences in family structure between the families of children born to teenage mothers and those of children born to older mothers. Data were taken from Cycle I (1973) of the National Survey of Family Growth (NSFG) conducted by the National Center for Health Statistics. The NSFG sample was composed of 9,797 women, of whom 3,856 were black, 5,864 were white and 77 were of other races. To be eligible, a woman had to be between the ages of 15 and 44 at the time of the interview and either married at least once or never married but raising a natural child. The NSFG was designed to provide information about fertility, family planning intentions and activity and other aspects of maternal and child health closely related to childbearing. Complete marriage histories are available for the women.

References

1. W. Baldwin and V. Cain, eds., *Adolescent Pregnancy and Childbearing*, U.S. Government Printing Office, Washington, D.C., 1980 (forthcoming).

2. W. Baldwin, "Adolescent Pregnancy and Childbearing—Growing Concerns for Americans," *Population Bulletin*, Vol. 31, No. 2, 1977 (updated reprint, 1980).

3. J. Menken, "The Health and Demographic Consequences of Adolescent Pregnancy and Childbearing," in W. Baldwin and V. Cain, eds., 1980, op. cit.

4. H. C. Chase, "Trends in Prematurity: United States, 1950–1967," *American Journal of Public Health*, **60**:1967, 1970.

5. J. Menken, 1975, op. cit.

6. B. R. Mednick, *Consequences of Family Structure and Maternal State for Child and Mother's Development*, progress reports to National Institute of Child Health and Human Development, DHEW (NICHD), Jan. 1979, and July 1979.

7. K. Niswander, M. Gordon et al., eds., *The Women and Their Pregnancies: The Collaborative Perinatal Study of the National Institute of Neurological Diseases and Stroke*, W. B. Saunders, Philadelphia, 1972.

8. H. M. Sandler, *Effects of Adolescent Pregnancy on Mother-Infant Relationships: A Transactional Model*, progress reports to NICHD, June 1977, Jan. 1978, May 1978 and May 1979; and M. D. Laney, H. M. Sandler, K. B. Sherrod and S. O'Connor, "Biologic Risks in Adolescent Mothers and Their Infants," 1979 (unpublished manuscript).

9. B. M. Lester, *Relations Between Teenage Pregnancy and Neonatal Behavior*, progress report to NICHD, Mar. 1978.

10. H. J. Osofsky, *The Pregnant Teenager: A Medical, Educational and Social Analysis*, Charles E. Thomas, Springfield, Ill., 1968; H. J. Osofsky, J. D. Osofsky, N. Kendall and R. Rajan, "Adolescents as Mothers: An Interdisciplinary Approach to a Complex Problem," *Journal of Youth and Adolescence*, **2**:233, 1973; J. Zackler, S.

Andelman and F. Bauer, "The Young Adolescent as an Obstetric Risk," *American Journal of Obstetrics and Gynecology*, **103**:305, 1969; and P. Sarrel and L. Klerman, "The Young Unwed Mother," *American Journal of Obstetrics and Gynecology*, **105**:575, 1969.

11. B. Mednick, U. Brock and R. Baker, "Infant Caretakers: In Praise of Older Women," paper presented at the annual meeting of the Western Psychological Association, San Diego, Apr. 6, 1979.

12. J. Marecek, *Economic, Social and Psychological Consequences of Adolescent Childbearing: An Analysis of Data from the Philadelphia Collaborative Perinatal Project*, final report to NICHD, Sept. 1979.

13. J. G. Dryfoos and L. Belmont, *The Intellectual and Behavioral Status of Children Born to Adolescent Mothers*, final report to NICHD, Nov. 1979.

14. F. F. Furstenberg, Jr., *Unplanned Parenthood: The Social Consequences of Teenage Childbearing*, Macmillan, New York, 1976.

15. J. Marecek, 1979, op. cit.

16. J. G. Dryfoos and L. Belmont, 1978, op. cit.

17. K. Davis, *Study of How Mother's Age and Circumstances Affect Children*, progress report to NICHD, Mar. 1979.

18. S. G. Kellam, *Consequences of Teenage Motherhood for Mother, Child, and Family in a Black, Urban Community*, progress reports to NICHD, July 1978 and June 1979; and S. G. Kellam, R. G. Adams, C. H. Brown and M. E. Ensminger, "The Long-term Evolution of the Family Structure of Adolescent and Older Mothers," paper presented at the annual meeting of the Society for the Study of Social Problems, Boston, Aug. 1979.

19. S. G. Kellam, M. E. Ensminger and R. J. Turner, "Family Structure and the Mental Health of Children," *Archives of General Psychiatry*, **34**:1012, 1977.

20. S. G. Kellam, 1978, op. cit.; and S. G. Kellam et al., 1979, op. cit.

21. J. Marecek, 1979, op. cit.

22. J. J. Card, *Long-term Consequences for Children Born to Adolescent Parents*, final report to NICHD, American Institutes for Research, Palo Alto, Calif., 1977.

23. H. B. Presser, "Social Factors Affecting the Timing of the First Child," in W. B. Miller and L. F. Newman, eds., *The First Child and Family Formation*, Carolina Population Center, Chapel Hill, N.C., 1978.

24. J. Menken and J. McCarthy, *Childhood Residence Patterns and Changes in Relation to Maternal Age at First Birth*, final report to NICHD, July 1979.

25. S. G. Kellam, 1978, op. cit.; and S. G. Kellam et al., 1979, op. cit.

26. C. Johnson, "Adolescent Pregnancy: Intervention into the Poverty Cycle," *Journal of Youth and Adolescence,* 9:391, 1974; and J. B. Hardy, D. W. Welcher, J. Stanley and S. K. Dallam, "Long-range Outcome of Adolescent Pregnancies," *Clinical Obstetrics and Gynecology,* 21:1215, 1978.

27. H. B. Presser, *The Social and Demographic Consequences of Teenage Childbearing for Urban Women,* final report to NICHD, National Technical Information Service, Washington, D.C. 1980.

28. T. Ooms et al., *Teenage Pregnancy and Family Impact,* The Family Impact Seminar, Washington, D.C., 1979.

29. Baldwin and Cain, 1980, op. cit.

18
Family Support: Helping Teenage Mothers to Cope

Frank F. Furstenberg, Jr., and Albert G. Crawford

Even under the most propitious circumstances, the formation of a new family is a complex transition. A growing body of research suggests that adolescent childbearing greatly complicates the process.[1] Early parenthood creates an immediate crisis for teenage parents and their families, and often initiates a chain of events which may result in long-term disadvantage for the young parents and their offspring. With increasing precision, researchers have been able to document the commonsensical notion that early and unscheduled childbearing curtails the life chances of the young mother, especially her prospects for educational, economic and marital well-being.[2] Less evidence exists on the impact of early childbearing on the father, but there are strong indications that the male's economic and family position may be damaged as well.[3] Carefully designed stud-

Material for this article was drawn from a background report prepared for a Conference on Perspectives on Policy Toward Teenage Pregnancy sponsored by the Family Impact Seminar. Seminar papers were commissioned by a grant from the Mott Foundation. The data were originally collected under a grant from MCHS (MC-R-420117-05-05) and the reanalysis was made possible by a contract from NICHD (NOI-HD-72822) to the Center for Research on the Acts of Man.

ies of the consequences of teenage childbearing for the offspring are extremely rare, though scattered results from related research point in the expected direction: The child of an adolescent parent is more likely to be physically and socially handicapped than are his peers.[4]

Researchers examining the situation of adolescent parents and their offspring have generally overlooked, however, the social context in which early childbearing takes place. There has been almost no analysis of how the family as a social unit is affected by an early pregnancy. It is widely assumed that many young mothers, even those who marry before or shortly after childbirth, but especially those who become single parents, rely on their own families to provide economic assistance, child-care services and psychological support.[5] It is believed that parents, siblings and, not infrequently, relatives outside the immediate family are drawn into the problematic life situation of the teenage mother.

Some researchers have suggested that early and out-of-wedlock childbearing is prevalent among low-income blacks because this pattern of family formation is more or less congruent with the matrifocal form of the family.[6] Relatives, so the argument goes, are willing to shoulder some of the responsibility for child care and child support in return for the adolescent's allegiance to the mother-centered household, for the economic resources she contributes through earnings or welfare, and for a share of the gratifications of childrearing.

None of these speculations has been tested empirically with systematic data. Whether or not they are correct, these hypotheses about the functional character of adolescent pregnancy direct our attention from an exclusive concern with individuals to a concern for collectivities. We shall consider how the family as an entity may be involved in helping the adolescent to cope with parenthood.

In addressing this issue, we hope to correct another shortcoming of existing studies on early childbearing. Researchers have been so preoccupied with demonstrating that early childbearing creates serious disadvantages that they have generally overlooked the fact that some young mothers overcome the obstacles associated with premature parenthood and even derive psychological benefits from the experience. Without minimizing the difficulties, we need to explore the circumstances which contribute to the successful management of adolescent parenthood.

This investigation represents a first step in that direction. In the following analysis, we look into the role played by kin in providing support and assistance to the young mother and her offspring. Our aim is to examine the proposition that the outcome of early childbearing is mediated by the family's involvement in the transition to parenthood.

Data and Methods

In 1966-1967, under the auspices of Sinai Hospital in Baltimore, a study was undertaken to evaluate the effectiveness of a comprehensive service program for adolescent mothers and their offspring. Though the initial purpose of this research was to assess the program, the study, even as it was originally conceived, was concerned with how the pregnancy affected the life situation of the young mother and her family. At the outset, data were obtained from both the adolescents and their mothers on the social and economic status of the family and on the structure of the household. Our sample consisted primarily of lower and working-class individuals. Most of the families had incomes near or below the poverty level; the median annual income was $3,000-$4,000. One out of four families was receiving welfare assistance at the time of the initial interview (1966-1967). Most of the families were black. About 50 percent of the adolescent mothers' families were headed by two parents, 40 percent by the mother, and the rest by another relative. *

Early parenthood was not an unfamiliar event in the families of the young women in the sample: Nearly one-half of the prospective grandmothers had borne their first child when they were younger than 18, and at least one-quarter had

*Because the sample is a purposive one, it is not easy to determine whether it provides a basis for generalization to the larger population of adolescent mothers in Baltimore. Efforts were made to compare the characteristics of our sample with those of teenagers who delivered in other Baltimore hospitals during the same period. In general, the results were reassuring. Our sample appeared to resemble the population of other teenagers below the age of 18 who delivered a child in Baltimore. The socioeconomic profiles of the families of our sample were also similar to the characteristics of the larger black population as reflected in census data on low-income families in the city. A detailed description of the sample, study design and content of the interviews can be found in F.F. Furstenberg, Jr., 1976 (see reference 2).

borne a child out of wedlock. Many of the siblings of the adolescents in the sample had also become pregnant while they were in their early teens.

All women younger than 18 who entered the hospital program were interviewed at the time of registration; their parents were interviewed in the home shortly thereafter. The initial interviews were conducted with 404 pregnant adolescents, of whom 87 percent were black, and with 350 of the prospective grandmothers. Nearly 95 percent of the adolescents were reinterviewed one year later (1967-1968), when the program evaluation had been completed. Because so little was known about the long-term careers of adolescent parents and their children, further funding was obtained to trace the impact of the teenage birth on educational, economic, marital and fertility behavior three years and five years after delivery. Data were also collected from a sample of former classmates of the adolescent mothers who did not get pregnant as teenagers (or did so later than the teenage mothers). The classmates were first interviewed in 1970, when the young mothers were interviewed for the third time (approximately three years after delivery) and again in 1972, when the final interview with the adolescent mothers took place. Sample attrition remained quite low throughout the study; nearly 82 percent of the original participants were reinterviewed at the five-year follow-up.

The interviews conducted three and five years after delivery provided additional data on the family situation of the young mother and her child (including an account of her residential situation), as well as selected information on economic aid provided by the family, participation by kin in child care, and psychological support, advice and information offered by relatives. An assessment of the impact of early childbearing on the organization of the family can be made by comparing the respective situations of the young mothers and their classmates at the final interview.

What makes the Baltimore data attractive is the longitudinal perspective they afford on the changing role of kin during the period of family formation. As the data make clear, provision of assistance by the family changes markedly over time. Consequently, a snapshot view at any point in time yields an incomplete picture of the aid rendered by the family. Only by tracing the changing pattern of family involvement do we begin to develop a sense of the flow of family assistance.

Having noted the advantages of the Baltimore data, we should also mention certain of their limitations. The principal defect is that the study was not designed to examine the questions posed in this article. Little systematic information was collected on the extent of the kinship involvement, especially in the early stages of the study; consequently, we are forced to make do with less than ideal indicators of family assistance. We do have careful records of household composition, and our analysis is based on this feature of the family support system. But even here we are confronted with certain difficulties. We have observations of the young mothers' household arrangements only at four separate points in time. No records exist of young mothers who moved out of and back into the same household during an interim period or who changed residential situations more than once in any given interval. Therefore, our results inevitably understate the changes that actually took place in family situations during the five-year period following delivery.

With these restrictions in mind, we may proceed to a consideration of what can be learned from the Baltimore study about the assistance rendered by the family and its consequences for the young mothers' adaptation to parenthood.

Attitudes Toward Family Formation

The conventional sequence for forming a family in our society begins with departure from one's family of origin, typically before, but sometimes concurrent with, entrance into marriage. Generally, marriage precedes parenthood, though in fact a substantial number of marriages have been and continue to be precipitated by pregnancy.* Establishment of a separate household generally happens before or at the same time as marriage, and infrequently succeeds childbearing.

Most of the teenage mothers in our study endorsed, at least verbally, this conventional schedule for family formation. In the final interview, when their median age was 21, nearly two-thirds said that becoming premaritally pregnant probably harms a couple's prospects for a successful marriage (although most approved of premarital sexual activity). Virtually all (96 percent) stated that living with relatives after marriage is likely to hurt a couple's chances for marital success. Almost no one regarded a premarital pregnancy or a postmarital extended-family arrangement as a desirable prelude to married life. Moreover,

the young mothers' standards were the same as those of their nonpregnant classmates, whose opinions, in turn, resembled the general values of the larger population of young adults regarding the appropriate schedule for family formation.

In practice, however, the young mothers' experience departed from the ideal pattern of family formation. Almost all became pregnant before marriage, thus disarranging and complicating the conventional sequence of family formation. What ensued were a number of distinct strategies for coping with these complications, which, as we shall see, reflect both personal predilections and the availability of material and psychological resources from family members.

Household Change Over Time

Households were classified† according to whether the adolescent mothers were married or unmarried, living with parents or other kin, or living alone or with their husbands in a separate household, or with their husbands in the family's home. The resulting fourfold typology is presented in Table 1, which displays the household arrangements of the young mothers at the four interview points, as well as the classmates' residential situations at the five-year follow-up in 1972. The data, when arrayed over time, point to several developments.

During the period from pregnancy to the five-year postpartum interview, a growing proportion of the young mothers predictably made their way out of the household of their parents. In 1966-1967, 88 percent of the pregnant

---

*The rate of births conceived premaritally in the 1970s is lower than in the immediately preceding decades, owing to the greater availability of abortion, but still, one-third of all teenage births occurring within marriage in 1972 were conceived out of wedlock. (See: P.J. Placek, "Trends in Legitimate, Legitimated by Marriage and Illegitimate First Births: United States, 1964-1966 and 1972," paper presented at the annual meeting of the American Statistical Association, Aug. 14-17, 1978, San Diego.)

---

† No standard formulation for classifying the household arrangements of family members exists other than the one developed by the Census Bureau. We use a modification of this scheme, adapted to the information available from the interviews.

**Table 1. Percentage distribution of adolescent mothers and a comparison group of class-
mates, by marital status and type of household in which they resided, 1966–1967 to 1972**

Marital status and household type	Adolescent mothers				Classmates, 1972	
	1966-1967 (N=370)	1967-1968 (N=374)	1970 (N=347)	1972 (N=312)	Early pregnancy (N=42)	No early pregnancy (N=158)
Currently unmarried						
Total	85	72	64	66	66	69
Never-married	85	64	48	36	57	58
Alone	2	5	8	11	21	9
With parents or kin	83	59	40	25	36	49
Ever-married	0	8	16	30	9	11
Alone	0	2	4	15	7	2
With parents or kin	0	6	12	15	2	9
Currently married						
Total	15	28	36	33	33	31
With spouse only	10	16	25	27	19	22
With spouse and parents or kin	5	12	11	6	14	9

Note: The Ns in this and the following tables vary because all questions were not answered by all respondents or because responses were unclear. Percents in this and subsequent tables may not add to 100 because of rounding.

adolescents (including both the married and the unmarried) were living with one or both parents, and/or other relatives. We suspect that the two percent of expectant mothers who were living alone had only moved from their families' household after becoming pregnant, although data to demonstrate this theory are not available. In effect, then, before childbirth, virtually all the pregnant adolescents resided with their parents or a parent surrogate and/or a spouse. In view of their youth, any other arrangement would have been surprising. It is noteworthy that few adolescents used the occasion of the pregnancy to leave their family of origin, probably because few were in an economic or psychological position to do so.

The second interview (1967-1968) takes us to the period approximately one

year after delivery, and reveals the impact of childbirth on the residential situation of the young mothers. As the table shows, a large but diminished proportion of the young mothers continued to live in their parents' or relatives' home (77 percent compared with 88 percent the previous year). Although 28 percent of the young mothers were currently married at this time (compared with 15 percent the year before), 43 percent of all those currently married were still living with parents (usually the woman's), an even larger proportion than the year before. Overall, the rate of marriage was even greater (36 percent had ever been married), but 22 percent of all marriages had already been dissolved. The breakup of marriage resulted either in the return of the young mother to her former household (six mothers) or in her establishment of a separate household (four mothers). Despite the frequency of marital breakup, only seven percent of the young mothers were living alone at the one-year follow-up. In contrast to the conventional pattern of family formation, disengagement from the parental household seldom took place among adolescent parents even *after* matrimony or childbearing.

About two years later, in 1970, there is evidence of some change, although the household constellations remain basically similar to those in previous periods. By this time, most of the young mothers were in their late teens and early 20s and 52 percent had been married (36 percent were currently married and an additional 16 percent were separated). Nonetheless, 63 percent of the entire sample continued to reside with one or both parents or other relatives. Of course, not all lived continuously with their family of origin since the outset of the study (as we shall see shortly from the longitudinal analysis), but residence with parents remained the modal arrangement. The number currently married had risen, but 31 percent of these couples continued to live with parents, again usually the woman's. Only a small proportion, 12 percent, of all the women had set up independent households.

At the final interview, when most young mothers were in their early 20s, a further shift had taken place in residential situation. By then, as the table shows, the proportion still living with their families had dropped to 46 percent, including married couples. The decline of this type of household arrangement did not result from a growth in the marriage rate, however. Indeed, the proportion of young mothers who were currently married actually decreased slightly during this period, from 36 percent to 33 percent. It has been reported elsewhere that there is a sharp rise in the propor-

tion of women of comparable age and socioeconomic status who are currently married at this stage of life.[7] But in the Baltimore sample, we observe a sizable increase in the proportion of women living alone, and only a slight increase in the proportion currently living with their spouses. The proportion of women living alone more than doubled between 1970 and 1972. Thus, the loss of parental assistance was not usually offset by a gain in conjugal support.

The extent to which early childbearing accelerates the movement away from the parental household, contributing to a separation from the family of origin, is highlighted by contrasting the residential situations of the young mothers with those of 200 of their classmates at the five-year follow-up. We have subdivided the classmates into two groups: Those who, like the young mothers, had become parents during adolescence, but at a later age (constituting 21 percent of the sample); and the remainder, who either had not yet become pregnant or had waited to do so until they were at least in their early 20s.[*] Data on these two subgroups of classmates are located in the last two columns of Table 1.

Now compare the early childbearers with the classmates who had not become pregnant or who had experienced a conception only after adolescence.[†] Virtual-

---

[*] In most respects, the 42 classmates who were teenage childbearers are virtually indistinguishable from the young mothers drawn from the clinic population. A higher proportion of the currently married classmates with children were still living with relatives, probably because their pregnancies had occurred more recently, allowing less time for a separate marital unit to be established.

[†] We grouped together the nulliparous classmates with those who delayed their first pregnancies until their 20s, as most of the latter had married prior to delivery, unlike the teenage childbearers. Moreover, the never-pregnant and later-pregnant women had similar household situations in 1972.

ly the same proportion of the classmates as of the young mothers were currently married at the five-year follow-up. (However, 63 percent of the young mothers had ever been married by this time, compared with just 42 percent of the classmates.) What distinguishes the women who delayed childbearing from the adolescent mothers was not their current marital situations but the residential situations of those who had remained single. A much greater proportion of those who had deferred childbearing were living with parents or other family members at the final interview. Fifty-eight percent were unwed and resided with parents at the final interview, compared with 38 percent of the early-childbearing classmates and 40 percent of the women in the clinic sample.

One other important difference emerges when we compare the early childbearers with their classmates who delayed conception. Only 11 percent of the childless classmates and those who had deferred childbearing were living alone, compared with 28 percent of the classmates who had had children later in adolescence, and 26 percent of the early childbearers. At least at this stage of life, teenage parenthood seems to result in an earlier establishment of a separate household unit, perhaps removing individuals from the amount of parental and family support which they might otherwise obtain.

Residence Patterns/Family Support

A pivotal problem, but one that we can only partially resolve, is what these early residential patterns imply for the subsequent flow of family assistance. We did not inquire about the specific provision of family support until the three-year follow-up; moreover, we neglected to collect detailed information on this sub-

ject until the final interview, making it impossible to examine data on the provision of family assistance over time. Incomplete as it is, however, the available evidence confirms the commonsense assumption that family support is more available to the young mother who remains with her parents or other relatives. Certain avenues of financial and emotional support are closed off to the young mother who leaves the family context; or, perhaps (as we shall later show) she departs because family support is not available to her.

At the one-year follow-up, the mothers were asked three questions relating to sources of child-care advice in particular and psychological support in general.[*] As the responses to these items were highly intercorrelated, they were combined into a single index, measuring the level of dependency on parents. Table 2 shows the extent of dependency expressed by the young mothers in the different residential contexts. According to expectation, the unmarried young mothers living with their parents or kin were more likely to be highly reliant on them than were the young mothers residing alone.

The unmarried young mother's parents and other kin play a key role in the determination of whether she will resume her education or go to work outside the home. At the one-year follow-up, when the young mothers were asked if they had received any help from their parents or kin in returning to school,

---

[*]The questions asked were as follows:
● "A lot of teenagers have personal problems from time to time. Suppose you had a serious personal problem, who would you go to for advice?"
● "Suppose you wanted some information about how to feed your baby, who would you go to for advice?"
● "Suppose your baby were ill, who then would you go to for advice about what to do?"

none of the unmarried women living apart from their parents reported that they had received such help, while 12 percent of the women living with their parents said they had received this assistance. Virtually none of the married women had received such aid, regardless of their residential situation.

Access to child-care support has significant consequences for the likelihood of finding stable employment.[8] At the three-year follow-up, the single young mothers living alone were almost twice as likely as those residing with parents or kin (42 percent vs. 22 percent) to say that they were not working because they had no one to care for their child. No such difference occurred, however, between the two groups of married young mothers.

In response to a question asked at the five-year follow-up about who spent the most time caring for their children, the unmarried respondents revealed that those who lived with their parents or other kin typically received more assistance from them than those living apart from them. In order to develop a measure which tapped various levels of support, we combined those cases where the grandmother or another female relative assumed greater child-care responsibility with the cases where the adolescent mother and that other woman assumed equal responsibility. Thus, we found that 43 percent of the unmarried mothers living with parents or other relatives reported that another woman was a principal caretaker; 33 percent of those no longer living with parents or relatives relied on them for child-care support. The young mothers living alone were correspondingly more likely than those living with family to take responsibility for child care themselves (52 percent vs. 43 percent), rather than to adapt by using other kinds of child care (15 percent vs.

Table 2. Among young mothers living in various types of households, percentage who obtained support from parents and other kin, by type of support; various years

Indicator of support	Household type			
	Alone	With parents or kin	With spouse	With spouse and parents or kin
Substantial reliance on parents or kin, 1967–1968				
(N)	(25)	(243)	(61)	(45)
%	12	25	7	9
Help from kin in returning to school, 1967–1968				
(N)	(25)	(243)	(61)	(45)
%	0	12	2	0
Not working because of lack of child care, 1970				
(N)	(40)	(182)	(88)	(37)
%	42	22	38	35
Various child-care arrangements, 1972				
(N)	(79)	(116)	(77)	(16)
Adolescent mother most (%)	52	43	53	62
Grandmother or other kin most or equally (%)	33	43	32	25
Other (friend, babysitter, day-care center) most or equally (%)	15	14	16	12
Receiving money from parents or kin, 1972				
(N)	(82)	(127)	(85)	(18)
%	18	20	12	22
Nonfinancial contributions from parents or kin, 1972				
(N)	(82)	(127)	(85)	(18)
%	12	64	6	33

14 percent). Their situation most closely resembled that of the married women, who received the least assistance with child care from relatives.

In the final interview, the women were asked whether they were currently receiving any financial assistance from their parents. Whether or not they responded affirmatively, they were also questioned about other forms of material aid provided by their parents, such as food, clothing or personal effects. Obviously, this open-ended question failed to yield complete information on assistance rendered, for many respondents undoubtedly neglected to report occasional gifts or forms of help that were taken for granted, such as room and board.

Very few of the young mothers, regardless of their residential situation, were receiving direct financial contributions from their parents at the five-year follow-up. Only 17 percent reported any form of cash allowance. And there was only a slight difference by household type in the unmarried women's chances of receiving such aid. Married women living with their parents or kin were more apt to receive money from them than were women living with their spouses alone (22 percent compared with 12 percent).

In addition to financial assistance, 33 percent of the women listed other forms of material support. Women living with their families were more likely to receive such assistance. Only six percent of the married women living in separate households with their husbands reported regular assistance from their families, whereas 33 percent of the married women residing with their parents or kin stated that they got regular help. Twelve percent of unmarried women living by themselves reported nonfinancial support, compared with 64 percent of the

single women who were living with a relative. Thus, while moving out of the home does not totally preclude receiving material assistance from parents, it certainly is associated with a decreased likelihood of receiving such aid.

In summary, we have found some consistent differences in the availability of family support by residential situation. Unmarried women living with their parents or other kin are generally more reliant on them for advice and support; their parents provide more aid, such as food, clothing and child care; and the young mothers take advantage of such aid in order to continue their educational and occupational careers. While some differences hold also for the married women, the differences are typically greater among the unmarried women, suggesting that marriage attenuates the supply of parental aid, perhaps because a spouse is able to provide the aid which otherwise comes from parents.

Differences in the availability of family support between women who remain in the household and those who leave their family of origin are probably sharpest around the time of delivery. Once patterns of child care and material assistance are initiated, they may continue even after the adolescent establishes a separate household. No doubt, many young mothers, both married and single, remain near their family of origin even after they move out of the household, and that proximity enables an exchange of services to continue.

Transitions in Family Formation

Having demonstrated that young mothers residing with their kin received greater benefits from their families in the form of advice, material aid and child care, we now face the task of explaining the circumstances which governed the

Table 3. Percentage of young mothers living in various types of households at the one-year follow-up who were living in the same or different type of household at the five-year follow-up, by type of household

Household at five-year follow-up	Mothers at five-year follow-up		% of mothers, by household at one-year follow-up			
	%	N	Alone (N=19)	With parents or kin (N=205)	With spouse (N=46)	With spouse and parents or kin (N=38)
Total	100	308	6	67	15	12
Alone	26	80	53	24	22	29
With parents or kin	41	126	21	49	17	34
With spouse	27	84	21	21	56	26
With spouse and parents or kin	6	18	5	5	4	11

residential careers of the young mothers. There are many ways of approaching this question, but we find it useful to begin our analysis with a longitudinal inspection of the data we presented earlier in our section on changes in residential situation over time. This longitudinal perspective provides a view of the dynamics of household change and an opportunity to pick up certain clues about the conditions underlying residential movement.

We have already learned from Table 1 that a sizable proportion of the young mothers altered their living situation during the course of the study, and that the pace of movement picked up slightly in the later phases of the study. By cross-tabulating the residential situation at each point in time with that at the successive point in time, we can introduce an element of animation into the four snapshot pictures depicted earlier. The text which follows summarizes the results of this analysis; however, for the sake of simplicity, we shall not show each separate turnover table. We present, instead, a summary table (Table 3) showing the pattern of movement from the one-year follow-up to the five-year follow-up. It captures most of the important residential changes that took place during the course of the study.*

While there is no simple way of summarizing in statistical terms the rate of movement from one interval to the next, some idea of the level of change which occurs can be obtained merely by examining the diagonal cells of the table, which represent stability. Between the one-year follow-up and the five-year follow-up, there was a modest level of residential stability, around 50 percent, in all but one of the four household arrangements (those who lived with spouse and parents). Among the women living alone, more than half, 53 percent, remained in that position. Just under half, 49 percent, of the unmarried women living with parents or other kin had the same living arrangement four years later. And more than half, 56 percent, of the married women living only with their spouses remained in this residen-

*The figures in the table are related to but are not identical with the amount of geographic movement that took place, for we are only recording residential movement which involved a change in household type.

tial situation at the final follow-up. However, among the married women living with their spouses and parents or relatives at the one-year follow-up, only four out of 38, 11 percent, remained in that kind of household. Apparently, this arrangement was a temporary convenience, permitting marriage to occur earlier than it otherwise could if a separate household had to be established prior to matrimony. Among the women who were married and living only with their spouses at the one-year follow-up, hardly any, four percent, were living with their relatives at the five-year follow-up interview.

One other finding not shown in Table 3 is of some importance. Single women who lived with families augmented by extended kin were no more likely to move out, either to marry or to establish an .independent household, after their child was born, than were those who lived in nuclear arrangements. However, movement from households with parents and kin occurred soon after the birth, suggesting that an additional family member may have placed more immediate strain on existing resources when the household was already augmented. In sum, the residential careers of single women were not greatly affected by their living arrangements when delivery occurred.

In a rather abbreviated fashion, we have tried to feature what may be thought of as typical transitions in family formation among the young mothers in our sample. As we found above in our cross-sectional analysis, almost all of the young mothers started out in the parental household and most remained there even after their child was born. The move to independent household headship did not occur for most even by the end of the study, although more than three out of five had ever married by this time. It bears reporting that marriage did

not invariably mean departure from the family of origin. Throughout the study, particularly in the early phases, a substantial proportion of the married couples continued to reside with their parents, and the women whose marriages broke up frequently returned to live with their parents.

A Typology of Residential Careers

Although it was theoretically possible for the young mothers to live in some 80 different residential situations in the course of the study, more than half of them followed one of four residential careers, two-thirds followed one of seven, and more than four-fifths followed one of 12 careers.°

The most common residential arrangement was for the young mother to be living with one or both parents or other kin throughout the first five years after delivery. Twenty-nine percent of the sample were sharing a household with their parents at each of the four interviews. While some may have spent a brief time outside the parents' or relatives' household during one or another interval, the young women in this category generally experienced a high degree of continuity in their residential situation.

The second most common sequence was to move from living with parents or relatives to living with a spouse for the rest of the time covered by the study. Twenty-four percent followed this route, though not all, as we have already seen, departed from their parents' household as soon as marriage occurred.

As we have previously observed, a number of unmarried mothers had established their own households by the con-

---

°Individuals residing with both spouse and parent(s) were coded as living with spouse, and those living only with siblings, cousins or children were considered to be living alone.

clusion of the study: Fifteen percent of the young mothers lived with their parents for some time after childbirth before moving to their own quarters, usually in the latter phase of the study.

Three other common residential sequences involved young mothers who married during the course of the study. Half of these women were no longer residing with their spouse at the five-year follow-up. Two-thirds (11 percent of the entire sample) had moved back into their parents' household, while the others had established their own separate household (four percent of the sample). A small segment of the married mothers, slightly more than six percent of the participants, were wed at the time of the initial interview and remained so throughout the study.

Only a tiny fraction of the sample, one percent, lived in independent households from the start.

Eleven percent of the sample did not conform to any of these patterns. Most of these women oscillated between a separate household, residence with parents and other kin, and marriage. While most women we studied experienced either no change in residential status (33 percent) or only one transition (40 percent) during the course of the study, all of the residual group made at least two moves and one-third of them had three recorded changes in their household situation during the five years following delivery.

The remainder of this article is devoted to an exploration of why these different residential strategies were adopted and what implications they had for adjustment to early parenthood. The initial objective of this analysis was to discover specific determinants of the young mother's decision to remain with or move away from her family. This decision, we believe, was dictated by two very general considerations—a woman's need for assistance and her family's ability to render aid. Using an economic analogy, we refer to the first as *demand* and the second as *supply*.

The Demand for Assistance

One obvious explanation for the variations in residential strategies is age and the aging process. This explanation, in fact, is deceptively simple, for age has manifold cultural, psychological and sociological implications. Following pregnancy, most young mothers would experience increasing pressure to set up an independent household, and the older the young mother, the more likely she would be to assert her independence from the family. Sociological conditions should reinforce this pattern, since older women in the study would be more likely to be of "marriageable age" or, at least, be old enough to meet the economic requirements of establishing a separate household if a marriage did not take place.

As we and others have discussed in some detail in previous publications, age is an important determinant of the timing of marriage.[9] A significantly higher proportion of the young mothers who were 21 and over at the conclusion of the study than of those younger than 21 had wed (71 percent vs. 56 percent), largely because the older women were in a position to marry immediately before the child was born. Although we have already seen that marriage does not automatically remove the young mother from the parental household, it typically has this effect. (Only 10 percent of the married women remained with their families throughout the study.)

Because of the link with marriageability, then, we would expect age to be inversely associated with continuous residence with parents throughout the study, and directly related to continuous residence with a spouse. It is true that among the never-married women, those under 21 were more likely to have remained with their parents throughout the study than were those 21 or over (69 percent vs. 59 percent). Nevertheless, there were no pronounced differences by age among the ever-married women in their likelihood of being married at the end of the study (50 percent vs. 45 percent). And, among the separated women, the younger women were *less* likely to be residing with their parents (39 percent vs. 56 percent). Possibly the age spread within the Baltimore sample is too narrow to account for much variation in residential arrangements.

We are not in a strong position to examine the influence of racial differences on the flow of family assistance, owing to the small number of whites in our sample. Nonetheless, we suspect there are sharp divergences between blacks and whites in the role the family plays after childbirth. As we have described in more detail elsewhere,[10] most of the whites in our study (70 percent) married soon after becoming pregnant, while most of the blacks (84 percent) deferred marriage until after childbirth. In part, these patterns reflect the disparate social meanings of out-of-wedlock childbearing for the two racial groups, but age and economic circumstances also enter into the differing strategies of accommodation to early pregnancy. The whites in the sample were generally older, and the fathers of the children, because of their higher economic status, were in a better position to enter marriage.*

---

*Recent qualitative interviews with white families suggest that when parents are willing to provide the resources, the white adolescent may elect to defer marriage as well. (See: P.C. Glick and A.J. Norton, "Marrying, Divorcing and Living Together in the U.S. Today," *Population Bulletin*, Vol. 32, No. 5, 1977.)

Young black women and their families frequently questioned the advantages of a rapid marriage, and with good reason, since their marriages tended to have lower rates of survival. Not only did deterrents to early marriage exist, but there were also decided incentives for remaining single. Most black parents were willing to provide subsidies to the young mother in the form of free room and board and often child care as well.

A major reason many young mothers postponed marriage was their desire to remain in school. The commitment to continuing their education was strongly voiced by both the young mothers (94 percent) and their parents (87 percent).[11] The women who stayed in school or resumed their education immediately after delivery were more likely to be living with their parents at the one-year and three-year follow-ups. It appears that the need for child-care assistance, and perhaps material support, led many young mothers to adopt a residential strategy which kept them close to their parents. In addition, our evidence suggests that aid was more likely to be provided when strong affective bonds existed between the young mother and her parents.

We mentioned earlier that an index of reliance on parents was constructed from several questions included at the one-year follow-up interviews concerning the degree to which the young mother looked to her parents for advice and support in childrearing matters. This index predicted, rather strongly, subsequent residential patterns. Whereas 52 percent of the women who never married during the course of the study indicated that they would look to their parents for help in each of the three hypothetical situations, 35 percent of the young mothers who married expressed this same level of dependency. This result reflects the fact that women who married before or shortly after delivery were much less likely to rely on their parents, turning instead to their spouse or boyfriend, a friend, or some other relative when they needed counsel.

Even if eventual marital status is held constant, we still find that the index of reliance on parents forecasts rather clearly the residential strategies from pregnancy to the five-year follow-up. Among the single mothers, 39 percent of those who expressed a low degree of reliance on their parents remained in the parental household, compared with 79 percent of those who acknowledged a high degree of reliance. Clearly, those who felt more independent during pregnancy were more likely to move out and establish their own households soon after their child was born.*

Reliance on parents also had some bearing on the residential decisions of the young mothers who married and subsequently separated. Approximately 50 percent of the young mothers who scored high on the index of reliance returned to live with parents after separation, compared with 32 percent of those who were less responsive to their families' opinions.

Thus, a reason for young women's accepting support from their families can be traced to bonds which antedate the pregnancy but which are sustained and perhaps deepened when a child is born. Obviously, for the women who remain single, pregnancy complicates the process of separation during late adolescence and early adulthood by offering real incentives for staying in the parental home. But it is also clear that these same incentives operate for many married women, perhaps reducing commitment to conjugal ties.†

From the evidence we have pieced together, it seems clear that the teenager derives a number of benefits from remaining with her parents during the early years of parenthood. Few teenage parents, especially those who remain single, have the skills or resources to establish an independent household, and the family provides an alternative to a hasty marriage. With the completion of their education and a diminished need for in-the-home child care, some of the young mothers in the study were ready to separate from their families by the five-year follow-up. How they felt about setting out on their own is a question that cannot be answered from the data at hand, but we have reason to suspect that pressures may have been building within the family which hastened their departure.

The Supply of Assistance

Thus far, we have considered only one side of the picture, the circumstances which increase the demand for family aid. We shall now try to show that the availability of assistance also shaped the young mothers' residential careers. In this section, we examine whether their families' desire to help and their resources to do so affected the young mothers' residential decisions.

Unfortunately, the initial interview, conducted in 1966-1967, does not pro-

---

* Of course, one cannot impose any one causal interpretation on these results. Very possibly, some young mothers who were highly reliant on their parents were more likely to voice their dependency precisely because they *expected* to remain in the parental household, while young mothers who had moved or were about to move into marriage accordingly gave less allegiance to their parents' views. Nevertheless, it is most certainly the case that women who experienced a high degree of dependency were less willing or able to move away from their parents.

---

† For a more detailed discussion of this problem, see: F. F. Furstenberg, Jr., 1978 (reference 2).

vide abundant information on the family's willingness or ability to provide assistance. The parents' initial reaction to the pregnancy had no effect on the residential strategies of the young mothers who never married during the course of the study. Parents who were extremely upset when the pregnancy occurred were actually slightly more likely to extend support to their daughters (70 percent vs. 66 percent)—an indication that few parents reacted punitively once the pregnancy occurred. On the other hand, among the separated young mothers, those whose parents were extremely upset about their pregnancy were less likely to return to their parents' household (38 percent vs. 52 percent). Apparently, these young mothers' marriage and inability to succeed in that marriage estranged them from their parents, complicating further what were already strained relations between them.

When asked whether the baby should be given up for adoption, 95 percent of the grandparents favored keeping the child. The tiny minority who counseled adoption were less likely to have their daughter and her offspring in the household at the follow-up interview. This pattern, however, may have as much to do with the availability of resources as with the reaction to the pregnancy.

We found little evidence that a prior history of early childbearing in the family promoted greater dependence on parents after delivery, or that female-headed families were more receptive to maintaining the mother and child in the home. Indeed, the contrary appears to hold true. Unmarried women were actually less likely to remain with the parents when other members of the family had borne a child out of wedlock (61 percent vs. 74 percent). Such a history of out-of-wedlock childbearing was highly cor-

related with female-headed families; such families were less likely than couple-headed households to retain the adolescent mother if she did not marry (60 percent vs. 83 percent) or if her marriage was dissolved (43 percent vs. 56 percent). One explanation, consistent with our data, for this result is that young mothers who were living in couple-headed households were more likely to look to their parents for advice and assistance (89 percent compared with 68 percent). It is also the case, however, that couple-headed households had more to offer in the way of material benefits than did female-headed households. Many of the female heads were already living on the economic margin and probably could not provide as much material assistance to their child and grandchild as could the household with two parents.

Our data confirm the supposition that the family's economic resources are critically important in determining the long-term supply of assistance to the young mother. The economic position of the family did not predict either early or eventual marriage of the young mother, but it did strongly influence the likelihood of her remaining with the family if marriage did not occur. Table 4 shows the residential patterns of the young mothers who remained single throughout the study and of those who married but separated, by the socioeconomic position of the parents.°

The better the family's economic situation at the outset of the study, the more likely the unmarried young mother was to remain in the home through the five-year follow-up. In families in which at

---

°Families in which one or both parents worked at skilled jobs were classified as being of high socioeconomic status; families in which neither parent worked at a skilled job were classified as being of low socioeconomic status.

least one of the parents worked at a skilled job, 73 percent of the unmarried young mothers remained in the household; where their parents' economic status was lower, only 57 percent of the women remained with their parents. Among the young mothers whose marriages had been dissolved, their families' economic status did not affect their likelihood of returning to live in the parental home. However, the separated women from poorer families were more likely to live alone than were those from families of higher economic status (32 percent vs. 16 percent).

There are too few cases to assess with any precision the independent effects of family form (that is, whether the household was headed by a couple or a single parent) and the economic position of the household head(s). However, it seems likely that both headship and economic standing independently affect the long-term supply of assistance to the young mother. Intact families are generally more economically secure, and economically secure families are more stable. Hence, each condition probably reinforces and augments the other.

Perhaps intervening circumstances relating to marriage, such as the economic status of the husband or the number of children produced, play a greater role in determining the fate of women in marital or postmarital situations.

Just as the transition to marriage often precipitates a move from the parental household, additional childbearing frequently forces the young mother and her family to reconsider the residential arrangement. The proportion of never-married women residing with their parents throughout the study drops from 71 percent to 62 percent when a second child is present, and declines to 50 percent when three or more children are present. Additional children also deter

Table 4. Percentage distribution of young mothers with various residential patterns, by parents' socioeconomic status, according to young mothers' marital status, 1972

Marital status and residential pattern	Socioeconomic status	
	High	Low
Never-married	(N=62)	(N=46)
Alone*	23	41
With parents or kin†	73	57
Other‡	5	2
Separated	(N=49)	(N=38)
Alone*	16	32
With parents or kin†	47	47
Other‡	37	21

*Alone throughout the study or from livng with families or spouse to living alone.

†With parents or kin throughout the study or from living alone or with spouse to families.

‡Two or more residential movements not coded otherwise.

the formerly married from resuming residence with their parents. As in the case of the never-married mothers, the sharing of a common household declines among the formerly married women as parity increases (from 50 percent of mothers with one or two children to 29 percent of those with three or more).

Available physical space may have had a good deal to do with the residential strategies which evolved during the course of the study. Although the size of the sample does not permit a definitive test of this interpretation, additional childbearing seems to precipitate a change in household situation because of lack of space. We computed a crude measure of crowding by taking the ratio of the total number of persons in the household to the total number of rooms; we then dichotomized this variable. Where crowding was more serious, only

45 percent of the unmarried adolescent mothers remained in the household of their parents or other kin; under less crowded conditions, 75 percent of the women remained. As we pointed out earlier, crowded conditions may also have forced the breakup of extended families of procreation and eventually may have forced some young mothers to move away from their families.

Our discussion has touched on only a few of the circumstances which explain residential patterns. We have examined both demand and supply conditions which promote and restrict the flow of family assistance, discovering that both psychological factors (such as dependency on parents) and material conditions enter into the decision of where and with whom to live after the child is born. In the final section of the article, we take up the question of how those residential decisions affect the well-being of the young mother.

Consequences of Family Help

Our examination of the impact of residential careers on the life chances of the young mother and her child offers, at best, only an introduction to this topic. The information at hand is not specific enough for us to carry out a refined analysis of the causal pathways which link family assistance to the subsequent economic outcomes or psychological sequelae. Moreover, our sample is not large enough for us to disentangle the complex sequence of familial and economic events which follow delivery; nor did we collect extensive qualitative information that might aid in the interpretation of the data. Nevertheless, it is possible to explore, albeit tentatively, whether remaining with parents enhanced the social prospects of the young mother and her child. Let us first consider some of the findings and then return to the difficulties in interpreting them.

As in the previous analysis, our results are clearer when we separate the young mothers who remained single from those who wed. Looking first at those who never married, we find a clear relationship between residential strategies and economic outcomes (see Table 5). Women who remained with their parents were somewhat more likely to return to school and to be graduated from high school; a much larger proportion were employed and a much smaller proportion were on welfare. (However, among those who were employed, a larger proportion of those who lived alone held skilled jobs.) Conversely, women who moved out of the home at the time of pregnancy or after the transition to parenthood were more likely to have dropped out of school and to have failed to return, a larger proportion were unemployed, and a larger proportion were receiving welfare at the time of the final interview. (It is notable that these data give no support to the conventional belief that teenagers have babies in order to get on welfare and escape from the parental home.)

For the women who married and subsequently separated, the findings are quite different. There are virtually no differences in socioeconomic status between the women who returned to live with their parents and the women who set up independent households. However, the women who remained married and lived with their spouses typically achieved somewhat higher socioeconomic levels than did the women who separated and set up independent households or who returned to the homes of their relatives.

The disparity in outcomes between the never-married and previously married lends plausibility to the interpretation that assistance from families may

Table 5. Five indicators of socioeconomic achievement of young women at the five-year follow-up, by marital status and residential pattern

Indicator	Never-married women				Ever-married women							
	Alone		With parents or kin		Alone		With parents or kin		With spouse		With spouse and parents or kin	
	%	N	%	N	%	N	%	N	%	N	%	N
Proportion who returned to school (excluding those who had already completed high school)	76	33	87	71	83	23	76	41	79	76	44	23
Proportion who completed high school	47	34	62	74	43	23	45	44	55	87	36	28
Proportion who were employed	41	32	60	68	43	23	43	44	51	85	36	28
Proportion who held skilled jobs, among those who were employed	31	13	24	41	10	10	11	19	23	43	10	10
Proportion who were on welfare	65	34	43	72	61	23	59	44	12	85	56	27

directly affect the economic prospects of the single mother. If the same outcome had occurred for both never- and ever-married mothers, we might have been convinced that the advantage in subsequent socioeconomic status was largely attributable to conditions that preceded the pregnancy and were associated with the family background of those women who resided with their parents. The fact that a favorable outcome occurred only among never-married women who remained with their parents throughout the study, and not among the women who returned home after marriage, suggests that the long-term provision of family assistance may have a part in shaping the economic career of the single mother. An intervening marriage, accordingly, attenuates the potential benefit of family support.

Even if we are correct in assuming

that assistance from families does promote the economic well-being of unmarried mothers, we cannot say for certain why this is so. Do these women fare better because they remain with their parents? Or do they remain with their parents because they are committed to advancing their educational and occupational careers? We suspect that both conditions are true, though not in equal measure in all families. Families who strongly support their daughters' educational efforts may be more likely to help out financially or provide child care so long as the young mother remains in school. If she drops out, there is less incentive for them to help and, thus, for her to remain in the home. Similarly, women who wish to advance educationally may be more likely to seek aid from their parents.

There is some evidence to substantiate

each of these interpretations. Adolescents who were more educationally ambitious were less likely to marry, and hence were more inclined to remain with their parents throughout the study. In turn, women who remained in the home were far more likely to attend school. Even at the five-year follow-up, when most women had completed their education, women living with their parents were more likely to be currently enrolled in school.[12] Probably, then, the relationship between family assistance and socioeconomic achievement is a reciprocal one. Women who receive family aid are more likely to advance economically, and those who most wish to improve their position are more likely to turn to their families for help.

Finally, we must point out that although our data are longitudinal, this study describes only a small slice of time in the lives of the young mothers. All the returns are not yet in. Many of the young mothers still living with their parents at the five-year follow-up may have been on the verge of moving out. Were the more successful ones to exit, the pattern reported here would disappear. Despite this qualification, our data strongly indicate that family support of single mothers improved their chances of returning to school, entering the labor force and finding employment.

Family Assistance and Parenting

We explored whether the young mothers who received support from their families in the early years of parenthood developed greater parenting skills than did the young mothers who did not receive such help. We also examined what effect, if any, such support had on the well-being of their children. Our data show that residential careers had little influence on childrearing patterns, and there

is no evidence that the provision of family support made any difference in the way the young mothers performed their maternal tasks. The quality of parent-child interaction seems not to have been affected by the child-care arrangements made by the young mothers.

Similarly, scrutiny of data gathered on the children's development showed little difference by the mothers' residential patterns. Only one measure, a test of cognitive skills, suggested that the children of unmarried mothers who resided in households with kin (usually, grandparents) outperformed those who lived with their mothers alone, even though the latter children were more apt to have gone to school. (However, the findings were not statistically significant.)

Conclusion

We have tried to show that the residential career of the teenage childbearer provides a means, albeit an imperfect one, of monitoring the flow of family support to the adolescent mother during the transition to parenthood. Most support received by the young mother is supplied by her nuclear family—her parents and siblings—in the form of free room and board and partly or wholly subsidized child care. The availability of material support is greater when the adolescent remains in the home, though even when she separates from her parents, she may continue to receive child-care assistance from a family member.

Our analysis suggests that the assistance rendered by family members significantly alters the life chances of the young mother, enhancing her prospects of educational achievement and economic advancement. It may also contribute to the well-being of her child, though the evidence we can marshall is limited.

If other studies, using richer data sets

than ours, reach the same conclusions regarding the benefits of family support in easing the transition to early parenthood, what implications will such conclusions have for policies and programs designed to ameliorate the adverse effects of early childbearing?

Present policies strike us as ill-conceived and shortsighted because many of the solutions devised for coping with early parenthood run counter to or undermine existing natural support systems. Nothing in the behavior of the young women in our study or their families suggests that they were alienated from one another. Quite the contrary, these predominantly low-income families provided support of all types, often at what must have been considerable sacrifice.

Public programs should build on the strengths inherent in these families. Financial assistance and other appropriate aid, such as child care, should be extended to families willing to help their young daughters to pick up the threads of their lives and advance their educational and occupational prospects. Assistance should go, as well, to the young fathers if they show interest in supporting the young women and their children. Assistance should be given, when needed, to young married couples to try to strengthen their marriages. Present welfare rules often guarantee the breakup of many of these marriages since assistance is usually provided only when there is no male head of household. This is shortsighted, punitive and self-defeating.

Where appropriate, support should go to those young women who desire to become independent. But the option of how to solve their residential problems should be theirs. They should not be pushed into premature independence to obtain the assistance they need.

Another illustration of the shortsight-

edness of public policies is in the formulation of programs intended to prepare the young mother for parenthood. There is widespread agreement among experts that the early childbearer is at some disadvantage in assuming the maternal role because of her psychological immaturity. Many young mothers are themselves still experiencing the developmental tasks of adolescence, consolidating their own interpersonal skills, working out life aims and achieving some sense of personal identity. It is widely believed that many young mothers lack the experience and skills to manage the complex obligations of motherhood. Based on these presuppositions, a number of programs serving teenage mothers have developed parent education courses designed to teach mothering skills. These programs operate on the erroneous assumption that the mother is the principal, if not the only, caretaker. If the results of our study are any indication, the family and the infant's father, not just the adolescent mother, should be targets of instruction as well.

In fact, many young parents are receiving a great deal of training on the job from parents, older siblings or more distant kin. Even though they may not always be residing with the young mothers and their children, the children's fathers, or father surrogates, too, may be performing important childrearing functions. Without taking into account the actual parenting structure, educational programs may be imparting wisdom that either cannot be applied or is ill-suited to fit the situations that young mothers typically face.

In citing ways the family adapts in order to ease the transition to early parenthood, however, we do not wish to dismiss the potential dysfunctions for the adolescent parent and her family members. These are discussed in some detail elsewhere.[13] Our data suggest that this kinship configuration may not be well designed to promote or reenforce conjugal ties. What is adaptive from one perspective, then, may be maladaptive from another. Furthermore, if we follow the logic of our longitudinal analysis, we must conclude that arrangements that are immediately functional for the young mother and her child are not always adaptive later in the life course. These qualifications serve to remind us of both the limitations of the present analysis and the urgent need for further studies of the impact of early childbearing on the family unit.

References

1. W.H. Baldwin, "Adolescent Pregnancy and Childbearing: Growing Concerns for Americans," *Population Bulletin*, Vol. 31, No. 2, 1976; and E.A. Crider, "School Age Pregnancy, Childbearing and Childrearing: A Research Review," 1976 (paper submitted to the Bureau of Elementary and Secondary Education, U.S. Office of Education, under Contract No. P00760271).

2. F.F. Furstenberg, Jr., *Unplanned Parenthood: The Social Consequences of Teenage Childbearing*, The Free Press (Macmillan), New York, 1976; ——, "Burdens and Benefits: The Impact of Early Childbearing on the Family," paper presented at the Conference on Perspectives on Policy Toward Teenage Pregnancy, Family Impact Seminar, Washington, D.C., Oct. 23–24, 1978; G. E. Hendershot and E. Eckard, "Unwanted Teenage Childbearing and Later Life Changes: Evidence from the National Survey of Family Growth," paper presented at the annual meeting of the Eastern Sociological Society, Philadelphia, Apr. 2, 1978; K. Moore, "The Social and Economic Consequences of Teenage Childbearing," paper presented at the Conference on Young Women and Employment, Washington, D.C., May 1, 1978; and H. B. Presser, "The Social and Demographic Consequences of Teenage Childbearing for Urban Women," paper presented at the National Institute of Child Health and Human Development Workshop on the Consequences of Adolescent Pregnancy and Childbearing, Bethesda, Jan. 12–13, 1978.

3. J. J. Card and L. L. Wise, "Teenage Mothers and Teenage Fathers: The Impact of Early Childbearing on the Parents' Personal and Professional Lives," chapter 13, above.

4. D. Nortman, "Parental Age as a Factor in Pregnancy Outcome and Child Development," *Reports on Population/Family Planning*, No. 16, Aug. 1974.

5. H.B. Presser, "Sally's Corner," paper presented at the annual meeting of the American Sociological Association, San Francisco, Sept. 4-7, 1978.

6. J.A. Ladner, *Tomorrow's Tomorrow: The Black Woman*, Doubleday, Garden City, N.Y., 1971; and L. Rainwater, *Behind Ghetto Walls*, Aldine, Chicago, 1971.

7. A. Cherlin, "Postponing Marriage: The Influence of Schooling, Working, and Work Plans for Young Women," paper presented at the annual meeting of the American Sociological Association, San Francisco, Sept. 4–8, 1978.

8. F. F. Furstenberg, Jr., 1976, op. cit.

9. A. Cherlin, 1978, op. cit.; F. F. Furstenberg, Jr., 1976, op. cit.; J. Modell, F. F. Furstenberg, Jr., and T. Hershberg, "Social Change and Transitions to Adulthood in Historical Perspective," *Journal of Family History*, 1:7, 1976; and J. Model, F. Furstenberg and D. Strong, "The Timing of Marriage in the Transition to Adulthood: Continuity and Change," *American Journal of Sociology*, 84 (Supp.):S120, 1978.

10. F.F. Furstenberg, Jr., 1976, op. cit.

11. Ibid.

12. Ibid.

13. F.F. Furstenberg, Jr., 1978, op. cit.

III
Locating the Problem /
Defining the Solution

Each article in the previous section described an array of adverse consequences resulting from early childbearing that shape the later lives of young parents, their children, and their families. While in some situations teenagers and their families may derive certain benefits from parenthood, most face a difficult adjustment when its inception is early and unplanned. The question raised in the readings that follow is what can be done to avoid the burdens imposed by premature parenthood.

Much social welfare literature on the topic of teenage parenthood concentrates on easing the transition to parenthood. However, most of the authors in this section have a different emphasis. They more or less assume that prevention is far less expensive and much more effective than the alternative, more passive, approach of constructing ameliorative social programs for young parents. Most of them undoubtedly concur with the policy recommendations in Section II, including educational continuation, day care, family support, and job training. But the authors of Section III are committed to a different strategy: preventing unwanted conceptions. They stress the urgency of sex education and the provision of contraception for sexually active teenagers.

In the present era of sexual enlightenment, most people vastly overestimate the level of sexual sophistication among the young. Young people are bombarded with information (not all of it factually correct) from radio and television, the print media, movies, and popular music. Much of the knowledge acquired from these diverse sources interferes with, rather than encourages, responsible sexual behavior.

The articles in this section document the level of knowledge about sexual functioning in general, and information about birth control methods in particular. In chapter 19, Paul Reichelt and Harriet Werley show that most teenagers are distressingly ill-informed when they begin to have sexual relations. This "learning failure" derives in large part from their restricted or selected access to information. There is no limit to the popular music that informs them of the desirability of sex, but the public tightly regulates information about contraception by overseeing the content of educational programs in the schools.

To be sure, the situation has improved substantially over the past decade or so. In a recent article not reprinted here, Melvin Zelnik reports that a majority of the females in the Zelnik/Kantner national survey had received some form of sex education in the schools, supplementing the information imparted by family, friends, and profession-als.[1] Zelnik's finding that seven out of every 10 adolescents reported classroom instruction is much higher than the level of 43 percent reported in a recent Gallup survey of 13–18-year-old males and females. The disparity in such findings suggests that instruction generally does not begin before high school, and that males are less likely to get such education than females (or it may reflect a difference in the pro-cedures of the two studies). Whether a majority or minority of teenagers have received some kind of formal education about sex probably is less significant than the fact, established by Zelnik, that most youngsters fail to learn much from the courses provided. Moreover, even the limited information young people are exposed to probably does not significantly alter their practices. Apparently, it is a case of teen-agers being given too little knowledge too late in their lives.

For example, information that is learned, it appears, is quickly forgotten. Harriet Presser tells us in chapter 20 that studies which measure the extent of sexual knowl-edge among teenagers invariably overestimate it by failing to take guessing into account. Although young people may possess a certain superficial acquaintance with birth control methods (having heard of the pill, diaphragm, or condom), they often lack both specific skills in using these methods properly and knowledge of where they may be obtained. As Madelon and David Finkel discovered, males are probably even less informed than females despite their high rates of sexual activity (chapter 21). It is difficult to avoid the conclusion that when it comes to birth control, most teenagers are "functional illiterates."

It is not that teenagers are incapable of learning sexual information. An impressive and consistent finding that emerges from this set of readings is the rapid increase in knowledge that occurs when teenagers come into contact with well-designed pro-grams of sexual instruction. Whether these programs impart a great deal of new information or crystallize existing latent knowledge is not so important. In either case, they do extend the scope of accurate information with a relatively brief exposure. What this knowledge means in practice is another matter, and a few authors raise the question whether more complete knowledge will by itself make a significant dent in the number of unplanned pregnancies.

The key to this problem, as perceived by several of the authors, is the reluctance on the part of society at large to acknowledge that teenagers are going to have sexual relations. The denial of this fact has, in the past, served to keep teenagers, especially females, innocent until marriage; currently, it keeps many innocent until pregnancy occurs. Some practitioners have described pregnancy as the "ticket of admission" to family planning clinics. As Presser observes in chapter 22, teenagers charac-teristically acquire information only after they are at risk of becoming pregnant, and not infrequently after conception or a "pregnancy scare." While efforts at primary prevention have markedly improved over the past few years, Warren Miller's descrip-tion of the early period of vulnerability to pregnancy still holds true today (chapter 23). Few teenagers are prepared for intercourse before it happens.

In resolving this issue, there are several distinct considerations that must be ad-dressed. Although sex is a social act, contraception is rarely thought of as a set of social skills. Thus, teenagers learn about the pill or the condom, but they do not learn how to apply this knowledge in social situations. This is most apparent in the context of the male/female relationship, which is governed by explicit and implicit understandings of appropriate, gender-related behavior. For example, "nice girls" don't tell their boyfriends to use a condom, because it means admitting that their sexual actions are premeditated. And we see in the Finkle and Finkle article that teenage males are uninformed, misinformed, and often apprehensive about sex. This state of uncertainty, no doubt, lessens their ability to exchange contraceptive information with their female partner. Even when males possess correct information, it is not at all clear whether they are in a position to apply this knowledge in their sexual conduct. To do so, they must possess the communicative skills to make effective use of their sexual information.

Whether increased levels of sexual information will translate into lower levels of unwanted pregnancy depends, finally, upon the character of the education provided. As Presser observes, family planning clinics may not provide detailed information about methods other than the one that is chosen. When the teenager abandons this method, for whatever reason, she (or occasionally, he) is not equipped to adopt any alternative. Obviously, our educational programs must be broader and more flexible, with periodic checkups and continuing sources of instruction. They must also develop some of the "social skills" that will enable contraceptive information to be put to solid use.

Ideally, teenagers can be reached by sex education and family planning programs before they incur the risk of pregnancy. As Jerome Evans, Georgiana Selstad, and Wayne Welcher show, many teenagers become pregnant without exposure to information about contraceptive techniques or access to them. Their study (chapter 24) is one of the few that have compared teenagers who followed different routes to resolving a pregnancy. One of their most important findings is that teenagers who elected to obtain an abortion are, if anything, more receptive to contraceptive information and services afterwards than are those who bring the pregnancy to term, or who had a pregnancy scare, but found that they were not pregnant.

Apart from this particular finding, their results suggest that program designers must be prepared to develop services tailored to meet the needs of very different groups of adolescents. Because of their similarity in age, there is some tendency to regard adolescent populations as homogeneous. In fact, as the article by Evans and his collaborators shows, teenage populations are diverse because of differences in sexual experience, psychological development, social background, and fertility goals. Programs that fail to take into account these differences as well as the differentiation that occurs after a first pregnancy are likely to encounter difficulties in serving their clients. The challenge for program planners is to provide an array of alternative approaches suited to the divergent demands of young people in need of services.

In chapter 22, Presser's study of the effect of birth timing on the transition to parenthood is especially informative about the unplanned character of the "decision" to have a first child. A substantial proportion of her sample just drifted into motherhood. While many did not strenuously attempt to avoid the role, neither did they enter it willingly and knowingly. Rather, they made their "choice" after they became pregnant. As we pointed out in the Overview, Presser's results suggest that if by some miracle of technology women had to take a pill only when they wished to become pregnant, early childbearing would become a rare event.

In the meantime, programs must face the fact that the available means of preventing unwanted pregnancies require a strong commitment to avoid conception. While many young people would certainly rather defer parenthood, most are unprepared to become effective and diligent contraceptors at the time they begin to have sexual relations. It is clear from this set of articles that we need to rethink the relatively passive approach we have followed in preparing young people for the responsibilities of sexual activity.

Chapter 25, by Laura Edwards and her collaborators, provides a model for introducing sexual education in the schools. While not arguing that such an approach is the only means of preventing unwanted pregnancies, it makes a persuasive case that educational settings are unusually well-suited to providing effective follow-up—the pervasive problem faced by many service delivery programs. The program developed in St. Paul represents a workable model for both pregnancy prevention and neonatal services for young mothers who have a child while still in school. While the high school program was clearly effective, there is evidence from the data assembled that a similar program reaching younger adolescents is advisable. (What is more, although the program also provides prenatal care and maternity services for pregnant adolescents, it is not allowed to provide abortion counseling—a decided handicap.) Many would argue that clinics, like the one established in St. Paul, reinforce teenage sexuality by lending institutional support to young people who wish to become sexually active. To some degree, they are probably right, though it is difficult to establish that such clinics "cause" teenagers to become sexually active. Yet, most persons who have studied the problem believe that the absence of such programs does not significantly deter teenagers from engaging in sex. The failure to provide services merely guarantees a steady rate of teenage pregnancy.

Reference

1. M. Zelnik, "Sex Education and Knowledge of Pregnancy Risk Among U.S. Teenage Women," *Family Planning Perspectives*, 11:355, 1979.

19

Contraception, Abortion and Venereal Disease: Teenagers' Knowledge and the Effect of Education

Paul A. Reichelt and Harriet H. Werley

What do teenagers know about contraception, abortion, venereal disease and the reproductive system? Can education improve their knowledge significantly? With evidence that more than two million unmarried women aged 15-19 are sexually active and at risk of an unintended pregnancy;[1] that approximately one-third of the legal abortions in the United States are performed on women under 20 years of age;[2] and that venereal disease among teenagers is pandemic, with the number of reported cases almost quadrupling between 1960 and 1972,[3] these questions are far from academic. Many teenagers recognize the hazards associated with unprotected coitus, as is demonstrated by the fact that substantial numbers are turning to family planning clinics for contraceptive services; in 1973, nearly three in 10 of the 3.2 million patients seen in organized family planning programs were teenagers.[4] At some centers, teenagers are seen along with adults in the regular clinic sessions. At others, special programs for teens have been established and, in these, education is an important component of the program.[5] Typical of the latter approach is the teen service of the Planned Parenthood League of Detroit. Its Youth Education on Sex Teen Center (YES) provides nonpre-scription contraception for teenage men and women, prescription contraception and related medical services for women under the age of 18, and sex education for adolescents of both sexes (the latter, a prerequisite for medical contraceptive services).

In an effort to provide data necessary for sex education program implementation, a two-part study was undertaken by the authors, with the cooperation of the Planned Parenthood League, to explore teen knowledge of contraception, abortion, reproduction and venereal disease, and to ascertain whether education in these specific areas results in improved knowledge.

The research upon which this article is based was conducted in collaboration with the Planned Parenthood League of Detroit while the authors were affiliated with the Wayne State University Center for Health Research in Detroit. It was supported in part by Division of Nursing Research Development Grant NU 00361 and Division of Research Resources General Research Support Grant RR 5718, both of the National Institutes of Health.

This article is adapted from presentations made by the authors at the 1974 annual meeting of the International Association of Applied Psychology held in Montreal, July 28-August 2, 1974, and at the Eighty-Second Annual Convention of the American Psychological Association held in New Orleans, August 30-September 3, 1974.

Confirming the experience of others who work with teenagers,[6] the study revealed that a large majority had intercourse prior to seeking contraception at the family planning clinic. The study also showed that most are either misinformed or uninformed about the various methods of contraception; that most obtain their information (and misinformation) from their peers or the mass media, with parents, educators and health professionals contributing only minimally; and that most are well-informed about abortion and venereal disease. Education, in the form of a single, informal rap session led by young professionals attuned to the psychosexual concerns of the teenagers, improved knowledge substantially in most areas.

Study Design

Each person who participated in a rap session during the nine-month period (from November 1972 to July 1973) of the study was asked to fill out a questionnaire before the start of the session. Participation in the study was voluntary, but teenagers were required by the Planned Parenthood League to attend a rap session prior to obtaining medical family planning services. Usable questionnaires were obtained from 1,327 persons of a total of 1,425—a response rate of 93 percent. Some of the nonrespondents declined to participate, and some did not arrive early enough to have enough time to complete the questionnaire before the rap session began. The respondents and nonrespondents were compared on several background variables, and there were no differences between the two groups on such factors as age, socioeconomic status, area of residence, highest grade completed, coital experience and use of birth control. Because the primary purpose of the research was to ascertain the knowledge of teenagers who had *not* already attended a rap session, the data are

based on the 1,190 respondents (148 males, 1,042 females) aged 13-19 who were attending such a rap session for the first time.

The questionnaire was composed of two sections. The first section elicited demographic and other background information; the second was primarily a test of knowledge, although it also contained some attitudinal questions. Because it was desirable to distinguish between teenagers who were uninformed and those who were misinformed, a three-point response scale was used for the second part of the questionnaire. The subjects could respond to each question by circling "true," "false," or "don't know." It required an average of 10 minutes to complete the questionnaire.

Demographic, Socioeconomic, Educational and Sexual Background

Almost nine out of 10 (88 percent) of the teenagers were women. While all the teen years were represented, the mean age was 16.3 years; six percent of the respondents were younger than 15, while eight percent were 18 years of age or older. Seven out of 10 were white; almost all the rest were black. Fifty-five percent were residents of Detroit and the rest came to the teen center from the surrounding metropolitan area where there are few facilities serving the birth control needs of teenagers. The majority of the respondents came from the middle and lower-middle socioeconomic classes, and 17 percent of them came from low-income families.*

As would be expected from the age distribution, the respondents clustered in the upper high school grades, with eight percent in the ninth or lower grades. Only four percent had dropped out of high

---

* As measured by Hollingshead's (1957) Two Factor Index of Social Position, which computes social position by occupation and level of education of the head of household.

school before graduation, and three percent were attending college.

Confirming the experience of other clinics serving teenagers,[7] a large majority of the respondents (84 percent) said that they had had sexual intercourse prior to coming to the teen center. About the same proportion (82 percent) came to the center for birth control; eight percent wanted a pregnancy test; and about one-third of those who came asked for sex education or counseling. Of the 993 sexually experienced teenagers, 675 (68 percent) said that they had used *some method* of contraception at least once. This can by no means be taken as an indication of the number of consistent contraceptors in the group. (Kantner and Zelnik found that although 86 percent of a national sample of teenagers said that they had ever used a contraceptive method, only 47 percent had used a method at last intercourse, and most of these used less-effective nonmedical methods.[8])

The teenagers major sources of information on matters relating to sex were friends and the mass media, with 45 percent of the 1,042 young women ranking their friends first and 23 percent ranking the mass media second. Among the 148 young men, just the opposite obtained, with 29 percent of them saying friends were their major source and 40 percent naming the mass media. Parents ranked third for the girls (19 percent) but last for the males (eight percent). Teachers, school counselors, physicians and nurses were rarely considered a major source of sex-related education by these young people.

Knowledge of Contraception

Twenty-five statements in the questionnaire concerned specific methods of birth control, including the pill, IUD, DIAphragm, condom, spermicides, withdrawal and rhythm; while five items dealt with reproduction.

As Table 1 shows, the teenagers were poorly informed in most areas, and lack of information rather than incorrect information was the principal problem. This distinction is important for two reasons. First, if the teenager is in a situation in which his or her behavior should be based on a particular piece of knowledge, but he or she does not possess that knowledge, the behavior will probably be fairly random (i.e., correct half the time and incorrect the other half, assuming there is an all right/all wrong response dichotomy). On the other hand, if the teenager incorrectly believes that he or she possesses the correct knowledge, the behavior will probably be incorrect most of the time. Second, the distinction has important implications for educational programs. If the teenager merely lacks information, it may be sufficient to provide only what is lacking. However, if the teenager has incorrect information, it is necessary to dispel the incorrect information and to provide the correct data—a more difficult task.

Despite the widespread publicity the birth control pill has received, a majority answered only two of the six items about the pill correctly, while a substantial majority simply did not know the answer to the four remaining items.

They did even more poorly on the IUD. Across the four items, only 20-39 percent of the teenagers knew the correct answers. Almost half did not know that the IUD remains in the uterus and does not have to be inserted before each act of coitus. They were better informed about the diaphragm (surprisingly, since this method is used by very few teenagers), with correct responses ranging from a low of 34 percent to a high of 55 percent. There appeared to be some confusion about the diaphragm and IUD since only four out of 10 respondents knew which device had to be

(text continued on page 310)

Table 1. Percent distribution of responses of teenagers to statements on contraception, reproduction and abortion, by questionnaire item, 1973 (N = 1,190)

Questionnaire item*	Percent, by type of response		
	Correct	Incorrect	Don't know
Orals			
The pill must be stopped every year for three months (F)	32	4	64
The pill is generally dangerous to use (F)	65	5	30
The pill may be taken along with other medications without decreasing its effectiveness (T)	31	8	61
The pill may be taken by a girl who uses alcohol and/or drugs (T)	33	13	54
The pill may not be taken if the woman has a history of certain illnesses (T)	39	4	57
The pill is the most effective method of birth control (T)	72	6	22
IUDs			
The IUD is inserted before each act of intercourse (making love) (F)	39	14	47
The IUD cannot be felt by the man or woman during intercourse (T)	37	7	56
The IUD is the second most effective method of birth control (T)	29	6	65
The IUD usually works best if the uterus (womb) has been stretched by a previous pregnancy (T)	20	7	73
Diaphragm			
The diaphragm must be worn at all times (F)	40	14	47
A diaphragm should be used only after having been fitted for it by a doctor (T)	55	5	40
The effectiveness of the diaphragm is increased when used with a cream or jelly (T)	34	6	61
The diaphragm cannot be felt by either the man or woman when properly in place (T)	44	3	53
Condom (rubber)			
A rubber should be tested before use (T)	55	14	31
Rubbers break easily (F)	19	48	33
The rubber should be held around the base of the man's penis when withdrawn (T)	48	5	48

* Correct answer in this and following tables is shown in parentheses following each statement. T = True; F = False.

Note: Percents may not add to 100 because of rounding.

Table 1 (continued)

Questionnaire item*	Percent, by type of response		
	Cor-rect	Incor-rect	Don't know
Spermicides (foams, creams, jellies)			
They should be inserted just *before each* intercourse (T)	68	6	26
They work by killing sperm (T)	63	5	32
They can be bought without a prescription in any drugstore (T)	67	6	27
When used with a rubber, they are a highly effective birth control method (T)	41	11	48
They should be washed out with a douche immediately after intercourse (F)	16	26	58
Miscellaneous Methods			
Rhythm is a highly effective method of birth control (F)	49	6	45
Withdrawal (pulling out) is a highly effective birth control method (F)	61	11	28
Douching after intercourse is a highly effective birth control method (F)	58	7	35
Reproduction			
Menstruation (monthly period) is a clearing of the uterus to prepare again for possible pregnancy (T)	74	9	16
A woman's fertile time (when she is most likely to become pregnant) covers the middle of the interval between her menstrual periods (T)	64	10	27
A girl can get pregnant the first time she has intercourse (T)	76	12	12
Sperm can live in the female's reproductive system for about 72 hours (three days) (T)	43	17	40
If a woman does not have an orgasm (climax) during intercourse, she can't get pregnant (F)	70	6	24
Abortion			
An abortion can be done safely and easily by a doctor during the first 12 weeks of pregnancy (T)	81	5	14
Having an abortion will make the woman sterile (unable to have children in the future) (F)	87	3	10
Anyone can tell if a girl has had an abortion (F)	85	1	14

* Correct answer in this and following tables is shown in parentheses following each statement. T = True; F = False.

Note: Percents may not add to 100 because of rounding.

Table 2. Percent distribution of responses of teenagers to statements on venereal disease, 1973 (N = 1,190)

Questionnaire item	Percent, by type of response		
	Correct	Incorrect	Don't know
Many cases of VD are caught by contact with toilet seats, drinking fountains and swimming pools (F)	73	14	13
If the symptoms of VD disappear by themselves, no treatment is needed (F)	87	2	12
Once you've had VD, you can't get it again (F)	75	11	15
VD is not really dangerous to your health (F)	91	4	5
VD can be treated in Michigan without parental consent (T)	68	5	28
Using a rubber can help prevent the spread of veneral disease (T)	66	11	23

Note: Percents may not add to 100 because of rounding.

inserted each time intercourse occurred and which remained in the uterus.

It was expected that most of the teenagers would know the correct answers to the items dealing with the condom both because it is the only male method and because it is available over-the-counter in pharmacies. However, only about half knew the correct answers to two of the three questions, while almost one-half the respondents answered one of the questions, "Rubbers break easily," incorrectly. This was the only statement where the number of incorrect responses was greater than the number of "don't know" responses. Such an incorrect belief may se-

riously and needlessly curtail the use of condoms by teenagers (and, as we shall see, teenagers appear to be so convinced of the correctness of their belief that they do not retain the correct information after it is supplied).

As Table 1 shows, the teenagers did fairly well on the section dealing with spermicides, except for one very important item. More than one out of four (26 percent) thought that spermicides "should be washed out with a douche immediately after intercourse," a dangerous misapprehension.

The teenagers were relatively well-informed about rhythm, withdrawal and douching, with from 49 percent to 61 percent responding correctly to the three statements. While they also did fairly well on the reproduction questions, one out of four did not know when the most fertile interval of the menstrual cycle occurs. As with incorrect information concerning the condom, this lack of knowledge could result in the occurrence of unprotected intercourse at precisely the most fertile time in the cycle.

As the final section of Table 1 shows, the teenagers were better informed about abortion than they were about birth control methods or reproduction. Few answered incorrectly, and only 10-14 percent didn't know the correct answers to these three items. Six items concerned venereal disease; one of these asked whether treatment could be obtained in Michigan without parental consent and one inquired about the prophylactic effect of condoms. Table 2 shows that while a majority of the teenagers knew the correct answers to all the questions, one out of three either did not know that venereal disease could be treated in their state without parental consent, or incorrectly thought it could not be; and the same proportion either did not know the protection that the condom affords against VD or believed it did not provide protection.

Table 3. Comparison of mean scores of teenagers for total knowledge and for birth control knowledge; 1973, by selected characteristics

Selected characteristic	Total knowledge*	Birth control knowledge†	Selected characteristic	Total knowledge*	Birth control knowledge†
Total sample	16.75	10.80	**Educational level**		
			7	7.75	5.63
Sex			8	7.90	4.37
Male	15.30	9.30	9	11.98	7.30
Female	17.31	11.02	10	14.72	8.97
			11	17.87	11.40
Age			12	19.01	12.14
13	8.46	5.36	College	20.11	13.75
14	11.13	6.56	Not in school — completed		
15	15.28	9.61	high school	18.16	11.57
16	17.00	10.75	Not in school — did not		
17	18.74	11.97	complete high school	14.54	8.96
18	17.72	11.03	**Sexually experienced**		
19	15.74	10.46	Yes	17.54	11.18
			No	14.74	9.05
Race					
Black	12.99	8.18	**Ever used birth control**		
White	18.76	11.91	Yes	19.18	12.46
Other	14.23	8.39	No	14.86	9.03
Socioeconomic status					
High	20.71	13.40			
	21.42	14.03			
	19.11	12.42			
	17.76	11.22			
Low	16.59	10.33			

* Based on 39 items concerning birth control, reproduction, abortion and venereal disease. Total score equals number correct minus number incorrect, with a weighting of zero for "don't know" or no response.

† Based on 30 birth control and reproduction items (a subset of the total knowledge scale). Scoring procedure is the same as that used for the total knowledge scale.

Overall Findings

In order to analyze teen knowledge by subgroup, two special scales were devised, one based on the replies to the 39 questions dealing with birth control, reproduction, abortion and venereal disease (the Total Knowledge Scale), and the second based on replies to the 30 items dealing with birth control alone (the Birth Control Knowledge Scale). The second scale is a subset of the Total Knowledge Scale. Table 3 presents the mean scores for each scale, with total score representing the number of correct answers minus

incorrect answers. It can be seen that the teenagers scored an average of 16.75 (or 42.9 percent) of a possible 39 in total knowledge, and 10.8 (or 36 percent) of a possible 30 in birth control knowledge. Teenagers with some college and those of high socioeconomic status scored a little more than 50 percent of the possible high score for total knowledge; but no subgroup came to within 50 percent of the possible high score for birth control knowledge.

The young women posted better scores

(text continued on page 314)

Figure 1. Comparison of teenagers' correct responses to questions* on contraception before and after the rap session, 1973 (N = 367)

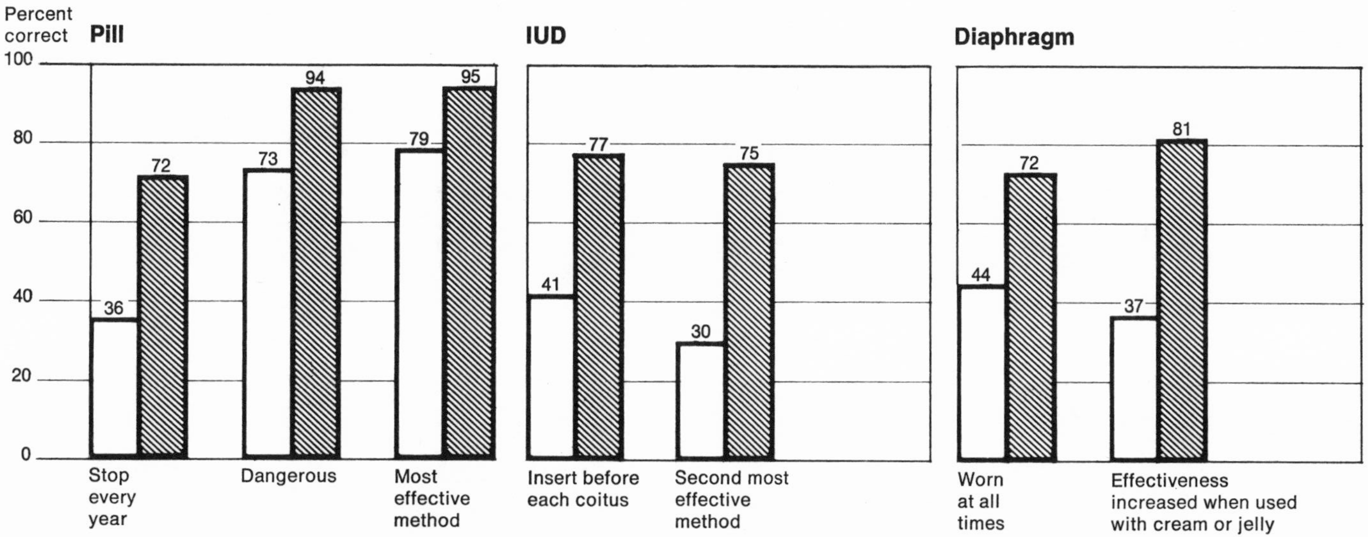

Figure 1 (continued)

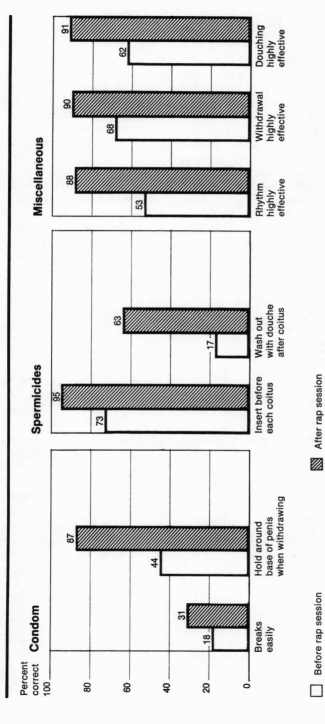

Percent correct

* Questions with strong program implications have been selected.

than the young men, indicating that it is obviously desirable to continue to include males in educational efforts. The scale scores by age increased up to age 17 and then fell off. This same pattern was reflected in the scores of the subgroups defined by educational level. With the exception of a minor reversal for seventh and eighth graders on birth control knowledge, the scale scores increased with grade level. However, high school graduates (who were necessarily an older group) scored lower than high school seniors. Teenagers who dropped out of school prior to graduation scored at the level of tenth graders. This is consistent with the fact that the modal highest grade completed by the drop-out group is tenth grade.

The results by race showed whites scoring the highest and blacks the lowest on this questionnaire. The scores for subgroups defined by socioeconomic status increased from low to high, except that the highest group performed slightly more poorly than the group immediately below it. As one would expect, or at least hope, those who had had intercourse were more knowledgeable than those who had not. And of the sexually experienced teenagers, those who had used birth control scored higher than those who had not.

Retest Results

Young women who had selected the pill as their preferred method returned for supplies approximately 10 weeks after they had attended a rap session.* At that visit

---

* After the rap session, teenagers who selected the pill were given an interim method such as condom and foam, and an appointment was made for them, usually within two weeks, for the required physical examination. After their physicals, they were provided with a two-month supply of pills. They were then required to return to the clinic for a supply visit. If all was well, they were given a five-month supply of pills.

they were asked to complete the same questionnaire again, but without the background questions; and over a nine-month period usable data were obtained from 367 girls aged 14-17. Analysis of the data from this series shows that the respondents were similar to the women in the previous group in every characteristic. A similar percentage was sexually experienced, but a slightly higher percentage of these young women had used some method of contraception at least once (76 percent compared with 68 percent) before seeking services at the center. In their responses to the prerap questionnaire, they displayed a similar level of knowledge in all areas and showed the same confusion about the IUD and diaphragm as the total group and the same incorrect perception about the sturdiness of the condom.

As Figure 1 shows, however, there was a striking improvement in knowledge in all areas subsequent to the rap session. On the pill, for example, 72 percent on the second test compared with 36 percent on the first knew that it is *not* true that pill-taking "must be stopped every year for three months." Ninety-four percent compared with 73 percent knew that it is *not* true that the pill "is generally dangerous to use." And 95 percent compared with 79 percent answered correctly that "The pill is the most effective method of birth control." Thus, even for a topic such as the pill, which has received widespread coverage in the mass media, there is a need for educational programs directed specifically at teenagers to give them a chance to integrate and clarify information they may have been exposed to previously.

Figure 1 also shows that there was not only great improvement in knowledge about the IUD and the diaphragm, but also that substantially more teenagers realized as a result of the rap session that the IUD remains in place after it has been inserted and that it does not have to be inserted before each act of coitus. The importance of using a spermicide along with the diaphragm was understood by 81 percent of the young women on the retest compared with only 37 percent who knew this on the original test.

In regard to the condom, however, the rap session did *not* succeed in convincing a majority of the teenagers that the condom is strong enough to be a reliable contraceptive. Almost one-half continued to believe that "rubbers break easily," while another 20 percent still said they did not know the answer to this question.

As for spermicides, considerably fewer (15 percent compared with 26 percent) continued to believe that they "should be washed out with a douche immediately after intercourse," but 21 percent (compared with 57 percent before) still did not know whether or not spermicides should be washed out. Thus, this is still an area for educational effort since such a degree of incorrect usage might result in substantial risk of unintended pregnancy.

While the general level of knowledge concerning rhythm, withdrawal, douching, reproduction, abortion and venereal disease was relatively high to begin with, it improved considerably following the rap session.

In view of these findings, it is not surprising that scores on both the Total Knowledge and the Birth Control Knowledge Scales improved sharply. For the sample that was retested, total knowledge rose from 18.5 to 28.3 (or from 47 percent to 72 percent of the highest possible score), and birth control knowledge rose to 20.9 from 11.9 (to 70 percent from 40 percent). The older the teenager, the higher the grade she was in, and the higher her socioeconomic level, the higher the mean score on each scale; as in the first test, black teenagers lagged behind white teenagers on both scales. The substantial increases in postrap scale scores are of roughly the same magnitude for all the various subgroups. For any given demographic variable, the postrap score for the subgroup that was lowest on the prerap measure exceeds the prerap score for the subgroup that was highest on the prerap measure. Thus, the rap session helped everyone increase knowledge to a level that exceeded the prerap session score of the most knowledgeable subgroup.

Conclusion

A distinguishing feature of the Detroit Teen Center, as compared with many other community service agencies that provide contraceptive services, is its requirement of attendance at an education session prior to the provision of birth control services. The wisdom of this policy is demonstrated, in our view, by the fact that prior to the education session not even a simple majority could provide the correct answer to two-fifths of the questionnaire items. After the rap session, there were only two items to which less than a majority knew the correct answer.

It is interesting to note that the item with the second lowest percentage of correct responses before and the lowest percentage correct after the rap concerns the strength of the condom. The teens are obviously rating condoms as much less reliable than studies in the professional literature indicate. This has obvious programmatic implications for those agencies aiming to meet the birth control needs of teenagers by serving males.

Because teenagers' major source of sex information is their peer group,[9] it is important to get correct information to as large a part of the teenage population as possible; the results presented here indicate that programs such as that provided by the Detroit Planned Parenthood League are both needed and valuable. However, voluntary agencies alone cannot be expected to provide this kind of education for all adolescents. More broadly based national programs channeled through the public school system are needed and are long overdue. There is evidence that the American public supports such school programs.[10]

References

1. J. G. Dryfoos, "A Formula for the 1970s: Estimating Need for Subsidized Family Planning Services in the United States," *Family Planning Perspectives*, 5:168, 1973, Table 32.

2. Center for Disease Control (CDC), *Abortion Surveillance, 1972*, Atlanta, Ga., 1974, p. 3.

3. CDC, *VD Fact Sheet, 1973*, Atlanta, Ga., 1974, Table 6, p. 16 and Table 7, p. 17.

4. M. Corey, "The State of Organized Family Planning Programs in the United States, 1973," *Family Planning Perspectives*, 6:15, 1974, Fig. 8.

5. S. Goldsmith, "San Francisco's Teen Clinic," *Family Planning Perspectives*, Vol. 1, No. 2, 1969,

p. 23; E. A. House and S. Goldsmith, "Planned Parenthood Services for the Young Teenager," *Family Planning Perspectives*, Vol. 4, No. 2, 1972, p. 27; and M. E. Lane, "Contraception for Adolescents," *Family Planning Perspectives*, 5:19, 1973.

6. D. S. Fordney Settlage, S. Baroff and D. Cooper, "Sexual Experience of Young Teenage Girls Seeking Contraceptive Assistance for the First Time," *Family Planning Perspectives*, 5:223, 1973.

7. S. Goldsmith, 1969, op. cit.; and D. S. Fordney Settlage et al., 1973, op. cit.

8. J. F. Kantner and M. Zelnik, "Contraception and Pregnancy: Experience of Young Unmarried Women in the United States," *Family Planning Perspectives*, 5:21, 1973.

9. H. D. Thornburg, "A Comparative Study of Sex Information Sources," *Journal of School Health*, 42:88, 1972.

10. G. Lipson and D. Wolman, "Polling Americans on Birth Control and Population," *Family Planning Perspectives*, Vol. 4, No. 1, 1972, p. 39.

20

Guessing and Misinformation About Pregnancy Risk Among Urban Mothers

Harriet B. Presser

Knowledge of the reproductive process is generally considered to be an important aspect of effective contraceptive practice. To estimate the prevalence of such knowledge, researchers have asked women when during the menstrual cycle they think they are most at risk of conceiving. Invariably, low proportions answer correctly that the time of greatest risk is about two weeks after their period begins. Only 41 percent of married women aged 18-39—50 percent of whites and 22 percent of blacks—correctly responded to this question in the 1965 National Fertility Study.[1] A 1976 national survey of 15-19-year-old women[2] found that 41 percent of unmarried teens—44 percent of whites and 24 percent of blacks—gave correct answers.*

Being misinformed about the facts of pregnancy risk could be especially hazardous for women who rely on coitally related methods of contraception, such as the condom or the diaphragm. If correctly informed, more of these women

(and their partners) might exercise particular caution during the time of maximum risk. If they are incorrectly informed or uninformed, the risk of unplanned pregnancy is enhanced.

There have been no studies that examine changes over time in the level of such knowledge among the same women. The various published estimates are all based on cross-sectional data, and correct responses are assumed to indicate actual knowledge. To the extent that people happen to guess correctly, we may be overestimating the level of knowledge; the situation may be worse than we think.

From the study we conducted in 1973 and 1974 of women who had recently become mothers for the first time, we have longitudinal data on the question of knowledge of the time of greatest pregnancy risk. Accordingly, we can ob-

---

*Sexually experienced teenagers were somewhat more likely to give correct answers (48 percent) than those who were still virgins (37 percent). This difference was found only among whites, however.

The research upon which this article is based was supported by the National Institutes of Health, DHEW, Contracts No. NO1-HD-2-2038 and NO1-HD-62836, with additional funding from The Population Council. The author gratefully acknowledges the assistance of Candace Clark and Helen Ginn in processing the data for this article.

serve change over time and make some assessment of the validity of this measure and of whether the interview itself may have an effect. Utilizing responses from separate interviews of the same women obtained in 1973 and 1974, we are able to obtain more refined estimates of the association of race, age and educational attainment with such knowledge. We also have information on the communication network that may determine such knowledge: whether the women have ever talked with others about how to keep from getting pregnant, whether they have had a class in high school that discussed contraception, and whether they have ever been to a hospital or clinic to obtain contraceptives. Finally, we are able to consider whether lack of information or misinformation is more common among those who are using less effective as opposed to more effective contraceptive methods.

It should be stated at the outset that although we are here considering women's knowledge of the relative risk of conception during the menstrual cycle, effective control of fertility may depend as much or more on the extent to which men are correctly informed. We would speculate that men are less knowledgeable than women, and do not consider the timing of sexual activity in relation to the menstrual cycle as much as women. Unfortunately, we do not have comparable data for men and women on this matter, nor do we know of any information that is available.

Study Design

The basic purpose of the overall study was to examine factors associated with mother's age at first birth. A sample was drawn from the birth records of women residing in the New York City boroughs of Brooklyn, the Bronx and Queens who had had their first child in July of 1970, 1971 or 1972. The sample was restricted to black or white mothers born on the U.S. mainland who had had singleton first births and were aged 15-29 at the time of their first birth.

A stratified random sample of women was drawn from those who met the above conditions. It included married and unmarried women of all economic statuses. A total of 541 eligible cases were located, and 408 were contacted (75 percent of those eligible). The fieldwork for both interviews was carried out by the National Opinion Research Center. We were able to reinterview 358 women, or 88 percent of the original sample. This is considered to be a high rate, given that 30 percent of the sample consists of unmarried mothers, a group that is especially difficult to locate.*

In this article, we shall limit our analysis to the 358 women who were interviewed in both 1973 and 1974. The question asked in both interviews was as follows:

> Now I want to ask about when a woman is most likely to become pregnant. When do you think this is?
> a. Right before her period
> b. During her period
> c. Right after her period
> d. About two weeks after her period begins
> e. Anytime during the month
> f. Don't know

For the first interview, all women were handed a card with these options and were asked to choose one of the alternatives. Since the second interview was

---

*For further discussion of the sample, see chapter 22, below.

Table 1. Percent distribution of second-interview responses given by mothers in the reinterview sample to the question on time of greatest pregnancy risk during the month, according to responses given in the first interview, New York City, 1973 and 1974

Responses in first interview (1973)	Responses in second interview (1974)							
	Right before period	During period	Right after period	About two weeks after period begins	Any-time during month	Don't know/no answer	Total	N
Total	**16**	**2**	**19**	**48**	**14**	**1**	**100**	**358**
Right before period	47	2	18	21	11	2	100	62
During period	0	0	100	0	0	0	100	3
Right before period	13	3	42	30	12	0	100	60
About two weeks after period begins	6	1	11	74	9	0	100	161
Anytime during month	15	2	18	24	35	6	100	54
Don't know/no answer	22	6	22	22	22	6	100	18

conducted mainly by telephone, women were read all of the options.

Differences in Response Over Time

As we reported in a previous article,[3] just 42 percent of all mothers responded correctly during the first (1973) interview to the question on pregnancy risk. Forty-five percent of those interviewed in both 1973 and 1974 correctly responded when first interviewed.[*] The low proportion is striking, since this is a sample of urban women, all of whom are mothers who recently have been in contact with physicians.

We anticipated that raising the question would lead some women to inquire among their friends, family or physicians about the correct response, and that they would be better informed at the time of the second interview just be-

cause of this interview effect. The change in the proportion correctly responding to the same question at the first and second interview was, however, minimal: from 45 percent to 48 percent.[†] What is more surprising is that 26 percent of women who gave correct responses when first interviewed gave incorrect responses a year later. Only 33 percent of the sample gave correct responses at both interviews. It thus appears that many correct responses were merely good guesses. Indeed, even the 33 percent may contain some women who simply guessed correctly twice.

Guessing is more evident, however, among those who initially gave incorrect answers. Table 1 shows, for each possible response to the question on time of greatest pregnancy risk, how the women who selected that response at the first interview answered the question at the second interview. As may be seen, most of the change in response was from one in-

[*] Disproportionately more of the 50 cases not reinterviewed than of those who were reinterviewed gave incorrect responses during the initial interview. Thus, by restricting our analysis here to those reinterviewed (since the focus is change over time), we are slightly overestimating the level of knowledge.

[†] The difference in method of interviewing (personal versus telephone) may be relevant, but we have no basis for evaluating its effect.

Table 2. Percent of mothers in reinterview sample responding correctly in both the first and second interview as to time of greatest pregnancy risk, by selected demographic characteristics, according to race, New York City, 1973 and 1974

Charac-teristics	All races		White		Black	
	% correct	N	% correct	N	% correct	N
Total	**33**	**358**	**48**	**219**	**11**	**139**
Age*						
16-20	10	103	12	33	9	70
21-23	29	134	40	89	7	45
24-32	58	121	66	97	25	24
Years of education*						
<12	9	93	13	38	6	55
12	33	167	46	104	13	63
≥13	56	98	66	77	19	21

*At first interview.

correct answer to another incorrect answer. Twenty-six percent of those initially incorrect gave correct responses the second time (not shown). The extent to which this represents better guessing or actual learning cannot be assessed.

It is evident from these data that a cross-sectional analysis of knowledge about the relative risk of conceiving during the menstrual cycle substantially overestimates the actual level of knowledge. Thus, in examining factors associated with such knowledge, we shall consider the more refined measure: those who were correct at *both* interviews.

Demographic Correlates

As shown in Table 2, there are marked differentials in the prevalence of knowledge among various subgroups of the sample. The difference by race is substantial: Only 11 percent of blacks answered correctly both times, in contrast to 48 percent of whites.

Table 2 also shows that age at first in-

terview is related to the prevalence of knowledge—the older the woman, the more likely she is to be correct. Only 10 percent of women under age 21 answered correctly both times, as compared to 58 percent of those 24 and older. Since black women in the sample are much younger than comparable white women, it may be that age explains much of the racial differential in knowledge. Table 2 shows, however, that substantial differences by race remain for those 21 years of age and older. Moreover, it may be seen that the relationship between age and knowledge is stronger for whites than for blacks.

Education, like age, is strongly related to knowledge about the time of month when a woman is most likely to become pregnant—the better educated the woman, the more likely she is to answer correctly. As is evident from Table 2, the differentials are similar to those noted for age: Only nine percent of those who did not graduate from high school answered correctly both times, as compared to 56 percent of those who had at least one year of college. Again, we see that the differential by race obtains when controlling for education, especially among those with a high school education or better.

How can we account for the strong association between race and knowledge about the time of maximum risk? Are there differences in access to correct information by race that are not compensated for by age or education?

The Communication Network

We hypothesized that discussion about contraception, especially with professionals, is positively associated with knowledge about the time of month a woman is most at risk of conceiving. Those who talk to others about con-

2

traception are more likely also to discuss the time of maximum risk and to be correctly informed—or so it would seem. To examine this relationship, we have selected for analysis the following questions asked of the women in this study:

• Did you ever have a class in high school where methods of contraception were discussed?
• Have you ever been to a hospital or clinic in order to obtain contraceptives?
• Now I'm going to read a list of different kinds of people, and I want you to tell me whether you have *ever* talked with any of them, or if they have *ever* talked with you, about how to keep from getting pregnant. The first one is your mother . . . a girl friend . . . a doctor.*

Table 3 reports our findings. First, it may be observed that blacks are *more* likely than whites to have had a class in high school in which contraception was discussed; thus, this factor cannot account for the greater lack of knowledge among blacks. Moreover, those who have had such a class show a *lower* prevalence of knowledge about the time of greatest pregnancy risk than those who have not had such a class.† This is the case for both blacks and whites. Zelnik and Kantner found in their 1976 study

Table 3. Percent of mothers in reinterview sample responding correctly in both the first and second interview as to time of greatest pregnancy risk, by selected communication variables, according to race, New York City, 1973 and 1974

Variable	All races		White		Black	
	% correct	N	% correct	N	% correct	N
Ever had class discussing contraception?						
Yes	13	91	26	27	8	64
No	40	267	50	192	14	75
Ever went to hospital or clinic for contraception?						
Yes	16	132	30	37	11	95
No	43	226	51	182	11	44
Ever talked to doctor about contraception?*						
Yes	36	275	51	176	10	99
No	22	83	31	42	13	40
Ever talked to mother about contraception?						
Yes	33	138	48	80	12	58
No	34	220	48	139	10	81
Ever talked to girl friend about contraception?						
Yes	36	253	51	162	10	91
No	26	105	37	57	13	48

*Excludes one case that did not answer this question.

*The list is much longer than the three people specified here. For more detailed findings concerning this question, see chapter 22.

†We considered the possibility that those who did not have such a class were more likely to be Catholic, and that Catholics might be more likely to know about the time of maximum risk of pregnancy (since rhythm is a Church-approved contraceptive method). However, we found little difference between Catholics and non-Catholics in the prevalence of such knowledge. This is consistent with findings from earlier studies (see reference 1 and J. F. Kantner and M. Zelnik, "Sexual Experience of Young Unmarried Women in the United States," *Family Planning Perspectives*, Vol. 4, No. 4, 1972, p. 9).

that unmarried teenagers who had had a sex education course in which the menstrual cycle was discussed were somewhat more likely to answer correctly the question about pregnancy risk—45 percent correct vs. 32 percent among those who had taken no course.[4] It may be that even when contraception was discussed in classes attended by the women in our study, this specific information was not covered—at least with sufficient emphasis or clarity. It also may be that students did not retain the information. Whatever the reason, the fact remains that an important component of effective contraceptive practice is not being communicated by high school teachers in a meaningful way, if at all.

The difference by race in attendance at a clinic or hospital to obtain contraceptives does not seem to be an explanatory factor either. Blacks are more likely to attend clinics than whites; but for blacks, attendance shows no relationship to knowledge. To some extent, the reason for this may be that those attending clinics overwhelmingly adopt the pill; and since the effectiveness of this method is not dependent upon knowledge of time of risk, such information may not be communicated or attended to in the clinic. For whites, the *higher* level of knowledge among those who did *not* attend a clinic may reflect a difference in socioeconomic status by clinic attendance; that is, the higher a woman's status, the less likely she is to attend a clinic and the more likely she is to be knowledgeable about specific aspects of the menstrual cycle (as is evident in our analysis of education). The socioeconomic differentials between those who attend and those who do not attend clinics may be greater for whites than blacks.

White mothers talk to doctors about contraception to a greater extent than black mothers. Does this explain why white mothers are more knowledgeable about the time of maximum risk? Our data indicate that for blacks, discussions with doctors about contraception are not associated with such knowledge, but are positively associated with such knowledge in the case of whites. Discussions about contraception with doctors are clearly no assurance that women will learn when during the menstrual cycle they are most at risk of conceiving.

In addition to discussions with professionals, we may consider whether talking with one's mother (or mother substitute) or girl friend about contraception is more common among whites, and whether this might explain differences

in knowledge by race. Table 3 shows that the majority of both blacks and whites have never talked to their mothers about contraception. For those who have talked to them, such discussions seem not to have contributed to their knowledge about the time of maximum risk. Talking with a girl friend about contraception is common among women of both races. Yet, a positive association between such discussions and knowledge of risk is evident for whites only.

In sum, it appears that classroom discussions about contraception, attendance at family planning clinics, and discussions with one's mother about contraception do not serve to enhance a woman's knowledge of when during the month she is most likely to become pregnant. White mothers seem more likely than black mothers to gain this knowledge if they discuss contraception with their doctors or girl friends, and this may partly explain differences in knowledge by race. Why might such discussions be more informative for whites than for blacks?

The nature of these discussions may vary by race. Whites, who are more likely to be private patients than blacks, may receive more time from doctors, including more lengthy discussions about the process of reproduction. Also, since the black mothers in our sample are much younger than the white mothers and more likely to be unmarried, physicians may restrict the scope of any discussion about contraception (perhaps in the mistaken fear that greater knowledge about sex and reproduction would encourage illegitimacy).

It is important to take into account the greater prevalence of incorrect responses among blacks than among whites when considering the positive association, for whites only, between talking with a girl friend about contraception and being knowledgeable about the time of maximum risk. Looking back at Table 1, we may observe that relatively few women reported they did not know or could not answer the knowledge question. Incorrect answers may be guesses, but they may also reflect misinformation. Many women may falsely think they are correct and may spread this incorrect information to others. Kantner and Zelnik found, in group discussions they had with 166 black females aged 15-49, that there was a general consensus that women were most likely to conceive five days before and five days after the menstrual period—and almost all of them had received some kind of formal sex education.[5] The authors comment: "It is known that older popular publications, those of a generation or more ago, had things exactly reversed. Whatever the origin of this misconception, it is amazingly resistant to correction."

Since blacks are more likely to be incorrect than whites, they may be involved to a greater extent in the exchange of misinformation (with little help from teachers or doctors to improve this situation).[*] Accordingly, whites talking with other whites may contribute more to learning about the reproductive process than do blacks talking to blacks. This may be the case for girl friends but not for mothers because of generational differences in knowledge and differences in the type of communication between peers and between generations. To gain some insight into the difficulties of obtaining this knowledge, we need only ask ourselves, How did we learn about the time of maximum risk? Was this a

Table 4. Percent of mothers in reinterview sample responding correctly in both the first and second interview as to time of greatest pregnancy risk, by current method of contraception as of the first interview (1973),[*] according to race, New York City, 1973 and 1974

Current method (1973)	All races		Whites		Blacks	
	% correct	N	% correct	N	% correct	N
Total	35	324	50	195	11	129
Pill or IUD	24	146	38	76	9	70
Other	53	97	60	79	22	18
None†	23	81	55	40	10	41

*Excludes those who were pregnant.

†Includes those not currently having sexual relations and those trying to become pregnant.

channel of information accessible to most people?

Contraceptive Practice

Knowledge about the relative risk of pregnancy during the month is less important in determining the use-effectiveness of the pill and the IUD than of other methods. But is knowledge thus related to the method of contraception used? Our data suggest that this is the case. Table 4 shows that those who, at first interview, were using methods other than the pill or the IUD were about twice as likely to be knowledgeable about pregnancy risk (53 percent) as women using the two medical methods (24 percent) or no method (23 percent).† The relationship holds for both blacks and whites.

These findings suggest that knowledge is influenced by the need to know.

---

[*]In an earlier article, we documented some of the myths that lead to unplanned first births, among them: "It was the time of the month I thought I couldn't become pregnant." In our sample, about 16 percent of those who did not want to become pregnant with their first child, but did not use contraception, gave this as their reason for nonuse (see chapter 22).

†Only five women were using rhythm at the time of the first interview. These women are grouped with those using "other methods." Zelnik and Kantner found in their 1976 study that teenagers who depended on the rhythm method were much more likely than others to be knowledgeable about pregnancy risk (see chapter 4, above).

Table 5. Percent of mothers in reinterview sample responding correctly in both the first and second interview as to time of greatest pregnancy risk, by methods of contraception used before the first birth and currently (1973),* according to race, New York City, 1973 and 1974

Current method (1973)	First method used before first birth																	
	All races						Whites						Blacks					
	Pill or IUD		Other		None		Pill or IUD		Other		None		Pill or IUD		Other		None	
	%	N	%	N	%	N	%	N	%	N	%	N	%	N	%	N	%	N
Total	45	65	39	193	11	66	53	49	56	119	19	27	19	16	12	74	5	39
Pill or IUD	29	35	32	75	3	36	38	24	54	36	6	16	9	11	13	39	0	20
Other	65	20	49	77	0	0	71	17	57	62	0	0	†	3	20	15	0	0
None‡	60	10	34	41	20	30	†	8	62	21	36	11	†	2	5	20	11	19

*Excludes those who were pregnant.

†Percentage not computed since base less than 10.

‡Includes those not currently having sexual relations and those trying to become pregnant.

But thus far we have been looking at current knowledge and current contraceptive use. Unfortunately, we cannot assess knowledge before the first child was born. It may well be that knowledge comes too late, a speculation that is consistent with our finding that effective contraceptive practice is often late: The majority of our sample had an unplanned first birth, following which they made a dramatic shift to the pill and the IUD.[6] We also find that women who planned their first child are much more likely to be currently knowledgeable about pregnancy risk (48 percent) than women who did not (22 percent).

Are women who used the pill or the IUD before their first birth also less knowledgeable about pregnancy risk than other women? The data do not permit analysis of all methods used before the first birth, but we can consider the first method used, if any. As may be seen in the "total" column of Table 5, the sharpest differential in knowledge occurs between those who used any method before their first child was born and those who used no method: Users are considerably more knowledgeable. There is little difference by method first

used. Similar patterns obtain for both blacks and whites, although one must be cautious with the small numbers in each cell for blacks.

Thus, current knowledge is associated with current pill and IUD use, but not with first method used prior to motherhood. When we examine simultaneously both first method and current method in relation to current knowledge, we find that it is those who went from no method before the first birth to the pill or IUD after the birth who are least knowledgeable—only three percent were correct. And it is those who began use of the pill or IUD prior to motherhood but are currently using other methods who are most knowledgeable—65 percent were correct. These women may be especially motivated to control fertility, but for some reason are dissatisfied with the pill or IUD, and thus seek out knowledge to minimize pregnancy risk with other, less effective methods. (Previous pill and IUD users who are currently not using any method are more difficult to interpret, since this group includes those not having sexual relations and those trying to become pregnant.)

In sum, we see that the low prevalence

of knowledge among current pill and IUD users is more pronounced for those who used no method before the birth of the first child. These women apparently were not highly motivated to control their fertility prior to motherhood, did not then know about the relative risk of pregnancy in order to minimize the risk of conception, and do not currently need to have such knowledge. Blacks are more likely than whites to have shifted from no method before the first birth to the pill and IUD afterwards (16 percent of blacks as compared to eight percent of whites); this may explain, in part, the racial difference in knowledge of pregnancy risk. It is of interest to note that among those women who did not use any contraception before the first birth, not one woman was currently using a traditional contraceptive method; they were using either the pill or IUD or no method.

Conclusion

Our data indicate that a cross-sectional view of knowledge about pregnancy risk overestimates the prevalence of such knowledge. A substantial minority of women simply guess correctly. Only one-third of our sample of urban mothers gave correct responses in both interviews, in contrast to 45 percent in the first interview.

The low prevalence of knowledge is striking. For urban women, we would expect exposure to the media to be substantial. Moreover, as mothers, they have all been in recent contact with physicians. Clearly, neither the media nor physicians are communicating this type of knowledge.

We observed marked differences by race, age and education in the percent of women who responded correctly to the knowledge question in both the first and the second interviews: Whites, older women, and those who are more highly educated are better informed. This may have to do with greater access to correct information among these subgroups.

It is surprising to find, however, that for both blacks and whites, classroom discussions about contraception, attendance at family planning clinics, and discussions with one's mother about contraception are not positively associated with knowledge about pregnancy risk. Only for whites is discussion with doctors or girl friends associated with higher levels of knowledge. We have speculated about the benefits of private medical care in this regard (more characteristic of whites than blacks) and the extent to which sharing of misinformation among peers may be taking place (more for blacks than whites).

The overall low prevalence of knowledge about pregnancy risk leads us to question whether such information is, indeed, of great practical significance. Should family planning clinics, for example, be concerned with improving the level of such knowledge? If all women began using the pill or IUD at the time they first had sexual intercourse, then the question would not be of practical importance. (Weighing the safety of these methods relative to alternatives would be the issue instead.) But such early use of highly effective methods is the exception rather than the rule.

It appears from our data that those women currently using less effective methods are more knowledgeable about pregnancy risk, perhaps because they have a greater need to know. The type of contraceptive used prior to the first birth, however, is not associated with current knowledge; those who never used contraception before their first birth show the lowest prevalence of knowledge. Knowledge apparently comes too late—

after motherhood that is often unplanned. Accordingly, it would seem that there is a need for clinics, physicians, teachers and the like to improve the level of such knowledge, especially among young women and men, and before parenthood begins.

References

1. N. B. Ryder and C. F. Westoff, *Reproduction in the United States: 1965,* Princeton University Press, Princeton, N.J., 1971.

2. M. Zelnik and J. F. Kantner, "Sexual and Contraceptive Experience of Young Unmarried Women in the United States, 1976 and 1971," chapter 4, above.

3. H. B. Presser, "Early Motherhood: Ignorance or Bliss?" chapter 22, below.

4. Chapter 3.

5. J. F. Kantner and M. Zelnik, "United States: Exploratory Studies of Negro Family Formation—Common Conceptions About Birth Control," *Studies in Family Planning,* Vol. 1, No. 47, 1969, p. 10.

6. Chapter 22.

21
Sexual and Contraceptive Knowledge, Attitudes and Behavior of Male Adolescents

Madelon Lubin Finkel and David J. Finkel

For more than half a century, organized family planning programs in the United States have concentrated on making contraception available to adult women, and it is only within the past five years that services to men, usually in the form of vasectomy clinics, have assumed a growing importance. Given this emphasis, it is hardly surprising that social research on sexual knowledge, attitudes and practice has also concentrated on the adult female. This concentration on the female now includes the adolescent woman as well, largely because of societal concern about teenage illegitimacy and venereal disease. Such concern has stimulated interest in the sexual behavior of teenage women, and has resulted in both small-scale[1] and national surveys[2] that have provided useful information on their sexual knowledge, behavior and contraceptive practice. With legal and policy constraints on serving teenagers eliminated or relaxed in many states, about 30 percent of the clients of organized family planning programs in 1974 were women younger than 20 years of age,[3] and one-third of legal abortions in 1973 were obtained by women in this age group.[4] However, the adolescent male has, for the most part, been ignored. Except for sporadic efforts to include him in clinic rap sessions and to provide him with free condoms, little has been done to bring organized services to the man younger than 20 years of age. Few data are available on his sexual and contraceptive knowledge, attitudes and practice.

This article seeks to delineate the knowledge of human reproduction and contraception of a selected sample of male high school students, the extent of their sexual activity and use of contraception, and the impact of a sex education class on their knowledge and behavior.

Methodology

A total of 421 male students enrolled in three high schools in a large, northeastern city completed a 46-item questionnaire administered in classrooms in the spring of 1974. Participation in the study was voluntary and the responses were confidential. All of the participants had taken or were going to take health education courses, a requirement for graduation. The schools were selected purposively and do not necessarily constitute a representative sample of high schools in the target area or in other sections of the country. The study does provide some data, how-

Table 1. Percent distribution of respondents according to sources of information on sexual intercourse and reproduction, by ethnicity

Source	Total	Black	His-panic	White
	(N= 403*)	(N= 116)	(N= 155)	(N= 132)
Male friends	37.3	31.6	33.5	46.0
Professionals†	22.6	19.0	28.9	19.0
Female friends	18.2	21.3	24.3	9.5
Brothers	7.8	10.3	4.6	9.0
Sisters	0.5	0.6	0.5	0.5
Fathers	9.1	10.9	6.4	10.4
Mothers	4.5	6.3	1.8	5.7
Total	100.0	100.0	100.0	100.0

* Not all the respondents answered the question.

† Refers to doctors and teachers.

Note: Percents may not add to 100 because of rounding.

Table 2. Number and percent of correct responses to statements on reproduction and contraception

Statement	No.	%
A douche (girl washing herself after sexual intercourse) is a good method to prevent pregnancies. (F)	272	66.3
A male's sperm lives less than one day inside a woman. (F)	278	67.8
Rubbers (scumbags, condoms, bags) help prevent unwanted pregnancies. (T)	376	90.2
A girl can most easily get pregnant just before her period begins. (F)	192	46.4
Rubbers (scumbags, condoms, bags) help prevent VD. (T)	313	75.4
During sexual intercourse, if a male takes out his penis *before* coming, his girl may get pregnant anyway. (T)	133	31.9

ever, on a population that has not previously been studied systematically. The questions were pretested on males of similar age and sociocultural characteristics as the target population, and were translated into Spanish by a team consisting of a nurse and sex educator of Hispanic descent and by one of the authors who speaks Spanish fluently.*

Findings

The sample of 421 males is almost evenly divided into three sociocultural categories: 30 percent (128) black; 38 percent (159) Hispanic†; and 32 percent (134) white. No deliberate stratification by ethnicity was undertaken; hence, the distributions by ethnic composition were relatively similar on the basis of random sampling. The mean age of the sample was 16.3 years and is homogeneous for each ethnic group. Ages ranged from 12 to 19 years. While 44 percent of 291 students responding to a question concerning family composition were living in families with both parents present, 43 percent were living in families headed by mothers, about three percent in families with fathers only, and the remainder with a variety of relatives. A large majority had siblings.

Sources of Sex Information

The students were asked to indicate two people from whom they had learned about sexual intercourse and human reproduction. A choice of seven persons was offered and the respondent was asked to circle two of them. As Table 1 shows, male friends were the most frequent

*Madelon Lubin Finkel.

†Refers to respondents of Puerto Rican, Cuban, Dominican or Haitian backgrounds.

Table 3. Number and percent distribution of respondents ranked according to number of knowledge statements answered correctly (from six correct to 0 correct), by ethnicity of respondents

Rank	Total No.	%	Black No.	%	Hispanic No.	%	White No.	%
6	23	5.5	4	3.1	13	8.2	6	4.5
5	83	19.7	23	18.0	31	19.5	29	21.6
4	137	32.5	44	34.4	47	29.6	46	34.3
3	117	27.8	37	28.9	43	27.0	37	27.6
2	54	12.8	17	13.3	21	13.2	16	11.9
1	5	1.2	2	1.6	3	1.9	0	0
0	2	0.5	1	0.8	1	0.6	0	0
Total	421	100.0	128	100.0	159	100.0	134	100.0

$X^2 = 5.7861$ df $= 8$ p$>$0.2; cells of 0-2 correct were collapsed.
Note: Percents may not add to 100 because of rounding.

source, followed by professionals (doctors and teachers) and female friends. Although male friends were cited most often by the respondents in each ethnic group, the second most frequent choice varied: Among Hispanic and white males, professionals were the second major source; among blacks, female friends ranked second. Less than 11 percent in each group learned about human reproduction and sexual intercourse from any family member.

Knowledge of Sex

Six statements were designed to elicit knowledge of human reproduction and contraception. As Table 2 shows, a large majority of those who responded knew that condoms can prevent unwanted pregnancies; far fewer, however, knew that condoms also help prevent venereal disease. Although two-thirds knew that a douche is not a reliable method of contraception, only about one-third knew that even if a male practices withdrawal, his partner may still become pregnant. While two-thirds knew that sperm can live longer than 24 hours after ejaculation, fewer than one-half could identify the

time during the menstrual cycle when conception is likeliest to occur. Each respondent was ranked by the number of statements answered correctly, receiving one point for each correct answer. (The range of points is from zero correct to six correct.) Table 3 illustrates the distribution of the respondents according to the number of points they scored. The table shows that almost 58 percent answered four or more statements correctly. In addition, just over one-quarter answered three statements correctly, while just under 15 percent scored only one or two points. Only two individuals did not answer any of the six statements correctly. There was no significant difference among the ethnic groups.*

Knowledge did *not* appear to increase with age (not shown). The majority within each age group scored between four and six points (not shown). It should be noted that the oldest group (18-19 years) and the youngest group (12-15 years) achieved almost identical scores when 4-6 points were grouped and when 0-2 points were grouped.

*Chi-square testing of distribution among the ethnic groups indicated nonsignificance (p$>$0.2).

Table 4. Number and percent distribution of respondents agreeing or agreeing strongly or disagreeing or disagreeing strongly with statements exploring attitudes toward sex and contraception, by statement

Statement	Agree		Agree strongly		Disagree		Disagree strongly		Total	
	No.	%	No.	%	No.	%	No.	%	No.	%
Teenagers have harder time getting birth control than adults.	166	39.8	96	23.0	125	30.0	30	7.2	417	100.0
Birth control makes sex seem preplanned.	194	47.0	63	15.3	124	30.0	32	7.7	413	100.0
Only the female should use birth control.	129	31.1	97	23.4	133	32.0	56	13.5	415	100.0
Intercourse okay even if couple not in love.	181	43.0	114	27.1	81	19.2	45	10.7	421	100.0
Male who uses a condom respects his partner.	163	39.1	81	19.4	130	31.2	43	10.3	417	100.0
Would not want friends to know I used condoms.	108	25.8	49	11.7	196	46.8	66	15.8	419	100.0
I have sex because most of my friends do.*	19	6.6	7	2.4	124	43.1	138	47.9	288	100.0

* Answered by sexually experienced respondents only.

Note: Percents may not add to 100 because of rounding.

Table 5. Number and percent of respondents who had experienced coitus, by ethnicity

Experience	Total		Black		Hispanic		White	
	No.	%	No.	%	No.	%	No.	%
Total	421	100.0	128	30.4	159	37.8	134	31.8
Sexually experienced	291	69.1	108	84.4	119	74.8	64	47.8
Not sexually experienced	130	30.9	20	15.6	40	25.2	70	52.2

$X^2 = 45.0366$ df $= 2$ p$<.001$.

Effect of Sex Education

The responses to the knowledge questions were analyzed according to whether the respondents had or had not yet taken the mandatory hygiene course that includes sex education. (Biological and social aspects of human reproduction were components of the course.)

Of the 285 students who had taken the course, almost 62 percent scored 4-6 points; while of the 132 who had not yet taken the course, 47 percent achieved that score. (Not all the respondents indicated whether or not they had taken the course.) Conversely, of those who had not taken the course, 17 percent scored 2-0 points as compared to 15 percent who had studied hygiene.[*]

Attitudes Toward Sex, Contraception

A number of statements explored attitudes toward sex and contraception, and respondents were asked to check whether they agreed or agreed strongly, or disagreed or disagreed strongly, with the statements. As Table 4 shows, more than six out of 10 agreed or agreed strongly that "sexually active teenagers have a

harder time getting birth control items . . . than do adults." A similar percentage agreed or agreed strongly that "birth control makes sex seem preplanned. . . ." More than half agreed or agreed strongly that "only the female should use birth control," but 46 percent rejected this point of view. Seven out of 10 respondents believed that sexual intercourse was "okay . . . even if two people are not really in love," but a sizable proportion (30 percent) did not accept this position. The meaning of contraceptive use was explored in the responses to the statement, "A male who uses a rubber . . . shows respect for his girl friend." Almost six out of 10 accepted this viewpoint, but slightly more than 40 percent disagreed, and 10 percent disagreed strongly. Although approval of the use of condoms was substantial, 38 percent did not want their friends to know they used them. This was so despite the fact that 93 percent of the 421 respondents denied that it was important to them to do what their friends do (not shown). Nine out of 10 of those respondents who were sexually experienced denied that they had had intercourse because most of their friends had done so.

Sexual Experience

Twelve questions explored the sexual experience of the 421 respondents. As Table 5 shows, 69 percent of the total sample reported that they were sexually experienced (having had at least one coital encounter). A large majority of the black

[*]Chi-square testing of the scores indicated a nonsignificant difference (p = 0.17), which means that there was a nonsignificant variation between those who had studied hygiene and those who had not. However, when scores 3-0 and scores 4-6 were compared, a Chi-square analysis confirmed that there was a statistically significant difference (0.001>p>0.01).

Table 6. Number and percent distribution of respondents according to age at first coitus, by ethnicity

Age	Total		Black		Hispanic		White	
	No.	%	No.	%	No.	%	No.	%
<12	104	35.7	59	54.6	37	31.1	8	12.5
13	40	13.7	19	17.6	15	12.6	6	9.4
14	59	20.3	17	15.7	27	22.7	15	23.4
15	52	17.9	6	5.6	30	25.2	16	25.0
16-17	36	12.4	7	6.5	10	8.4	19	29.7
Total	291	100.0	108	100.0	119	100.0	64	100.0

$X^2 = 59.0100$ df $= 8$ p$<$.001.

and Hispanic males in the sample were sexually experienced, while almost half (48 percent) of the whites reported themselves to be sexually experienced.

The mean age at first coitus for the sexually experienced males was 12.8 years, with a range from age five to age 17. Of those who reported that they were sexually active, almost 15 percent were nine years old or younger when they had their first sexual experience. All but three percent of the sexually experienced males had their first coital experience before the age of 17.

Table 6 illustrates the distribution by age at first coitus. Just under 36 percent had their first intercourse at 12 years of age or less; 34 percent at 13-14 years of age; and the rest at 15-17 years of age. The majority of black males had their first coital experience between the ages of five and 12 years. There was a bimodal distribution in age at first coitus in the Hispanic group (ages 5-12 and age 15). The majority of white males had their first coital experience between the ages of 15 and 17.

Differences in mean age at first coitus were apparent among the three sociocultural groups. Black and Hispanic males had their first coital experience at the earliest ages: Mean age at first coitus for black males was 11.6 years and for Hispanic males it was 13.0 years. The white

males began their coital activity at a much later age, 14.5 years.

When asked if the female with whom they had first had sexual intercourse was older, younger or the same age as they were, 53 percent said their partner was older, about 35 percent said she was the same age and 12 percent said she was younger (not shown).

Frequency of Coitus

The mean frequency of sexual intercourse in the week prior to the survey was 0.93 times, and the range was from zero to seven times. Sexual activity appears to be sporadic, since more than half the respondents (55.3 percent) did not have sexual intercourse in the week prior to the survey: 58 percent of the Hispanic, 64 percent of the white and 47 percent of the black males did not engage in sexual activity (not shown).

When asked whether their sexual activity in the past week was usual in terms of coital frequency, 65 percent said that their activity was the same as usual; 19 percent, that they were less active than usual; and 16 percent, that they were more active than usual. Of those who reported no sexual activity in the past week, 74 percent said that that was usual.

In the previous month, the respondents

Table 7. Number and percent distribution of respondents according to contraceptive utilization at last coitus, by ethnicity

Method	Total		Black		Hispanic		White	
	No.	%	No.	%	No.	%	No.	%
Condom	81	28.1	24	22.4	22	18.8	35	54.7
Female (pill, loop, foam)	49	17.0	19	17.8	27	23.1	3	4.7
Withdrawal/douche	86	29.9	35	32.7	38	32.5	13	20.3
None	72	25.0	29	27.1	30	25.6	13	20.3
Total	288	100.0	107	100.0	117	100.0	64	100.0

$X^2 = 32.4651$ df $= 6$ p$<$.001.
Note: Not all the respondents answered the questions on contraceptive use.

reported that they had had intercourse an average of 3.6 times with 1.5 partners.

Contraceptive Utilization

Four categories of contraceptive use at last coitus were formulated on the basis of three questions: use of condom; female use of birth control (pill, loop, foam); use of withdrawal or douche; and no use of birth control. Table 7 illustrates the distribution of contraceptive utilization at last coitus. More than half (55 percent) had relied on withdrawal or douche or had used nothing. Just over one-quarter (28 percent) had used a condom. Seventeen percent reported that their partner had used the pill, loop or foam.

Differences in contraceptive use were evident when sociocultural group was controlled. The findings suggest that white males were more consistent in their use of the condom than were their black or Hispanic counterparts. That is, 55 percent of the white males had used the condom at last coitus, compared with 22 percent of the black males and 19 percent of the Hispanic males. Moreover, almost 60 percent of the black and Hispanic males had relied on ineffective (or no) methods of contraception compared with 41 percent of the white males. Far larger proportions of the partners of black and His-

panic males had used the pill, loop or foam than had the partners of white males, while far fewer partners of whites had used douche/withdrawal than had partners of the other two ethnic groups.

Seventy-two percent of the sexually active respondents reported that they had *not* used the condom at last coitus, 32 percent of them because they didn't have one with them; 26 percent because they didn't feel it was important to use birth control; and 16 percent because they didn't think their partner could become pregnant at that time. About one-quarter said they hadn't used a condom because they believed their partner was using some kind of contraception. Of all sexually active males, only 15 percent said they used a condom every time they had intercourse, while 50 percent said they hardly ever or never used one (not shown).

Discussion

A profile of the sexually active male teenager can be inferred from these data. Male adolescents begin sexual activity at an early age, the mean age in this study being 12.8 years. However, the activity is sporadic in nature, with more than half reporting that they had not engaged in sexual intercourse in the week prior to the survey. Furthermore, a majority stated

334   FINKEL AND FINKEL

that the absence of sexual activity during that week was usual. When frequency of coitus in the past week was examined by present age, the mean frequency increased as age increased; however, the variance was high.

The use of contraceptives appears to be haphazard. Of those who used a condom at last coitus (28 percent), 92 percent always or sometimes used it. This finding suggests that those who used a condom at last coitus are more inclined to use it generally during sexual intercourse. Of those whose female partners had used birth control (the pill, loop or foam) at last coitus (17 percent), 63 percent stated that they hardly ever or never used a condom. Because their female partner used a reliable method of birth control at last coitus, they probably saw no need to use a condom themselves. However, it is not known whether the female used birth control consistently, since the question referred to last coitus only. Studies detailing contraceptive use by teenage women have also shown it to be haphazard, with reliance on the ineffective methods of birth control.[5]

Of those who relied on the douche or withdrawal (30 percent) at last coitus, 57 percent hardly ever or never used a condom. Of the 25 percent who did not use any method of birth control at last coitus, 80 percent hardly ever or never used a condom. It remains unclear what motivates some adolescents to use effective methods of birth control and others to use ineffective methods when knowledge about contraception appears to be widespread.

Policy Implications

This study found that sexual activity had begun for about half the sexually active group by 13 years of age. Therefore, sex education offered in high school comes rather late and may be inappropriate to this group's needs. Birth control programs should reach out to younger male (as well as female) adolescents.

If sex education were offered in the junior high schools, more adolescents might obtain correct information about sexual intercourse and contraceptive use before, rather than after, they began having sexual relations.

Those who oppose the distribution of contraceptives to sexually active adolescents argue that the result of such a program would be an increase in promiscuity in the adolescent population. As has been pointed out, "access to effective medically supervised contraception and abortion is no more likely to encourage teenage promiscuity than denial of access has been to discourage adolescent sexual activity."[6] Such access might help avert unwanted pregnancies and abortion. While no program or policy decision can hope to prevent premarital coitus, such programs can at the very least educate adolescents about the risks involved in unprotected coitus, and the methods available to reduce the risks.

References

1. S. Goldsmith, M. O. Gabrielson, I. Gabrielson, V. Mathews and L. Potts, "Teenagers, Sex and Contraception," *Family Planning Perspectives*, Vol. 4, No. 1, 1972, p. 32; F. F. Furstenberg, "Preventing Unwanted Pregnancies Among Adolescents," *Journal of Health and Social Behavior*, 12:340, 1971; A. M. Vener and C. S. Stewart, "Adolescent Sexual Behavior in Middle America Revisited: 1970-1973," *Journal of Marriage and the Family*, 36:728, 1974; and J. Jekel, L. V. Klerman and D. R. E. Bancroft, "Factors Associated With Rapid Subsequent Pregnancies Among School Age Mothers," *American Journal of Public Health*, 63:769, 1973.

2. J. F. Kantner and M. Zelnik, "Sexual Experience of Young Unmarried Women in the United

States," *Family Planning Perspectives*, Vol. 4, No. 4, 1972, p. 9; and "Contraception and Pregnancy: Experience of Young Unmarried Women in the United States," *Family Planning Perspectives*, 5:21, 1973.

3. M. Corey, "U.S. Organized Family Planning Programs in FY 1974," *Family Planning Perspectives*, 7:98, 1975.

4. Center for Disease Control, DHEW, *Abortion Surveillance, Annual Summary 1973*, Atlanta, 1975, p. 3.

5. J. F. Kantner and M. Zelnik, 1973, op. cit.

6. P. Cutright, "The Teenage Sexual Revolution and the Myth of an Abstinent Past," *Family Planning Perspectives*, Vol. 4, No. 1, 1972, p. 24.

22
Early Motherhood: Ignorance or Bliss?

Harriet B. Presser

Motherhood is often defined as the most sacred of women's roles; but, ironically, it is the social role women are most likely to adopt unintentionally. The great majority of women do plan to become mothers at some time: they have been socialized to motherhood from infancy.* But little stress has been placed on the importance of planning when to begin having children. Many doctors do not initiate discussion of contraception with patients who have not already borne children.[1] And most family planning programs emphasize reaching women in the postpartum (or postabortion) period when, it is believed, they are most moti-

vated to control their fertility.[2] What is more, U.S. couples have been found to use contraception most consistently and most effectively after they have reached (or exceeded) their intended family size.[3] Possibly the most ineffective contraceptors are sexually active teenagers who have never been married and, if female, never been pregnant.[4]

Why are women relatively poor contraceptors before they experience their first pregnancy? Do they not know that there are effective methods to control fertility before this time? Are the modern medical contraceptive methods generally inaccessible to them before they become mothers? Or is the problem motivation? Do women who have not yet achieved the (wanted) status of motherhood care enough about delaying childbirth to take positive, effective action to avert it?

Data from a survey of New York City women bear directly on these questions. The study was designed to explore the processes whereby the roles of women affect the age at which they first give birth, and the effect of age at first birth on women's subsequent roles and fertility. As a first step, we sought to determine the

---

* Increasingly, women are challenging socialization for motherhood, and are choosing social roles which may exclude parenthood altogether. As yet, however, few women choose to be and remain childless over a lifetime. (See: U.S. Bureau of the Census, "Birth Expectations and Fertility: June 1972," *Current Population Reports*, Series P-20, No. 240, 1972.)

The research upon which this article is based was performed pursuant to Contract No. NO1-HD-2-2038 with the National Institutes of Health, DHEW. The author wishes gratefully to acknowledge the research assistance of Emira Habiby, Norma Agatstein and Louise Conklin at various stages of the study.

extent to which certain aspects of fertility control are experienced prior to the onset of motherhood, and how these relate to age at first birth. This article focuses on our findings.

Procedures

Our analysis is based on a sample of 408 urban women from all economic strata who recently became mothers for the first time. This sample was drawn from the birth records of women residing in three boroughs of New York City (Brooklyn, the Bronx and Queens) who had their first child in July of 1970, 1971 or 1972. Only women who were born in the mainland United States were eligible; this excluded first-generation migrants from Puerto Rico and elsewhere. Nonwhites other than blacks were excluded. Women whose first birth was a twin were considered ineligible, as were women whose first child was not residing with them. About 90 percent of first births in New York City occur to women aged 15-29, and our sample was restricted to this group of mothers.

Among the total of New York City mothers meeting the above sampling criteria, 38 percent were black and 30 percent of all first births were illegitimate. This population was stratified by race and legitimacy status (as well as by age at first birth) so that the sample would be representative in this regard. Women were not proportionately drawn into the sample, however, by year of birth. The sample was designed to include about 25 percent whose first birth was in July 1970, about 25 percent in July 1971 and about 50 percent in July 1972. (A major consideration here was the difficulty in locating women whose addresses, obtained from their birth records, were over a year

old.) Women were interviewed in person during the period January 15-March 14, 1973. For about one-half of the sample, then, their first child was about seven months old at the time the mother was interviewed; the remainder of the sample was divided between those whose first child was about one-and-one-half years old and those whose first child was about two-and-one-half years old at the time of the interview.

The field work was conducted by the National Opinion Research Center (NORC). We systematically put 709 cases into the field in order to obtain a minimum of 400 completed interviews. NORC was successful in locating all but 38 (five percent) of the 709 mothers, despite the fact that 330 (47 percent) of them were not at the address shown on the birth record. Eighty-eight (12 percent) of the 709 women had moved outside New York City and, thus, would not be interviewed, and an additional 42 (six percent) were ineligible for other reasons (e.g., first child not residing with mother). Seventy-three women (10 percent) refused to participate and an additional 60 (eight percent) were not at home, even after repeated call-backs. The completed interviews totaled 408, a total of 58 percent. These 408 respondents represent 76 percent of the 541 located eligible cases.

A comparison of data from the 709 birth records showed little difference between those interviewed and those not interviewed with regard to race, legitimacy status of first birth, age of mother and father at first birth, education of mother and father at first birth, and whether or not the mother was born in New York City. The exclusion of women who moved out of the city or who were not interviewed for other reasons does

Table 1. Percent distribution of New York City mothers, by planning status of first birth, according to age at first birth, 1970-1972

Planning status of first birth	Percent, by age (in years) at first birth			
	15-29 (N= 408)	15-19 (N= 129)	20-23 (N= 154)	24-29 (N= 125)
Total	100	100	100	100
Planned	44	19	44	70
Unplanned	56	81	56	30
(Used contraception during month consistently)	(6)	(8)	(7)	(4)
(Used contraception during month inconsistently)	(6)	(5)	(6)	(6)
(Did not use contraception during month)	(44)	(68)	(43)	(20)

not appear to introduce a serious bias. A subsequent comparison of the 408 completed interviews with the birth records showed a remarkably high level of comparability between these two sources of data on the variables specified above.

Planning Status and Age at First Birth

The modal ages at first birth for women in our sample are 21 and 22; the median age is 21.9. For the purpose of analysis, we grouped age at first birth into three categories: ages 15-19 years; ages 20-23; and ages 24-29. The percent of the total sample in each age group is 31, 38 and 30, respectively.

A first step toward understanding the transition to motherhood is considering whether the first birth was planned or unplanned. Planning status was deter-

mined by asking respondents whether contraception was consistently practiced during the month the woman became pregnant with her first child and, if contraception was not employed, the reason or reasons. A card listing several possible reasons was provided; it included an "other" category in which additional reasons could be volunteered. First births to women who indicated that at least one of the reasons that they did not use contraception was that they were trying to have a baby (a specified option) were classified as planned. All other first births were classified as unplanned.*

As shown in Table 1, over one-half of the women in the sample (56 percent) reported that they did not plan their first birth — that is, they did not deliberately try to become pregnant. Some of the unplanned births were undoubtedly contraceptive failures, since six percent of the sample said they consistently used contraception during the month they became pregnant. An additional six percent said they used contraception, but not consistently, during that month, although they were not trying to have a baby. Most of the unplanned first births, however, were a consequence of not using contraception at all during the month they became pregnant — 44 percent of the total sample.

It may also be seen from Table 1 that age at first birth is strongly related to the planning status of the birth. Fewer than two in 10 of first births among teenage mothers were planned, as compared with more than four in 10 of those aged 20-23, and seven in 10 of those aged 24-29.

The fact that most first births to teenagers are unplanned is undoubtedly related to the fact that most first concep-

---

* For other reasons stated for not using contraception, see Table 6.

tions among this age group occur to unmarried women, only some of whom marry by the time the child is born.* Table 2 shows that 60 percent of teenage mothers had first births out of wedlock, declining sharply to 15 percent of mothers aged 20-23, and nine percent of mothers aged 24-29. In addition to the 27 percent of first births that were born to unmarried women, seven percent were born to married women but were conceived prior to marriage. Premarital conceptions that are legitimated by marriage are associated here with early motherhood.

Contraceptive Experience

Whereas only about two-fifths (44 percent) of the women planned their first birth, nearly two-thirds (66 percent) said they had used some form of contraception at some time prior to the onset of motherhood. As indicated in Table 3, most women who used contraception prior to their first birth used a method at the time of first sexual intercourse. One-third of the mothers *never* used any method of contraception prior to motherhood. After the first birth,† an additional 22 percent of the women in the sample initiated contraceptive practice. Twelve percent of the interview sample (of whom 45 percent are Catholic‡) report that they never used contraception.

* Only seven of the 110 women who were not married at the time the first child was born were married at the time of the interview. It can be determined for three cases that the respondent married the child's father, and in one case that she married someone else; for the remaining three cases, this cannot be determined.

† This was seven months prior to interview for about half the women and either 1.6 or 2.6 years before for the other half.

Table 2. Percent distribution of New York City mothers, by legitimacy and conception status of first birth, according to age at first birth, 1970-1972

Legitimacy and conception status of first birth	Percent, by age (in years) at first birth			
	15-29 (N= 408)	15-19 (N= 129)	20-23 (N= 154)	24-29 (N= 125)
Total	100	100	100	100
Illegitimate	27	60	15	9
Legitimate	73	40	85	91
(Premaritally conceived)	(7)	(14)	(6)	(2)
(Maritally conceived)	(66)	(26)	(79)	(90)

Note: Percents may not sum because of rounding.

Table 3. Percent distribution of New York City mothers, by timing of first contraceptive use in relation to first birth, 1970-1972

Timing of first contraceptive use	Percent	Number of cases
Total	100	408
Prior to first birth	66	271
(At first sexual intercourse)	(52)	(214)
(After first sexual intercourse)	(14)	(57)
After first birth	22	90
Never used	12	47

‡ An analysis of the 47 cases who report they never used contraception reveals that 51 percent were Catholic, a proportion not much higher than for the total sample; this suggests that religion is not of critical importance in this regard. (See: C. F. Westoff and L. L. Bumpass, "The Revolution in Birth Control Practices of U.S. Roman Catholics," *Science*, 179:41, 1973.)

Table 4. Percent distribution of New York City mothers who have ever used contraception, by first contraceptive method used, according to timing of first contraceptive use in relation to first birth, 1970-1972

First contraceptive method used*	Percent, by timing of first contraceptive use		
	Total (N=361)	Prior to first birth (N=271)	After first birth (N=90)
Total	100	100	100
Pill/IUD	38	28	68
Condom/ Diaphragm	49	59	19
Other methods	13	13	13

* If more than one method was reported, the most effective method was considered.

There are marked differences in contraceptive use prior to the first birth, according to age at first birth (not shown in Table 3). Thus, 55 percent of women who had their first births at ages 15-19 had never used any contraceptive method prior to the birth. This contrasts with 32 percent for those aged 20-23, and 13 percent for those aged 24-29.

Table 4 shows the increase in use of the most effective methods of contraception, the pill and the IUD,° after the first birth. Only 28 percent of the mothers who first used contraception prior to the first birth used one of these physician-prescribed methods, as compared with 68 percent of those who first used contraception after having a first — often unplanned — child. (It is probably also true that those who initiate contraceptive use prior to the first

° Sterilization is excluded from the most effective methods considered here, since it is not a childspacing method, and is, therefore, seldom employed by women in these age groups who have not yet had any children.

birth shift to more effective methods after the first birth. For the 268 sexually active women who were not pregnant at the time of the interview and were currently using contraception, 60 percent were using the pill or the IUD, 31 percent, the condom or diaphragm, and the remaining nine percent, other methods. When multiple methods are cited, only the most effective method is considered.)

The consequences of the risks entailed in using less effective methods may be more keenly realized after the birth, increasing the mother's motivation to control her fertility. These data may also reflect the fact that it takes a birth, planned or unplanned, to bring most women into the medical system which controls prescription of the most effective methods, the pill and the IUD. The diaphragm is also a medically prescribed method, but very few of the women grouped as "condom/diaphragm"† users prior to the first birth reported using the diaphragm. The first method most commonly used by those who employ contraception before the first birth is the condom. The pattern of change may also be seen as a shift from male to female methods. It suggests that after the first birth, women tend to choose a method where they are not dependent on the male to provide contraception.

The postpartum approach of family planning programs may be seen from Table 5. Thirty-six percent of the respondents indicate they had at some time obtained contraceptives from a hospital or clinic, but only eight percent did so *prior* to the first birth. Infrequent use of clinics

† The condom and diaphragm are grouped together because they have about the same failure rate in actual use, as reported in the 1970 National Fertility Study. (See: N. B. Ryder, "Contraceptive Failure in the United States," *Family Planning Perspectives*, 5:133, 1973.)

before the first birth seems to be characteristic of mothers of all ages. However, *after* the first birth, younger mothers are much more likely to attend clinics than older mothers. Indeed, most of the teenage mothers (54 percent) obtained contraceptives from a hospital or clinic after their first birth. (DHEW's National Reporting System for Family Planning Services shows that nine out of 10 teenage clinic patients adopt the pill or the IUD as their method.[5])

Abortion and Miscarriage

Should contraception fail, or fail to be used, induced abortion is an alternative method to prevent an undesired birth. A very liberal abortion law took effect in New York State in July 1970, and was highly publicized; three-quarters of the mothers in our study conceived at a time when they would have been eligible for a legal abortion in New York City. Indeed, about 65,000 New York City women who had never before given birth did take advantage of the law between July 1970 and July 1972 to terminate their pregnancies.[6] Among the respondents in this study, only 20 (five percent) reported that they had ever had an induced abortion before the first birth. This is not a surprising statistic, considering that this is a sample of young women, about half of them Catholics, who recently carried a pregnancy to term. The women who did report a previous induced abortion tended to be older at the time of first birth (median age, 24) than those who did not (median age, 22). (This is to be expected since termination of pregnancy serves to postpone motherhood.)

Ten percent of the respondents reported a miscarriage or stillbirth prior to the first birth. As an indirect way of assessing whether induced abortions among these

Table 5. Percent distribution of New York City mothers, by whether and when they obtained contraceptives from a hospital or clinic, according to age at first birth, 1970-1972

Obtained contraceptives from hospital or clinic	Percent, by age (in years) at first birth			
	15-29 (N=407)*	15-19 (N=129)	20-23 (N=153)	24-29 (N=125)
Total	100	100	100	100
Before first birth	8	10	8	6
After first birth	28	54	21	10
Never	64	36	71	84

* Excludes one case of no answer.

young women who recently demonstrated their ability to carry a pregnancy to term were being misreported as miscarriages, we examined whether Catholics were more likely than non-Catholics to report a miscarriage; this was not the case. The median age at first birth for women who experienced a miscarriage or stillbirth prior to the first birth is 22.8; for those who have not, it is 21.9.

It appears, then, that young mothers prior to their first birth were more inexperienced in methods of controlling their fertility than older mothers. Although most women had at some time used contraception prior to their first birth, young mothers (and their partners) were very likely to be ineffective or nonusers. This may be related to the fact that most rely on the condom, which must be used at the time of intercourse. Use of the most effective methods, the pill and the IUD (which are not coitus-related), requires contact with the medical system; and, as we have seen, there is little use of organized clinic programs — an important source of effective contraception for those who, like most of the young mothers studied, are of

Table 6. Percent distribution of reasons why New York City mothers, who have ever used contraception and who were not trying to become pregnant, did not use contraception during month they became pregnant and had first birth in 1971-1972

Reason for not using contraception	%	No. of cases
Total	100*	148*
Didn't mind if I became pregnant	39	58
It was the time of the month I thought I couldn't become pregnant	16	23
Didn't have contraceptives available and didn't expect to have sex at that time	14	21
Didn't think I had intercourse often enough to become pregnant	13	19
Stopped taking pill or using IUD because of side effects and didn't use anything else	7	10
Husband (partner) objected to using contraception	7	10
Felt sex wouldn't be as much fun if used contraception	6	9
Other reasons	22	32

* The percentages total to more than 100 and the number of cases to more than 148 because 26 women gave two or more answers.

Table 7. Percent distribution of New York City mothers, by knowledge of when during month they are most at risk of becoming pregnant, according to age at first birth, 1970-1972

When most at risk of pregnancy	Percent, by age (in years) at first birth			
	15-29 (N= 408)	15-19 (N= 129)	20-23 (N= 154)	24-29 (N= 125)
Total	100	100	100	100
Right before period	18	27	18	8
During period	1	2	1	0
Right after period	17	24	15	11
About two weeks after period begins	42	19	45	63
Any time during month	15	22	14	11
Don't know*	7	7	8	6

* Includes one case of no answer.

Note: Percents may not add to 100 because of rounding.

low income. Induced abortion was an infrequent experience prior to the first birth for young and older mothers alike. Miscarriages — an involuntary means of postponing birth — were more common.

Knowledge vs. Motivation

To what extent are unplanned first births the consequence of inadequate knowledge, or access or of low motivation? Let us consider, for women who were not trying to become pregnant with their first

child when they did, why they did not use contraception.*

The reasons cited by respondents for not using contraception in the month they became pregnant, as shown in Table 6, indicate that knowledge, accessibility *and* motivation, as well as interpersonal barriers, present problems relating to nonuse of contraception. Low motivation is suggested by the replies of nearly two-fifths of the respondents that they "didn't mind" if they became pregnant (although it is not possible to determine what proportion, if any, of such response represented ex

* This analysis excludes women who reported consistent use of contraception during the month they became pregnant with their first child as well as women who said that they never had used contraception, as they were not asked why they did not use a method at this particular time.

post facto rationalization). A substantial proportion of the women (16 percent) took risks because of lack of knowledge, as reflected in the response: "It was the time of month when I thought I couldn't become pregnant."* Lack of knowledge is also reflected in the reason cited by an additional 13 percent of respondents that one must have intercourse "often" to become pregnant. The unavailability of contraceptives when needed was cited by 14 percent of the women. Ten women (seven percent) volunteered that they stopped taking the pill or had their IUD removed because of side effects, and got pregnant before they adopted an alternative method. Interpersonal barriers to effective contraception are suggested by such reasons as: "Husband [partner] objected to using contraception" (seven percent), and "Felt sex wouldn't be as much fun" (six percent).

Some of the reasons cited suggest that many women are poorly informed about the reproductive process. All respondents were asked when during the month they thought that they were most at risk of becoming pregnant. Table 7 shows that fewer than half of all mothers correctly reported this to be about two weeks after the beginning of the last menstrual period. If we also include as a possible correct answer, "any time during the month," to allow for those that may have missed the emphasis of the question on *most* at risk, still only a bare majority answered correctly. This is quite a low proportion considering that all of these women are mothers who have been in contact with physicians. It may also be seen in Table 7 that

---

* These women did not check rhythm or the "safe period" as a contraceptive method they had ever used; only six women among all 408 in the interview sample said that they were using rhythm when they became pregnant with their child.

Table 8. Percent of New York City mothers (whose first birth was in 1970-1972) who discussed with other persons how to keep from getting pregnant, by category of person and timing of discussion

Category of person	No. of cases	Percent, by timing of discussion			
		Total	Before first birth	After first birth	Never
Mother (or substitute)	407*	100	29	9	62
Father (or substitute)	359†	100	3	2	95
Sister	286‡	100	32	12	56
Brother	298§	100	5	1	94
Girlfriend	408	100	53	14	33
Boyfriend	104**	100	30	11	59
Husband	304††	100	59	17	24
Doctor	408	100	38	36	26
Nurse	408	100	11	15	74
Druggist	408	100	2	1	97
Social worker	408	100	3	7	90
Clergyman	408	100	3	0	97
Teacher, other school personnel	408	100	8	2	90

* For those with a mother or mother substitute.
† For those with a father or father substitute.
‡ For those with at least one sister.
§ For those with at least one brother.
** For those who were never-married.
†† For those married at least once.

younger mothers are much more misinformed about the time of greatest risk than older mothers — only one-fifth of teenage mothers gave a correct answer to this question. *Prior* to their first birth it

Table 9. Percent distribution of New York City mothers, by planning status of first birth, according to attitude toward timing of first birth, 1970-1972

Planning status	No. of cases	Percent, by attitude toward timing of first birth			
		Total	Wanted child sooner	Right time or didn't matter	Wanted child later or never
Total	408	100	7	61	32
Planned	178	100	14	82	4
Unplanned	183	100	0	38	62
(Didn't mind if became pregnant)	(53)	(100)	(0)	(64)	(36)
(Other reasons*)	(130)	(100)	(1)	(27)	(72)
Never used contraception	47	100	9	68	23

* Excludes women who said they "didn't mind" *and* gave other reasons.

may be assumed that even fewer knew when the risk of pregnancy was greatest.

From whom does one learn about the reproductive process and how to prevent conception? Women in the study were asked whether they had ever talked with specific categories of individuals, or whether these people had talked with them, about how to keep from getting pregnant. Table 8 reports their answers. Before the first birth, exceedingly small proportions of women discussed how to prevent pregnancy with fathers, brothers, druggists, social workers, clergymen, and teachers or other school personnel. About one-tenth of the women had spoken with a nurse. The proportion is only one-third for mother, sister, boyfriend (for the never-married) or doctor. Girlfriends and husbands (for the ever-married) show the highest percentages, with more than half indicating they had discussed ways of preventing pregnancy with one or the other prior to the first birth. Nevertheless, it is striking that the figures are not higher. More than 40 percent of those ever-married did *not* speak with their husbands about ways of preventing pregnancy prior to their first birth and, at the time of the

survey (after the women had become mothers), one-fourth of the ever-married women still had not discussed this with their husbands. It may also be seen from Table 8 that doctors are the most important source of information about contraception *after* the first birth. Yet, even after childbirth, one-fourth had never discussed contraception with a doctor.

Attitude Toward Timing of First Birth

We asked the women in the study how they felt about the timing of their first birth. At the time they had the child, did they wish that it had been born sooner? later? Had it been born at just about the right time, or had they wished not to have any children at all?* Sixty percent of the women said the birth came at "the right time," and 30 percent said they had wanted the child to come "later."

The planning status of the first birth is

* This question was repeated in the reinterview of women approximately one year later. We shall be analyzing the extent to which attitudes toward the timing of the first birth change over time.

highly correlated to attitudes toward its timing. Table 9 shows that 96 percent of planned first births were wanted at that time or sooner. This is not the case for unplanned births. Sixty-two percent of the women who became pregnant with their first child, when they were not deliberately trying to do so, wished they had had their first child later or never.* Among women whose firstborn was unplanned, those who said they "didn't care" if they became pregnant are only half as likely to report they wish they had delayed the birth than those who gave other reasons for not using contraception prior to conception (36 vs. 72 percent). Since the other reasons cited most often relate to inadequate knowledge about the reproductive process or lack of accessibility to contraceptive services, it would seem that tackling these problems might serve to postpone motherhood for many women.

Table 10 shows the relationship between age at first birth and attitude toward the timing of the first birth. Nearly half of the teenagers report that they had wanted to postpone the first birth or remain childless. This is a remarkably high proportion, considering that women can be expected to rationalize a birth as wanted after it has occurred, even if the birth was unintended. With increasing age at first birth, the proportions who report that they had wanted their first birth at the time it occurred, or sooner, increases, and the proportion who wished it to come later, or not at all, decreases. Thus, of the mothers who gave birth at ages 24-29, 18 percent wanted the child later or never, and 82 percent said it came at the right time or not soon enough.

Although there is a marked decline with increasing age in the percent wishing

* For the total sample, only eight women said they didn't want any children at all.

Table 10. Percent distribution of New York City mothers, by attitude toward timing of first birth, according to age at first birth, 1970-1972

Attitude toward timing	Percent, by age (in years) at first birth			
	15-29 (N=408)	15-19 (N=129)	20-23 (N=154)	24-29 (N=125)
Total	100	100	100	100
Wanted child sooner	7	2	7	13
Right time	60	48	62	69
Wanted child later	30	44	30	17
Didn't want any children	2	4	1	1
Didn't matter when	1	2	0	0

they had postponed their first birth, it is noteworthy that a substantial proportion of women who became mothers in their late twenties felt this way. It should also be noted that 13 percent of those who became mothers at ages 24-29 wanted to have their first child *sooner* than when the birth occurred. Since most of these women were trying to become pregnant when they conceived, it may be assumed that many *began* trying even sooner.

The high proportion of teenage mothers who say they wish that they had postponed their first birth suggests that the legitimacy status of the birth is related to attitudes toward timing. A strong relationship is apparent in Table 11. However, it may be noted that *conception* status is a more relevant consideration than *legitimacy* status. The distribution in attitudes toward timing is similar for out-of-wedlock first births and first births which occurred inside marriage, but were premaritally conceived. More than two-fifths of the women who conceived their firstborn out of wedlock wished that the child was born

Table 11. Percent distribution of New York City mothers, by attitude toward timing of first birth, according to legitimacy status of first birth, 1970-1972

Attitude toward timing	Percent, by legitimacy status		
	Illegitimate (N=110)	Legitimate	
		Premaritally conceived (N=30)	Maritally conceived (N=268)
Total	100	100	100
Wanted child sooner	3	3	9
Right time	47	43	67
Wanted child later	44	50	23
Didn't want any children	5	3	1
Didn't matter when	2	0	0

Note: Percents may not add to 100 because of rounding.

later, as compared with one-fourth of the women whose first child was conceived during marriage.

Discussion

Most women want to become mothers. But a substantial proportion (one-third in our study of urban mothers) wish that their first child had come later. This is especially true if the firstborn is unplanned, conceived out of wedlock, or born while the mother was still in her teens. In our study, nearly six in 10 first births were unplanned, more than one-third were conceived out of wedlock, and one-third were born to teenagers. For 22 percent of the mothers in our study, all three conditions obtained.

When those who regretted the timing of their first birth were asked their reasons, the reason most often volunteered was that having an infant restricted their life choices far more than they had anticipated. For example, one woman who had conceived her first child prior to marriage, but subsequently married the child's father, explains:

> I didn't want to get married just yet and of course having the baby now stops me from doing all the things I'd like to do. I'd like to go back to school.

Another women whose first birth was conceived in the course of marriage says:

> I wasn't ready to have babies when I did. I was doing fine. I was working and I had to stop and take care of the baby. It stopped me in my tracks.

For the unmarried woman, an unplanned first birth has often meant having to go to work. One such woman explains her feelings about wishing her first child had been born later:

> Because I wasn't married or settled yet, I didn't have a job or a place to stay. I was living with my sister and she had a family to support and couldn't afford another head in the house. So I had to find a job and a place as soon as the baby came, and that wasn't easy.

What can be done to help young women postpone these often unplanned, often illegitimate, often regretted early first births? It would appear, from the data in this study, that a combination of approaches is required which would improve knowledge about the risks of pregnancy, improve access to effective contraceptive services *before* the first birth, improve contraceptive technology and strengthen motivation to seek out and use contraception.

Making family planning services accessible to women before they give birth was urged by Arthur A. Campbell in 1968. In discussing the relationship between family planning and poverty, Campbell said:

> ... many of the publicly supported family-planning programs now in operation first reach the mother when she is in the hospital to give birth to a child. Although there are many good reasons for taking advantage of the maternity ward setting, there should be additional programs to reach the potential mother before she has her first birth. In a very real sense, it may be more important to delay the first child than to prevent the seventh. The timing of the first birth is of crucial strategic importance in the lives of young women because the need to take care of a baby limits severely their ability to take advantage of the opportunities that might have changed their lives for the better. . . . The girl who has an illegitimate child at the age of 16 suddenly has 90 percent of her life's script written for her.[7]

Our data provide empirical support for this argument. The provision of birth control services to teenagers, however, is not necessarily very popular, politically. For example, President Nixon's only response to the dozens of population-related recommendations of the U.S. Commission on Population Growth and the American Future was to reject its conclusions that abortion laws should be liberalized and that contraceptive information and services should be made available to minors.[8] The President based his opposition to extending family planning services to teenagers on his belief that it would weaken family relationships. Our data suggest that it is the lack of birth planning information and services that may weaken the family, since three-quarters of births to teenagers are conceived outside of marriage. Illegitimacy has never been associated with strong families, nor have shotgun weddings. Political controversy is likely to dwindle in light of clear evidence that from 57 percent to 75 percent of Americans favor the provision of birth control services to teenagers who want them.[9] By the end of 1973, 43 states and the District of Columbia had affirmed the right of unmarried girls aged 18 or older to consent to their own contraceptive care, and in 23 states and the District of Columbia, girls may consent at considerably younger ages, or with no age restriction.[10]

Policy Implications

In light of this changing legal situation, what can be done to avert unintended early motherhood?

Since young people who have unintended first births tend to have a seriously distorted understanding of those aspects of human reproduction related to risk of pregnancy, it would appear that high schools and junior high schools could help close this knowledge gap. Courses which teach the biology of human reproduction are not likely to solve the problem unless an accurate notion of the risks of pregnancy is stressed, and practical advice on effective contraception offered.

Organized family planning programs could reach out to young people who have not yet had babies, rather than concentrating on the postpartum approach. Special teen clinics have been highly successful where they have been organized.[11] Some of the self-help clinics which are being established by feminist groups may focus on the importance of preventing early unintended motherhood, and generate interest among teenagers at the grassroots level.

The most effective available methods —the pill and the IUD—are unacceptable to many individuals because of their undesirable side effects. Abortion, even as a backup method, may be feared or regarded as immoral. Development of an effective, convenient, safe method of post-coital contraception (such as a pill which would induce menses) would be desirable, especially to meet the needs of the unmarried, who have intercourse less regularly and predictably than most married couples.

One alternative to promoting the practice of birth control to prevent unintended motherhood would be to discourage sexual activity outside of marriage. It would, to say the least, be a far more difficult task to motivate individuals not to have sexual intercourse prior to marriage than to motivate them to practice birth control when they have sexual relations and do not want to have a child.

But knowledge, accessibility and contraceptive technology are not the only problems. Our data show that many of the mothers in our study whose firstborn was unintended said they had not used contraception because they didn't care whether they became pregnant or not. For some of these women, neither increased knowledge, nor increased accessibility, nor improved technology is likely to change this situation. They do not have the motivation to take advantage of the opportunities to control their fertility. To alter motivation would require major social changes involving the early socialization of females, and the opportunities for women in the society. We shall be exploring both of these factors in future work emerging from this study, as we relate the roles of women to the timing of the first birth and subsequent fertility.

As women move through the reproductive span, those poorly motivated to control their fertility will undoubtedly become more highly motivated. Their knowledge about the reproductive process will increase, and they will become more efficient and effective in their birth control prac-

tice. But, for many women, these changes will occur too late to have any real effect on their choice of roles outside the family. Early first births mean early child care responsibilities for most women. These often have a very restrictive effect on women's day-to-day activities for years to come. Thus, in the current efforts to assess the need for expanding family planning services as well as the need for structural change,[12] it seems meaningful to distinguish the needs of women prior to and following the first birth. On the basis of our findings, it seems that policy decisions relating to the period preceding motherhood merit priority.

References

1. M. A. Silver, "Birth Control and the Private Physician," Family Planning Perspectives, Vol. 4, No. 2, 1972, p. 42; N. H. Wright, G. Johnson and D. Mees, "Report of a Survey of Physicians' Attitudes in Georgia Toward Family Planning Services, Prescribing Contraceptives, Sex Education and Therapeutic Abortion," Advances in Planned Parenthood, Vol. III, S. Lewit, ed., Excerpta Medica, Princeton, N. J., 1968, p. 37; and S. S. Spivack, "The Doctor's Role in Family Planning," Journal of the American Medical Association, 188:152, 1964.

2. H. C. Taylor, "A Family Planning Program Related to Maternity Service," in B. Berelson, et al., eds., Family Planning and Population Programs, University of Chicago Press, Chicago, 1966, p. 433.

3. L. L. Bumpass and C. F. Westoff, The Later Years of Childbearing, Princeton University Press, Princeton, N. J., 1970, p. 73.

4. J. F. Kantner and M. Zelnik, "Contraception and Pregnancy: Experience of Young Unmarried Women in the United States," Family Planning Perspectives, 5:21, 1973.

5. Center for Family Planning Program Development, Data and Analyses for 1974 Revision of DHEW Five-Year Plan for Family Planning Services, Planned Parenthood-World Population, New York, 1974.

6. C. Tietze, "Two Years' Experience with a Liberal Abortion Law: Its Impact on Fertility Trends in New York City," *Family Planning Perspectives*, 5:36, 1973.

7. A. A. Campbell, "The Role of Family Planning in the Reduction of Poverty," *Journal of Marriage and the Family*, 30:236, 1968.

8. C. F. Westoff, "The Commission on Population Growth and the American Future: Its Origins, Operations and Aftermath," *Population Index*, 39:491, 1973.

9. J. Blake, "The Teenage Birth Control Dilemma and Public Opinion," *Science*, 180:708, 1973; and R. Pomeroy and L. C. Landman, "Public Opinion Trends: Elective Abortion and Birth Control Services to Teenagers," *Family Planning Perspectives*, Vol. 4, No. 1, 1972, p. 39.

10. "Girls Under 18 Can Consent to Birth Control Services in 40% of the States," *Family Planning Digest*, Vol. 1, No. 6, 1972, Table 1, p. 1; and updated from *Family Planning/Population Reporter*, 2:25, 29, 50, 57, 61, 93, 110, 1973.

11. E. A. House and S. Goldsmith, "Planned Parenthood Services for the Young Teenager," *Family Planning Perspectives*, Vol. 4, No. 2, 1972, p. 27.

12. J. Blake and P. Das Gupta, "The Fallacy of the Five Million Women: A Reestimate," *Demography*, 9:569, 1972; P. Cutright, "Reactions to Blake and Das Gupta's 'The Fallacy of the Five Million Women: A Reestimate'," *Demography*, 10:663, 1973; and R. W. Osborn, "Further Reactions to Blake and Das Gupta's 'The Fallacy of the Five Million Women: A Reestimate'," *Demography*, 10:673, 1973.

23
Psychological Vulnerability to Unwanted Pregnancy

Warren B. Miller

Many women become unintentionally pregnant at some time during their lives, mistiming a conception that they had intended to have at a more propitious time, or failing to prevent a conception which they did not want to have then or ever. Some of these unintended pregnancies are terminated by abortion; others are carried through to delivery. Experience with women coming for abortion and prenatal care to the Stanford University Medical Center over the past four years has shown that, not only did women seeking abortion have unwanted pregnancies, but many of the women seeking care prior to delivery have pregnancies which were not fully wanted at time of conception. Why do women have unwanted pregnancies? And why do such unwanted pregnancies seem to recur at certain specific times during the life cycle of fertile women? Our experience indicates that there are stages in a woman's reproductive career when she is especially vulnerable psychologically to unwanted pregnancy. I have identified, among the women we have seen at Stanford, eight stages of the life cycle when such vulnerability tends to occur.

First, it might be useful to enumerate five aspects of ego psychology which may bear on the occurrence of unwanted

pregnancies, and may improve understanding of the origin of these life cycle stages:

● *The conscious wish for a child* is evident in a small number of women who request abortion. That is, the woman initially wanted to have a child but subsequently changed her mind because of changes in her personal life, or because the negative aspect of a basic ambivalence toward having a child asserted itself after she had conceived.

● *The preconscious or unconscious wish for a child* involves a desire for a child which is latent in the psychology of the woman, but which can be brought out by careful self-exploration or when certain conflicting or repressive forces are removed. It is very difficult to tease out how important such a wish actually is in influencing behavior. I think that psychiatrists and other clinicians have tended to overemphasize the importance of such preconscious and unconscious wishes.

● *Risk-taking* is another factor. In the broad sense, this refers to the fact that a woman must evaluate the potential for good and bad of various alternative behaviors, and then make a decision about how much risk she is willing to take. Sometimes, an unwanted pregnancy occurs as the result of a calculated risk or a risk taken on impulse.

• *Learning failure* involves several phenomena. One obvious example occurs when the woman has not acquired the knowledge of how conception occurs, under what conditions it occurs, what the probabilities are that it will occur under those conditions, and what methods are available for altering those probabilities. Another example lies in the failure to develop *contraceptive vigilance:* The practice of contraception is not a natural process. We must learn to attend to the likelihood that unprotected intercourse will result in an unwanted pregnancy. We commonly see adolescent girls and women who request abortion after having failed to acquire this contraceptive vigilance, at least to the extent that it will work automatically and effectively for them.

• *Integrative breakdown of the ego* is another factor leading to unintended pregnancy. That is, under certain circumstances, the integrative, executive function of the ego breaks down, either under a particular stress or when an individual moves from a fairly stable situation into a new and unfamiliar environment.

Vulnerable Stages in the Life Cycle

Every individual goes through a sequence of events in his or her lifetime based upon an unfolding of internal biological factors as well as a change of expectations from the self and from society. The five factors discussed above operate to make a woman especially vulnerable psychologically to unwanted pregnancy at recurrent periods during that part of her life cycle, from puberty to menopause, which encompasses her sexual and reproductive career.

• The first vulnerable stage occurs during early adolescence, when the girl is still subfecund or sterile. She is in a transition period between a time when she does not have to worry about getting pregnant and a time when this possibility must be a real concern. During that transition there must be a change of attitude towards the self as a biologically fertile person. A new level of personal responsibility must be achieved. This is especially difficult because the point at which contraceptive behavior is necessary is not clearly or reliably demarcated. The transition from low to high fecundity is gradual. In such a setting, with the risks changing, the learning and use of contraceptive vigilance is difficult.

• The second vulnerable stage occurs at about the time a woman first becomes sexually active. At this point, a woman characteristically develops new feelings about herself and others. The change is rarely made without at least some turmoil and such stress disposes the woman towards vulnerability. Nowadays, this second stage frequently occurs in mid-adolescence, thus corresponding in time with the first stage.

Some women who request abortion become pregnant during their first experience of intercourse. Almost all women, however, have been exposed to an initial period of unprotected intercourse. After the first few sexual experiences, the woman usually becomes fully aware that she is a sexually active person, that she probably will continue to be so, and realizes, at some psychological level, that she must make a decision about contraception. A large proportion of these women then seek out contraceptive help and adopt a method. Some women, however, cannot fully accept themselves as sexually active. They deny to themselves that they are going to continue sexual activity, and have sexual relations for months without adequate contraception. Often, they become pregnant.

Table 1. Eight vulnerable stages in the sexual careers of women at which time they are especially susceptible to an unwanted pregnancy

1. During early adolescence: a. when fecundity is absent or low but increasing, and, as a consequence, contraceptive vigilance is incompletely developed.	**5. In relation to marriage:** a. Just before or just after, when contraceptive vigilance is commonly relaxed; b. during conflict and/or separation (same as 3b); c. after separation or divorce (same as 3c).
2. At the start of the sexual career: a. at the time of the first few acts of intercourse, for which there is typically no contraceptive preparation; b. during the three to six months afterwards, until the woman recognizes and acknowledges the beginning of her sexual career.	
3. In relation to a stable sexual partner: a. while the relationship is in the stage of development, before a stable sexual and contraceptive pattern has been established; b. during conflict and/or separation, when patterns of communication and cooperation are disrupted and the sense of interpersonal loss may be acute; c. after breakup with a partner with whom a particular sexual and contraceptive pattern has been established— • when situationally reexposed to the old partner but without access to the previous contraceptive method, • when exposed to new partners with different sexual and contraceptive styles.	**6. After each pregnancy:** a. during the postpartum period, when there is subfecundity, altered sexual activity, and, often, the use of interim contraceptive methods; b. when a new level of contraceptive vigilance is required as a result of the demands brought about by a new baby; c. after abortion, when there is guilt or ambivalence. **7. In relation to the end of childbearing:** a. when the decision to stop having children is being dealt with.
4. As a result of geographic mobility: a. when there are major changes in the social field such that sexual and contraceptive norms and opportunities change— • after moving away from home and the nuclear family, • after moving to a new sociocultural area.	**8. During menopause:** a. when fecundity is decreasing and, as a consequence, contraceptive vigilance is waning.

Source: Adapted from the author's chapter, "The Psychological and Psychiatric Aspects of Population Problems," in D. A. Hamburg and H. K. Brodie, eds., *American Handbook of Psychiatry*, Vol. IV, Basic Books, 1973.

• The third stage of vulnerability occurs with unmarried women as they become involved with one man and develop an ongoing, stable sexual relationship. At the beginning, they are working out the patterns and understandings of this sexual relationship, including the nature of their need for contraception, their contraceptive preferences, and who, ultimately, will take responsibility for contraception. Contraceptive practice, it must be emphasized, is an ongoing, two-party affair and in the beginning of every sexual relationship (every stable relationship in particular), there are important negotiations that take place. In this early phase, when the woman and her partner are sexually involved, but have not yet worked out their contraceptive pattern, there is increased vulnerability to unintended conception.

Once a couple's pattern of interaction has become stable, women seem most likely to be subject to unwanted pregnancy at times of crisis in the relationship. This is the period when integrative breakdown of the ego frequently occurs. Even though two partners may have developed a working pattern of communication and cooperation regarding contraception, either one may forget or simply abandon this previously established routine under the stress of a serious argument. The conscious or preconscious wish to become pregnant may also occur at this time—when a woman sees pregnancy as a way of coping with, or even preventing, disruption of the relationship.

There is a third vulnerable substage which occurs after a couple has separated. For example, as a result of the breakup, the woman may have suspended sexual activity and discontinued oral contraception. A surprise weekend or a late effort to repair the broken relationship may find the woman contraceptively unprepared.

These three substages recycle for a woman with each subsequent sexual partner. Although a woman acquires a certain kind of contraceptive routine or pattern with one partner, this process of developing a new pattern of communication and cooperation, with its associated negotiations, is necessary again when the woman becomes involved with a new individual. Thus, the woman is returned to the first substage of vulnerability.

• The fourth vulnerable stage occurs in relation to geographic mobility. Here again, integrative breakdown of the ego may occur under the pressure of change.

Two kinds of geographic change are seen most frequently: One involves the adolescent girl who moves out of her parents' home where there may have been little opportunity for sexual activity. When she moves into an apartment of her own or with a group of girlfriends, there is a new set of opportunities and social pressures to which she is exposed.

Sometimes an individual moves from one subcultural or psychosocial area where sexual standards are conservative to another where there is more sexual freedom and more opportunity, and she is not familiar nor prepared to cope with the social demands and expectations placed on her.

• A fifth vulnerable stage occurs in relation to marriage. As the marriage date approaches, contraceptive vigilance tends to decline because the consequences of an unplanned pregnancy are not so grave. We have observed a number of women who had an unintended conception sometime after they became engaged, or just after they got married (if they waited for marriage to begin sexual activity). For these women, even an accidental pregnancy may be acceptable because they are married or soon to become so. Often, such individuals will continue with the pregnancy rather than seek an abortion. But in a very important sense this may be an unplanned, undesired pregnancy. Once within marriage, the same set of principles applies to the marital partner as applies to the stable sexual partner prior to marriage.

• A sixth vulnerable stage occurs after completion of each pregnancy, whether terminated by delivery or by induced or spontaneous abortion. Following delivery, there is a natural period of subfecundity, usually lasting about eight weeks. During this time, the couple's usual sexual behavior is altered and they commonly follow a pattern of contraception different from that to which they had been accustomed prior to the pregnancy. These changes set the stage for a transition period during which unwanted pregnancies often occur. In addition, after each baby is born, a woman's desire to delay the next one is presumably greater, and she will have to achieve a new level of contraceptive vigilance to realize her intention—often necessitating new contraceptive precautions. These changes add to the vulnerability of the postpartum stage.

Following abortion, some women are subject to real conflict and they become pregnant again as a form of restitution. Other women may become pregnant initially when they are very ambivalent about having a child. If they have an abortion, the other side of the ambivalence asserts itself and they may become pregnant again. Either of these two situations may lead to another pregnancy soon after an abortion.

• The seventh vulnerable stage occurs toward the end of the childbearing period. For many couples, there develops at this time a conflict about ending childbearing. At such a time preconscious and sometimes fully conscious motivations to have 'one more child' may lead to an unplanned pregnancy if the woman's ambivalence about stopping her procreative career has been inadequately resolved.

• The last stage of vulnerability occurs during menopause. It corresponds to the first stage during early adolescence in that it is also psychologically based on subfecundity. During menopause, a woman naturally begins to suspect that she is not fecund anymore as her periods become less regular. She is more willing to take the risk of omitting contraception than she was at the height of her fecund years. As a consequence, we see a small but definite number of women who apply for abortion when they are in their early or midforties.

24

Teenagers: Fertility Control Behavior and Attitudes Before and After Abortion, Childbearing or Negative Pregnancy Test

Jerome R. Evans, Georgiana Selstad and Wayne H. Welcher

More than one million teenagers become pregnant every year, and more than 325,000 such pregnancies are terminated by legal abortion.[1] Some 600,000 pregnancies are carried to term,[*][2] often cutting short both the education and training for future employment of the adolescent mothers.[3] Evidence from several studies suggests that ignorance about human reproduction, lack of readily accessible, reliable contraception, and chance taking are among the causes of this pregnancy epidemic.[4]

This article presents data from a study carried out between 1972 and 1974 of 333 unwed adolescents, 297 of whom were pregnant and 36 of whom believed they had conceived, but turned out to have negative pregnancy tests.

Methodology

Four groups of never-married, never-pregnant 13-19-year-old Anglos or Mexican-Americans who were residents of Ventura County,[†] California, comprised the study population. All had come to a variety of health providers for pregnancy-related assistance, some seeking abortions, some pregnancy tests, some prenatal care.[‡] All agreed to be interviewed

twice, once prior to abortion or delivery (or at the time of the pregnancy test), and again six months after abortion, delivery or the initial interview. Of the total number, 184 chose to terminate their pregnancies by legal abortion; 68 decided to continue their pregnancies but to remain single; 45 married before their pregnan-

---

[*]More than 100,000 teenage pregnancies end in miscarriages.

[†]Ventura County is located north of Los Angeles in Southern California. The population of 445,000 is approximately 80 percent Anglo and 20 percent of other ethnic backgrounds, principally Mexican-American. Family incomes tend to be above the national average. Agriculture, light manufacturing and oil production are among the most common industrial activities.

[‡]Prospective subjects were approached in a wide variety of settings, including the county hospital, a private community hospital (where 75 percent of the area's abortions are performed), free clinics, public health clinics, the offices of private physicians and several county high schools with programs for pregnant students.

The authors gratefully acknowledge the assistance of Christine Cooke, Rima Rackauskas and Gina Manchester. The study upon which this article is based was supported by Grant No. HD06830 from the National Institute of Child Health and Human Development, DHEW, and a grant from the Medical Research Foundation, Ventura County.

Table 1. Percent distribution of four groups of 13-19-year-olds who sought pregnancy-related assistance, by selected characteristics, Ventura County, California, 1972-1974

Characteristic	%, by group			
	Abortion	Negative pregnancy	Term-single	Term-married
	(N=184)	(N=36)	(N=68)	(N=45)
Total	100	100	100	100
Age				
13-15	12	22	21	11
16-17	38	42	53	65
18-19	50	36	26	24
Ethnic background				
Anglo	92	92	53	69
Mexican-American	8	8	47	31
Parental religion				
Protestant	50	50	31	40
Catholic	34	33	57	42
Other	3	3	3	2
None	14	14	9	16
Parental divorce				
Yes	20	22	38	36
No	80	78	62	64
No. of siblings				
0	5	6	4	0
1-3	63	61	41	49
4-6	29	28	38	40
≥7	3	6	16	11
Mother's education				
0-11	24	14	66	48
12	51	61	22	39
≥13	25	25	12	14
Father's education				
0-11	22	14	57	46
12	42	37	28	35
≥13	36	49	15	19
Father's occupation				
Major professional	17	28	3	3
Minor professional or sales	48	33	25	31
Skilled manual	27	25	49	38
Unskilled-unemployed	8	14	24	29

Note: Percents may not add to 100 due to rounding.

cies came to term; and 36 who suspected they were pregnant subsequently found out they were not.

All the adolescents were interviewed in private for about one hour by one of three young, female interviewers. (More time was taken with subjects who were uneasy with the questioning.) The same interviewer conducted the initial and follow-up sessions.

At both interviews, questions were asked concerning socioeconomic background, school performance, religious and social activities, sources of financial support, opinions about abortion, knowledge of conception, attitudes toward and use of contraception, and reasons for nonuse of contraceptives. At the follow-up interviews, additional questions dealt with the young women's satisfaction with the decisions they had made about resolution of their first pregnancies.

Background Characteristics

As Table 1 shows, the teenagers in the abortion group were older than the young women in the term groups, and were more apt to be Anglos and Protestants, to come from intact families, and to have a total of three or fewer siblings. Except for their slightly younger age, the adolescents with negative pregnancy tests closely resembled those in the abortion group. The parents of the young women in both these groups were better educated, and the fathers more often held professional or sales jobs than those of the adolescents whose pregnancies went to term.

The adolescents in the term groups resembled each other more than they resembled those in the other two groups. A majority of the young women who delivered their babies and remained single were aged 16-17, as were two-thirds of those who married. A larger proportion

Table 2. Percent distribution of four groups of 13-19-year-olds at time of initial and follow-up interviews, by school attendance and grades

School attendance and grades	%, by group							
	Initial interview				Follow-up interview			
	Abor-tion (N=184)	Negative pregnancy (N=36)	Term-single (N=68)	Term-married (N=45)	Abor-tion (N=184)	Negative pregnancy (N=36)	Term-single (N=68)	Term-married (N=45)
Total	100	100	100	100	100	100	100	100
Attending school?								
Yes	70	78	63	69	68	72	50	11
No	30	22	37	31	32	28	50	89
Not attending because:								
Graduated	76	75	40	36	75	90	32	18
Dropped out*	23	25	60	64	25	10	68	82
Of those attending, grade average:								
A	9	14	0	3	16	16	4	20
B	55	61	19	52	62	60	70	60
C	32	25	70	42	22	24	23	20
D	4	0	12	3	1	0	4	0

*These adolescents had dropped out of school prior to their becoming pregnant or knowing that they were pregnant. The reasons they gave for dropping out were poor grades, poor attendance, lack of interest, belief that they could get jobs.

Note: Percents may not add to 100 because of rounding.

of both term groups were Mexican-American and Catholic, had parents who were divorced, and came from families with four or more children. Their parents had less education, and the fathers were more often employed in skilled manual jobs than as professionals or sales persons; more of them were unemployed at the time of the study than were the fathers of the adolescents in the other two groups.

Education and Financial Support

As Table 2 shows, *before* they became pregnant or suspected a pregnancy, most of the young women were attending school, but more who were to carry to term had already dropped out of school.° Among the total group in school, those in the abortion and negative pregnancy groups had earned

significantly better grades than teenagers in the term groups; adolescents who became unwed mothers had the poorest grades of all.

At the six-month follow-up, school attendance was significantly higher among those who had had abortions or who had proved not to be pregnant. Teenagers who married prior to delivery showed the lowest rate of school enrollment. Significant declines in enrollment occurred only in the two term groups, but this was not because they had graduated; rather, it was because they had dropped out. Although they were not specifically asked why they had dropped out, it is reasonable to assume that school discontinuation was precipitated by childbirth

°The policy of Ventura County schools is to encourage attendance whether a girl is pregnant, is a mother or is married.

Table 3. Percent distribution of four groups of 13-19-year-olds at time of initial and follow-up interviews, by living arrangements and sources of support

Living arrangements and support	%, by group							
	Initial interview				Follow-up interview			
	Abortion (N=184)	Negative pregnancy (N=36)	Term-single (N=68)	Term-married (N=45)	Abortion (N=184)	Negative pregnancy (N=36)	Term-single (N=68)	Term-married (N=45)
Total	100	100	100	100	100	100	100	100
Living with parents?								
Yes	79	83	98	93	72	81	56	36
No	21	17	2	7	28	19	44	64
Financial support from parents or relatives?								
Yes	82	86	97	96	68	81	53	22
No	18	14	3	4	32	19	47	78
Financial support from welfare or Med-i-cal?								
Yes	3	3	13	2	5	3	75	22
No	97	97	87	98	95	97	25	78
Any money from outside job?								
Yes	43	47	28	22	67	64	13	33
No	57	53	72	78	33	36	87	67

and the problems of child care and support. In contrast to the initial differences between the teenagers in school performance, however, by the six-month follow-up, approximately similar grades had been earned by those in each of the four groups, with the sharpest improvements in grades occurring among the women in the term groups. This convergence in grade averages probably occurred because the term patients who stayed in school were highly motivated to continue their education despite the problems imposed by childbearing.

Table 3 shows that at time of the initial interview, a large majority of all the groups were living in the parental home, were being supported by parents or relatives, and were not on welfare. However, adolescents in the abortion and negative pregnancy groups were far more likely to be earning some money from employment. They were more independent of parental support, since they were somewhat less likely to be living at home or to be receiving financial help from parents. A significantly larger proportion (though still a small minority) of young women who planned to deliver and remain single had been receiving financial support from welfare prior to their pregnancies.

By the time of the second interview, important changes in economic support had occurred, as Table 3 shows. Because significantly larger numbers of adolescents in the term groups had moved out of their parents' homes, those who had had abortions or negative pregnancy tests appeared to be more dependent on their families at follow-up. Direct financial aid from parents declined for all groups, but more sharply for the teenagers who delivered—who, instead, became more reliant on welfare. Thus, being an adolescent mother, whether married or single, increased rather than decreased dependency. The single mother, because of the demands of caring for her child, was less able to take a job than she had been prior to delivery; the young woman who married and delivered, however, was more likely to be working than previously, perhaps because the shared responsibility for child care made it possible for her to do so.

Approval of Abortion

The attitudes of these adolescents toward abortion are shown in Table 4. Their initial opinions were given when those who were to have their pregnancies terminated had already decided on abortion, when women in the negative pregnancy group had learned their pregnancy test results, and after the term-married and term-single groups had declared their respective plans for delivery. Presentation of the same statements at follow-up made it possible to determine whether the young women's experiences had modified their opinions about abortion.

Approval of abortion varied with both the group of adolescents under study[*] and the particular question they were asked.[†] Initially, the overwhelming majority of all the groups accepted abortion as a legitimate means of ending a pregnancy if a woman's health were endangered, if she had been raped, if she were very young, or if the child might be born defective. (In this regard, they are part of the mainstream of adult opinion on abortion, as numerous polls have shown.[5]) Adolescents who were to have abortions felt significantly more favorably about pregnancy termination under these conditions than the term group. Abortion motivated by financial, family or other considerations was less acceptable to all the young women. But while substantial numbers in the abortion and negative pregnancy groups remained in favor of abortion under such circumstances, a large majority of the young women who carried to term were opposed.

At the follow-up interviews, the respondents' opinions remained quite similar to their initial views.

Choices and Conception Knowledge

Each teenager was also asked at both interviews to indicate what course of action was her first choice in solving the problem of her out-of-wedlock pregnancy, and to rank the other possible options. The alternatives were to have an abortion; to become a single parent; to marry and deliver; or to deliver and give the baby up for adoption. Initially, a majority in each group preferred the alternative to which they were committed, as Table 5 shows, but substantial minorities in each indicated that they would favor another option if circumstances permitted. The largest of these minorities was found in the term-single group, 35 percent of whom indicated a preference for marriage.

On follow-up, all of the teenagers had another opportunity to rank the alternatives, but this time against the background of all that had transpired from conception to the six-month interview. Satisfaction with the resolution actually chosen had increased, as Table 5 shows. There were no significant differences between groups. Similar proportions (13-20 percent) in each said they would favor another choice in handling their pregnancy if they had it to do over again.

---

[*] Because the two sets of term patients did not differ much in their attitudes, their data are combined.

[†] Statistical analysis used the chi-square test, with significance defined as p<.05, unless otherwise indicated.

Table 4. Percent distribution of three groups of 13-19-year-olds at time of initial and follow-up interviews, by attitudes toward abortion

Question: Is abortion all right?	%, by group					
	Initial interview			Follow-up interview		
	Abortion (N=184)	Negative pregnancy (N=36)	Term* (N=113)	Abortion (N=184)	Negative pregnancy (N=36)	Term* (N=113)
Total	100	100	100	100	100	100
If the woman has been raped?						
Yes	99	94	88	98	92	90
No	1	6	11	1	8	8
Undecided	0	0	2	1	0	2
In the case of a very young person?						
Yes	98	86	64	96	89	66
No	1	11	34	3	11	28
Undecided	1	3	3	1	0	6
If the pregnancy seriously endangered the woman's health?						
Yes	99	92	96	98	97	93
No	†	5	4	1	3	5
Undecided	†	3	1	1	0	2
If there is a good reason to believe the child might be born deformed or mentally defective?						
Yes	88	69	72	81	83	62
No	10	25	27	17	14	30
Undecided	2	6	1	2	3	8
If she felt she couldn't afford to take care of the child?						
Yes	75	53	24	76	61	21
No	21	44	73	21	40	73
Undecided	4	3	3	3	0	6
If having the child would destroy her relationship with her family?						
Yes	74	53	14	68	47	11
No	23	44	84	28	44	86
Undecided	3	3	2	4	8	3
If she wanted the abortion for any reason that seemed important to her?						
Yes	63	47	9	62	42	10
No	32	47	88	34	58	87
Undecided	5	6	4	4	0	3

*Because the two sets of term patients did not differ much, their data are combined.

†Less than one percent.

Note: Percents may not add to 100 because of rounding.

Table 5. Percent distribution of three groups of 13-19-year-olds at time of initial and follow-up interviews, by first-choice ranking of specific alternatives in resolving their out-of-wedlock pregnancies

Alternative	%, by group					
	Initial interview			Follow-up interview		
	Abortion (N=184)	Term-single (N=68)	Term-married (N=45)	Abortion (N=184)	Term-single (N=68)	Term-married (N=45)
Total	100	100	100	100	100	100
Abortion	66	6	2	80	10	2
Delivery and become a single parent	16	56	18	14	87	16
Marriage and delivery	14	35	78	2	3	80
Delivery and release baby for adoption	4	3	2	4	0	2

A significant number of adolescents in the abortion group who had initially favored another alternative came to believe that abortion was the right choice for them. A similar significant increase in acceptance of being a single parent occurred among those women in the term-single group who had initially expressed the desire to marry before delivery. No doubt, after-the-fact rationalizations influenced these opinion changes. There was little change in preference among the term-marrieds.

Within the abortion group, 36 young women (20 percent) indicated at the follow-up interview that they wished they had chosen to deliver. A special analysis of the data shows that they were younger, were more often Mexican-American, and tended to have divorced parents with significantly poorer educational-occupational backgrounds (not shown in tables). These teenagers had earned poorer grades in school and were less likely to have been earning any money prior to their pregnancies. They were also more conservative in their opinions about abortion than were those who were satisfied with the decision to obtain an abortion, and they were more likely to

have stated at the outset that abortion was not their first choice.

Numerous studies have shown that teenagers are typically misinformed about the menstrual cycle and its relationship to conception;[6] that many become sexually active prior to obtaining effective contraception;[7] that they know something about the various birth control methods (although few use them);[8] and that the older the teenager, the more likely she is to use contraception.[9] These findings apply to the young women in this study.

Asked at the initial interview about the time of month when a woman is most likely to become pregnant, between one-third and one-half of the adolescents simply said they did not know. Those in the abortion group, however, were significantly more likely to know the correct answer (57 percent compared with 42 percent of the negative pregnancy test group, and 46-51 percent of the term groups).

At the six month follow-up, each adolescent was asked the same question about conception, but in the interval all the pregnant teenagers had received family planning counseling and the neg-

Table 6. Percent distribution of four groups of 13-19-year-olds at time of initial and follow-up interviews, by knowledge and opinions about contraception

Knowledge and opinion	%, by group							
	Initial interview				Follow-up interview			
	Abortion (N=184)	Negative pregnancy (N=36)	Term-single (N=68)	Term-married (N=45)	Abortion (N=184)	Negative pregnancy (N=36)	Term-single (N=68)	Term-married (N=45)
Total	100	100	100	100	100	100	100	100
Effective knowledge of contraceptive methods								
0 methods	0	0	8	4	0	0	0	0
1-3 methods	12	8	38	25	3	3	13	0
4-6 methods	35	47	44	51	20	19	35	22
≥7 methods	53	45	10	20	77	78	53	78
In your opinion, which contraceptive method would be best for you?								
Don't know	6	3	16	9	2	0	7	2
Rhythm, douche, withdrawal	1	3	0	9	2	3	2	2
Foam, condom, diaphragm	3	6	2	0	2	3	6	0
Pill, IUD	90	89	82	82	94	94	85	96

Note: Percents may not add to 100 because of rounding.

ative pregnancy test group had been referred to clinics with educational programs and contraceptive assistance. One to two out of every five were still misinformed, with those in the abortion group still significantly more knowledgeable. Although there had been some improvement in knowledge of conception, none of the groups showed a statistically significant change from the initial to follow-up interview. Differences in knowledge were not a function of age, as differences between age groups were not statistically significant.

Contraceptive Knowledge, Attitudes

Table 6 presents the interviewer's assessment of each group's knowledge of contraceptive methods. To earn credit on this question, the teenager had to have known the name of an accepted method and must have had a general idea of its application. The young women in the abortion and negative pregnancy groups were much more knowledgeable about contraceptive methods at the initial interview than those who were to deliver; the latter groups were comparable to one another in contraceptive sophistication.

On follow-up, the adolescents in the abortion, negative pregnancy test and term-married groups were equal in their understanding of contraception, and they knew more than those in the term-single group. All showed significant improvement in contraceptive knowledge.

A special analysis revealed that the older adolescents knew significantly more about contraception than the younger ones at both the initial and follow-up interviews (not shown in table). This may explain why those who had abortions and negative pregnancy tests were more knowledgeable initially.

Table 6 also shows the teenagers' opinions about the best means for them of avoiding conception. At the initial interview, significantly larger numbers of adolescents who were to become unwed mothers said they didn't know which method was best. These differences all but disappeared by the time of the follow-up interview.

Seeking Help

In order to determine the extent of each young woman's initiative in seeking accurate information about pregnancy prevention, she was asked about contacts with physicians and family planning professionals *prior* to suspecting her own pregnancy. The majority had not talked with a trained person, although 27 percent of the abortion and 36 percent of the negative pregnancy groups had done so, compared with nine percent of term-singles and 18 percent of term-marrieds.

By the time of the follow-up interview, those who had delivered were much more likely to have sought recent family planning advice, but since significant increases had occurred in all the groups, a majority of the adolescents said they had received such counseling. However, more than two out of five of the young women in the negative pregnancy test group had not done so.

Age was an important determinant in the decision to seek professional help prior to becoming pregnant or suspecting pregnancy. Before pregnancy, 35 percent of the 18- and 19-year-olds sought such assistance, compared to 17 percent of the 16- and 17-year-olds and just eight percent of those aged 13-15. This may also explain the superior knowledge of contraceptive methods demonstrated by the abortion and nega-

tive pregnancy groups. Obtaining post-pregnancy advice was not a function of age, probably because of the entry gained to the medical delivery system through seeking pregnancy-related care.

Contraceptive Practice

Table 7 shows the teenagers' use of contraceptives, and the effectiveness of the methods used, during the six months preceding both the initial and follow-up interviews. Responses from the initial interview revealed that the adolescents in the abortion and negative pregnancy groups were more likely than those in the term groups to have used some method (regardless of reliability).

By the follow-up, more than 95 percent in the abortion and term groups combined had practiced birth control, and nearly 80 percent had been consistent users of the pill or IUD. Among the adolescents who had never conceived, only 59 percent had used contraception, and just 20 percent had used the pill or IUD regularly. On the whole, many more adolescents in all four groups were using the most effective methods by the time of the six-month interview.

A separate analysis of the data showed that contraceptive effectiveness was a function of the adolescents' age. As Table 8 shows, those aged 18-19 were significantly more likely at initial interview to be using highly or moderately reliable techniques. Thus, age may account for group differences at the initial interview. Even though age continued to be related to effective practice on follow-up, such factors as postnatal medical care were also influential, since the term-married women who were relatively young, used more effective contraception than the somewhat older adolescents who had negative pregnancy tests (see Table 7).

Table 7. Percent distribution of four groups of 13-19-year-olds at time of initial and follow-up interviews, by use of contraceptives in previous six months and effectiveness* of method used

Use and effec- tiveness	%, by group							
	Initial interview				Follow-up interview†			
	Abor- tion (N=184)	Negative pregnancy (N=36)	Term- single (N=68)	Term- married (N=45)	Abor- tion (N=166)	Negative pregnancy (N=32)	Term- single (N=63)	Term- married (N=45)
Total	100	100	100	100	100	100	100	100
Used contraceptives?								
Yes	46	61	22	33	97	59	92	98
No	54	40	78	67	3	41	8	2
Effectiveness*								
High	1	0	0	0	81	20	67	83
Moderate	5	12	1	4	9	11	10	13
Low	40	49	21	29	7	28	15	2

*Interviewer's judgment. High is use of pill or IUD; moderate is use of pill or IUD sometimes, or foam/condoms/diaphragm always; low is use of foam/condoms/diaphragm sometimes, or withdrawal, douching, rhythm.

†The number of cases at the follow-up interview is smaller because adolescents who reported they were no longer sexually active are excluded.

Note: Percents may not add to100 because of rounding.

Table 8. Percent distribution of adolescents aged 13-15, 16-17 and 18-19 at time of initial and follow-up interviews, by effectiveness of contraceptive method used

Effectiveness*	%, by age					
	Initial interview			Follow-up interview†		
	13-15 (N=50)	16-17 (N=149)	18-19 (N=134)	13-15 (N=45)	16-17 (N=138)	18-19 (N=123)
Total	100	100	100	100	100	100
High	0	1	1	64	74	83
Moderate	6	4	18	9	14	9
Low or none	94	95	81	27	12	8

See note to Table 7.

†Excludes adolescents who reported they were no longer sexually active.

Factors Related to Contraceptive Use

An adolescent's use of contraception depends on whether she has had or plans to have intercourse, wants to conceive or not, and a host of other factors—most of which have received little systematic examination. Contraceptive motivation was examined in this project in two ways: First, all of the adolescents were asked the principal reason they had not used any method regularly;° second, a statistical study was conducted of the abortion group only in which the initial interview responses of these teenagers

° Excludes those who, at the time of the initial interview, were using any method regularly.

Table 9. Percent distribution of four groups of 13-19-year-olds at time of initial and follow-up interviews, by specific reason for not using contraception regularly or at all

Reason	%, by group							
	Initial interview*				Follow-up interview†			
	Abortion (N=156)	Negative pregnancy (N=25)	Term-single (N=64)	Term-married (N=42)	Abortion (N=38)	Negative pregnancy (N=22)	Term-single (N=19)	Term-married (N=7)
Total	100	100	100	100	100	100	100	100
Use of contraception								
Not using regularly	15	31	6	7	77	31	70	84
Not using at all	85	69	94	93	23	69	30	16
Reason for nonuse								
Not having intercourse regularly	51	36	30	26	71	54	42	29
Contraception unavailable or inconvenient	24	32	6	10	16	27	10	29
Patient, family or boyfriend opposed to contraception	16	16	14	5	3	9	21	14
Did not object to becoming pregnant	10	16	50	60	10	9	26	29

*Excludes those using any method regularly.

†Excludes those using any method regularly or those who said they were sexually abstinent. Abstainers included 18 women in the abortion group, five in the negative pregnancy group and four in the term-single group. None of the young married women abstained.

Note: Percents may not add to 100 because of rounding.

were compared with their postpregnancy use of highly effective contraception.

In the first analysis, the reasons given for not using contraception were subsequently assigned to one of four categories (see Table 9). A majority of the adolescents in the abortion and negative pregnancy groups explained at the initial interview that they had not practiced birth control prior to suspecting a pregnancy because they weren't having intercourse often and, therefore, didn't really anticipate becoming pregnant, or because they did not have access to accept-

able methods. (These were also the two main reasons given by adolescents in a large national study.[10]) By way of contrast, those who carried to term were more likely to claim that they had avoided using contraceptives because they did not object to becoming pregnant. Their second reason, however, was that they had not anticipated the need for contraception. These differences in reasons given for not practicing contraception were highly significant statistically.

Once the suspected or actual pregnancy had been resolved, the largest propor-

Table 10. Percent distribution of four groups of 13-19-year-olds, by whether they had become pregnant by the time of the follow-up interview

Pregnancy status	Total (333)	Abortion (184)	Neg. preg. (36)	Termsing. (68)	Termmarr. (45)
Total	100	100	100	100	100
Yes	8	5	17	15	4
No	92	95	83	85	96

tion of each group who were still not using a contraceptive method explained that they were not having intercourse with any regularity. For all but the term-single women, the second reason was that contraceptives were not easily available to them. A significantly larger number of single nonusers who had already delivered gave as their second reason the lack of any objection to another pregnancy. Many of the young women in the negative pregnancy test group continued not to use contraception in the belief that they did not need it because they had not become pregnant the first time.

The statistical analysis of the abortion group showed that age, grades and initial opinions on abortion and contraceptive methods best predicted the subsequent effectiveness of the young women as contraceptors. Lower postabortion use of reliable contraceptive methods was found among adolescents in the youngest age group (13-15 years); among those who had had average to below-average prepregnancy grades; among those who were somewhat more conservative in their opinions about the acceptability of abortion; and among those who had initially favored the least effective means of contraception (not shown in tables).

Repeat Pregnancies

Eight percent of all the teenagers had confirmed pregnancies during the six-month interval following resolution of the initial pregnancies or suspected pregnancies. As Table 10 shows, significantly more conceptions occured among adolescents in the negative pregnancy and term-single groups than in the other groups.* This finding appears to confirm other reports that those who have abortions do not come to rely on the procedure as a method of contraception.[11] It also confirms the previously reported observation that teenagers who once escape becoming pregnant following unprotected coitus may again be willing to take the same risk.[12]

Summary and Conclusions

Being pregnant or suspecting pregnancy is usually an intensely stressful experience for the unmarried adolescent. It is self-evident that no single solution is right for all young women who find themselves in this situation. This study examined the differential impact over time of various means of resolving pregnancy on such variables as education, religious commitment, social behavior, economic dependency, knowledge of conception risks, and knowledge and practice of contraception. Statistical analysis of the data provided some information about which sociodemographic factors play a role in decision making regarding pregnancy resolution. Among the overall findings are the following:

• *Education.* Adolescents who had

---

*It seems puzzling at first that the term-single group had about the same proportion of repeat pregnancies as the negative pregnancy test group, although more of the former used contraception—and more effective contraception—than the latter. (Actually, none of the term-singles who used highly effective contraception subsequently became pregnant.) This finding is apparently due to the fact that relatively more of the term-singles were seeking pregnancy or didn't mind getting pregnant, and relatively more of the negative pregnancy group were not having intercourse regularly (see Table 9).

abortions were doing quite satisfactorily in school before their pregnancies, and their performance did not alter significantly during the six months following termination. In this regard, they were much like their sexually active, but non-pregnant, counterparts. The young women who carried their pregnancies to term were, to some extent, struggling with school before they knew they were pregnant, and for many the delivery was associated with abandonment of academic work. Other studies have shown, however, that such abandonment is due more to the burdens of caring for their infants than it is to lack of interest in continuing their education.[13] The women who did return to school after delivery of their babies seemed to do quite well, probably because they were extremely motivated to complete their education.

• *Economic dependence.* At the time of the initial interview, a large majority of all these sexually active teenagers lived with and were supported by their parents. Many more of the adolescents in the abortion and negative pregnancy groups than in the term groups earned some of their income from regular employment outside the home. The only ones dependent upon welfare to any extent were the young women in the term group who were to become unwed mothers.

In the six-month interval after the abortion, delivery or initial interview, the most notable changes in economic status occurred among the adolescents in both term groups. Far fewer were living at home with their parents or were being supported by them. Three-quarters of the single mothers and one-fifth of those who had married were receiving welfare assistance. The problems attendant upon being an unwed mother are highlighted by the employment experience of the women in this group. Only half as many were earning money after they delivered

compared with the proportion employed before delivery. Among the married group, however, 50 percent more were employed at least part-time, presumably because there was someone to share the baby-care responsibility.

• *Abortion attitudes.* Most of the adolescents in all the study groups believed abortion was "all right" if the physical well-being of the woman was in jeopardy, if the pregnancy had resulted from rape, or if a very young woman was involved. Those who had abortions or negative pregnancy tests were also likely to favor abortion if economic hardship were involved, if the child might be defective, or if the birth might destroy family relationships. Most of the adolescents who delivered opposed abortion for these last three reasons. For the most part, the teenagers' experiences with abortion or delivery did not appreciably modify their initial attitudes.

• *Resolution of pregnancy.* Six months after their abortions, about one teenager in five said she wished she had not terminated her pregnancy. For these adolescents, the dilemma brought on by pregnancy was not resolved by abortion, but continued on in the form of regret and ambivalence. Teenagers who had abortions but did not subsequently accept them as the best solution for themselves could be identified prior to surgery by their relative youth, by various social and academic factors, and by their ambivalence towards pregnancy interruption.

• *Initial knowledge and attitudes.* Many teenagers in all the groups were not clear on when they were most likely to become pregnant and were unsophisticated in their contraceptive practice. One-third of those who had abortions and 42-51 percent of the others simply didn't know what the relationship is between conception risk and their monthly cycles. Even though nine out of 10 who had abortions or negative pregnancy tests, and substantial (though lesser) majorities of the teenagers who went to term, could name and describe contraceptive methods, and although most indicated a preference for the more reliable techniques, a majority had not sought professional advice on birth control, and indicated that they had engaged in intercourse with no contraceptive protection. When a contraceptive was used, the teenagers typically used methods of lesser effectiveness.

When compared with adolescents who carried their pregnancies to term, those in the abortion and negative pregnancy groups showed themselves initially to be superior in knowledge of conception and contraception, acceptance of the more reliable contraceptive methods, initiative in seeking out professional advice on birth control, and effectiveness of contraceptive practice. In part, this superiority may be a function of age. Abortion patients were older, and three of the study's six variables related to contraceptive knowledge and effectiveness were correlated positively with age. The young women who obtained abortions were more closely matched in age and other characteristics with the teenagers who suspected they were pregnant, but discovered that they were not. These two groups did not differ from one another on any of the six initial interview variables.

• *Follow-up knowledge and attitudes.* Six months after termination, about one out of every five abortion patients was still in doubt about the relationship between conception and the menstrual cycle, an improvement but not a statistically significant increase in knowledge. Only slight improvement among the other groups was observed, so members of the abortion group remained in a position of relatively greater understanding of conception on follow-up.

Teenagers who had obtained abor-

tions had also improved their knowledge about contraceptive methods when they were questioned the second time. Three-quarters could then name and describe numerous techniques. The other groups had also improved significantly, but adolescents who became unwed mothers had made smaller gains, and therefore were significantly poorer in contraceptive knowledge. By the time of the six-month interview, a large majority of the girls in all four groups expressed the opinion that the pill and IUD were the best contraceptive methods. Those who had delivered had altered their opinions sufficiently so that they were about as accepting of reliable methods as the young women who had terminated their pregnancies.

The data on knowledge and opinions can be interpreted as indicating a general improvement in the direction of greater birth planning competence among most of the women under study. The initial superiority among abortion patients, due perhaps to the fact that they were older, appeared to have been offset by the exposure of the other groups to contraceptive information given and to the positive attitudes toward birth control expressed by service deliverers.

• *Contraceptive practice.* In order to determine whether knowledge affected behavior, teenagers in the present study were asked about their efforts to consult physicians on the proper use of contraceptives and about their attempts to avoid conception.

Approximately two-thirds of the abortion patients stated that they had talked at least once with a professional person about contraception subsequent to their surgical aftercare. Physician contacts were significantly more numerous than in their prepregnancy days, when fewer than one-third had such conferences. Even larger gains were observed among the women who went to term.

The abortion and term patients

showed much improvement in the use of contraceptives during the follow-up interval. Almost all reported using some method, compared to fewer than half initially. Teenagers who experienced only a pregnancy scare—those in the negative test group—did not show any improvement in birth control use. The young women's use of effective methods followed this same pattern, with significant improvement for all except the negative pregnancy group. Teenagers whose first pregnancies were terminated by abortion increased their use of effective contraception from a very low preconception level to one where more than four out of five sexually active adolescents reported using a highly reliable method consistently. Their contraceptive use was on a par with that of the term groups, and was significantly superior to the practice of birth control by sexually active, never-pregnant adolescents of comparable age and social status. Such results, which are consistent with findings from studies of older women who have abortions, indicate that rather than exhibiting a tendency to rely on abortion as a means of preventing birth young women who obtain abortions go on to become more competent in avoiding conception.

With appropriate postabortion counseling, as was provided the teenagers in the present study, most of the adolescents were in a position to avoid another unwanted pregnancy. The one in five who, after their abortions, were still having sex and were still relying on less reliable contraceptive methods were characterized by their relative youth (13-15 years), poorer scholastic records, and a tendency to favor carrying a pregnancy to term.

Implications for Counseling

The counselor discussing the alternatives available to an unmarried pregnant adolescent in resolving her pregnancy is obligated to provide information on the advantages and disadvantages of each option. As far as abortion is concerned, most adolescents comparable to those in this study could be informed that neither their educational, religious and social lives nor their economic condition is likely to be adversely affected, and that their initial positive feelings about abortion will probably strengthen with the passage of time. For the adolescent who is an applicant for abortion, but is ambivalent about or opposed to termination of pregnancy, the risk of subsequent dissatisfaction appears to be clearly documented. Whether these particular teenagers should avoid abortion or not is beyond the scope of this study; nevertheless, there can be no question about the pregnancy counselor's obligation to inform them of the possible negative feelings they may experience following pregnancy termination.

Single parenthood or marriage for the pregnant unwed adolescent certainly are not ideal solutions either, and teenagers who deliver babies are as likely to be unhappy with their decision as those who choose abortion. For some teenagers, delivery is associated with interruption of education, and increased financial dependency. The counselor's obligation to point this out is clear. There is no risk-free solution to the problems brought on by an adolescent's pregnancy; the data presented in this study may provide a somewhat firmer foundation from which the counselor can assist young women in making satisfactory decisions about what course to take if they find themselves pregnant or, indeed, if the pregnancy test proves negative.

Contraceptive Availability

Following the lives of the 333 young persons described in this study, the investigators were witness to personal and family life crises, and to a range of human emotional experiences which left them with a greatly increased sensitivity to the special needs of the unmarried pregnant teenager. In the face of so much anxiety, doubt and denial, it seems only natural to ask the question, "Could these particular human struggles have been avoided?" In response, it is essential first to come to terms with the reality of sexual activity among today's youth. The trend toward sexual expression among unmarried adolescents has a history and place in our culture which is unlikely to be reversed. The only practical alternative for those young persons who have chosen to engage in sex, but are responsible enough to want to avoid conception, is prevention of pregnancy.

While effective contraception may have been available to married and to older unmarried women in the Ventura area, teenagers have not had the same privilege of free access. At the time this study began in 1972, young people under age 16 could not legally obtain contraception without parental consent; and this meant informing parents about their sexual activity. In addition, if they went to a government-funded "family planning" clinic (the very name is enough to turn most teenagers off), they would have been required to document parental income to obtain subsidized services. Given the guilt and ambivalence surrounding the introductory phase of sexual activity, it is not surprising that many younger teenagers chose, under these circumstances, to engage in sexual intercourse without contraception and take their chances with pregnancy. If an adolescent in such emotionally conflicted circumstances is to seek out and obtain an effective method to prevent pregnancy, she cannot be expected to clear a series of difficult hurdles in the process. Because of their temporarily conflicted

psychological state, these individuals must be provided with access to contraception that is characterized by a particularly high degree of understanding and privacy.

Family conferences and the traditional large group-service programs are much too provocative of the mixed feelings about sexuality so commonly observed in teenagers. In the investigators' opinion, community plans for making contraceptive information and supplies available to women will be incomplete and, therefore, less effective if these plans are not designed with consideration for the distinctive requirements of persons under 18.

References

1. F. S. Jaffe and J. G. Dryfoos, "Fertility Control Services for Adolescents: Access and Utilization," paper prepared for Conference on Determinants of Adolescent Pregnancy and Childbearing, sponsored by the Center for Population Research, National Institute of Child Health and Human Development, Belmont, Md., May 3-5, 1976.

2. National Center for Health Statistics, DHEW, "Advance Report: Final Natality Statistics, 1974," *Monthly Vital Statistics Report*, Vol. 24, No. 11, Supplement 2, 1976.

3. H. B. Presser, "Social Consequences of Teenage Childbearing," in W. Petersen and L. Day, eds., *Social Demography: The State of the Art*, Harvard University Press, Cambridge, Mass., 1977.

4. P. A. Reichelt and H. H. Werley, "Contraception, Abortion and Venereal Disease: Teenagers' Knowledge and the Effect of Education," chapter 19, above; D. S. F. Settlage, S. Baroff and D. Cooper, "Sexual Experience of Younger Teenage Girls Seeking Contraceptive Assistance for the First Time," *Family Planning Perspectives*, 5:223, 1973; and H. B. Presser, "Early Motherhood: Ignorance or Bliss?" chapter 22, above.

5. W. R. Arney and W. H. Trescher, "Trends in Attitudes Toward Abortion, 1972–1975," *Family Planning Perspectives*, 8:117, 1976.

6. J. F. Kantner and M. Zelnik, "Sexual Experience of Young Unmarried Women in the United States," *Family Planning Perspectives*, Vol. 4, No. 4, 1972, p. 9.

7. J. F. Kantner and M. Zelnik, "Contraception and Pregnancy: Experience of Young Unmarried Women in the United States," *Family Planning Perspectives*, 5:21 1973.

8. Chapter 19.

9. J. F. Kantner and M. Zelnik, 1973, op. cit.

10. Ibid.

11. C. Tietze, "The 'Problem' of Repeat Abortions," *Family Planning Perspectives*, 6:148, 1974; and J. Pakter, F. Nelson and M. Svigir, "Legal Abortion: A Half-Decade of Experience," *Family Planning Perspectives*, 7:248, 1975.

12. K. Luker, *Taking Chances: Abortion and the Decision Not to Contracept*, University of California Press, Berkeley, 1975.

13. Chapter 22.

25
Adolescent Pregnancy Prevention Services in High School Clinics

Laura E. Edwards, Mary E. Steinman, Kathleen A. Arnold and Erick Y. Hakanson

Problems associated with adolescent child-bearing have been well identified; workable solutions have not. The St. Paul Maternal and Infant Care (MIC) Project has offered comprehensive, multidisciplinary health care to adolescents since 1968. In 1973, the MIC Project opened a health clinic in a local junior-senior high school. This article describes the development of the school clinic program, details the services offered and attempts to evaluate its impact.

Background

Teenagers 17 or younger comprise 44 percent of the MIC Project's population and are responsible for 25 percent of all pregnancies experienced by project participants. Most of these teenagers' pregnancies are unplanned and frequently can be traced to a lack of knowledge about the risk of pregnancy or how to prevent it, or to the unavailability of

The study upon which this article is based was partially funded by the Maternal and Infant Care Project #549 from DHEW; the Minnesota Department of Health; the Minnesota Family Planning and Special Project Funds; and the Medical Education and Research Foundation. The authors wish to thank Jeanne Arnold for her assistance in data collection and data analysis.

services designed for adolescents. Because of the poor obstetric outcomes experienced by adolescents, the MIC Project has intensified efforts to provide high-quality educational, counseling and family planning services to teenagers to prevent adolescent pregnancy.

In order to address the total health care needs of adolescents, the MIC Project has developed a comprehensive medical and educational program which was initially offered in an inner city junior-senior public high school. Planning and implementation of this program took almost two years because of questions and objections voiced by the school administration, the school board, faculty, parents and students. Many expressed concern that the clinic would create a "negative image" for the school. Others claimed that the clinic would take money, energy and space that could otherwise be used for classroom education. Some predicted that students would be hesitant to use the clinic for fear of being identified as sexually active. Parents expressed concern that services were going to be provided without parental consent; students feared that their parents would be notified if they visited the clinic.

Three presentations were made to the St. Paul Board of Education. In Februrary 1973, after hearing reports, objections and clarifications, the school board voted unanimously to approve the school program—provided that the school principal would be responsible for the project, that school space would not be used to the detriment of existing educational programs, and that the program would be reevaluated at the end of the one-year funding period. Community members objected to dispensing of contraceptives in the school, so students were given contraceptives by the school clinic staff at a special evening adolescent clinic at St. Paul-Ramsey Hospital. In addition, a community advisory committee was formed to be involved in the program on an ongoing basis.

The clinic was first opened in a former storage room off the cafeteria. Initially, services offered included prenatal and postpartum care, VD testing and treatment, pregnancy testing, Pap smears and contraceptive information and counseling. Despite informal discussions between numerous students and the nurse clinician, only a few patients registered for care during the spring term. Later in the year, the clinic was moved to an attractive renovated classroom, and services were expanded to include athletic, job and college physicals, immunizations and a weight-control program. These changes resulted in a more positive attitude among faculty, parents and students, and provided a measure of anonymity for the sexually active student; use of the clinic grew rapidly.

Current Services

The junior-senior high school in which this clinic was initiated closed at the end of the 1975–1976 school year, by which time the clinic was being used by about two-thirds of 12th grade students and by more than nine in 10 pregnant students. As the result of widespread use of services and high rates of contraceptive continuation, fertility rates among female students fell by 56 percent between 1973 and 1976—from 79 to 35 births per 1,000. The MIC Project obtained funds to open clinics in the two senior high schools to which the ninth, 10th and 11th grade students from the original school were transferred.*

Each school has its own team providing a wide range of health-related services. The family planning nurse practitioner is the team leader. She is responsible for taking health histories of all new family planning patients, and is the primary nurse for all prenatal patients. She performs simple laboratory tests, including pregnancy tests, on site. This service not only expedites pregnancy diagnosis, but helps identify those in need of family planning services. She conducts a group or individual educational session before the initial examination, and performs follow-up family planning examinations. Each patient initiating contraception is contacted by the nurse practitioner within a week of the first visit to go over the selected method, and is contacted at least once every month thereafter to discuss problems relating to contraceptive use. Immunizations are provided for students referred to the clinic by the school nurse.

The clinic attendant routes all patients and prepares them for examination. Students needing follow-up are located through class schedules and attendance records. To date, all patients with abnormal laboratory test results (such as positive GC tests and abnormal Pap smears) have been followed up. The clinic attendant is always available to listen to students' problems and complaints and to encourage them to share their concerns with other appropriate staff.

The emotional concerns of adolescents are as important to them as medical concerns, and frequently are even more important. Each family planning patient is seen by the clinic social worker prior to the initial exam to

---

*Students from the lower grades were transferred to other junior high schools, and were followed up in those schools by the MIC clinic team.

discuss such concerns as her relationship with her male partner or her family. The social worker is available to work with the male partner or to intervene with parents, but only at the student's request.

Other MIC team members provide services on a weekly or biweekly basis. The obstetrician-gynecologist provides services one morning a week at each school. Initial examination of students interested in contraception, evaluation of those believed to be pregnant, and follow-up of all abnormal findings are provided. Prenatal and postpartum patients are also followed closely.

The pediatric staff, consisting of a pediatrician and a pediatric nurse associate, provide health examinations for jobs, college, and school sports. This service, like the immunization service, has become an important means of identifying sexually related needs in a setting and under circumstances which ensure anonymity and confidentiality. In working with adolescents, it is important to meet a need when it is a concern. The family planning nurse practitioner, who is always on site, can immediately provide information and services and arrange for ongoing care for both male and female students who utilize the clinic for any reason and who indicate interest in contraceptive services.

Family planning counseling, education, examinations and follow-up are provided at the school clinics. As with the initial clinic, by agreement with the St. Paul Board of Education, students wishing contraceptive supplies and devices are referred to the after-school and evening teen birth control clinic at St. Paul-Ramsey Medical Center to obtain them. This clinic is staffed by the high school clinic staffs (nurse practitioners, social workers and gynecologist), and the pediatrician conducts a teen health clinic in the adjacent area, so that students see familiar faces.

The team nutritionist provides screening and education for all new family planning patients, emphasizing nutrition-related aspects of family planning methods. (For exam-

ple, she points out that pills do not contain calories and that weight gain is a poor reason for discontinuing oral contraceptives.)

All patients are given appointments to see the dental hygienist, who provides counseling, oral hygiene screening, and referral for more extensive services, if needed.

The day-care director is in charge of the day-care center located within the school. This is an early-education program for the children of registered students, who may bring their infants starting at six weeks of age. The objective of the day-care program is to give the adolescent parents an opportunity to complete high school, and at the same time learn good parenting skills. The day-care director also helps identify those student-parents in need of information, supplies or counseling to ensure correct contraceptive usage.

MIC staff also provide education in prenatal care, parenting, family life and human sexuality to students in both project high schools, as well as in additional high schools and junior high schools in the school district. The health educator coordinates the health education program, teaches many of the classes and writes curricula for high school and junior high school classes.

Analysis of Data

The records of all students who received family planning services in the initial junior-senior high school project and in the two current senior high school projects, and the records of pregnant students who received prenatal care and subsequently delivered at St. Paul-Ramsey Medical Center, were reviewed retrospectively. The study period covered the six-year interval from the opening of the first school clinic in April of 1973 through May 31, 1979. Four hundred and three students had received initial family planning educational, medical and counseling services in the three MIC school clinics. After initial examination and evaluation, these students had been referred to the MIC hospital-based adolescent clinic for contraceptive supplies or devices. Follow-up care had been instituted and continued in the school clinics. All students who had obtained contraceptive services were followed until they were 18 years of age or until they were graduated from high school, at which time they were referred to other sources of care for further contraceptive assistance.

Contraceptive usage was evaluated by calculating termination and continuation rates using the Tietze life-table method.[1] In addition, the high school family planning patients were compared (as to age, race, gravidity, parity, contraceptive method, continuation and loss to follow-up) with the entire group of 1,762 adolescents who received services during the same period in the MIC hospital-based teen contraceptive clinic.

The records of the 85 pregnant students who delivered at St. Paul-Ramsey Medical Center after having received their care at the MIC school clinics were also reviewed retrospectively; characteristics, complication rates and newborn outcomes were compared with those of MIC patients who had not received prenatal care at the school clinics. Information was obtained from obstetric summary sheets compiled by the Project Director for all patients delivered through the MIC project.

Fertility rates for the female student population of the schools served were calculated for each year that the school clinics were in operation.

Results

Although use of the original school clinic was initially low, by the end of the third year (1976), 50 percent of the entire student body had attended the clinic at least once and 92 percent of the pregnant students had obtained prenatal services. The school dropout rate after delivery was reduced from 45 percent in 1973 to 10 percent in 1976. Furthermore, no repeat pregnancies occurred

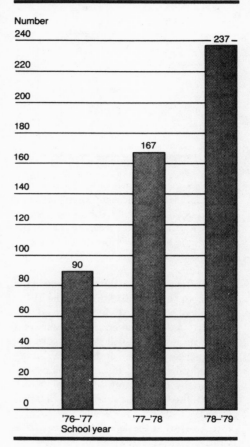

Figure 1. Number of students obtaining contraception from two project high school clinics, St. Paul, 1976–1977 to 1978–1979

among those students who delivered with the project and returned to school. The 12-month contraceptive continuation rate for the three years was 86.4 per 100 women.* The fertility rate for the school population fell from 79 per 1,000 to 35 per 1,000.

A study comparing the obstetric events and newborn outcomes of patients who received care in the school clinic with those of

*Calculated by the life-table method.

Figure 2. Percentage of female students obtaining contraception from the two project high school clinics, 1976–1977 to 1978–1979

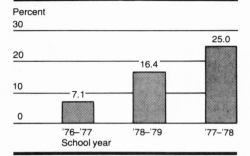

matched adolescents who attended a weekly nonschool MIC adolescent prenatal clinic has also been reported.[2] This study showed that those patients who received care in the school clinic had a lower incidence of obstetric problems as well as better outcomes for their infants.

From the time of the initial opening of the first school clinic in 1973 through the 1978–1979 school year, 403 students received contraceptive medical and educational services, and 85 students received prenatal care and subsequently delivered at the St. Paul-Ramsey Medical Center.° Results of the experience in the original project school, which covered the first three years of the program (1973–1976), have been previously reported.[3] During the last three years (1976–1979), these two categories of patients represented 19 percent of the total number of patients served in the senior high school clinics.

The two senior high school project clinics have been in operation since the closing of the original project school in 1976. During the three-year period that these clinics have been operational, utilization of clinic services

has steadily increased. In the 1978–1979 school year, 1,465 students (75 percent of the entire student body in the two schools) utilized clinic services, as compared to 748 students (32 percent of the total student population) in 1976–1977.

The utilization of the two clinics for family planning services has also increased each year. During the 1978–1979 school year, 237 students received services, nearly three times the number obtaining contraception in 1976–1977 (see Figure 1). Furthermore, the percentage of the female student population enrolling for family planning services has increased each year (see Figure 2). In 1976–1977, seven percent of the female students came to the high school clinic for family planning services; in 1978–1979, this figure grew to 25 percent, with 21 percent of the female students in one school and 30 percent of those in the second school utilizing the family planning services.

The ages of all 403 high school family planning patients at the first visit ranged from 13 to 19, with a mean age of 16.0. The mean age in the larger MIC teen contraceptive group was 16.2; the age distribution was similar to that of the high school group.

The racial distribution of the high school contraceptors is shown in Figure 3. Sixty-seven percent were white, 26 percent black, six percent Spanish American and two percent American Indian and other. When the racial distribution of the high school group was compared to that of the overall MIC teen clinic population (not shown), it was found that significantly more of the high school clinic group belonged to minority races—33 percent as against 15 percent (p<0.001).

As may be seen in Figure 4, of the 403 teenage family planning patients seen in the original project clinic and in the two senior high school clinics, 304 (75 percent) had never been pregnant. Twenty-four (six percent) had had a previous abortion, 66 (16 percent) had had one or more live births, and

° The 85 students subsequently joined one of the high school family planning clinics, and so are a part of the 403 served in that program.

Figure 3. Percentage distribution of project school clinic contraceptors, by race and ethnic group, 1973–1979

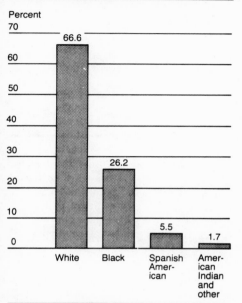

Figure 4. Percentage distribution of project school clinic contraceptors, by prior pregnancy status, 1973–1979

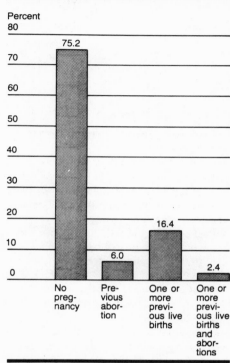

10 (two percent) had had at least one baby *and* one abortion. When the study group was compared to the overall MIC teen contraceptive clinic population (not shown), it was found that the percentage of never-pregnant contraceptors was significantly lower in the school group—75 percent compared to 89 percent ($p<0.001$). Of the student group, 19 percent had delivered at least one viable infant, whereas six percent of those in the overall teenage MIC group had done so.

Eighty-five percent of the project school clinic contraceptors chose oral contraceptives as their initial method, 10 percent chose IUDs, and five percent picked other methods. The distribution was similar for those in the overall MIC teenage clinic population.

Table 1 shows net cumulative contraceptive termination and continuation rates at 12, 24, 36 and 48 months for students from all

three schools. (Patients were followed up for a maximum of 53 months, for a total of 3,744 woman-months of use.) The 12-month life-table continuation rate of 92.8 per 100 women was similar to that for all the MIC teen clinic patients (92.3). However, continuation rates of the project school students at 24, 36 and 48 months were higher than those for the MIC teen clinic patients, although these differences were not statistically significant. Of the six terminations for unplanned pregnancy, one was due to an IUD method failure. The remaining unplanned pregnancies occurred when patients temporarily discontinued pills, mainly for personal reasons.

Of the 403 family planning patients, 23 (six

Table 1. Adolescents obtaining contraception at school clinics and MIC teen clinics: net cumulative continuation and termination rates per 100 women,* 1973–1979

Event	12 months		24 months		36 months		48 months	
	School	MIC	School	MIC	School	MIC	School	MIC
Continuation	**92.8**	**92.3**	**89.9**	**85.0**	**86.6**	**79.1**	**86.6**	**79.1**
Termination	**7.2**	**7.7**	**10.1**	**15.0**	**13.4**	**20.9**	**13.4**	**20.9**
Pregnancy	(1.3)	(2.0)	(3.2)	(4.5)	(6.4)	(6.3)	(6.4)	(6.3)
Medical	(1.7)	(0.8)	(1.7)	(1.6)	(1.7)	(2.6)	(1.7)	(2.6)
Personal	(4.2)	(4.9)	(5.2)	(8.9)	(5.3)	(12.0)	(5.3)	(12.0)

*Based on 3,744 woman-months of observation among school clinic users, and 15,602 woman-months among MIC teen clinic users.

percent) were lost to follow-up, primarily because they dropped out of school. Of these, five (one percent) were lost to follow-up after one visit only, leaving 18 patients (five percent) who were lost to follow-up after two or more visits. Significantly fewer were lost to follow-up in the school-based clinic group than in the overall MIC teen clinic group—six percent compared to 22 percent, and five percent compared to 12 percent after two or more visits (p<0.001). The relative effectiveness of the school-based clinics is clearly related to the ease with which the young people can be followed up without endangering the confidentiality of the relationship. (That is, it is often difficult to follow adolescent clinic patients who have not informed their parents about their participation; but in the school program, the young people can be reached without communications to the home.)

A total of 190 patients left the program as active contraceptors. Of these, 168 (88 percent) were 18 years of age or had graduated and were referred by the program to other sources of family planning care. Nineteen (10 percent) moved away and three (two percent) transferred to other sources of care. When compared to the overall MIC teen clinic population, a slightly higher proportion of those who left the program from the project school

clinic group did so because they either had graduated or were 18 years of age (88 percent compared to 85 percent in the overall MIC group).

Pregnant Adolescents

As with the original pilot school clinic, utilization of the two senior high school clinics by pregnant students increased during the first three years of operation; 66 percent of the pregnant students in one school and 70 percent of those in the second school came to the MIC clinics for prenatal and postpartum services in the 1978–1979 school year. Additionally, almost all of those who received medical care elsewhere utilized one or more of the high school clinic's educational, social, dental and nutritional services.

The mean age of the 85 students who delivered was 16.4. Forty-five percent were white, 41 percent black and nine percent Spanish American; five percent belonged to other races. Eighty-four percent had never before been pregnant, nine percent had had one or more previous abortions, and seven percent had had one or more previous live births.

Eighty-five percent were unmarried at the time of delivery. When evaluated according to the project's risk-scoring system, 61 per-

Figure 5. Number of deliveries in the two project high schools, 1976–1977 to 1978–1979

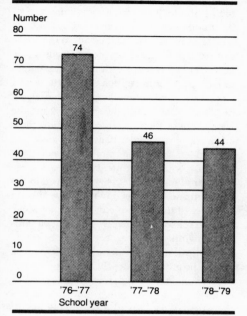

Figure 6. Births per 1,000 females in the two project high schools, 1976–1977 to 1978–1979

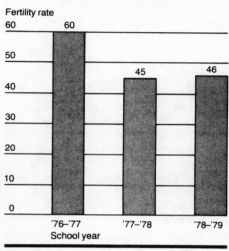

cent were found to be at high risk of neonatal morbidity and fetal and neonatal mortality.* Prenatal care was begun before the third trimester by 94 percent. All but six percent had at least five prenatal visits.

Review of the pregnancy complications experienced by the young women revealed that 15 percent had mild or severe preeclampsia, more than two times the proportion (seven percent) found among the older MIC population (mean age, 21.6). Gonorrhea was diagnosed in 12 percent, also more than two times the proportion (five percent) found among the older MIC population. A higher

incidence of anemia (<11 grams) was found among the high school students who gave birth than among the older MIC pregnant women—20 percent compared with 11 percent.

The incidence of premature delivery and low-birth-weight-infants among the pregnant high school students was no different from that among the older MIC population. Of the 85 students who delivered, 11 percent delivered prematurely and seven percent had low-birth-weight-infants (<2,500 g).

As may be seen in Figure 5, the number of deliveries in the two senior high schools currently served has fallen over the three-year period (1976–1977 to 1978–1979). The 44 deliveries in the 1978–1979 school year represent a decline of over 40 percent from the number in the 1976–1977 school year.

The fertility rate in the combined female population of the two currently served senior high schools, shown in Figure 6, has de-

---

*Risk was calculated on the basis of 67 demographic, obstetric, medical and miscellaneous factors. (See: L. E. Edwards, M. L. Barrada, R. W. Tatreau and E. Y. Hakanson, "A Simplified Ante-Partum Risk-Scoring System," *Obstetrics and Gynecology*, 54:237, 1979.

clined from 60 births per 1,000 to 46 per 1,000 over the three-year period. This 23 percent decline, though substantial, is considerably less than the 56 percent fertility-rate decline over three years recorded in the original junior-senior high school.

Discussion

Teenage contraceptive programs have reported widely varying continuation rates. These are not always comparable since clinic populations differ and different methods are used to calculate the rates. Relatively few studies have calculated teenage continuation rates using the life-table method. One such study of clinics in three communities reported 12-month continuation rates of 72.6 per 100 patients among IUD users and 50.0 per 100 patients among oral contraceptive users who were 19 years of age or younger.[4] In the present study, a 12-month continuation rate of 92.8 per 100 women was found among the high school clinic family planning patients; a similar rate was found for the larger group of all MIC teen clinic patients. Factors contributing to these high continuation rates include consistency of staff offering personalized services with guaranteed confidentiality; accessibility of free services; and provision of educational and social services prior to the medical encounter, including involvement of the male partner and parents if the patient so desires.

At 24, 36 and 48 months, continuation rates for the high school clinic patients were better than those of the MIC teen clinic population. Protocols for prompt follow-up contribute to better long-term contraceptive continuation. Students are contacted in the high school setting by the nurse practitioner within a week after initiating contraception in order to review the selected method. They are then contacted monthly in order to discuss any problems or questions regarding

contraception, and are scheduled for medical follow-up every three months. In addition, clinic staff are available daily and are accessible within the high school, providing care for the students in familiar surroundings. A team approach is utilized by the staff to deal with the students' varied problems, focusing on needs and fears and offering encouragement to continue contraception. Since these services are provided together with generalized health services within the school setting, the anonymity of the sexually active teenager is ensured, and confidentiality of follow-up is maintained since communication need not be made with the student's home. A large number of male students are involved in the program and are helped to recognize the importance of the male role in family planning.

High school clinic family planning patients were significantly less likely to be lost to follow-up than were the adolescents served in the hospital-based MIC teenage contraceptive clinic. The high school clinic patients could be contacted much more frequently than was possible in the hospital clinic, so that any problems associated with contraceptive usage could be discussed. Since class schedules and absentee lists were available to the clinic staff, patients who missed appointments could be more easily located. Additionally, staff were available daily to deal with problems or questions as they arose.

A number of studies have indicated that contraceptive usage is poorer and the incidence of premarital conception and childbirth is higher among nonwhite than among white adolescents.[5] In the present study, however, the long-term contraceptive continuation rates were higher among patients receiving services in the high school clinic than in the MIC teen clinic, although the percentage of the former group who were black or belonged to other minority groups was significantly greater than in the overall teen clinic group. This suggests that the manner in which contraceptive services are delivered, regardless of the patients' racial status, is an important determinant of adolescent contraceptive usage.

Zelnik and Kantner have reported an impressive improvement in teenage contraceptive practice, both in the regularity of use and in the use of more effective methods, between 1971 and 1976.[6] In the two national surveys, the proportion of adolescents who always used contraception increased from 18 percent to 30 percent. Similarly, the proportion of those using contraception at the time of last intercourse increased from 45 percent to 64 percent. The dramatic shift to use of oral contraception in this group in recent years may be explained in part by the fact that the enrollment of teenagers in clinics more than doubled between 1971 and 1975. Zelnik and Kantner suggest that this improved quality and consistency of contraceptive usage among sexually active unmarried teenagers is due to increased federal funds supporting the provision of family planning services and to the significant liberalization of laws and policies affecting teenagers' access to contraceptive services.

Despite improved contraceptive use, however, Zelnik and Kantner found that the proportion of women aged 15–19 who experienced a premarital first pregnancy increased from nine percent to 12 percent,[7] a rise explained by the increased prevalence of premarital intercourse among teenagers.

Our findings show that the fertility rate in the two high schools currently served has declined from 60 per 1,000 in 1976 to 46 per 1,000 in 1979. The pilot school, which closed in 1976, was a junior-senior high school. The fact that the two schools currently served are senior high schools may account for the smaller decline in fertility experienced there in comparison with the pilot school, where the students were reached at an earlier age. It is hoped that a new junior high school sexuality curriculum, as well as the expansion of the clinics to include the younger

sexually active teenagers in junior high schools, will contribute to better contraceptive usage and decreased fertility rates. Additionally, the possibility that the St. Paul school system may be reorganized to incorporate the ninth grade in the high school level may result in better access to contraceptive services for the younger teenagers, who have been shown to be poorer contraceptors than older teenagers and at especially high risk of pregnancy and its most adverse effects.[8]

References

1. C. Tietze and S. Lewit, "Recommended Procedures for the Statistical Evaluation of Intrauterine Contraception," *Studies in Family Planning*, 4:35, 1973.

2. M. Berg, B. Taylor, L. E. Edwards and E. Y. Hakanson, "Prenatal Care for Pregnant Adolescents in a Public High School," *Journal of School Health*, 49:32, 1979.

3. L. E. Edwards, M. E. Steinman and E. Y. Hakanson, "An Experimental Comprehensive High School Clinic," *American Journal of Public Health*, 67:765, 1977.

4. C. Tietze and S. Lewit, "Use-Effectiveness of Oral and Intrauterine Contraception," *Fertility and Sterility*, 22:508, 1971.

5. M. Zelnik, Y. J. Kim and J. F. Kantner, "Probabilities of Intercourse and Conception Among U.S. Teenage Women, 1971 and 1976," *Family Planning Perspectives*, 11:177, 1979; L. Morris, "Estimating the Need for Family Planning Services Among Unwed Teenagers," *Family Planning Perspectives*, 6:91, 1974; and M. Zelnik and J. F. Kantner, "The Resolution of Teenage First Pregnancies," *Family Planning Perspectives*, 6:74, 1974.

6. M. Zelnik and J. F. Kantner, "Sexual and Contraceptive Experience of Young Unmarried Women in the United States, 1976 and 1971," chapter 4, above.

7. M. Zelnik and J. F. Kantner, "First Pregnancies to Women Aged 15–19: 1976 and 1971," chapter 6, above.

8. L. S. Zabin, J. F. Kantner and M. Zelnik, "The Risk of Adolescent Pregnancy in the First Months of Intercourse," chapter 8, above.

IV
Sources of Resistance and Change

Few observers, however well-informed or insightful, could have foreseen the magnitude of the institutional change that has taken place in public response to adolescent sexual behavior and pregnancy during the past two decades. From surveys of sexual attitudes and behavior as well as from vital records, there is every reason to believe that a substantial minority of teenagers were sexually active in the late 1950s and early 1960s. Yet, in many states it was against the law for unmarried individuals, especially minors, to have sexual intercourse. Teenagers were barred from family planning clinics, restricted from purchasing drugstore methods of contraception, and, of course, denied access to abortion. Twenty years ago, there were virtually no programs of sex education in the schools, no discussions of teenage pregnancy and childbearing in the mass media, and few organized interests promoting the rights of young people to receive information about sexual matters.

Surveying the changes which have occurred in the past two decades, it is perhaps not hyperbole to use the term "revolution." Certainly the old order, maintained by tradition and enforced by legal sanction, has broken down, despite the fact that many people, especially the elderly, still endorse the ideal of premarital chastity. Sexual behavior is no longer linked to matrimony, and the inception of intercourse is increasingly left up to individual discretion. Legal prohibitions against premarital sexuality have crumbled, creating a more hospitable climate for sex education and family planning programs for youth. Sex instruction is rapidly gaining favor in many communities as educators, clergy, political leaders, and parents, even if they do not openly welcome it, begin to see that its absence is harmful. Though, as we noted in the introduction to Section III, there is some disagreement about the precise figures, it is evident that a growing number of students now receive some form of classroom instruction about sex.

Not everything has changed. There are, as the articles in this and earlier sections state, serious institutional barriers limiting the information that teenagers receive about sexual options. Sex education is still controversial and is the object of bitter opposition in many localities. Programs may sprout up all over the country, but they are frequently challenged on moral grounds. Often, too, they languish or disappear because of indifference or an absence of material resources.

Despite both intense opposition and passive resistance, sex education has become a reality. Now the debate has shifted from *whether* sex information should be provided to teenagers, to *what* and *how much* should be provided. In her brief analysis of the informational materials available to pregnant teenagers (chapter 26), Linda Ambrose raises some serious questions about the nature of the commitment by public and private agencies to realistic instruction. Her review indicates a paucity of materials, especially those designed to help pregnant young women to make responsible decisions regarding their welfare and the well-being of their children. The style and content of the existing materials is also a problem. Her survey indicates that books and pamphlets intended to reach pregnant women may, in fact, be designed to turn adolescents off. The overall tone is moralistic and proscriptive, the idiom adopted is stilted and insensitive to the teenager, and the messages contained in them are frequently unrealistic and ill-informed. If Ambrose's recent inventory is any indication, we are woefully unprepared to instruct or inform pregnant teenagers, much less their nonpregnant peers, through our printed media.

No comparable analysis of the visual media exists, but some stock-taking is certainly in order. Casual observation of materials presented on television suggests that a good deal of emotionally-loaded information is imparted in soap operas and serials about teenage sexual behavior, but relatively few educational programs have been undertaken. Those few which have been aired tend to raise the issue of the need for sex education, but rarely offer much in the way of actual help. If they are too explicitly didactic, they may be vulnerable to political pressure. For example, an educational documentary, made for a Midwestern public television station, was edited to remove "controversial" portions that cited the advantages and disadvantages of various methods of contraception. So, it is clear that the "sexual revolution" has been more successful in bringing down the old order than in constructing a new one.

This conclusion is supported as well by the overview of services conducted by Joy Dryfoos and Toni Heisler and described in chapter 27. To be sure, the network of services available to teenagers has expanded enormously. Services, which were virtually nonexistent in the mid-1960s, have been extended to well over a million teenagers in recent years. That is the bright side of the picture. In a less optimistic vein, Dryfoos and Heisler also report that a majority of teenagers at risk of pregnancy still do *not* receive family planning services from public or private agencies or private physicians. This fact helps to explain the findings in earlier sections of this book that most teenagers are ill-informed about birth control and ill-equipped when they first have intercourse.

Not only is there a need for more clinics nationwide to serve the expanding population of sexually experienced teenagers, but, as was demonstrated by Laura Edwards and her colleagues in St. Paul, clinics must deliver their services differently if they are to attract and hold an adolescent clientele. Programs designed to suit the convenience of the health provider may not suit their clients. Evening and weekend hours, outreach programs that check up and follow up in the neighborhood, services to accommodate unscheduled visits may be inconvenient to the service deliverers, but they are likely to be attractive to their clients. As Dryfoos and Heisler demonstrate, there is still a wide gap between the promise of preventive services for teenagers and its effective implementation.

Long a source of resistance to change, the legal system during the past decade has been a principal agent of it. When in 1971 Harriet Pilpel and her collaborator, Nancy Wechsler, first reviewed the law governing the provision of contraception and sexual information to minors, they stressed the legal obstacles in the way of expanding services. The great majority of states prohibited the medical treatment of minors, including the provision of contraception, without parental consent. At that time, the authors foresaw a growing trend toward recognition of the right of mature minors (that is, those able to understand the nature and consequences of medical treatment such as contraception and abortion) to make their own decisions about reproductive health care. Subsequent articles, updating the current status of minors' legal rights, have supported their forecast that legal barriers to fertility control would come down. During the 1970s there has been a steady trend of judicial opinion and legislative liberalization favoring the doctrine of the "mature minor." Up until the recent Supreme Court ruling in *Baird* v. *Belotti*, the status of young adolescents was cloudy. A number of states had imposed parental consent requirements before a minor could receive an abortion. But as Paul and Pilpel observe in chapter 28, the matter has more or less been laid to rest. The rights of a mature minor to consent to an abortion or receive medical contraceptive services have been firmly established. States may establish procedures for determining the capacity of a minor to make such decisions, and the court has left open the possibility for parents to participate in the adolescent's decision to seek an abortion, but regulations cannot require parental consent. Thus, the law has come full circle from providing a stiff barrier to pregnancy prevention just a few short years ago, to its current prohibition of such legal restrictions. To what extent resolution of the legal issues will remove the de facto obstacles to preventing unplanned and unwanted pregnancies is a matter not yet settled. It remains to be seen how effectively the law will be implemented, and to what extent most providers, who are not bound by law to do so, will provide services to mature minors on their own consent. A recent study, not included in this volume, shows that two-fifths of abortion facilities and one-fifth of family planning clinics require consent or notification of parents of female patients 17 and under.[1] Although most teenagers already tell their parents about their decision to obtain contraception, there is evidence that the substantial minority who do not would abandon effective contraception and risk pregnancy if their parents had to be told. Nevertheless, it seems likely that obstructive efforts will continue to come from those who oppose family planning and abortion.

It would be unfortunate if the thrust of the judicial rulings were to remove parents completely from the role of sexual socializers. Among some people in the family planning movement, it has become fashionable to view parents as culturally backward, and in their counseling efforts they have either covertly or overtly attempted to bypass the family, directing services exclusively to the teenagers. We believe this policy is unwise and unwarranted. It is true that parents are often confused about how to train their children to become sexually responsible, and it is probably also the case that most parents look to other agencies for support in this task. Nevertheless, parents are not asking to abdicate their training role, and many would probably welcome the opportunity to collaborate with family planning agencies. As we mentioned in the Overview, school sex education programs have, for the most part, not responded to the challenge of reaching out to the family of the teenager.

We return, then, to a question of whether, and how quickly, a consensus could emerge about the norms governing teenage sexuality. The old order which inextricably linked sexual intercourse to marriage no longer exists, but a new standard to replace it has yet to be formed.

Reference

1. A. Torres, "Telling Parents about Adolescents' Use of Family Planning and Abortion Services:Clinic Policies and Teenage Behavior," *Family Planning Perspectives*, **12**, no. 6, 1980.

26
Misinforming Pregnant Teenagers

Linda Ambrose

More than four million teenage women in the United States are sexually active, over one million get pregnant, and about 600,000 give birth each year. Two-thirds of the pregnancies and half the births are unintended.[1] One reason for such a large number of accidental pregnancies is teenagers' ignorance and misinformation concerning the basic facts about reproduction, the risk of pregnancy and contraception; misinformation is especially prevalent among teenage mothers,[2] and contributes to the relatively high incidence of subsequent unintended pregnancies: One in five adolescent mothers have had two or more births.[3]

Background

Despite the Carter administration's clamor for a "teenage initiative" to deal with the adverse consequences of adolescent pregnancy, there has been no organized national effort to educate pregnant young women about contraception, the symptoms of pregnancy, and the importance of early prenatal care or, alternatively, of early abortion. (Indeed, the administration focuses only on "alternatives to abortion" in its teenage initiative.) For adolescents who carry their pregnancies to term, the schools and the health care system have done little to provide information that professionals and young mothers agree is vital for the health and social and economic adjustment of the young mother and her child.

Service programs for pregnant teenagers reach only a handful of those who need assistance.° Lack of coordination, varying funding sources and contradictory purposes guarantee that the educational components of such programs are, at best, of uneven quality. Some indication of the kind of 'education' currently

---

°In its *National Directory of Services for School-Age Parents* (Washington, D.C., 1976), the National Alliance Concerned with School-Age Parents identifies some 1,200 agencies. Many of the organizations listed, however, are merely information or referral agencies, or child welfare advocacy groups. It is not known how many of the listed programs provide comprehensive services, including sex education, or even how many of them are intended primarily to serve school-age parents. The Directory's authors suggest that earlier research documenting the scarcity and inadequacy of services to adolescent mothers is still valid (see: H.M. Wallace, E.A. Gold, H. Goldstein and A.C. Oglesby, "A Study of Services and Needs of Teenage Pregnant Girls in the Large Cities of the United States," *American Journal of Public Health*, 63:5, 1973).

available to teenage parents may be found by looking at the contents of the periodicals, leaflets and informational pamphlets published for distribution through physicians' offices, school programs for pregnant students, prenatal clinics and governmental and charitable agencies.

A survey by this author of such materials available in the spring of 1977 indicates that few resources exist that deal with pregnancy, and virtually none of these are well-suited to the pregnant adolescent's needs. There are many materials dealing with child development and parental responsibilities; but the physiological aspects of labor and delivery, pregnancy prevention and the mechanics of human reproduction are, at best, covered only briefly in the few booklets devoted to prenatal care.

According to Lucy Eddinger of the National Alliance Concerned with School-Age Parents, "Program people [working with pregnant teenagers] complain frequently about the difficulty of finding material suitable for teenagers, especially black teenagers or those living in rural areas."[4] Nancy M. Boykin, Director of Continuing Education for Girls in the Detroit public schools, comments, "What we're doing, really, is scrambling for materials and making the best of what supplementary materials we can find."[5]

The Materials Available

The U.S. Office of Education and the National Institute of Education have implicitly recognized the widespread reliance on informal, nontextbook sources of information for teenage parents by financing the preparation of two bibliographies identifying more than 1,500 "resources considered most helpful to those working with adolescent parents."[6]

In addition to baby care books by Dr. Spock and others, these bibliographies list hundreds of pamphlets and brochures intended for free or low-cost distribution. However, the overwhelming majority of the entries are devoted to child development, parental responsibilities, the stages of infant growth, money and household management, needs of handicapped children and parent-child relations. About one-dozen can be said to deal in any way with pregnancy. Both these bibliographies were published in 1975; recognizing that new materials may have been published since that time, this author wrote or telephoned 33 national voluntary and professional organizations, medical societies, pharmaceutical companies, manufacturers of maternity and infant products, social welfare agencies and federal government offices that were thought to have responsibility or concern for some aspect of teenage pregnancy and motherhood. From all sources, fewer than two dozen items were located.* Sponsors in-

---

*These include, in addition to the materials on pregnancy discussed in this article, the following publications: Public Health Service, Health Services Administration, DHEW, *The Hassles of Becoming a Teenage Parent*, U.S. Government Printing Office, Washington, D.C., stock no. 017–031–00008–2, 1975; Nutrition Department, General Mills, Inc., *Meal Planning During Pregnancy*, Minneapolis, 1972; Nutrition Section, Michigan Department of Public Health, *Food While You're Pregnant*, Lansing, 1973; Maternity Center Association, *Preparation for Childbearing*, New York, 1973; E. Ogg, *Preparing Tomorrow's Parents*, Public Affairs Committee, New York, Mar. 1975; National Foundation–March of Dimes, *Be Good to Your Baby Before It Is Born*, White Plains, N.Y., 1973; Ross Laboratories, Columbus, Ohio, *Becoming A Parent*, May 1976, *There Will Be a New Baby at Your House*, June 1974, *What To Do About Minor Discomforts of Pregnancy*, Dec. 1975; Medical Department, Carnation Company, *Pregnancy in Anatomical Illustrations*, Los Angeles, 1962; Parents Magazine Films, Inc., *Prenatal Care: Preparing for Parenthood* (script booklets accompanying filmstrips and recordings are included in the same set), New York, 1974;

clude commercial publishing houses, government agencies, social welfare agencies, baby food companies and feminist organizations.

Only three booklets were specifically addressed to pregnant teenagers, and only one offered detailed information about pregnancy testing and the alternative choices of induced abortion and full-term delivery (as well as information about miscarriage). This 37-page booklet, *What Now?! Under 18 and Pregnant*, was prepared in 1976 (too late for inclusion in either of the bibliographies) by a group of teenagers enrolled in a federally supported summer job program, and was published under the auspices of a Salem, Massachusetts, women's center.[7] The cover consists of a crudely hand-drawn maze, with the title hand-lettered above it. Inside, the typewritten text includes direct quotations from a diverse group of young women between the ages of 12 and 18 who delivered a baby, had a miscarriage or obtained an abortion.

What Now?! focuses on the pregnant teenager's legal rights, her options and her needs. Without suggesting that the choices will be easy, the booklet points out that the teenager has the right to remain in school, to obtain medical care and to decide about abortion or, if she delivers the baby, whether to keep it or release it for adoption. Speaking of teenagers who delivered their babies, the authors conclude:

Did the women we talked to regret going through their pregnancies?

There was no one answer. Some felt happy with their decisions. They wanted the baby or else they felt and still feel abortion is wrong for them. Some felt they might have done differently if they had to do it again. Some were not sure.

You must trust the decision you make. The only way you'll ever know is to experience what you think is right. Most of the women managed to make it through their pregnancies pretty well and the ones who kept their babies are still trying to make the best of it.

While *What Now?!* does not discuss birth control (beyond suggesting "using a method of birth control or waiting to have sex until you are older . . .") or the menstrual cycle and the risks of pregnancy, it is by far the most comprehensive of the booklets we have been able to locate, and is also one of the least available. (Only about 1,000 copies were distributed in the year after its publication.)

Most of the available materials tend to deal with a single aspect of pregnancy—especially the importance of adequate nutrition. The most widely distributed publications appear to be *Prenatal Care,* a 70-page handbook from DHEW which is not specifically addressed to teenagers,[8] and *For the Young Mother-to-Be,* a 19-page pamphlet published by a pharmaceutical company and addressed to "the young girl who did not plan or want to become pregnant at this time";[9] the latter is one of the very few publications that direct information and advice specifically to pregnant teenagers and adolescent mothers. The pamphlet has been distributed since 1974 to clinics, hospitals and other institutions serving pregnant women. According to the company's marketing office, more than 100,000 copies were distributed in 1976.

Unlike *What Now?!,* this popular pam-

American Baby magazine (12 issues between Apr. 1976 and Mar. 1977 were examined), New York; Education Development Center, EDC School and Society Programs, *Exploring Childhood: Program Overview and Catalog of Materials,* Newton, Mass., 1976; American College of Obstetricians and Gynecologists, *Food, Pregnancy and Family Health,* Chicago, Feb. 1976; and American Medical Association, *Prenatal Care,* Chicago, 1977.

phlet stresses the benefits of unplanned teenage pregnancies:

> Unwanted pregnancy has caused problems for women since the beginning of time. Every year, thousands of young girls become pregnant. . . . The important thing for you to understand is that you are not alone. Pregnancy, under any conditions, is one of the most significant and wonderful experiences a woman can have. You must not let your experience be marred by the problems that surround it.

Following illustrations and textual discussions of the female reproductive organs, conception, fetal development, health and dietary needs during pregnancy, the booklet identifies the benefits of pregnancy more specifically:

> During the next nine months, you will be your healthiest, and with just a little care you can be prettier than you have ever been in spite of your changing figure. Your skin will be clear and radiant, and your eyes will sparkle with excitement and anticipation.

Finally, after seven pages of discussion of labor, delivery and the postpartum period, the pamphlet concludes:

> By the end of the postpartum period . . . the young girl who previously existed will be gone. In her place can be a young woman capable of making mature decisions and directing her own life.
>
> You can have learned to limit your own desires in consideration of others, to think through a decision before you act, and to live with your decisions without regret. . . . The past is yesterday. The future is tomorrow. Today is the time for a new beginning.

There is no suggestion that in real life, the consequences of childbirth for the teenager may include curtailed schooling, limited job opportunities and a life in poverty for the mother and her child.

Given its rosy view of teenage pregnancy outcome, of course, this booklet finds no need to discuss the alternative of abortion, or the risk of future unplanned pregnancies, or the need to use contraception to avert them.

Bypassing Teen Concerns

For the most part, publications about pregnancy and prenatal care are aimed at women past their teens. They tend to bypass topics that specifically interest teenagers, but that older women are presumed to know already—for example, the various contraceptive methods, how to identify early symptoms of pregnancy, how to obtain a pregnancy test, what the pelvic examination and other gynecological procedures are like, and what experiences and practices may be expected in the delivery room.

A baby food company publishes a 16-page *Expectant Mother's Guide* that, typically, limits information about reproductive physiology to conception ("when one successful sperm merges with the ovum, fertilization has occurred") and fetal development.[10]

Virtually all of these publications (with the exception of *What Now?!*) assume that a pregnancy uniformly results in a birth even though almost one in seven teenage pregnancies end in spontaneous miscarriage and more than one in four are terminated by induced abortion.[11] Failure to acknowledge the alternative of adoption is further indication of the orientation toward older, middle-class mothers.

In addition to omitting a number of topics altogether, the publications frequently incorporate information and attitudes that are remote from the needs, experiences and circumstances of adolescent mothers. *When Your Baby Is on the Way,* an illustrated leaflet published by DHEW's Office of Child Development, for example, is set firmly in the mold of traditional family life.[12] The booklet is dominated by sketches of an adult, apparently middle-class couple whose facial features are inexplicably absent. A section entitled "Fathers Have Their Special Ways of Helping" advises, "Find out from her doctor what your wife needs to do. Help her in doing what he says. . . . Plan well ahead how you are going to pay for the hospital. Decide how you are going to get your wife there."

DHEW's *Prenatal Care,* first published by the Children's Bureau in 1913, has replaced references to "husbands" with "your mate," "your male partner," "men" and "the baby's father."[13] But the new terminology frequently seems contrived and the advice somewhat dated. For example, under the topic "What Can the Family Do to Help?" the following suggestions are made: "Men, this is for YOU. You are very special during this time. Give that girl of yours a hand with things around the house. . . . Do something special on those 'blue' days by taking your lady out to a movie, drive, or if the budget can stand it, out to dinner. Take her out. Go for a walk together." However, the section "Birth Control—Is Spacing Children Necessary?" does include one of the few discussions of alternative methods of contraception.

In the eyes of an unhappily pregnant adolescent, instructions in several brochures may appear simplistic or authoritarian. Without further explanation, a leaflet published by a company that manufactures infant formula directs, "Rest during the day when you are tired. Get a good, long sleep at night. . . . Have your teeth checked by a dentist.

During pregnancy there are times when it is unwise to have sexual relations. Ask your doctor."[14]

Several publications include brief discussions of diet and nutrition that carry a tone of obligatory responsibility which may ultimately be as likely to induce feelings of guilt or uncertainty as to improve eating habits. Thus, a recent DHEW publication begins, "If you are a teenage girl who is going to have a baby, you probably know that your baby takes body-building materials from what you eat during the nine months of your pregnancy. It's up to you to eat enough food to provide for your baby's growth."[15] A widely distributed leaflet of the National Foundation–March of Dimes, *Nutrition and Pregnancy,* comments, "Although your greatest concern has always been to feed the others in your family even if you were left with less than enough, the baby within you must be fed first and it can only be nourished through the foods you eat. You must not deprive yourself."[16] Even *What Now?!* adopts a somewhat scolding tone, admonishing the pregnant teenager that "your baby will be what you eat. . . . The health of your child before and after birth will depend on how well you take care of yourself during pregnancy. . . . Smoking, drinking (alcohol), and drugs are all bad things for both you and your child."[17]

Conclusions

The educational and informational materials available to adolescents who are pregnant or the parents of a newborn infant are few and, for the most part, inappropriate. It is time that commercial companies, government agencies and public and charitable organizations that publish "new mother" materials review them with an eye toward the needs of the one million teenagers who become pregnant each year. Do their booklets deal with choice of abortion in an evenhanded way? Do they explain how birth control methods work and where to obtain them? Do they discuss the early symptoms of pregnancy, and how to get a pregnancy test? Do they talk about the possibility of miscarriage? Do they identify resources for job, child care and educational counseling, as well as sources of medical care and economic help? Do they explain reproductive physiology, especially its relationship to the risk of pregnancy, and the various gynecological and obstetrical procedures the young woman is likely to undergo in the course of her pregnancy?

Although it is not surprising that commercial and charitable institutions emphasize subjects in their publications that correspond to their own interests, and that they try to avoid controversy, we can expect them also to be straightforward in delineating the rights of pregnant women, and the options open to them.

But even if all the currently available materials were appropriately rewritten, the supply would still fall drastically short of the need. New materials are needed from DHEW to be distributed through maternal and child health clinics, community health centers, child and youth projects, family planning agencies, junior and senior high schools, youth organizations and other programs that have contact with young persons.

It would seem reasonable for such publishing and distribution activities to be incorporated into community sex education efforts, which the Carter administration has advocated as a necessary part of a federal "initiative on adolescent pregnancy."[18] Full implementation of such a program would require cooperation by the state departments of education and by local school officials. Curriculum and textbook reforms would be particularly timely since many state education departments and local school districts are currently in the process of modifying their policies and practices to conform to federal regulations prohibiting schools from expelling, suspending or otherwise discriminating against students on the basis of pregnancy or parenthood.[19] Furthermore, however "controversial" sex education for all young people might appear to school officials, it seems less likely that they would object to providing information that enables pregnant students to deal knowledgeably and realistically with the circumstances that confront them.

Ideally, of course, sex-related health and educational services should be provided to teenagers *prior* to pregnancy. Making educational materials available to already-pregnant adolescents would seem to be the very least that could be done pending the implementation of adequate sex education programs in the nation's schools.

References

1. National Center for Health Statistics, DHEW (NCHS), "Teenage Childbearing: United States, 1966–75," *Monthly Vital Statistics Report*, Vol. 26, No. 5, Supplement, 1977; and The Alan Guttmacher Institute (AGI), *11 Million Teenagers: What Can Be Done About the Epidemic of Adolescent Pregnancies in the United States*, Planned Parenthood Federation of America, New York, 1976.

2. M. Zelnik and J. F. Kantner, "Sexual and Contraceptive Experience of Young Unmarried Women in the United States, 1976 and 1971," Chapter 4, above; J. R. Evans, G. Selstad and W. H. Welcher, "Teenagers: Fertility Control Behavior and Attitudes Before and After Abortion, Childbearing or Negative Pregnancy Test," chapter 24, above; and H. B. Presser, "Early Motherhood: Ignorance or Bliss?" chapter 22, above.

3. NCHS, "Advance Report: Final Natality Statistics, 1975," *Monthly Vital Statistics Report*, Vol. 25, No. 10, Supplement, 1976.

4. L. Eddinger, personal interview, May 1977.

5. N.M. Boykin, personal interview, May 1977.

6. Southwest Educational Development Laboratory, *Parenting in 1975: A Listing from the Parenting Materials Information Center*, Austin, Tex., June 1975 (report of a project supported by the National Institute of Education, DHEW); and National Alliance Concerned with School-Age Parents, *Parenting Guide: Selected Resources and Materials, 1965–1975*, Washington, D.C., Oct. 1975 (report of a project performed under contract with the Office of Education, DHEW). See also: Food and Nutrition Services, U.S. Department of Agriculture, *Audiovisual and Print Materials, Special Supplemental Food Program for Women, Infants and Children*, Washington, D.C., Mar. 1976 and Oct. 1976 (mimeo); and Bureau of Elementary and Secondary Education, DHEW, *Audiovisual Materials Available at the U.S. Office of Education*, Washington, D.C. (mimeo, undated).

7. L. Carroll, D. LaBelle, V. Wooldridge and L. Zarkowsky, *What Now?! Under 18 and Pregnant*, Origins, Inc., Salem, Mass., 1976.

8. Office of Child Development, DHEW (OCD), *Prenatal Care*, U.S. Government Printing Office, Washington, D.C. (GPO), stock no. 1791–00187, 1973.

9. E. Cowart and W. Liston, *For the Young Mother-to-Be*, Mead Johnson Laboratories, Evansville, Ind., 1974.

10. Gerber Products Company, *Expectant Mother's Guide*, Fremont, Mich., 1974.

11. AGI, 1976, op. cit., p. 10.

12. OCD, *When Your Baby Is on the Way*, GPO, stock no. 017–091–00080–8, 1975.

13. OCD, *Prenatal Care*, 1973, op. cit.

14. Carnation Company, *When You're Going to Have a Baby*, Los Angeles (undated).

15. Public Health Service, Health Services Administration, DHEW, *Food for the Teenager During Pregnancy*, GPO, stock no. 1726.00036, 1976.

16. National Foundation–March of Dimes, *Nutrition and Pregnancy*, White Plains, N.Y. (undated).

17. L. Carroll et al., 1976, op. cit.

18. H. Aaron and P. Schuck, "Memorandum: Initiative to Address Adolescent Pregnancy and Related Issues," Office of the Secretary, DHEW, Aug. 4, 1977 (mimeo); and J.A. Califano, transcript of press conference of June 24, 1977, Office of the Secretary, DHEW (mimeo).

19. *Code of Federal Regulations*, Vol. 45, Section 86.40.

27
Contraceptive Services for Adolescents: An Overview

Joy G. Dryfoos and Toni Heisler

Unintended teenage pregnancy is now generally recognized as one of America's critical personal and social problems. It has been well documented that for each of the past several years, more than one million pregnancies have occurred to women under the age of 20, two-thirds conceived out of wedlock, and a large majority, unintended.[1] Concern about adolescent pregnancy has stimulated the Carter Administration to launch what it describes as a "comprehensive initiative . . . to help prevent unwanted initial and repeat pregnancies among adolescents and to decrease the likelihood that they will become dependent on welfare."[2] Unfortunately, the "comprehensive initiative" launched with much fanfare by the Department of Health, Education and Welfare's Secretary, Joseph A. Califano, Jr., in January 1978, stresses provision of services to pregnant teenagers and their babies, while providing little new support for preventive services for the majority of sexually active unmarried teenagers who

This article is adapted from *Contraceptive Services for Adolescents: United States, Each State and County, 1975*, The Alan Guttmacher Institute, New York, 1978.

have neither experienced pregnancy nor begun to use effective contraception. Much of the Administration's rhetoric and most of its proposed funding are intended to provide "alternatives to abortion" rather than "alternatives to pregnancy." The implicit assumption is that once a girl is pregnant, her only choice is to bear the child. Many teenagers, however, when given the option, have chosen to prevent unintended pregnancy: In 1975, some 1.2 million of them (as we will show) sought and received contraceptive services from family planning clinics throughout the United States; approximately the same number are estimated to have received contraception from private doctors.

In an effort to find out to what extent and where family planning services were available in 1975 to the estimated four million sexually active teenagers in need of contraception, The Alan Guttmacher Institute (AGI) conducted a county-by-county analysis, the findings of which we summarize in this article. Among other things, we were interested in testing some of the conventional wisdom about teenagers and birth control services: Are public agencies more resistant to serving teenagers than private agencies? Are more teenagers served in states with laws and policies affirming the right of minors to consent to their own health care? Will adolescents use contraception once it is made available and accessible? Are teenage birth control needs so different from those of adults that a special service-delivery system needs to be set up for them?

Methodology

The estimates of adolescent women at risk of unintended pregnancy are based on census data updated to 1975, and adjusted for sexual activity and pregnancy intention. The county estimates* of teenagers in need of services† include women aged 15-19 who, according to national studies, are sexually active and neither intentionally pregnant nor trying to become pregnant.[3]

Service statistics come directly from reports from family planning provider agencies, either through the National Reporting System for Family Planning Services (NRSFPS)—a national, uniform data-collection system operated in 1975 by DHEW's National Center for Health Statistics—or through AGI surveys of agencies not covered by reporting systems. Data problems were solved through hundreds of follow-up telephone calls to family planning programs, and the final results for each state were reviewed by knowledgeable sources in each state. We believe that the findings of this study are reasonably accurate, considering the size of the universe under examination.

The Need

Just over four million of the nation's adolescent women were at risk of unintended pregnancy in 1975, about 40 percent of all U.S. females aged 15-19. About 58 percent were from families with incomes above 200 percent of the federal poverty level,‡ 75 percent were white, more than 40 percent were aged 17 or younger, almost 30 percent resided in nonmetropolitan areas, and a large proportion lived in suburban communities outside central cities.

In addition, there were an estimated 375,000 sexually active girls aged 13 and 14 (not included in area need estimates). Of the 10.6 million young men who were aged 15-19 in 1975, about 65 percent, or 6.9 million, are estimated to have been sexually active.

The geographic distribution of young women aged 15-19 at risk followed population patterns fairly consistently, with large concentrations in the major metropolitan counties and small numbers dispersed over large, rural, more remote areas. A small number of counties (159) with 5,000 or more teenagers in need accounted for more than half of all the adolescents at risk; while 1,174 counties, each with fewer than 300 such women, contained about five percent of all teenagers at risk.

Contraceptive Services for Teens

A total of 1.2 million women under the age of 20 received contraceptive services from family planning clinics in 1975;

---

*County-level data refer to women residing in a county whether or not they receive family planning services in the county. Some women obtain services in areas other than their place of residence.

†For details on how need was defined and estimated, see: J. G. Dryfoos, "Women Who Need and Receive Family Planning Services: Estimates at Mid-Decade," *Family Planning Perspectives*, 7:172, 1975.

‡ Defined in 1975 as a family income of over $11,000 for a nonfarm family of four.

Table 1. Estimated total number of patients aged 15–44, and number and percent aged 15–19, served by family planning clinics, 1969–1975 (numbers in 000s)

Year	No. aged 15–44	No. aged 15–19	% aged 15–19	Increase in teen patients No.	%
FY 69	1,070	214	20	na	na
FY 70	1,410	300	21	86	40
FY 71	1,889	460	24	160	53
FY 72	2,612	691	27	231	50
FY 73	3,089	855	28	164	24
FY 74	3,282	945	29	90	11
FY 75	3,813	1,125	29	180	19
CY 75*	3,924	1,175	30	50	4

*Between FY 1975 and CY 1975 there is an overlap period from Jan. 1, 1975–June 30, 1975.

Note: In this and subsequent tables, na=not applicable.

Sources: The Alan Guttmacher Institute (AGI), *Data and Analyses for 1977 Revision of DHEW Five-Year Plan for Family Planning Services*, New York, 1977; AGI, *Contraceptive Services for Adolescents: United States, Each State and County, 1975*, New York, 1978; and reference 6.

Table 2. Estimated number of new patients aged 15–19 served by family planning clinics, and percent of patients aged 15–19 who were new, 1972–1975 (numbers in 000s)

Year	No. of patients reported as new	% of patients who were new
FY 72	531	77
FY 73	591	69
FY 74	627	66
CY 75*	700	60

*Includes entire calendar year.

these women comprised 30 percent of the 3.9 million patients in organized family planning programs. Private physicians also provided contraceptive services to adolescents, but detailed information about the quantity and components of these services does not exist. From several national studies, it has been concluded that about 1.2–1.3 million teenagers received contraception from the private sector in 1975.[4]

Utilization of family planning clinic programs by women aged 19 or younger has increased dramatically over the years, as Table 1 shows. Rapid growth began in the early 1970s, when substantial federal funds for family planning services became available. At the same time, organized programs, reflecting liberalization of restrictive state laws on provision of services to unwed minors, began to provide services to them on their own consent.[5]

Each year beginning in 1972, most of the 15–19-year-olds enrolled in family planning clinics were new patients. As may be seen in Table 2, in 1975, 700,000 patients were new to the reporting clinic. However, 18 percent had previously used another clinic; therefore, 574,000 were newly enrolled in the organized program (not shown in table). Data from previous years suggest that family planning clinics have the capacity to enroll at least one-half million new teenage patients annually.

At the clinics, young women obtained the most effective methods. Data from the NRSFPS show that in 1975, only 32 percent of new teenage patients had used the pill prior to enrollment; afterward, 81 percent were using it. Prior to enrollment, half the teenagers were using no method; this proportion declined to seven percent at the time of their last clinic visit (data not shown).[6]

Family planning services for adolescents have been identified in four out of five of the 3,072 U.S. counties. However, in 592 counties, no such services are provided; 153 of these no-service counties each have more than 300 adolescents in need of contraceptive care. While the counties without services are widely scattered around the nation, they represent more than one-half of the counties in each of seven states.* In four additional states,† one-third to one-half of the counties have no identified family planning clinic services for adolescents, our data show.

Family Planning Provider Agencies

Altogether, 3,089 different agencies participate in the delivery of organized family planning services to adolescents. These consist of 630 hospitals, 1,693 health departments, 172 Planned Parenthood affiliates and 594 other agencies. Not all of them deliver services directly; 595 assist provider agencies with space, staff or supplies. Almost half of the hospitals, compared to 14 percent (at most) of all other agencies, participate in joint programs, in which they typically supply space while other agencies provide personnel.

Table 3 shows the number and percent distribution of 15-19-year-olds served by the various types of providers. Health departments served by far the largest proportion of the adolescent case load in 1975—42 percent—followed by Planned Parenthood affiliates, which served 28 percent. Hospitals served 13 percent, while a variety of other agencies—poverty programs, neighborhood health centers and free clinics—served the remaining 17 percent. The mix of providers varied with metropolitan status, as the table shows. Nonmetropolitan health departments served almost twice the proportion of adolescents as metropolitan

* Kansas, Montana, Nebraska, North Dakota, South Dakota, Utah and Wyoming.

† Colorado, Idaho, Illinois and Indiana.

Table 3. Percentage distribution of patients aged 15–19 and 20–44, by metropolitan status and type of agency providing services, 1975 (numbers in 000s)

Agency and status	% aged 15–19	% aged 20–44
U.S. total	N=1,175	N=2,749
Hospitals	13	15
Health department	42	44
Planned Parenthood	28	25
Other	17	16
Metropolitan	N=905	N=2,050
Hospitals	16	19
Health departments	35	36
Planned Parenthood	33	30
Other	16	15
Nonmetropolitan	N=270	N=699
Hospitals	2	4
Health departments	67	65
Planned Parenthood	12	11
Other	19	20

health departments, while nonmetropolitan hospitals served fewer than two percent of all 15-19-year-old patients, compared with 16 percent served by metropolitan hospitals.

The distribution of teenage patients closely mirrors that of adult patients served by the clinics: Planned Parenthood affiliates and other agencies served only a slightly higher proportion of teenagers than of older patients, and hospitals and health departments, a slightly lower proportion, but the differences were slight.

There were marked differences, both regionally and among states, in the use of provider agencies by teenage contraceptive patients (not shown). In the northeastern states, patients tended to rely upon hospitals and Planned Parenthood affiliates; in the South, where health departments tend to be responsible for the health care of the poor, teen-

Table 4. Number and percentage distribution of women aged 15–19 at risk of unintended pregnancy, and number and percent served by organized family planning programs, by federal region* and state, according to metropolitan status, 1975 (numbers in 000s)

Region and state	At risk			Served			
	No.	% distribution of total at risk		No.	% of women at risk who were served		
		Metro	Nonmetro		Total	Metro	Nonmetro
U.S. total	4,076	72	28	1,175	29	31	23
Region I	218	78	22	51	24	23	26
Region II	451	90	10	131	29	30	21
Region III	453	74	26	129	28	31	21
Region IV	683	56	44	253	37	39	34
Region V	897	76	24	188	21	24	10
Region VI	448	66	34	124	28	29	24
Region VII	225	51	49	63	28	41	14
Region VIII	122	52	48	29	24	31	16
Region IX	448	90	10	152	34	34	37
Region X	130	57	43	54	42	49	32
Alabama	78	61	39	22	28	32	22
Alaska	7	na	100	4	50	na	50
Arizona	39	72	28	16	42	48	25
Arkansas	42	38	62	11	26	32	23
California	384	93	7	127	33	32	41
Colorado	46	80	20	16	35	35	29
Connecticut	56	85	15	13	23	25	11
Delaware	12	69	31	4	39	38	41
D.C.	13	100	na	9	68	68	na
Florida	130	82	18	46	35	35	39
Georgia	101	55	45	44	43	44	43
Hawaii	15	81	19	5	35	30	53
Idaho	16	15	85	4	23	50	19
Illinois	217	82	18	41	19	22	7
Indiana	108	66	34	22	20	27	5

*Region I: Connecticut, Maine, Massachusetts, New Hampshire, Rhode Island and Vermont; Region II: New Jersey and New York; Region III: Delaware, District of Columbia, Maryland, Pennsylvania, Virginia and West Virginia; Region IV: Alabama, Florida, Georgia, Kentucky, Mississippi, North Carolina, South Carolina and Tennessee; Region V: Illinois, Indiana, Michigan, Minnesota, Ohio and Wisconsin; Region VI: Arkansas, Louisiana, New Mexico, Oklahoma and Texas; Region VII: Iowa, Kansas, Missouri and Nebraska; Region VIII: Colorado, Montana, North Dakota, South Dakota, Utah and Wyoming; Region IX: Arizona, California, Hawaii and Nevada; Region X: Alaska, Idaho, Oregon and Washington.

agers obtained care primarily from this source. In the absence of local public health facilities in the midwestern states, teenagers relied more upon Planned Parenthood affiliates for services; in the West Coast states, with a fairly wide variety of provider agencies, 15-19-year-olds obtained services from a mix of agencies.

With the exception of Planned Parenthood programs, which served an average of 1,964 adolescent patients each in 1975, most agencies had small case loads, ranging from a mean of 431 teenage patients per hospital program to a mean of 338 per health department program. About 36 percent of all agencies had adolescent case loads of 100 or fewer patients. Only 11 percent served more than 1,000 teenagers in 1975.

Many family planning agencies operate more than one clinic, so that adolescents had access to some level of contraceptive services at 5,272 separate loca-

Table 4 (continued)

Region and state	At risk			Served			
	No.	% distribution of total at risk		No.	% of women at risk who were served		
		Metro	Nonmetro		Total	Metro	Nonmetro
Iowa	57	37	63	13	23	37	15
Kansas	45	45	55	11	24	38	12
Kentucky	70	46	54	20	28	29	28
Louisiana	85	60	40	25	30	30	29
Maine	20	27	73	6	29	34	37
Maryland	79	85	15	28	36	36	38
Massachusetts	102	97	3	21	20	20	27
Michigan	188	82	18	43	23	23	19
Minnesota	78	62	38	23	30	40	11
Mississippi	53	24	76	19	35	42	34
Missouri	94	66	34	31	34	43	14
Montana	16	25	75	4	24	38	20
Nebraska	30	43	57	7	24	40	12
Nevada	10	79	21	4	39	45	21
New Hampshire	14	30	70	3	25	22	26
New Jersey	131	94	6	31	23	24	18
New Mexico	25	31	69	8	31	43	26
New York	320	88	12	100	31	32	21
North Carolina	109	43	57	31	29	32	26
North Dakota	14	10	90	1	10	29	8
Ohio	218	80	20	51	23	25	15
Oklahoma	53	56	44	16	31	30	32
Oregon	41	59	41	19	46	50	38
Pennsylvania	221	80	20	48	22	24	13
Rhode Island	17	82	18	5	29	31	18
South Carolina	59	45	55	22	38	36	39
South Dakota	15	14	86	2	15	21	12
Tennessee	83	63	37	49	59	63	50
Texas	244	78	22	64	26	28	19
Utah	24	79	21	4	17	21	3
Vermont	9	na	100	4	41	na	41
Virginia	93	63	37	34	36	42	38
Washington	66	72	28	28	43	48	28
West Virginia	36	36	64	6	16	15	16
Wisconsin	88	60	40	8	9	23	3
Wyoming	7	na	100	2	21	na	21

tions. Thus, there were an average of 773 adolescents at risk for each available clinic site in 1975. However, differences in access among states were significant: There were 2,108 adolescents at risk per site in Illinois, compared to 264 in Mississippi.

Adolescents Served and Unserved

With just over four million adolescents at risk of unintended pregnancy, and about 2.4 million served by organized family planning programs and private physicians combined, a minimum of 1.6 million adolescents at risk did not receive family planning services from either source in 1975. Some of these young women may have been using methods purchased from drugstores, while others were using rhythm, withdrawal, folk methods or no method. According to the major national study of adolescent contraceptive practices, only one-third of sexually active teenagers reported using the pill or IUD at last intercourse, and 37 percent reported using no method at all.[7] The same study has shown that sexually active teenagers who never used contraceptives were more than five times as likely to become pregnant as those who always used a method, and 10 times as likely to get pregnant as those who always used a medical method.[8]

Because we have no data on the distribution of teenage women served by private physicians, we will focus in the remainder of this article on the young women at risk who were served and not served by family planning clinic programs. This procedure should provide a reasonably accurate picture of differences in access to clinic services, a factor over which the public and voluntary sectors can exercise some control by expanding or contracting existing programs or by initiating new ones. The little available information on the use of private physicians suggests that access is more uniform and that the nature of this type of service delivery renders it less subject to intervention by outside agencies.

Table 4 shows that of the approximately four million 15-19-year-olds at risk, 72 percent lived in metropolitan counties. In 1975, 1.2 million women aged 15-19, 29 percent of all U.S. adolescents at risk of unintended pregnancy, were served by organized programs—31 percent of those at risk in metropolitan counties and 23 percent of those at risk in nonmetropolitan counties. In the northwestern states (Region X), 42 percent of those in need were served, twice the proportion (21 percent) served in the Great Lakes area (Region V). The differences among states are even greater: Fifty-nine percent of teenagers at risk were served in Tennessee and 68 percent in the District of Columbia, but only 10 percent were served in North Dakota, and only nine percent in Wisconsin. In seven states,[*] more than 40 percent of the adolescents at risk of unintended pregnancy were served, while in eight others,[2†20] percent or fewer were served. Neither the geographic location of the state, nor the size of the need, nor the demographic characteristics of the population appeared to be a factor in the percentage of the adolescents at risk who were served; however, as we will show, the relative number of clinic locations apparently was.

In general, counties with the largest *number* of adolescents at risk contained clinic programs that served the largest *proportion* of teenagers at risk (data not shown). In 159 counties (about five percent of the nation's total), more than 60 percent of the adolescents at risk were served by clinic programs, and in 745 counties (about 25 percent of the total), 30-60 percent were served. In the majority of counties, however, service case loads were smaller than the national average. In 1,548 counties, fewer than 30 percent of those at risk were served, and in 592 counties, no services were provided to meet the needs of some 160,000 15-19-year-olds. In contrast, in 28 counties, it appears that all the adolescents at risk were provided with contraceptive services by organized programs in 1975.[‡]

More than 2.9 million teenagers at risk—71 percent of all 15-19-year-olds at

---

[*]Alaska, Arizona, Georgia, Oregon, Tennessee, Vermont and Washington.

[†]Illinois, Indiana, Massachusetts, North Dakota, South Dakota, Utah, West Virginia and Wisconsin.

[‡]Since intercensal data are not available, it is possible that the need has been underestimated in selected counties, especially if they contained a university with a highly mobile adolescent population.

risk—remained unserved by the organized program.* In the Great Lakes area (Region V), there were almost three-quarters of a million adolescents at risk who were not served by organized clinics, and almost 200,000 of them lived in nonmetropolitan areas (not shown). In the southern states comprising Region IV, there were more than 400,000 teenagers left unserved, largely in rural areas. In eight states, there remained 100,000 or more teenagers at risk who were not served by clinic programs. These include California and New York, with 257,000 and 220,000 at risk but not served, respectively. (It should be noted, however, that each of these states served more teenagers in need—127,000 in California and 100,000 in New York—than any other state.) In no region were 50 percent of teenagers at risk served.

As may be seen in Table 5, almost two million adolescents, two-thirds of the young women not served by organized clinics, lived in 594 metropolitan counties where some services were currently provided. The 239 metropolitan counties with more than 3,000 teenagers in need, and with existing services, accounted for 82 percent of women not served in metropolitan areas.

More than three-quarters of a million adolescents who did not visit a family planning clinic lived in 1,886 nonmetropolitan counties with existing services. A total of 251 large nonmetropolitan counties can be identified with more than 1,000 teenagers in need and an existing family planning clinic; these counties contained 292,000, or 33 percent, of the adolescents not accounted for by the organized delivery system.

The 592 counties with no family plan-

ning services were mostly small and nonmetropolitan; however, 12 metropolitan and eight nonmetropolitan counties with more than 1,000 adolescents in need were included in those 592. About 123,000 teenagers lived in the 556 nonmetropolitan counties with no family planning services; many of these counties were sparsely populated—183 contained fewer than 100 adolescents in need.

Program Characteristics

The wide range in the proportions of adolescents at risk provided with contraceptive services in the various counties suggests that some states and communities may be more responsive to the needs of sexually active adolescents than others. In order to explain these differences, several factors have been examined: availability of contraceptive services to low- and marginal-income women at risk; types of provider agencies; number of clinic locations related to number in need; legal barriers to services for adolescents at the state level. Since the objectives of the study were quantitative—to determine how many teenagers were and were not being served by family planning programs—no qualitative measures, such as the existence of specialized teen sessions, were included.

Analysis of the survey data suggests that the principal determinant of a program's success in serving adolescents is its success in serving large numbers of low- and marginal-income adult women in need. The Spearman rank correlation coefficient between the percentage of teenagers served by organized programs in counties and the percentage of all low- and marginal-income adult women in need served was extraordinarily high, .901. That is, 81 percent of the variance

Table 5. Distribution of counties and of women aged 15–19 at risk and not served by organized programs,* by metropolitan status and number of women at risk, 1975

No. at risk	Total		Metro		Nonmetro	
	Counties	Women not served (000s)	Counties	Women not served (000s)	Counties	Women not served (000s)
All counties	**3,072**	**2,907**	**630**	**2,023**	**2,442**	**884**
Counties with services						
Total	2,480	2,747	594	1,986	1,886	761
≥20,000	22	592	22	592	0	0
10,000–19,999	51	451	51	451	0	0
5,000–9,999	85	400	84	396	1	4
3,000–4,999	87	234	82	221	5	13
2,000–2,999	106	192	73	130	33	62
1,000–1,999	332	340	120	127	212	213
500–999	563	295	101	56	462	239
300–499	499	143	31	9	468	134
100–299	648	96	29	4	619	92
<100	87	4	1	†	86	4
Counties without services						
Total	592	160	36	37	556	123
≥20,000	0	0	0	0	0	0
10,000–19,999	0	0	0	0	0	0
5,000–9,999	1	5	1	5	0	0
3,000–4,999	0	0	0	0	0	0
2,000–2,999	4	10	3	8	1	2
1,000–1,999	15	22	8	12	7	10
500–999	55	38	13	9	42	29
300–499	78	30	4	2	74	28
100–299	255	45	6	1	249	44
<100	184	10	1	†	183	10

*Approximately 1.2 million of the women not served by organized programs visited private physicians for contraceptive care in 1975, but their distribution is unknown.

†Fewer than 500 women.

in the proportion of teenagers at risk who were served by clinics is explained by the variation in the proportion of low- and marginal-income women in need who were served.

At the same time, high levels of adolescent services are directly associated with the number of clinic locations and the diversity of the delivery network. As Table 6 shows, in counties with more than 5,000 adolescents at risk per clinic site, only 12 percent were served; in counties with fewer than 1,000 at risk per site, 35 percent or more were served.

Similarly, the greater the number of *types* of providers, the more adolescents who are served (see Table 7). Thus, in counties with only one type of provider (typically a health department), only 24 percent of teenagers at risk were served, compared to 38 percent in counties with four types of providers.

Table 6. Number and percentage distribution of counties and of women aged 15–19 at risk and not served, and percent of total at risk served and not served by clinic programs, according to number at risk per clinic site, 1975

No. at risk per clinic site	Counties		Women aged 15–19					
			At risk		Not served		% of total at risk	
	No.	%	No. (000s)	%	No. (000s)	%	Served	Not served
Total	3,072	100	4,076	100	2,907	100	29	71
*	592	19	160	4	160	6	0	100
†	57	2	39	1	36	1	7	93
≥ 5,000	14	1	102	2	90	3	12	88
3,000–4,999	25	1	166	4	138	5	17	83
1,000–2,999	349	11	1,858	46	1,363	47	27	73
500–999	568	18	1,047	26	672	23	36	64
300–499	541	18	408	10	255	9	37	63
100–299	806	26	282	7	184	6	35	65
1–99	120	4	14	‡	9	‡	38	62

*No clinic sites.   †Patients served outside of resident county.   ‡<0.5 percent.

Table 7. Number and percentage distribution of counties and of women aged 15–19 at risk, and percent of women at risk served and not served by clinic programs, by type of delivery system, 1975

Type of delivery system	Counties		Women aged 15–19					
			At risk		Not served		% of total at risk	
	No.	%	No. (000s)	%	No. (000s)	%	Served	Not served
Total	3,072	100	4,076	100	2,907	100	29	71
No agencies	592	19	160	4	160	6	0	100
Single agency	2,142	70	1,780	44	1,354	46	24	76
Multiagency	338	11	2,136	52	1,393	48	35	65
Two types	241	8	759	18	517	18	32	68
Three types	57	2	492	12	323	11	34	66
Four types	40	1	885	22	553	19	38	62

The relative consistency in the proportion of the total case load aged 15-19 is shown in Table 8; the case load ranged from 21 percent (in West Virginia) to 38 percent (in Oregon), but most states were close to the national level of 30 percent. Within the 15-19 age group, the proportion aged 17 or younger appeared to make a difference in the proportion of teenagers served, at least at the state level.* In the nation as a whole, 38 percent of the teenage patients were aged 17 or under. Among the states most 'successful' in serving those in need (i.e., serving more than 30 percent of those at risk), 15

*The age distribution of patients under 18 and 18-19 was not available at the county level.

Table 8. Percent of total patients aged 15–19 and percent of 15–19-year-old patients under 18 and 18–19, by state, 1975

State	Patients aged 15–19			State	Patients aged 15–19		
	% of total patients	% distribution			% of total patients	% distribution	
		<18	18-19			<18	18-19
U.S. total	**30**	**38**	**62**	Missouri	35	39	61
				Montana	29	34	66
Alabama	28	42	58	Nebraska	34	34	66
Alaska	31	45	55	Nevada	31	37	63
Arizona	28	35	65	New Hampshire	34	37	63
Arkansas	29	43	57				
California	30	39	61	New Jersey	32	35	65
Colorado	28	37	63	New Mexico	23	34	66
Connecticut	36	36	64	New York	27	35	65
Delaware	35	41	59	North Carolina	28	40	60
D.C.	28	36	64	North Dakota	26	17	83
Florida	33	43	57	Ohio	35	36	64
				Oklahoma	26	32	68
Georgia	30	46	54	Oregon	38	44	56
Hawaii	31	34	66	Pennsylvania	30	35	65
Idaho	35	41	59	Rhode Island	23	23	77
Illinois	33	40	60				
Indiana	34	32	68	South Carolina	31	44	56
Iowa	37	36	64	South Dakota	26	22	78
Kansas	30	31	69	Tennessee	32	42	58
Kentucky	26	37	63	Texas	23	34	66
Louisiana	25	42	58	Utah	37	22	78
Maine	32	40	60	Vermont	29	41	59
				Virginia	31	48	52
Maryland	29	44	56	Washington	36	39	61
Massachusetts	29	29	71	West Virginia	21	27	73
Michigan	37	40	60	Wisconsin	27	29	71
Minnesota	37	33	67	Wyoming	29	36	64
Mississippi	29	43	57				

had case loads of adolescents under 18 exceeding the U.S. average, while only seven of the less successful states reached that level.

The percentage of adolescents at risk who were served by clinics varied directly with age, as Table 9 shows. Thirty-three percent of the 18-19-year-olds at risk were served, compared with nine percent of the 15-year-olds and only 3-4 percent of the 13- and 14-year-olds. More than half of the adolescents in need who were not served were aged 17 or younger, and because of their youth,

they may have encountered greater problems in gaining access to contraceptive services than did older adolescents.

While the presence or absence of state policies regarding parental consent were not highly related to successful state programs, this factor did seem to have a bearing on the proportion of adolescent patients who were aged 17 or younger. Of the 26 states that had laws affirming the right of minors to consent to their own family planning services (not shown), 17 had a higher proportion of patients under age 18 than the U.S. aver-

Table 9. Number of women under age 20 at risk, and number and percent served and not served by clinic programs, according to age, 1975

Age	No. at risk	Served		Not served	
		No.	%	No.	%
<15	375	13	3	362	97
13	117	3	3	114	97
14	258	10	4	248	96
15–19	4,076	1,175	29	2,907*	71
15	385	37	9	351*	91
16–17	1,472	405	28	1,067	72
18–19	2,219	733	33	1,489*	67

*Number not served does not equal number at risk minus number served in organized programs because in 28 counties, the number of adolescents served appears to exceed the number of adolescents at risk.

age; in only five states that did not have such affirmative laws were more than 38 percent of the adolescent patients under age 18.

Adolescent Abortion Services

Although the primary aim of the study was to document the need for contraceptive services among teenagers, and to identify the family planning service pattern in each state and county, the availability of abortion services to meet adolescent needs was also examined. About one-third of the one million legal abortions occurring in the United States in 1975 were obtained by teenagers,[9] and this proportion did not vary widely among states. That is, no matter how many, or how few, abortions were provided, the percentage of abortions obtained by teenagers was fairly constant, ranging from 22 percent (in Hawaii) to 41 percent (in Nebraska and Kansas).

A more important measure of utilization is the age-specific rate of abortions obtained per 1,000 women. The adoles-

cent abortion rate, 32 per 1,000 women aged 15-19, compares to a rate of 19 per 1,000 women aged 20-44, indicating the importance of legal abortion for reducing unintended childbearing among teenagers. State abortion rates varied substantially, from just one abortion per 1,000 women aged 15-19 in Mississippi to 57 per 1,000 in California. Ratios of abortions per 1,000 live births show similar variations by state.

Since adolescent behavior is not likely to differ radically from state to state, the most likely explanation for such enormous differences in abortion rates and ratios must be availability. Because of the concentration of abortion services in one or two large metropolitan areas in most states, and the difficulties experienced by teenagers in traveling outside of their home communities to obtain abortions, differences at the local level are even more striking. It has been estimated that as many as 138,000 teenage women in need of abortions were unable to obtain them in 1975, probably a conservative figure considering that approximately 40-45 percent of the 582,000 live births experienced by teenagers in that year were unintended.[10]

Implications

This study shows that in most parts of the nation, there are family planning clinics to which adolescents can go for contraceptive services, and adolescents will use contraception—and choose the most effective methods—when the services are made available. It is doubtful whether any other preventive health program reaches more than one million adolescent patients in a 12-month period, of whom at least one-half million are new enrollees.

During this research, it became clear that adolescents are willing to accept services from agencies providing care for women of all ages. There are few agencies with exclusively teen programs. Of the 2,494 direct provider agencies identified, only six percent had a patient population more than half of which was aged 15-19; fewer than one percent served a case load with 90 percent or more teenagers. At the same time, virtually every family planning agency served some adolescents. Public health agencies appeared to carry a large share of the adolescent case load; in fact, five of the 10 agencies with the largest volume of teenage patients were local health departments (of the remainder, four were Planned Parenthood affiliates and one was a poverty program).

The study shows that most of the teenagers not currently served by organized family planning clinics live in or near places with programs that could be expanded to accommodate them, and the remainder—a small number—live in communities which probably contain a potential family planning clinic site, such as a hospital.

Creation of a new delivery system to provide adolescents with contraceptive services does not appear to be required. However, the current system which serves adolescents and older women with almost equal success (or lack of success) needs additional support if it is to develop the capacity to care for the additional young women who need and want family planning services.

Whether or not adolescents *want* specialized clinic sessions just for people their age has not been addressed in this research. However, a recent assessment of the need for improving services for adolescents suggests that teenagers are more interested in the quality of care than in the setting.[11] That study reported

that adolescent patients were concerned primarily about waiting time in clinics, confidentiality and convenience in scheduling and location. Only the very young patients (15 or under) wanted specialized care and counseling.

The AGI study shows that the number of clinic locations is an important factor in serving the population in need, regardless of age. For teenagers, access may be a relatively more severe problem, especially in suburban areas with little public transportation. A large number of the most underserved counties are in the outer rings of metropolitan areas, where few public health facilities exist and community recognition or acceptance of the need for services is limited.

Many family planning provider agencies already operate more than one clinic. Much less effort is required of an existing provider agency to offer family planning services in a new location than to organize a new agency to deliver such services. Opening new clinic locations (and possibly closing or relocating some existing ones) appears to be a first order of business in order to meet the need in counties with inadequate service networks. In other counties, expansion of services for adolescents can be accomplished by increasing clinic staffs and the number of sessions and by adding an outreach component. Simply scheduling clinic sessions during more convenient hours could also increase utilization.

The 592 counties which, in 1975, had no family planning programs should receive priority attention from program planners interested in reaching teenagers with contraceptive services. Although many of these counties are remote and rural, with small numbers of teenagers at risk, 153 of them each have 300 or more young women at risk, a number sufficient to warrant consideration of the initiation of family planning services. Altogether, these 153 counties contain 106,300 teenagers and 203,300 older low- and marginal-income women at risk of unintended pregnancy. Although no programs exist, there are potential providers: In all but 21 of the counties, there are hospitals—a total of 200 of them, including 75 public institutions. More than half the priority counties are in the Midwest, heavily concentrated in Illinois and Indiana.

Priority should also be given to those counties with large numbers of teenagers at risk and few served. There are 106 counties with 300,000 teenagers at risk who remain unserved, and only 18,000 teenagers who are served. Services are provided primarily by one agency, usually a health department. However, all but five of the counties have non-Catholic general hospitals that are not involved in family planning. Of the 270 such hospitals, 46 are public.

Many hospitals do not perceive or acknowledge that they may be potential sites for organized family planning clinics. They require assistance from another agency to initiate a program. Such an agency may be located within the same county as the hospital, or it may be situated outside. In many areas, Planned Parenthood affiliates and health departments use local hospital outpatient facilities as clinic sites, or conduct postpartum recruitment in maternity wards.

Agencies capable of operating clinics across county lines should be invited to help provide services where local agencies cannot or will not do so. For example, Planned Parenthood affiliates operate without geographic restrictions or catchment areas. State health departments usually have the authority to stimulate local health departments to initiate and expand programs, while nonprofit statewide coordinating councils have, as a primary function, the identification of underserved areas and the allocation of funds for equalizing access to family planning services. Almost every state has some variant of a lead agency which could take the initiative in expanding the delivery network for adolescents and for low- and marginal-income women.

Private physicians can participate even more fully than they now do in the delivery network. More of them could staff clinics or join organized referral programs.

The cost of adding the capacity to clinic programs to serve one-half million additional adolescents each year has been estimated at $35 million for 1979, $74 million for 1980 and $118 million for 1981.[12] Given the well-documented long-term adverse consequences of an unintended birth for the teenage mother and her baby, the cost to individuals, and to society, of *not* adding this capacity is enormous.

Access to birth control is not, of course, a panacea for unintended adolescent pregnancy. Women of all ages will continue to experience failure as long as methods remain as imperfect as they are. Adolescents will continue to conceive if they do not understand the risk of conception from unprotected intercourse. Some teenagers (even as some adults) will, with full knowledge of the risks, take chances and have intercourse without using contraception.

Family planning clinics cannot solve all of these problems, nor can they solve such adolescent problems as lack of employment opportunities, inadequate education and alienation from society. They can, however, provide young women and men with one critical option, the choice of when in the life cycle to become a parent, an event whose timing sets the framework for many other of life's decisions. Unlike some social, educational and health programs, the family planning program is already functioning on a broad scale and requires only increased financial support to expand its current capacity to encompass the contraceptive needs of the majority of adolescents not currently being served.

References

1. The Alan Guttmacher Institute (AGI), *11 Million Teenagers: What Can Be Done About the Epidemic of Adolescent Pregnancies in the United States,* Planned Parenthood Federation of America, New York, 1976.

2. DHEW, *The Fiscal Year 1979 Budget,* Washington, D.C., Jan. 23, 1978.

3. M. Zelnik and J. F. Kantner, "Sexual and Contraceptive Experience of Young Unmarried Women in the United States, 1976 and 1971," chapter 4, above;——, "First Pregnancies to Women Aged 15-19: 1976 and 1971," chapter 5, above; L. Morris, "Estimating the Need for Family Planning Services Among Unwed Teenagers," *Family Planning Perspectives,* 6:91, 1974; and J. F. Kantner and M. Zelnik, "Contraception and Pregnancy: Experience of Young Unmarried Women in the United States," *Family Planning Perspectives,* 5:21, 1973.

4. AGI, *Data and Analyses for 1976 Revision of DHEW Five-Year Plan for Family Planning Services,* New York, 1976, Appendix E.

5. E. W. Paul, H. F. Pilpel and N. F. Wechsler, "Pregnancy, Teenagers and the Law, 1974," *Family Planning Perspectives,* 6:142, 1974.

6. National Reporting System for Family Planning Services, Annual Tables and Special Tabulations, 1975.

7. Chapter 4.

8. M. Zelnik and J. F. Kantner, "Contraceptive Patterns and Premarital Pregnancy Among Women Aged 15-19 in 1976," chapter 6, above.

9. Center for Disease Control, DHEW, *Abortion Surveillance, Annual Summary, 1975,* Atlanta, 1977.

10. National Center for Health Statistics, DHEW, "Advance Report: Final Natality Statistics, 1975," *Monthly Vital Statistics Report,* Vol. 25, No. 10, 1976; and M. Zelnik and J. F. Kantner, "The Resolution of Teenage First Pregnancies," *Family Planning Perspectives,* 6:74, 1974, Table 9.

11. Urban and Rural Systems Associates, *Improving Family Planning Services for Teenagers,* DHEW, Washington, D.C., June 1976.

12. National Family Planning Forum et. al., *Planned Births, the Future of the Family and the Quality of American Life: Towards a Comprehensive National Policy and Program,* New York, June 1977.

28

Teenagers and Pregnancy: The Law in 1979

Eve W. Paul and Harriet F. Pilpel

Since January 1976, when we last reviewed state laws and policies affecting the right of teenagers to consent for their own birth control and other reproductive health care,[1] the U.S. Supreme Court has in effect issued at least a partial bill of reproductive rights for minors. In three landmark cases—two involving abortion and one dealing with contraception—the Court has laid down a federal constitutional framework with which all future laws and regulations must comply. In so doing, the Court has rendered obsolete many of the laws we previously described that had restricted access of young people to fertility control services, and has clarified the rest. Thus, out of the old patchwork of statutes, case law, attorneys generals' opinions and administrative rulings there is finally emerging a coherent body of law based on two fundamental principles:

• the constitutional right of mature minors to obtain reproductive health services on their own consent, and

• the constitutional right of all minors to have an alternative to parental involvement in implementing their decisions about such health care.

By 1976, liberalization of state laws and reduction of the age of majority had established the right of unmarried women aged 18 or older to consent for most aspects of their own medical care in at least 45 states and the District of Columbia. In 48 states and the District, they could consent for most pregnancy-related health services, including abortion. In a number of states, however, minors still encountered obstacles to obtaining contraceptive services or terminating unwanted pregnancies without the consent of their parents.

Abortion and Parental Consent

When the Supreme Court ruled in 1973 (in *Roe* v. *Wade*[2] and *Doe* v. *Bolton*[3]) that women have a constitutional right (with the concurrence of their physicians) to obtain abortions, it left open the question of the validity of laws that required minors to secure the consent of their parents in order to obtain the procedure. A number of states enacted statutes requiring such consent for unmarried minors. These laws have been challenged in the courts on the ground that adolescent women, like adults, have a right of privacy which entitles them to decide, in consultation with their physicians, whether or not to terminate an unwanted pregnancy.

On July 1, 1976, the U.S. Supreme Court decided the cases of *Planned Parenthood of*

Central Missouri v. *Danforth* [4] and *Bellotti* v. *Baird*.[5] These decisions firmly established the principle that minors have rights—though not necessarily identical with those of adults—to access to sex-related health care. In the *Danforth* case, the Court was called upon to decide the constitutionality of a Missouri statute which required the written consent of a parent or person acting in place of a parent before an unmarried woman younger than 18 could obtain a first-trimester abortion, unless "the abortion [was] certified by a licensed physician as necessary in order to preserve the life of the mother." The Court ruled that this law was unconstitutional, because a state may not "impose a blanket provision . . . requiring the consent of a parent or person *in loco parentis* as a condition for abortion of an unmarried minor during the first 12 weeks of her pregnancy." It added that a state "does not have the constitutional authority to give a third party an absolute, and possibly arbitrary, veto over the decision of the physician and his patient to terminate the patient's pregnancy, regardless of the reason for withholding the consent."

Parental-consent statutes invalidated by the *Danforth* decision included those in Arkansas, Illinois, Indiana, Kentucky, Louisiana, Nebraska, Nevada, New Mexico, North Dakota, Ohio, Pennsylvania, South Dakota and Virginia. Some of these statutes, however, remained on the books and were not formally challenged, causing concern to physicians and others who did not realize that what the Supreme Court decides is indeed the applicable law in every state.

At the same time that it decided the *Danforth* case, the Court considered the constitutionality of a Massachusetts statute which stipulated that an abortion could not be performed on an unmarried woman under the age of 18 without the written consent of both parents (*Bellotti* v. *Baird*). The Massachusetts statute also provided, however, that if one or both parents refused, consent could be given by a judge of the Superior Court. The U.S. Supreme Court sent the case back to the Massachusetts Supreme Judicial Court for a clearer interpretation, indicating that the statute might be constitutional if it were construed in a way "that permits a mature minor capable of giving informed consent to obtain, without undue burden, an order permitting the abortion without parental consultation, and, further, permits even a minor incapable of giving informed consent to obtain an order without parental consultation where there is a showing that the abortion would be in her best interests."

When the state court gave the law a very strict interpretation, the case was appealed again all the way to the U.S. Supreme Court, and on July 2, 1979, the Court in an 8-1 decision ruled the statute unconstitutional.[6]

The eight justices did not agree on the reasons for the ruling, and two different opinions were written—one, by Justice Lewis F. Powell for himself and three other justices (Chief Justice Warren E. Burger and Justices Potter Stewart and William H. Rehnquist); the other opinion, by Justice John Paul Stevens for himself and three other justices (Justices Thurgood Marshall, William J. Brennan and Harry A. Blackmun).

The Stevens opinion was based on the principles laid down in *Danforth*: It viewed the alternative to parental consent provided in the Massachusetts law—a lawsuit initiated by the minor—as inadequate because it gave the judge who heard the case an absolute veto over the minor's decision. The judge's decision was to be based on his or her judgment of the minor's best interest, no matter how mature the minor might be, or how capable of making an informed decision. Justice Stevens further pointed out that "as a practical matter, . . . the need to commence judicial proceedings in order to obtain a legal abortion would impose a burden at least as great as, and probably greater than, that imposed on the minor child by the need to obtain the consent of a parent."

Justice Powell and the three concurring justices held that the Massachusetts statute was invalid because it violated the constitutional right of a mature minor to decide with her physician whether or not to have an abortion and because it imposed an unconstitutional requirement of parental notification in all cases. Consequently, they found the Massachusetts statute unconstitutional as well with respect to minors who are not mature, because it required parental consultation or notification in every instance, without affording the pregnant minor an opportunity to receive an independent judicial determination either that she is mature enough to consent or, if she is not, that an abortion would be in her best interest.

However, while Justice Powell decided that the Massachusetts law violated minors' rights, he made it clear that in his view the constitutional rights of children cannot be equated with those of adults, for three reasons: "the peculiar vulnerability of children; their inability to make critical decisions in an informed, mature manner; and the importance of the parental role in childrearing." In an unusual procedure, he spelled out guidelines which a state wishing to enact a constitutional parental-consent law for abortion might follow. Such a law, according to Justice Powell and the three concurring justices, would be constitutional if it gave the minor an alternative procedure in the event she could not obtain—or was unwilling to seek—parental consent. The minor would be entitled to a court or administrative proceeding to show "(1) that she is mature enough and well enough informed to make her abortion decision, in consultation with her physician, independently of her parents' wishes; or (2) that even if she is not able to make this decision independently, the desired abortion would be in her best interest." Justice Powell said that a state may require

the consent of both parents, at least when the parents are together and the minor is living at home, but that an alternative procedure must be provided; it would have to be confidential and quick enough to allow time for an abortion to be obtained. Justice Powell suggested that a state could delegate this alternative procedure to an administrative agency or officer.

Justice Byron White disagreed with the other eight justices, and found the Massachusetts law valid.

The 1979 *Bellotti* decision (*Bellotti II*) thus makes clear that the state laws which now require parental consent for abortions provided to minors are invalid. These include statutes enacted after *Danforth*, such as those in Florida, Illinois, Louisiana, Missouri and North Dakota. These statutes, designed to meet the standards set in *Danforth* and in the earlier *Bellotti* opinion, clearly fall short of the standards set in *Bellotti II*.

For example, on July 13, 1979, 11 days after *Bellotti II* was decided, a federal district court judge invalidated a Florida statute which provided that a minor seeking an abortion who could not obtain or did not wish to seek parental consent could obtain an abortion by getting permission from a court.[7] The statute was deficient in several ways under the *Bellotti II* standards. First, it allowed the judge to make the determination based on "the best interest of the minor," regardless of her maturity. Second, the statute failed to set up a judicial proceeding which would guarantee confidentiality and sufficient speed for an abortion to be obtained.

One cannot predict what the Court will finally do when presented with an actual case; a statute drawn along the lines suggested by Justice Powell could be challenged if it were shown that it failed to provide the speed and confidentiality that the Court has mandated. Barring such a showing, however, it appears likely that a statute drawn along such lines would be approved also by

Justice White and thus would be supported by five of the nine justices—a majority.

Abortion and Parental Notification

Bellotti II also invalidates statutes requiring that parents be notified in all cases before an abortion is performed on their minor daughter. A number of states and cities have such laws, many of them currently under court injunctions or temporary restraining orders. Montana and Utah require parental notification for all unmarried minors seeking abortions. In Nebraska, the law was recently changed to require all minors seeking an abortion to sign a statement certifying that they have consulted with their parents, but enforcement of that law has been enjoined.[8] A North Dakota provision, which is part of an ordinance generally restricting abortion, has also been enjoined by a federal district court.[9] In Maine, a statute that took effect September 1, 1979, requires a physician to notify the parents of an unemancipated minor before performing an abortion. A Maryland statute requires parental notification before an abortion is performed on an unmarried minor unless the physician believes the minor would suffer physical or emotional harm if her parents were informed. A Tennessee statute requires a physician or abortion facility to notify the parents of an unmarried minor two days before the abortion but permits notice to be waived if the abortion is necessary to preserve the minor's life or health. Parental notification requirements have also been included in abortion ordinances in Louisville, Kentucky, Niagara County, New York, and Akron, Ohio.[10] Enforcement of all these ordinances is currently enjoined. The Akron ordinance, which has been the model for similar laws and bills around the country, was permanently enjoined on August 22 by a federal district court on the grounds cited in *Bellotti II*.

Justice Powell and the three justices concurring with him in *Bellotti II* recognized that "there are parents who would obstruct and perhaps altogether prevent the minor's right to go to court." On the other hand, Justice Stevens's opinion, in which three other justices concurred, contained a footnote suggesting that the question of a parental-notification requirement was still open. However, it seems highly unlikely (in the light of the views those other three justices have expressed in other abortion cases) that they would approve a blanket requirement of parental notification. In other words, it is probable that six of the present members of the Supreme Court would regard an absolute requirement of parental notification as unconstitutional.*

The *Danforth* and *Bellotti* decisions have important implications for the law of medical malpractice. The Supreme Court in effect approved in *Danforth* the rule that minors sufficiently mature and intelligent to understand the nature of a medical problem and the risks and benefits of the treatment may give effective consent for abortion. More explicitly, the Court held in *Bellotti II* that states "cannot constitutionally permit disregard of the abortion decision of a minor who has been determined to be mature and fully competent to assess the implications of the choice she has made."[11] This affirmation of the mature minor rule indicates that damages cannot be assessed against a physician or other health care provider for performing an abortion on a mature minor without parental consent, since such an award would violate the minor's constitutionally established right to privacy in the same way as would a state law requiring parental consent.

---

*Chief Justice Burger and Justices Powell, Stewart, Brennan, Marshall and Blackmun. Justice Rehnquist is excluded from this group because, although he joined in the Powell opinion, he also wrote a separate concurring opinion stating his desire to reconsider the Court's ruling in the *Danforth* case.

Contraception: A Minor's Right?

A New York statute which forbade nonphysicians to distribute contraceptives to anyone under the age of 16 was declared unconstitutional with respect to "nonhazardous" (i.e., nonprescription) contraceptives by the U.S. Supreme Court in 1977 (*Carey* v. *Population Services International* [12]). However, the Court did not rule on whether minors could obtain prescription contraceptives (such as the pill or IUD) on their own, because the state of New York had conceded that physicians were not covered by the law and could prescribe such contraceptives for their minor patients of any age.

As in *Bellotti II*, the Supreme Court in *Population Services* was divided on the question of minors' rights. The plurality opinion was delivered by Justice Brennan, joined by three other justices (Stewart, Marshall and Blackmun). Justices Stevens, White and Powell concurred, but wrote three separate opinions stating their reasons.

Justice Brennan began by reaffirming the principle that minors possess constitutional rights, including the right of privacy in decisions affecting procreation. He went on to say that state restrictions inhibiting privacy rights of minors are valid only if they serve "any significant state interest . . . that is not present in the case of an adult." Since the Court had already ruled that a state may not impose a blanket prohibition, or even a blanket requirement of parental consent, on the choice of a minor to terminate her pregnancy, Justice Brennan held that a blanket prohibition against the distribution of contraceptives to minors was not permissible. A state's interests in protecting the health of the pregnant minor and in protecting potential life, he said, are clearly more involved in the decision to have an abortion than in the decision to use a nonhazardous contraceptive.

New York State argued that significant state interests were served by restricting minors' access to nonprescription contraceptives, because their free availability would lead to increased sexual activity among the young, in violation of New York's policy to discourage such behavior. While he did not question the assumption that the state may regulate the sexual behavior of minors, Justice Brennan said it would be unreasonable if the state "prescribed pregnancy and the birth of an unwanted child (or the physical and psychological dangers of an abortion) as punishment for fornication." Moreover, New York State had conceded that "there is no evidence that teenage extramarital sexual activity increases in proportion to the availability of contraceptives."

Justice Stevens did not agree that the Constitution provides the same measure of protection to the minor's right to use contraceptives as to the pregnant woman's right to obtain an abortion. The options available to the already pregnant minor, he wrote, are fundamentally different from those available to the nonpregnant minor. "The former must bear a child unless she aborts," he said, "but persons in the latter category can and generally will avoid childbearing by abstention." New York State had contended that the law had symbolic importance in that it communicated disapproval of adolescent sexual activity. Justice Stevens concluded that "an attempt to persuade by inflicting harm on the listener is an unacceptable means of conveying a message that is otherwise legitimate. . . . It is as though a state decided to dramatize its disapproval of motorcycles by forbidding the use of safety helmets."

Justice White based his concurrence in the decision on New York State's failure to demonstrate that prohibiting the distribution of contraceptives to minors deterred them from having sexual intercourse. Justice Powell concurred because, in his view, the statute infringed the privacy interests of married females between the ages of 14 and 16 and the privacy interests of parents who wished to distribute contraceptives to their children.

Contraception and Parental Consent

No state has enacted a statute specifically requiring parental consent for contraception. In a number of states (such as Indiana and Texas), attempts have been made to persuade the courts to construe ambiguously worded statutes that enable *some* minors to consent for their own medical care as barring other minors from doing so. Moreover, as with abortion, physicians and other health care providers have been concerned about remnants of an old common law rule under which providing medical services without parental consent might constitute malpractice or even, under a still older theory, assault and battery.

The *Population Services* case did not deal directly with the issue of parental consent or of prescription contraceptives. However, it seems to follow from the Supreme Court's decisions in the *Danforth, Bellotti* and *Population Services* cases that at least a majority of the present Supreme Court justices would agree that mature minors have a constitutional right to obtain prescription as well as nonprescription contraceptives on their own consent, and that any absolute requirement of parental consent or notification with reference to the prescribing of contraceptives for minors of any age would be unconstitutional.

A number of considerations support this conclusion. In the first place, since it has been shown that a blanket requirement of parental consent or notification for prescribed contraceptives would not deter young people from sexual activity, no "significant state interest" would be served. The Supreme Court has already rejected the idea that pregnancy may be used as "punishment" for fornication. Additionally, the risks attached to the use of prescription contraceptives are demonstrably lower than those related to no use of birth control.[13]

This means that, as with abortion, neither minors nor their parents should be able, in the absence of negligence, to successfully sue a physician or other health services provider for having rendered medical contraceptive services to a mature minor without parental consent. This principle, which had been explicitly affirmed by 30 states and the District of Columbia as early as October 1976,[14] has now been endorsed by the Supreme Court, whose decisions apply everywhere in the nation. The right of a 16-year-old woman to obtain contraceptive services from a county clinic without parental consent has been upheld in West Virginia, one of the 20 states that had not previously upheld such a right.[15]

Federal law has already recognized the right to contraceptive services of minors eligible under the Medicaid and AFDC federal assistance programs. In 1976, the Supreme Court affirmed a decision of a three-judge federal district court invalidating Utah regulations which required parental consent for family planning services on the ground that the regulations were inconsistent with the federal Social Security Act.[16] Since then, the Court has recognized the constitutional rights of minors with reference to sex-related health services in the decisions we have discussed above.

Contraception and Parental Notification

The Supreme Court decision in *Bellotti II* has made unconstitutional all statutes requiring that parents be notified in every case before an abortion is performed on their minor daughters. The reasoning behind this ruling suggests that it is equally applicable to contraception. There are lawsuits pending in at least three states—Michigan, Ohio and Hawaii—brought by parents who claim it is their right to be notified before contraceptives are prescribed for their minor daughters. In the Michigan case, a district court judge ruled in 1977 that the parents had a constitutional right to be notified in every case by a county-operated and state-funded family planning clinic which dispensed contraceptives to their children. The judge's decision was sent back to him by the court of appeals for reconsideration in light of the Supreme Court's *Population Services* decision. The district court judge again, however, held for the parents, and the county family planning center again appealed to the court of appeals.[17] *Bellotti II* provides a firm basis for the center's argument that parental notification cannot constitutionally be required in all cases.

The Mature Minor and Informed Consent

Since the U. S. Supreme Court and the federal courts have said that mature minors may obtain abortions (and, by implication, medically prescribed contraceptives) on their own consent, the determination of what makes a minor mature is very important.

The legal concept of the mature minor is closely related to the concept of informed consent. Clinicians are legally required to inform all patients of the risks and benefits involved, and obtain their consent, before beginning any type of medical treatment.[18] No person can give informed consent unless he or she is sufficiently intelligent and mature to understand the situation and the explanation. A minor who can understand the nature and consequences of a medical procedure that is for the minor's benefit, and can weigh alternatives to the procedure, is considered (for these purposes) mature. It has been widely accepted in the family planning field that medical professionals or trained counselors can determine maturity through their discussion with the minor patient.

The Powell opinion in *Bellotti II* states that if the maturity of a minor seeking an abortion is in question, and if the minor refuses to seek or cannot get parental consent, the state may require that a court or administrative agency determine maturity. The reason, according to Justice Powell, is "the unique nature of the abortion decision, especially when made by a

minor." In areas other than abortion, Justice Powell said, the state "generally may resort to objective, though inevitably arbitrary, criteria such as age limits, marital status, or membership in the armed forces for lifting some or all of the legal disabilities of minority."

It is not clear whether prescription contraception, which we believe is analogous to abortion in that it affects the minor's ability to control her fertility, would be included under this rubric. It seems likely that the Court would agree that contraception, like abortion, is a special situation. It is most unlikely, however, that a majority of the present justices would uphold a requirement that every minor seeking medical contraception must go through a court proceeding. Difficult as such a procedure might be for the already pregnant minor, it would be totally impractical for the literally millions of sexually active teenagers who seek prescription contraceptives.

The courts are likely to seek criteria for the determination of maturity in the context of contraception that are less arbitrary than age limits, but more practical than judicial proceedings. The physician prescribing a contraceptive, we believe, is one of the persons most qualified to determine the maturity of the individual minor. Justice Powell in *Bellotti II* explicitly refused to entrust this responsibility to physicians with respect to abortion, apparently because of the minor's possible inability to recognize "ethical, qualified physicians" and because of evidence that, at some abortion clinics, the physician has little if any prior contact with the minor. One alternative that courts may approve for medical contraception and, indeed, for abortion is the delegation of the determination of maturity as well as counseling to trained professionals, possibly following state guidelines. This alternative has the advantage of assuring not only that the minor will be giving informed consent but also that the medical professional will be able to check the medical history and background of the minor.

The Immature Minor

The Supreme Court in *Bellotti I* and Justice Powell's opinion in *Bellotti II* made it clear that even a minor lacking the maturity necessary to decide to have an abortion must be able to obtain the procedure without parental involvement if a court decides that the abortion is in her best interest. The Court recognized that a youngster not mature enough to consent to an abortion is obviously not old enough to have a baby—the only alternative. The need for medical contraception of a minor believed to be too immature to give informed consent may appear to be somewhat less compelling, since the *Population Services* case affirmed the right of all minors—irrespective of level of maturity—to obtain nonprescription contraceptives on their own consent. Nevertheless, the availability of medical methods to young teenagers may be extremely important. Young adolescents have been shown to be at the highest risk of incurring an unintended pregnancy soon after beginning sexual activity— precisely because they are least likely to use contraception, especially the most effective medical methods.[19] From a physiological and socioeconomic viewpoint, such pregnancies are most devastating to these young teens.[20] Young teenagers overwhelmingly opt for the pill when they have the opportunity, apparently because they are unwilling to carry condoms, diaphragms or foam, which are evidence of premeditation of sex and more easily discoverable by parents. When the pill is not available, they are likely to "take a chance" or to depend on unreliable methods such as withdrawal. Here, as with abortion, a requirement of parental consent or notification may not be in the young person's best interest. Although most young teenagers apparently share their decision to seek contraceptive help with their parents, there are many who feel that they cannot do so.[21] A requirement of parental consent or notification clearly is not in the best interest of such young people. However, a request for a prescription contraceptive by an immature minor does require specialized counseling to assure that the young patient knows how to use the prescribed method effectively, knows how to recognize any method-related complications that may ensue, and understands the importance of coming promptly for treatment of any such complications. In cases where parental consent is impractical, the minor could be asked to involve another, more understanding family member (such as an aunt or older sister) who is in close contact with the patient, or some other responsible adult (such as a teacher, clergyman or group leader). Such involvement may well help to reinforce both the young person's motivation to use a method consistently and her awareness of untoward side effects, and be an important source of information for the clinician about personal or family history which may contraindicate use of one or another method.

Providers and the Law

Agencies providing medical contraceptive services that receive funds under Title XX (Social Services) and under Title XIX (Medicaid) of the Social Security Act are required to provide such services to eligible persons, including "minors who can be considered to be sexually active," without regard to age or marital status.

The most recent statement of congressional policy in this area is the Adolescent Pregnancies Act, which took effect November 10, 1978.[22] The Act opens with a summary of congressional committee findings that adolescents are at especially high risk of unwanted pregnancy. It notes that "pregnancy and childbirth among adolescents, particularly young adolescents, often result in severe adverse health, social, and economic consequences." One of the stated purposes of the statute is "to expand and improve the availability of, and access to, needed comprehensive community services which assist in preventing unwanted initial and repeat pregnancies among adolescents," as well as to assist those adolescents who are already pregnant or parents.

The Secretary of Health, Education and Welfare is authorized to make grants for the provision of adolescent services. Grant applications must contain "assurances that unemancipated minors requesting services . . . will be encouraged, whenever feasible, to consult with their parents with respect to such services." The clear implication of this provision is that parental consultation may not be required as a condition of rendering service. However, the final regulations issued by the Secretary effective July 23, 1979, state that "an applicant may not condition the provision of services on [parental] consultation or on parental notification, unless state law requires it to do so."[23] This last clause is totally unjustified by the legislative history, and its effect may well be contrary to the Secretary's explanation that the regulations are intended to be "consistent with the purpose of the Act, to increase access by adolescents to such services." Indeed, the clause appears vulnerable to challenge as inconsistent with the purpose of the Act it is supposed to implement. Furthermore, under the Supremacy Clause of the Constitution, federal law automatically supersedes any contrary state law.[24]

Elsewhere in the new regulations, DHEW recognizes the importance of confidentiality in serving adolescents. Thus, when eligible young people are unable to pay for services without financial assistance from their parents or legal guardians, and are unwilling to seek that assistance, DHEW grantees are required to provide services gratis, regardless of the annual income of the parents or guardians. The new regulations provide that all personal data obtained by the project staff about patients shall be held confidential. Some states, like New York and California, have statutes which require that family planning services be provided to *all* needy persons, regardless of age or parental consent.[25]

Of course, a private provider of health care has much greater leeway than a public health care provider in determining whether to serve minors without parental consent or consultation. In the absence of a specifically applicable statute, the private provider that receives no public funds is under no obligation to respect either the constitutional right of a minor to receive sex-related health services on her own consent or any right alleged by a parent to be notified before such services are rendered to his or her minor daughter.

Voluntary Sterilization of Minors

Few adolescents request sterilization, except in the unusual cases where any pregnancy would endanger their health or when they are carriers of a serious hereditary disease. However, there are women who have as many children as they want before they are 21. These women may no longer obtain sterilizations from federally funded projects or programs, because of DHEW regulations that took effect February 6, 1979. These regulations—which also prohibit the sterilization of mentally incompetent persons, and set up numerous safeguards for voluntary sterilization of mentally competent individuals aged 21 and older—were promulgated to stem sterilization abuse, the subject of a six-year public and legal controversy. Although most states have reduced the age of majority to 18, DHEW has imposed 21 years as the minimum age at which sterilizations can be obtained from a federally funded project. The regulations make no exception for medically necessary procedures.

Even when there is no federal funding, the right of minors to consent for sterilization procedures remains unclear. Nine states—Arkansas, Colorado, Georgia, North Carolina, Oklahoma, Rhode Island, Tennessee, Virginia and West Virginia—and New York City have minimum age requirements for sterilization. Even with parental consent, sterilization cannot be performed on a person under the age limit. In addition, statutes enabling minors to consent to birth control and/or medical services in California, Kentucky, Maryland, Nebraska and the District of Columbia specifically exclude sterilization. The Massachusetts medical care statute permits only married, widowed or divorced minors to consent to sterilizations.

Since voluntary sterilization is generally irreversible, and because female sterilization may be a relatively major surgical procedure, courts are likely to treat it differently from contraceptive services and abortion. It is much more likely that a requirement of minimum age or of parental consent or notification would be sustained for sterilization than for contraceptive services or abortion. In addition, we believe that a challenge to federal regulations prohibiting federally funded sterilization for persons under 21 would probably succeed with respect to those procedures that are medically necessary, but the outcome of a suit involving elective procedures is unclear.

Conclusions

In a case which preceded the landmark decisions discussed in this article, and in a different context, the Supreme Court stated that "neither the 14th Amendment nor the Bill of Rights is for adults alone."[26] Yet, until recently, the Court addressed the subject of minors' rights only sporadically and inconclusively. However, in the last decade, the Court has made it clear that minors do have constitutional rights; and in the past four years, the Court has extended these rights from the areas of constitutional safeguards against abuses in the criminal justice system

and against arbitrary actions by school authorities to protection of minors' rights to obtain sex-related health services such as contraception and abortion. In *Danforth* and *Bellotti*, it was ruled that mature minors have a right to obtain an abortion on their own consent, and that immature minors seeking abortion must be provided with a swift and confidential alternative to parental involvement. In the *Population Services* decision, the Court established that minors of any age have a right to purchase nonprescription contraceptives. It follows from *Bellotti* and *Danforth* that mature minors also have the right to obtain medically prescribed contraceptives on their own consent. The right of an immature minor to obtain prescribed contraceptives without parental involvement is a more complex and sensitive issue. It would seem to call for a test similar to the one laid down in *Bellotti II*—namely, a determination of whether the provision of such contraception would be in the young person's best interest. It seems highly unlikely, however—as well as impractical and unworkable—that a court or administrative agency would have to be involved in procedures to determine the maturity of a minor seeking medically prescribed contraception without parental consent, or, if the minor is deemed immature, in procedures to determine whether such a prescription is in her best interest. The attending physician may well be the best judge of a minor's maturity. When the physician believes that mature judgment may be lacking, intensive counseling of the young person and involvement of an adult closely connected with the minor or of at least two adults in the "helping professions" may be in order to ensure that the minor's interests are protected.

As a result of these Supreme Court rulings, physicians and other health care providers can render sex-related medical services to minors mature enough to give informed consent (and can give nonprescription contraceptives to any minor) without fear of being successfully sued for damages by the young patient or her parents because parental consent was not obtained. Nor can such suits be successful if abortion services or prescription contraceptives are provided without parental involvement to an immature minor if it is determined that such provision is in the young person's best interest.

Finally, it should be emphasized that the Powell opinion in *Bellotti II* that states may require parental consent for abortion if a swift and confidential alternative is available does *not* mean that states *must* institute parental-consent procedures of any kind. A number of states have instituted policies, and others no doubt will do so, which permit minors to make their own decisions about sex-related medical care, and have provided safeguards or assistance to minors which do not include *any* requirement of parental consent.

It has taken a long time for the law to recognize the rights of young people, and there remain many grey areas, even in this internationally recognized Year of the Child. There appears, however, to be something irresistible in the growth of human freedom, whatever temporary setbacks it may encounter. We may hope that freedom of reproductive choice will in the not too distant future be secured for all Americans, of whatever age and economic status.

References

1. E. W. Paul, H. F. Pilpel and N. F. Wechsler, "Pregnancy, Teenagers and the Law, 1976," *Family Planning Perspectives*, 8:16, 1976.

2. 410 U.S. 113.

3. 410 U.S. 179.

4. 428 U.S. 52.

5. 428 U.S. 132.

6. 99 S. Ct. 3035.

7. *Jones* v. *Smith*, Case No. 79–6403–CIV–SMA, U.S.D. Ct. S.D. Fla. (July 13, 1979).

8. *Women's Services* v.*Thone*, Case No. C.V. 79–L–85, U.S.D. Ct. Neb. (Dec. 29, 1978).

9. *Leigh* v. *Olson*, Civ. No. A3–79–78, U.S.D. Ct. N.D. (July 9, 1979).

10. *Wolfe* v. *McConnell*, Case No. 78 CI 0710, Jefferson Circuit Ct., Div. 15, Ky. (Aug. 31, 1978); *Susan B.* v. *Clifford*, Case No. CIV–78–823, U.S.D. Ct. W.D. N.Y. (Dec. 15, 1978); *Akron Center for Reproductive Health* v. *City of Akron*, C78–155A, U.S.D. Ct. N.D. Ohio (Aug. 22, 1979).

11. 99 S. Ct. 3035.

12. 431 U.S. 678.

13. C. Tietze and S. Lewit, "Life Risks Associated with Reversible Methods of Fertility Regulation," *International Journal of Gynaecology and Obstetrics*, 16:456, 1979.

14. The Alan Guttmacher Institute, *Family Planning and Abortion: An Analysis of Laws and Policies in the United States*, U.S. Government Printing Office, Washington, D.C. (GPO), 1979.

15. *Doe* v. *Pickett*, Case No. 79–3222H, U.S.D. Ct. S.D. W. Va. (Sept. 6, 1979).

16. *T. H.* v. *Jones*, 425 F. Supp. 873 (D. Utah 1975), aff 'd in part 425 U.S. 986.

17. *Doe* v. *Irwin*, 428 F. Supp. 1198 (W.D. Mich. 1977), vacated and remanded, 559 F.2d 1219 (6th Cir.), aff 'd on remand, 441 F. Supp. 1247 (W.D. Mich. 1977).

18. E. W. Paul and G. Scofield, "Informed Consent for Fertility Control Services," *Family Planning Perspectives*, 11:159, 1979.

19. L. S. Zabin, J. F. Kantner and M. Zelnik, "The Risk of Adolescent Pregnancy in the First Months of Intercourse," chapter 8, above.

20. W. Baldwin and V. Cain, *Adolescent Pregnancy and Childbearing*, GPO, 1980 (forthcoming).

21. A. Torres, "Does Your Mother Know . . . ?" *Family Planning Perspectives*, 10:280, 1978.

22. Title VI of Pub. L. No. 95–626 (42 U.S.C. 300a–21 et seq.).

23. *Federal Register*, 44:43226, 1979.

24. U.S.Const. VI, §2.

25. N.Y. Soc. Serv. Law §131-e and D.S.S. Reg. §386.16; Cal. Welf. and Inst. Code §10053.2.

26. In re Gault, 387 U.S. 1, 13 (1967).

Contributors

Linda Ambrose is senior communications specialist at Aetna Life & Casualty, Hartford, Connecticut.

Kathleen A. Arnold is a family-planning nurse-practitioner with the St. Paul Maternal and Infant Care Project, St. Paul-Ramsey Hospital, St. Paul, Minnesota.

Wendy Baldwin is chief of the Social and Behavioral Sciences Branch of the Center for Population Research, National Institute of Child Health and Human Development, U.S. Department of Health and Human Services, Bethesda, Maryland.

Beth Berkov is a demographic analyst with the California State Department of Health, San Francisco.

Virginia S. Cain is a psychologist in the Social and Behavioral Sciences Branch of the Center for Population Research, National Institute of Child Health and Human Development, U.S. Department of Health and Human Services, Bethesda, Maryland.

Steven B. Caldwell is assistant professor of sociology at Cornell University and is a consultant with The Urban Institute, Washington, D.C.

Josefina J. Card is a research scientist at the American Institutes for Research, Palo Alto, California.

Albert G. Crawford is a research associate at the Center for Research on the Acts of Man, Philadelphia.

Phillips Cutright is professor of sociology at Indiana University, Bloomington.

Joy G. Dryfoos is a fellow with The Alan Guttmacher Institute, New York City.

Laura E. Edwards is director of the St. Paul Maternal and Infant Care Project, St. Paul-Ramsey Hospital, St. Paul, Minnesota, and assistant professor of obstetrics and gynecology at the University of Minnesota.

Jerome R. Evans is children's services coordinator of mental health services for the county of Ventura, California.

David J. Finkel is a research associate in the department of sociology/anthropology at Fordham University, New York City.

Madelon Lubin Finkel is a research associate in the Department of Public Health, The New York Hospital-Cornell Medical Center, New York City.

Frank F. Furstenberg, Jr., is professor of sociology at the University of Pennsylvania.

Erick Y. Hakanson is chairman of the department of obstetrics and gynecology at St. Paul-Ramsey Hospital and professor of obstetrics and gynecology at the University of Minnesota.

Toni Heisler is a former planning associate with The Alan Guttmacher Institute.

John F. Kantner is professor and chairman of the department of population dynamics at The Johns Hopkins University School of Hygiene and Public Health, Baltimore.

James McCarthy is assistant professor of population dynamics at The Johns Hopkins University School of Hygiene and Public Health, Baltimore.

Jane Menken is professor of sociology and assistant director of the Office of Population Research at Princeton University.

Warren B. Miller is principal research scientist at the American Institutes for Research, Palo Alto, California.

Kristin A. Moore is a research associate with the Program of Research on Women and Family Policy of The Urban Institute, Washington, D.C.

Maurice J. Moore is chief of the Fertility Statistics Branch of the Population Division, U.S. Bureau of the Census.

Martin O'Connell is a statistician with the Fertility Statistics Branch of the Population Division, U.S. Bureau of the Census.

Eve W. Paul is vice president for legal affairs of the Planned Parenthood Federation of America, Inc., New York City.

Harriet F. Pilpel is a senior partner in the law firm of Greenbaum, Wolff and Ernst, and is general counsel to the Planned Parenthood Federation of America, Inc., New York City.

Harriet B. Presser is professor of sociology at the University of Maryland, College Park.

Paul A. Reichelt is associate professor at the College of Nursing of the University of Illinois and Medical Center, Chicago.

Georgiana Selstad is a member of the staff of the Ventura County, California, Health Services Agency.

The late June Sklar was assistant research demographer, International Population and Urban Research, University of California, Berkeley.

Mary E. Steinman is nurse-clinician with the St. Paul Maternal and Infant Care Project, St. Paul-Ramsey Hospital, St. Paul, Minnesota.

Christopher Tietze is senior consultant with The Population Council, New York City, where he directs that organization's abortion research activities.

James Trussell is associate professor of economics and public affairs, Woodrow Wilson School, and faculty associate of the Office of Population Research, Princeton University, Princeton, New Jersey.

Wayne H. Welcher is a member of the staff of the Ventura County, California, Health Services Agency.

Harriet H. Werley is associate dean at the School of Nursing of the University of Missouri-Columbia.

Charles F. Westoff is director of the Office of Population Research and Maurice During '22 Professor of Demographic Studies and Sociology at Princeton University.

Lauress L. Wise is director of Project TALENT, a large prospective study of boys and girls who were students in U.S. high schools in 1960.

Laurie Schwab Zabin is vice chairperson, The Alan Guttmacher Institute, New York City and is assistant professor in the department of gynecology and obstetrics, The Johns Hopkins School of Medicine, Baltimore.

Melvin Zelnik is professor of population dynamics at The Johns Hopkins University School of Hygiene and Public Health, Baltimore.